# Working with Microfit

Interactive Econometric Ana

# Working with Microfit 4.0
## Interactive Econometric Analysis

M. HASHEM PESARAN

and

BAHRAM PESARAN

OXFORD UNIVERSITY PRESS

*Oxford University Press, Great Clarendon Street, Oxford OX2 6DP*

*Oxford New York*
*Athens Auckland Bangkok Bogota Bombay Buenos Aires*
*Calcutta Cape Town Dar es Salaam Delhi Florence Hong Kong Istanbul*
*Karachi Kuala Lumpur Madras Madrid Melbourne Mexico City*
*Nairobi Paris Singapore Taipei Tokyo Toronto Warsaw*

*and associated companies in*
*Berlin Ibadan*

*Oxford is a trade mark of Oxford University Press*



*ISBN 0 19 268530 9*

*3 5 7 9 10 8 6 4*

*Typeset by Dobbie Typesetting Limited*
*Printed in Great Britain by*
*Redwood Books, Trowbridge, Wiltshire*

To Caroline and Marian.

# Preface

*Microfit* 4.0 has taken over four years to complete and represents a major advance over the earlier versions of the package. It contains many new features and covers a number of recent developments in the areas of univariate and multivariate time series analysis. *Microfit* 4.0 is available for both DOS and for Windows. The present volume is for the Windows version. There is also a companion volume for the DOS version.

This volume describes how to install and run the package, and how to use its various menus, options, formulae, and commands. In addition, it contains detailed reviews of the underlying econometric and computing methods, together with 76 tutorial lessons using more than 25 different data sets, including the original time series data used by Cobb–Douglas, A.W. Phillips, and Almon. It is hoped that this volume can serve as an interactive tool in the teaching of time series econometrics, supplementing recent econometric texts by, for example, Greene (1993), Davidson and MacKinnon (1993), and Hamilton (1994).

This volume is in six parts:

Part I (Chapters 1 and 2) gives an introduction to the package and shows how to install and run it on personal PCs or on networks.

Part II (Chapters 3 to 5) deals with reading/saving of data and graphics files, management and processing of data, and preliminary data analysis.

Part III (Chapters 6 and 7) gives an account of the estimation menus and the various single and multiple equation options that are available in *Microfit* 4.0.

Part IV (Chapters 8 to 17) is devoted to tutorial lessons covering many different issues and problems, ranging from data management and data processing to linear and non-linear regressions, univariate time series analysis, GARCH modelling, Probit and Logit estimation, unrestricted VAR modelling, cointegration analysis, and SURE estimation.

Part V (Chapters 18 and 19) provides a review of the underlying econometric techniques for the analysis of single and multiple equation models.

Part VI (Appendices A to C) gives information on the size limitations of the package, error messages, and tables of critical values.

In developing *Microfit* 4.0 we have benefited greatly from comments and suggestions from many *Microfit* users, students, and colleagues, particularly those at Cambridge University, UCLA, the University of Pennsylvania, the

University of Southern California and the Bank of England, as well as the participants in the 'Working with *Microfit*' courses, organized by Cambridge Econometrics and Camfit Data, and the Geneva courses on 'Forecasting Techniques for Financial Markets' organized by the International Center for Monetary and Banking Studies.

We are also grateful to the beta testers of the package for their helpful comments and suggestions on a preliminary version: Heather Anderson, Anil Bera, Roberto Golinelli, Terry Haines, Sangwhan Kim, Mike McAleer, Colin McKenzie, Les Oxley, Adrian Pagan, Kerry Patterson, John Samuel, Ron Smith, Pravin Trivedi, Farshid Vahid, and Michael Wickens.

Brian Holley made valuable suggestions with respect to *Microfit*'s installation program, particularly for networks. Melvin Weeks commented on the Logit and Probit options, and provided us with the data set used in Lesson 14.1. Francesca Massone went through all the tutorial lessons and checked them for consistency and accuracy. She also helped us with lesson 9.14 and provided the data file used in this lesson. Silvia Fabiani supplied the data used in the lessons in Chapter 15.

Our special thanks go to Yongcheol Shin and Ron Smith for their generous help with the preparation of this volume. Ron Smith provided the materials for Lessons 10.12, 13.5, and 16.1, and made a number of valuable suggestions. Yongcheol Shin helped us with the compilation of the references and the lessons on univariate time series and cointegration analysis. He also read the whole of this volume in its manuscript form, identifying many errors and ambiguities. We are also grateful to Francesca Massone, James Mitchell, and George Kapetanios for careful proof-reading of the finished manuscript, and to Gill Smith for liaising with the publishers and those involved at the many stages of production of the program, particularly Delia Gallagher of the OUP.

The interface of the Windows version owes much to the dedication and hard work of Catherine Rees-Lay of Polyhedron Software. She has been responsible for programming the interface and for skilfully linking it up to the codes of the DOS version of the program. Kati Hamza has done an excellent job of copy-editing and preparing the help files for the Windows version.

Finally, we are most grateful to Ann Widdop for skilful keyboarding of this manuscript. There is no doubt that without her dedication and hard work the publication of *Microfit* 4.0 would have been delayed even further!

M. Hashem Pesaran — Cambridge
Bahram Pesaran — London

May 1996
April 1997 (Windows version)

# Contents

# List of Figures

# List of Tables

# PART I

# Introduction to *Microfit*

# 1
# Introduction

## 1.1 What is *Microfit*?

*Microfit* is an interactive econometric software package written for microcomputers, and is designed specifically for the econometric modelling of time series data. It is suitable for classroom teaching of undergraduate and postgraduate courses in applied econometrics. It has powerful features for data processing, file management, graphic display, estimation, hypothesis testing, and forecasting under a variety of univariate and multivariate model specifications. These features make *Microfit* 4.0 one of the most powerful time series econometric packages currently available.

*Microfit* for Windows is even easier to use than the DOS version, and generates output in carefully set out tables and graphs in a matter of seconds. Output from *Microfit* can be sent directly to a printer, saved in a disk file to be printed subsequently, or used in a text file as part of a printed report.

*Microfit* accepts comma delimited files (CSV), text (TXT), and AREMOS (TSD) files. It also allows extension, revision, and merging of data files. Small data sets can also be pasted into *Microfit* from the clipboard. Data on *Microfit*'s workspace can be exported to spreadsheet packages in CSV and TSD formats. Other software in the operating system can be accessed easily. For routine and repetitive data processing tasks, *Microfit* employs commands close to conventional algebraic notation.

The strength of the package lies in the fact that it can be used at different levels of technical sophistication. For experienced users of econometric programs it offers a variety of univariate and multivariate estimation methods, and provides a large number of diagnostic and non-nested tests not readily available on other packages. The interaction of excellent graphics and estimation capabilities in *Microfit* allows important econometric research to be carried out in a matter of days rather than weeks.

## 1.2 New features of *Microfit* 4.0

*Microfit* 4.0 represents a major advance over the earlier versions of the package. It makes more intensive use of screen editors and window facilities for data entry, for model specification, and for easy storage and retrieval of data and result files. Using the new version you can run regressions up to 102 regressors (as compared to 42 in *Microfit* 3.0) and 3,000 observations. You can also move readily between drives, directories, and subdirectories for retrieving and saving data input and output files. Scrolling within a result screen is also possible. All files created using *Microfit* 3.0 can be used in *Microfit* 4.0.

*Microfit* 4.0 allows you to read data files in comma delimited (CSV), PRN (Lotus print files), text (TXT), and AREMOS (TSD) formats, complete with their variable names and their descriptions (if any). Data on *Microfit*'s workspace can be easily exported into spreadsheet packages such as *Excel*. It comes with an extensive system of help facilities, providing easy on-line access to the *Microfit* manual. The graphic features of the package have been upgraded further, and now allow the graphs produced in *Microfit* to be imported into word-processing packages, or printed on a variety of printers.

For data analysis, *Microfit* 4.0 has a large number of additional time series and econometric features; these include new functions and commands, new single-equation options, and new multivariate time series techniques.

### 1.2.1 New functions and commands

New functions included in *Microfit* 4.0 are:

- The RATE(X) function, which computes the percentage change in variable X.
- The MEAN(X) function, which computes the mean of X.
- The STD(X) function, which computes the standard deviation of X.
- The MAV(X, $p$) function, which computes a $p$th order moving average of X.
- The Hodrick and Prescott Filter, HPF(X, $\lambda$), which runs the variable X through the Hodrick–Prescott filter using the parameter $\lambda$, chosen by the user depending on the frequency of Y.
- The Pesaran and Timmermann test statistic, PTTEST(Y, X), which computes a non-parametric measure of association between Y, and X.

New commands in *Microfit* 4.0 are:

- REORDER X, which activates a complete reordering of the observations in the variables list according to the ordering of X. This command is particularly useful when using *Microfit* in cross-sectional analysis.
- RESTORE, which restores the ordering of the observations to their original state before the use of the command REORDER.

### 1.2.2 New single-equation estimation techniques

The new single-equation options in *Microfit* 4.0 include:

**Estimation of conditionally heteroscedastic models:** Maximum likelihood estimation of regression models under a variety of conditionally heteroscedastic error specifications, such as ARCH, GARCH, GARCH in mean, absolute value GARCH, absolute value GARCH in mean, exponential GARCH, and exponential GARCH in mean. The ARCH and GARCH models can be estimated for two different specifications of the conditional distribution of the errors, namely normal and the student's t-distributions.
**Logit and probit estimation.**
**Phillips–Hansen's fully modified OLS estimation:** This procedure provides single-equation estimates of the cointegrating relations.
**Autoregressive-distributed Lag (ARDL) estimation procedure:** This procedure provides estimates of a single cointegrating relation on the basis of an ARDL model selected by means of model selection procedures such as Akaike, Schwarz, Hannan and Quinn, and $\bar{R}^2$. This approach also readily allows for the inclusion of time trends, seasonal dummies, and other deterministic/exogenous regressors in the cointegrating relation (see Pesaran and Shin 1995a).
**New non-nested tests:** Tests of linear versus log-linear models, level-differenced versus log-differenced models, and other non-linear specifications of the dependent variable are now included in *Microfit* 4.0.

### 1.2.3 New system equation estimation techniques

*Microfit* 4.0 provides an integrated tool-box for the analysis of multivariate time series models. The estimation and testing procedures cover the following models:

**Estimation of unrestricted VAR models:** This option provides estimates of the coefficients in the VAR model, together with various diagnostic test statistics for each equation in the VAR model, separately. It allows automatic order selection in the VAR using Akaike, Schwarz, and likelihood-ratio procedures, Granger (1969) block non-causality tests, orthogonalized (Sims 1980) and generalized impulse response in VAR models (Koop et al. 1996), and orthogonalized and generalized forecast error variance decomposition in unrestricted and cointegrating VAR models. The generalized impulse responses are new and, unlike the orthogonalized responses, do not depend on the ordering of the variables in the VAR model.
**Estimation of seemingly unrelated regression equations:** Estimation and hypothesis testing in systems of equations by the seemingly unrelated regression equations (SURE) method (see Zellner 1962). ML estimation and hypothesis testing in systems of equations subject to parametric restrictions.

The restrictions can be homogeneous or non-homogeneous, and involve coefficients from different relations (i.e. cross-equation restrictions).

**New cointegration tests in VAR models:** These tests allow for deterministic linear trends in the underlying VAR model both with and without restrictions on the trend coefficients, and enable the user to carry out the cointegration tests when one or more of the I(1) variables are exogenously determined. *Microfit* 4.0 automatically provides appropriate critical values for all of these tests, a feature not available elsewhere.

**Long-run structural modelling:** This estimation procedure allows you to estimate and test more than one cointegrating relation subject to identifying and over-identifying restrictions on the long-run (or cointegrating) relations. The restrictions can be homogeneous or non-homogeneous, and can involve coefficients from different cointegrating relations. Long-run structural modelling also allows analysis of sub-systems where one or more of the I(1) variables are exogenously determined (see Pesaran and Shin 1995b, and Pesaran et al. 1996a, 1996b).

**Impulse response analysis and forecast error-variance decomposition:** The program now allows computations of orthogonalized and generalized impulse response functions, and forecast error variance decomposition in the case of cointegrating VAR models. It also produces estimates of the persistence profiles for the effect of system-wide shocks on the cointegrating relations (see Pesaran and Shin 1996).

**Computation of multivariate dynamic forecasts:** Multivariate dynamic forecasts for various horizons can be readily computed using *Microfit* 4.0, for unrestricted and cointegrating VAR models, and for seemingly unrelated regression equations with and without parametric restrictions.

## 1.3 Tutorial lessons

Important features of *Microfit* are demonstrated throughout this book by means of 67 tutorial lessons, using data files supplied with the program. There are lessons in data management; data transformation; graphics (plotting time series, scatter diagrams, histograms); displaying, printing, and saving results; estimation; hypothesis testing and forecasting, using a variety of univariate and multivariate econometric models. These lessons and the details of econometric methods provided in Chapters 18 and 19 are intended to complement the more traditional econometric texts used in quantitative economic courses, and to help further establish the concept of interactive econometric teaching in the profession.

## 1.4 Other features of *Microfit* 4.0

Many useful features of *Microfit* 3.0 have either been retained or have been greatly enhanced, particularly as far as interface and graphics are concerned. A summary of these features follows.

### 1.4.1 Data management

*Microfit* can be used to input data directly from the keyboard, from raw ASCII data files, or from special *Microfit* files prepared and saved previously. The data can be input as undated series or as monthly, quarterly, half-yearly, or yearly frequencies. Integral parts of the data management system of *Microfit* are the facilities provided for the extension, revision, and merging of the data files. These data management facilities allow the user to extend an existing data file by adding more observations and/or more variables to it. It is also possible to input and output raw data files in ASCII formats to and from *Microfit*.

### 1.4.2 Data transformation

*Microfit* allows the user to compute new series as algebraic transforms of existing data using standard arithmetic operators, such as + – / *, and a wide range of built-in functions including MAX, MIN, SIGN, RANK, and ORDER. Time trends, seasonal dummies, and random numbers from UNIFORM and NORMAL distributions can also be generated easily by *Microfit*.

### 1.4.3 High-resolution graphics

*Microfit* can be used to produce high-quality scatter diagrams and graphs of variables plotted against time or against another variable, with the option of adding headings to the graph. A hard copy of the graphs can be produced on any IBM-compatible dot-matrix printer, and on a large number of printers including PostScript and HP LaserJet printers. *Microfit* can also automatically produce graphs of actual and fitted values, residuals, histograms with superimposed normal and t-distribution in the case of the ARCH and GARCH options, as well as graphs of forecasts and concentrated log-likelihood functions.

*Microfit* 4.0 allows the graphs to be saved for importation into word-processing programs such as Microsoft Word, Scientific Word, and Word Perfect. It allows you to save graphics in bitmap (BMP) or Windows Metafile (WMF) format, or in the special *Microfit* graphics format (MFW). You can also paste a graph into another Windows application via the clipboard.

### 1.4.4 Batch operations

*Microfit* allows the user to run batch jobs containing formulae, samples and simulation commands. This facility is particularly useful when the same transformations of different or revised data sets are required.

### 1.4.5 General statistics

*Microfit* allows the user to compute:

- Means and standard deviations
- Skewness and Kurtosis measures
- The coefficient of variation
- Correlation coefficients of two or more variables
- Minimum and Maximum of a series
- The autocorrelation coefficients and their standard errors
- Estimates of the spectral density function and their standard errors using Bartlett, Tukey, and Parzen windows.

### 1.4.6 Dynamic simulation

Important facilities in *Microfit* are the SIM and SIMB commands, which allow the user to simulate dynamically any non-linear difference equation both forwards and backwards.

### 1.4.7 Other single-equation estimation techniques

*Microfit* 4.0 estimates regression equations under a variety of stochastic specifications. The estimation techniques carried over from *Microfit* 3.0 include:

- Ordinary least squares
- Generalized instrumental variables
- Two stage least squares
- Recursive and rolling estimation by the least squares and instrumental variables methods
- Non-linear least squares and non-linear two-stage least squares
- Cochrane–Orcutt iterative technique
- Maximum likelihood estimation of regression models with serially correlated errors (both for AR and MA error processes)
- Instrumental variable estimation of models with serially correlated errors (both for AR and MA error processes)
- Maximum likelihood estimation of ARMA or ARIMA processes
- Maximum likelihood estimation of cointegrated systems.

Models with autocorrelated errors of up to order 12 can be estimated, both when the pattern of residual autocorrelation is unrestricted and when it is subject to zero restrictions. The estimation results are compactly tabulated and provide parameter estimates and other statistics of interest including t-statistics, standard errors, Durbin–Watson statistic, Durbin's h-statistic (when relevant), $\bar{R}^2$, and more.

Alternative estimates of the variance-covariance matrix of the parameter estimates, namely White's heteroscedasticity-consistent estimates and Newey–West adjusted estimates with equal weights, Bartlett weights, and Parzen weights, can also be obtained with *Microfit* for the cases of linear and non-linear least squares and instrumental variables methods.

*Microfit* enables the user to list and plot the actual and fitted values, as well as the residuals. The fitted values and the residuals can be saved for use in subsequent econometric analysis.

### 1.4.8 Model respecification

The specification of equations in *Microfit* can be changed simply by using a screen editor to add and/or delete regressors, or to change the dependent variable. The equations and variable lists can be saved to a file for later use. It is possible to re-estimate the same regression equation over different time periods and under different stochastic specifications simply by selecting the relevant choices from the menus.

### 1.4.9 Diagnostic tests and model selection criteria

*Microfit* supplies the user with an array of diagnostic statistics for testing residual autocorrelation, heteroscedasticity, autoregressive conditional heteroscedasticity, normality of regression disturbances, predictive failure, and structural stability. It automatically computes:

- Lagrange multiplier tests for serially correlated residuals in the case of OLS and IV estimation methods
- Ramsey's RESET test of functional form misspecification
- Jarque–Bera's test of normality of regression residuals
- Heteroscedasticity test
- Predictive failure test
- Chow's test of stability of regression coefficients
- Unit roots tests
- ARCH test
- The CUSUM and the CUSUM of squares tests for structural stability
- $\bar{R}^2$, Akaike, Schwarz, and Hannan–Quinn model selection criteria
- Generalized $\bar{R}^2$ for models estimated by Instrumental Variables method (see Pesaran and Smith 1994).

### 1.4.10 Variable addition and variable deletion tests

*Microfit* has options for doing variable addition and variable deletion tests. These facilities are very helpful in the process of model construction and enable users to follow either of the two basic modelling strategies, namely specific-to-general or general-to-specific. Variable addition is particularly useful as it allows the user to carry out further diagnostic tests, such as higher order RESET or ARCH tests, or to test for the independence between the disturbances and the regressors of the regression equation.

### 1.4.11 Cointegration tests

*Microfit* provides a user-friendly method of testing for cointegration among a set of at most 12 variables by the Johansen's maximum likelihood method. Both versions of Johansen's tests, namely the maximal eigenvalue and the trace tests, are computed. These features have been extensively enhanced in *Microfit* 4.0.

### 1.4.12 Testing for unit roots

*Microfit* automatically computes augmented Dickey–Fuller statistics and gives the appropriate critical values at the 10 per cent and the 5 per cent levels. Unit root test statistics for regression residuals, together with their critical values, are automatically supplied by *Microfit*.

### 1.4.13 Tests of linear and non-linear restrictions

Tests of linear and non-linear restrictions on the parameters of the regression model (both the deterministic and the stochastic parts of the model) can be carried out using *Microfit*. It is also possible to compute estimates of functions (possibly non-linear ones) of the parameters of the regression model, together with their asymptotic standard errors for all the estimation methods. This facility is particularly useful for the analysis of long-run properties, such as estimation of long-run responses, mean lags, and computation of persistence measures.

### 1.4.14 Non-nested tests

*Microfit* provides a number of non-nested statistics proposed in the literature for tests of non-nested linear regression models. These include Godfrey and Pesaran's small sample-adjusted Cox statistic, Davidson and MacKinnon's J-test, and the encompassing F-statistic based on a general model. It also contains options for testing linear versus log-linear models, and for testing ratio models versus log-linear and linear models. A number of important model selection criteria such as Akaike's information criterion and Schwarz's Bayesian criterion are also computed in the case of non-nested models.

### 1.4.15 Static and dynamic univariate forecasts

*Microfit* generates one-period-ahead (static) and dynamic forecasts of single-equation regression models. It gives forecast errors and a number of useful summary statistics. If lagged dependent variables are included in the regression, *Microfit* automatically computes dynamic forecasts, otherwise it generates static forecasts. The plot of actual and forecast values is also provided, with the possibility of saving forecast values and forecast errors on a file for later analysis.

Missing values are fully supported by *Microfit*, and when a transformation (including leading and lagging) results or involves undefined values, the undefined values are set to *NONE*. At the Estimation/Testing/Forecasting stage *Microfit* looks for *NONE* values and adjusts the specified sample period automatically so that beginning and end periods with missing values are discarded. If missing values are encountered in the middle of the estimation and/or forecast periods the Estimation/Testing/Forecasting will not take place and the user is informed of this. The value *NONE* is displayed whenever the computations involve operations that cannot be carried out, such as taking the square root or the logarithm of a negative number.

## 1.5 Installation and system configuration

*Microfit* can be installed easily both on personal computers and on networks of PCs. It can be configured to suit the taste and the needs of the user. It automatically configures itself to the particular type of graphics adaptor installed on the PC, and allows the user to adjust the way in which windows are displayed. Print setup options allows you to cater for paper of different lengths.

## 1.6 System requirements for *Microfit* 4.0

*Microfit* 4.0 for Windows runs on an IBM PC (or full compatible) with 80386, 80486, or Pentium processor and the following specifications:

- At least 8 Mb free RAM, although 16 Mb free RAM is recommended
- Maths 80386SX, or 80486SX co-processors
- DOS 3.0 or higher
- Windows 3.1 or higher, including Windows 95 and NT

- At least 12 Mb free hard-disk space plus an additional 4 Mb free hard-disk space for initial installation of program files
- VGA or SVGA monitor
- Microsoft mouse or compatible
- IBM (or compatible) dot-matrix, PostScript, or HP Laserjet printer for producing hard copies of graphs and regression results (optional).

*Microfit* 4.0 allows running regressions with up to 102 regressors and up to 3000 observations.[1] In the case of the unrestricted VAR option *Microfit* allows for up to 12 variables in the VAR model and a maximum lag order of 24. In the cointegration option it allows a maximum of 12 endogenous I(1) variables and five exogenous I(1) variables, and 18 deterministic and/or exogenous I(0) variables. See Appendix A for further information on the size limitations of the program.

*Important warning:* When *Microfit* 4.0 is loaded with less than the required free RAM and hard-disk space specified above, the program may crash without due warning!

## 1.7 *DETS*: a new data retrieval package

*Data Extractor for Time Series* (*DETS*) is a companion program which greatly simplifies the input of data from data banks and spreadsheet packages into *Microfit*. The extracted series can be saved for later analysis in *Microfit* or other programs.

The program presents the user with a list of available databases; all or some of these may be searched very rapidly for specified keywords and for a specified frequency (monthly, quarterly, or annual). Individual series can then be viewed in numeric or simple graphical form; they can also be selected for output to a file.

*DETS* can currently output files in *Microfit*, spreadsheet, and raw text formats.

*DETS* works with a special internal format. Published databases can be converted from their source form into *DETS* format, which is compact, and contains an internal index to enable rapid searches to be made. The module includes conversion programs for OECD, CITIBASE, CSO, World Bank, Penn World Tables, and other data sources. Conversion programs for sources not currently supported may be developed as required.

*DETS* helps to overcome the problem of extracting data when data is supplied in a variety of different formats. It is envisaged that companies and

[1] *Microfit* 4.0 can be modified to allow for more regressors and observations. Those interested in such a customized version of *Microfit* should contact Camfit Data Limited, 283 Hills Road, Cambridge CB2 2RP, ENGLAND, E-mail: Camfit@INTECC.CO.UK or visit the Internet site, http://www.INTECC.CO.UK/Camfit/

educational or governmental institutions will use the conversion programs once when the data is received, but from then on will use *DETS* as a means of extracting subsets.

*DETS* was developed by Brian Holley who is the Senior Computer Officer at the Faculty of Economics and Politics, University of Cambridge.

# 2

# Installation and Getting Started

The Windows version of *Microfit* 4.0 is supplied on three 3.5-inch floppy disks. Disk 1 should contain the file SETUP.EXE and Disks 2 and 3 should contain the files SETUP.W02 and SETUP.W03 respectively. For the student version, follow the same installation instructions outlined below. For details on the limitations of the student version, see Appendix A.

## 2.1 Installation

To work with *Microfit* you first need to install it on your machine. To install *Microfit* 4.0, place Disk 1 in your floppy-disk drive and make sure Windows is running. Select Run... from the File Menu (Windows 3.1) or choose Start, Run... (Windows 95 or Windows NT). Into the edit field, type

A: SETUP ↩

(where A is the letter of your floppy-disk drive). Follow the instructions given by the installation program. You will be presented with a choice between installing the program on a stand-alone computer or on a network workstation.

### 2.1.1 Installing *Microfit* on a single PC

If you want to install Microfit on a stand-alone computer, make sure the stand-alone option is checked and click OK. Follow the instructions given by the installation program. When the Select components to install dialog appears, make sure you check the Tutorial files option if you want to install the tutorial files as well as the program (many of the worked examples in this book make use of the tutorial files).

At the end of the installation procedure you will be asked to enter a researcher name and make certain choices about results printouts. Type the researcher name in the Name of researcher field.

The default number of lines per printed page is 60. You can change this, if you wish, by typing another number into the input box. By default, page numbers and the researcher name are added to printed results. If you do not want printed output to feature either or both of these, uncheck the appropriate checkbox(es). When you are satisfied with your printing choices, click OK.

### 2.1.2 Installing *Microfit* on a network of PCs

To install *Microfit* on a multiple-user client-server network, the system administrator should run SETUP/N in the usual way by typing:

A: SETUP/N ↩

where A: is the letter of your floppy-disk drive. To install a personal copy on a network computer, run the installation program as described in Section 2.1.1. The installation program will check whether you have write access to the Windows SYSTEM directory. If you do not, the relevant files will be installed in the WINDOWS directory. A copy installed in this way will run on your computer only.

To install *Microfit* on a peer-to-peer network, the first user should install a full version of the program as described in Section 2.1.1. Subsequent users should follow the steps described in Section 2.1.1, choosing Workstation installation instead of Stand-alone installation when prompted.

## 2.2 Starting and ending a session

### 2.2.1 Running *Microfit*

To load *Microfit* in Windows 3.1, Windows 95 or NT, double click the Microfit for Windows icon. In Windows 95 or NT, you can also choose Start, Programs, Microfit for Windows.

### 2.2.2 Quitting *Microfit*

To quit *Microfit*, do one of the following:

- Click the [icon] button
- Choose Exit from the File Menu
- Double click the Control-menu box (Windows 3.1) or the *Microfit* icon (Windows 95) on the left of the title bar
- Click the Control-menu box or the *Microfit* icon on the left of the title bar once, and choose CLOSE
- Press ALT+F4
- Click the Close button (Windows 95 only).

You are warned that all unsaved data will be lost. If you are sure you have saved all your data, choose OK. If not, click CANCEL, save any unsaved data, and quit again.

## 2.3 Using windows, menus, and buttons

You work your way through a *Microfit* 4.0 session using a combination of windows, menus, and buttons. At the heart of the application are several menus and sub-menus for processing your data. Each menu contains a selection of up to nine options with one of the options (usually the most common) already selected.

A simple method of familiarizing yourself with *Microfit* and what it can do is to learn about its main menus and their interrelationships, as shown in Chart 1.

The rest of this manual describes the various components of *Microfit* and shows you how to input and process data, and to estimate/test/forecast using a number of univariate and multivariate time series models.

### 2.3.1 The main window

The main window is your workspace. From here you can access all the main functions of the program: the Variables window, the Data Editor, the Command Editor, the Single Equation Estimation window, and the System Estimation window.

### 2.3.2 Main menu bar

Many of the program's functions are controlled using the menus on the main menu bar.

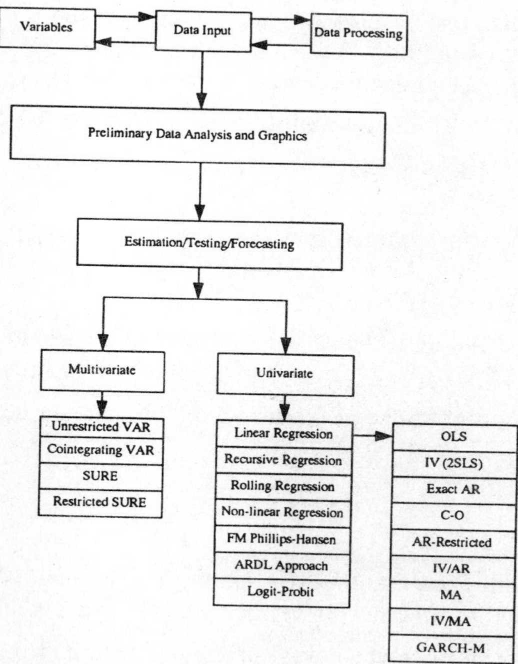


Chart 1: The flow chart of functions in *Microfit*

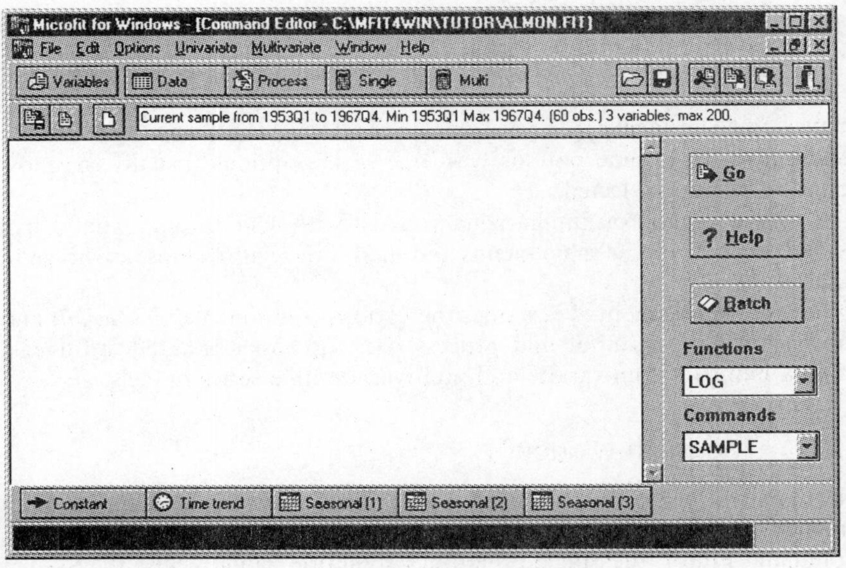


Figure 2.1: The main window

*File Menu*

**New...** Allows you to enter a new data set from the keyboard (see Section 3.1.1).

**Open...** Opens an existing data file saved in any of the following formats: ASCII (DAT), *Microfit* (.FIT), comma delimited values (CSV), AREMOS time series data (.TSD). The button equivalent of this function is [open button].

**Add...** Adds a *Microfit* file to existing data in *Microfit* (see Section 3.2).

**Save** Saves a file you have already saved once using the Save as... option (see Section 3.4)

**Save as...** Saves your data in a new file in special *Microfit*, ASCII, comma delimited values, or AREMOS format (see Section 3.4). Its button equivalent is [save button].

**View...** Opens a file and allows you to examine its contents (see Section 4.2.1).

**Exit** Quits the program (see Section 2.2.2). The button equivalent of this function is [exit button].

*Edit Menu*

**Cut**, **Copy**, and **Paste** Allow you perform standard Windows editing functions. They have the button equivalents [cut button], [copy button], and [paste button] respectively.

**Paste Data** Imports data which was copied to the clipboard using a standard spreadsheet package such as Microsoft Excel. (See Section 3.1.7.)

**Font...** Changes the font style, colour, and size of text displayed in *Microfit* (see Section 2.3.4).

In the Command Editor (see Section 4.2) several additional options are available:

**Constant (intercept) term** Creates a constant (see Section 4.1.1). Its button equivalent is [→ Constant].

**Time trend** Creates a time trend (see Section 4.1.2). Its button equivalent is [Time trend].

**Seasonal dummies** Creates seasonal dummies (see Section 4.1.3 to 4.1.5). Its button equivalents are the [Seasonal (1)], [Seasonal (2)], and [Seasonal (3)] buttons.

*Options Menu*

**Startup...** Specifies startup options such as the size of the main window and the size and position of the Variables window (see Section 2.3.4).

**Graphics...** Allows you to make choices about graphic display and printing options (see Section 2.3.4).

**Bubble help...** Switches bubble help on and off (see Section 2.3.4).

**Results printing...** Allows you to make choices about how results are printed out (see Section 2.3.4).

**Editor defaults...** Specifies the size, style, and colour of default text in editor and results windows (see Section 2.3.4).

*Univariate Menu*

This is the Single Equation Estimation Menu (see Section 6.4) from which all the single-equation estimation options may be accessed. These are discussed in detail in Chapter 6.

*Multivariate Menu*

This is the System Estimation Menu (see Section 7.3) from which all the multiple equation estimation options may be accessed. These are discussed in detail in Chapter 7.

*Windows Menu*

**Tile** Displays all open windows in a tile arrangement (see Section 2.3.4).

**Cascade** Displays all open windows in an overlapping arrangement (see Section 2.3.4).

**Arrange icons** If any windows are minimized to an icon, this option rearranges them (see Section 2.3.4).

1, 2, 3, etc. Switches between open windows.

*Help Menu*

Accesses the program's help functions (see Section 2.3.5).

### 2.3.3 Buttons

The buttons in the main window control the most common program functions:

| **Button** | **Function** |
|---|---|
| Variables | Switches to the Variables window where the current list of variables and their descriptions are displayed, and may be edited (see Section 3.1.1). |
| Data | Moves to the Data Editor where you can edit your data (see Section 3.1.1). |
| Process | Moves to the Command Editor where you process your data (see Section 4.2). |
| Single | Switches to the Single Equation Estimation window (see Section 6.4). The Single Equation Estimation options can also be accessed from the Univariate Menu. |
| Multi | Switches to the System Estimation window (see Section 7.3). The System Estimation options can also be accessed from the Multivariate Menu. |
| | Opens an existing data set (see Section 3.1.2). This is the equivalent of Open... from the File Menu. |
| | Cuts highlighted text to the clipboard (see Section 3.3). Its equivalent is Cut from the Edit Menu. |
| | Copies highlighted text to the clipboard (see Section 3.3). Copy from the Edit Menu is its menu equivalent. |
| | Pastes text from the clipboard into the current *Microfit* window (see Section 3.3). Alternatively, use Paste from the Edit Menu. |
| | Quits *Microfit*. |
| | Saves the contents of the current editor to disk (see Section 4.2.1). |
| | Loads a LST or EQU file you saved earlier into the current box editor (see Section 4.2.1). |
| | Clears the contents of the current box editor (see Section 3.3). |

### 2.3.4 Program options

Various aspects of the program may be customized to personal preference using the Edit, Options, and Window Menus.

### *Startup options*

Use the Startup... option to control how *Microfit* is displayed each time you start the program. By default the main window is displayed at a default size on startup. If you want to retain any changes you made to the window size between sessions, make sure the Use previous values option is selected.

The Variables window is treated as a child (subsidiary) window by default. This means that if you switch from it to another window, the new window is automatically brought to the top. You can ensure the Variables window always stays on top by clicking the Always on top option. If you want to retain any changes you made to the Variables window size between sessions, make sure the window's Use previous values option is selected (otherwise the window will revert to its default size).

### *Graphics options*

The Graphics... option from the Options Menu is used to specify graph display and printing options. For printing colour or greyscale (depending on your printer) is used by default. You can switch to using black and white symbols or patterns instead by selecting the Use black and white symbols... option, if you wish. Multiple-line graphs are displayed using thick and thin lines by default. You have the option to display them using patterned lines. The last data point in a graph is automatically labelled. If you do not want this to happen uncheck the Force labelling of last data point checkbox.

### *Bubble help*

You can display bubble help on *Microfit*'s buttons and editors, by selecting Bubble help... from the Options menu and checking the Bubble help checkbox. To display help on an item, simply move the cursor over it.

### *Results printing options*

To specify how your results are printed out, choose Results printing... from the Options Menu, or (if the Options dialog is already open) click the Results printing page tab. When you first install *Microfit* you are prompted to enter the name of the current researcher (user). To edit or replace the name click on the Name of researcher field and edit (or delete) the name as necessary. Print page numbers

Page numbers are added to your results printout by default. To exclude them, uncheck the Print page numbers option. The date of your results and the name of the researcher are added to results printouts by default. To exclude them, uncheck the Print date and researcher name option.

### *Changing font*

You have two choices when specifying how the contents of *Microfit* editors and results windows are displayed. You can either change the font in the current window or change the default font for all editor/results windows.

To change the font style, size, or colour in which the current editor or results window is displayed, select Font... from the Edit Menu and choose an alternative font, size, and/or colour from the Font dialog. The default font option is System. The default colour and size of *Microfit* text are black 10 point. In some windows there is a button equivalent to this menu option: **A**.

To change the default fonts, choose Editor defaults... from the Options Menu, or (if the Options dialog is already open) click the Editor defaults page tab.

The default font used in the Data Editor, Command Editor, Single Equation Estimation window, etc. is System. The default colour and size are black 10 point. To change the default font, click the **A** button next to the default (or current) font name and choose an alternative font, size, and/or colour from the Font dialog box. Then click OK.

The changes you have made will be implemented *the next time you start Microfit*.

The default font used in results windows is black Courier New 10 point. To change the default font, click the **A** button next to the default (or current) font name and choose an alternative font, size, and/or colour from the Font dialog box. Then click OK. (To ensure the correct display of results, only the fixed fonts available on your computer are listed.)

*Rearranging windows*

When several windows are displayed at once you can rearrange them in a tiled or overlapping display using the Tile or Cascade function from the Window Menu. To rearrange any windows reduced to icons, choose Arrange icons from the Window Menu.

## 2.3.5 Help

*Microfit* has an extensive on-line help facility. For help on the part of the application you are currently using, press F1 or, if relevant, click the HELP button.

Alternatively, use the Help Menu. This has several options.

**Overview** Displays general information on using *Microfit* help. Click on a topic highlighted in green to move there.

**Contents** Displays a list of help topics. Click on a topic highlighted in green to move there.

**Search For Help On...** Searches for help on a particular topic. Type the information you want to find into the top field. The index moves to the closest matching topic. Double click on a topic to view it.

**How To Use Help...** Gives help on using Help.

**About...** Gives copyright information about *Microfit* for Windows.

# PART II

# Processing and Data Management

# 3

# Inputting and Saving Data files

Data can be input into *Microfit* directly from the keyboard, from ASCII files, from special *Microfit* files saved previously, from CSV files, and from AREMOS (TSD) files.[1] Data on the workspace of *Microfit* can be saved as ASCII (text) files, as special *Microfit* files, as TSD files or as Comma Delimited (CSV) files. It is also possible to paste (copy) *small* data sets from (to) the clipboard to (from) *Microfit*.

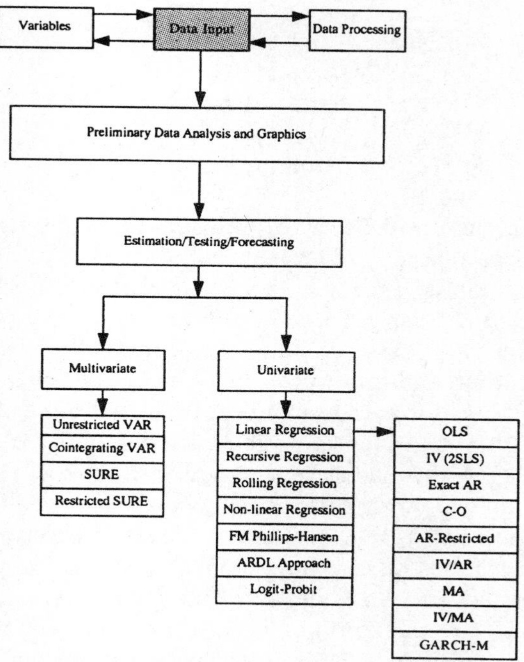


Chart 1: The flow chart of functions in *Microfit*

[1] *Excel* is the trade mark of Microsoft

To input and save data, use the options in the File Menu. You can also use the Add... option in the File Menu to add new variables (already saved in a special *Microfit* file) to your current data set.

## 3.1 Inputting data

When you start a new session with *Microfit*, you can either input a new data set directly from the keyboard or load an existing data set.

### 3.1.1 Inputting data from the keyboard

Inputting data directly from the keyboard is the most basic method of entering data. Before entering new data, make sure you know the frequency of your data (i.e. whether your data are undated, or have annual, half-yearly, quarterly, or monthly frequencies), the number of variables in your data set, and the sample period of your observations.

To input a new data set, choose New... from the File Menu. This opens the New data set dialog. The data frequency fields are at the top of the dialog, with fields for start and end dates, and number of variables below.

The following data frequency options are available. To choose one, click the appropriate radio button:

Undated
Annual
Half-yearly
Quarterly
Monthly

**Entering undated observations:** This option is often relevant for entering cross-sectional observations, and when it is chosen *Microfit* assumes that the observations are unordered, and asks how many observations you have. An observation refers to the individual unit on which you have data. For example, if you have cross-section data containing variables such as employment, output, and investment on a number of firms, then each firm represents an observation and the number of observations will be equal to the number of firms in your data set. If you have time series data covering the period from 1960 to 1970 inclusive, and you wish to enter them as undated data, then the number of observations in your data set will be equal to 11.

**Entering annual, half-yearly, quarterly, or monthly observations**: If any of these options are chosen, the program supplies the dates and you do not need to type them in. You are, however, asked to type the dates for the start and end of your data into the appropriate field. For example, if your data are annual and cover the period 1960–1985 inclusive, you need to enter 1960 into the Start field and 1985 into the End field. You can type the year in its full (1960) or abbreviated (60) form. However, if your data go beyond the year 1999 you must enter the dates in their full forms, namely 2000, 2025, etc.

If your data are quarterly and cover the period from the first quarter of 1970 to the last quarter of 1980 inclusive, you need to enter 70 into the Start field and 1 into the adjacent quarter field, then 80 into the End field, specifying 4 as its quarter.

Similar figures will be required if your data are half-yearly or monthly.

**Entering number of variables:** This refers to the number of data items that you have for each observation. Set as appropriate.

When you have finished entering the information, click OK. This opens the Variables window.

**Entering variable names:** The Variables window contains the default variable names X1, X2, X3, etc. For example, if you specify that you have ten variables, the Variables window appears with the following default variable names:

X1 X2 X3 X4 X5 X6 X7 X8 X9 X10

You can enter your own choice of variable names and/or add a description if you wish. Move to the appropriate field and edit or add text using standard Windows editing functions.

A valid variable name is alphanumeric, can be at most nine characters long, and must begin with a letter. Lower- and upper-case letters are treated as equivalent. The underscore character '_' is allowed anywhere in a variable name. Examples of valid variable names are:

GDPUK OUTPUT X2Y3 DATA261 Y_1

Variable names such as $GDP, 123, 2X, W# are not allowed. Note that function and command names used in the Command Editor cannot be used as variable names. The full list of function and command names can be found in Chapter 4. Variable descriptions can be up to 80 characters long. You can return to the Variables window to edit your data at any stage by clicking the [VARIABLES] button. Variables can also be given an optional description of up to 80 characters in the Command Editor by means of the command ENTITLE. See Chapter 4 on how to use this and other commands.

When you are satisfied with the changes you have made, click [GO].

When you have finished either:

**Entering Data:** When you have completed listing your variable names, you are presented with the Data Editor. This is where you enter observations on your variables. Initially, all the observations on this screen are set to *NONE*, indicating 'missing' values.

To enter your data, move to each cell in turn and type in your data. Continue until all the observations are entered. If the observations do not fit into the window, use the **PgUp** and **PgDn** keys to move up or down a screen page. To move to the top or bottom of the table, press **Ctrl + Home Ctrl + End**. When you have finished entering your observations, click [CLOSE].

### 3.1.2 Loading an existing data set

You can input data from an existing file in any of the following formats: special *Microfit*, ASCII, comma delimited (CSV), or AREMOS (TSD).

To load an existing file, choose Open... from the File Menu or click the [open] button. This displays the Open dialog. Select one of the file types from the drop-down list at the base of the dialog, choose your file from the appropriate drive and directory in the usual way, and click [OK].

If the data are in *Microfit*, CSV, or TSD file formats, the data are loaded automatically.

If the data are in another file format, you will be asked to confirm how the data in the file are structured before they are loaded in.

You are then presented with the Command Editor. To view or edit the variable names or descriptions, click the [VARIABLES] button. To edit the data, click the [DATA] button.

*Notes*

1. To read other spreadsheet files use the companion *Data Extractor for Time Series* (*DETS*) package (also available from Oxford University Press) to convert your spreadsheet data file into a special *Microfit* file. The *DETS* package can also be used to convert data from one type of frequency (e.g. monthly) to another (e.g. quarterly).
2. If the package fails to open the file, because the file is in use by another program or application, because the filename does not exist or is misspelt, or because the file is of the wrong type, you will get an error message. Click OK to return to the Open dialog and start again. You need to choose the correct drive, directory, and filename.

### 3.1.3 Inputting data from a raw data (ASCII) file

An ASCII (i.e. text) file may be extracted from an existing data bank, typed in directly using spreadsheets or other data processing packages, or transferred from another computer package. The file is expected to contain numbers only. A missing value is represented by the number 8934567.0.

Once you have specified a filename successfully (see Section 3.1.2), you will need to specify the frequency of your data, their coverage, and the names for the variables that they contain. These specifications are the same as those described above in Section 3.1.1, and require similar action. In addition, you need to specify whether your data is arranged variable by variable, or by observations, and whether its format is free or fixed.

**Data is organized by variable:** This option should be chosen if all the observations on the first variable appear in the file before the observations on the second variable are entered, and so on.

**Data is organized by observations:** This option should be chosen if the first observations on all of the variables appear in the file before the second observations are entered, and so on.

As an example, suppose you have the following data on variables VAR1 and VAR2 over the period 1980 to 1983 inclusive on your file:

| Period | VAR1 | VAR2 |
|---|---|---|
| 1980 | 23 | 45 |
| 1981 | 26 | 50 |
| 1982 | 30 | 52 |
| 1983 | 40 | 60 |

If your data appear on the file as

```
23 26 30 40
45 50 52 60
```

then your data are organized by variable. But if your data appear on the file as

```
23 45
26 50
30 52
40 60
```

then your data are organized by observations.

**Free format:** Choose this option if the data appear in the file with one item separated from another by a space, a comma, or an end of line.

**Fixed format:** The only time you need to choose this option is when the data are packed into the file without any such spacing, or have a particular layout specified according to one of the FORTRAN format statements. Users who are not familiar with formatted data are advised to consult a FORTRAN manual.

Once you have made all your choices, click OK. The program starts reading the data from the file and, if successful, presents you with the Command Editor. However, if the information on the file does not match what has been supplied, then you will get an error message. Click OK to return to the Open dialog and start again.

### 3.1.4 Inputting data from a special *Microfit* file saved previously

You are likely to load this type of file the second or subsequent time you use *Microfit*, assuming you have previously saved a file as a special (i.e. 'non-text') *Microfit* file. If a correct filename is specified, the file is loaded and you are presented with the Command Editor.

*Warning:* A special *Microfit* data file must have the file extension .FIT. Special .FIT files created on earlier versions of *Microfit* can be read in *Microfit* 4.0, but the reverse is not possible: special *Microfit* files created using the current version of the package *cannot* be read into *Microfit* versions 3.0 to 3.24.

### 3.1.5 Inputting data from CSV files

These files are in ASCII (text) formats and are usually created by spreadsheet packages. Before they can be read into *Microfit* they must have the following structure:

1. The file should be organized so that columns are variables and rows are observations.
2. The first row of the file must contain the variable names, followed by optional descriptions and separated by spaces. Alternatively, the first row could contain the variable names, with their descriptions given on a second row immediately below the variable names.
3. The first column of the file must contain dates or if undated the observation numbers. Acceptable examples of dates are:

   1990, 70H1, 1983Q2, 76M12, 30/7/83, 34-7-2001, May-90, 951103

   Note that the separator for the values/observations for each row in the above files can be a comma, a tab, or spaces.

### 3.1.6 Inputting data from AREMOS (TSD) files

Files created by the AREMOS package are in the time series data (TSD) format.

Note that only TSD files containing data with the same frequency, namely annual, half-yearly, quarterly, or monthly observations, can be read into *Microfit*.

### 3.1.7 Pasting data into *Microfit* from the clipboard

Data copied from a standard Windows spreadsheet package, such as Microsoft Excel, to the clipboard, can be pasted from the clipboard into *Microfit*.

To paste data from the clipboard into the Data Editor, choose Paste Data from the Edit Menu.

This opens the New data set dialog. The data frequency fields are at the top of the dialog, with fields for start and end dates, and number of variables below.

Choose the frequency of your data by clicking the appropriate radio button (e.g. quarterly), and enter the start and end dates (giving a figure for half years, quarters, or months, if necessary). For undated observations, enter the number of observations.

For example, if monthly data from March 1979 to August 1996 are to be input via the clipboard, enter the start year 1979 and the start month 3; then enter the end year 1996 and the end month 8. (For more information on data frequency choices, see Section 3.1.1.)

You also need to specify the number of variables being imported into *Microfit*. Type the number into the Number of variables field.

When you have finished entering your information, click OK.

You are now required to specify whether the variable names (up to nine characters) and/or variable descriptions (up to 80 characters for each variable) have also been copied to the clipboard. You need to specify whether the first column on the clipboard consists of dates (or observation numbers in the case of undated data).

This relates to the format in which your data appear on the clipboard. The information on the clipboard could consist of numbers only, such that each column represents observations on a particular variables. Alternatively, the variables names could be supplied in the first row and (optionally) the second row could include the descriptions of the variables. If the first column consists of dates or observation numbers, *Microfit* needs to know about it (although in that case the information in the first column does not get used by *Microfit*.)

*Note:* It is always possible to switch back and forth to the spreadsheet application in order to inspect or change the contents of the clipboard so that the necessary information can be supplied to *Microfit*.

The data are pasted in to the Data Editor. Move to the Data Editor (click DATA) to check that the data have been correctly formatted. If you are satisfied, click CLOSE. If not, try to paste in the data again, making different choices about how they are formatted.

*Warning:* It is not possible to import/export more than approximately 32K of data via the clipboard. For importing large data sets, use your spreadsheet package to save the data in a comma delimited values (.CSV) file, then load it into *Microfit* using the Open... option from the File Menu: see Section 3.1.5.)

### 3.1.8 Copying data from *Microfit* to the clipboard

To copy a data set from the Data Editor to the clipboard, move to the Data Editor and choose Copy from the Edit Menu. A dialog appears giving you various choices about how much of the data you want to copy and in what format.

The complete data set is selected by default. If you want to copy less than the full set, specify the first and last variable and/or observation by clicking on the appropriate field and choosing an option from the list.

By default, variable names are copied to the first row of the clipboard and variable descriptions are copied to the second row. If you want to disable either of these options, uncheck the appropriate checkbox.

When you are satisfied with all the choices you have made, click OK.

*Warning:* It is not possible to import/export more than approximately 32K of data via the clipboard. For importing large data sets, use your spreadsheet package to save the data in a comma delimited values (.CSV) file, then load it into *Microfit* using the Open... option from the File Menu: see Section 3.1.5.)

## 3.2 Adding two data files

You can add two *Microfit*t files containing the same variables or add the variables from one *Microfit* file to another.

To add two files, load the first file into *Microfit* in the usual way. Then select Add... from the Edit Menu, and choose the file you want to add to your existing file from the Open dialog.

If the file contains the same variables, data frequency, and differently dated observations (or any number of undated observations), the data are combined.

If the file contains different variables, but the same data frequency, the data are added to one another.

If the data are incompatible in any way, a warning message is displayed.

### 3.2.1 Adding two special *Microfit* files containing the same variables

Adding two data files containing different observations on the same variables is particularly useful for extension and/or revision of data in either direction (i.e. backward or forward), and for stacking of undated (e.g. cross-sectional) data. In the case of files containing dated and overlapping observations the second file that you specify should contain the most recent information. The content of the first file which overlaps with the second file will be overwritten.

As an example, suppose you have a special *Microfit* file (SET1.FIT) which contains annual observations for the period 1970 to 1978 inclusive on the variables C, S, and Y:

| Obs | C | S | Y |
|---|---|---|---|
| 1970 | 57814.0 | 0.0908 | 63585.0 |
| 1971 | 59724.0 | 0.0747 | 64544.0 |
| 1972 | 63270.0 | 0.0989 | 70214.0 |
| 1973 | 66332.0 | 0.1163 | 75059.0 |
| 1974 | 65049.0 | 0.1215 | 74049.0 |
| 1975 | 60000.0 | 0.1429 | 70000.0 |
| 1976 | 60000.0 | 0.1429 | 70000.0 |
| 1977 | 60000.0 | 0.1429 | 70000.0 |
| 1978 | 60000.0 | 0.1429 | 70000.0 |

Consider now a second special *Microfit* file called SET2.FIT which contains revised and updated observations on the same variables C, S, and Y over the period 1975 to 1980.

| Obs | C | Y | S |
|---|---|---|---|
| 1975 | 64652.0 | 74005.0 | 0.1264 |
| 1976 | 64707.0 | 73437.0 | 0.1189 |
| 1977 | 64517.0 | 72288.0 | 0.1075 |
| 1978 | 68227.0 | 78259.0 | 0.1282 |
| 1979 | 71599.0 | 83666.0 | 0.1442 |
| 1980 | 17550.0 | 84771.0 | 0.1560 |

Starting with file SET1.FIT and adding the file SET2.FIT to it creates the following 'combined' data set:

| Obs | C | Y | S |
|---|---|---|---|
| 1970 | 57814.0 | 63585.0 | 0.0908 |
| 1971 | 59724.0 | 64544.0 | 0.0747 |
| 1972 | 63270.0 | 70214.0 | 0.0989 |
| 1973 | 66332.0 | 75059.0 | 0.1163 |
| 1974 | 65049.0 | 74049.0 | 0.1215 |
| 1975 | 64652.0 | 74005.0 | 0.1264 |
| 1976 | 64707.0 | 73437.0 | 0.1189 |
| 1977 | 64517.0 | 72288.0 | 0.1075 |
| 1978 | 68227.0 | 78259.0 | 0.1282 |
| 1979 | 71599.0 | 83666.0 | 0.1442 |
| 1980 | 71550.0 | 84771.0 | 0.1560 |

Notice that the observations for the period 1975 to 1978 in the first file (SET1.FIT) which overlap with the observations in the second file (SET2.FIT) are overwritten by the corresponding observations in the second file. Also note that the order of variables in the combined data set is the same as that of the second file. *Remember to save the combined data set as a special Microfit file!*

In the case of data files with non-overlapping observations, the data gaps (if any) will be shown by the string *NONE*, indicating missing observations. For example, combining the files

| First file | | | Second file | | |
|---|---|---|---|---|---|
| Obs | X1 | X2 | Obs | X1 | X2 |
| 1960 | 2.0 | 10.0 | 1965 | 10.0 | 25.0 |
| 1961 | 3.0 | 20.0 | 1966 | 20.0 | 35.0 |
| 1962 | 4.0 | 30.0 | 1967 | 22.0 | 45.0 |

gives the combined data set

| Obs | X1 | X2 |
|---|---|---|
| 1960 | 2.0 | 10.0 |
| 1961 | 3.0 | 20.0 |
| 1962 | 4.0 | 30.0 |
| 1963 | *NONE* | *NONE* |
| 1964 | *NONE* | *NONE* |
| 1965 | 10.0 | 25.0 |
| 1966 | 20.0 | 35.0 |
| 1967 | 22.0 | 45.0 |

In the case of data files containing undated observations (e.g. cross-sectional data), the use of this option has the effect of stacking the observations in the two special *Microfit* files. This facility is particularly useful for pooling cross-sectional and time series data. For example, combining the following two special *Microfit* files containing *undated* observations:

| First file | | | Second file | | |
|---|---|---|---|---|---|
| Obs | PU | PS | Obs | PU | PS |
| 1 | 3.0 | 66.0 | 1 | 16.0 | 71.0 |
| 2 | 3.0 | 66.0 | 2 | 25.0 | 64.0 |
| 3 | 9.0 | 62.0 | 3 | 24.0 | 64.0 |
| 4 | 9.0 | 64.0 | 4 | 22.0 | 64.0 |
| | | | 5 | 12.0 | 70.0 |
| | | | 6 | 13.0 | 66.0 |

results in a data set which appends the observations in the second file to the end of the observations in the first file.

Only *Microfit* files with the same data frequencies can be combined. For example, a data set containing annual observations cannot be combined with a data set containing quarterly or monthly observations.

### 3.2.2 Adding two *Microfit* files containing different variables

Combining two files containing different variables but the same data frequency allows you to add new variables to your current data set. The new variables should already have been stored in a special *Microfit* file. If you wish to add variables to your data set from the keyboard, you should use the ADD command in the Command Editor and then use the DATA button to input values for the new variable just added to the workspace.[2]

When using this option the following points are worth bearing in mind:

1. The current data set and the special *Microfit* file to be added to it should have the same data frequencies, otherwise an error message will be displayed.
2. The current data set and the special *Microfit* file need not cover the same time periods.

[2]See Chapter 4 for details of data processing using the Command Editor.

As an example, suppose your current data set contains

| Obs | X | Y |
|---|---|---|
| 1960 | 34.0000 | 76.0000 |
| 1961 | 25.0000 | 84.0000 |
| 1962 | 76.0000 | 90.0000 |

and you have a special *Microfit* file containing variables A and B over the period 1959 to 1963.

The special *Microfit* file to be added to the current data set contains

| Obs | A | B |
|---|---|---|
| 1959 | 20.0000 | 72.0000 |
| 1960 | 40.0000 | 98.0000 |
| 1961 | 50.0000 | 76.0000 |
| 1962 | 30.0000 | 45.0000 |
| 1963 | 56.0000 | 87.0000 |

If you now add the files the above special *Microfit* file is added to your current data set, and your new current data set is

| Obs | X | Y | A | B |
|---|---|---|---|---|
| 1959 | *NONE* | *NONE* | 20.0000 | 72.0000 |
| 1960 | 34.0000 | 76.0000 | 40.0000 | 98.0000 |
| 1961 | 25.0000 | 84.0000 | 50.0000 | 76.0000 |
| 1962 | 76.0000 | 90.0000 | 30.0000 | 45.0000 |
| 1963 | *NONE* | *NONE* | 56.0000 | 87.0000 |

## 3.3 Using the box (screen) editors in *Microfit*

At various stages during the processing of your data you will need to enter text into an on-screen editor box, such as the Command Editor. Text can be edited in the usual way, using the Cut, Paste, and Copy options from the Edit Menu or their equivalent buttons , , and .

To scroll through the contents of the current editor, use the mouse or the cursor keys. To scroll up or down a screen page, press **PgUp** or **PgDn**. To scroll to the top or bottom of the editor text, press **Ctrl+Home** or **Ctrl+End**.

When you have finished using the current editor, click the GO, START, or OK button as appropriate.

You can change the font of text displayed in the box editors using the Font... option from the Edit menu (see Section 2.3.4).

To clear a box editor completely, click .

## 3.4 Saving data

You can save your current data set (the data on *Microfit*'s workspace), in several different formats: in an ASCII (or text) file, in a special *Microfit* file for use in subsequent *Microfit* sessions, in a comma separated values (CSV) file for exporting data into spreadsheet packages such as Microsoft *Excel*, or in an AREMOS (TSD) file.

To save your current data file, select Save as... from the File Menu or click the [save] button.

When the Save as dialog appears, select the typeof file in which you want to save your data from the drop-down list at the base of the dialog, choose the drive and directory in which you want to save the data, and type in a filename in the usual way. Click OK.

If you are working with a file you have already saved once, you save it again by choosing Save from the File Menu.

### 3.4.1 Saving data in a raw data (ASCII) file

You can save your data in an ASCII (i.e. text) file for the purpose of exporting it to other programs or computers that are not capable of reading CSV files (see Section 3.4.3). If you choose this option you are asked to type the start and finish of the subset of observations to be saved, whether you want to save your data variable by variable or by observations, and whether you want to save your data in fixed or free format.

*Notes*

1. The start and the finish of the subset of observations to be saved should fall within the specified range (i.e. between the minimum and maximum values).
2. *Microfit* will automatically affix the extension .DAT. An alternative cannot be used.
3. A raw data file does not contain any information on the frequency of your data, variable names, or their descriptions. It only contains numbers or 'raw' data.
4. When saving raw data files *Microfit* replaces missing data, i.e. *NONE* values, by the number 8934567.0.

### 3.4.2 Saving data in a special *Microfit* file

You can save your data in a special *Microfit* file for use in subsequent sessions. In addition to data, special *Microfit* files also contain other important information, namely on data frequency, time periods, variable names and their descriptions (if any).

*Notes*

1. If you specify a file that already exists, you will be prompted to confirm that you wish to overwrite it.

2. *Microfit* automatically affixes the file extension FIT to files saved as special *Microfit* files. An alternative cannot be used.
3. Special *Microfit* files saved using earlier versions of *Microfit* (versions 3.24 and lower) can still be used in *Microfit* 4. However, special *Microfit* files created in *Microfit* 4.0 cannot be used in the earlier versions.

### 3.4.3 Saving data in a comma separated values (CSV) file

This file format is useful when you wish to export the data on *Microfit*'s workspace to *Excel* or other software programs. *Microfit* automatically gives the file the extension .CSV. An alternative extension cannot be used. The CSV files created by *Microfit* 4.0 contain information in ASCII (raw text) on data frequencies (undated, yearly, quarterly, etc.), variable names, and their descriptions (if any).

### 3.4.4 Saving data in an AREMOS (TSD) file

You can save data from *Microfit*'s workspace as a time series data (TSD) file for export into the AREMOS package. The file extension .TSD is given by default. An alternative extension cannot be used.

## 3.5 Starting with a new data set

Suppose you wish to abandon your current data set and start with a new data set without exiting *Microfit*. To enter your data from the keyboard, choose New... from the File Menu. To open an existing file, click the [open] button or choose Open... from the File Menu.

*Warning:* Before starting with a new data set make sure that your current data set is saved. To save your data, use the Save or the Save as... option from the File Menu.

# 4

# Data Processing and Preliminary Data Analysis

When your data has been successfully read in *Microfit*, the program opens the Command Editor. This is *Microfit*'s gateway to data transformations and preliminary data analyses. The main part of the screen is where you enter your commands. Various buttons appear along the top, the base, and to the right of the editor box. To return to the Command Editor if it is not displayed on screen, click the Process button.

The rectangular buttons across the top of the Command Editor are used to access other parts of the application.

To view your variables, and edit their names and/or descriptions, click the Variables button. To return to the Data Editor to edit your data, click the Data button.

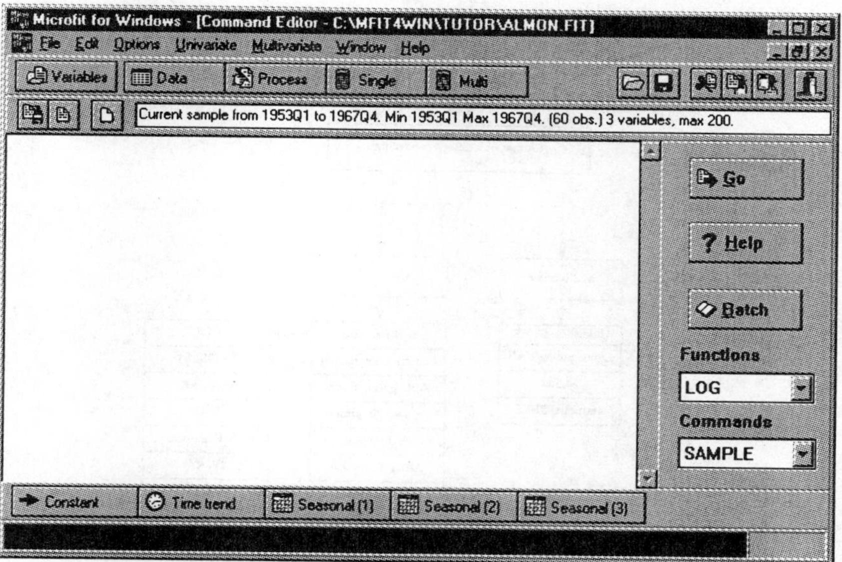


Figure 4.1: The Command Editor

To access the Single Equation Estimation window, click the [Single] button. The Single Equation Estimation options can also be accessed directly using the Univariate Menu option on the main menu bar. (For more information on these estimation options, see Chapter 6.)

To access the System Estimation window, click the [Multi] button. The System Estimation functions can also be accessed directly using the Multivariate Menu option on the main menu bar. (For more information on these estimation options see Chapter 7.)

The buttons along the base of the screen allow you to create constants, time trends, and seasonal dummies. These functions can also be accessed via the Edit Menu; they are described in Section 4.1.

You can type formulae and commands directly into the Command Editor (see Section 4.2). The different formulae need to be separated by semicolons (;).

You can see lists of available functions and commands using the drop-down lists on the right of the editor. Click on the appropriate box to view its list. To select a function or command, highlight it in the list by clicking on it and press **Enter**. Functions and commands are discussed in Sections 4.3 and 4.4.

## 4.1 Creating constant terms, time trends, and seasonal dummies

The buttons along the base of the Command Editor allow you to create constants, time trends, and seasonal dummies. Equivalent options are found in the Edit Menu.

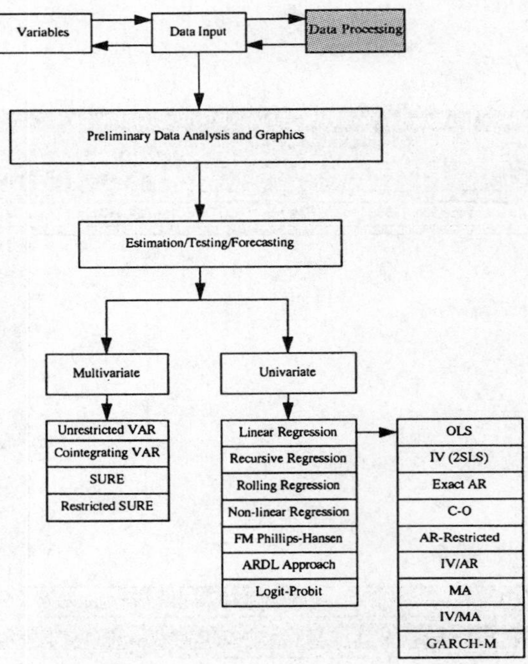


Chart 1: The flow chart of functions in *Microfit*

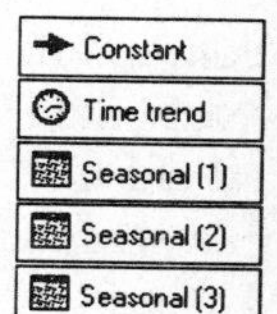


Click here to create a constant.
To create a time trend, use this button.
Click this button to create (0,1) seasonal dummies.
Creates centred seasonal dummies.
Creates seasonal dummies relative to the last season.

These options enable you to create a constant (or an intercept) term, a linear time trend, or seasonal dummies with the frequency of your choice, for use with quarterly or monthly observations.

### 4.1.1 Creating a constant (intercept) term

To create a constant (intercept) term, click the [Constant] button or choose Constant (intercept) term from the Edit Menu. *Microfit* creates a constant term (i.e. a variable with all its elements equal to unity) and asks you to supply a name for it.

### 4.1.2 Creating a time trend

If you click [Time trend] or choose Time trend from the Edit Menu, *Microfit* creates a time trend and asks you to supply a name for it. The time trend variable begins with the value of one at the start of the sample and increases in steps of one.

### 4.1.3 Creating (0, 1) seasonal dummies

To create traditional (0, 1) seasonal dummies, click the [Seasonal (1)] button or choose Seasonal dummies (0, 1) from the Edit Menu. Each seasonal dummy created has the value of unity in the season under consideration and zeros elsewhere. In the case of quarterly observations seasonal dummies created by this option will be

| Obs | S1 | S2 | S3 | S4 |
|---|---|---|---|---|
| 80q1 | 1 | 0 | 0 | 0 |
| 80q2 | 0 | 1 | 0 | 0 |
| 80q3 | 0 | 0 | 1 | 0 |
| 80q4 | 0 | 0 | 0 | 1 |
| 81q1 | 1 | 0 | 0 | 0 |
| 81q2 | 0 | 1 | 0 | 0 |
| 81q3 | 0 | 0 | 1 | 0 |
| 81q4 | 0 | 0 | 0 | 1 |

When you choose this option, you are asked to specify the periodicity of your seasonal variables. When your data are undated or are ordered annually you can choose any periodicity. But for other data frequencies the program automatically creates seasonal dummies with periodicities equal to the frequency of your data, and presents you with a screen editor containing default names for the seasonal dummies. For example, for half-yearly data the periodicity will be 2 and the default variable names S1 and S2; for quarterly data the periodicity will be 4 and the default variable names S1, S2, S3, and S4; and for monthly data the periodicity will be 12 and the default variable names, S1, S2, . . ., S12.

Notice that in each case the sum of the seasonal dummies will add up to unity, and their inclusion in a regression equation containing an intercept (constant) term will cause regressors to be perfectly multicollinear. To avoid this problem, drop one of the seasonal dummies, or use the seasonal dummies created using the [Seasonal (3)] button (see section 4.1.5).

### 4.1.4 Creating centred seasonal dummies

Clicking the [Seasonal (2)] button, or choosing the Seasonal dummies, Centred option from the Edit Menu, generates seasonal dummies centred at zero. For example, in the case of quarterly observations the centred seasonal dummies will be:

| Obs | SC1 | SC2 | SC3 | SC4 |
|---|---|---|---|---|
| 80q1 | 0.75 | −0.25 | −0.25 | −0.25 |
| 80q2 | −0.25 | 0.75 | −0.25 | −0.25 |
| 80q3 | −0.25 | −0.25 | 0.75 | −0.25 |
| 80q4 | −0.25 | −0.25 | −0.25 | 0.75 |
| 81q1 | 0.75 | −0.25 | −0.25 | −0.25 |
| 81q2 | −0.25 | 0.75 | −0.25 | −0.25 |
| 81q3 | −0.25 | −0.25 | 0.75 | −0.25 |
| 81q4 | −0.25 | −0.25 | −0.25 | 0.75 |

When you choose this option you will be presented with a screen editor containing the default names SC1, SC2, etc. Click [OK] to accept or edit the default variable names and then click [OK].

### 4.1.5 Creating seasonal dummies relative to the last season

Clicking the [Seasonal (3)] button, or choosing Seasonal dummies, Relative to last season from the Edit Menu, creates seasonal dummies relative to the last season, which are transformations of (0,1) seasonal dummies. For example, in the case of quarterly observations it generates the following seasonal dummies:

$$SR1 = S1 - S4$$
$$SR2 = S2 - S4$$
$$SR3 = S3 - S4$$

where S1, S2, S3, S4 are the (0, 1) dummies created using the [Seasonal (1)] button. These relative seasonal dummies can be included along with a constant (intercept) term in a regression equation and their coefficients provide estimates of the first three seasonal effects (say $\alpha_1, \alpha_2$, and $\alpha_3$). The effect of the last season can be computed as $-(\alpha_1 + \alpha_2 + \alpha_3)$. This procedure restricts the sum of the seasonal effects to be zero. A similar logic also applies to monthly or half-yearly observations. For monthly observations, 11 relative seasonal dummies defined as SR1 = S1 – S12, SR2 = S2 – S12, etc. will be created. Once again S1, S2, etc. are (0, 1) monthly seasonal dummies, which can be created using, for example, the Seasonal (1) button (see Section 4.1.3).

## 4.2 Typing formulae in *Microfit*

The Command Editor is automatically displayed in the main window when you open a data set. To return to the Command Editor from another part of the application, click the Process button. The Command Editor is where you can type one or more formula(e) or command(s). The different formulae need to be separated by semicolons (;). The formulae can be as complicated as you wish and, with the help of nested parentheses, you can carry out complicated transformations on one line, using standard arithmetic operators such as +, −, /, *, and a wide range of built-in functions. For example, to create a new variable (e.g. XLOG) which is the logarithm of an existing variable (e.g. X), you need to type

XLOG = LOG(X)

into the box editor. You can then execute the formula by clicking the GO button. This operation places the natural logarithm of X in XLOG. The program adds the extra variable (XLOG) to the list of variables; click the Variables button to display the list in the Variables window. To view the values for XLOG, click the Data button. Scroll through the data to find the new variable if necessary. To exit the Variables window and return to the Command Editor, click CLOSE.

In this version of *Microfit* it is also possible to enter two or more formulae/commands in the box editor before carrying out the operations. Suppose you have annual observations on US output (USGNP) over the period 1950 to 1994, and you wish to compute the percentage rate of change of the variable USGNP, and compute its mean and standard deviations over the period 1970 to 1990. You need to type the following operations in the box editor:

g = 100 * (USGNP – USGNP(– 1))/USGNP(– 1);
**SAMPLE** 1970 1985; **COR** g

and then click GO to carry out the required operations. Notice that mistakes can be corrected with little effort. *Microfit* does not automatically clear the Command Editor so you can edit any mistakes that you find without having to retype all the formulae or commands. You can save the content of the

Command Editor in a file for later use (see Section 4.2.1). To clear the editor completely, click [icon].

The following points are worth bearing in mind when entering formulae/ commands:

1. Upper- and lower-case letters are equivalent. So, the above operation could be put into effect by typing

   xlog = log(x) GO

2. The new variable XLOG is added to the list of variables on the workspace, but needs to be saved in a special *Microfit* file if you wish to use it in subsequent sessions. (See Section 3.4.2 on how to save a file as a special *Microfit* file.)
3. If one or more observations of X are negative, the program still creates the new variable XLOG but enters the symbol *NONE* for the negative observations.
4. If you attempt to take the logarithm of a non-existent variable you will see the error message

   *Error in formula or command OR ";" missing*

Examples of other data transformation are as follows:

Y = 2 * X + (Z/3) − 5 GO

This creates a new variable called Y which is equal to twice X plus a third of Z minus 5. An error message is generated if X and/or Z do not exist

Y = X^3.25 GO

This raises X to the power 3.25 and places the result in Y (on some keyboards the symbol ↑ is used in place of ^).

X1 = X(−1) GO

This generates first-order lagged values of X and places the results in the variable X1. The initial value, if undefined, will be set equal to *NONE*. For higher order lagged values of X, you need to specify the order in parentheses. For example, to create third-order lagged values of X in X3, you should type

X3 = X(−3) GO

It is also possible to generate lead values of a variable of any arbitrary order. For example,

XF2 = X(+2) GO

creates the second-order lead of X and places the results in variable XF2. In this example the undefined final two observations of XF2 will be set equal to *NONE*

INPT = 1 GO

This creates a constant (intercept) term called INPT with all its elements equal to 1.

You can also create linear or quadratic time trends in the Command Editor. Suppose you have a set of monthly observations over the period 1965m1 to 1995m12, and you wish to create a linear trend variable, say T, starting with the value of 1 in January of 1974. Type

**SAMPLE** 74m1 95m12; T = CSUM(1) GO

The variable T now contains the values of 1, 2, 3, etc. for the months 74m1, 74m2, 74m3, etc. The values of T for the months prior to 1974 will be set to *NONE*, unless you specify otherwise. CSUM(•) is the 'cumulative sum function' described below in Section 4.3.4.

### 4.2.1 Printing, saving, viewing, and copying files

You can save the content of the Command Editor or any other box editor in a file for later use by clicking the button. Such a file will be saved with extension .EQU. To load a file you saved previously, click the button. You are presented with an Open file dialog displaying the files with the extension .EQU. Choose the location and name of the file in the usual way.

To view, copy, or save the contents of a saved file (without loading it into the editor), choose the View... option from the File Menu. Choose the file you want from the dialog in the usual way. It is displayed in the View window.

To print the contents of the View window, click and make the appropriate selections from the Print dialog.

You can copy text from the View window to the clipboard or to a new file of the same type. First, highlight the text you want to copy. To save it to a file, click the button and specify a name and location for your saved file. To copy it to the clipboard, click the button.

To edit the font of text displayed in the window, click the A button. A standard Windows font dialog is displayed. Make your choices in the usual way and click OK.

## 4.3 Using built-in functions in *Microfit*

Standard mathematical functions, namely LOG (logarithm function), EXP (exponential function), COS (cosine function), SIN (sine function), SQRT (square roots operator), and ABS (absolute value operator), can also be used in a formula.

In addition to the above standard functions, several other functions can also be used in a formula. A brief description is given in Sections 4.3.1 to 4.3.23. For a list of available functions, click the Functions field to the right of the Command Editor box and scroll through the drop-down list. To copy a function from the list to the Command Editor box, highlight it by clicking on it and press **Enter**.

### 4.3.1 Function ABS

The absolute value function. Example:

$$Y = 2 + 3 * ABS(X) \quad \boxed{GO}$$

### 4.3.2 Function COS

The cosine function. Example:

$$Y = 2 + 3.5 * COS(5 + 2 * X) \quad \boxed{GO}$$

### 4.3.3 Function CPHI

This is the cumulative standard normal function so that CPHI(X) represents the integral between minus infinity to X of the standard normal distribution. Examples:

$$Y = CPHI(0.0) \quad \boxed{GO}$$

returns the value of 0.5 for Y.

$$Y = CPHI(w + 2 * (z1/z2)) \quad \boxed{GO}$$

first computes the expression inside the brackets, and then returns the values of the integral of the standard normal distribution from minus infinity to $w + 2 * (z1/z2)$.

### 4.3.4 Function CSUM

This function, when applied to the variable X, calculates the cumulative sum of X. For example, if X = (6, 2, − 1, 3, 1), then typing the formula

$$Y = CSUM(X) \quad \boxed{GO}$$

will result in Y = (6, 8, 7, 10, 11).

The argument X can itself be a function of other variables as in the following example:

$$Y = CSUM((z - (SUM(z)/SUM(1))^2) \quad \boxed{GO}$$

Here SUM(•) is the function SUM described below (see Section 4.3.22).

### 4.3.5 Function EXP

This function takes the exponential of the expression that follows in the brackets. Example:

$$Y = 2 + 3.4 * \text{EXP}(1.5 + 4.4 * X) \quad \boxed{\text{GO}}$$

The general form of EXP(•) is given by

$$\text{EXP}(x) = 1 + x + x^2/2! + x^3/3! + \ldots$$

### 4.3.6 Function HPF

This function has the form

$$Y = \text{HPF}(X, \lambda) \quad \boxed{\text{GO}}$$

and runs the variable X through a Hodrick–Prescott filter using the parameter $\lambda$. In this function X is a vector, and $\lambda$ is a non-negative scalar (i.e. a vector with all its elements equal to $\lambda \geqslant 0$). This filter is used extensively in the real business cycle literature as a de-trending procedure (see Hodrick and Prescott 1980).

The choice of $\lambda$ depends on the frequency of the time series X. For quarterly observations Hodrick and Prescott set $\lambda = 1600$. The argument X could also be specified to be a function of other variables in the variables list. Harvey and Jaeger (1993) show that for $\lambda = 1600$ the transfer function for the HP filter peaks around 30.14 quarters (approximately 7.5 years). This suggests using the value of $\lambda = 7$ for annual observations, and $\lambda = 126\,400$ for monthly observations.[1] But in general, the optimal choice of $\lambda$ will depend on the particular time series under consideration.

For example, suppose USGNP contains quarterly observations on US aggregate output. The trend series (in logarithms) are given by

$$YT = \text{HPF}(\log(\text{USGNP}), 1600) \quad \boxed{\text{GO}}$$

To compute the filtered, or de-trended series, you need to type

$$YD = \log(\text{USGNP}) - YT \quad \boxed{\text{GO}}$$

### 4.3.7 Function INVNORM

This function computes the inverse of the cumulative standard normal distribution so that, for a given probability $p$, Y = INVNORM($p$) computes Y such that the area under the standard normal curve between minus infinity to Y is equal to $p$.

$$Y = \text{INVNORM}(0.975) \quad \boxed{\text{GO}}$$

In this example, Y is set to 1.9600, the 95 per cent critical value of the standard normal distribution. Note that $0 < p < 1$.

[1] We are grateful to Michael Binder for the estimates of $\lambda$ in the case of annual and monthly observations.

### 4.3.8 Function LOG

This function takes logarithm to the base $e$ (natural logarithm) of the expression that follows in brackets. Example:

$$Y = 2.4 + 3.5 * LOG(X + 3) \quad \boxed{GO}$$

For negative or zero values of X, this function returns the missing values *NONE*.

### 4.3.9 Function MAX

This function has the form

$$Y = MAX(X, Z) \quad \boxed{GO}$$

and places the maximum of X and Z in Y. For example, if X = (1, 7, 2, 3, 6) and Z = (6, 2, − 1, 3, 1), then Y will be set to (6, 7, 2, 3, 6).

### 4.3.10 Function MAV

This function has the form

$$Y = MAV(X, p) \quad \boxed{GO}$$

and places the $p$th order moving-average of the variable X in Y, namely

$$Y_t = \frac{1}{p}(X_t + X_{t-1} + \ldots + X_{t-p+1}).$$

Variable X could be any of the variables in the variables list or a function of them. If $p$ is not an integer, *Microfit* chooses the nearest integer to $p$ in order to carry out its computations. If $p$ is negative, this function returns the missing value *NONE*.

### 4.3.11 Function MEAN

This function, when applied to a variable X, calculates the mean of X over the specified sample period. For example,

**SAMPLE** 1970 1995; $Y = (X - MEAN(X))$ $\boxed{GO}$

generates deviations of variable X from its mean computed over the sample period 1970 to 1995 inclusive.

Note that the value of MEAN(X) will be set to *NONE* (i.e., missing) if one or more values of X are missing over the specified sample period.

### 4.3.12 Function MIN

This function has the form

Y = MIN(X, Z) [GO]

and places the minimum of X and Z in Y. The arguments X and Z themselves could be functions of other variables, as in the following example:

y = MIN((G1/G2) + 1, (H1/H2) − 1) [GO]

### 4.3.13 Function NORMAL

This function can be used to generate independent standardized normal variates (i.e. with zero means and unit variances). The function should be used in the form of NORMAL($j$) within a formula, where $j$ represents the 'seed' for the quasi-random numbers generated, and must be an integer in the range $0 < j < 32000$. By changing the value of $j$ different quasi-random number series can be generated. Examples of the use of this function are:

X = NORMAL(1); Y = 2 + 3.5 * NORMAL(124) + Z [GO]

*Warning:* The function UNIFORM and NORMAL must not be used in SIM or SIMB commands!

### 4.3.14 Function ORDER

This function has the form

Y = ORDER(X, Z) [GO]

and orders X according to the sorting implied by Z, where Z is sorted in an ascending order. The result is placed in Y. For example, if X = (1, 7, 2, 3, 6) and Z = (6, 2, − 1, 3, 1), then Y will be set to (2, 6, 7, 3, 1).

Clearly, as in the case of other functions, the arguments of the function, namely X and Z, could themselves be functions of other variables.

### 4.3.15 Function PTTEST

This function has the form

T = PTTEST(Y, X) [GO]

and returns the Pesaran–Timmermann (1992) statistic for a non-parametric test of association between the variables Y and X. Under the null hypothesis that X and Y are distributed independently, PTTEST(X, Y) has a standard normal distribution in large samples. For example, for a two-sided test, the hypothesis that Y and X are statistically independent will be rejected if PTTEST is larger than 1.96 in absolute value. This function returns the value of *NONE* if the observations in Y and/or X do not change signs over the specified sample period.

### 4.3.16 Function RANK

This function, if applied to the variable X, gives the ranks associated with the elements of X, when X is sorted in an ascending order. For example, if $X = (6, 2, -1, 3, 1)$ then typing the formula:

$$Y = \text{RANK}(X) \quad \boxed{\text{GO}}$$

will give $Y = (5, 3, 1, 4, 2)$.

### 4.3.17 Function RATE

This function has the form

$$\text{PIZ} = \text{RATE}(Z) \quad \boxed{\text{GO}}$$

and computes the percentage rate of change of Z and places the result in PIZ. More specifically, PIZ will be computed as:

$$\text{PIZ} = 100 * (Z - Z(-1))/Z(-1)$$

with its initial value set equal to *NONE*.

An alternative approximate method of computing rate of change in a variable would be to use changes in logarithms, namely

$$\text{PIZX} = 100 * (\log(Z/Z(-1)) \quad \boxed{\text{GO}}$$

Both approximations are reasonably close to one another for values of PIZ and PIZX around 20 per cent or less.

The argument of this function, namely $Z$, can itself be a function of other variables, as in the following example:

$$Y = \text{Rate}(W + U/V) \quad \boxed{\text{GO}}$$

### 4.3.18 Function SIN

This function takes the sine of the expression that follows in brackets. Example:

$$Y = 2 + 3 * \text{SIN}(5 + 7 * X) \quad \boxed{\text{GO}}$$

### 4.3.19 Function SORT

This function, when applied to the variable X, will sort X in an ascending order. For example, if X = (6, 2, − 1, 3, 1) then typing

$$Y = \text{SORT}(X) \quad \boxed{\text{GO}}$$

will set Y = (−1, 1, 2, 3, 6), while:

$$Z = -\text{SORT}(-X) \quad \boxed{\text{GO}}$$

will sort X in descending order in Z so that Z = (6, 3, 2, 1, − 1).

In the example

$$Y = \text{SORT}(2 + w/z) \quad \boxed{\text{GO}}$$

the expression 2 + w/z will be first computed and the resultant expression will be sorted in Y as above.

### 4.3.20 Function SQRT

This function takes the square root of the expression that follows in the brackets. Example:

$$Y = 3 + 5 * \text{SQRT}(X) \quad \boxed{\text{GO}}$$

For negative values of X, this function returns the missing values *NONE*.

### 4.3.21 Function STD

This function, when applied to the variable X, calculates the standard deviation of X over the specified sample period. For example,

**SAMPLE** 1970 1995;

$$Z = (X - \text{MEAN}(X))/\text{STD}(X) \quad \boxed{\text{GO}}$$

places the standardized values of X over the period 1970 to 1995 (inclusive) in the variable Z.

Note that the value of STD(X) will be set to *NONE* (i.e. missing) if one or more values of X are missing over the specified sample period.

### 4.3.22 Function SUM

This function first calculates the expression specified within closed brackets immediately following it, and then computes the sum of the elements of the result over the relevant sample period. Examples of the use of this function are:

**SAMPLE** 1960 1970; XBAR = SUM(X)/SUM(1);
XD = X − XBAR; YBAR = SUM(Y)/SUM(1); YD = Y − YBAR;
BYX = SUM(XD * YD)/SUM(XD * XD) [GO]

In the above examples, SUM(X) is a vector with all its elements equal to the sum of the elements of X over the period 1960 to 1970. SUM(1) is equal to the number of observations in the sample period (i.e., 11). XBAR is, therefore, equal to the arithmetic mean of X, computed over the specified sample period. XD and YD are deviations of X and Y from their respective means and BYX is the ordinary least squares (OLS) estimate of the coefficients of X in the regression of Y on X (including an intercept term).

### 4.3.23 Function UNIFORM

This function can be used to generate independent random numbers from a uniform distribution within the range 0 to 1. The function should be used in the form of UNIFORM($j$) within a formula, where $j$ represents the 'seed' for the quasi-random numbers generated, and must be an integer in the range $0 < j < 32000$. By changing the value of $j$, different quasi-random number series can be generated.

Examples of the use of this function are:

X = UNIFORM(1) [GO]
Y = 2 + 3.5 * UNIFORM(124) + Z [GO]

*Warning:* The functions UNIFORM and NORMAL must not be used in SIM or SIMB commands!

## 4.4 Using commands in *Microfit*

For a list of available commands, click the Commands field to the right of the Command Editor box and scroll through the drop-down list. To select a command from the list and copy it to the Command Editor box, highlight it and press **Enter**.

### 4.4.1 Command ADD

This command enables you to add a new variable to the list in the Variables window.

The form of this command is

**ADD** XNEW [GO]

where XNEW is the name of the new variable.

The variable is added to the Variables list and to the data in the Data Editor with all its values set to *NONE*. To add a description to your variable, click [Variables] to move to the Variables window and type in your description. To insert the values for your variable, click the [Data] button to move to the Data Editor, then click on each of the relevant cells in turn and type in the value you want.

Note that this command allows you to add one new variable at a time. If you want to add the variables from an existing *Microfit* file to your current data set, you should use the Add... option from the File Menu instead: see Section 3.2.2.

Remember to save the data set with the added variable(s) as a special *Microfit* file if you wish to use it in subsequent *Microfit* sessions.

### 4.4.2 Command ADF

This command, when followed by a variable name, displays the Dickey–Fuller (DF) and the augmented Dickey–Fuller (ADF) statistic for testing the unit root hypothesis together with the associated critical values. See Dickey and Fuller (1979) and Lesson 11.1.

For example,

**SAMPLE** 75Q1 87Q1; **ADF X** [GO]

computes the DF and the ADF test statistics of up to order 4 (i.e. the periodicity of the data) for the variable X, and displays the statistics together with their 95 per cent critical values on screen.

For models with no trends the ADF test statistic is computed as the *t*-ratio of $\rho$ in the ADF($p$) regression

$$\Delta X_t = a_0(1-\rho) - \rho X_{t-1} + \sum_{i=1}^{p} \gamma_i \Delta X_{t-i} + u_t$$

where $\Delta X_t = X_t - X_{t-1}$, and $p$ is the order of augmentation of the test. In the case of models with a deterministic linear trend, the $p$th order ADF test statistic is given by the t-ratio of $\rho$ in the ADF regression

$$\Delta X_t = a_0 + (1-\rho)a_1 T_t - \rho X_{t-1} + \sum_{i=1}^{p} \gamma_i \Delta X_{t-i} + u_t$$

where $T_t$ is a linear time trend. *Microfit* computes the ADF statistic both with and without a time trend, and also provides the Akaike information and Schwarz Bayesian criteria for selecting the order of augmentation in the ADF tests. The 95 per cent critical values for the test computed using the response surface estimates given in MacKinnon (1991, Table 1) are given at the foot of the result tables.

The ADF command can also be used to compute the augmented Dickey–Fuller test statistics, up to an order of augmentation specified by the user. The desired order should be specified in parentheses immediately after the variable name. For example,

**ADF** X(12) [GO]

gives the ADF test statistics for the variable X up to the order 12, assuming, of course, that there are enough observations.

### 4.4.3 Command BATCH

This command has the form

**BATCH** [GO]

or

**BATCH** < filename > [GO]

A shortcut to entering this command is to use the [BATCH] button. If you enter the command BATCH on its own and then click [GO] or if you click the [BATCH] button, the names of the batch files in your default directory will appear on the screen. When the batch command is followed by a filename, the instructions in the file will be carried out on the current variables list. A batch filename must have the extension .BAT.

This command allows you to place a number of commands in a file so that they are subsequently obeyed in batch mode. The legitimate instructions can either be one or more mathematical formulae and/or commands SAMPLE, DELETE, KEEP, ENTITLE, SIM, SIMB, REORDER, RESTORE, and $. When you use the command ENTITLE in batch mode you need to enter the descriptions of the variables on separate lines in exactly the same order that the variables are typed after the command. You can also write in comments in your batch file by starting your comments with the dollar sign $. Anything entered on the same line after the $ sign in the batch file will be ignored.

An example of a simple batch file is given below:

```
$ Space for comments
SAMPLE 70M1 78M5
INPT = 1
Z = X + LOG(Y)
W = X - Y
SAMPLE 75M1 78M5
ENTITLE X Y
Consumption Expenditures
Labour Income
 $ The end of BATCH file
```

Running this file with the BATCH command creates variables INPT, Z, and W from the data series X and Y, and gives the titles 'Consumption Expenditures' and 'Labour Income' to the variables X and Y respectively.

This is a useful command enabling you to carry out the same operations on different data sets or on revisions of the same data set. You can check the contents of a batch file using the View... command from the File Menu. When the dialog appears, choose Batch files from the List files of type box and select the file you want. It is displayed in the View window (see Section 4.2.1).

Notice that in *Microfit*, the commands COR, LIST, SPECTRUM, HIST, PLOT, XPLT, SCATTER, ADD, ADF, and TITLE cannot be included in the batch file.

### 4.4.4 Command COR

This command has different effects depending on whether it is followed by one variable or more. When only one variable is specified after COR, as in the example

**SAMPLE** 1 20; **COR** X [GO]

summary statistics for X (i.e. mean, standard deviation, coefficient of variation, skewness, kurtosis, minimum and maximum values) and its auto-correlation coefficients of up to the order of a third of the number of specified observations are shown on screen. If you have a graphics adaptor, the plot of the auto-correlation function will also be displayed.

The COR command can also be used to compute auto-correlation coefficients up to an order specified by the user. The desired order should be specified in parentheses immediately after the variable. For example,

**COR** X(12) [GO]

gives the auto-correlation coefficients for the variable X up to the order of 12 (assuming, of course, that there are enough observations). When the COR command is followed by two or more variables, as in the example

**COR** X Y Z [GO]

then summary statistics and the correlation coefficients for these variables, over the specified sample period, will be provided.

For the relevant formulae and appropriate references to the literature, see Section 18.1.

### 4.4.5 Command DELETE

This command enables you to delete one or more variables from the current variables list. The names of the variables to be deleted should follow the command, separated by spaces. For example,

**DELETE** X Y Z [GO]

deletes the variables X, Y, and Z from the list of existing variables. If you wish to delete a single variable, you can also type

X = [GO]

This operation has the effect of deleting variable X.

### 4.4.6 Command ENTITLE

This command allows you to enter or change the description of one or more of the variables on your work. For example, if you type

**ENTITLE** X Y Z [GO]

you are asked for the titles (or descriptions) of the variables X, Y, and Z, in that order. Note that the description of a variable can be at most 80 characters. If you type in a title which is more than 80 characters long, only the first 80 characters will be saved. If you enter the command ENTITLE on its own, namely

**ENTITLE** [GO]

you will be asked to give titles for those variables in the list which do not have them.

When a new variable is generated using the data transformation facilities, the first 80 characters after the equality sign will be automatically used as the title of the generated variable. When the variable XNEW is created by the formula

XNEW = XOLD [GO]

the title of the variable XOLD, if any, will be passed on to the new variable XNEW.

*Note:* In earlier versions of *Microfit* the maximum number of characters allowed for a description of a variable was 39.

### 4.4.7 Command HIST

When followed by a variable name, the command displays the histogram of the variable. For example

**SAMPLE** 1 20; **HIST** X [GO]

The number of bands is automatically chosen as between 6 and 15 according to the formula

$$\text{Min}\{15,\ \text{Max}(n/10, 6)\}$$

where $n$ is the total number of observations.

The HIST command can be used to plot the histograms for any numbers of intervals chosen by the user. The desired number of classes should be specified in parentheses immediately after the variable. For example:

**HIST** X(12) [GO]

See Section 5.2 for information on altering, printing, saving, or retrieving graphs.

### 4.4.8 Command KEEP

This command deletes all the variables in the variables list except those specified. For example, suppose you have 10 variables named X1, X2, . . ., X10 in your variables list, and you wish to keep only the variables X1 and X2. Type

**KEEP** X1 X2 [GO]

to keep the variables X1 and X2 only. See also command DELETE (Section 4.4.5).

### 4.4.9 Command LIST

This command allows you to inspect your data on screen and/or to save them in a file to be printed out later. If the command LIST is typed on its and you then click [GO], the values of all the variables will be displayed over the current sample period set by the SAMPLE command. If the command LIST is followed by one or more variable names, then only the values of the specified variables will be listed.

For example,

**SAMPLE** 1940 1980;
**LIST** [GO]

displays all the existing variables over the period 1940 to 1980.

**SAMPLE** 80Q1 85Q2;
**LIST** X Y Z [GO]

displays the observations on the variables X, Y, Z over the period from the first quarter of 1980 to the second quarter of 1985 inclusive.

See Chapter 5 on how to print or save the displayed observations in a result file.

### 4.4.10 Command PLOT

This command produces a line graph of up to a maximum of 50 variables against time. You must specify at least one variable name. For example

**SAMPLE** 1950 1970;
**PLOT** X [GO]

produces a plot of variable X against time over the period 1950 to 1970.

**PLOT** X1 X2 X3 X4 X5 X6 X7 X8 X9 X10 [GO]

produces a plot of the ten variables X1 to X10 against time.

*Warning*: There is a combined limit of 6000 points on any graph. This means that a graph with one line can have up to 6000 points, a graph with two lines can have up to 3000 points, and so on.

See Section 5.2 on how to alter the display of graphs.

### 4.4.11 Command REORDER

This command enables a complete reordering of *all* the observations in the variables list according to the ordering of the variable that follows the command. For example,

**REORDER** X [GO]

produces a reordering of observations according to the ordering of the observations in variable X. This command is particularly useful when analysing cross-sectional observations where you wish to carry out regression analysis on a subset of the observations. The exact nature of the particular subset of interest is defined by the ordering of the observations in the variable X.

As an example, suppose that the *undated* observations in the variables list refer to both male and female indexed by 0 and 1 respectively, stored in the variable SEX. Issuing the command

**REORDER** SEX [GO]

reorders the observations so that observations referring to females appear first. The number of such observations is equal to SUM(SEX). See the SUM function described in Section 4.3.22.

### 4.4.12 Command RESTORE

This command should be used after the REORDER command. It restores the ordering of the observations to their *original* state (i.e. before REORDER was used).

### 4.4.13 Command SAMPLE

This command can be used to change the sample period for subsequent data analysis in the Command Editor, but does not carry over to the other parts of the program. An example of the use of this command for undated observations is

**SAMPLE** 3 26 [GO]

For annual observations:

**SAMPLE** 1972 1986 [GO]

For half-yearly data:

**SAMPLE** 50H2 72H1 [GO]

For quarterly data:

**SAMPLE** 75Q1 78Q2 [GO]

For monthly data:

**SAMPLE** 70M1 80M11 [GO]

*Note:* The default century for half-yearly, quarterly, and monthly observations is taken to be the 20th century. This can be overwritten.

### 4.4.14 Command SCATTER

This command can be used to produce scatter diagram of one variable against another. When issuing this command, you must specify the two variable names exactly. For example

**SCATTER** X Y [GO]

produces a scatter plot of the variable X against the variable Y.

See Section 5.2 for details concerning adding text to, saving, retrieving, and printing graphs. Also see the *Warning* given in Section 4.4.10.

### 4.4.15 Command SIM

This is a simulation command and enables you to solve numerically any general univariate linear or non-linear difference equation. For example, to solve the non-linear difference equation

$$X(t) = 0.2X(t-1) + 0.7\log(X(t-2)) + Z$$

for $t = 3, 4, \ldots, 20$, with initial values $X(1) = 0.05$ and $X(2) = 0.10$, you need to issue the following commands:

**SAMPLE** 1 1; X = 0.05;
**SAMPLE** 2 2; X = 0.10;
**SAMPLE** 3 20; **SIM** X = .2 * X(−1) + .7 * LOG(X(−2)) + Z;
**SAMPLE** 1 20; **PLOT** X [GO]

The first four commands in the above example set the initial values for X, which are used to simulate the values of X for observations 3, 4, . . ., 20.

The following points should be borne in mind when using the SIM command:

1. When the SIM command is used, the values of the simulated variable are overwritten. To avoid this problem, one possibility would be to create a

new variable called, for example, XNEW, which contains the appropriate values, but is otherwise undefined for other periods. The SIM command can then be applied to XNEW over the sample period for which XNEW is undefined. A typical example of this procedure would be (assuming that the specified sample period runs from 1950 to 1980)

> **SAMPLE** 1950 1950; XNEW = 0.05;
> **SAMPLE** 1951 1980;
> **SIM** XNEW = 4 * XNEW(−1) * (1 − XNEW(−1)) [GO]

The above will solve the well-known chaotic bifurcation equation

$$X_t = 4X_{t-1}(1 - X_{t-1})$$

starting with the initial value $X_{1950} = 0.05$ over the period 1951 to 1980.

2. Choose your sample period carefully and make sure that well-defined initial values exist for the simulation. Otherwise, all the values of the variable being simulated will be set equal to *NONE*.
3. In the case of unstable difference equations, the use of the SIM command may cause an overflow. When the value of the simulated variable exceeds 10 to the power of 50, to prevent the program from crashing, all subsequent values will be set equal to *NONE*.

### 4.4.16 Command SIMB

This is a simulation command which allows you to solve numerically any general univariate linear or non-linear difference equation involving lead (not lagged) values of the left-hand side variable. The difference equation is solved backwards over the specified sample period. For example, to solve the linear difference equation

$$X(t) = 1.2 * X(t+1) + Z(t), \quad \text{for} \quad t = 20, 19, \ldots, 1$$

with a terminal value of 30.5 at observation 20, the following commands should be issued:

> **SAMPLE** 20 20; X = 30.5;
> **SAMPLE** 1 19; **SIMB** X = 1.2 * X(+1) + Z;
> **SAMPLE** 1 20; **PLOT** X [GO]

For more information, see the description of the SIM command in Section 4.4.15.

### 4.4.17 Command SPECTRUM

This command, when followed by a variable name, displays the estimates of the standardized spectral density function of the variable and their estimated standard errors using Bartlett, Tukey, and Parzen lag windows as in the following example:

**SAMPLE** 1 120; **SPECTRUM** X [GO]

The window size will be taken to be twice the square root of the number of specified observations. The plot of the different spectral density functions and the associated standard error bands will also be displayed.

The SPECTRUM command can be used to estimate the spectrum for a window size specified by the user. The desired window size should be specified in parentheses after the variable. For example:

**SPECTRUM** X(12) [GO]

See Section 5.2 on how to alter the display of graphs.

The algorithms used to compute the different estimates of the spectral density and the relevant references to the literature are given in Section 18.2.

### 4.4.18 Command TITLE

This command generates a list of the names of your variables, together with their descriptions, if any. If you type

**TITLE** [GO]

the names and descriptions (if any) of all your variables will be displayed. To view the description of some of your variables only, you can either type TITLE followed by the list of the variables you are interested in, or simply type the list of variables and click [GO]. For example,

**TITLE** X Y Z W [GO]

has the same effect as

X Y Z W [GO]

and generates a list and description (if any) of the variables X, Y, Z, and W.

### 4.4.19 Command XPLOT

This command can be used to plot up to a maximum of 50 variables against another variable. When issuing this command you must specify at least two variable names. For example:

**XPLOT** X Y [GO]

produces a plot of the variable X against the variable Y.

**XPLOT** X1 X2 X3 X4 X5 X6 Y [GO]

produces a plot of the variables X1, X2, X3, X4, X5, and X6 against the variable Y.

See Section 5.2 for details concerning adding text to, saving, retrieving, and printing graphs. Also see the *Warning* given in Section 4.4.10

### 4.4.20 Command &

This command is useful when preparing batch files for use with *Microfit*. It enables you to continue the list of variables appearing after the commands DELETE, KEEP, TITLE, ENTITLE, LIST, and COR on a new line. To continue the list of variables on a new line, type

**KEEP** X Y Z&
W D

This example applies the KEEP command to the variables X, Y, Z, W, and D. Similarly, the command

**COR** A B C D&
X Z

This example applies the COR command to all variables A, B, C, D, X, and Z, and computes the correlation matrix for these variables.

# 5

# Printing/Saving Results and Graphs

Output from *Microfit* appears on your screen in the form of text and graphs. These can be output to a variety of printers attached to your PC, or saved to a file for later printing or importation as a text file into word-processing packages such as Word Perfect, Microsoft Word, and Scientific Word. *Microfit* 4.0 also allows you to save regression results in equation format, which is suitable for use with modelling or simulation packages.

## 5.1 Result screens

Text output is displayed inside a results window. Scroll through the window in the usual way using the mouse and scroll bar and/or the **PgUp/Dn**, **Ctrl + Home/End** keys.

Use standard Windows editing functions to edit the contents of the results window if you wish. To copy text to the clipboard, highlight the text you want by clicking and dragging with the mouse, and click the [copy] button.

To edit the font of text displayed in the window, highlight the text you want to change, and click the [A] button. A standard Windows font dialog is displayed. Make your choices in the usual way and click [OK].

To exit the results window, click [CLOSE].

### 5.1.1 On-line printing of results

The content of each result screen can be printed separately by clicking the [print] button. Make any choices about the number of copies etc. and click [OK].

### 5.1.2 Saving results

When saving results you can save them either in 'report file' format or in 'model file' format. The former saves the content of the result screen in a text (ASCII) file for use with word-processing editors. The latter saves only the estimated coefficients in the form of a linear/non-linear regression equation.

**Saving results to a report file:** To save your results in a report file, click the [?] button. When the Save as... dialog appears, specify a filename, drive, and directory. Report files in *Microfit* are given the extension .OUT, and if you have any such files in your default directory you should see them in the list.

Suppose now that you have already opened a result file called RESULT.OUT. To add the results displayed on the screen to this existing report (or output) file, click the [+] button. You will be asked to confirm whether you wish to overwrite the file RESULT.OUT or add to it.

To view the contents of a results file, use the View... option from the File Menu. Choose the file you want from the Open dialog to display it in the View window (see Section 4.2).

The result files created on *Microfit* are in text (ASCII) format and can be edited/printed using a text editor or word-processing package.

**Saving equation specifications to a model file:** This function applies only when the displayed results contain coefficients of an estimated relation/model.

To save your results in a model or an equation file, click the [?] button. When the Save as... dialog appears, specify a filename, drive, and directory in the usual way. A menu appears giving you a choice of model file types; choose the type most suited to the package into which you want to import the file.

Model files are in text (ASCII) format and can be imported to other econometric or modelling software packages. All model files are given the extension .MOD automatically.

Once you have saved your file once, and while it is still open, you can save any further modifications to it using the [+] button.

## 5.2 Printing, saving, and retrieving graphs

The graphic facilities in *Microfit* 4.0 are considerably enhanced in comparison with earlier versions of the package. In order to take full advantage of these facilities you need at least a LaserJet or PostScript printer.

Note that there is a combined limit of 6000 points on a graph, regardless of how many lines it plots. For example a graph with one plotted line may have up to 6000 points, a graph with two plotted lines may have up to 3000 points, and so on.

### 5.2.1 Altering the display of graphs

The default graph display may be edited using the Graph Control facility. Click the [ ] button to access it.

Graph Control contains numerous options for adjusting the background, colour, axes, style, titles, etc. of your graph. Each option (e.g. Background) has its own property page; click the appropriate page tab to view it. Each property page contains a number of options; use the appropriate buttons, checkboxes, etc. to make your changes. To apply a change you have made without closing Graph Control, click the APPLY NOW button. To apply a change you have made, close Graph Control, and return to your graph, click the OK button. To exit Graph Control without implementing your changes, click CANCEL.

To minimize the graph window and reduce it to an icon, click the MINIMIZE button.

To close the window, click CLOSE.

Graph Control has its own on-line Help facility which gives detailed information about all the options available. Access it by clicking the HELP button. This Help is not *Microfit*-specific, however, so the most common functions you may want to use with *Microfit* are described here. (Headings refer to the pages which are accessed by clicking the appropriate tab.)

*Note:* There are some global settings for the graphics defaults available on the Graphics page of the Options dialog. These allow you to force a label for the last point and to use patterned lines instead of thick/thin lines (this may come out better on some printers).

**Markers:** In this page you can set the line thickness, pattern, and colour. Note that you cannot have both thick and patterned lines simultaneously. If you want some lines thick and others thin, turn thick lines on and then reduce the thickness for individual lines as required. Similarly if you want only some lines patterned, turn patterns on and set the pattern for some lines to a solid line. You should note that if you change the colour of one line, all the others will turn black and you will have to set a colour explicitly for every line.

To change the data set so that you can set colours etc. for all sets, click on the appropriate line in the box. However, it can be very difficult to select the required data set if you have a large number of points. To get around this, go to the Data page. Note the number of points in Data Dimension, and reduce this (15 is a good number to use here). Now go back to the Markers page and set up the colours etc. for all the sets. You should now return to the Data page and set Points back to the value you noted earlier.

**Style:** This allows you to set markers at each data point if required. This is only effective visually for small numbers of points. Note that if all options are switched off, you get a line graph. If you want to plot one variable against another and use markers at each point, a more effective way is to use the Microfit command SCATTER (see Section 4.4.14).

**Background:** This allows you to customize the location and appearance of elements of the graph such as the legend. If you are planning to print your graph you should note that complex shading often looks better on the screen than on a printout!

**Fonts:** Use this page to set the font and size for legends, titles etc.

**Titles:** This page allows you to change the top and bottom titles of the graph, and to add left and right titles if required.

**Axis:** Use this page to turn tick marks, labels, etc. on and off for each axis independently. Note that for some graph types, and especially if there are large numbers of points, certain operations on the x-axis may have no effect or may produce undesirable effects (for instance, a grid of 1500 lines does not look particularly good!).

*Note:* If you have more than 550 observations, by default your graphs will be plotted with the x-axis labels turned off. This is to avoid a problem observed on some computers where these graphs were plotted very slowly or not at all. You can turn the axis labels on yourself by going to the Axis page, selecting the x-axis, and checking the Show checkbox in the Labels field.

The other pages may not be as useful in conjunction with Microfit. There is no reason why you should not experiment with these settings; however, it is possible to confuse the Graph Control and appear to lose all but one set of data. If this happens to you:

1. Do not panic! Your data is still there.
2. Try resizing the graph window. This may force Graph Control to redraw all the data.

   If this doesn't work, save the graph file as a special *Microfit* graph (.MFW) file using the [icon] button.
3. Close the graph window, then reload the .MFW file using View... from the File Menu. Your graph will be redrawn using the default settings. (If you have already saved the graph as an .MFW file, the Save option is not available. Just shut the window and reload the .MFW file using View... from the File Menu.)

## 5.2.2 Printing graphs

To obtain a hard copy of the displayed graph, click the [icon] button. Make any choices about number of copies etc. and click OK.

## 5.2.3 Saving graphs

A displayed graph can be saved as a bitmap (BMP) or Windows metafile (WMF). It can also be saved as a special *Microfit* graphics file with the extension .MFW.

To save the graph as a bitmap or Windows metafile, click the [icon] button. Choose the file type you want from the drop-down list and enter a filename and location for your file before clicking OK. The graph's image only is saved.

To save the graph as a special *Microfit* graph file, click the [icon] button. Specify a filename and location, and click OK. The complete file is saved and can be loaded into *Microfit* at a later date for further editing (see Section 5.2.4).

### 5.2.4 Retrieving graphs

To retrieve a graphic file, choose View... from the File Menu. In the Open dialog, select Graph files from the List files of type box, find the location and name of the file you want, and click OK. Graphs saved in *Microfit* format in earlier versions of the program can be retrieved into *Microfit* 4.0, but you must first change their extensions from .GRP to .MFW. (This change has been made to ensure compatibility with the Windows version of the program.)

### 5.2.5 Capturing graphs to the clipboard

It is possible to capture the displayed graph to the Windows clipboard. Click the button. From the clipboard the graph may be pasted into another application in the usual way, using the special Paste option available in word processing packages such as Microsoft Word or Scientific Word.

## 5.3 Exercises using graphs

### 5.3.1 Exercise 5.1

Carry out Lesson 9.5, copy the plot of C and Y against time to the clipboard, and then try to paste it into Microsoft Word or Scientific Word. When you see the graph click the button to add a title to the graph, resize, and print.

Note that any text that you wish to add to the graph must be added in *Microfit* using Graph Control (see Section 5. 2.1). Once a graph is imported into a word-processing package you cannot add text inside the graphic box; you can only give it a title.

### 5.3.2 Exercise 5.2

Carry out Lessons 9.9 and 9.10, and save the results from both lessons in *one* file. Add titles and other descriptions to this result file by editing it and then print the file.

# PART III
# Estimation Menus

# 6

# Single-Equation Options

In this chapter we show how *Microfit* can be used to estimate a large number of single-equation econometric models, to compute diagnostic statistics for them, to carry out tests of linear or non-linear restrictions on their parameters, and to use them in forecasting. But first we review briefly the classical linear regression model and the likelihood approach that underlie the various estimation options in *Microfit*. The more technical details of the econometric methods and the computational algorithms used are given in Chapter 18 where further references to the literature can also be found.

## 6.1 The classical normal linear regression model

The econometric model underlying the linear regression estimation options in *Microfit* is the classical linear regression model. This model assumes that the relationship between $y_t$ (the dependent variable) and $x_{1t}, x_{2t}, \ldots, x_{kt}$ (the $k$ regressors) is a linear one:

$$y_t = \sum_{i=1}^{k} \beta_i x_{it} + u_t, \qquad t = 1, 2, \ldots, n \tag{6.1}$$

where $u_t$s are unobserved 'disturbance' or 'error' terms, subject to the following assumptions:

**A1: Zero mean assumption**. The disturbances $u_t$ have zero means:

$$E(u_t) = 0, \quad t = 1, 2, \ldots, n$$

**A2: Homoscedasticity assumption**. The disturbances $u_t$ have a constant conditional variance:

$$V(u_t | x_{1t}, x_{2t}, \ldots, x_{kt}) = \sigma^2, \quad \text{for all } t$$

**A3: Non-autocorrelated error assumption**. The disturbances $u_t$ are serially uncorrelated:

$$Cov(u_t, u_s) = E(u_t u_s) = 0, \qquad \text{for all } t \neq s$$

**A4: Orthogonality assumption**. The disturbances $u_t$ and the regressors $x_{1t}, x_{2t}, \ldots, x_{kt}$ are uncorrelated:

$$E(u_t | x_{1t}, x_{2t}, \ldots, x_{kt}) = 0, \quad \text{for all } t$$

**A5: Normality assumption**. The disturbances $u_t$ are normally distributed.

Adding the fifth assumption to the classical model yields the classical linear normal regression model. The latter model can also be derived using the *joint* distribution of $y_t$, $x_{1t}$, $x_{2t}$, . . ., $x_{kt}$, and by assuming that this distribution is a multivariate *normal* with constant means, variances, and covariances. In this setting the regression of $y_t$ on $x_{1t}$, $x_{2t}$, . . ., $x_{kt}$ is defined as the mathematical expectation of $y_t$ conditional on the realized values of the regressors and will be linear in the regressors. The linearity of the regression equation follows from the joint normality assumption and need not hold if this assumption is relaxed. Both of the above interpretations of the classical normal regression model have been used in the literature. (See, for example, Spanos (1986)).

In time series analysis the critical assumptions are A3 and A4. Assumption A3 is particularly important when the regression equation contains lagged values of the dependent variable, namely $y_{t-1}$, $y_{t-2}$, etc. However, even if lagged values of $y_t$s are not included among the regressors, the breakdown of assumption A3 can lead to misleading inferences; a problem recognized as early as the 1920s by Yule (1926), and known in the econometrics time series literature as the spurious regression problem.[1] The orthogonality assumption, A4, allows the empirical analysis of the relationship between $y_t$ and $x_{1t}$, $x_{2t}$, . . ., $x_{kt}$ to be carried out without fully specifying the stochastic processes generating the regressors or the 'forcing' variables. Assumption A1 is implied by A4 if a vector of ones is included among the regressors. It is therefore important that an intercept is always included in the regression model, unless it is found to be statistically insignificant. Assumption A2 specifies that $u_t$s have constant variances both conditionally and unconditionally. The assumption that the error variances are constant unconditionally is likely to be violated when dealing with cross-sectional regressions. The assumption that the conditional variance of $u_t$ is constant is often violated in analysis of financial and macro-economic time series, such as exchange rates, stock returns, and interest rates. The normality assumption A5 is important in small samples, but is not generally required when the sample under consideration is large enough. All the various departures from the classical normal regression model mentioned here can be analysed using the options that are available in *Microfit*.

### 6.1.1 Testing the assumptions of the classical model

*Microfit* enables the user to test the assumptions that underlie the classical model in a simple and straightforward manner. This type of diagnostic testing is an essential component of any applied econometric research.

[1]Champernowne (1960), and Granger and Newbold (1974) provide Monte Carlo evidence on the spurious regression problem, and Phillips (1986) establishes a number of theoretical results.

However, it is important that the outcomes of such diagnostic testing exercises are properly interpreted and acted upon.

## Guidelines

You may find the following broad guidelines useful when working with *Microfit*:

1. Rejection of a hypothesis against an alternative does not necessarily imply that the alternative hypothesis is acceptable or that it should necessarily be adopted. Rejection of a given hypothesis could be due to a number of different interlocking factors, and it is therefore important that a variety of nested and non-nested alternative explanations are considered before a firm conclusion, as to the appropriate choice of the alternative hypothesis, is reached. For example, when assumption A3 (the non-autocorrelated error assumption) is rejected it may be due to any one or a mixture of the following model misspecifications: omitted variables, structural change, misspecified dynamics, or aggregation across heterogenous groups. Rejection of the normality assumption may be due to the presence of outliers or non-linearities. Rejection of the orthogonality assumption could arise because of simultaneity, expectational effects, omitted variables, and/or misspecified dynamics.
2. A regression equation that passes all the diagnostic tests generated by *Microfit* is not necessarily a statistically adequate model, and should not be regarded as the 'true' data generating process! It is quite possible for two rival (or non-nested) models to pass all the diagnostic tests produced by *Microfit*, but for one of the models still to be rejected by the other and not vice versa.[2] The non-nested test options in *Microfit* can be used to deal with such eventualities. Even then there could be other possible models that may not have been considered or thought out by the investigator. A satisfactory econometric model should satisfy a number of quantitative and qualitative criteria, and can at best represent a reasonable approximation of one or more aspects of the reality that the investigator is interested in analyzing. Pesaran and Smith (1985) summarize these different criteria under the heading 'relevance', 'consistency', and 'adequacy'.
3. The $t$-tests on individual regression coefficients should be carried out with great care, particularly when the regressors exhibit a high degree of collinearity. It is a good practice to combine the $t$-tests on individual coefficients with F-tests of *joint* restrictions on the coefficients. It is important that the results of the individual $t$-tests (also known as separate-induced tests) and the joint tests are not in conflict. Otherwise, inferences based on individual $t$-tests can be misleading. For a

[2]As an example, see the comparative empirical analysis of the Keynesian and the neoclassical explanations of US unemployment in M. H. Pesaran (1982a, 1988), and Rush and Waldo (1988).

demonstration of this point see Lesson 10.4 on the multicollinearity problem.

### 6.1.2 Estimation of the classical linear regression model

Under the classical assumptions (A1 to A4), the estimation of the regression coefficients $\beta_1, \beta_2, \ldots, \beta_k$ is carried out by minimizing the sum of squares of the errors, $u_t$, with respect to $\beta_1, \beta_2, \ldots, \beta_k$. Writing (6.1) in matrix notations we have

$$\mathbf{y} = \mathbf{X}\boldsymbol{\beta} + \mathbf{u} \tag{6.2}$$

where

$$\underset{n\times 1}{\mathbf{y}} = \begin{bmatrix} y_1 \\ y_2 \\ \vdots \\ y_n \end{bmatrix}, \qquad \underset{n\times 1}{\mathbf{u}} = \begin{bmatrix} u_1 \\ u_2 \\ \vdots \\ u_n \end{bmatrix}$$

$$\underset{n\times k}{\mathbf{X}} = \begin{bmatrix} x_{11} & x_{21} & \cdots & x_{k1} \\ x_{12} & x_{22} & \cdots & x_{k2} \\ \vdots & \vdots & & \vdots \\ x_{1n} & x_{2n} & \cdots & x_{kn} \end{bmatrix}$$

and $\boldsymbol{\beta} = (\beta_1, \beta_2, \ldots, \beta_k)$ is a $k \times 1$ vector of unknown coefficients. The sum of squares of the errors can now be written in matrix notations as

$$Q(\boldsymbol{\beta}) = \sum_{t=1}^{n} u_t^2 = \mathbf{u}'\mathbf{u} = (\mathbf{y} - \mathbf{X}\boldsymbol{\beta})'(\mathbf{y} - \mathbf{X}\boldsymbol{\beta}) \tag{6.3}$$

The first-order conditions for minimization of $Q(\boldsymbol{\beta})$ with respect to $\boldsymbol{\beta}$ are given by

$$\frac{\partial Q(\boldsymbol{\beta})}{\partial \boldsymbol{\beta}} = -2\mathbf{X}'(\mathbf{y} - \mathbf{X}\boldsymbol{\beta}) \tag{6.4}$$

The ordinary least squares (OLS) estimator of $\boldsymbol{\beta}$ is obtained by solving the normal equations in $\hat{\boldsymbol{\beta}}_{\text{OLS}}$:

$$\mathbf{X}'(\mathbf{y} - \mathbf{X}\hat{\boldsymbol{\beta}}_{\text{OLS}}) = \mathbf{0}$$

For these equations to have a unique solution it is necessary that $\mathbf{X}'\mathbf{X}$ has a unique inverse, $(\mathbf{X}'\mathbf{X})^{-1}$. When $\mathbf{X}$ is rank deficient any one of the columns of $\mathbf{X}$ can be written as exact linear combinations of the other columns, and it is said that the regressors are *perfectly multicollinear*. In what follows we make the following assumption:

**A6:** The observation matrix $\mathbf{X}$ has a full column rank, i.e. $Rank(\mathbf{X}) = k$.

Under this assumption the OLS estimator of $\boldsymbol{\beta}$ is given by:

$$\hat{\boldsymbol{\beta}}_{\text{OLS}} = (\mathbf{X}'\mathbf{X})^{-1}\mathbf{X}'\mathbf{y} \tag{6.5}$$

Under the classical assumptions (A1 to A4), $\hat{\boldsymbol{\beta}}_{\text{OLS}}$ is unbiased (i.e. $E(\hat{\boldsymbol{\beta}}_{\text{OLS}}) = \boldsymbol{\beta}$), and among the class of linear unbiased estimators it has the least variance. (This result is known as the Gauss Markov theorem.)

Under the normality assumption A5, the maximum likelihood (ML) estimator of $\boldsymbol{\beta}$ is identical to the OLS estimator, and the log-likelihood function is given by

$$\ell(\boldsymbol{\beta}, \sigma^2) = -\frac{n}{2}\log(2\pi\sigma^2) - \frac{1}{2\sigma^2}(\mathbf{y} - \mathbf{X}\boldsymbol{\beta})'(\mathbf{y} - \mathbf{X}\boldsymbol{\beta}) \tag{6.6}$$

where $\sigma^2$ stands for the variance of $u_t$. The ML estimator of $\sigma^2$ is given by

$$\tilde{\sigma}^2 = n^{-1}(\mathbf{y} - \mathbf{X}\hat{\boldsymbol{\beta}}_{\text{OLS}})'(\mathbf{y} - \mathbf{X}\hat{\boldsymbol{\beta}}_{\text{OLS}}) \tag{6.7}$$

and is biased. In fact

$$E(\tilde{\sigma}^2) = \left(\frac{n-k}{n}\right)\sigma^2 \tag{6.8}$$

The unbiased estimator of $\sigma^2$, which we denote by $\hat{\sigma}^2$, is defined by

$$\hat{\sigma}^2 = (n-k)^{-1}\left(\mathbf{y} - \mathbf{X}\hat{\boldsymbol{\beta}}_{\text{OLS}}\right)'\left(\mathbf{y} - \mathbf{X}\hat{\boldsymbol{\beta}}_{\text{OLS}}\right) \tag{6.9}$$

The variance matrix of $\hat{\boldsymbol{\beta}}_{\text{OLS}}$, together with a number useful summary statistics for regression analysis, are given in Section 18.5.1.

## 6.1.3 Testing zero restrictions and reporting probability values

Consider the problem of testing the 'null' hypothesis that

$$H_0: \beta_i = \beta_i^0$$

against

$$H_1: \beta_i \neq \beta_i^0$$

where $\beta_i$ is the $i$th element of $\boldsymbol{\beta}$ in (6.2). The relevant test statistic is given by the $t$-ratio

$$t_i = \frac{\hat{\beta}_i - \beta_i^0}{\sqrt{\hat{V}(\hat{\beta}_i)}} \tag{6.10}$$

where $\hat{\beta}_i$ is the $i$th element of $\hat{\boldsymbol{\beta}}_{\text{OLS}}$, and $\hat{V}(\hat{\beta}_i)$ is the estimator of the variance of $\hat{\beta}_i$ and is given by the $i$th diagonal element of the variance matrix defined by (18.4) in Chapter 18. Since the alternative hypothesis, $H_1$, is two-sided, the absolute value of $t_i$ should be compared with the appropriate critical value of the student-$t$ distribution with $n - k$ degrees of freedom. *Microfit* reports the probability of falsely rejecting the null hypothesis that $\beta_i = 0$

against $\beta_i \neq 0$ in square brackets next to the $t$-ratios. These probability values are valid under assumptions A1 to A5 for two-sided tests and give an indication of the level of significance of the test. For example, if the probability value reported for $\beta_i$ is equal to 0.025, it means that the probability of falsely rejecting $\beta_i = 0$ is at most equal to 0.025. Therefore, the null hypothesis that $\beta_i = 0$ against $\beta_i \neq 0$ is rejected at the 2.5 per cent significance level. The probability values are applicable even if the normality assumption is violated, so long as the sample is large enough.

## 6.2 The maximum likelihood approach

Many of the estimation options in *Microfit* compute estimates of the regression coefficients when one or more of the classical assumptions are violated. For example, the AR and the MA options discussed in Sections 6.8–6.13 below, compute estimates of $\boldsymbol{\beta}$ under a variety of assumptions concerning the autocorrelation patterns in the disturbances. To deal with such departures, *Microfit* makes use of two general principles: the likelihood principle and the instrumental variables method, which is a special case of the generalized method of moments (GMM). Here we briefly review the likelihood principle.

Let $L(\boldsymbol{\theta})$ be the likelihood function of the $k \times 1$ vector of unknown parameters, $\boldsymbol{\theta}$, associated with the joint probability distribution of $\mathbf{y} = (y_1, y_2, \ldots, y_n)'$, conditional (possibly) on a set of pre-determined variables or regressors. Assume that $L(\boldsymbol{\theta})$ is twice differentiable and satisfies a number of regularity conditions. See, for example, Davidson and MacKinnon (1993, Ch 8).

The maximum likelihood (ML) estimator of $\boldsymbol{\theta}$ is that value of $\boldsymbol{\theta}$ which globally maximizes $L(\boldsymbol{\theta})$. Let $\tilde{\boldsymbol{\theta}}$ be the ML estimator of $\boldsymbol{\theta}$, then it must also satisfy the first order condition

$$\left.\frac{\partial \log L(\boldsymbol{\theta})}{\partial \boldsymbol{\theta}}\right|_{\boldsymbol{\theta}=\tilde{\boldsymbol{\theta}}} = 0$$

### 6.2.1 Newton–Raphson algorithm

The computation of the ML estimators in *Microfit* is generally carried out using the Newton–Raphson algorithm. Denote the estimator of $\boldsymbol{\theta}$ in the $j$th iteration by $\tilde{\boldsymbol{\theta}}_{(j-1)}$, then the iterative algorithm used is given by

$$\tilde{\boldsymbol{\theta}}_{(j)} = \tilde{\boldsymbol{\theta}}_{(j-1)} + d\left[-\frac{\partial^2 \log L(\boldsymbol{\theta})}{\partial \boldsymbol{\theta} \partial \boldsymbol{\theta}'}\right]^{-1}_{\boldsymbol{\theta}=\tilde{\boldsymbol{\theta}}_{(j-1)}} \left[\frac{\partial \log L(\boldsymbol{\theta})}{\partial \boldsymbol{\theta}}\right]_{\boldsymbol{\theta}=\tilde{\boldsymbol{\theta}}_{(j-1)}} \tag{6.11}$$

where $d$ is a scalar 'damping factor'. In cases where convergence of the numerical algorithm may be problematic *Microfit* allows the user to start the iterations with different choices for the initial estimates, $\tilde{\theta}_{(0)}$ and the value of the damping factor in the range [0.01–2.00]. The iterations are terminated if

$$\sum_{i=1}^{k} \left| \tilde{\theta}_{i,(j)} - \tilde{\theta}_{i,(j-1)} \right| < k\epsilon$$

where $\tilde{\theta}_{i,(j)}$ is the $i$th element of $\tilde{\boldsymbol{\theta}}_{(j)}$, and $\epsilon$ is a small positive number usually set equal to 1/10,000. In some cases the program also checks to ensure that at termination the maximized value of the log-likelihood function, is at least as large as the log-likelihood values obtained throughout the iterations.

### 6.2.2 Properties of the maximum likelihood estimators

The optimum properties of ML estimators are asymptotic; that is, they are valid in large samples. Assuming certain regularity conditions are satisfied and, in particular, $\mathbf{y_t}$ is a stationary process, then $\tilde{\boldsymbol{\theta}}$, the ML estimator of $\boldsymbol{\theta}$ has the following properties:[3]

1. $\tilde{\boldsymbol{\theta}}$ is a consistent estimator of $\boldsymbol{\theta} = (\boldsymbol{\theta}_1, \boldsymbol{\theta}_2, \ldots, \boldsymbol{\theta}_k)'$; that is

$$\lim_{n\to\infty} \Pr\{|\tilde{\theta}_i - \theta_{i0}| < \epsilon\} = 1, \qquad \text{for} \quad i = 1, 2, \ldots, k$$

   where $\theta_{i0}$ is the true value of $\theta_i$ and $\epsilon(> 0)$ is a small positive number.
2. Asymptotically (i.e. as $n \to \infty$), $\sqrt{n}(\tilde{\boldsymbol{\theta}} - \boldsymbol{\theta}_0)$ has a multivariate normal distribution with zero means and the variance matrix $\boldsymbol{\Sigma}$, where

$$\boldsymbol{\Sigma}^{-1} = E\left\{-\frac{1}{n}\cdot\frac{\partial^2 \log L(\boldsymbol{\theta})}{\partial\boldsymbol{\theta}\partial\boldsymbol{\theta}'}\right\}, \qquad \text{or} \qquad \boldsymbol{\Sigma}^{-1} = \operatorname*{Plim}_{n\to\infty}\left\{-\frac{1}{n}\cdot\frac{\partial^2 \log L(\boldsymbol{\theta})}{\partial\boldsymbol{\theta}\partial\boldsymbol{\theta}'}\right\}$$

3. $\tilde{\boldsymbol{\theta}}$ attains the Cramer–Rao lower bound asymptotically.
4. $\tilde{\boldsymbol{\theta}}$ is an asymptotically unbiased estimator of $\theta$, that is

$$\lim_{n\to\infty} E(\tilde{\boldsymbol{\theta}}) = \boldsymbol{\theta}_0.$$

5. $\tilde{\boldsymbol{\theta}}$ is an asymptotically efficient estimator. That is, $\tilde{\boldsymbol{\theta}}$ has the lowest asymptotic variance in the class of all asymptotically unbiased estimators.

### 6.2.3 Likelihood-based tests

There are three main likelihood-based test procedures that are commonly used in econometrics for testing linear or non-linear parametric restrictions on a maintained model. They are:

[3]Many of these properties continue to hold even if the stationary assumption is relaxed. For general results in the case of the ML estimation of models with unit root processes see Chapters 7 and 19.

1. The likelihood ratio (LR) approach.
2. The Lagrange multiplier (LM) approach.
3. The Wald (W) approach.

All these three procedures yield asymptotically valid tests, in the sense that they will have the correct size (i.e. the type $I$ error) and possess certain optimal power properties in large samples. They are asymptotically equivalent, although they can lead to different results in small samples. The choice between them is often made on the basis of computational simplicity and ease of use.

**The likelihood ratio test procedure**

Suppose that the hypothesis of interest to be tested can be written as a set of $r$-independent restrictions (linear and/or non-linear) on $\boldsymbol{\theta}$. Denote these $r$ restrictions by[4]

$$
\begin{aligned}
\phi_1(\theta_1, \theta_2, \ldots, \theta_k) &= 0 \\
\phi_2(\theta_1, \theta_2, \ldots, \theta_k) &= 0 \\
\vdots \qquad & \quad \vdots \\
\phi_r(\theta_1, \theta_2, \ldots, \theta_k) &= 0
\end{aligned}
$$

which can be written compactly in vector notations as

$$H_0 : \boldsymbol{\phi}(\boldsymbol{\theta}) = 0$$

where $\phi(\cdot)$ is an $r \times 1$ twice differentiable function of the $k \times 1$ parameter vector, $\boldsymbol{\theta}$. Consider the two-sided alternative hypothesis

$$H_1 : \boldsymbol{\phi}(\boldsymbol{\theta}) \neq 0$$

The log-likelihood ratio (LR) statistic for testing $H_0$ against $H_1$ is defined by

$$LR = 2\{\log[L(\tilde{\boldsymbol{\theta}}_U)] - \log[L(\tilde{\boldsymbol{\theta}}_R)]\} \tag{6.12}$$

where $\tilde{\boldsymbol{\theta}}_U$ is the *unrestricted* ML estimator of $\boldsymbol{\theta}$, and $\tilde{\boldsymbol{\theta}}_R$ is the *restricted* ML estimator of $\boldsymbol{\theta}$. The latter is computed by maximizing $L(\boldsymbol{\theta})$ subject to the $r$ restrictions $\boldsymbol{\phi}(\boldsymbol{\theta}) = 0$. Under the null hypothesis, $H_0$, and assuming that certain regularity conditions are met, the statistic LR is asymptotically distributed as a chi-squared variate with $r$ degrees of freedom. The hypothesis $H_0$ is then rejected if the log-likelihood ratio statistic, LR, is larger than the relevant critical value of the chi-squared distribution.

The LR approach requires that the maintained model, characterized by the likelihood function $L(\theta)$, be estimated both under the null and the alternative hypotheses. The other two likelihood-based approaches to be presented below require the estimation of the maintained model either under the null or under the alternative hypothesis, but not under both.

---

[4]The assumption that these restrictions are independent require that the $r \times k$ matrix of the derivatives $\partial\phi/\partial\theta'$ has a full rank, namely that $Rank(\partial\phi/\partial\theta') = r$.

**The Lagrange multiplier test procedure**

The Lagrange multiplier (LM) procedure uses the restricted estimators, $\tilde{\boldsymbol{\theta}}_R$, and requires the computation of the following statistic:

$$LM = \left\{\frac{\partial \log L(\boldsymbol{\theta})}{\partial \boldsymbol{\theta}'}\right\}_{\boldsymbol{\theta}=\tilde{\boldsymbol{\theta}}_R} \left\{-\frac{\partial^2 \log L(\boldsymbol{\theta})}{\partial \boldsymbol{\theta} \partial \boldsymbol{\theta}'}\right\}^{-1}_{\boldsymbol{\theta}=\tilde{\boldsymbol{\theta}}_R} \left\{\frac{\partial \log L(\boldsymbol{\theta})}{\partial \boldsymbol{\theta}'}\right\}_{\boldsymbol{\theta}=\tilde{\boldsymbol{\theta}}_R} \tag{6.13}$$

where

$$\left\{\frac{\partial \log L(\boldsymbol{\theta})}{\partial \boldsymbol{\theta}}\right\}_{\boldsymbol{\theta}=\tilde{\boldsymbol{\theta}}_R}$$

and

$$\left\{\frac{\partial^2 \log L(\boldsymbol{\theta})}{\partial \boldsymbol{\theta} \partial \boldsymbol{\theta}'}\right\}_{\boldsymbol{\theta}=\tilde{\boldsymbol{\theta}}_R}$$

are the first and the second derivatives of the log-likelihood function which are evaluated at $\tilde{\boldsymbol{\theta}} = \tilde{\boldsymbol{\theta}}_R$, the *restricted* estimator of $\boldsymbol{\theta}$. Recall that $\tilde{\boldsymbol{\theta}}_R$ is computed under the null hypothesis, $H_0$, which defines the set of restrictions to be tested. The LM test was originally proposed by Rao (1948) and is also referred to as Rao's score test, or simply the 'score test'.

**The Wald test procedure**

The Wald test (W) makes use of the unrestricted estimators, $\tilde{\boldsymbol{\theta}}_U$, and is defined by

$$W = \phi'(\tilde{\boldsymbol{\theta}}_U)\{\hat{V}[\phi(\tilde{\boldsymbol{\theta}}_U)]\}^{-1}\phi(\tilde{\boldsymbol{\theta}}_U) \tag{6.14}$$

where $\hat{V}[\phi(\tilde{\boldsymbol{\theta}}_U)]$ is the variance of $\phi(\tilde{\boldsymbol{\theta}}_U)$ and can be estimated consistently by:

$$\hat{V}[\phi(\tilde{\boldsymbol{\theta}}_U)] = \left\{\frac{\partial \phi(\boldsymbol{\theta})}{\partial \boldsymbol{\theta}'}\right\}_{\boldsymbol{\theta}=\tilde{\boldsymbol{\theta}}_U} \left\{-\frac{\partial^2 \log L(\boldsymbol{\theta})}{\partial \boldsymbol{\theta} \partial \boldsymbol{\theta}'}\right\}^{-1}_{\boldsymbol{\theta}=\tilde{\boldsymbol{\theta}}_U} \left\{\frac{\partial \phi(\boldsymbol{\theta})}{\partial \boldsymbol{\theta}}\right\}_{\boldsymbol{\theta}=\tilde{\boldsymbol{\theta}}_U} \tag{6.15}$$

Asymptotically (namely as the sample size, $n$, is allowed to increase without a bound), all the three test procedures are equivalent. Like the LR statistic, under the null hypothesis, the LM and the W statistics are asymptotically distributed as chi-squared variates with $r$ degrees of freedom. We can write:

$$LR \underset{\sim}{a} LM \underset{\sim}{a} W$$

where $\underset{\sim}{a}$ stands for 'asymptotic equivalence' in distribution functions.

Other versions of the LM and the W statistics which replace

$$\left\{\frac{\partial^2 \log L(\boldsymbol{\theta})}{\partial \boldsymbol{\theta} \partial \boldsymbol{\theta}'}\right\}$$

in (6.13) and (6.15) by a consistent estimate of

$$n\text{Plim}_{n\to\infty}\left\{n^{-1}\frac{\partial^2 \log L(\boldsymbol{\theta})}{\partial\boldsymbol{\theta}\partial\boldsymbol{\theta}'}\right\}$$

are also used in *Microfit*. This would not affect the asymptotic distribution of the test statistics, but in some cases could simplify the computation of the statistics.

The various applications of the likelihood approach to single-equation econometric models are reviewed in Chapter 18.

## 6.3 Estimation menus in *Microfit*

*Microfit*'s gateways to econometric analysis are the Single Equation Estimation Menu (shortened to Univariate Menu on the menu bar) and the System Estimation Menu (shortened to Multivariate Menu on the menu bar).

The Univariate Menu option opens the Single Equation Estimation Menu (see Section 6.4) which provides you with a large number of options for estimation of linear and non-linear single-equation models.

The Multivariate Menu option opens the System Estimation Menu (see Section 7.3) which allows you to estimate unrestricted vector autoregressive models (VAR), cointegrating VAR models with exactly identifying and

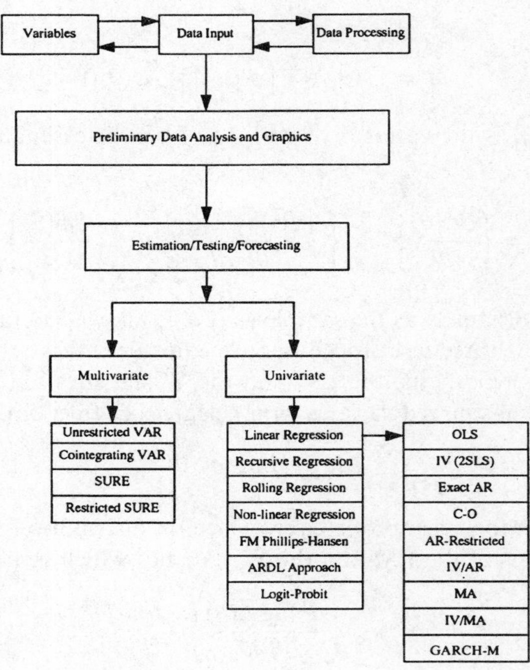


Chart 1: The flow chart of functions in *Microfit*

over-identifying restrictions on the long-run relations, system of seemingly unrelated equations (SURE), with and without restrictions. These multiple-equation estimation options are described in Chapter 7.

Alternatively, use the [Single] or [Multi] button to move to the Single Equation Estimation window or the System Estimation window respectively. The window opens with the last menu option you chose (or the first option in the menu) selected by default.

Before any of the estimation options are used, it is important that the data are correctly entered, along with all the variables to be included in the regression equation, such as the constant (the intercept term), time trends, seasonal dummies, or transformations of your existing variables (for example, their first differences or logarithms). See the data processing functions described in Chapter 4.

## 6.4 Single Equation Estimation Menu

The Single Equation Estimation Menu (abbreviated to Univariate Menu in the menu bar) contains the following options:

1. Linear Regression Menu
2. Recursive Linear Regression Menu
3. Rolling Linear Regression Menu
4. Non-linear Regression Menu
5. Phillips-Hansen Estimation Menu
6. ARDL Approach to Cointegration
7. Logit and Probit Models

In Microfit each of these options is regarded as a menu in its own right. When you choose any of these options, or their submenu options, you will be asked to enter the specification of your econometric model in the editor window on the screen.

**Option 1** allows you to estimate linear regression models by a variety of methods: ordinary least squares (OLS), instrumental variables (IV) or two-stage least squares (2SLS), Maximum Likelihood (ML) estimates for regression models with serially correlated errors (AR, CO, MA), IV estimates of regression models with serially correlated errors (IV/AR and IV/MA options), and ML estimates of a variety of conditionally heteroscedastic models (such as ARCH, GARCH, exponential GARCH, absolute GARCH, GARCH in mean models both for normally and student-*t* distributed errors).

**Options 2** and **3** compute recursive and rolling regressions estimated by the OLS and the IV methods.

**Option 4** enables you to estimate non-linear regression equations by the least squares or the two-stage least squares method.

**Option 5** can be used to obtain fully-modified OLS (FM-OLS) estimators of a single cointegrating relation proposed by Phillips and Hansen (1990).

**Option 6** implements the autoregressive-distributed lag (ARDL) approach to estimation of a single long-run relationship advanced by Pesaran and

Shin (1995a), with automatic order selection using any one of the four model selection criteria, namely $\bar{R}^2$, the Akaike information criterion (AIC), the Schwarz Bayesian criterion (SBC), and the Hannan and Quinn criterion (HQC).

**Option 7** can be used to estimate univariate binary quantitative response models for normal and logistic probability distributions (namely, the Probit and Logit models).

## 6.5 Linear Regression Menu

This is the main menu for estimation of single-equation linear regression models. It contains the following options:

1. Ordinary Least Squares
2. Gen. Inst. Var. Method
3. AR Errors (Exact ML) J< =2
4. AR Errors (Cochrane-Orcutt) J< =12
5. AR Errors (Gauss-Newton)
6. IV with AR Errors (Gauss-Newton)
7. MA Errors (Exact ML) J< =12
8. IV with MA Errors J< =12
9. Garch-M Estimation

The options in this menu can be used to compute estimates of a linear regression equation under a number of different stochastic specifications of the disturbances. To start your calculations once they have been set up, click START. All the options in this menu assume that the observation matrix of the regressors has a full rank (that is, assumption A6 is satisfied and the specified regressors are *not perfectly* multicollinear). If this condition is not satisfied *Microfit* gives an error message and invites you to click OK, whereupon you will be presented with the Backtracking Menu (see Section 6.25).

To access the Linear Regression Estimation Menu choose Option 1 in the Single Equation Estimation Menu (the Univariate Menu: see Section 6.4), and then follow up the instructions below to specify your regression equation and the estimation period.

### 6.5.1 Specification of a linear regression equation

When you choose Options 1 to 3 in the Single Equation Estimation Menu (Univariate Menu: see Section 6.4) you will be asked to type the name of your dependent variable followed by the list of your regressors, separated by spaces, in the box editor that appears on the screen. For example, to specify the regression

$$YFOOD_t = a_0 + a_1 XL_t + a_2 XC_t + u_t$$

you need to type

YFOOD INPT XL XC [START]

where YFOOD is the dependent variable and INPT, XL, and XC are the regressors. The variable INPT here stands for the intercept (or constant) term and can be created either by using the [→ Constant] button (see Section 4.1.1) or by typing the formula

INPT = 1 [GO]

into the Command Editor. Before running this regression you must make sure that all the four variables YFOOD, INPT, XL, and XC are in the variables list by clicking the [Variables] button (see Chapter 4).

In specifying the regression equation the following points are worth bearing in mind:

1. It is possible to specify lagged or lead values of the dependent variable or other variables as regressors by giving the order of lags or leads enclosed within brackets immediately after the relevant variables. For example, to specify the regression equation,

$$y_t = \alpha + \phi_1 y_{t-1} + \phi_2 y_{t-2} + \phi_3 y_{t+1} + \beta_0 x_t + \beta_1 x_{t-1} + u_t$$

when asked to list your regression equation you can type

Y INPT Y(−1) Y(−2) Y(+1) X X(−1) [START]

where INPT stands for an intercept term (a vector of ones), Y(− 1) and Y(−2) represent the first and second-order lags of the dependent variable (i.e. Y), respectively, Y(+1) stands for the first-order lead of Y, and X(−1) is the first-order lag of X. The variables Y(−1), Y(−2), Y(+1), and X(−1) are created temporarily for use only in the estimation/testing/forecasting stage of the program. This is a useful facility and allows you to include lags of variables in the regression equation without having to create them explicitly as new variables in the Command Editor. When the specified equation contains lagged variables, the information in the order of lags will also be used in the calculation of dynamic forecasts (see the forecast option in the Post Regression Menu in Section 6.21). However, if lagged values of the dependent variable are created in the Command Editor, before entering the estimation/testing/forecasting stage, these lagged values will be treated like any other regressors, and static forecasts will be calculated. For example, suppose Y1, Y2, and X1 are created in the Command Editor as

Y1 = Y(−1); Y2 = Y(−2); X1 = X(−1) [GO]

The regression of Y on

INPT Y1 Y2 X1

will generate the same results as the regression of Y on

INPT Y(−1) Y(−2) X(−1)

except for the forecasts which will be static (see options 8 and 9 in Section 6.21).

2. Also, in the regression of Y on

INPT Y(−1) X

the program recognizes that only the first-order lag of the dependent variable, namely Y(−1), is specified amongst the regressors, and automatically includes Durbin's *h*-statistic in the OLS regression results. But if the regression is specified as Y on INPUT Y1 X the program treats Y1 like any other regressor and does not report the *h*-statistic.

3. In specifying distributed lag functions it is often convenient to use the new facility introduced in *Microfit* 4.0 that allows the user to include a number of lagged values of a variable without having to type all of their names in full. For example, to include the variables

$$x_t, x_{t-1}, x_{t-2}, x_{t-3}, x_{t-4}, x_{t-5}, z_{t-10}, z_{t-11}, z_{t-12}$$

among your regressors you simply need to type

X{0 − 5} Z{10 − 12}

As another example, suppose you wish to include the following regressors in your model:

$$w_t, w_{t-2}, w_{t-5}, w_{t-8}, w_{t-9}, w_{t-10}$$

You need to type

W{0 2 5 8 − 10}

4. Note that except for Phillips–Hansen's fully-modified OLS estimator (option 5 in the Single Equation Estimation Menu – the Univariate Menu), *Microfit* does not automatically include an intercept term in the regression equation, and you need to include it explicitly amongst your regressors.

### 6.5.2 Specification of the estimation period

You need to specify the estimation period once you have set up the model (see Section 6.5.1). By default, all available observations are chosen, and the start and finish for the estimation period are the same as the minimum and maximum dates (or observations) displayed on the screen.

You may, however, wish to choose a subset of available observations for estimation, perhaps saving some of the observations for the predictive failure and structural stability tests, or for forecasting. In this case you should enter the start and finish of your estimation period, by clicking on the Start and End boxes in turn and choosing a date from the drop-down list.

If there are observations at the end of the sample period which have not been included in the estimation period, in the case of the OLS option you will also be asked to specify the number of observations to be used in the predictive failure/structural stability tests. Enter your desired sample period and then press.

In specifying the estimation period the following points are worth bearing in mind:

1. The estimation period cannot fall outside the period defined by the minimum and maximum dates (or observations).
2. The program automatically adjusts the chosen estimation period to allow for missing observations (i.e. *NONE* values) at the beginning and at the end of the sample period. For example, if the available observations run from 1960 to 1980, but the observations on the dependent variable and/or one of the regressors are missing for the years 1960, 1961, and 1980, then the default estimation period will be 1962 to 1979.
3. The estimation will not be carried out if one or more observations on the dependent variable and/or on the regressors are missing in the middle of the specified estimation period. In such an event an error message will appear on the screen.

## 6.6 OLS option

The (OLS) option computes the ordinary least squares estimates of $\beta$ together with the corresponding standard errors, $t$-ratios, and probability values (see Sections 6.1.2 and 6.1.3). It also computes a number of summary statistics and diagnostic test statistics (with probability values) aimed at checking for possible deviations from the classical normal assumptions (**A1** to **A5**). The summary statistics include $R^2$, $\bar{R}^2$, Akaike information criterion (AIC), Schwarz Bayesian criterion (SBC), residual sum of squares, standard error of regression, and the maximized value of the log-likelihood function. The formulae used for the computation of these and other statistics are given in Sections 18.5 and 18.6.

The diagnostic statistics included in the OLS regression results are for testing the following hypotheses:

- Residual serial correlation
- Functional form misspecification
- Normality of residuals
- Heteroscedasticity
- Predictive failure
- Structural stability.

For each of these hypotheses the program computes two test statistics: a Lagrange multiplier (LM), or score statistic, and an F statistic. The LM statistic is asymptotically distributed as a chi-squared ($\chi^2$) variate. For a comprehensive review of the use of LM tests in econometrics see Godfrey

(1988). The F statistic, also known in the literature 'LM F' or 'modified LM' statistic is taken approximately to have the F distribution: see Harvey (1981, p. 277). The LM and the F statistics have the same distribution asymptotically. But, on the basis of Monte Carlo results, Kiviet (1986) has shown that in small samples the F version is generally preferable to the LM version. In what follows we provide a brief account of these diagnostic tests. For further details of the econometric methods involved and the relevant references to the literature, see Section 18.5.2.

### 6.6.1 Tests of residual serial correlation

The program provides the following tests of the non-autocorrelated error assumption, A3:

- Durbin–Watson (DW) test (1950, 1951)
- Durbin's (1970) *h*-test
- Lagrange multiplier (LM) tests[5]

The program always supplies the DW statistic, but reports the *h*-statistic only when the regression equation is explicitly specified to include a single, one-period lag of the dependent variable. The LM statistic is included in the diagnostic tests table, and is applicable to models with and without lagged dependent variables (Godfrey 1987a, 1987b). It is applicable to testing the hypothesis that the disturbances, $u_t$, are serially uncorrelated against the alternative hypothesis that they are autocorrelated of order $p$ (either as autoregressive or moving average processes). In the diagnostic tests table the following values are chosen for $p$:

$p = 1$ for undated and annual data
$p = 2$ for half-yearly data
$p = 4$ for quarterly data
$p = 12$ for monthly data

Other values for $p$ can be specified using Option 1 in the Hypothesis Testing Menu (see Section 6.24).

### 6.6.2 Ramsey's RESET test for functional form misspecification

The Ramsey (1969) RESET test reported in the diagnostic tests table refers to the simple case where only the square of fitted values (i.e. $\hat{y}_t^2$) are included in the extended regression of $e_t = y_t - \mathbf{x}_t' \hat{\beta}$ (or $\hat{y}_t$) on $\mathbf{x_t}$ and $\hat{y}_t^2$. A $p$th order RESET test can be carried out by using Option 6 in the Hypothesis Testing

[5]For example, see Godfrey (1987a, 1987b), Breusch and Pagan (1980), Breusch and Godfrey (1981).

Menu (section 6.24), with $\hat{y}_t^2, \hat{y}_t^3, \ldots, \hat{y}_t^p$ specified as additional variables. Notice that to carry out such a test, you first need to save the fitted values of the regression of **y** on **X** by means of option 7 in the Display/Save Residuals and Fitted Values Menu (see Section 6.22).

### 6.6.3 The normality test

This is the test proposed by Bera and Jarque (1981) for testing the normality assumption, A5, and is valid irrespective of whether the regression equation includes an intercept term or not.

### 6.6.4 Heteroscedasticity test

This is a simple test of the (unconditional) homoscedasticity assumption, A4, and provides an LM test of $\gamma = 0$ in the model

$$E(u_t^2) = \sigma_t^2 = \sigma^2 + \gamma(\mathbf{x}_t'\beta)^2, \qquad t = 1, 2, \ldots, n$$

See Koenker (1981), where it is also shown that such a test is robust with respect to the non-normality of the disturbances.

### 6.6.5 Predictive failure test

This is the second test discussed in Chow (1960), and is applicable even if the number of available observations for the test is less than the number of unknown parameters. As shown in Pesaran *et al.* (1985), the predictive failure test can also be used as a general specification error test.

### 6.6.6 Chow's test of the stability of regression coefficients

This is the first test discussed in Chow (1960), and tests the equality of regression coefficients over two sample periods conditional on the equality of error variances. In the statistics literature this test is known as the analysis of covariance test: see Scheffe (1959). The program computes this test if the number of observations available after the estimation period is greater than $k$, the number of regressors included in the model.

### 6.6.7 Measures of leverage

In the classical linear regression model (6.2), the leverage (or the influence) of points in the regression design is measured by the diagonal elements of the matrix:[6]

[6]Since matrix **A** maps **y** into $\hat{\mathbf{y}} = \mathbf{A}\mathbf{y}$, the matrix **A** is also known in the literature as the 'hat' matrix.

$$\mathbf{A} = \mathbf{X}(\mathbf{X}'\mathbf{X})^{-1}\mathbf{X}' = (a_{ij}). \tag{6.16}$$

The relevance of the leverage measures, $a_{ii}$, $i = 1, 2, \ldots, n$, in regression analysis has been discussed in detail by Belsley *et al.* (1980, Chapter 2), and Cook and Weisberg (1982, Chapter 2).

The program provides plots of $a_{ii}, i = 1, 2, \ldots, n$ and allows you to save them for subsequent analysis. In the plot of the leverage measures, the average value of $a_{ii}$, which is equal to $k/n$, is also displayed.[7]

The leverage measures also provide important information on the extent of small sample bias that may be present in the heteroscedasticity-consistent estimators of the covariance matrix of $\hat{\beta}_{OLS}$ (see Section 18.22). As shown by Chesher and Jewitt (1987), substantial downward bias can result in the heteroscedasticity-consistent estimators of the variance of the least squares estimators, if regression design contains points of high leverage.

## 6.7 Generalized Instrumental Variable Method option

Option 2 (the IV or 2SLS option) in the Linear Regression Menu (see Section 6.5) enables you to obtain consistent estimates of the parameters of the regression model when the orthogonality assumption, A4, is violated.[8] The breakdown of the orthogonality assumption could be due to a variety of problems, such as simultaneity, measurement errors, sample selection bias, or it could be because actual values are used as a proxy for expectational variables under the rational expectations hypothesis. For example, see Sargan (1958), McCallum (1976), Wickens (1982), and Pesaran (1987a). A unified account of the IV method can be found in Pesaran and Smith (1990).

The IV option can also be used to compute two-stage least squares (2SLS) estimates of a single equation from a simultaneous equation system. Notice, however, that the computations of the 2SLS estimates require that all the predetermined variables of the simultaneous equation model be specified as instrumental variables.

When you choose this option, you will be asked to list your instrumental variables separated by spaces. The number of instruments should be at least as large as the number of regressors. In the case of exact collinearity amongst the instruments and/or the regressors, the program displays an error message and invites you to click OK to continue.

If you specify fewer instruments than regressors, the program shows the minimum number of required instruments (i.e. the number of regressors) and asks you to try again.

The estimation results for the IV option are summarized in two tables. The first table gives the parameter estimates, their estimated asymptotic standard errors, and $t$-ratios, as well as Sargan's statistic for a general test of

[7]Note that since $Tr(\mathbf{A}) = \sum_{i=1}^{n} a_{ii} = k$, then the simple average of $a_{ii}, i = 1, 2, \ldots, n$ will be equal to $k/n$.

[8]A test of the orthogonality assumption can be carried out by computing the Wu–Hausman statistic $T_2$, (Wu 1973, Hausman 1978), using the variable addition test option in the Hypothesis Testing Menu (see Section 6.24). See also Lesson 10.10.

misspecification of the model and the instruments. This test statistic is asymptotically distributed as $\chi^2$ with $s-k$ degrees of freedom, where $s$ represents the number of instruments and $k$ the number of the regressors ($s > k$) (see Section 18.9.3). This table also reports probability values, the values of the IV minimand, $R^2$, $\bar{R}^2$, $GR^2$, $\overline{GR}^2$, F, and DW statistics and a few other summary statistics. But, note that these statistics in the case of the IV option do not have the usual OLS interpretations. For example, $R^2$, $\bar{R}^2$ are not valid for regressions estimated by the IV method, and can lead to misleading results. Appropriate measures of overall fit for IV regressions are given by the generalized R-bar-squared statistics ($GR^2$ and $\overline{GR}^2$) proposed in Pesaran and Smith (1994) (see Section 18.9.2). The same also applies to the DW statistic. For tests of residual serial correlation the appropriate statistic is the LM statistic reported in the diagnostic tests table. Finally, note that the probability values reported are only valid asymptotically.

The second table supplies diagnostic statistics (with the associated probability values) for the tests of residual serial correlation, functional form misspecification, non-normal errors, and heteroscedasticity. The tests of residual autocorrelation and functional form misspecification are both based on the statistics in (18.67), originally due to Sargan (1976) using different specifications for the **W** matrix. In the case of the test of residual autocorrelation, the **W** matrix is defined by (18.68), with $p$, the order of the test, being

$p = 1$ for undated and annual data

$p = 2$ for half-yearly data

$p = 4$ for quarterly data

$p = 12$ for monthly data

Other values for $p$ can be specified using Option 1 in the Hypothesis Testing Menu (see Section 6.24). The statistic for the test of functional form misspecification is computed using (18.67) with the **W** matrix specialized to

$$\mathbf{W} = (\hat{y}^2_{1,IV}, \hat{y}^2_{2,IV}, \ldots, \hat{y}^2_{n,IV})'$$

where $\hat{y}_{t,IV} = \mathbf{x}'_t\hat{\beta}_{IV}$ are the IV fitted values.

The statistics for normality and the heteroscedasticity tests are computed as in the OLS case, with the difference that the IV fitted values and the IV residuals are used in place of the OLS ones (see Section 18.5.2).

The details of the algorithms used to compute the IV estimators and the associated test statistics are given in Section 18.9.

## 6.8 AR Errors (Exact ML) option

Option 3 in the Linear Regression Menu (see Section 6.5) computes exact maximum likelihood estimators of the regression equation (6.1) under the assumption that the disturbances, $u_t$, follow a stationary autoregressive process with stochastic initial values. This option differs from the

Cochrane–Orcutt option (option 4 in the Linear Regression Menu), which estimates the AR-error regression model under the assumption of fixed initial values. The idea of allowing for initial values in the estimation of AR(1) error models was first put forward in econometrics by Hildreth and Lu (1960). The method was then subsequently extended to higher order AR-error models by Pesaran (1972), and Beach and MacKinnon (1978). The details of algorithms for this estimation method can be found in Section 18.10. When you choose this option you will also be asked to specify initial parameter estimates for the start of iterations. See Section 6.13.1 for more details.

When you click the START button to begin the calculation you need to specify the order of the AR-error process. You can either choose the AR(1) specification

$$\text{AR(1):} \quad u_t = \rho u_{t-1} + \epsilon_t$$

or the AR(2)-error specification

$$\text{AR(2):} \quad u_t = \rho_1 u_{t-1} + \rho_2 u_{t-2} + \epsilon_t$$

For example, to choose the AR(2)-error specification, when prompted, type 2 and click OK.

The estimation results are displayed in a table in two parts. At the top are the estimates of the regression coefficients, their (asymptotic) standard errors, and other summary statistics such as $R^2$, $\bar{R}^2$, standard errors of regression ($\hat{\sigma}_\epsilon$) are given. At the bottom (use the scroll bar if necessary) is the second part of the results which gives the parameter estimates of the AR-error process, together with the associated $t$-ratios computed on the basis of the (asymptotic) standard errors (see Sections 18.10.1 and 18.10.2 for the relevant formulae). The program also reports the log-likelihood ratio statistics for the test of AR(1) against the non-autocorrelated error hypothesis, and for the test of the AR(2)-error specification against the AR(1)-error specification. The latter statistic is reported only in the case of the AR(2) option. These statistics are computed according to the formulae set out in Section 18.10.4.

In case of the AR(1) option, you will also be given the opportunity to see the plot of the concentrated log-likelihood function in terms of the parameter of AR(1)-error process over the range $|\rho| < 1$: see (18.75) in Section 18.10.1. The plot of the concentrated log-likelihood function is particularly useful for checking the possibility of multiple maxima.

*Notes*

1. In the case of this option the standard errors (and hence $t$-ratios) reported for the estimates of the regression coefficients and the parameters of the AR-error process are valid (asymptotically) if the regression equation does not contain lagged dependent variables. When your equation includes lagged dependent variables, try other AR options, namely options 4 to 6 in the Linear Regression Menu.

2. The iterations, if convergent, always converge to a stationary solution. This is a particular feature of the exact ML/AR option and does not apply to the other AR options.
3. If the estimation method fails to converge within 40 iterations, a sub-menu will be displayed. The options in this sub-menu allow you to terminate the iterations and start with a different set of initial parameter estimates, or to increase the number of iterations in steps of 20 until convergence is reached. If you choose option 0 (Abandon estimation), you will be presented with another menu for you to specify a new set of initial parameter estimates and another chance to try the iterations again (see Section 6.13.1 for more details). In situations where the convergence cannot be attained even after, say, 100 iterations, and for different sets of initial parameter estimates, it is perhaps best to terminate the iterations and try other AR options in the Linear Regression Menu. Notice, however, that in the case of option 3 where a first-order error process is specified, the iterations are certain to converge (see Section 18.10.1).

## 6.9 AR Errors (Cochrane–Orcutt) option

Option 4 in the Linear Regression Menu (see Section 6.5) computes estimates of the regression equation (6.1) under the following AR($m$) error process ($m \leqslant 12$)

$$\text{AR}(m): \quad u_t = \sum_{i=1}^{m} \rho_i u_{t-i} + \epsilon_t \tag{6.17}$$

using a generalization of the Cochrane–Orcutt (CO) iterative method (1949). This method assumes that the initial values $u_1, u_2, \ldots, u_m$ are given (or fixed). Notice, however, that if the AR($m$) process is stationary the Cochrane–Orcutt option yields estimates that are asymptotically equivalent to the exact ML estimators that explicitly allow for the distribution of the initial values.

The results for the CO option are summarized in a table, the top half giving the estimates of the regression equation (6.1), and the bottom half giving the estimates of the error process (6.17). The details of the computations can be found in Section 18.11.

*Notes*

1. For the case where $m = 1$, the program provides you with the option of seeing the plot of the concentrated log-likelihood function given by (18.100) in Section 18.11.
2. The estimated standard errors computed under the CO option are valid (asymptotically) even if the regression equation contains lagged values of the dependent variable.

3. The program displays a warning if the estimates of $\rho_1, \rho_2, \ldots, \rho_m$ result in a non-stationary error process. In such a case, inferences based on the reported standard errors can be misleading.
4. The program allows you to increase the number of iterations interactively, or to change the choice of the initial parameter estimates for the start of the iterations, if the method fails to converge within 40 iterations. (For details see note 3 in Section 6.8.)

## 6.10 AR Errors (Gauss–Newton) option

Option 5 in the Linear Regression Menu (see Section 6.5) provides estimates of (6.1) and (6.17) when the AR($m$) process is subject to zero restrictions. For example, it allows estimation of (6.1) under

$$u_t = \rho_4 u_{t-4} + \epsilon_t \tag{6.18}$$

or under

$$u_t = \rho_1 u_{t-1} + \rho_4 u_{t-4} + \rho_{15} u_{t-14} + \epsilon_t \tag{6.19}$$

When this option is chosen you will be prompted to type the non-zero lags in the AR-error process (6.17) in an ascending order separated by space(s). To choose, for example, specification (6.18), you need to type

4↵

To choose specification (6.19), you need to type

1 4 15↵

In the case of example (6.18), the order of the AR-error process is $m = 4$, but there is only one unknown parameter in the AR-error process. Similarly, in example (6.19), $m = 15$, but the number of unknown parameters of the AR-error process is equal to $r = 3$. The following restrictions apply

$$r \leqslant 12$$

and

$$n > m + k + r.$$

where

$n \equiv$ the number of observations in the chosen sample period

$k \equiv$ the number of regressors in the regression equation

$m \equiv$ the order of the AR-error process

$r \equiv$ the number of non-zero coefficients in the AR-error process.

See Section 18.12 for more details. Notice, however, that in the case of this option, the plot of the concentrated log-likelihood function can be obtained if $r = 1$, irrespective of the value specified for $m$.

## 6.11 IV with AR Errors (Gauss–Newton) option

Option 6 in the Linear Regression Menu (see Section 6.5) is appropriate for the estimation of a regression equation with autocorrelated disturbances when one or more of the regressors are suspected of being correlated with the disturbances. The estimation method which is due to Sargan (1959) is, however, applicable if there exists a sufficient number of instrumental variables that are uncorrelated with the current and past values of the transformed disturbances, $\epsilon_t$ in (6.17), but at the same time are asymptotically correlated with lagged disturbances, $u_{t-1}, u_{t-2}, \ldots, u_{t-m}$. This option also enables you to compute IV/AR estimates when the AR-error process is subject to zero restrictions (see Section 18.12.1 for details). The econometric methods underlying this option are briefly described in Section 18.13. Other relevant information can be found in Sections 18.13.1 and 18.13.2.

When you click START you will be asked first to type the non-zero lags in the AR process (as in Section 6.10). You will then be presented with a screen editor to type the list of your instruments. At least $k+m$ instruments are needed for this option. The program provides a number of useful error messages if the instruments and/or regressors are exactly collinear or if the number of instruments supplied is insufficient (see also Section 6.7). You can save your instrument lists for use in subsequent sessions using the button.

*Notes*

1. In the absence of adequate initial observations, the program automatically adjusts the estimation period to allow for the specification of lagged values of the dependent variable and/or the regressors as instruments. In the case of the IV regressions only the generalized $R^2$ measures are appropriate for this option.
2. The Sargan misspecification test statistic reported in the case of this option is computed using (18.109), and is useful as a general test of misspecification. It is asymptotically distributed as a chi-squared variate with $s-k-r$ degrees of freedom, where $s$ is the number of specified instruments, $k$ is the number of regressors, and $r$ is the number of unknown parameters of the AR-error process (see Section 18.13.1).
3. The $R^2$, $\bar{R}^2$, $GR^2$, and $\overline{GR}^2$ statistics reported for this option are based on adjusted residuals and prediction errors, respectively. The relevant formulae are given in Section 18.13.2. Notice that in the case of the IV regressions only the generalized $R^2$ measures are appropriate for this option.
4. When $r=1$, the program gives you the option of plotting the minimized values of the IV minimand, (18.107), in terms of the unknown parameter of the AR process. This is useful for checking the possibility of multiple minima.

5. The program enables you to increase the number of iterations interactively if the methods fails to converge within 40 iterations (for details, see note 3 in Section 6.8).
6. The program gives a warning if the method converges to a non-stationary AR process (see note 3 in Section 6.9).
7. In the case of this option, the estimated standard errors are valid (asymptotically) even if the regression equation contains lagged values of the dependent variable.

## 6.12 MA Errors (Exact ML) option

Option 7 in the Linear Regression Menu (see Section 6.5) allows you to estimate the regression equation (6.1) under the following *MA*($q$) error specification,

$$u_t = \sum_{i=0}^{q} \gamma_i \epsilon_{t-i}, \qquad \gamma_0 = 1 \tag{6.20}$$

Like option 5, this allows you to impose zero restrictions on the MA parameters, $\gamma_i$. The estimation is carried out by the exact ML method described in B. Pesaran (1988), and does not require the MA process to be invertible. For a description of the method, see Section 18.14. The MA option can also be used to estimate univariate ARMA or ARIMA processes.

*Notes*

1. The estimation of high-order MA-error processes (with $q > 6$) can be time-consuming, especially in the case of regression equations with a large number of regressors and observations.
2. The standard errors of the parameter estimates obtained under the MA (or the IV/MA) options are valid asymptotically so long as the estimated MA process is invertible: that is when all the roots of $\Sigma_{i=1}^{q} \gamma_i z^i = 0$ fall outside the unit circle. *Microfit* displays a warning if the estimated MA process is non-invertible.

   See also the notes to Section 6.11.

## 6.13 IV with MA Errors option

This is the MA version of the IV/AR option described in Section 6.11. It differs from the IV/AR option in the following important respects:

1. Following Hayashi and Sims (1983), the IV/MA estimates are computed using 'forward filter' transformation of the regressors and

the dependent variable (but not the instruments) to correct for the residual serial correlation. In effect, the IV/MA option is an iterated version of the Hayashi–Sims procedure: see Pesaran (1987a, Section 7.6.2). It is particularly useful for the estimation of linear rational expectations models with future expectations of the dependent variable, where the $u_t$s may be correlated with the future values of the instruments.

2. The IV minimand for the IV/MA option contains an additional Jacobian term. Although, in the case of invertible processes this additional term is asymptotically negligible, our experience suggests that its inclusion in the IV minimand helps the convergence of the iterative process when the roots of the MA part are close to the unit circle. The details of the algorithm and the rationale behind it can be found in B. Pesaran (1990). A similar procedure has also been suggested by Power (1990) for the first-order case. A description of the underlying econometric method can be found in Section 18.15.
3. The $R^2$, $\bar{R}^2$, $GR^2$, and $\overline{GR}^2$ statistics are computed using the formulae in Section 18.15.1. Only the generalized $R^2$ statistics are appropriate for this option.

## 6.13.1 Specification of initial estimates for the parameters of the AR/MA error process

When you choose the AR/MA options in the Linear Regression Menu (see Section 6.5) and click START, you will be presented with a menu[9] which gives you the choice of starting the iterations with initial estimates supplied either by the program or by you. In the case of the AR and MA options with $r = 1$ (i.e. when the error process depends only on one unknown parameter), you will also be presented with an option to see the plot of the concentrated log-likelihood function or the IV minimand.

To enter the initial estimate for the first-order lag coefficient, type your choice into the appropriate cell of the table. Repeat this process until all the initial estimates are supplied. Then click OK to start the iteration.

Since there is no guarantee that the iterative procedures will converge on the global maximum (minimum) of the likelihood function (the IV minimand), we recommend that you check the computations by starting the iterations from a number of different initial values. In the case of error processes with only one unknown parameter, the plot of the concentrated log-likelihood function or the IV minimand can be used to see whether the global optimum has been achieved.

---

[9]There is an exception. The AR(1) error specification in Option 3 of the Linear Regression Menu does not give you a choice for the specification of the initial parameter value of the AR(1) process. The iterative method used does not require it, and is always sure to converge.

## 6.14 GARCH-M Estimation option

Option 9 in the Linear Regression Menu (see Section 5) enables you to estimate a variety of conditional heteroscedastic models. When you click START you will be presented with the GARCH Estimation Menu containing the following options:

0. Move to Backtracking Menu
1. GARCH, Auto-Regressive Conditional Heteroscedasticity
2. GARCH-M, GARCH in Mean
3. AGARCH, Absolute value GARCH
4. AGARCH-M, Absolute value GARCH in Mean
5. EGARCH, Exponential GARCH
6. EGARCH-M, Exponential GARCH in Mean

**Option 0** takes you to the Backtracking Menu (see Section 6.25).

**Option 1** allows you to estimate the class of autoregressive conditional heteroscedastic (ARCH) models proposed by Engle (1982) and Bollerslev (1986). The econometric specification underlying this option is given by

$$y_t = \boldsymbol{\beta}'\mathbf{x}_t + u_t \tag{6.21}$$

$$V(u_t|\Omega_{t-1}) = h_t^2 = \alpha_0 + \sum_{i=1}^{q} \alpha_i u_{t-i}^2 + \sum_{i=1}^{p} \phi_i h_{t-i}^2 + \boldsymbol{\delta}'\mathbf{w}_t \tag{6.22}$$

where $h_t^2$ is the conditional variance of $u_t$ with respect to the information set $\Omega_{t-1}$, and $\mathbf{w}_t$ is a vector of predetermined variables assumed to influence the conditional error variances in addition to the past squared errors. The generalized ARCH model of Bollerslev, or GARCH($p$,$q$) for short, is a special case of (6.22) where $\boldsymbol{\delta} = 0$. In what follows we refer to $\Sigma_{i=1}^{q}\alpha_i u_{t-i}^2$ and $\Sigma_{i=1}^{p}\phi_i h_{t-i}^2$ in (6.22) as the MA and the AR parts of the GARCH($p$,$q$) model, respectively. See Section 18.16.1 for further details and the relevant algorithms.

**Option 2** enables you to compute ML estimates of the following GARCH($p$,$q$)-in-mean model:

$$y_t = \boldsymbol{\beta}'\mathbf{x}_t + \gamma h_t^2 + u_t \tag{6.23}$$

where the conditional error variance $h_t^2 = V(u_t|\Omega_{t-1})$ is defined by (6.22). The variables $\mathbf{x_t}$ and $\mathbf{w_t}$ must be in the variables list and can include lagged values of $y_t$ (see Section 18.16.1).

**Option 3** enables you to compute ML estimates of the following absolute value GARCH($p$,$q$) model where the conditional standard error of the disturbances, $u_t$ in (6.21), is specified by

$$h_t = \sqrt{V(u_t|\Omega_{t-1})} = \alpha_0 + \sum_{i=1}^{q} \alpha_i |u_{t-i}| + \sum_{i=1}^{p} \phi_i h_{t-i} + \boldsymbol{\delta}'\mathbf{w}_t \tag{6.24}$$

Once again, $\Sigma_{i=1}^{p}\phi_i h_{t-i}$ will be referred to as the AR part of the

AGARCH($p,q$) model, and $\Sigma_{i=1}^{q}\alpha_i|u_{t-i}|$ as its MA part. See Section 18.16.1 for more details.

**Option 4** enables you to estimate the absolute value GARCH-in-mean model (or AGARCH($p,q$)-M for short) specified by (6.23) and (6.24). This model has been introduced in the literature by Heutschel (1991). See Section 18.16.5 for more details.

**Option 5** allows you to compute ML estimates of the exponential GARCH($p,q$) model where the logarithm of the conditional variance of the errors has the following specification:

$$\log h_t^2 = \alpha_0 + \sum_{i=1}^{q}\alpha_i\left(\frac{u_{t-i}}{h_{t-i}}\right) + \sum_{i=1}^{q}\alpha_i^*\left(\left|\frac{u_{t-i}}{h_{t-i}}\right| - \mu\right) + \sum_{i=1}^{p}\phi_i \log h_{t-i}^2 + \delta'\mathbf{w}_t \tag{6.25}$$

where $\mu = E(|\frac{u_t}{h_t}|)$.

The value of $\mu$ depends on the density function assumed for the standardized disturbances, $\epsilon_t = u_t/h_t$. This model, which is due to Nelson (1991), allows for the possible asymmetric effects of past errors on the conditional error variances.

**Option 6** enables you to estimate the EGARCH($p,q$)-in-mean model given by (6.23) and (6.25). See Section 18.16.4 for more details.

### 6.14.1 Specification of the GARCH, AGARCH, and EGARCH models

When you choose any one of the estimation options in the GARCH Estimation Menu you will be presented with the following sub-menu:

0. Return to GARCH Estimation Menu
1. Estimate assuming a normal distribution for conditional errors
2. Estimate assuming a $t$-distribution for conditional errors

This gives a choice between a conditional normal density and a conditional standardized Student-$t$ distribution for the disturbances.[10] Once you have selected one of these two conditional distributions you will be asked to specify the orders of the GARCH($p,q$) in the box editor that appears on the screen. You need to type the non-zero lags in the AR and the MA parts of the GARCH specification, respectively.

Separate the two sets of numbers by ;.

Each set of numbers should be in ascending order.

A set can contain only a single 0.

Examples:

[10]The use of the Student-$t$ distribution for the standardized errors $\epsilon_t = u_t/h_t$ has been suggested by Bollerslev (1987).

To specify an ARCH(1) type: 0 ; 1 [OK]
To specify a GARCH(2,1) type: 1 2 ; 1 [OK]
To specify a restricted ARCH(4) type: 0 ; 4 [OK]
To specify OLS/ML estimation type: 0 ; 0 [OK]

Notice that the same rules apply when you specify the AGARCH and EGARCH class of models.

Once you have specified the orders of your GARCH model, the program asks you to specify the list of the variables $\mathbf{w}_t$ (if any) to be added to the specification of the conditional variance equations: see (6.22), (6.24), and (6.25). If you do not wish to include any other variables in the equation for the conditional variances, simply click OK to move to the next stage of the program where you will be asked to supply initial estimates for the parameters of the GARCH-M models.

### 6.14.2 Specification of the initial parameter values for the GARCH, AGARCH, and EGARCH models

Once you have completed the specification of your conditional heteroscedastic model, you will be asked to supply initial estimates for the parameters of your model. Type your choice and click OK. You will now be asked to choose a damping factor in the range [0.01, 2.0]. This damping factor is multiplied by the Hessian matrix in the Newton–Raphson algorithm (see Section 6.2.1). An appropriate choice for the initial estimates and the damping factor is often critical for a successful convergence of the numerical algorithm used to compute the ML estimates. This is particularly important in the case of generalized ARCH models with a non-zero AR component.

*Notes*

1. The algorithm often fails to converge if you try to estimate a GARCH model when there is in fact no statistically significant evidence of an ARCH effect in the data. After running an OLS regression to check for the presence of an ARCH effect in your regression, use option 2 in the Hypothesis Testing Menu (see Section 6.24).
2. It is often advisable not to choose initial values which are on the boundary of the feasible set. For example, in the case of the GARCH specification (6.22), the values of $\alpha_i$ and $\phi_i$ should be such that $\Sigma_{i=1}^{q}\alpha_i + \Sigma_{i=1}^{p}\phi_i$ is not too close to unity. It is important that *positive non-zero* values are chosen for these parameters.
3. Make sure that the residuals in the underlying regression model are not serially correlated. The presence of significant residual serial correlation can create problems for the ML estimation of the GARCH model.

4. Initially, try to see whether convergence can be achieved with a small damping factor. If not, try other values. The default value for the damping factor in *Microfit* is 0.01.
5. The algorithm may fail to converge if the observations on the dependent variable are very small. Scale up these observations and re-estimate the GARCH model.

### 6.14.3 Estimation results for the GARCH-M options

The estimation results for the GARCH-M options are summarized in a table. The top half gives the ML estimates of the regression coefficients, $\beta$, and the estimate of $\gamma$ (when a GARCH-in-mean model is estimated), their estimated asymptotic standard errors and $t$-ratios, as well as a number of summary statistics and model selection criteria. The bottom of the table table gives the ML estimates of the parameters of the conditional variance model together with their asymptotic standard errors.

After the estimation results you are presented with the Post Regression Menu. This contains a number of options described in detail in Section 6.21. In particular, you can plot/save estimates of the conditional standard errors, $\hat{h}_t$, and save their forecasts, if any. (To compute forecasts of $h_t$ you need to choose options 8 or 9 in the Post Regression Menu.) You can also plot the histogram of the standardized (or scaled) residuals, $\hat{\epsilon}_t = \hat{u}_t/\hat{h}_t$. To access these options select option 3 in the Post Regression Menu after the GARCH estimation results.

## 6.15 Recursive regression options

Option 2 in the Single Equation Estimation Menu (Univariate Menu: see Section 6.4) is the Recursive Linear Regression Menu with the following options:

1. Recursive Least Squares
2. 2-stage Recursive Least Squares

**Option 1** enables you to estimate a linear regression equation recursively using the OLS method.

**Option 2** allows you to estimate a linear regression equation recursively using the 2SLS (or the IV) method. When you choose this option you will be prompted to list at least as many instruments as there are regressors in your model.

Specify the estimation period and your linear regression equation as described in Sections 6.5.1 and 6.5.2. When the computations are completed you will be presented with the Recursive OLS (or IV) Regression Results Menu described in Section 6.15.1. For details of the algorithms used in carrying out the necessary computations, see Section 18.17.

### 6.15.1 Recursive OLS Regression Results Menu

This menu has the following options:

0. Move to Backtracking Menu
1. Plot recursive coefficients and their standard errors
2. Plot standard errors of recursive regressions
3. Save recursive coefficients
4. Save standard errors of recursive coefficients
5. Save standard errors of the recursive regressions
6. Save standardized recursive residuals
7. Save recursive predictions based on existing regressors
8. Save recursive predictions based on variables to be specified
9. Save adaptive coefficients

**Option 0** takes you to the Backtracking Menu (see Section 6.25).

**Option 1** allows you to plot the recursive coefficients, $\hat{\beta}_r$, $r = r^*, r^* + 1, \ldots, n$, and their standard error bands (computed as $\hat{\beta}_r$ plus or minus twice their standard errors). To avoid the large uncertainties that are associated with the initial estimates, only the final $\frac{3}{4}$ of the estimates for each coefficient are displayed; namely $r^*$ is set equal to $\frac{1}{4}n + \frac{3}{4}(k + 1)$. When you choose this option you are presented with the variable names for your regressors and are asked for the name of the regressor whose coefficient estimates you wish to see plotted. See Sections 18.17.3 and 18.17.5.

**Option 2** plots the standard errors of the recursive regressions, defined by $\hat{\sigma}_r^2, r = r^*, r^* + 1, \ldots, n$, computed using the formulae (18.151) and (18.156) for the OLS and the IV options, respectively. To avoid the uncertain initial estimates, the plots are displayed for $r^* = \frac{1}{4}n + \frac{3}{4}(k + 1)$.

**Option 3, 4,** and **5** allow you to save all the estimated recursive coefficients, their standard errors, and the standard errors of the recursive regressions as variables in *Microfit*.

**Option 6** enables you to save standardized recursive residuals defined by (18.149) and (18.154) for the OLS and the IV options, respectively.

**Option 7** enables you to save recursive predictions and their standard errors. See Section 18.17.8.

**Option 8** allows you to save recursive predictions and their standard errors obtained with respect to the variable $\mathbf{w}_t$, which may differ from the regressors, $\mathbf{x}_t$: see (18.159) in Section 18.17.8. When you choose this option you will be prompted to list the variable names in $\mathbf{w}_t$ to be used in the calculations of the recursive predictions. You *must* specify exactly the same number of variables as there are regressors in your regression equation.

**Option 9** enables you to save the adaptive coefficients defined by (18.157).

## 6.16 Rolling Linear Regression Menu

Option 3 in the Single Equation Estimation Menu (see Section 6.4) is the Rolling Linear Regression Menu. This menu has the following options:

1. Rolling least squares
2. Rolling 2-stage least squares

**Option 1** allows you to estimate the coefficients of a linear regression equation by the OLS method over successive rolling periods of a fixed length.

**Option 2** allows you to estimate the coefficients of a linear regression equation by the 2SLS (or IV) method over successive rolling periods of a fixed length (set using option 1). If you choose this option, you will be prompted to list at least as many instruments as there are regressors in your equation.

Specify the estimation and your regression equation as usual. You will be asked to type in the length of the window to be used in the estimation.

### 6.16.1 Rolling Regression Results Menu

This menu has the following options:

0. Move to Backtracking Menu (Rolling Regression)
1. Plot rolling coefficients and their standard errors
2. Plot standard errors of rolling regressions
3. Save rolling coefficients
4. Save standard errors of rolling coefficients
5. Save standard errors of rolling regressions

**Option 0** takes you to the Backtracking Menu (see Section 6.25).

**Option 1** allows you to plot the rolling regression coefficients and their standard errors. See also the description of option 1 in the Recursive Regression Results Menu in Section 6.15.1.

**Option 2** allows you to plot the standard errors of the rolling regressions.

**Options 3**, **4**, and **5** enable you to save the rolling coefficients, their standard errors, and the standard errors of the rolling regressions in *Microfit*.

## 6.17 Non-linear Regression Menu

The Non-linear Regression Menu is option 4 in the Single Equation Estimation Menu (Univariate Menu: see Section 6.4). It contains the following options:

1. Non-linear least squares
2. Non-linear 2-stage least squares

**Option 1** allows you to estimate your specified non-linear equation by the least squares method.

**Option 2** allows you to estimate your specified non-linear equation by the 2SLS (or IV) method. When you choose this option you will be prompted to list at least as many instruments as there are unknown parameters in your non-linear model.

*Notes*

1. See Section 6.17.1 on how to specify/modify a non-linear equation.
2. Special care needs to be exercised with respect to the choice of initial parameter estimates. An inappropriate choice of initial estimates can hamper the convergence of the iterative process, and may lead to error messages which can be difficult to decipher at first. For example, suppose you are interested in estimating the following non-linear equation

$$C_t = A_0 + A_1 \exp(Y_t/A_2)$$

where $C$ is real consumption expenditure, Y is the real disposable income, and $A_0$, $A_1$, and $A_2$ are unknown parameters. If you start the iterations with $A_2 = 0$, you will see an error message stating that there are insufficient observations to estimate. This is because with $A_2$ initially set equal to zero, all the values of $Y_t/A_2$, being undefined, will be set equal to *NONE*.

   Another problem that arises frequently in the estimation of non-linear regression models concerns the scaling of the regressors. In the case of the above examples, unless the $Y_t$s are reasonably small, exponentiation of $Y_t$ can result in very large numbers, and the computer will not be able to handle the estimation problem. When this arises you will see an error message on the screen.
3. A similar problem can arise when the initial value chosen for $A_2$ is too small, even if the $Y_t$s are reasonably small. In some applications the use of zero initial values for the parameters can result in an error message. It is always advisable to think carefully about the scale of your regressors and the choice of the initial parameter values before running the non-linear regression option.
4. When estimating a linear regression equation via the non-linear regression option, it is all right to use zeros as initial values for the parameters.
5. The least squares and the IV options in the Non-linear Regression Menu allow you to estimate a linear or a non-linear regression, subject to linear or non-linear parametric restrictions. For example, to estimate the ARDL model

$$y_t = \alpha + \lambda y_{t-1} + \beta_1 x_t + \beta_2 x_{t-1} + u_t$$

subject to the common factor restrictions

$$\beta_1 \lambda + \beta_2 = 0$$

you need to type the following formula.

$$Y = A0 + A1 * Y(-1) + A2 * X - A1 * A2 * X(-1) \quad \boxed{\text{START}}$$

6. The non-linear 2SLS option can also be used to estimate Euler equations, namely the first-order conditions for intertemporal optimization problems under uncertainty. For an example, see Lesson 13.2.

### 6.17.1 Specification of a non-linear regression equation

Enter the specification of your non-linear equation; type the formula for the equation in the box editor provided on the screen. You can type your formula using standard arithmetic operators such as +, −, /, and *, and any one of the built-in functions set out in Section 4.2. For example, suppose you are interested in estimating the following Cobb–Douglas production function with additive errors:

$$Y_t = AL_t^{\alpha}K_t^{\beta} + u_t$$

where $Y_t$ is output, $L_t$ and $K_t$ are labour and capital inputs, and $u_t$ is a disturbance term. The unknown parameters are represented by $A$, $\alpha$, and $\beta$. Then you need to type

Y = A0 * (L ^ A1) * (K ^ A2) [START]

As another example, suppose you wish to specify the following non-linear regression:

$$z_t = \alpha_1 e^{\beta_1 x_{1t}} + \alpha_2 e^{\beta_2 x_{2t}} + u_t$$

In the box editor which appears on the screen you need to type

Z = a1 * exp(b1 * X1) + a2 * exp(b2 * X2) [START]

When specifying a non-linear regression, the following points are worth bearing in mind:

1. In the case of the above two examples, it is assumed that the variables Y, K, and L, and z, x1, and x2 are in the variables list and that A0, A1, A2, B1, and B2 are parameters to be estimated, and are not, therefore, in your list of variables. (Note that in *Microfit* upper- and lower-case letters are treated as identical.)
2. You need to watch for two important types of mistakes: using an existing variable name to represent a parameter value, and including a non-existent variable in the specification of the non-linear equation. *Microfit* is not capable of recognizing these types of mistakes. But you should be able to detect your mistakes at a later stage when you will be asked to give initial estimates for the unknown parameters of your equation (see Section 6.17.2). If, by mistake, you use a variable name to present a parameter, you will not be asked to supply an initial estimate for the parameter in question, and most likely the computations will fail to converge. In the opposite case, where a non-existent variable is included in the regression equation, *Microfit* treats the non-existent variable as an

unknown parameter and asks you to supply an initial estimate for it! *To reduce the probability of making such mistakes we recommend that you reserve the names $A0, A1, A2$, etc. and $B0, B1, B2$, etc. for parameter values, and try not to use them as names for the variables in the variables list.*

3. Mistakes in typing the regression formula are readily detected by *Microfit*. But you need to fix the problem by carefully checking the non-linear formula that you have typed, and by making sure that you have not inadvertently mixed up variable names and parameter values!
4. The list of variables specified under the various estimation options, including the non-linear equation specified under option 4, can be saved in a file for use at a later stage using the [icon] button. The variable lists are saved in files with the extension .LST, and the non-linear equations are saved in files with the extension .EQU. To retrieve a file you saved earlier, click the [icon] button.

## 6.17.2 Specification of initial parameter estimates

The non-linear estimation option and the other estimation methods that use iterative techniques will require you to supply initial values for the unknown parameters in your specified econometric model. In such cases you will be presented with a screen containing the names of the known parameters, all of which are initially set equal to zero. You can change these initial settings by moving the cursor to the desired position and typing your own choice of the initial estimate. These initial parameter values can be changed if the estimation method fails to converge.

## 6.17.3 Estimation results for the non-linear regression equation

Once the estimation of the non-linear equation is successfully complete, you will be presented with the estimation results in a format similar to that given for the OLS and the IV options in the case of linear regression (see Section 6.5). *Microfit* also automatically computes diagnostic statistics for tests of residual serial correlation, functional form misspecification, non-normality of disturbances, and heteroscedasticity in the case of non-linear equations estimated by the least squares or the IV methods. These statistics are computed using the same procedures as outlined in Sections 18.5.2 and 18.9, with the matrix $\mathbf{X}$ replaced by the matrix of first derivatives (of the non-linear equation with respect to the unknown parameters) evaluated at the parameter estimates obtained on convergence. The non-linear options do not compute statistics for structural stability and predictive failure tests.

The relevant formulae for the non-linear estimation options are given in 18.21.

## 6.18 Phillips–Hansen Estimation Menu

This menu allows you to estimate the parameters of a *single* cointegrating relation by the fully-modified OLS (FM–OLS) procedure proposed by Phillips and Hansen (1990). The underlying econometric model is given by

$$y_t = \beta_0 + \beta_1' \mathbf{x}_t + u_t,\ t = 1, 2, \ldots, n \tag{6.26}$$

where $y_t$ is an $I(1)$ variable, and $\mathbf{x}_t$ is a $k \times 1$ vector of $I(1)$ regressors, assumed not to be cointegrated among themselves.[11] It is also assumed that $\mathbf{x}_t$ has the following first-difference stationary process:

$$\Delta \mathbf{x}_t = \boldsymbol{\mu} + \mathbf{v}_t,\ t = 2, 3, \ldots, n \tag{6.27}$$

where $\boldsymbol{\mu}$ is a $k \times 1$ vector of drift parameters, and $\mathbf{v}_t$ is a $k \times 1$ vector of $I(0)$, or stationary variables. It is also assumed that $\boldsymbol{\xi}_t = (u_t, \mathbf{v}_t')'$ is strictly stationary with zero mean and a finite positive-definite covariance matrix, $\Sigma$.

The OLS estimators of $\boldsymbol{\beta} = (\beta_0, \boldsymbol{\beta}_1')'$ in (6.26) are consistent even if $\mathbf{x}_t$ and $u_t$ (equivalently $\mathbf{v}_t$ and $u_t$) are contemporaneously correlated: see, for example, Engle and Granger (1987), and Stock (1987). But in general the asymptotic distribution of the OLS estimator involves the unit-root distribution and is non-standard; carrying out inferences on $\boldsymbol{\beta}$ using the usual $t$-tests in the OLS regression of (6.26) will be invalid. To overcome these problems appropriate corrections for the possible correlation between $u_t$ and $\mathbf{v}_t$ and their lagged values is required. The Phillips–Hansen FM-OLS estimator takes account of these correlations in a semi-parametric manner. But it is important to recognize that the validity of this estimation procedure critically depends on the assumption that $\mathbf{x}_t$s are $I(1)$ and are not themselves cointegrated. For Monte Carlo evidence on small sample properties of the FM-OLS estimators see Pesaran and Shin (1995a). For details of the computational algorithms see Section 18.18.

To access this menu, select option 5 in the Single Equation Estimation Menu (Univariate Menu: see Section 6.4). It contains the following options:

1. None of the regressors has a drift
2. At least one regressor is $I(1)$ with drift

You need to choose option 1 if $\boldsymbol{\mu}$ in (6.27) is zero. Otherwise you should select option 2. List the dependent variable, $y_t$, followed by the $I(1)$ regressors, $x_{1t}, x_{2t}, \ldots, x_{kt}$, in the box editor on the screen. Do not include intercept or time trends among the regressors. Specify your estimation period and the length of your lag window. When you press START you will be presented with the following menu for selecting the lag window for the estimation of the long-run variances used in the estimation procedure:

[11]A variable is said to be $I(1)$ if it must be differenced once before it can be rendered stationary. A random walk variable is a simple example of an $I(1)$ variable. A set of $I(1)$ variables are said to be cointegrated if a linear combination of them exists which is $I(0)$, or stationary. For further details see, for example, Engle and Granger (1991).

0. Move to Backtracking Menu
1. Equal weights lag window
2. Bartlett lag window
3. Tukey lag window
4. Parzen lag window

The use of the equal weights (or uniform) lag window may result in negative standard errors, and when this happens you need to choose one of the other three lag windows. We recommend the Parzen lag window.

Once the lag window is chosen you will be asked to specify the length of the lag window (if this has not been done already), and are then presented with the estimation results. You can also carry out tests of linear and non-linear restrictions on the cointegrating coefficients $\boldsymbol{\beta} = (\beta_0, \boldsymbol{\beta}_1')'$, using the options in the Post Regression Menu (see Section 6.21).

## 6.19 ARDL approach to cointegration

Option 6 in the Single Equation Estimation Menu (Univariate Menu: see Section 6.4) allows you to estimate the following ARDL($p, q_1, q_2, \ldots, q_k$) models:

$$\phi(L,p)y_t = \sum_{i=1}^{k} \beta_i(L,q_i)\mathbf{x}_{it} + \delta'\mathbf{w}_t + u_t \tag{6.28}$$

where

$$\begin{aligned} \phi(L,p) &= 1 - \phi_1 L - \phi_2 L^2 - \ldots - \phi_p L^p \\ \beta_i(L,q_i) &= 1 - \beta_{i1} L - \beta_{i2} L^2 - \ldots - \beta_{iq_i} L^{q_i}, \text{ for } i = 1, 2, \ldots, k \end{aligned} \tag{6.29}$$

$L$ is a lag operator such that $Ly_t = y_{t-1}$, and $\mathbf{w_t}$ is a $s \times 1$ vector of deterministic variables such as the intercept term, seasonal dummies, time trends, or exogenous variables with fixed lags. *Microfit* first estimates (6.28) by the OLS method for *all* possible values of $p = 0, 1, 2, \ldots, m$; $q_i = 0, 1, 2, \ldots, m$; $i = 1, 2, \ldots, k$: namely a total of $(m+1)^{k+1}$ different ARDL models. The maximum lag, $m$, is chosen by the user, and all the models are estimated on the same sample period, namely $t = m+1, m+2, \ldots, n$.

In the second stage the user is given the option of selecting one of the $(m+1)^{k+1}$ estimated models using one of the following four model selection criteria: the $\bar{R}^2$ criterion, Akaike information criterion (AIC), Schwarz Bayesian criterion (SBC), or the Hannan–Quinn criterion (HQC).[12] The program then computes the long-run coefficients and their asymptotic standard errors for the selected ARDL model. It also provides estimates of the error correction model (ECM) which corresponds to the selected ARDL

[12]These model selection criteria are described in Section (18.6).

model. For further details and the relevant formulae for the computation of the long-run coefficients and the associated ECM, see Section 18.19.

### 6.19.1 Specification of an ARDL regression equation

Specify the estimation period and maximum lag order $m(m < 24)$ for your ARDL specification before specifying your equation. The list of the variables to be included in the ARDL model should be typed in followed by deterministic regressors such as the intercept term, time trends, and regressors with fixed lags. The two sets of variables should be separated by &. The dependent variable should be the first variable in the list. The first set of variables should not appear in lagged or lead form, and it should not contain an intercept term or time trends.

As an example, suppose you wish to specify the following ARDL model:

$$\phi(L,s)y_t = \alpha_0 + \alpha_1 T_t + \alpha_2 z_t + \beta_1(L,s)x_{1t} \\ + \beta_2(L,s)x_{2t} + u_t$$

where $\phi(L,s)$, $\beta_i(L,s)$, $i = 1, 2$ are polynomial lag operators of the maximum order equal to $s$; $T_t$ is a deterministic time trend, and $z_t$ is an exogenous regressor. Once presented with the box editor you need to type

Y X1 X2 & INPT T Z [START]

It is important to note that even in the case of ARDL models with a small number of regressors (say $k = 2$), the number of ARDL models to be estimated could be substantial, if $m$ is chosen to be larger than 6. In the case where $k = 2$, and $m = 6$, the total number of ARDL models to be estimated by the program is equal to $(6 + 1)^3 = 343$. If the number of ARDL models to be estimated exceeds 125, you will be presented with a warning that the computation may take a long time to complete. If you choose to go ahead, *Microfit* carries out the necessary computations and presents you with the ARDL Order Selection Menu (see Section 6.19.2).

### 6.19.2 ARDL Order Selection Menu

This menu has the following options:

0. Move to Backtracking Menu
1. Choose maximum lag to be used in model selection
2. R-BAR Squared
3. Akaike Information Criterion
4. Schwarz Bayesian Criterion
5. Hannan–Quinn Criterion
6. Specify the order of the ARDL model yourself

**Option 1** allows you to change the maximum lag order, *s*, to be used in the computations.

**Option 2** selects the orders of the ARDL($p, q_1, q_2, \ldots, q_k$) model, namely the values of $p, q_1, q_2, \ldots, q_k$ using the $\bar{R}^2$ criterion.

**Option 3** selects the orders of the ARDL model using the Akaike information criterion.

**Option 4** selects the orders of the ARDL model using the Schwarz Bayesian criterion.

**Option 5** selects the orders of the ARDL model using the Hannan–Quinn criterion.

**Option 6** allows you to specify your own choice of the lag orders, $p, q_1, q_2, \ldots, q_k$. When you choose this option you will be asked to specify exactly $k+1$ integers representing the order of the lag on the dependent variable, followed by the order(s) of the lag(s) on the *k* regressor(s). *Microfit* works out the maximum value of these orders which can be chosen by the user given the sample size available.

Once the orders $p, q_1, q_2, \ldots, q_k$ are selected either using one of the model selection criteria (options 2 to 5) or by specifying them yourself (option 6), you will be presented with the Post ARDL Model Selection Menu (see Section 6.19.3).

### 6.19.3 Post ARDL Model Selection Menu

This menu has the following options:

0. Return to ARDL Order Selection Menu
1. Display the estimates of the selected ARDL regression
2. Display long run coefficients and their asymptotic standard errors
3. Display Error Correction Model
4. Compute forecasts from the ARDL model

**Option 0** returns you to the ARDL Order Selection Menu (see Section 6.19.2).

**Option 1** gives the estimated coefficients of the ARDL model, together with the associated summary and diagnostic statistics. This option also allows you to make use of all the options available under the OLS method for hypothesis testing, plotting fitted values, residuals, leverage measures, etc. (see Section 6.6).

**Option 2** presents you with a table giving the estimates of the long-run coefficients, their asymptotic standard errors, and the associated *t*-ratios. The orders $\hat{p}, \hat{q}_1, \hat{q}_2, \ldots, \hat{q}_k$ selected for the underlying ARDL model are also specified at the top of the table.

**Option 3** displays a result table containing the estimates of the error correction model (ECM) associated with the selected ARDL model. These estimates are computed using the relations in Section 18.19, and allow for possible parametric restrictions that may exist across the long-run and the short-run coefficients. The estimated standard errors also take account of such parametric restrictions.

**Option 4** computes computes forecasts based on the selected ARDL model, and asks you whether you wish to see forecasts of the levels or the first-differences of $y_t$. You will then be presented with the ARDL Forecast Menu (see Section 6.19.4).

### 6.19.4 ARDL Forecast Menu

This menu appears on the screen if you choose option 4 in the Post ARDL Model Selection Menu (see Section 6.19.3). It contains the following options:

0. Choose another variable
1. Display forecasts and forecast errors
2. Plot of in-sample fitted values and out of sample forecasts
3. Save in-sample fitted values and out of sample forecasts

**Option 0** enables you to alter your choice of the levels or the first-differences of $y_t$ that you may wish to forecast.

**Option 1** displays the forecasts and the forecast errors for $y_t$ (or $\Delta y_t$) computed on the basis of the selected ARDL model. It also provides a number of summary statistics computed for both the estimation and the prediction periods.

**Option 2** plots the actual values of $y_t$ (or $\Delta y_t$), and the fitted and forecast values of $y_t$ (or $\Delta y_t$) over the estimation and the forecast periods, respectively.

**Option 3** allows you to save the fitted values of $y_t$ (or $\Delta y_t$) over the estimation period, and the forecast values of $y_t$ (or $\Delta y_t$) over the forecast period.

## 6.20 Logit and Probit models

The Logit and Probit options are appropriate when the dependent variable $y_i$, $i = 1, 2, \ldots, n$ takes the value of 1 or 0. In econometrics such models naturally arise when the economic agents are faced with a choice between *two* alternatives (for example, whether to use public transportation, or to purchase a car), and their choice depends on a set of $k$ explanatory variables or factors. The models are also referred to as 'qualitative' or 'limited dependent' variable models. In the biological literature they are known as 'quantal variables' or as 'stimulus and response models'.

Comprehensive surveys of the literature on binary response models can be found in McFadden (1976) and Amemiya (1981). Other useful references are Maddala (1983), Judge *et al.* (1985, Chapter 18), Cramer (1991), and Greene (1993, Chapter 21).

### 6.20.1 Specification of the Logit/Probit model

To access the Logit and Probit estimation options choose option 7 in the Single Equation Estimation Menu (Univariate Menu: see Section 6.4). You will then be asked to list the dependent variable, $y_i$, followed by the regressors (or the explanatory) variables, $x_{i1}, x_{i2}, \ldots, x_{ik}$. The dependent variable must contain only ones and zeros. The explanatory variables could contain both continuous and discrete variables. Select a sample period for estimation. If the dependent variable in your model contains values other than ones and zeros you will be presented with an error message to that effect; click OK to continue. This will take you to the Backtracking Menu for the Logit/Probit estimator.

### 6.20.2 Logit/Probit Estimation Menu

You will be presented with this menu when you have successfully specified the list of the variables in the Logit/Probit model and the estimation period (see Section 6.20.1). The Logit/Probit Estimation Menu contains the following options:

0. Move to Backtracking Menu
1. Estimate/Test/Forecast with a Logit model
2. Estimate/Test/Forecast with a Probit model

**Option 0** takes you to the Backtracking Menu (see Section 6.25) for the Logit/Probit estimation.

**Option 1** computes ML estimates of the coefficients assuming the logistic probability model:

$$\Pr(y_i = 1) = \Lambda(\boldsymbol{\beta}'\mathbf{x}_i) = \frac{e^{\boldsymbol{\beta}'\mathbf{x}_i}}{1 + e^{\boldsymbol{\beta}'\mathbf{x}_i}}, \quad i = 1, 2, \ldots, n \tag{6.30}$$

where $\boldsymbol{\beta} = (\beta_1, \beta_2, \ldots, \beta_k)'$ is the $k \times 1$ vector of unknown coefficients, and $\mathbf{x}_i$ is a $k \times 1$ vector of explanatory variables, possibly containing a vector of ones (the intercept term). The effect of a unit change in the $j$th element of $\mathbf{x}_i$ on $\Pr(y_i = 1)$ is given by

$$\frac{\partial \Pr(y_i = 1)}{\partial x_{ij}} = \beta_j \Lambda_i(1 - \Lambda_i), \quad \text{for} \quad j = 1, 2, \ldots, k \quad \text{and} \quad i = 1, 2, \ldots, n \tag{6.31}$$

where $\Lambda_i = \Lambda(\boldsymbol{\beta}'\mathbf{x}_i)$. The ML estimation is carried out using the iterative method of scoring: see (18.195).

**Option 2** computes ML estimates of the coefficients assuming the normal probability model

$$\Pr(y_i = 1) = \Phi(\boldsymbol{\gamma}'\mathbf{x}_i) = \int_{-\infty}^{\boldsymbol{\gamma}'\mathbf{x}_i} \frac{1}{\sqrt{2\pi}} \exp\{-\tfrac{1}{2}t^2\} \mathrm{d}t \tag{6.32}$$

where, as in option 1 above, $\gamma$ is a $k \times 1$ vector of unknown coefficients and $\mathbf{x_i}$ is a $k \times 1$ vector of explanatory variables. In the case of this option the effect of a unit change in the $j$th element of $\mathbf{x_i}$ on $\Pr(y_i = 1)$ is given by

$$\frac{\partial \Pr(y_i = 1)}{\partial x_{ij}} = \beta_j \phi(\beta' \mathbf{x}_i), \quad \text{for} \quad j = 1, 2, \ldots, k, \quad \text{and} \quad i = 1, 2, \ldots, n \tag{6.33}$$

where $\phi(\cdot)$ stands for the standard normal density

$$\phi(\beta' \mathbf{x}_i) = (2\pi)^{-1/2} \exp\{-\tfrac{1}{2}(\beta' \mathbf{x}_i)^2\}$$

### 6.20.3 Estimation results for Logit and Probit options

The estimation results for both the Logit and Probit options are set out in a table with two parts. The top part gives the ML estimates of coefficients together with their (asymptotic) standard errors and the $t$-ratios. The bottom part of the table gives the factor

$$\Lambda(\hat{\beta}' \bar{\mathbf{x}}_i)(1 - \Lambda(\hat{\beta}' \bar{\mathbf{x}}))$$

or

$$\phi(\hat{\beta}' \bar{\mathbf{x}}_i)$$

needed to compute the marginal effects (6.31) and (6.33) for different coefficients evaluated at sample means, a number of summary statistics, test statistics, and model selection criteria. Here $\bar{\mathbf{x}}$ refers to the sample mean of the regressors. The details of these are given in Section 18.20.3.

Since under both probability models the log-likelihood function is concave, the computations usually converge very quickly to the unique ML estimators (when they exist). Also note that the variances of the logistic and normal distributions that underlie the Logit and Probit options differ and are given by $\pi^2/3$ and 1, respectively. As a result, to ensure comparability of the ML estimates obtained under these two options, the ML estimates using the Probit option must be multiplied by $\pi/\sqrt{3} \approx 1.814$ to make them comparable with those computed using the Logit option.

The problem of choosing between the Probit and Logit models can be approached either by application of model selection criteria (such as the Akaike information criterion or the Schwarz Bayesian criterion) or by means of non-nested hypothesis testing procedures. In cases where the Logit and Probit options are used on the same set of regressors, $\mathbf{x}_i$, the applications of the various model selection criteria are reduced to a simple comparison of the maximized log-likelihood values. In practice these log-likelihood values will be quite close, particularly if the estimates of $\beta' \mathbf{x}_i$ (or $\gamma' \mathbf{x}_i$) lie in the range $(-1.6, 1.6)$. In these circumstances the application of the non-nested testing methods is more appropriate: see Pesaran and Pesaran (1993).

### 6.20.4 Logit/Probit Post Estimation Menu

You will be presented with this menu when you have finished with the estimation results table (see above). This menu has the following options:

0. Return to Logit/Probit Estimation Menu
1. Display results again
2. List actual and fitted values, and fitted probabilities
3. Plot actual values and fitted probabilities
4. Save fitted probabilities (and forecasts if any)
5. Wald test of linear/nonlinear restrictions
6. Estimate/test functions of parameters of the model
7. Compute forecasts

**Option 0** takes you back to the Logit/Probit Estimation Menu (see Section 6.20.2).

**Option 1** enables you to see the ML estimation results again (see Section 6.20.3).

**Option 2** lists actual values $y_i$, the fitted values $\hat{y}_i$, and the fitted probability values, $\Phi(\hat{\beta}'\mathbf{x}_i)$ and $\Lambda(\hat{\beta}'\mathbf{x}_i)$, for the Probit and Logit options, respectively (see Section 18.20.2).

**Option 3** plots actual values $y_i$ and the fitted values, $\Phi(\hat{\beta}'\mathbf{x}_i)$ and $\Lambda(\hat{\beta}'\mathbf{x}_i)$, for the Probit and Logit options, respectively.

**Option 4** allows you to save fitted probability values and their forecasts (if any). Use option 7 to compute forecasts of probability values.

**Option 5** enables you to carry out Wald tests for linear and non-linear restrictions on the coefficients $\beta$. Also see option 7 in the Hypothesis Testing Menu (see Section 6.24). For the relevant formulae, see Section 18.25.

**Option 6** allows you to estimate linear and non-linear functions of the coefficients $\beta$. Also see option 5 in the Post Regression Menu (see Section 6.21). For the relevant formulae, see Section 18.24.

**Option 7** computes forecasts of the probability values and the associated forecasts of $y$ using the formulae in Section 18.20.4. This option also gives a number of summary statistics computed over the estimation and forecast periods.

## 6.21 Post Regression Menu

This menu appears on the screen immediately after the estimation results for the single equation linear and the non-linear estimation options. The Probit and Logit estimation option has its own Post Estimation Menu (see Section 6.20.4). The Post Regression Menu contains the following options:

0. Move to Backtracking Menu
1. Display regression results again
2. Move to Hypothesis Testing Menu
3. List/plot/save residuals and fitted values

4. Standard, White and Newey-West adjusted variance menu
5. Estimate/test (possibly non-linear) functions of parameters
6. Plot the leverage measures of the regression (OLS)
7. Save the leverage measures of the regression (OLS)
8. Forecast
9. Plot of forecast values only

These options enable you to study the properties of your specified regression equation in more detail. The default selection is option 2 in the case of the least squares and the IV methods; otherwise it is option 1.

**Option 0** takes you to the Backtracking Menu, where a new estimation period and/or a regression equation can be specified (see Section 6.25).

**Option 1** enables you to see your regression results again.

**Option 2** takes you to the Hypothesis Testing Menu (see Section 6.24).

**Option 3** takes you to the Display/Save Residuals and Fitted Values Menu (see Section 6.22).

**Option 4** takes you to the menu for the computation of alternative estimators of the variance matrices (see Section 6.23).

**Option 5** allows you to estimate linear or non-linear functions of the parameters of your regression model. In the case of linear regressions *Microfit* assigns $A1$, $A2$, . . ., to the regression coefficients and $B1$, $B2$, . . ., to the parameters of the AR/MA error processes. For non-linear regression, *Microfit* works directly in terms of the parameter names that you have specified. When you choose this option you will be asked to type your functions individually in the box editor that appears on the screen, separating the functions by a semicolon (;). The program computes and displays the estimates of the functions and the estimates of their (asymptotic) variance-covariance matrix. The relevant formula for the variance-covariance matrix of the parameter estimates is given in Section 18.24.

**Option 6** provides plots of the measures of the leverage (or the influence) of points in the regression design, together with a horizontal line representing the average value of the leverage measures. (See Section 6.6.7 for more details and relevant references to the literature.)

**Option 7** allows you to save the leverage measures for subsequent analysis.

**Option 8** computes static or dynamic forecasts of the dependent variable conditional on the observed values of the regressors over the forecast period, if any, together with forecast errors, and the standard errors of the forecast. Dynamic forecasts will be computed if the lagged values of the dependent variable are explicitly included among the regressors (see note 1 in Section 6.5.1). When you choose this option you will be asked to specify the final observation in your forecast period. Type in the observation number, or the relevant date, and click OK. To choose all the available observations in the forecast period, click OK. (See Section 18.26 for details of the computations.)

**Option 9** provides a plot of actual and forecast values. The emphasis in this plot is on the forecast values and, in contrast to the plot provided under option 8, it does not, in general, cover the whole of the estimation period.

## 6.22 Display/Save Residuals and Fitted Values Menu

This is a sub-menu of the Post Regression Menu and contains the following options:

0. Return to Post Regression Menu
1. List residuals and fitted values
2. Plot actual and fitted values
3. Plot residuals
4. Plot the autocorrelation function and the spectrum of residuals
5. Plot the histogram of residuals
6. Save residuals (and forecast errors if any)
7. Save fitted values (and forecasts if any)

**Option 0** takes you back to the Post Regression Menu (see Section 6.21).

**Option 1** displays the residuals and fitted values, together with the actual values of the dependent variable. In the case of the AR and MA options (i.e. options 3 to 8 in the Linear Regression Menu), adjusted residuals and fitted values are reported.

**Option 2** provides a plot of actual and (adjusted) fitted values.

**Option 3** provides a plot of (adjusted) residuals, together with a standard error band. The band represents $\pm 2\hat{\sigma}_\epsilon$, where $\hat{\sigma}_\epsilon$ is the estimated standard error of the regression.

**Option 4** displays graphs of the autocorrelation function and the standardized spectral density function of the residuals estimated using the Parzen window. To obtain estimates that utilize other windows or to compute the standard errors of these estimates, you can apply the COR and the SPECTRUM commands to the residuals, after saving them using option 6 in this menu.

**Option 5** displays a histogram of the residuals. If you wish to produce a histogram with a different number of bands, save the residuals using option 6 in this menu and then apply the HIST command to the saved residuals in the Command Editor.

**Option 6** allows you to save the residuals and forecast errors (if any) in a variable for use in subsequent analyses. When you select this option, you will be asked to specify a variable name for the residuals to be saved. Type in the variable name followed by an optional description and click OK.

**Option 7** allows you to save fitted and forecast values (if any) in a variable for use in subsequent analyses (see option 6 of this menu for more details).

## 6.23 Standard, White and Newey–West Adjusted Variance Menu

This menu has the following options:

0. Return to Post Regression Menu
1. Standard variance-covariance matrix

2. White heteroscedasticity adjusted
3. Newey–West adjusted with equal weights
4. Newey–West adjusted with Bartlett weights
5. Newey–West adjusted with Tukey weights
6. Newey–West adjusted with Parzen weights

**Option 0** returns you to the Post Regression Menu (see Section 6.21).

**Option 1** displays the conventional variance-covariance matrix of the estimated coefficients. This option applies to all the methods available for the estimation of linear and non-linear regression models. It also computes and displays the covariance matrix of the regression coefficients and the parameters of the AR and MA error processes.

**Option 2** computes and displays a 'degree of freedom adjusted' version of White's (1980, 1982) heteroscedasticity-consistent estimates of the variance-covariance matrix of the parameter estimates in the case of the OLS, the IV, the non-linear least squares, and the non-linear IV options. (See Section 18.22 for the relevant formulae.) If you click CLOSE, you are presented with the following choices:

0. Return to White and Newey–West Adjusted Variance Menu
1. Display regression results for the adjusted covariance matrix
2. Display the adjusted covariance matrix
3. Wald test of restrictions based on adjusted covariance matrix
4. Estimate/test functions of parameters based on adjusted matrix

The options in this sub-menu allow you to test hypotheses on the regression coefficients using the heteroscedasticity-consistent estimates of the variance-covariance matrices.

**Options 3** to **6** compute a 'degree of freedom adjusted' version of the Newey–West (1987) heteroscedasticity and autocorrelation consistent estimates of the variance-covariance matrix of the parameter estimates, in the case of the linear and non-linear least squares and IV options for different choices of lag windows (see Section 18.23). Newey and West use the Bartlett weights but in general the Parzen weights are preferable. The 'equal weights' option is relevant when the residual serial correlation can be approximated by a finite order MA process. When you choose any of these options you are prompted to specify the size of the lag window. We recommend that you do not specify a window size which is in excess of one third of the available observations. *Microfit* then computes and displays the estimates of the Newey–West adjusted variance-covariance matrices. If you click CLOSE, you are presented with the same choices as in the case of option 2 (White heteroscedasticity adjusted variance-covariance matrix) described above.

*Note:* The formula for the White standard errors is a special case of the Newey–West formula and can also be obtained using options 3 to 6 by setting the window size equal to zero.

## 6.24 Hypothesis Testing Menu

This menu contains the following options:

0. Return to Post Regression Menu
1. LM tests for serial correlation (OLS, IV, NLS, & IV-NLS)
2. Autoregressive conditional heteroscedasticity tests (OLS & NLS)
3. Unit root tests for residuals (OLS & NLS)
4. CUSUM and CUSUMSQ tests (OLS)
5. Variable deletion test (OLS & IV)
6. Variable addition test (OLS & IV)
7. Wald test of linear/nonlinear restrictions
8. Non-nested tests against another linear regression (OLS)
9. Non-nested tests for models with different LHS variables

and allows you to subject your chosen linear and non-linear regression model to additional tests.

**Option 0** takes you back to the Post Regression Menu (see Section 6.21).

**Option 1** allows you to carry out a $p$th order test of residual serial correlation ($p \leqslant 12$). In the case of the least squares option (OLS and NLS), it provides (asymptotic) $t$-ratios for individual coefficients of the AR-error process as well as the LM, the F, and the log-likelihood ratio statistics. When this option is chosen you will be asked to specify the order of the test. Type in your answer (an integer between 1 and 12) and click OK. In the case of the least squares options, the program computes the LM and the F version of Godfrey's test statistic given respectively by (18.17) and (18.19). For the IV options, the program computes Sargan's test statistic given by (18.67).

**Option 2** allows you to compute the autoregressive-conditional heteroscedasticity (ARCH) test statistic due to Engle (1982). For an (ARCH) test of order $p$, the program computes the LM statistic for the test of $\delta_i = 0$, $i = 1, 2, ..., p$ in the auxiliary regression

$$e_t^2 = \text{intercept} + \sum_{i=1}^{p} \delta_i e_{t-i}^2 + \text{Error}$$

estimated over the period $t = p + 1,\ p + 2, \ldots, m$, where $e_t$ are the OLS residuals. See also Section 18.16.7.

**Option 3** allows you to carry out the Dickey–Fuller and augmented Dickey–Fuller tests of the unit root hypothesis in the residuals (see the ADF command for more details). This test is discussed in Engle and Granger (1987) and Engle and Yoo (1987) as a test of cointegration. The program also displays the 95 per cent critical values, using the results in MacKinnon (1991). Note that these critical values differ from those supplied with the ADF command. They depend on the number of $I(1)$ variables in the underlying regression (excluding the intercept term and the time trend), and on whether or not the regression model includes a time trend. *Microfit* checks the regressions and reports the correct critical values. If an intercept term is not included in the original regression, a warning is displayed. It is important to note that, in view of the above considerations, the direct application of the ADF command to saved residuals will generate incorrect critical values for the test, and must be avoided.

**Option 4** enables you to carry out the cumulative sum (CUSUM) and the CUSUM of squares (CUSUMSQ) tests of structural stability proposed by Brown *et al.* (1975). When you choose this option, *Microfit* displays two graphs, one giving the plot of the CUSUM statistic (18.144), and the other giving the plot of the CUSUMSQ statistic (18.146). Each graph also displays a pair of straight lines drawn at the 5 per cent level of significance defined by equations (18.145) and (18.147), respectively. If either of the lines is crossed, the null hypothesis that the regression equation is correctly specified must be rejected at the 5 per cent level of significance. The CUSUM test is particularly useful for detecting systematic changes in the regression coefficients. The CUSUMSQ test is useful in situations where the departure from the constancy of the regression coefficients is haphazard and sudden.

**Option 5** enables you to test for the statistical significance of deleting one or more regressors from your linear regression model.

**Option 6** enables you to test the statistical significance of adding one or more regressors to your linear regression model.

**Option 7** allows you to carry out a Wald test of linear or non-linear restrictions on the parameters of your model. When you choose this option, you will first be prompted to specify the number of the restrictions that you wish to test, and then the restrictions themselves.

*Notes*

1. Restrictions must be linearly independent and should not exceed the number of unknown parameters in your model.
2. In the case of linear regressions, *Microfit* assigns $A1$, $A2$, . . ., to the regression coefficients and $B1$, $B2$, . . ., to the parameters of the AR/MA error processes. For example, to test the hypothesis that in the regression of C on INPT, Y, Y(−1), C(−1) the long-run response of C to Y is equal to 1, you need to specify either $(A2+A3)/(1-A4)=1$, or $A2+A3+A4=1$. Both are mathematically equivalent and in large samples give the same results. In small samples, however, they could give very different results: see Gregory and Veall (1985, 1987). The linear form of the restriction is preferable and should be used in practice.
3. Another method of testing restrictions would be to use option 5 in the Post Regression Menu (see Section 6.21).
4. The relevant expression for the test statistic is given by (18.211).

**Option 8** enables you to compute a number of test statistics proposed in the literature for the test of non-nested linear regression models. This option also computes a number of useful summary statistics, including Akaike and Schwarz Bayesian information criteria. (See Section 18.7 for details, and for relevant references to the literature.)

**Option 9** allows you to carry out non-nested tests of the following linear regression models:

$$M_1: \mathbf{f(y)} = \mathbf{X}\beta_1 + \mathbf{u}_1, \qquad \mathbf{u}_1 \sim N(0, \sigma^2\mathbf{I}_n)$$
$$M_2: \mathbf{g(y)} = \mathbf{Z}\beta_2 + \mathbf{u}_2, \qquad \mathbf{u}_2 \sim N(0, \omega^2\mathbf{I}_n)$$

where $\mathbf{f(y)}$ and $\mathbf{g(y)}$ are known transformations of the $n \times 1$ vector of observations on the underlying dependent variable of interest, $\mathbf{y}$; and $\mathbf{X}$ and $\mathbf{Z}$ are $n \times k_1$ and $n \times k_2$ observation matrices for the models $M_1$ and $M_2$, respectively. In what follows we refer to $\mathbf{f(y)}$ and $\mathbf{g(y)}$ as the right-hand-side (RHS) variables.

When you choose this option, you will be prompted to list the regressors of model $M_2$. The currently specified regression equation will be treated as model $M_1$. Then you will be presented with the following menu, asking you to specify the nature of the transformation of the dependent variable for model $M_1$:

0. Move to Hypothesis Testing Menu
1. Linear form
2. Logarithmic form
3. Ratio form
4. Difference form
5. Log-difference form
6. General non-linear form to be specified by you

**Options 1** to **5** allow you to specify the following transformations of the dependent variable under model $M_1$:

| | |
|---|---|
| Linear form | $\mathbf{f(y)} = \mathbf{y}$ |
| Logarithmic form | $\mathbf{f(y)} = \log(\mathbf{y})$ |
| Ratio form | $\mathbf{f(y)} = \mathbf{y}/\mathbf{z}$ |
| Difference form | $\mathbf{f(y)} = \mathbf{y} - \mathbf{y}(-1)$ |
| Log-difference form | $\mathbf{f(y)} = \log \mathbf{y} - \log \mathbf{y}(-1)$ |

where $\mathbf{z}$ is another variable in the variables list. Notice that $\log(\mathbf{y})$ refers to a vector of observations with elements equal to $\log(y_t)$, $t = 1, 2, \ldots, n$. Also $\mathbf{y} - \mathbf{y}(-1)$ refers to a vector with a typical element equal to $y_t - y_{t-1}$, $t = 1, 2, \ldots, n$.

**Option 6** in this sub-menu allows you to specify your own particular functional form for $\mathbf{f(y)}$. See note 4 below for more details.

Once one of these options is chosen, the program presents you with a similar menu to identify the functional form, $\mathbf{g(y)}$, for the RHS variable under model $M_2$. Having specified the functional forms for the dependent variables of the two models, the program asks you to give the number of replications, $R$, to be used in the simulations, and computes the following test statistics: $P_E$ test statistic due to MacKinnon *et al.* (1983), the Bera-McAleer (1989) test statistic, the double-length regression test due to Davidson and MacKinnon (1984), and the simulated Cox test statistic, $SC_c$, proposed in Pesaran and Pesaran (1995). Furthermore, it reports Sargan's (1964) and Vuong's (1989) likelihood criterion for the choice between the three models (see Section 18.8 for details). Using this option it is possible, for example, to test linear versus log-linear models, first-difference models versus models in log-differences, and models in ratio forms against models in logarithms.

*Notes*

1. In the case of testing linear versus log-linear models (or first-difference versus log-difference models) the program first computes the probability of drawing a negative value of $y$ under the linear model, and displays a warning if this probability is larger than 0.0001. In such an event, the Cox statistic for testing the log-linear versus the linear model cannot be computed, and the program only computes the Cox statistic for testing the linear versus the log-linear model. See Pesaran and Pesaran (1995).
2. The results are displayed in a table in two parts. The first part gives the OLS estimates of the models $M_1$ and $M_2$, as well as the quasi-maximum likelihood estimators of the parameters of model $M_1$ and $M_2$, and vice versa. The different test statistics are displayed in the subsequent part.
3. Our experience suggests that for most problems 150 to 200 replications should be enough for achieving accuracies of up to two decimal places in the computation of the simulated Cox statistic. Nevertheless, we recommend that you try different numbers of replications to check the robustness of the results.
4. You need to choose option 6 when the functional forms **f(y)** or **g(y)** are not among the menu choices. When you choose this option you will be presented with a box editor, asking you to specify the functional forms for the RHS variable, their inverse functions, and their derivatives, for each of the non-nested models separately. You need to provide the required information first for model $M_1$ and then for model $M_2$, separating them by a semicolon (;). For example, suppose you wish to specify the functions

$$f(y_t) = \frac{y_t - y_{t-1}}{z_t}$$
$$g(y_t) = \log(y_t/z_t)$$

for the non-nested regression models $M_1$ and $M_2$, respectively. You need to type

F = (Y − (Y(−1)))/Z;  Y = Z ∗ F + Y(−1);  DFY = 1/Z;
G = log(Y/Z);  Y = Z ∗ Exp(G);  DGY = 1/Y  [OK]

Notice that the variables F, Y, G, and Z should exist in the variables list, but the variables DFY and DGY should not.

## 6.25 Backtracking Menu

The Backtracking Menu enables you to edit your regression equation, specify a new sample period for estimation, or access the other estimation menus (see Section 6.3).

The Backtracking Menu contains the following options:

1. Return to Single Equation Estimation Window
2. Choose estimation method for existing equation & sample
3. Define new sample period for existing equation
4. Edit regression equation & estimate over existing sample period
5. Define & estimate new equation over a new sample period

**Option 1** takes you to the Single Equation Estimation window (see Section 6.4). Notice that each of the estimation menus has its own Backtracking Menu, albeit with the same options. You only need to choose this option if you need to try a different estimation menu.

**Option 2** returns you to the estimation option from which the backtracking has been initiated. This option enables you to choose a different estimation method (within the currently active estimation module) for your existing regression model and sample period.

**Option 3** enables you to define a new estimation period for your regression (see Section 6.5.2).

**Option 4** takes you to the screen editor for modifying or replacing the regression equation to be estimated over the existing sample period.

**Option 5** allows you to specify a new regression equation as well as a new estimation period (see Sections 6.5.1 and 6.5.2).

# 7

# Multiple Equation Options

This chapter deals with the multiple (system) equation options in *Microfit* and covers estimation, hypothesis testing, and forecasting in the context of unrestricted vector autoregressive (VAR) models, seemingly unrelated regression equations (SURE), and cointegrating VAR models. The chapter also shows how to compute/plot orthogonalized and generalized impulse response functions, forecast error variance decompositions, and persistence profiles for the analysis of the effect of system-wide shocks on the cointegrating relations. There are also important new options for long-run structural modelling, enabling the user to estimate and test models with multiple cointegrating relations subject to general linear, (possibly) non-homogeneous restrictions. The details of the econometric methods and the computational algorithms which underlie the multivariate options are set out in Chapter 19, where references to the literature can also be found.

## 7.1 The canonical multivariate model

The multivariate estimation options in *Microfit* are all based on the following augmented vector autoregressive model of order $p$, or AVAR($p$) for short:

$$\mathbf{z}_t = \mathbf{a}_0 + \mathbf{a}_1 t + \sum_{i=1}^{p} \mathbf{\Phi}_i \mathbf{z}_{t-i} + \mathbf{\Psi}\mathbf{w}_t + \mathbf{u}_t \tag{7.1}$$

where $\mathbf{z}_t$ is an $m \times 1$ vector of jointly determined (endogenous) variables, $t$ is a linear time trend, $\mathbf{w}_t$ is a $q \times 1$ vector of exogenous variables, and $\mathbf{u}_t$ is an $m \times 1$ vector of unobserved disturbances assumed to satisfy the following assumptions:[1]

**B1: Zero Mean Assumption**. The $m \times 1$ vector of disturbances, $\mathbf{u}_t$, has zero means:

$$E(\mathbf{u}_t) = \mathbf{0}, \qquad \text{for} \quad t = 1, 2, \ldots, n$$

[1]These assumptions are the multivariate generalizations of those underlying the univariate classical linear regression model described in Section 6.1.

**B2: Homoscedasticity Assumption.** The $m \times 1$ vector of disturbances, $\mathbf{u}_t$, has a time-invariant conditional variance matrix

$$E(\mathbf{u}_t\mathbf{u}_t' | \mathbf{z}_{t-1}, \mathbf{z}_{t-2}, \ldots, \mathbf{w}_t, \mathbf{w}_{t-1}, \ldots) = \Sigma$$

where $\Sigma = (\sigma_{ij})$ is an $m \times m$ symmetric positive definite matrix.

**B3: Non-autocorrelated Error Assumption.** The $m \times 1$ vector of disturbances, $\mathbf{u}_t$, is serially uncorrelated:

$$E(\mathbf{u}_t\mathbf{u}_s') = 0 \qquad \text{for all} \qquad t \neq s$$

**B4: Orthogonality Assumption.** The $m \times 1$ vector of disturbances, $\mathbf{u}_t$, and the regressors, $\mathbf{w}_t$, are uncorrelated:

$$E(\mathbf{u}_t | \mathbf{w}_t) = 0 \qquad \text{for all } t$$

**B5: Stability Assumption.** The augmented VAR($p$) model (7.1) is stable. That is, all the roots of the determinantal equation

$$| \mathbf{I}_m - \Phi_1\lambda - \Phi_2\lambda^2 - \cdots - \Phi_p\lambda^p | = 0 \tag{7.2}$$

fall outside the unit circle.

For maximum likelihood estimation, the following normality assumption is also needed:

**B6: Normality Assumption.** The $m \times 1$ vector of disturbances has a multivariate normal distribution.

The VAR specification is chosen for its flexibility and computational ease, and it is hoped that by choosing $p$ (the order of the VAR) high enough, the residual serial correlation problem can be avoided. The conditional homosedasticity assumption, B2, is likely to be violated in the case of financial time series at monthly or higher frequencies. But there are no options in *Microfit* 4.0 to deal with multivariate GARCH models. Assumption B2 does, however, allow for contemporaneous correlation across the errors in different equations, and therefore also accommodates instantaneous feedback between the different variables in $\mathbf{z}_t$.

The canonical multivariate model (7.1) also forms the basis of the seemingly unrelated regression equations (SURE) and the restricted SURE options in *Microfit*. The general SURE model results when one allows for different lag orders and/or exogenous variables in different equations in (7.1) (see Section 7.6).

Finally, the cointegrating VAR options discussed in Section 7.5 are based on (7.1) but allow one or more roots, of the determinantal equation (7.2) to fall on the unit circle.

### 7.1.1 The log-likelihood function of the multivariate model

The available multivariate estimation options in *Microfit* compute maximum likelihood (ML) estimators of the parameters of (7.1) subject to appropriate parametric restrictions. The log-likelihood function of (7.1), conditional on $\mathbf{w}_1, \mathbf{w}_2, \ldots, \mathbf{w}_n$ and the initial values, $\mathbf{z}_0, \mathbf{z}_{-1}, \ldots, \mathbf{z}_{-p+1}$, is given by

$$\ell_n(\varphi) = \frac{-nm}{2} \log 2\pi - \frac{n}{2} \log|\Sigma| - \tfrac{1}{2}\sum_{t=1}^{n} \mathbf{u}_t' \Sigma^{-1} \mathbf{u}_t \tag{7.3}$$

where $\varphi$ stands for all the unknown parameters of the model. Stacking the $n$ observations on the $m$ equations in (7.1), the log-likelihood in (7.3) can also be written in matrix form as

$$\ell_n(\varphi) = \frac{-nm}{2} \log 2\pi - \frac{n}{2} \log|\Sigma| - \tfrac{1}{2} Tr(\Sigma^{-1}\mathbf{U}\mathbf{U}') \tag{7.4}$$

where $Tr(\cdot)$ stands for the trace of a matrix, and

$$\mathbf{U} = \mathbf{Z} - \tau_n \mathbf{a}_0' - \mathbf{t}_n \mathbf{a}_1' - \sum_{i=1}^{p} \mathbf{Z}_{-i}\Phi_i' - \mathbf{W}\Psi' \tag{7.5}$$

$$\underset{n\times m}{\mathbf{U}} = (\mathbf{u}_1, \mathbf{u}_2, \ldots, \mathbf{u}_n)', \quad \underset{n\times m}{\mathbf{Z}} = (\mathbf{z}_1, \mathbf{z}_2, \ldots, \mathbf{z}_n)' \tag{7.6}$$

$$\underset{n\times m}{\mathbf{Z}_{-i}} = (\mathbf{z}_{-i+1}, \mathbf{z}_{-i+2}, \ldots, \mathbf{z}_{-1+n})', \quad \underset{n\times q}{\mathbf{W}} = (\mathbf{w}_1, \mathbf{w}_2, \ldots, \mathbf{w}_n)' \tag{7.7}$$

$$\underset{n\times 1}{\tau_n} = (1, 1, \ldots, 1)', \quad \underset{n\times 1}{\mathbf{t}_n} = (1, 2, \ldots, n)' \tag{7.8}$$

The particular computational algorithm used to carry out the maximization of the above log-likelihood function depends on the nature of the restrictions on the parameters of the model, and are set out in detail in Chapter 19. In this chapter our focus will be on how to use the various multiple estimation options.

## 7.2 General guidelines

Before proceeding any further, the following points are worth bearing in mind when using the multiple equation options in *Microfit*:

1. The order of the VAR, $p$, often plays a crucial role in empirical analysis and in selecting it, special care must be taken to ensure that it is high enough that the disturbances, $\mathbf{u}_t$, in (7.1) are not serially correlated and that, for the $p$ chosen, the remaining sample for estimation is large enough for the asymptotic theory to work reasonably well. This involves a difficult balancing act. For VAR order selection, *Microfit* automatically generates the Akaike information criterion (AIC) and the Schwarz Bayesian criterion (SBC), as well as a sequence of log-likelihood ratio statistics. In practice, their use often leads to different choices for $p$; it is up to you to decide the best choice of $p$ for the problem in hand.

2. Multivariate techniques are often highly data intensive, particularly when $m$, the number of jointly determined variables, is large. For example, when $m = 10$, $p = 4$, and $q = 2$, each equation in the AVAR model (19.25) contains $s = mp + q + 2 = 44$ unknown coefficients. For such a specification our experience suggests that sample sizes of 200 or more are often needed if any sensible results are to be obtained. It is, therefore, important that the multivariate options in *Microfit* are applied in cases where $n$ is sufficiently large.[2]
3. Cointegrating VAR options presume that the variables $\mathbf{z}_t$ are $I(1)$, *and* that the user already knows the nature of the *unconditional* mean of the variables in the underlying VAR model, namely whether the variables $\mathbf{z}_t$ have non-zero means or are trended, and whether the trend is linear. Therefore, it is important that the variables in $\mathbf{z}_t$ are tested for unit roots (for example using the ADF command in the Command Editor), and that the nature of the trends in $\mathbf{z}_t$ is ascertained, for example, by plotting each elements of $\mathbf{z}_t$ against time! Econometric techniques are not often powerful enough to identify the nature of the trends in the variables being modelled.
4. Before using the long-run structural modelling options described in Section 7.5.3, you need to specify the number of cointegrating (or long-run) relations of your model. The maximum eigenvalue and the trace statistics advanced by Johansen (1988, 1991) can be employed for this purpose (see Section 7.5). However, the results of these tests are often ambiguous in practice, and it may be necessary for the number of cointegrating relations to be chosen on the basis of *a priori* information; for example from the long-run predictions of a suitable economic model: cf. Pesaran (1997).
5. Another important issue in the use of long-run structural modelling options concerns the nature of the just-identifying restrictions on long-run relations. This invariably requires an explicit formulation of the long-run economic model that underlies the empirical analysis. *Microfit* invites you to specify the cointegration or the long-run relations of your model at two different stages. At the first stage you will be asked to specify the cointegrating relations that are just-identified. Once such a just-identified model is successfully estimated, you will be prompted to specify your over-identifying restrictions (if any). For the ML estimation procedure to converge, it is important that the over-identifying restrictions are introduced one at a time, starting with those that are less likely to be rejected. The asymptotic standard errors, computed for the estimated coefficients of the exactly identified cointegrating relations, can be used as a guide in deciding which over-identifying restriction to impose first, which to impose second, and so on.
6. Since the cointegration analysis focuses on the long-run properties of the economic model, it is important to combine it with some additional information on how the long-run relations of the model respond to

[2]Size limitations in the case of the multivariate estimation options are set out in Appendix A.

shocks. For example, it may be of interest to know whether there are over-shooting effects, and how long, on average, it will take for the economy to settle back into its long-run state after being shocked. To shed light on these and other related issues, we recommend the use of the generalized impulse response functions for characterizing the time-profiles of the effects of variable-specific shocks on long-run relations, and the persistence profiles for characterizing the effects of system-wide shocks on cointegrating relations. See Sections 19.8.4 to 19.8.6.

## 7.3 System Estimation Menu

All the multivariate options in *Microfit* can be accessed from the System Estimation Menu (the Multivariate Menu) or the MULTI button. When you use the button the currently selected menu option (e.g. Unrestricted VAR) is automatically selected.

The Multivariate Menu option opens the System Estimation Menu which contains the following options:

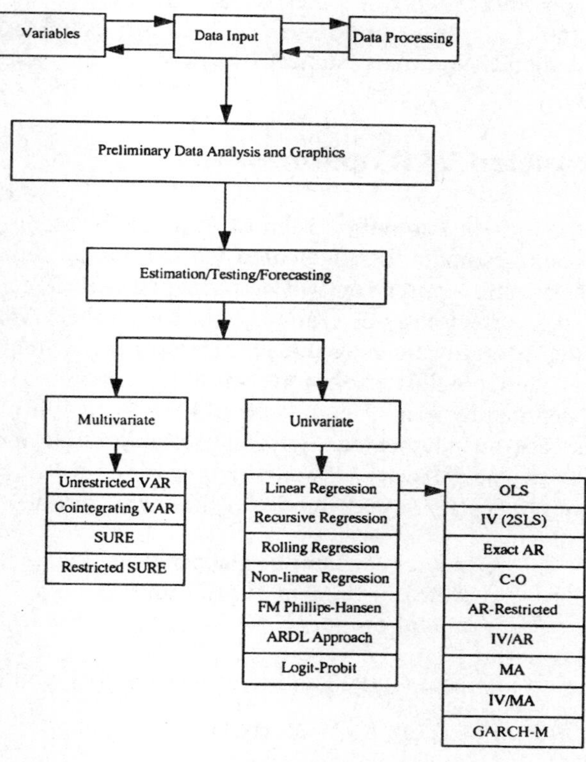


Chart 1: The flow chart of functions in *Microfit*

1. Unrestricted VAR
2. Cointegrating VAR Menu
3. SURE Method
4. Restricted SURE Method

**Option 1** enables you to estimate unrestricted VAR models, test a number of restrictions on their parameters, and compute multivariate, multi-step forecasts. You can also use this option to estimate univariate AR models. However, if you wish to estimate univariate ARMA models, you need to choose the MA option in the Linear Regression Menu (see Sections 6.5 and 6.12).

**Option 2** enables you to carry out cointegration analysis in a VAR framework; distinguishing between $I(1)$ jointly determined variables, $I(1)$ exogenous variables, and $I(0)$ exogenous variables. This option also allows you to choose between five different specifications of intercepts and/or trends in the underlying VAR model.

**Option 3** allows you to estimate a system of seemingly unrelated regression equations (SURE) by the full maximum likelihood method (cf. Zellner 1962).

**Option 4** provides an important extension of the SURE estimation method of option 3, and allows estimation of SURE models subject to linear restrictions, possibly involving coefficients from different regression equations in the model. This option can be used, for example, to estimate systems of demand equations subject to homogeneity and symmetry restrictions.

## 7.4 Unrestricted VAR option

Option 1 in the System Estimation Menu (Multivariate Menu: see Section 7.3) enables you to estimate the augmented VAR($p$) model defined by (7.1). When you choose this option you will be presented with screen 7.1, which prompts you to list the jointly determined variables in the VAR, namely $\mathbf{z}_t$, followed by the deterministic/exogenous variables, namely intercepts, trend terms (if any), and possibly exogenous variables determined outside the VAR model, denoted by $\mathbf{w}_t$ in (7.1). It is possible to specify only one variable in $\mathbf{z}_t$. In this case an augmented *univariate* autoregressive model will be estimated. The two sets of variables must be separated by &.

For example, to specify a VAR model in the three variables

C ≡ Real consumption expenditure
I ≡ Real invetment expenditure
Y ≡ Real output

including in it an intercept (INPT) and a linear trend (T), you need to type

C I Y & INPT T

in the box editor shown in Screen 7.1. Type in the start and finish of your estimation period, and the order of the VAR model ($p \leqslant 24$), and then click

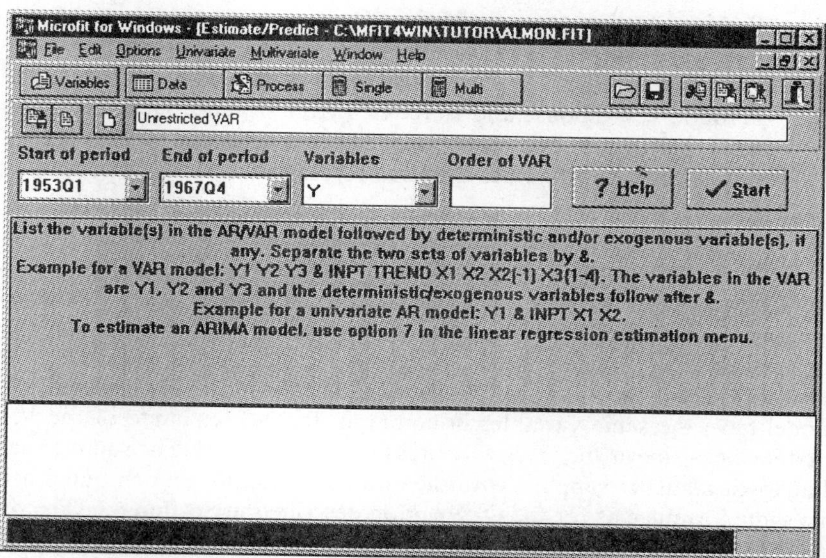


Screen 7.1: The System Estimation window with the Unrestricted VAR option selected

START. *Microfit* carries out the necessary computations and presents you with the Unrestricted VAR Post Estimation Menu (see Section 7.4.1).

*Notes*

1. The ordering of the variables in the VAR is important only as far as computation of the orthogonalized impulse responses and orthogonalized error variance decompositions are concerned. See Sections 19.4 and 19.5.
2. Lagged values cannot appear among the set of jointly determined variables, $\mathbf{z}_t$. However, they could be included in the second set, namely $\mathbf{w}_t$, so long as these are not lagged values of the first set!
3. If a lagged variable, say C(−1), is included as one of the variables in the VAR by mistake, *Microfit* will present you with an error message.
4. If you include lagged values of the jointly determined variables as an exogenously determined variable, no error messages will appear on the screen initially, but at the stage of computation the program will encounter a perfect multicollinearity problem and issue an error message.

## 7.4.1 Unrestricted VAR Post Estimation Menu

The Unrestricted VAR Post Estimation Menu appears on the screen when the estimation of the VAR model is complete. It contains the following options:

0. Move to Backtracking Menu
1. Display single equation estimation results
2. Display system covariance matrix of errors
3. Impulse Response and Forecast Error Variance Decomposition
4. Hypothesis testing and lag order selection in the VAR
5. Compute multivariate dynamic forecasts

**Option 1** enables you to see estimation results for individual equations in the VAR model. When you choose this option you will be asked to select the equation to be displayed. Select the variable whose equation you wish to inspect and click OK. The estimation results for the selected equation should now appear on the screen. Since all the equations in the unrestricted VAR model have the same variables in common, the ML estimate of the VAR model is the same as the OLS estimates (see Section 19.3). The summary and diagnostic statistics supplied with the estimation results are computed using the same formulae as for the OLS option described in Section 6.6. The only additional information provided is the maximized value of the system log-likelihood function given at the bottom right-hand corner of the first result table that appears on the screen: see (19.30).

As in the case of the OLS option, after the estimation results you will be presented with the Post Regression Menu (see Section 6.21), which provides you with a number of options for further analysis of the residuals and hypothesis testing. For example, you can compute White and Newey–West adjusted standard errors for the parameter estimates or carry out tests of linear/non-linear restrictions on the coefficients of the chosen equation in the VAR. However, to carry out tests of restrictions that involve parameters of different equations in the VAR model, you need to choose the SURE and restricted SURE options described in Sections 7.6.1 and 7.6.2.

**Option 2** presents you with the unbiased estimates of $\Sigma$, given by $\hat{\Sigma}$ in (19.31).

**Option 3** takes you to the Unrestricted VAR Dynamic Response Analysis Menu, from where you can compute and plot orthogonalized and generalized impulse responses and forecast error variance decompositions for unit shocks to the *i*th equation in the VAR model (7.1): see Section 7.4.2.

**Option 4** moves you to the VAR Hypothesis Testing Menu, where you can select the order of the VAR, test for the statistical significance of the exogenous/deterministic variables, $\mathbf{w}_t$, and finally test for non-causality of a subset of jointly determined variables, $\mathbf{z}_t$, in the VAR model defined by (7.1): see Section 7.4.3.

**Option 5** enables you to compute forecasts of the jointly determined variables, $\mathbf{z}_t$ in (7.1), for given values of the exogenous/deterministic variables, $\mathbf{w}_t$, over the forecast period. When you select this option you will be asked first to specify the forecast period, and second to choose the variable you wish to forecast. For each variable you choose you have the option of forecasting the levels of the variable or its first-differences. The program then computes the forecasts and presents you with the Multivariate Forecast Menu (see Section 7.4.4).

### 7.4.2 Unrestricted VAR Dynamic Response Analysis Menu

This menu has the following options:

0. Return to VAR Post Estimation Menu
1. Orthogonalized IR of variables to shocks in equations
2. Generalized IR of variables to shocks in equations
3. Orthogonalized forecast error variance decomposition
4. Generalized forecast error variance decomposition

When you choose any one of options 1 to 4, you will be asked to choose the equation to be shocked. Each equation is designated by its left-hand-side variable. Choose a variable name (equation) and click OK. You will now be asked to specify the horizon (denoted in Chapter 19 by N) for the impulse responses (or forecast error variance decomposition). The default value is set to 50, otherwise you need to type your desired value of N (with $N \leqslant 150$) and then click OK. Once you have specified the horizon, the program carries out the computations and presents you with a list of impulse responses (or forecast error variance decompositions) at different horizons.

To plot or save the results click CLOSE to move to the Impulse Response Results Menu. This menu has the following options:

0. Move back
1. Display results again
2. Graph
3. Save in a special Microfit file

**Option 0** returns you to the Unrestricted VAR Dynamic Response Analysis Menu.

**Option 1** enables you to see the results of the impulse response analysis and forecast error variance decompositions again.

**Option 2** enables you to plot the impulse responses (or the forecast error variance decompositions) for one or more of the variables in the VAR at different horizons.

**Option 3** allows you to save the impulse responses (or the forecast error variance decompositions) for all the variables in a special *Microfit* file for subsequent analysis.

It is worth noting that the orthogonalized impulse responses, and the orthogonalized forecast error variance decompositions, usually depend on the ordering of the variables in the VAR, but their generalized counterparts do not. The orthogonalized and the generalized impulse responses exactly coincide either for the first variable in the VAR or if $\Sigma$ is diagonal. An account of these concepts and the details of their computation are set out in Sections 19.4 and 19.5.

### 7.4.3 VAR Hypothesis Testing Menu

This menu appears on the screen when option 4 in the Unrestricted VAR Post Estimation Menu is chosen (see Section 7.4.1). It has the following options:

0. Return to VAR Post Estimation Menu
1. Testing and selection criteria for order (lag length) of the VAR
2. Testing for deletion of deterministic/exogenous variables in the VAR
3. Testing for block non-causality of a subset of variables in the VAR

**Option 0** returns you to the Unrestricted VAR Post Estimation Menu (see Section 7.4.1).

**Option 1** computes the Akaike (AIC) and Schwarz Bayesian (SBC) model selection criteria for selecting the order of the VAR($p$), for $p = 0, 1, 2, \ldots, P$, where $P$ represents the maximum order selected by the user (see Section 7.4).

The selection procedure involves choosing the VAR($p$) model with the highest value of the AIC or the SBC. In practice, the use of the SBC is likely to result in selecting a lower order VAR model than when using the AIC. However, in using both criteria it is important that the maximum order chosen for the VAR is high enough for high-order VAR specifications to have a reasonable chance of getting selected, if they happen to be appropriate.

This option also computes log-likelihood ratio statistics and their small sample adjusted values, which can be used in the order-selection process.

The log-likelihood ratio statistics are computed for testing the hypothesis that the order of the VAR is $p$ against the alternative that it is $P$, for $p = 0, 1, 2, \ldots, P-1$. Users interested in testing the hypothesis that the order of the VAR model is $p$ against the alternative that it is $p+1$, for $p = 0, 1, 2, \ldots, P-1$, can construct the relevant log-likelihood statistics for these tests by using the maximized values of the log-likelihood function given in the first column of the result table corresponding to this option. For example, to test the hypothesis that the order of the VAR model is 2 against the alternative that it is 3, the relevant log-likelihood ratio statistic is given by

$$\mathrm{LR}(2{:}3) = 2(\mathrm{LL}_3 - \mathrm{LL}_2) \tag{7.9}$$

where $LL_p$, $p = 0, 1, 2, \ldots, p$ refers to the maximized value of the log-likelihood function for the VAR($p$) model. Under the null hypothesis, LR(2:3) is distributed asymptotically as a chi-squared variate with $m^2(3-2) = m^2$ degrees of freedom, where $m$ is the dimension of $\mathbf{z_t}$ in (7.1). For further details and the relevant formulae, see Section 19.3.1.

**Option 2** computes the log-likelihood ratio statistic for testing zero restrictions on the coefficients of a subset of deterministic/exogenous variables in the VAR. For example, to test the hypothesis that the VAR specification in (7.1) does not contain a deterministic trend, the relevant hypothesis will be $\mathbf{a_1} = \mathbf{0}$. In general, this option can be used to test the validity of deleting one or more of the exogenous/deterministic variables from the VAR. When you choose this option you will be asked to list the deterministic/exogenous variable(s) to be dropped from the VAR model. Type in the variable name(s) in the box editor and click OK to process. The test results should now appear on the screen; they give the maximized values of the log-likelihood function for the unrestricted and the restricted model, and the log-likelihood ratio statistic for testing the restrictions. The degrees of freedom and the rejection probability of the test are given in round ( ) and square [ ] brackets, respectively. For further details and the relevant formulae, see Section 19.3.2.

**Option 3** computes the log-likelihood ratio statistic for testing the null hypothesis that the coefficients of a subset of jointly determined variables in the VAR are equal to zero. This is known as the 'block Granger non-causality' test and provides a statistical measure of the extent to which lagged values of a set of variables (say $\mathbf{z}_{2t}$) are important in predicting another set of variables (say $\mathbf{z}_{1t}$) once lagged values of the latter set are included in the model.

More formally, in (7.1), let $\mathbf{z}_t = (\mathbf{z}'_{1t}, \mathbf{z}'_{2t})'$, where $\mathbf{z}_{1t}$ and $\mathbf{z}_{2t}$ are $m_1 \times 1$ and $m_2 \times 1$ subsets of $\mathbf{z}_t$, and $m = m_1 + m_2$. Consider now the following block decomposition of (7.1):

$$\mathbf{z}_{1t} = \mathbf{a}_{10} + \mathbf{a}_{11}t + \sum_{i=1}^{p} \mathbf{\Phi}_{i,11}\mathbf{z}_{1,t-i} + \sum_{i=1}^{p} \mathbf{\Phi}_{i,12}\mathbf{z}_{2,t-i} + \mathbf{\Psi}_1\mathbf{w}_t + \mathbf{u}_{1t} \quad (7.10)$$

$$\mathbf{z}_{2t} = \mathbf{a}_{20} + \mathbf{a}_{21}t + \sum_{i=1}^{p} \mathbf{\Phi}_{i,21}\mathbf{z}_{1,t-i} + \sum_{i=1}^{p} \mathbf{\Phi}_{i,22}\mathbf{z}_{2,t-i} + \mathbf{\Psi}_2\mathbf{w}_t + \mathbf{u}_{2t}$$

The hypothesis that the subset $\mathbf{z}_{2t}$ do not 'Granger-cause' cause $\mathbf{z}_{1t}$ is defined by

$$H_G\colon \mathbf{\Phi}_{12} = 0$$

where $\mathbf{\Phi}_{12} = (\mathbf{\Phi}_{1,12}, \mathbf{\Phi}_{2,12}, \ldots, \mathbf{\Phi}_{p,12})$. When you choose this option you will be asked to list the subset of variable(s) on which you wish to carry out the block non-causality test, namely $\mathbf{z}_{2t}$, in the above formulation. The program then computes the relevant log-likelihood ratio statistic and presents you with the test results, also giving the maximized log-likelihood values under the unrestricted (i.e. $\mathbf{\Phi}_{12} \neq \mathbf{0}$) and the restricted (i.e. $\mathbf{\Phi}_{12} = \mathbf{0}$) models. For further details and the relevant formulae, see Section 19.3.3. Note that the Granger non-causality test may give misleading results if the variables in the VAR contain unit roots (namely when one or more roots of (19.26) lie on the unit circle). In such a case, one must ideally use either VAR models in first differences or cointegrating VAR models if the underlying variables are cointegrated. See the discussion in Canova (1995, p. 104) and the references cited therein.

### 7.4.4 Multivariate Forecast Menu

This menu appears on the screen when Option 5 in the Unrestricted VAR

Post Estimation Menu (see Section 7.4.1) is selected. It contains the following options:

0. Choose another variable
1. Display forecast and forecast errors
2. Plot of in-sample fitted values and out of sample forecasts
3. Save in-sample fitted values and out of sample forecasts

**Option 0** enables you to inspect forecasts of the level or first-differences of another variable in the VAR.

**Option 1** lists the actual values, multivariate forecasts, and forecast errors. In cases where actual values for the jointly determined variables over the forecast period are not available, it is still possible to generate multi-step ahead forecasts so long as observations on the exogenous/deterministic variables in the VAR (namely $\mathbf{w}_t$, intercepts, and trends) are available over the forecast period. In addition to listing the forecasts, this option also computes a number of standard summary statistics for checking the adequacy of the forecasts over the estimation and forecast periods.

**Option 2** enables you to see plots of the actual and forecast values for the selected variable. You need to specify the period over which you wish to see the plots.

**Option 3** allows you to save the fitted and forecast values of the selected variable on the workspace in a new variable to be used in subsequent analysis.

## 7.5 Cointegrating VAR options

The econometric model that underlies the cointegrating VAR options is given by the following general vector error correction model (VECM):

$$\Delta \mathbf{y}_t = \mathbf{a}_{0y} + \mathbf{a}_{1y}t - \mathbf{\Pi}_y \mathbf{z}_{t-1} + \sum_{i=1}^{p-1} \mathbf{\Gamma}_{iy} \Delta \mathbf{z}_{t-i} + \mathbf{\Psi}_y \mathbf{w}_t + \mathbf{u}_{ty} \tag{7.11}$$

where

$$\mathbf{z}_t = \begin{pmatrix} \mathbf{y}_t \\ \mathbf{x}_t \end{pmatrix}$$

This model distinguishes between four categories of variables:

1. $\mathbf{y}_t$ which is an $m_y \times 1$ vector of jointly determined (or endogenous) $I(1)$ variables.[3]
2. $\mathbf{x}_t$ which is an $m_x \times 1$ vector of $I(1)$ exogenous variables.
3. $\mathbf{w}_t$ which is a $q \times 1$ vector of $I(0)$ exogenous variables.
4. Intercepts and deterministic linear trends.

---

[3]Vector $\mathbf{y}_t$ is said to be $I(1)$ if all its elements *must* be differenced to achieve stationarity.

The implicit VAR model for the $I(1)$ exogenous variables, $\mathbf{x}_t$, is given by

$$\Delta \mathbf{x}_t = \mathbf{a}_{0x} + \sum_{i=1}^{p-1} \mathbf{\Gamma}_{ix} \Delta \mathbf{x}_{t-i} + \mathbf{\Psi}_x \mathbf{w}_t + \mathbf{v}_t \tag{7.12}$$

and assumes that $\mathbf{x}_t$s are not themselves cointegrated. Notice also that despite the fact that (7.12) does not contain a deterministic trend, the levels of $\mathbf{x_t}$ will be trended due to the drift coefficients, $\mathbf{a}_{0x}$.

Combining (7.11) and (7.12) we obtain

$$\Delta \mathbf{z}_t = \mathbf{a}_0 + \mathbf{a}_1 t - \mathbf{\Pi} \mathbf{z}_{t-1} + \sum_{i=1}^{p-1} \mathbf{\Gamma}_i \Delta \mathbf{z}_{t-i} + \mathbf{\Psi} \mathbf{w}_t + \mathbf{u}_t \tag{7.13}$$

where

$$\mathbf{u}_t = \begin{pmatrix} \mathbf{u}_{ty} \\ \mathbf{v}_t \end{pmatrix}, \quad \mathbf{a}_0 = \begin{pmatrix} \mathbf{a}_{0y} \\ \mathbf{a}_{0x} \end{pmatrix}, \quad \mathbf{a}_1 = \begin{pmatrix} \mathbf{a}_{1y} \\ \mathbf{0} \end{pmatrix}$$

$$\mathbf{\Pi} = \begin{pmatrix} \mathbf{\Pi}_{0y} \\ 0 \end{pmatrix}, \quad \mathbf{\Gamma}_i = \begin{pmatrix} \mathbf{\Gamma}_{iy} \\ \mathbf{\Gamma}_{ix} \end{pmatrix}, \quad \mathbf{\Psi} = \begin{pmatrix} \mathbf{\Psi}_y \\ \mathbf{\Psi}_x \end{pmatrix}$$

which is a restricted vector error correction form of (7.1).

In estimating (7.11) *Microfit* distinguishes between five cases depending on whether (7.11) contains intercepts and/or time trends, and on whether the intercepts and the trend coefficients are restricted. Ordering these cases according to the importance of deterministic trends in the model, we have:

**Case I:** $\mathbf{a}_{0y} = \mathbf{a}_{1y} = \mathbf{0}$ (no intercepts and no deterministic trends).
**Case II:** $\mathbf{a}_{1y} = \mathbf{0}$, and $\mathbf{a}_{0y} = \mathbf{\Pi}_y \boldsymbol{\mu}_y$ (restricted intercepts and no deterministic trends).
**Case III:** $\mathbf{a}_{1y} = \mathbf{0}$, and $\mathbf{a}_{0y} \neq \mathbf{0}$ (unrestricted intercepts and no deterministic trends).
**Case IV:** $\mathbf{a}_{0y} \neq \mathbf{0}$, and $\mathbf{a}_{1y} = \mathbf{\Pi}_y \boldsymbol{\gamma}_y$ (unrestricted intercepts and restricted deterministic trends).
**Case V:** $\mathbf{a}_{0y} \neq \mathbf{0}$, and $\mathbf{a}_{1y} \neq \mathbf{0}$ (unrestricted intercepts and trends).

The intercept and the trend coefficients, $\mathbf{a}_{0y}$ and $\mathbf{a}_{1y}$, are $m_y \times 1$ vectors; $\mathbf{\Pi}_y$ is the long-run multiplier matrix of order $m_y \times m$, where $m = m_x + m_y$, $\mathbf{\Gamma}_{1y}, \mathbf{\Gamma}_{2y}, \ldots, \mathbf{\Gamma}_{p-1,y}$ are $m_y \times m$ coefficient matrices capturing the short-run dynamic effects; and $\mathbf{\Psi}_y$ is the $m_y \times q$ matrix of coefficients on the $I(0)$ exogenous variables.

The VECM (7.11) represents an important generalization over the model underlying the cointegrating options in *Microfit* 3.0. Firstly, (7.11) allows for a sub-system approach in which the $m_x$ vector of random variables, $\mathbf{x_t}$, are treated as structurally exogenous, in the sense that there are no error correction feedbacks in the equations explaining $\Delta \mathbf{x}_t$. Models of this type naturally arise in empirical macroeconomic analysis of small open economies where, for the purpose of modelling the domestic macroeconomic relations, foreign prices, interest rates and foreign incomes can often be treated as exogenous $I(1)$ variables. Secondly, the model (7.11) explicitly allows for the possibility of deterministic trends, which again could be an important consideration in macroeconomic applications.

The importance of distinguishing between the five cases above is discussed in Section 19.6. In the case where $\mathbf{a}_0$ and $\mathbf{a}_1$ are both unrestricted (i.e. case V), $\mathbf{y}_t$ will be trend-stationary when the rank of $\mathbf{\Pi}_y$ is full, but when $\mathbf{\Pi}_y$ is rank deficient, the solution of $y_t$ will contain quadratic trends, unless $\mathbf{a}_{1y}$ is restricted as in case IV. Similarly, in case III, when $\mathbf{\Pi}_y$ is rank deficient then $y_t$ will contain a linear deterministic trend, unless $\mathbf{a}_{0y}$ is restricted as in case II. Case I is included for completeness and is unlikely to be of relevance in economic applications.

It is also worth noting that in

**Case IV:** where $\mathbf{a}_{1y} \neq 0$, the cointegrating vectors contain a deterministic trend.

**Case II:** where $\mathbf{a}_{0y} \neq 0$, the cointegrating vectors contain intercepts.

Under the assumption that $\text{rank}(\mathbf{\Pi}_y) = r$, that is when there exists $r$ cointegrating relations among the variables in $\mathbf{z_t}$, we have

$$\mathbf{\Pi}_y = \boldsymbol{\alpha}_y \boldsymbol{\beta}' \tag{7.14}$$

where $\boldsymbol{\alpha}_\mathbf{y}$ and $\boldsymbol{\beta}$ are $m_y \times m$ and $m \times r$ matrices, each with full column rank, $r$. The $r$ cointegrating relations are then given by

$$\boldsymbol{\beta}'\mathbf{z}_t = \boldsymbol{\beta}'\mathbf{z}_0 + (\boldsymbol{\beta}'\mathbf{C}^*(1)\mathbf{a}_1)t + \boldsymbol{\eta}_t \tag{7.15}$$

where $\mathbf{z}_0$ is the initial value of $\mathbf{z}_t$; $\mathbf{C}^*(1) = \mathbf{C}_0^* + \mathbf{C}_1^* + \mathbf{C}_2^* + \cdots$, defined by the recursive relations (19.75), and $\boldsymbol{\eta}_t(\boldsymbol{\eta}_0 = \mathbf{0})$ is an $r \times 1$ vector of a mean-zero $I(0)$ disturbance vector, representing the covariance stationary components of the cointegrating relations.[4] In the case where the trend coefficients, $\mathbf{a}_{\mathbf{1y}}$, in the underlying VECM are restricted (i.e. case IV), we have $\boldsymbol{\beta}'\mathbf{C}^*(1)\mathbf{a}_1 = \boldsymbol{\beta}'\boldsymbol{\gamma}$, where $\boldsymbol{\gamma}$ is an $r \times 1$ vector of unknown coefficients. In this case, the trend coefficients enter the cointegrating relations and we have

$$\Delta\mathbf{y}_t = \mathbf{a}_{0y} - \boldsymbol{\alpha}_y\boldsymbol{\beta}'(\mathbf{z}_{t-1} - \boldsymbol{\gamma}t) + \sum_{i=1}^{p-1}\mathbf{\Gamma}_{iy}\Delta\mathbf{z}_{t-i} + \mathbf{\Psi}_y\mathbf{w}_t + \mathbf{u}_{ty} \tag{7.16}$$

where $\boldsymbol{\beta}'(\mathbf{z}_{t-1} - \boldsymbol{\gamma}t)$ will be a covariance stationary process with a constant mean. In this case the presence of a deterministic trend in the cointegrating relations can be empirically tested by testing the $r$ 'co-trending' restrictions:

$$\boldsymbol{\beta}'\boldsymbol{\gamma} = 0 \tag{7.17}$$

In the case V where $\mathbf{a}_{1y}$ is unrestricted, the deterministic trends in the error correction model (7.11) are specified outside the cointegrating relations. One could test for their presence in the error correction model by means of standard $t$-tests. Similar considerations also apply when comparing models

[4]For a derivation and an explicit expression for $\boldsymbol{\eta}_t$, see Section 19.6.1. Also see Park (1992) and Ogaki (1992).

with restricted and unrestricted intercepts, but with no deterministic trends (i.e. cases II and III). In case II, the intercepts in the underlying error correction model will appear as a part of the cointegrating relations, while in case III, the unrestricted intercepts appear as a part of the error correction specification.

In most macroeconomic applications of interest, where $\mathbf{y}_t$ and $\mathbf{x}_t$ contain deterministic trend components, and $\mathbf{\Pi}_y$ is rank deficient, the appropriate VECM is given by case IV, where the trend coefficients are restricted. In cases where $(\mathbf{y}_t, \mathbf{x}_t)$ do not contain deterministic trends, case II is the appropriate error correction model.

### 7.5.1 Specification of the cointegrating VAR model

The Cointegrating VAR Menu is option 2 in the System Estimation Menu (Multivariate Menu: see Section 7.3). The menu contains the following choices for the inclusion of intercepts/trends in the VAR model:

1. No intercepts or trends
2. Restricted intercepts, no trends
3. Unrestricted intercepts, no trends
4. Unrestricted intercepts, restricted trends
5. Unrestricted intercepts, unrestricted trends

**Options 1** to **5** refer to cases I to V set out above, and correspond to different specifications of intercept/trend in the underlying VAR model. Option 2 is appropriate when the jointly determined variables do not contain a deterministic trend. Option 4 (which corresponds to case IV) is appropriate when the jointly determined variables in the VAR have a linear deterministic trend.

**Options 3** and **5** can lead to error correction models with different trend properties depending on the number of cointegrating relations.

You need to list the $I(1)$ variables in your model, namely variables $\mathbf{z}_t$, followed by the list of your $I(0)$ variables, $\mathbf{w}_t$, if any, separating them by &. The division of $I(1)$ variables into the jointly determined variables, $\mathbf{y}_t$, and the exogenously determined variables, $\mathbf{x}_t$, is done by using the semicolon character (;) as a separator. For example, suppose you wish to estimate a cointegrating VAR model containing the following variables:

| | | |
|---|---|---|
| P | ≡ | Domestic price level |
| PF | ≡ | Foreign price level |
| E | ≡ | Exchange rate |
| R | ≡ | Domestic interest rate |
| RF | ≡ | Foreign interest rate |
| DPO | ≡ | Changes in real oil prices |
| DPO(−1) | ≡ | Lagged changes in real oil prices |

where P, E, and R are endogenous $I(1)$ variables; PF and RF are exogenous

$I(1)$ variables; and DPO is the exogenous $I(0)$ variable in the model. Then you need to type:

P E R; PF RF & DPO DPO(−1)

You should not include an intercept or a deterministic trend term among these variables.

You need to specify the order of the VAR model (i.e. $p \leqslant 24$), and then click [START] to begin the calculatations. *Microfit* presents you with the trace and maximum eigenvalue statistics for testing a number of hypotheses concerning the rank of the long-run matrix, $\mathbf{\Pi}_y$, in (7.11), together with the relevant 90 and 95 per cent critical values (see Sections 19.7, 19.7.1, and 19.7.2).

The program also gives the maximized values of the log-likelihood function of the cointegrating VAR model, Akaike, Schwarz, and Hannan and Quinn model selection criteria, for the different values of $r$, the rank of the long-run matrix, $\mathbf{\Pi}_y$ (see Section 19.7.3).

The above test results and model selection criteria can be used to determine the appropriate number of cointegrating relations that are likely to exist among the $I(1)$ variables. Before moving to the next stage of the cointegration analysis, you *must* choose a value for $r$. It is only meaningful to continue with the cointegration analysis if your choice of $r$ lies strictly between 0 and $m_y$.

## 7.5.2 Cointegrating VAR Post Estimation Menu

This menu appears on the screen after the cointegration test results, and has the following options:

0. Move to Backtracking Menu
1. Display cointegration tests again
2. Specify r, the number of cointegrating vectors (CV's)
3. Display CV's using Johansen's just-identifying restrictions
4. Display system covariance matrix of errors
5. Display matrix of long-run multipliers for the specified r
6. Long-run structural modelling, IR Analysis and Forecasting
7. Compute multivariate dynamic forecasts

**Option 0** takes you to the Backtracking Menu for the Cointegrating VAR Analysis (see Section 7.5.4).

**Option 1** enables you to see the cointegration test results again.

**Option 2** allows you to specify your choice of $r$, the number of cointegrating or long-run relations among the $I(1)$ variables. Notice that $r$ cannot be zero. If $r$ is chosen to be equal to $m_y$, the dimension of $\mathbf{y_t}$, the estimation results will be the same as using the unrestricted VAR option.

**Option 3** displays the ML estimates of the cointegrating vectors under Johansen's exact identifying restrictions. These estimates lack any meaningful economic interpretations when $r > 2$. In the case where $r = 1$,

Johansen's estimates (when appropriately normalized) will be the same as those obtained using option 6 in this menu.

**Option 4** displays the estimates of $\Sigma$, the variance matrix of the errors in the cointegrating VAR model, assuming the rank of $\mathbf{\Pi_y}$ is equal to $r$.

**Option 5** displays the ML estimates of $\mathbf{\Pi_y}$, the matrix of the long-run coefficients defined by (7.14), subject to the cointegrating restrictions. Notice that by construction, the rank of $\hat{\mathbf{\Pi}}_y$ is equal to $r$.

**Option 6** moves you to the Long Run Structural Modelling Menu (see Section 7.5.3) and enables you to estimate the cointegrating vectors subject to general linear restrictions, possibly involving parameters across the cointegrating vectors, and to test over-identifying restrictions (if any). This option is also the gateway to computation of impulse response functions, forecast error variance decompositions, persistence profile analysis, and multivariate forecasting, with the cointegrating vectors, $\boldsymbol{\beta}$, being subject to (possibly) over-identifying restrictions. See Section 7.5.3.

**Option 7** enables you to compute multivariate dynamic forecasts of $\mathbf{y_t}$, the jointly determined variables, for given values of $\mathbf{x}_t$ and $\mathbf{w}_t$ over the forecast period, and assuming that $\text{rank}(\mathbf{\Pi}_y) = r$. The forecasts obtained under this option implicitly assume that the cointegrating vectors, $\boldsymbol{\beta}$, are *exactly* identified. To compute multivariate forecasts when $\boldsymbol{\beta}$ is subject to over-identifying restrictions, you must use option 5 in the Impulse Response Analysis and Forecasting Menu (see Section 7.5.5). When you choose this option you will be asked first to specify the forecast period, and then to choose the variable you wish to forecast. For each variable you choose you will be given a choice of forecasting the levels of the variable or its first differences. The program then computes the forecasts and presents you with the Multivariate Forecast Menu (see Section 7.4.4).

### 7.5.3 Long Run Structural Modelling Menu

This menu can be accessed by selecting option 6 in the Cointegrating VAR Post Estimation Menu (see Section 7.5.2). It contains the following options:

0. Move to Cointegrating VAR Post Estimation Menu
1. Likelihood ratio test of fixing some cointegrating vectors (CV's)
2. Likelihood ratio test of imposing same restriction(s) on all CV's
3. Likelihood ratio test of imposing restriction(s) on only one CV
4. Likelihood ratio test of imposing general restrictions on CV's
5. Use CV's obtained under Johansen's just-identifying restrictions
6. Fix all the cointegrating vectors

**Option 0** returns you to the Cointegrating VAR Post Estimation Menu (see Section 7.5.2).

**Options 1** to **3** represent different ways of testing simple homogeneous restrictions on the cointegrating vectors. Since the same restrictions can be imposed and tested using option 4, we will not discuss these options here.

The interested user should consult the manual for *Microfit* 3.0 where these tests are described in detail (see Pesaran and Pesaran 1991, pp. 88–89).

**Option 4** enables you to estimate the VAR model subject to general (possibly) non-homogeneous restrictions on the cointegrating (or the long-run) coefficients, and compute log-likelihood ratio statistics for testing over-identifying restrictions on the long-run coefficients. However, when you first choose this option you will be asked to specify exactly $r$ restrictions on each of the $r$ cointegrating vectors to just-identify the long-run restrictions. For example, if the number of cointegrating relations, $r$, is equal to 4, a typical set of just-identifying restrictions could be:

$$\begin{aligned} &A1 = 1;\ A2 = 0;\ A3 = 0;\ A4 = 0; \\ &B1 = 0;\ B2 = 1;\ B3 = 0;\ B4 = 0; \\ &C1 = 0;\ C2 = 0;\ C3 = 1;\ C4 = 0; \\ &D1 = 0;\ D2 = 0;\ D3 = 0;\ D4 = 1 \end{aligned}$$

The files CO2.EQU, CO3.EQU to CO10.EQU in the *Microfit* TUTORIAL directory contain such just-identifying restrictions for $r = 2, 3, \ldots, 10$, respectively. The above type of just-identifying restrictions could be made relevant to your particular application by suitably ordering the variables in the VAR.[5] Once you have successfully estimated the model subject to the just-identifying restrictions, you can add over-identifying restrictions at a later stage (see option 0 in Section 7.5.5). The econometric and computational details are set out in Section 19.8.

**Option 5** sets the cointegrating vectors equal to Johansen's estimates, $\hat{\beta}_J$, which are obtained subject to the just-identifying restrictions defined by (19.98) and (19.99).

**Option 6** enables you to fix the cointegrating vectors by specifying all their elements.

Options 1 to 6 in the menu, once successfully implemented, take you to the Impulse Response Analysis and Forecasting Menu (see Section 7.5.5).

### 7.5.4 Backtracking Menu for the Cointegrating VAR Analysis

This menu contains the following options:

1. Return to System Estimation Window
2. Choose intercept/trend in the underlying VAR
3. Define new sample period for existing equation
4. Edit regression equation & estimate over existing sample period
5. Define & estimate new equation over a new sample period

[5]Notice that except for the results on orthogonalized impulse response functions and the orthogonalized forecast error variance decomposition, the cointegration tests and the ML estimates are invariant to the ordering of the variables in the VAR.

**Option 1** returns you to the System Estimation menu (see Section 7.3).

**Option 2** returns you to the menu for specifying the nature of intercept/ trend in the cointegrating VAR (see Section 7.5.1).

**Option 3** enables you to change the estimation/forecast periods of your specified cointegrating VAR specification (see Section 7.5.1).

**Option 4** allows you to move back in the program and change the specification of the variables in the cointegrating VAR model (see Section 7.5.1).

**Option 5** enables you to change the specification of the underlying VAR model, and the estimation and forecast periods.

### 7.5.5 Impulse Response Analysis and Forecasting Menu

This menu appears on the screen after the successful implementation of options 1 to 6 in the Long Run Structural Modelling Menu (see Section 7.5.3). It contains the following options:

0. Return to identify/test cointegrating vectors
1. Impulse Response of variables to shocks in equations
2. Forecast Error Variance Decomposition analysis
3. Impulse Response of CV's to shocks in equations
4. Persistence Profile of CV's to system-wide shocks
5. Compute multivariate dynamic forecasts
6. Display restricted/fixed CV's again
7. Display error correction equations
8. Display system covariance matrix of errors

**Option 0** enables you to estimate/test (further) over-identifying restrictions on the cointegrating or long-run coefficients. The restrictions could involve parameters from different long-run relations: see Section 19.6 and option 4 in the Long Run Structural Modelling Menu described in Section 7.5.3. When you choose this option you will be asked to confirm whether you wish to test over-identifying restrictions on the long-run relations. If you choose 'No', you will be returned to the Long Run Structural Modelling Menu (see Sections 19.8.1 to 19.8.3). If your answer is in the affirmative, you will be presented with a box editor to specify your over-identifying restrictions. *Our recommendation is to introduce these restrictions gradually (ideally one by one), starting with the ones that are less likely to be rejected.* The asymptotic standard errors reported below the just-identified estimates could provide a good guide as to which over-identifying restrictions to impose first, second, etc.

Once your over-identifying restrictions are added successfully to the existing set of restrictions (including the just-identifying ones), you will be presented with a screen containing initial values for all the long-run coefficients. These are the estimates obtained under the previous set of restrictions. We recommend that you accept these initial estimates.[6]

If you now click OK to accept the initial values, you will be presented with a small menu giving you a choice between the 'back substitution algorithm' and the 'modified Newton–Raphson algorithm'. The default is always the latter, which is the one that we recommend.[7] If you choose the modified Newton–Raphson algorithm, you will also be given a choice of a damping factor in the range [0.01 to 2.0]. We recommend starting with the value of 0.01, unless you experience difficulties with getting the algorithm to converge.

Once the damping factor is chosen, the program starts the computations and, if the iterative process converges successfully, presents you with the ML estimates of the long-run relations subject to the over-identifying restrictions, together with their asymptotic standard errors in round brackets. *Microfit* also generates log-likelihood ratio statistics for testing the over-identifying restrictions, which are asymptotically distributed as $\chi^2$ variates with degrees of freedom given by $k - r^2$, where $k$ is the total number of restrictions and $r^2$ is the number of just-identifying restrictions. (See Section 19.8.3.)

**Option 1** computes and displays orthogonalized and generalized impulse responses of variable-specific shocks on the different variables in the cointegrating VAR model, (possibly) subject to over-identifying restrictions on the long-run coefficients.

**Option 2** computes and displays orthogonalized and generalized forecast error variance decompositions for the cointegrating VAR model, (possibly) subject to restrictions on the long-run relations.

The algorithms used to carry out the necessary computations for options 1 and 2 are given in Section 19.8.4. See also Section 7.4.2 for instructions on how to display and/or save the results obtained when using these options.

**Option 3** computes and displays orthogonalized and generalized impulse responses to the effect of variable-specific shocks on the $r$ cointegrating relations.

**Option 4** computes and displays the time profile of the effect of system-wide shocks on the cointegrating relations, referred to as 'persistence profiles'.

The algorithms used to carry out the computations for options 3 and 4 are set out in Sections 19.8.5 and 19.8.6, where references to the literature can also be found.

**Option 5** enables you to compute multivariate, multi-step ahead forecasts (of levels and of first-differences) of $\mathbf{y}_t$ conditional on values of $\mathbf{x}_t$ and $\mathbf{w}_t$. The forecasts obtained using this option and those obtained using option 7 in the Cointegrating VAR Post Estimation Menu will be identical under just-identifying restrictions on the cointegrating relations, and differ only

[6]You can, of course, edit the initial estimates if you experience difficulties with the convergence of the interative algorithm.

[7]For a detailed account of these two algorithms, see Section 19.8.2.

when there are over-identifying restrictions on $\beta$. (See Section 7.4.4, and option 7 in Section 7.5.2.)

**Option 6** displays the ML (or fixed) estimates of the cointegrating vectors again.

**Option 7** displays error correction equations for each of the jointly determined $I(1)$ variables in the model. These estimates are followed by diagnostic statistics and the other options available after the OLS option (see Section 6.6).

**Option 8** displays the degrees-of-freedom adjusted system covariance matrix of the errors in the underlying VAR model (7.11). The adjustments are made by dividing the cross-product of residuals from different equations by $n-s$, where $s$ is the total number of coefficients estimated for each equation in the VAR. This adjustment does not take account of the cross-equation restrictions on the long-run coefficients, $\mathbf{\Pi}_y$, implicit in the cointegrating restrictions. These estimates will be identical to those obtained using option 4 in the Cointegrating VAR Post Estimation Menu, if the cointegrating vectors, $\beta$, are not subject to over-identifying restrictions (see Section 7.5.2.)

## 7.6 SURE options

There are two options in *Microfit* for estimation of seemingly unrelated regression equations (SURE) models. Both options can be accessed from the System Estimation Menu (see Section 7.3). Option 3 in this menu enables you to compute ML estimates of the parameters of the following SURE model:

$$y_{it} = \beta_i' \mathbf{x}_{it} + u_{it}, \qquad i = 1,2, \ldots, m \tag{7.18}$$

where $y_{it}$ is the $i$th dependent variable in the model composed of an equation; $\mathbf{x}_{it}$ is the $k_i \times 1$ vector of regressors in the $i$th equation; $\beta_i$ is the $k_i \times 1$ vector of unknown coefficients of the $i$th equation; and $u_{it}$ is the disturbance term. The disturbances (shocks), $u_{it}$, $i = 1, 2, \ldots, m$, are assumed to be homoscedastic and serially uncorrelated, but are allowed to be contemporaneously correlated (i.e. $\text{Cov}(u_{it}, u_{jt}) = \sigma_{ij}$, need not be zero for $i \neq j$).

Option 4 in the System Estimation Menu allows you to compute ML estimates of (7.18) when $\beta_i$s are subject to the following general linear restrictions:

$$\mathbf{R}\beta = \mathbf{b} \tag{7.19}$$

where $\mathbf{R}$ and $\mathbf{b}$ are $r \times k$ matrix and $r \times 1$ vector of known constants, and $\beta = (\beta_1', \beta_2', \ldots, \beta_m')'$ is a $k \times 1$ vector of unknown coefficients $k = \Sigma_{i=1}^m k_i$. When there are no cross-equation restrictions, we have

$$\mathbf{R}_i \beta_i = \mathbf{b}_i \tag{7.20}$$

where $\mathbf{R}_i$ and $\mathbf{b}_i$ are the $r_i \times k_i$ and $r_i \times 1$ matrix vector of restrictions applicable only to the coefficients of the $i$th equation in the model. (See Section 19.2 for more details.)

### 7.6.1 Unrestricted SURE option

This is option 3 in the System Estimation Menu (see Section 7.3). When you choose this option you need to specify the equations in the SURE model. You should list the endogenous variable, $y_{it}$, followed by its regressors, $\mathbf{x}_{it}$, for each equation, separating the different equations by a semicolon (;). The program then automatically works out the number of equations in the SURE model, namely $m (m \leqslant 12)$. A simple example of a SURE specification is

W1 INPT W1(−1) LP1 LP2 LP3 LRY;
W2 INPT W2(−1) LP1 LP2 LP3 LRY; START

where INPT is an intercept term; W1 and W2 could be budget shares of two different commodity groups; LP1, LP2, and LP3 the logarithm of price indices; and LRY the logarithm of real income. It is also possible to estimate restricted VAR models using the SURE option. For example, suppose you wish to estimate the following restricted VAR(4) model:

$$x_{1t} = a_1 + \sum_{j=1}^{4} b_{1j} x_{1,t-j} + c_{11} x_{2,t-1} + d_{11} x_{3,t-1} + u_{1t},$$

$$x_{2t} = a_2 + \sum_{j=1}^{4} b_{2j} x_{2,t-j} + c_{21} x_{1,t-1} + d_{21} x_{3,t-1} + u_{2t},$$

$$x_{3t} = a_3 + \sum_{j=1}^{4} b_{3j} x_{3,t-j} + c_{31} x_{1,t-1} + d_{31} x_{2,t-1} + u_{3t}$$

You need to specify the SURE model as

X1 INPT X1{1 − 4} X2(−1) X3(−1);
X2 INPT X2{1 − 4} X1(−1) X3(−1);
X3 INPT X3{1 − 4} X1(−1) X2(−1) START

For specification of VAR models with linear non-homogeneous and/or cross-equation parametric restrictions, you need to use the restricted SURE option (see Section 7.6.2).

Remember to specify the period over which you wish to estimate the model using the Start of period and End of period fields. *Microfit* then starts to compute the ML estimators of the parameters using the numerical procedure described in Section 19.1.1 and, if the iterations converge successfully, presents you with the SURE Post Estimation Menu (see Section 7.6.3).

### 7.6.2 Restricted SURE option

This estimation method can be accessed using option 4 in the System Estimation Menu (see Section 7.3). Specify the estimation period as usual and enter the equations in the SURE model (see Section 7.6.1 on how to specify the SURE model) into the box editor, then click START. When you have done this you will be presented with another box editor for you to specify coefficients of the SURE model. These restrictions must be linear, but can include cross-equation restrictions. For example, suppose you are interested in estimating the following system of equations:

$$Y_{it} = \alpha_i + \beta_i X_{it} + \gamma_i W_{it} + u_{it}$$

for $i = 1, 2, \ldots, 4$, and $t = 1, 2, \ldots, n$, assuming the homogeneity of the slope coefficients, namely $\beta_i = \beta$, and $\gamma_i = \gamma$, for $i = 1, 2, \ldots, 4$. In the System Estimation window (which is on screen when you choose option 4), type

```
Y1  INPT  X1  W1;
Y2  INPT  X2  W2;
Y3  INPT  X3  W3;
Y4  INPT  X4  W4  START
```

In the second box editor, type the restrictions

```
A2 = B2;   B2 = C2;   C2 = D2;
A3 = B3;   B3 = C3;   C3 = D3  OK
```

Note that *Microfit* assigns the coefficients A1, A2, and A3 to the parameters of the first equation, B1, B2, and B3 to the parameters of the second equation, C1, C2 and C3 to the parameters of the third equation, and so on. Therefore,

$$\alpha_1 = \text{A1}, \quad \beta_1 = \text{A2}, \quad \gamma_1 = \text{A3};$$
$$\alpha_2 = \text{B1}, \quad \beta_2 = \text{B2}, \quad \gamma_2 = \text{B3}$$

and so on.

When this is done, *Microfit* starts the task of computing ML estimators of the parameters of the SURE model subject to the restrictions. The technical details and the relevant formulae are given in Section 19.2. When the algorithm converges you will be presented with the SURE Post Estimation Menu (see Section 7.6.3), with options for displaying the ML estimates and their standard errors, carrying out tests on the parameters of the model, and computing multivariate forecasts.

### 7.6.3 SURE Post Estimation Menu

This menu appears on the screen after a SURE model or a restricted SURE model has been successfully estimated (see Sections 7.6.1 and 7.6.2). It contains the following options:

0. Move back to System Estimation Window
1. Edit the model and estimate
2. Display individual equation estimation results
3. Display system covariance matrix of errors
4. Wald tests of hypotheses on the parameters of the model
5. Estimate/test functions of parameters of the model
6. Compute multivariate dynamic forecasts

**Option 0** returns you to the System Estimation Menu (see Section 7.3).

**Option 1** allows you to edit the equations in the SURE model and estimate the revised model.

**Option 2** enables you to see the ML estimates of the coefficients of the equations in the SURE model. When you choose this option you will be asked to select the equation in the model which you wish to inspect. You will then be presented with estimation results together with a number of summary statistics, including the values of the Akaike information criterion (AIC) and the Schwarz Bayesian criterion (SBC) for the SURE model (see Sections 19.1 and 19.2 for computational details). If you click CLOSE you are presented with the Post Regression Menu, with a number of options including plotting/listing/saving residuals and fitted values, and displaying the estimates of the covariance matrix of the coefficients of the chosen equation (see the OLS option in Section 6.6 for further details). Notice, however, that if you wish to test restrictions on the coefficients of the SURE model, estimate known functions of the parameters, or compute dynamic forecasts, you need to use options 4 to 6.

**Option 3** displays the estimates of the variance matrix of the error, namely $\hat{\Sigma}$, given by (19.23) and (19.24).

**Option 4** enables you to compute Wald statistics for testing the general linear/non-linear restrictions

$$H_0: \quad \mathbf{h}(\boldsymbol{\beta}) = \mathbf{0}$$

against

$$H_1: \quad \mathbf{h}(\boldsymbol{\beta}) \neq \mathbf{0}$$

where $\boldsymbol{\beta} = (\boldsymbol{\beta}_1', \boldsymbol{\beta}_2', \ldots, \boldsymbol{\beta}_m')'$ and $\mathbf{h}(\cdot)$ is a known $r \times 1$ vector function with continuous partial derivatives (see Section 19.1.2).

**Option 5** allows you to compute ML estimates of known (possibly) non-linear functions of the coefficients, $\boldsymbol{\beta} = (\boldsymbol{\beta}_1', \boldsymbol{\beta}_2', \ldots, \boldsymbol{\beta}_m')'$.

**Option 6** enables you to compute multivariate forecasts of the dependent (left-hand-side) variables in the SURE model. When the regressors include lagged values of the dependent variables, the program computes multivariate *dynamic* forecasts. When you choose this option you will need to specify the forecast period, and then to choose the variable you wish to forecast. For each variable that you choose you will be given a choice of forecasting the levels of the variables or their first-differences. *Microfit* then computes the forecasts and presents you with the Multivariate Forecast Menu (see Section 7.4.4).

# PART IV

# Tutorial Lessons

# 8
# Lessons in Data Management

The tutorial lessons in this chapter demonstrate the input/output features of *Microfit*. We start these lessons with an example of how to read a raw data (ASCII) file using the file UKSTOCK.DAT. This contains monthly observations on a number of financial series for the UK economy. Before attempting the lessons make sure that you have gone through the steps set out in Chapter 2; that *Microfit* 4.0 is properly installed on your system, and that the various tutorial data files are on your hard disk (or accessible from a floppy disk). In what follows we assume that the tutorial data files are in the subdirectory

C:\MFIT4WIN\TUTOR

Make sure that the tutorial files supplied with *Microfit* are copied into this subdirectory.

## 8.1 Lesson 8.1: Reading in the raw data file UKSTOCK.DAT

Load *Microfit* 4.0, and click [open icon] or choose Open... from the File Menu. This displays the Open file dialog with a list of files on the left. Using the List files of type field, you can choose to display tutorial files in a number of different formats (see Section 3.1).

Initially, we suggest that you try to load into *Microfit* the data file UKSTOCK.DAT which is in ASCII format. This file contains seven economic time series for the UK economy organized by observations over the period 1970m1 to 1995m5, where m means that the data are monthly and the integers 1, 2, . . ., 12 denote the months starting with January = 1. All variables refer to the last trading day of the month. The seven variables are arranged in the file in the following order:

1. Financial Times 500 composite share index.
2. FT30 dividend yield.
3. Money supply (M0).
4. Three-month treasury bill rate (end of period).
5. Average gross redemption yield on 20-year government securities.
6. Exchange rate: US dollar to 1 pound sterling (spot rate).
7. Retail (consumer) price index.

To load (read) the data, choose ASCII/raw data files from the List files of type box, then double click on the file UKSTOCK.DAT. You should now see the New data set dialog on the screen. This prompts you to provide information about the frequency and sample period of the data as well as the number of variables included in the file.

For frequency of the data choose monthly. For the sample period choose the start year and month as 70 and 1, and the end year and month as 95 and 5. For the number of variables type 7. Choose to organize your data by observation, make sure the Free format radio button is selected, then click OK.

*Microfit* assigns the variable names X1, X2, X3, X4, X5, X6, and X7 to your variables by default. To change these variables, move to each cell of the table in turn and type in the variable names:

ukftidx ukftdy ukm0 uk3tbr uk20yr ukexch ukcpi

and then click GO.

If the data are read in unsuccessfully, you will see an error message. Read Section 3.1 carefully and start the lesson again!

After the raw data file has been read in successfully it is good practice first to inspect the data in the Data Editor to ensure that they have been read in correctly. To check the data, click the DATA button. You should see the list of the monthly observations on all the seven variables on the screen. You can use the scroll bars, and the **Pg Up/Dn**, **Ctrl + Home/End** keys to move around the list.

To save the data in a binary format for subsequent use with *Microfit*, you need to click the [save] button (see Lesson 8.2).

## 8.2 Lesson 8.2: Saving your current data set as a special *Microfit* file

Once you have satisfied yourself that the raw data file has been read in correctly, you may wish to save it as a special *Microfit* file for use in subsequent sessions. Special *Microfit* files are saved as binary files and give you rapid access to your data from within *Microfit*.

To save your current data set in a special *Microfit* file, click the [save] button or choose Save as... from the File Menu (see Section 3.4). This takes you to a Save as dialog. Make sure Microfit data files is selected in the List files of type box, enter the filename UKSTOCK.FIT, and click OK. Since the file UKSTOCK.FIT already exists, you will be asked if you want to replace it. Choose No to return to the Save as dialog. (If you wanted to overwrite the file UKSTOCK.FIT, you would choose Yes.)

## 8.3 Lesson 8.3: Reading in the special *Microfit* file UKSTOCK.FIT

The file UKSTOCK.FIT is the special *Microfit* file corresponding to the raw data file UKSTOCK.DAT. To read UKSTOCK.FIT, you need to click [open] or choose Open... from the File Menu and choose the file UKSTOCK.FIT from the list by double clicking on it. The program starts reading the data from the file and, assuming that the data have been read in successfully, it displays the Command Editor (see Chapter 4).

## 8.4 Lesson 8.4: Combining two special *Microfit* files containing different variables

Suppose you wish to add the variables in the *Microfit* file UKSTOCK.FIT to the variables in another special *Microfit* file, USSTOCK.FIT. First read in the file UKSTOCK.FIT (see Lesson 8.3). Once this has been done successfully, choose Add... from the File Menu and when the Open file dialog appears select USSTOCK.FIT. If the two files are combined successfully, a message confirming this is displayed.

Click [OK] to return to the Command Editor. To make sure that the variables in USSTOCK.FIT (USLGR, USCPI, USM1, US3TBR, USSIDX, and USDY) are correctly added to the current variables (namely the variables in UKSTOCK.FIT), click the [Variables] button to display the list of variables. There should be 13 variables (seven from UKSTOCK.FIT) and six from USSTOCK.FIT on your workspace. Use the [save] button to save this combined data set under a different filename before proceeding further.

## 8.5 Lesson 8.5: Combining two special *Microfit* files containing the same variables

One of the tutorial files, the special *Microfit* file EJCON1.FIT, contains annual observations (1948 to 1981) on the following eight variables[1]

AB : Personal bond holdings
AM : Net liquid assets net of house loans
AS : Personal share holdings
BP : Bond prices
C : Real consumption expenditures
PC : Nominal consumption expenditures
SP : Share prices
Y : Real disposable income

Suppose you wish to update and extend this data set with observations on the same variables over the period 1970 to 1985, saved in the special *Microfit* file EJCON2.FIT. First read in the file EJCON1.FIT, then choose Add... from the File Menu and choose the file EJCON2.FIT. The program augments the data contained in EJCON1.FIT using the new and additional observations

[1]For a description and sources of this data set, see Pesaran and Evans (1984) and the manual for *Microfit* 3.0 (Pesaran and Pesaran 1991).

from the file EJCON2.FIT in the manner described in Section 3.2.1. To inspect the combined data set, click the Data button. The data set displayed on the screen should now contain observations on the eight variables C, PC, Y, AS, AB, AM, SP, and BP over the *extended* period from 1948 to 1985 inclusive. Notice also that observations for the period 1970 to 1981 contained in the file EJCON1.FIT are now overwritten by the corresponding observations in the file EJCON2.FIT. To save this revised and extended data set in a special *Microfit* file, see Lesson 8.2. We have already saved this data set in the file EJCON.FIT and this file should be in your tutorial directory or on your *Microfit* disks.

## 8.6 Lesson 8.6: Extending the sample period of a special *Microfit* file

By combining two files you can extend the sample period of an existing special *Microfit* file. Suppose you wish to extend the period of the data set UKSTOCK.FIT from 1970(1)–1995(5) to 1965(1)–1996(12). First start with a new data set by choosing New... from the File Menu (see Section 3.1.1). Choose the monthly data frequency, and enter the start year and month as 1965 and 1, and the end year and month as 1996 and 12. For the number of variables choose 0. Save your file as a special *Microfit* file under a name of your choice. Choose Add... from the File maneu and find the file UKSTOCK.FIT. Click OK. Back in the main window, click the DATA button. You should see the observations on the variables UKFTIDX,UKFTDY,UKM0,UK3TBR,UK20YR,UKEXCH and UKCPI, now extended over the period 1965(1) to 1996(12). The values of all these variables over the periods 1965(1) to 1969(12) and 1995(6) to 1996(12) will be set equal to *NONE*. You can replace some or all these *NONE* values by actual observations by clicking on the relevant cells and typing in new values.

## 8.7 Lesson 8.7: Reading the CSV file UKCON.CSV into *Microfit*

The file UKCON.CSV is a comma delimited values file containing quarterly observations on the following seven variables obtained from the UK Central Statistical Office (CSO95) data bank:

AIIWQA Personal disposable income £m (seasonally adjusted)
AIIXQA Consumers' expenditure: total £m CURR SA
CAABQA Consumers' expenditure: total £m CONS (1990 prices) SA
CCBHQU Consumers' expenditure: total £m CONS (1990 prices) NSA
CECOQU Real personal disposable income at 1990 prices (seasonally unadjusted)

CECPQA Real personal disposable income at 1990 prices (seasonally adjusted)
DQABQU Tax and prices index (January 1987 = 100)

The variable names and their descriptions are the same as those in the CSO95 data bank.

If you read this file into *Excel* you will see that the data on the worksheet are arranged in columns with the first column being the dates, and the first row containing the variable names, followed by their descriptions, separated by spaces. The last column contains observations on 'tax and prices index', but only over the period 1987(1) to 1995(1).

To read this file into *Microfit*, click [Open] or choose Open... from the File Menu. In the Open dialog, choose Comma delimited files from the List files of type box and select UKCON.CSV by double clicking on it. You will be presented with an information screen. Click the [OK] button to proceed. *Microfit* attempts to read in the file and, if successful, displays the message

*Text file imported successfully. Please check the imported data carefully before using it!*

Click [OK] to move to the Command Editor, then click the [Variables] button to see the seven variables in the file UKCON.CSV and their descriptions.

To see the observations on all the variables, click the [Data] button. Inspect the data carefully and make sure that they are imported into *Microfit* correctly. Note that the missing values of DQABQU (Tax and prices index) over the period 1955(1) to 1986(4) are set to *NONE*.

## 8.8 Exercises in data management

### 8.8.1 Exercise 8.1

The raw data file USSTOCK.TXT contains monthly observations covering the period 1973m3 to 1995m6 (inclusive) on the following variables

Yield on Long-term US government bonds
US consumer price index
US money supply (M1 definition)
Three-month US treasury bill rate
US share prices–Standard and Poor 500 (SP500) composite index
Dividend yield on SP500

These observations are arranged 'variable-by-variable' in the file in free format. Input this file into *Microfit*, check that it is correctly read in, and save it as a special *Microfit* file.

### 8.8.2 Exercise 8.2

Load the file EJCON.FIT containing the variables AB, AM, AS, BP, C, PC,

SP, and Y into *Microfit* and add to it the file EU.FIT, containing annual observations on the following variables:

E Employees in employment (1000s)
U Unemployed including school leavers

### 8.8.3 Exercise 8.3

Repeat the steps in Lesson 8.7 and read the comma delimited (CSV) file UKCON.CSV into *Microfit*. Save them in a *Microfit* file and add the five variables in the file UKCON.FIT to the variables on the workspace. Check that the observations on the variables C and CAABQA are in fact identical.

### 8.8.4 Exercise 8.4

Load the file UKSTOCK.FIT into *Microfit*, and then save the variables in this file as a CSV file. Exit *Microfit* and read the CSV file created by *Microfit* into *Excel*. Are the observations exported correctly?

# 9

# Lessons in Data Processing

The lessons in this chapter show how to carry out data transformations in the workspace by issuing commands and formulae in the Command Editor. It is assumed that the data files used in this chapter are in the subdirectory

C:\MFIT4WIN\TUTOR

Before proceeding any further, make sure that all the tutorial data files supplied with *Microfit* are copied into this subdirectory.

## 9.1 Lesson 9.1: Doing interactive data transformations

You can carry out the transformations which you require on your data in two ways: interactively, or by executing an already prepared batch/equation file. Suppose you wish to analyse the quarterly movements in aggregate consumption expenditures in the UK. First read in the special *Microfit* file UKCON.FIT (see Lesson 8.3). You should see the Command Editor on the screen in which you can type a formula to carry out data transformations on your existing variables, or issue one of the commands described above. For example, if you type

INPT = 1; P = CNOM/C; LY = LOG(Y); LC = LOG(C);
PI = LOG(P/P(−1)); DLY = LY − LY(−1);
DLC = LC − LC(−1) [GO]

the program generates seven new variables:

INPT Intercept term (a vector with all its elements equal to unity)
P Implicit price deflator of consumption expenditures (1990 = 1.00, on average)
LY Logarithm of Y
LC Logarithm of C
PI Inflation rate (measured as the change in log of P)
DLY Change in log of Y
DLC Change in log of C

These new variables are now added to the list of your existing variables; to see them, click the [Variables] button. Edit the variables' descriptions if you wish.

*Note:* The content of the box editor can be saved as an equation file (with the extension .EQU) and retrieved at a later stage. Click [save icon] to save the content of the box editor, enter the filename, and click OK. We have already saved this file as UKCON.EQU; it should be in your tutorial directory (typically C:\MFIT4WIN\TUTOR\).

## 9.2 Lesson 9.2: Doing data transformations using the BATCH command

A convenient method of carrying out data transformations is first to create a batch file (using your preferred text editor before running *Microfit*), containing the instructions (i.e. formulae and commands) that you wish carried out, and then to run this batch file interactively by means of the BATCH command. The file UKCON.BAT on the tutorial directory is an example of such a batch file. The content of the file UKCON.BAT is reproduced as Table 9.1. You can also see the content of this file on the screen by using View... from the File Menu and then double clicking on UKCON.BAT.

To run the batch file UKCON.BAT, first make sure that the file UKCON.FIT is loaded into *Microfit* and that the Command Editor is clear. Then enter the following command

**BATCH** UKCON [GO]

Alternatively, you can click on the [BATCH] buttton on the Command Editor

**Table 9.1:** Content of the batch file UKCON.BAT

```
$ BATCH file UKCON.BAT, to be used in conjunction
$ with the special Microfit file UKCON.FIT
$
$
$ Generate an intercept term
Inpt=1
$ Generate implicit price deflator of consumer expenditures
p=cnom/c
$ Take (natural) logarithms
ly=log(y)
lc=log(c)
$ Generate rates of change of the variables computed as log-changes
pi=log(p/p(-1))
dly=ly-ly(-1)
dlc=lc-lc(-1)
$ Generate rates of change of the variables computed as
$ percentage change
rp=rate(p)
ry=rate(y)
rc=rate(c)
$ Note that rate(y) is computed as 100*(y-y(-1))/y(-1)
s=(y-c)/y
$ End of the BATCH file.
```

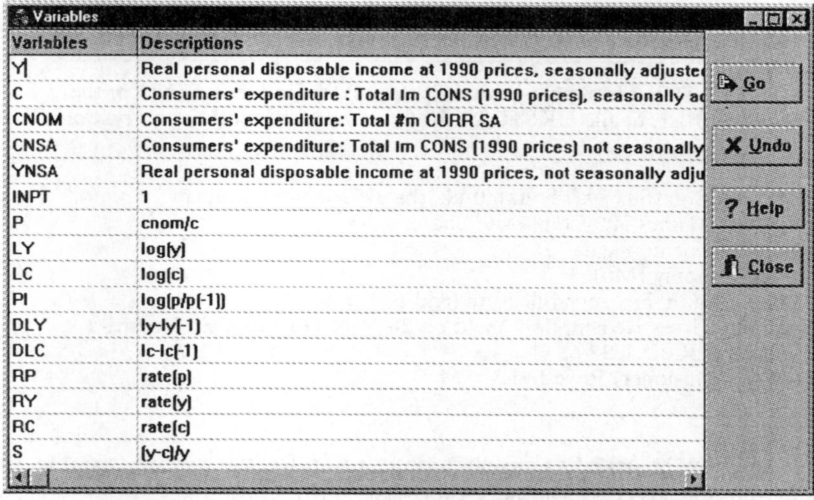


Screen 9.1: The Variables dialog

screen, and then select the desired batch file from the list of file names by double clicking the file UKCON.BAT.

Wait until the computations are completed and the message

*Operations on batch file completed successfully.*

appears on the screen. If you now click OK and then click the Variables button, you will see the list of the five original variables together with 11 more variables created by the program in the process of executing the instructions contained in the batch file UKCON.BAT. The Variables dialog should now look like Screen 9.1.

The variables in this list will be used in other lessons on preliminary data analysis, estimation, hypothesis testing, and forecasting.

## 9.3 Lesson 9.3: Adding titles (descriptions) to variables

Suppose you wish to give titles to the seven variables in the special *Microfit* file UKSTOCK.FIT (see Lesson 8.3). This can be done either interactively or by means of a batch file. Read in the file UKSTOCK.FIT and click the VARIABLES button. Move to each of the variables' description fields in turn and type in a title. Alternatively, in the Command Editor, type

**ENTITLE** UKFTIDX UKFTDY UKM0
UK3TBR UK20YR UKEXCH UKCPI

and click GO. You will be prompted to give the title for UKFTIDX. Simply type the title (a description not more than 80 characters long) that you wish to give to this variable, say,

Financial Times 500 Composite Share Index ↩

**Table 9.2:** Content of the batch file UKNAMES.BAT

```
$ This BATCH file supplies titles (descriptions) for the variables in the
$ special Microfit file UKSTCOK.FIT (containing monthly observations).
$
$
ENTITLE ukftidx ukftdy ukm0 uk3tbr uk20yr ukexch ukcpi
Financial Times 500 Composite Share Index
FT30 Dividend Yield
Money Supply (M0)
Three Month Treasury Bill Rate (end of period)
Average Gross Redemption Yield on 20-Year Government Securities
Exchange Rate: US$ to £1
Retail (Consumer) Price Index
```

You will now be asked to supply a description for the second variable after the command ENTITLE, namely UKFTDY, and so on.

Another alternative is to run the batch file UKNAMES.BAT. The content of this file is listed in Table 9.2. In the Command Editor type

**BATCH** UKNAMES [GO]

You need to ensure that the file UKNAMES.BAT is in your default directory. Otherwise you will see an error message on the screen. If you do not recall the directory where the UKNAMES.BAT file is resident, type

**BATCH** [GO]

Alternatively, you can click the [BATCH] button on the Command Editor screen. You will be presented with an Open file dialog to help you search for the file UKNAMES.BAT on your PC.

## 9.4 Lesson 9.4: Creating dummy variables

In this lesson we will describe how to construct a dummy variable in *Microfit*. Suppose that your current sample period is 1948 to 1981 and that you wish to construct the following dummy variable:

$$D_t = 0, \text{ for } 1948, 1949$$
$$D_t = 1, \text{ for } 1950, \ldots, 1955$$
$$D_t = 2, \text{ for } 1956, \ldots, 1960,$$
$$D_t = 3, \text{ for } 1961, \ldots, 1970,$$
$$D_t = 4, \text{ for } 1971, \ldots, 1981.$$

Read in the file EJCON1.FIT. Into the Command Editor type

**SAMPLE** 1948 1981; D = 0;
**SAMPLE** 1950 1955; D = 1;
**SAMPLE** 1956 1960; D = 2;
**SAMPLE** 1961 1970; D = 3;
**SAMPLE** 1971 1981; D = 4;
**SAMPLE** 1948 1981; [GO]

The program now creates the variable D with the following values:

| OBS | D | OBS | D |
|---|---|---|---|
| 1948 | 0 | 1965 | 3 |
| 1949 | 0 | 1966 | 3 |
| 1950 | 1 | 1967 | 3 |
| 1951 | 1 | 1968 | 3 |
| 1952 | 1 | 1969 | 3 |
| 1953 | 1 | 1970 | 4 |
| 1954 | 1 | 1971 | 4 |
| 1955 | 1 | 1972 | 4 |
| 1956 | 2 | 1973 | 4 |
| 1957 | 2 | 1974 | 4 |
| 1958 | 2 | 1975 | 4 |
| 1959 | 2 | 1976 | 4 |
| 1960 | 2 | 1977 | 4 |
| 1961 | 3 | 1978 | 4 |
| 1962 | 3 | 1979 | 4 |
| 1963 | 3 | 1980 | 4 |
| 1964 | 3 | 1981 | 4 |

As another example, suppose you wish to create a variable which takes the value of zero over the period 1948 to 1968 (inclusive) and then increases by steps of unity from 1969 onward. You need to type

**SAMPLE** 1948 1968; TD = 0;
**SAMPLE** 1969 1981; **SIM** TD = TD(−1) + 1;
**SAMPLE** 1948 1981; **LIST** TD [GO]

The variable TD should now have the following values

| OBS | TD | OBS | TD |
|---|---|---|---|
| 1948 | 0 | 1956 | 0 |
| 1949 | 0 | 1966 | 0 |
| 1950 | 0 | 1967 | 0 |
| 1951 | 0 | 1968 | 0 |
| 1952 | 0 | 1969 | 1 |
| 1953 | 0 | 1970 | 2 |
| 1954 | 0 | 1971 | 3 |

| | | | |
|---|---|---|---|
| 1955 | 0 | 1972 | 4 |
| 1956 | 0 | 1973 | 5 |
| 1957 | 0 | 1974 | 6 |
| 1958 | 0 | 1975 | 7 |
| 1959 | 0 | 1976 | 8 |
| 1960 | 0 | 1977 | 9 |
| 1961 | 0 | 1978 | 10 |
| 1962 | 0 | 1979 | 11 |
| 1963 | 0 | 1980 | 12 |
| 1964 | 0 | 1981 | 13 |

Alternatively you can use the cumulative sum function CSUM(•) to construct this trend (see Section 4.3.4). Type

**SAMPLE** 1948 1968; TD = 0;

**SAMPLE** 1969 1981; TD = CSUM(1);

**SAMPLE** 1948 1981; **LIST** TD [GO]

## 9.5 Lesson 9.5: Plotting variables against time and/or against each other

Suppose you have loaded in the special *Microfit* file UKCON.FIT and wish to plot the variables C (real consumption expenditures) and Y (real disposable income) against time on the same screen. In the Command Editor type

**PLOT** C Y [GO]

for the graph to appear on the screen. (See Figure 9.1 below)

You can alter the display of the graph, print, or save it. To alter the display, click [icon] and choose one of the options. For more information, see Section 5.2.1. To print the displayed graph click [icon]. You will be presented with a standard Windows Print dialog.

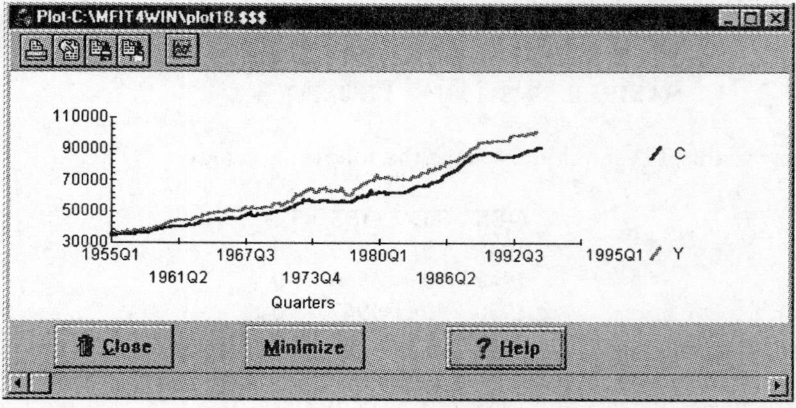


**Figure 9.1:** Real consumption expenditure and real disposable income in the UK

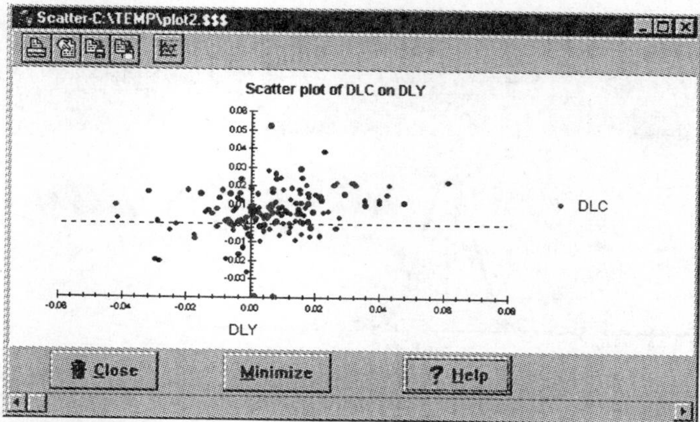


**Figure 9.2**: Scatter plot of DLC on DLY (sample from 1955Q2 to 1994Q4)

You can also save the image of the displayed graph as a bitmap or Windows metafile using the button, or save the graph as a *Microfit* graphics file using the button. You can also copy the displayed graph to the clipboard for pasting into other programs. For this purpose you need to click on (see Section 5.2 for further details).

Suppose now that you wish to obtain a scatter plot of the rate of change of real consumption (DLC) against the rate of change of real disposable income (DLY). Move back to the Command Editor (click PROCESS) and clear it (click ), then type

**BATCH** ukcon; **SCATTER** dlc dly GO

to see the scatter plot on your screen (see Figure 9.2). (Recall that lower- and upper-case letters are treated as identical in *Microfit*.) Clearly there seems to be a high degree of association between the rate of change of consumption expenditure and the real disposable income.

## 9.6 Lesson 9.6: The use of the command XPLOT in generating probability density function

The command XPLOT can be used for a variety of purposes, including plotting probability distributions and Lorenz (or concentration) curves. For example, to generate a plot of the standard normal distribution and the Cauchy distribution on the same graph, use the button to read in the special *Microfit* file X.FIT. This file should be in the TUTOR directory and contains the variable X, $\{x_t = (t - 100)/10,\ t = 1, 2, \ldots, 200\}$. (See Lesson 8.3 on how to read in a special *Microfit* file.) In the Command Editor type

MEU = 0; ZIG = 1;
**BATCH** DENSITY GO

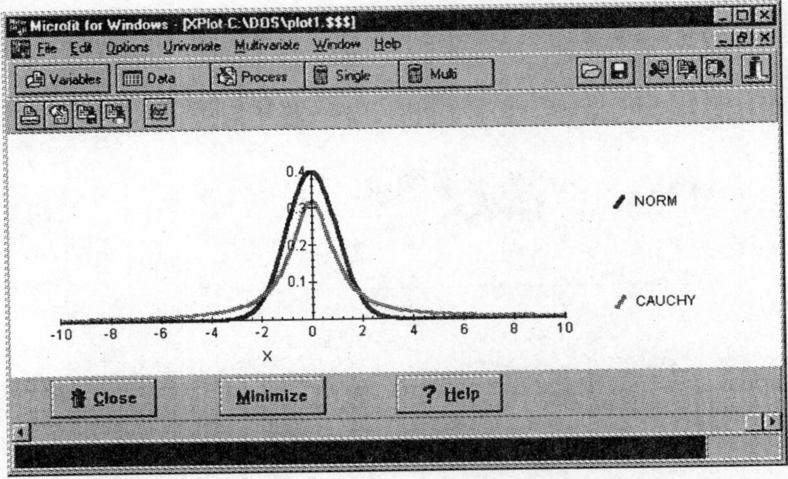


**Figure 9.3:** Plot of Normal and Cauchy distributions

When the operations in the batch file are completed successfully, clear the editor and then type

**XPLOT** norm cauchy x [GO]

You will see the plot of the standard normal and Cauchy distributions on the screen (see Figure 9.3).

## 9.7 Lesson 9.7: Histogram of US stock market returns

The HIST command can be used to generate histograms and check the extent to which the empirical distribution function of a given variable deviates from the normal distribution. For instance, suppose you are interested in obtaining the histogram of the return on the US stock market. The special *Microfit* file USSTOCK.FIT contains 270 monthly observations over the period 1973(1) to 1995(6) on the following variables:

- USDTBR US three-month treasury bill rate (per cent, per annum)
- USCPI Consumer price index
- USDY Dividend yield: ratio of dividends to share prices (per cent, per annum)
- USLGR Yield of long-term US government bond (per cent, per annum)
- USM1 Money supply M1
- USSIDX Share prices index — standard and poor 500 composite (beginning of the month)

The monthly rate of return on the standard and poor 500 (SP500) share index is defined as the sum of the capital gains/losses, i.e. $(P_t - P_{t-1})/P_{t-1}$ plus the dividend yield, i.e. $D_{t-1}/P_{t-1}$. Since in USSTOCK.FIT observations on the dividend yield variable (USDY) are measured in per cents and at annual

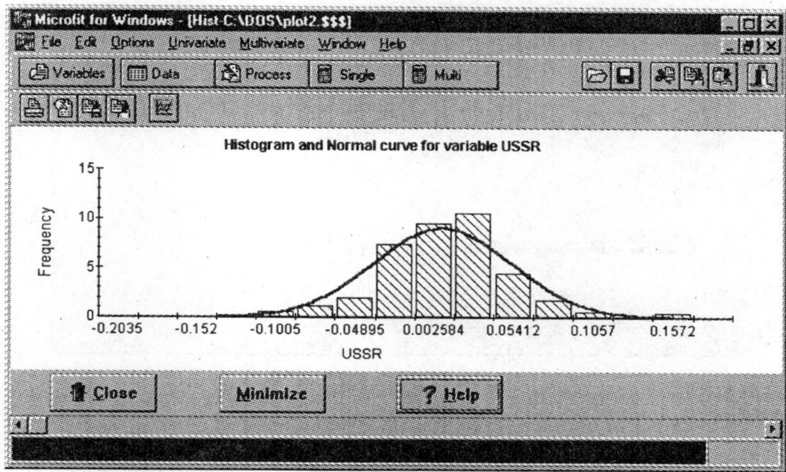


**Figure 9.4:** Histogram and normal curve for variable USSR (sample from 1973M1 to 1995M6)

rates, we first need to compute the dividends paid on SP500 per month. To carry out the necessary computations, read the file USSTOCK.FIT into *Microfit* and in the Command Editor type:

USDIV = (USDY ∗ USSIDX)/1200;
USSR = (USSIDX − USSIDX(−1) + USDIV(−1))/USSIDX(−1);
**HIST** USSR [GO]

You should see a histogram with 15 bands on the screen. If you wish to draw a histogram with a specific number of bands, say 20, you need to type

**HIST** USSR(20) [GO]

The result should match Figure 9.4. Compared with the normal distribution, which is given in the background of the histogram, the distribution of USSR is a little skewed and has fat tails, i.e. it displays excess kurtosis. There also seems to be an 'outlier', showing a 21.6 per cent decline in monthly returns, which refers to the October 1987 stock market crash.

## 9.8 Lesson 9.8: Hodrick–Prescott filter applied to UKGDP

The HP filter is routinely used as a method of de-trending aggregate output in the real business cycle (RBC) literature. In this lesson we use the function HPF(·, ·) described in Section 4.3.6 to de-trend the logarithm of the UK GDP.

The special *Microfit* file GDP95.FIT in the TUTOR directory contains the following variables:

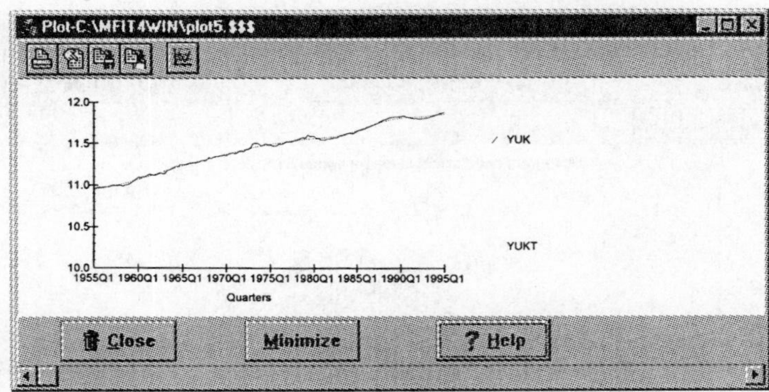


**Figure 9.5:** Plot of logarithm of the UK GDP and its trend estimated using the Hodrick–Prescott filter with $\lambda = 1600$

UKGDPGDP(A) at constant market prices (1990 prices £ million)
USGNP GROSS NATIONAL PRODUCT (BILL.1987$) (T1.10)
average

The sample periods for the US and UK output series are 1960(1) to 1995(1) and 1955(1) to 1995(1), respectively. Read this file into *Microfit* (see Lesson 8.3) and into the Command Editor type:

YUK = log(UKGDP);
YUKT = HPF(YUK, 1600);
**PLOT** YUK YUKT [GO]

You should now see the plot of the logarithm of UK GDP and its trend computed using the HP procedure with $\lambda = 1{,}600$ on the screen (see Figure 9.5). The de-trended series can now be computed as

YUKD = YUK − YUKT; **PLOT** YUKD [GO]

You should see Figure 9.6. To check the sensitivity of the HP de-trending procedure to the choice of $\lambda$, try other values of $\lambda$ and plot the results. Notice that for most part, the trend series are not very sensitive to the value of $\lambda$ in the range [600, 3600].

Repeat the above exercise with the USGNP. Remember to reset the sample to 1960(1) to 1995(1), as US output series are not defined outside this period and the application of the HP function will result in *NONE* values for the trend.

## 9.9 Lesson 9.9: Summary statistics and correlation coefficients of US and UK output growths

As a part of your preliminary data analysis you may be interested to see the summary statistics and correlation matrix of some of the variables in the

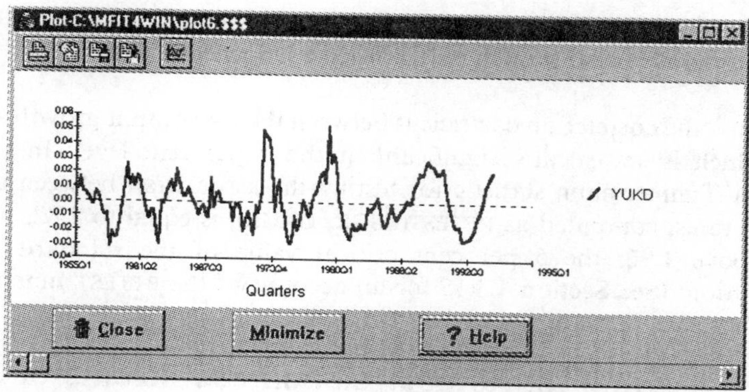


**Figure 9.6** Plot of de-trended UK output series using the Hodrick–Prescott filter with $\lambda = 1600$

variables list. For example, suppose you have read in the file GDP95.FIT and you wish to compute summary statistics and correlation coefficients for the variables USGR (US output growth) and UKGR (UK output growth). Type in the Command Editor

> **SAMPLE** 1960Q1 1994Q4;
> USGR = Rate (USGNP); UKGR = Rate (UKGDP);
> **COR** USGR UKGR [GO]

First, you should see the summary statistics for the two variables USGR and UKGR on the screen. If you click [CLOSE], the correlation matrix for these variables will be displayed (see Table 9.3). The result in Table 9.3 shows that the US economy has enjoyed a slightly higher growth than the UK over the 1960 to 1994 period. The US economy has grown around 2.9 per cent per annum as compared to an average annual rate of 2.3 per cent in the UK.

**Table 9.3:** Summary statistics for UK and US output growth (sample period 1960Q2 to 1994Q4)

| Variable(s) | USGR | UKGR |
|---|---|---|
| Maximum | 2.9980 | 4.8923 |
| Minimum | −2.6335 | −2.6096 |
| Mean | 0.7276 | 0.5716 |
| Std. Deviation | 0.9035 | 1.1160 |
| Skewness | −0.5616 | 0.5461 |
| Kurtosis-3 | 1.5262 | 2.3304 |
| Coefficient of Variation | 1.2417 | 1.9526 |

Estimated Correlation Matrix of Variables

| | USGR | UKGR |
|---|---|---|
| USGR | 1.0000 | 0.2198 |
| UKGR | 0.2198 | 1.0000 |

Output growth has been relatively more variable in the UK. The coefficients of variation of output growth is 1.24 for the US as compared to 1.95 for the UK.

Finally, the correlation coefficient between the two output growth series is 0.22 which is statistically significant at the 5 per cent level. In fact the Pesaran–Timmermann statistic for testing the association between the two growth rates, computed as PTTEST(USGR, UKGR), is equal to 2.82, which is well above 1.96, the 5 per cent critical value of the standard normal distribution. (See Section 4.3.15 for an account of the PTTEST function.)

## 9.10 Lesson 9.10: Autocorrelation coefficients of US output growth

Suppose you are interested in computing the autocorrelation coefficients of up to order 14 for the variable USGR (the quarterly growth rate of US GNP). Carry out the steps in Lesson 9.9, and when presented with the Command Editor, type

**SAMPLE** 1960Q1 1994Q4;
DYUS = log(USGNP/USGNP(−1));
**COR** DYUS(14) [GO]

The program first computes the logarithmic rate of change of the US real GNP, and then displays the summary statistics (i.e. mean, standard deviation, etc.) for the variable DYUS. If you now click [CLOSE], the autocorrelation coefficients, the Box–Pierce and Ljung–Box statistics will be displayed (see Table 9.4).

Clicking [CLOSE] now yields a plot of the autocorrelation coefficients (see Figure 9.7). The default value for the maximum order of the computed autocorrelation coefficients is equal to $\frac{1}{3}$ of the sample size. For example, if you compute the autocorrelation coefficients over the period 1985(1) to 1990(4), only the first eight autocorrelation coefficients will be computed (see the COR command in Section 4.4.4).

The command COR applied to a variable, say X, also computes the Q statistic due to Box and Pierce (1970) and its modified version, the Q* statistic, due to Ljung and Box (1978) for X (see Section 18.1.1). These statistics can be used to carry out general tests of serial correlation. The Ljung–Box Q* statistic tends to be more reliable in small samples. The figures in square brackets refer to the probability of falsely rejecting the null hypothesis of no serial correlation. A small *p*-value provides evidence against the null hypothesis that the variable X is serially uncorrelated. In the case of the results in Table 9.4, there is clear evidence of serial correlation in US output growth. The first- and second-order autocorrelation coefficients 0.31864 and 0.23792 are large relative to their standard errors (the *t*-ratios for these autocorrelation coefficients are 3.76 and 2.56 which are above the critical value of the standard normal distribution at a level of 5 per cent). The remaining autocorrelation coefficients are not statistically significant.

**Table 9.4:** Summary statistics and autocorrelation coefficients for US output growth

| | |
|---|---|
| Sample period | 1960Q2 to 1994Q4 |
| Variable(s) | DYUS |
| Maximum | 0.029539 |
| Minimum | −0.026688 |
| Mean | 0.0072099 |
| Std. deviation | 0.0089935 |
| Skewness | −0.60515 |
| Kurtosis-3 | 1.6251 |
| Coef of Variation | 1.2474 |

| Variable DYUS | | Sample from 1960Q2 to 1994Q4 | | |
|---|---|---|---|---|
| Order | Autocorrelation coefficient | Standard error | Box–Pierce statistic | Ljung–Box statistic |
| 1 | 0.31864 | 0.084819 | 14.1132[.000] | 14.4200[.000] |
| 2 | 0.23792 | 0.093033 | 21.9812[.000] | 22.5178[.000] |
| 3 | 0.044503 | 0.097312 | 22.2565[.000] | 22.8032[.000] |
| 4 | 0.056147 | 0.097458 | 22.6947[.000] | 23.2609[.000] |
| 5 | −0.057294 | 0.097691 | 23.1510[.000] | 23.7410[.000] |
| 6 | 0.028012 | 0.097932 | 23.2601[.001] | 23.8566[.001] |
| 7 | −0.071426 | 0.097990 | 23.9692[.001] | 24.6141[.001] |
| 8 | −0.14831 | 0.098364 | 27.0268[.001] | 27.9051[.000] |
| 9 | −0.067555 | 0.099960 | 27.6612[.001] | 28.5931[.001] |
| 10 | 0.042191 | 0.10029 | 27.9086[.002] | 28.8636[.001] |
| 11 | −0.0054286 | 0.10042 | 27.9127[.003] | 28.8681[.002] |
| 12 | −0.17486 | 0.10042 | 32.1626[.001] | 33.5865[.001] |

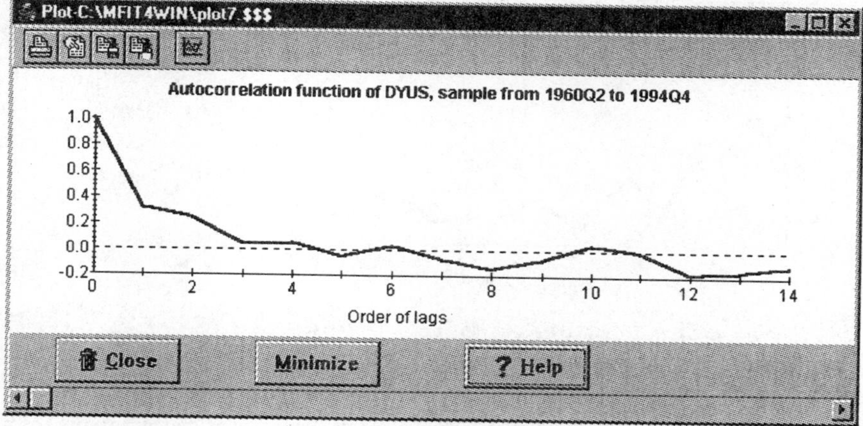


**Figure 9.7:** Autocorrelation function of DYUS (sample from 1960Q2 to 1994Q4)

## 9.11 Lesson 9.11: Spectral density function of US output growth

The SPECTRUM command (see Section 4.4.17) can be used to obtain different estimates of the standardized spectral density function. As an example, consider the problem of estimating the spectral density function for the rate of change of the US real GNP.

Use the button to read the GDP95.FIT file into *Microfit*, and in the Command Editor create the variables (using the full sample)

DYUS = log(USGNP/USGNP(−1)) GO

Then clear the editor and type

**SPECTRUM** DYUS GO

You should see three different estimates of the standardized spectral density function of DYUS on the screen. These estimates, and their asymptotic standard errors, are based on Bartlett, Tukey, and Parzen windows (see Section 18.2 for the details of the algorithms and the relevant references to the literature). The window size is set to the default value of $2\sqrt{n}$, where $n$ is the number of observations. In the present application, $n = 139$ and the window size is equal to 24 (to override the default value for the window size, see the SPECTRUM command: see Section 4.4.17). The estimates of the spectral density are scaled and standardized using the unconditional variance of DYUS, and if evaluated at zero frequency give a consistent estimate of Cochrane's (1988) measure of persistence. Click ? to save these estimates in a result file, or to print. If you click CLOSE, you will be presented with four screens. The first three give the plots of the alternative estimates of the spectral density function (under Bartlett, Tukey, and Parzen windows) and their standard error bands. For the purpose of comparing the different windows, the fourth screen displays all the three estimates of the spectral density function in one graph (see Figure 9.8).

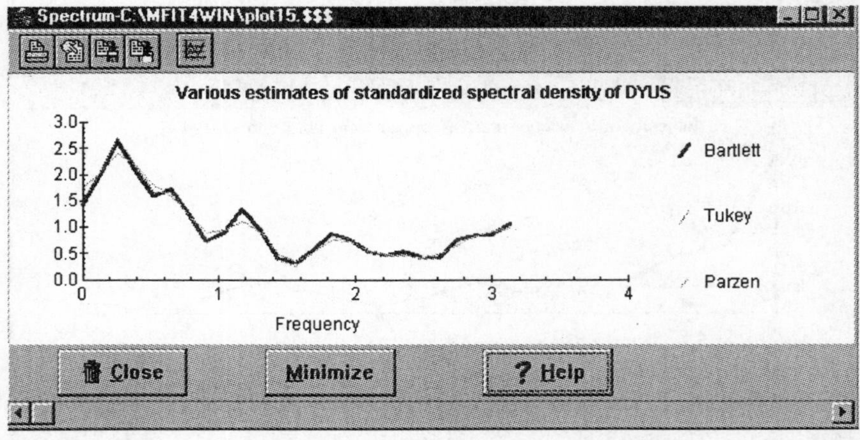


**Figure 9.8:** Various estimates of standardized spectral density of DYUS (sample from 1960Q2 to 1994Q4)

Notice that the spectrum peaks at frequency 0.26, suggesting a cycle with periodicity equal to 24 quarters or 6 years.

## 9.12 Lesson 9.12: Constructing a geometrically declining distributed lag variable: using the SIM command

Suppose you are interested in constructing a geometrically declining distributed lag function of the UK inflation rate, stored in the special *Microfit* file UKCON.FIT. Let $\Pi_t$ be the inflation rate and denote its geometric distributed lag function by $\Pi_t^e$. Then

$$\Pi_t^e = (1-\lambda)\sum_{i=0}^{\infty} \lambda^i \Pi_{t-i-1}, \qquad \text{for} \quad t = 1960(1), \ldots, 1995(1) \tag{9.1}$$

with $\lambda = 0.8$, and $\Pi_{1960(1)}^e = \Pi_{1960(1)}$. First notice that (9.1) can also be written recursively as

$$\Pi_t^e = \lambda \Pi_{t-1}^e + (1-\lambda)\Pi_{t-1}, \qquad \text{for} \quad t = 1960(1), \ldots, 1995(1)$$

or

$$\Pi_t^e - \Pi_{t-1}^e = (1-\lambda)(\Pi_{t-1} - \Pi_{t-1}^e), \qquad \text{for} \quad t = 1960(1), \ldots, 1995(1)$$

The last equation is immediately recognized as the first-order adaptive expectations model.

To compute $\Pi_t^e$, for $t = 1960(1), \ldots, 1995(1)$, load the special *Microfit* file, UKCON.FIT, and when presented with the Command Editor, type

```
BATCH     UKCON;
SAMPLE    60Q1 95Q1;   PIE = PI;
SAMPLE    60Q2 95Q1;
SIM       PIE = 0.8 * PIE(−1) + 0.2 * PI(−1);
SAMPLE    60Q1 95Q1  [GO]
```

The variable PIE (i.e. $\Pi_t^e$) will now be created (you can see it added to the list of your existing variables by clicking VARIABLES). For a graphical presentation of the relationship between the inflation rate (PI), and the adaptively formed inflation expectations (PIE), type

**PLOT** PI PIE [GO]

You should see the plot of PI and PIE against time on the screen (Figure 9.9). It can be clearly seen from this graph that the adaptive expectations tend to underestimate the actual rate of inflation when inflation is accelerating, and to overestimate it when inflation is decelerating. A proof of this phenomenon can be found in Pesaran (1987a, pp. 18–19).

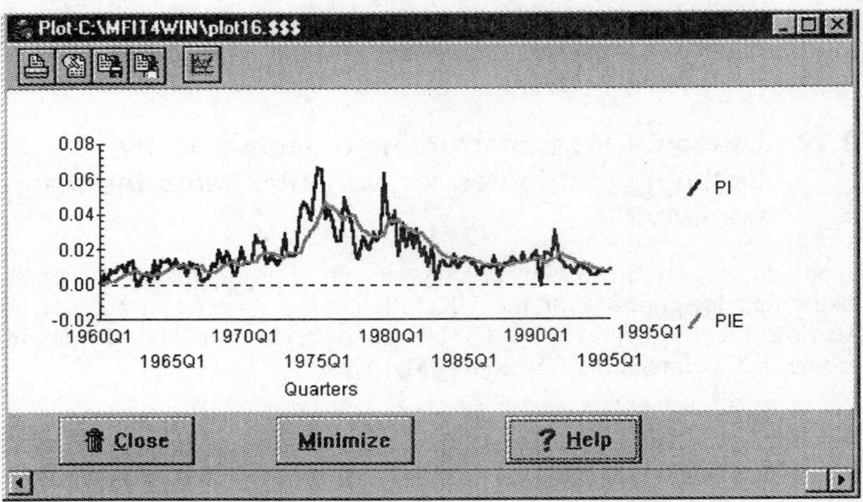


**Figure 9.9:** Actual and (adaptive) expected inflation in the UK (with adaptive coefficient = 0.80)

## 9.13 Lesson 9.13: Computation of OLS estimators using formulae and commands

In this lesson we show how the function SUM, described in Section 4.3.22, can be used to compute OLS estimators of the coefficients of a simple regression equation from first principles. This is particularly useful for undergraduate courses in statistics and econometrics where students need to be shown the details of the various steps involved in the computations.

Suppose you are interested in computing the OLS estimates of the regression of C (the real consumption expenditure) on Y (the real disposable income) using quarterly UK observations over the period 1960(1) to 1994(4):

$$C_t = \alpha + \beta Y_t + u_t, \quad t = 1, 2, \ldots, n \tag{9.2}$$

where $u_t$ is the error term. The OLS estimators of the coefficients $\alpha$ and $\beta$ in (9.2) are given by

$$\hat{\beta} = \sum_{t=1}^{n}(Y_t - \bar{Y})(C_t - \bar{C}) \bigg/ \sum_{t=1}^{n}(Y_t - \bar{Y})^2$$

$$\hat{\alpha} = \bar{C} - \hat{\beta}\bar{Y}$$

where $\bar{C}$ and $\bar{Y}$ are the arithmetic means of C and Y, respectively.

To carry out the necessary computations, read in the special *Microfit* file UKCON.FIT, and type the following instructions in the Command Editor

```
Sample 60Q1 94Q4; n = sum(1); cbar = sum(c)/n;
cd = c – cbar; ybar = sum(y)/n; yd = y – ybar;
bhat = sum(yd * cd)/sum(yd^2);
ahat = cbar – bhat * ybar                    [GO]
```

The variables AHAT and BHAT will now contain the OLS estimates of $\alpha$ and $\beta$, respectively. You can list these estimates using the LIST command.

**Table 9.5:** The batch file OLS.BAT

```
$ Contents of the file OLS.BAT on the Tutorial Directory.
$ This is an example of a batch file for the direct
$ computation of the OLS regression, C = a + b Y + u,
$ estimated over the sub-period 1960(1)-1994(4), using the
$ special Microfit file, UKCON.FIT. This file contains
$ quarterly observations on C (consumption) and Y (income),
$ over the period 1955(1)-1995(1).
$
$
sample 60q1 94q4
$ Setting the sample size (n)
n=sum(1)
$ Computing sample means of C and Y and storing the results in
$ cbar and ybar
cbar=sum(c)/n
ybar=sum(y)/n
$ Computing deviations of C and Y from their sample means
cd=c-cbar
yd=y-ybar
$ Computing variances of Y and C in yvar and cvar
yvar=sum(yd^2)/(n-1)
cvar=sum(cd^2)/(n-1)
$ Computing OLS estimates of the coefficients a and b
bhat=sum(cd*yd)/sum(yd^2)
ahat=cbar-bhat*ybar
$ Computing OLS residuals (e)
e=c-ahat-bhat*y
$ Computing R-Squared, R-BAR-Squared, standard error of
$ the regression, and the Durbin-Watson statistic
rsq=1-sum(e^2)/sum(cd^2)
zigsq=sum(e^2)/(n-2)
zigma=sqrt(zigsq)
rbarsq=1-(zigsq/cvar)
seahat=zigma*sqrt(sum(y^2))/sqrt(n*sum(yd^2))
sebhat=zigma/sqrt(sum(yd^2))
dummy=1
sample 60q2 94q4
dummy=0
sample 60q1 94q4
e1sq=sum(dummy*(e^2))
sample 60q2 94q4
dw=sum((e-e(-1))^2)/(sum(e^2)+e1sq)
$ Re-setting the sample back to its full range
sample 55q1 95q1
$ End of the BATCH file
```

You can also use the SUM function to compute other statistics, such as the estimates of the standard error of the OLS estimates, the squared multiple correlation coefficient ($R^2$), the adjusted squared multiple correlation coefficient ($\bar{R}^2$), and the Durbin–Watson statistic. (The formulae for these statistics can be found in Section 18.5.1). The batch file OLS.BAT in the TUTOR directory contains the necessary instructions for carrying out these computations. It is reproduced in Table 9.5. To run this batch file, first make sure that the variables C and Y are in the list of variables (click [Variables]), then type

**BATCH** OLS [GO]

If the operations are successful, you should see the following additional variables in the list of variables (click [Variables] to view if necessary):

| | | |
|---|---|---|
| AHAT | ≡ | OLS estimate of $\alpha$ |
| BHAT | ≡ | OLS estimates of $\beta$ |
| SEAHAT | ≡ | Estimate of the standard error of ahat($\hat{\alpha}$) |
| SEBHAT | ≡ | Estimate of the standard error of bhat($\hat{\beta}$) |
| ZIGMA | ≡ | $\hat{\sigma}$, the standard error of regression |
| RSQ | ≡ | $R^2$, the square of the multiple correlation coefficient |
| RBARSQ | ≡ | $\bar{R}^2$, the adjusted $R^2$, |
| DW | ≡ | Durbin–Watson statistic |
| E | ≡ | OLS residuals |

You can now use either the LIST or the COR command to list/print the various estimators/statistics computed by the batch file OLS.BAT. If you type,

**COR** c y cbar ybar cvar yvar ahat seahat
bhat sebhat zigma rsq rbarsq dw n [GO]

you should get the results shown in Table 9.6.

As we shall see in Chapter 10 (see Lesson 10.1), the same results (and more) can be computed using the OLS option in the Linear Regression Menu.

## 9.14 Lesson 9.14: Construction of indices of effective exchange rates and foreign prices

In this lesson we provide an example of how a batch file can be used to compute the indices of the effective exchange rate (EER) and foreign prices (PF) for a given 'home' country (which we denote by '$j$' ) with respect to its main trading partners.

Denote the effective exchange rate index of the $j$th country by $E_{jt}$. Then

$$E_{jt} = \sum_{i=1}^{N} w_{ji} \left[ \frac{E_{jit} * 100}{E_{ji,85}} \right]$$

where $w_{ji}$ is the share of country $j$th trade with the $i$th country, so that $\sum_{i=1}^{N} w_{ji} = 1$, and $E_{jit}$ is the market rate of exchange of the $j$th currency in terms of the $i$th currency, computed as

$$E_{jit} = \left[ \frac{j\text{th country national currency}}{\text{US dollar}} \right] \times \left[ \frac{\text{US dollar}}{i\text{th country national currency}} \right]$$

$E_{ji,85}$ is the average value of the $E_{jit}$ variable over the quarters in 1985,

**Table 9.6:** OLS regression results using the batch file OLS.BAT

**Sample period 1960Q2 to 1994Q4**

| Variable(s) | C | Y | CBAR | YBAR | CVAR | YVAR |
|---|---|---|---|---|---|---|
| Maximum | 90399.0 | 100831.0 | 61143.5 | 67763.6 | 2.43E+08 | 3.06E+08 |
| Minimum | 39059.0 | 42059.0 | 61143.5 | 67763.6 | 2.43E+08 | 3.06E+08 |
| Mean | 61301.6 | 67954.1 | 61143.5 | 67763.6 | 2.43E+08 | 3.06E+08 |
| Std. Deviation | 15546.1 | 17400.8 | 0.1095E−9 | 0.1606E−9 | 0.2991E−6 | 0.9571E−6 |
| Skewness | 0.46381 | 0.40399 | 1.00000 | −1.00000 | 1.00000 | 1.000 |
| Kurtosis-3 | −1.0111 | −0.99184 | −2.0000 | −2.0000 | −2.0000 | −2.0000 |
| Coef of Variation | 0.25360 | 0.25607 | 0.0000 | 0.0000 | 0.0000 | 0.000 |

**Sample period 1960Q2 to 1994Q4**

| Variable(s) | AHAT | SEAHAT | BHAT | SEBHAT | ZIGMA | RSQ |
|---|---|---|---|---|---|---|
| Maximum | 954.1058 | 513.2711 | 0.88823 | 0.0073359 | 1512.2 | 0.99067 |
| Minimum | 954.1058 | 513.2711 | 0.88823 | 0.0073359 | 1512.2 | 0.99067 |
| Mean | 954.1058 | 513.2711 | 0.88823 | 0.0073359 | 1512.2 | 0.99067 |
| Std. Deviation | 0.0000 | 0.0000 | 0.0000 | 0.00 | 0.0000 | 0.000 |
| Skewness | *NONE* | *NONE* | *NONE* | *NONE* | *NONE* | *NONE* |
| Kurtosis-3 | *NONE* | *NONE* | *NONE* | *NONE* | *NONE* | *NONE* |
| Coef of Variation | 0.0000 | 0.0000 | 0.0000 | 0.00 | 0.0000 | 0.000 |

**Sample period 1960Q2 to 1994Q4**

| Variable(s) | RBARSQ | DW | N |
|---|---|---|---|
| Maximum | 0.99061 | 0.44194 | 140.0000 |
| Minimum | 0.99061 | 0.44194 | 140.0000 |
| Mean | 0.99061 | 0.44194 | 140.0000 |
| Std. Deviation | 0.0000 | 0.0000 | 0.00 |
| Skewness | *NONE* | *NONE* | *NONE* |
| Kurtosis-3 | *NONE* | *NONE* | *NONE* |
| Coef of Variation | 0.0000 | 0.0000 | 0.00 |

$$E_{ji,85} = \tfrac{1}{4} \sum_{t=85q1}^{85q4} E_{jit}$$

Let $PF_j$ be the $j$th country foreign price index, defined as the weighted average of the wholesale price indices of the main trading partners of the $j$th country,

$$PF_{jt} = \sum_{i=1}^{N} w_{ji} P_{it}$$

where $P_{it}$ is the wholesale price index (WPI) of the $i$th country.

The batch file G7EXCH.BAT contains the instructions for computing the variables EER and PF for the UK. But it can be readily modified to compute these variables for any other G7 country (see below). Table 9.7 reproduces this batch file. The data needed to run the batch file are stored in the file G7EXCH.FIT. This file contains the variables $E_i$ and $P_i$, with i = 1, 2, . . ., 10, where

$E_1$ = Japan market rate (yen versus US$)
$E_2$ = Germany market rate (DM versus US$)
$E_3$ = France market rate (FF versus US$)
$E_4$ = UK market rate (UK£ versus US$)
$E_5$ = Italy market rate (Ilira versus US$)
$E_6$ = Canada market rate (Can$ versus US$)
$E_7$ = The Netherlands market rate (NGuil versus US$)
$E_8$ = Switzerland market rate (SF versus US$)
$E_9$ = Belgium market rate (BF versus US$)
$E_{10}$ = Austria market rate (AS versus US$)

and

$P_0$ = USA WPI
$P_1$ = Japan WPI
$P_2$ = Germany WPI
$P_3$ = France CPI (1972–79), WPI (1980–92)
$P_4$ = UK WPI
$P_5$ = Italy WPI
$P_6$ = Canada WPI
$P_7$ = The Netherlands WPI
$P_8$ = Switzerland WPI
$P_9$ = Belgium WPI
$P_{10}$ = Austria WPI

**Table 9.7:** Content of the batch file G7EXCH.BAT

```
$ This batch file computes the indices of effective
$ exchange rates (EER) and foreign prices (PF) for currency j
$
$ Setting the sample period
SAMPLE 72Q1 92Q3
$ Defining the Pound Sterling/Dollar rate as the currency j
EJ = E4
$ Setting the UK's major trading partners' currencies
EJ0 = E4
EJ1 = EJ/E1
EJ2 = EJ/E2
EJ3 =  EJ/E3
EJ4 = EJ/E4
EJ5 = EJ/E5
EJ6 = EJ/E6
EJ7 =  EJ/E7
EJ8 = EJ/E8
```

*continued*

*continued*

```
EJ9=EJ/E9
EJ10=EJ/E10
$ Constructing the dummy variable, D85, equal to zero except
$ for the four quarters in 1985 where it is set equal one
D85=0
SAMPLE 85Q1 85Q4
D85=1
SAMPLE 72Q1 92Q3
$ Computing the currency weights in the base year, 1985
D0= SUM(EJ0*D85)/4
D1=SUM(EJ1*D85)/4
D2= SUM(EJ2*D85)/4
D3= SUM(EJ3*D85)/4
D4= SUM(EJ4*D85)/4
D5= SUM(EJ5*D85)/4
D6= SUM(EJ6*D85)/4
D7= SUM(EJ7*D85)/4
D8= SUM(EJ8*D85)/4
D9= SUM(EJ9*D85)/4
D10= SUM(EJ10*D85)/4
$ Exchange rate indices with 1985 = 100
EJ0IND=(EJ0*100)/D0
EJ1IND=(EJ1*100)/D1
EJ2IND=(EJ2*100)/D2
EJ3IND=(EJ3*100)/D3
EJ4IND=(EJ4*100)/D4
EJ5IND=(EJ5*100)/D5
EJ6IND=(EJ6*100)/D6
EJ7IND=(EJ7*100)/D7
EJ8IND=(EJ8*100)/D8
EJ9IND=(EJ9*100)/D9
EJ10IND=(EJ10*100)/D10
$ Setting the values of the trading weights (for the UK)
WJ0=0.2281
WJ1=0.0530
WJ2=0.2276
WJ3=0.1552
WJ4=0.0
WJ5=0.0814
WJ6=0.0349
WJ7=0.1422
WJ8=0.0
WJ9=.0776
WJ10=0.0
$ Computing the EER index
EER=WJ0*EJ0IND+WJ1*EJ1IND+WJ2*EJ2IND+WJ3*EJ3IND+&
WJ4*EJ4IND+WJ5*EJ5IND+WJ6*EJ6IND+WJ7*EJ7IND+WJ8*EJ8IND+&
WJ9*EJ9IND+WJ10*EJ10IND
$ Computing the PF index.
PF=WJ0*P0+WJ1*P1+WJ2*P2+WJ3*P3+WJ4*P4+WJ5*P5+&
WJ6*P6+WJ7*P7+WJ8*P8+WJ9*P9+WJ10*P10
$ Giving titles to the variables
ENTITLE EER PF
```

*continued*

*continued*

UK Effective Exchange Rate index
UK Foreign Price index
$ Deleting unnecessary variables
DELETE EJ EJ0 EJ1 EJ2 EJ3 EJ4 EJ5 EJ6 EJ7 EJ8 EJ9 EJ10 &
D85 D0 D1 D2 D3 D4 D5 D6 D7 D8 D9 D10 &
EJ0IND EJ1IND EJ2IND EJ3IND EJ4IND EJ5IND EJ6IND &
EJ7IND EJ8IND EJ9IND EJ10IND WJ0 WJ1 WJ2 WJ3 WJ4 WJ5 &
WJ6 WJ7 WJ8 WJ9 WJ10
$ End of batch file.

The chosen home country, $j$, in the batch file G7EXCH.BAT is the UK, so that $j = 4$, $P_j = P_4$, $E_j = E_4$. The eight main trading partners are taken to be the USA, Japan, Germany, France, Italy, Canada, the Netherlands and Belgium. However, the batch file G7EXCH.BAT can be modified to compute the EER and PF indices for the other G7 countries. You simply need to edit it so that EJ is set to the currency of your choice and the main trading weights in the construction of the indices are adjusted appropriately. The relevant weights for the G7 countries are given in Table 9.8.

**Table 9.8:** Trading weights of the G7 countries

| Main trading partners | USA | Japan | Germany | France | UK | Italy | Canada |
|---|---|---|---|---|---|---|---|
| USA | — | 0.7232 | 0.1513 | 0.1355 | 0.2281 | 0.1634 | 0.8546 |
| Japan | 0.2996 | — | 0.0493 | 0.0345 | 0.0530 | 0.0262 | 0.0613 |
| Germany | 0.0948 | 0.0778 | — | 0.2654 | 0.2276 | 0.3024 | 0.0201 |
| France | 0.0504 | 0.0256 | 0.1951 | — | 0.1552 | 0.2432 | 0.0111 |
| UK | 0.0841 | 0.0488 | 0.1422 | 0.1376 | — | 0.1084 | 0.0286 |
| Italy | 0.0473 | 0.0171 | 0.1362 | 0.1762 | 0.0814 | — | 0.0098 |
| Canada | 0.3601 | 0.0726 | 0.0156 | 0.0151 | 0.0349 | 0.0164 | — |
| The Netherlands | 0.0366 | 0.0197 | 0.1803 | 0.0927 | 0.1422 | 0.0767 | 0.0820 |
| Belgium | 0.0261 | 0.0151 | 0.1301 | 0.1431 | 0.0776 | 0.0632 | 0.0061 |

To compute the two indices for the UK, load the file G7EXCH.FIT into *Microfit*. Check the definitions of the variables $E_i$, $P_i$, by clicking the VARIABLES button. Run the batch file G7EXCH.BAT by typing

**BATCH** G7EXCH [GO]

in the Command Editor. If the operations are successful, you should see the following additional variables in the variables list:

$$\text{EER} \equiv \text{UK effective exchange rate index}$$

$$\text{PF} \equiv \text{UK foreign price index}$$

To see a time-plot of these indices, type

**PLOT** EER PF [GO]

Figure 9.10 should now appear on your screen.

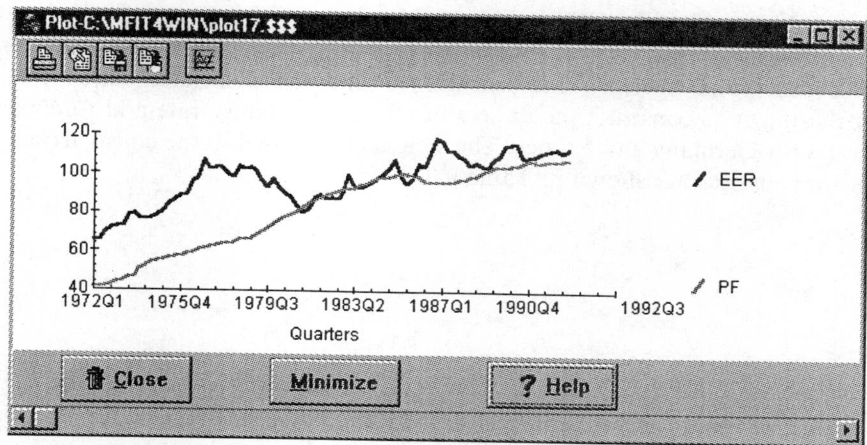


**Figure 9.10** Effective and weighted foreign price indices for the UK (1985 = 100)

## 9.15 Exercises in data processing

### 9.15.1 Exercise 9.1

Combine the two Special *Microfit* files UKSTOCK.FIT and USSTOCK.FIT and compute the rates of change of consumer prices (say USPI and UKPI) in the two countries. Compare the histograms, estimated autocorrelation functions, and spectrums of the two inflation rates. Comment on their differences and similarities.

### 9.15.2 Exercise 9.2

Load the file USCON.FIT into *Microfit* and retrieve the file USCON.EQU into the Command Editor. Process the content of the editor, and then plot the scatter of the rate of change of real non-durable consumption on the rate of change of real disposable income. Using the function RATE(·), compute the average growth of UK real disposable income over the four sub-periods 1960(1) to 1969(4), 1970(1) to 1979(4), 1980(1) to 1989(4), and 1990(1) to 1994(4). Comment on your results. Repeat these calculations by computing the quarterly rate of change of real disposable income as first differences of the logarithm of the real disposable income. Are your conclusions affected by the method used to compute the average growth rates?

### 9.15.3 Exercise 9.3

Load the file UKCON.FIT into *Microfit* and compute the Pesaran–Timmermann non-parametric statistic for testing the degree of association between the rates of change of consumption expenditure and real disposable income. Compare the results of this test with that based on the correlation coefficient between these variables.

### 9.15.4 Exercise 9.4

Use the special *Microfit* file G7EXCH.FIT and the associated batch file G7EXCH.BAT to construct the indices of effective exchange rate and foreign prices for Germany and France. The weights to be used in the construction of these indices are shown in Table 9.8.

# 10

# Lessons in Linear Regression Analysis

The lessons in this chapter are concerned with estimation, hypothesis testing, and prediction problems in the context of linear regression models. They use a variety of time series and cross-sectional observations to show how the options in *Microfit* can be used to test for residual serial correlations, heteroscedasticity, non-normal errors, structural change, and prediction failure. They also show how to carry out estimation of models with serially correlated errors, compute recursive and rolling regressions, test linear and non-linear restrictions on the regression coefficients, and detect when multicollinearity is likely to be a problem.

## 10.1 Lesson 10.1: OLS estimation of simple regression models

When you have finished your data transformations you can estimate, test, or forecast using a variety of estimation methods. You will need to specify your regression equation, the period over which you wish your regression to be estimated, and, in the case of linear regression, the number of observations you would like to set aside for predictive failure/structural stability tests.

In this lesson we shall consider two applications: first, we estimate the simple regression equation (9.2) already estimated in Lesson 9.13 by running a batch file containing formulae and commands. Later we estimate a more complicated regression. Here we show how the computations can be carried out more simply using the OLS option. The relevant data is in the special *Microfit* file UKCON.FIT (see Lessons 9.1 and 9.2). Load this file (using the [folder icon] button), and in the Command Editor create an intercept term by typing

INPT = 1 [GO]

Click the Univariate Menu option on the main menu bar, choose Linear Regression Menu, and make sure option 1 Ordinary Least Squares is selected. Type the specifications of the regression equation in the box editor:

C  INPT  Y

Now enter the sample period

1960Q1 1994Q4

into the Start and End fields. Click START; you will be presented with the OLS results reproduced in Table 10.1a. Compare these estimates with those in Table 9.6.

Consider now the estimation of a slightly more complicated consumption function involving lagged values, namely the ARDL(1,1) specification in logarithms.[1]

$$\log c_t = \beta_1 + \beta_2 \log c_{t-1} + \beta_3 \log y_t + \beta_4 \log y_{t-1} + u_t \qquad (10.1)$$

For empirical analysis it is often more appropriate to consider an 'error correction' form of (10.1) given by:

$$\Delta \log c_t = \alpha_1 + \alpha_2 \Delta \log y_t + \alpha_3 \log c_{t-1} + \alpha_4 \log y_{t-1} + u_t \qquad (10.2)$$

**Table 10.1a:** OLS estimates of a simple linear consumption function

Ordinary Least Squares Estimation

Dependent variable is C
140 observations used for estimation from 1960Q1 to 1994Q4

| Regressor | Coefficient | Standard Error | T-Ratio[Prob] |
|---|---|---|---|
| INPT | 954.1058 | 513.2711 | 1.8589[.065] |
| Y | .88823 | .0073359 | 121.0796[.000] |

| | | | |
|---|---|---|---|
| R-Squared | .99067 | R-Bar-Squared | .99061 |
| S.E. of Regression | 1512.2 | F-Stat. F( 1, 138) | 14660.3[.000] |
| Mean of Dependent Variable | 61143.5 | S.D. of Dependent Variable | 15602.7 |
| Residual Sum of Squares | 3.16E+08 | Equation Log-likelihood | −1222.6 |
| Akaike Info. Criterion | −1224.6 | Schwarz Bayesian Criterion | −1227.6 |
| DW-statistic | .44194 | | |

Diagnostic Tests

| Test Statistics | LM Version | F Version |
|---|---|---|
| A:Serial Correlation | CHSQ( 4)= 90.9952[.000] | F( 4, 134)= 62.2049[.000] |
| B:Functional Form | CHSQ( 1)= 4.6340[.031] | F( 1, 137)= 4.6899[.032] |
| C:Normality | CHSQ( 2)= 3.6022[.165] | Not applicable |
| D:Heteroscedasticity | CHSQ( 1)= 25.5183[.000] | F( 1, 138)= 30.7606[.000] |

A:Lagrange multiplier test of residual serial correlation
B:Ramsey's RESET test using the square of the fitted values
C:Based on a test of skewness and kurtosis of residuals
D:Based on the regression of squared residuals on squared fitted values

[1] In most applications the log-linear specification performs better than the linear specification. The coefficients of the log-linear specification, being elasticities, and hence scale-invariant, are also much easier to interpret. For a formal test of the linear versus the log-linear specification and *vice versa*, see Lesson 10.9.

where $\Delta \log c_t = \log c_t - \log c_{t-1}$; $\Delta \log y_t = \log y_t - \log y_{t-1}$; $\alpha_1 = \beta_1$; $\alpha_2 = \beta_3$; $\alpha_3 = -(1 - \beta_2)$; and $\alpha_4 = \beta_4 + \beta_3$. To run the regression (10.2) first return to the Command Editor (click CLOSE, choose CANCEL in the next two menus, then click Process) to generate the following variables:

LC = log(C); LY = log(Y); INPT = 1;

DLC = LC − LC(−1); DLY = LY − LY(−1) GO

Alternatively, you can either retrieve the equation file UKCON.EQU into the Command Editor or run the batch file UKCON.BAT. Once the above variables have been generated, choose Linear Regression Menu from the Univariate Menu and choose option 1 Ordinary Least Squares for the specification of the regression equation. Type the dependent variable, DLC, followed by the regressors:

DLC INPT DLY LC(−1) LY(−1)

Choose the start and end dates 1955Q1 and 1992Q4 from the drop-down lists. Click START. You can save the variable list for future use in a file by using the button.

Since the observations 1993(1) to 1994(4) are not used up in the estimation, you will now be asked to specify the number of observations to be used in the predictive failure/structural stability tests. Type in 8 to choose all the eight remaining observations (note that the observation 1995(1) for $y_t$ is missing) and click OK. The results given in Table 10.1b should now appear on the screen. The diagnostic statistics that follow the estimation results suggest statistically significant evidence of residual serial correlation and non-normal errors.

To leave the OLS result screen, click CLOSE. You will now be presented with the Post Regression Menu (see Section 6.21), giving a number of options to analyse your regression results further. For example, suppose you wish to test the hypothesis that in (10.2) $\alpha_3 = \alpha_4 = 0$. Choose option 2 in this menu and then option 5 in the Hypothesis Testing Menu (see Section 6.24) that follows, and after clearing the content of the box editor if necessary (by clicking the button), type

LC(−1) LY(−1) OK

The results in Table 10.1c should now appear on the screen.

The various statistics for testing the joint restrictions $\alpha_3 = \alpha_4 = 0$ are given at the lower end of Table 10.1c. For example, the likelihood ratio (LR) statistic is 3.0191. Notice that the critical value of this test depends on whether $\log y_t$ is integrated or not: see Pesaran *et al.* (1996b) and Lesson 16.5 for further details. However, in the present application, the value of the LR statistic is small enough for us to safely conclude that the hypothesis that $\alpha_3 = \alpha_4 = 0$ cannot be rejected. Therefore, the ARDL(1,1) specification in (10.1) does not provide a stable long relationship between real disposable income and consumption in the UK.

To see a plot of the actual and fitted values choose option 3 in the Post Regression Menu and when presented with the Display/Save Residuals and

**Table 10.1b:** Error correction form of the ARDL(1,1) model of consumption and income in the UK

Ordinary Least Squares Estimation

Dependent variable is DLC
151 observations used for estimation from 1955Q2 to 1992Q4

| Regressor | Coefficient | Standard Error | T-Ratio[Prob] |
|---|---|---|---|
| INPT | .044746 | .040844 | 1.0955[.275] |
| DLY | .27680 | .062296 | 4.4433[.000] |
| LC(−1) | −.072844 | .042586 | −1.7105[.089] |
| LY(−1) | .068540 | .040599 | 1.6882[.093] |

| | | | |
|---|---|---|---|
| R-Squared | .11929 | R-Bar-Squared | .10131 |
| S.E. of Regression | .011589 | F-Stat. F( 3, 147) | 6.6366[.000] |
| Mean of Dependent Variable | .0061324 | S.D. of Dependent Variable | .012225 |
| Residual Sum of Squares | .019743 | Equation Log-likelihood | 460.8790 |
| Akaike Info. Criterion | 456.8790 | Schwarz Bayesian Criterion | 450.8445 |
| DW-statistic | 2.3424 | | |

Diagnostic Tests

| Test Statistics | LM version | F Version |
|---|---|---|
| A:Serial Correlation | CHSQ( 4)= 13.5294[.009] | F( 4, 143)= 3.5184[.009] |
| B:Functional Form | CHSQ( 1)= .017570[.895] | F( 1, 146)= .016990[.896] |
| C:Normality | CHSQ( 2)= 62.5209[.000] | Not applicable |
| D:Heteroscedasticity | CHSQ( 1)= 1.1656[.280] | F( 1, 149)= 1.1591[.283] |
| E:Predictive Failure | CHSQ( 8)= .84989[1.00] | F( 8, 147)= .10624[.999] |
| F:Chow Test | CHSQ( 4)= .27225[.992] | F( 4, 151)= .068063[.991] |

A:Lagrange multiplier test of residual serial correlation
B:Ramsey's RESET test using the square of the fitted values
C:Based on a test of skewness and kurtosis of residuals
D:Based on the regression of squared residuals on squared fitted values
E:A test of adequacy of predictions (Chow's second test)
F:Test of stability of the regression coefficients

**Table 10.1c:** Statistical significance of the level variables in the ARDL(1,1) model of income and consumption in the UK

Variable Deletion Test (OLS case)

Dependent variable is DLC
List of the variables deleted from the regression:
LC(−1) LY(−1)
151 observations used for estimation from 1955Q2 to 1992Q4

| Regressor | Coefficient | Standard Error | T-Ratio[Prob] |
|---|---|---|---|
| INPT | .0045088 | .0010256 | 4.3962[.000] |
| DLY | .23859 | .058154 | 4.1026[.000] |

Joint test of zero restrictions on the coefficients of deleted variables:

| | |
|---|---|
| Lagrange Multiplier Statistic | CHSQ( 2)= 2.9891[.224] |
| Likelihood Ratio Statistic | CHSQ( 2)= 3.0191[.221] |
| F Statistic | F( 2, 147)= 1.4844[.230] |

Fitted Values Menu (see Section 6.22), click OK. You should see Figure 10.1 on the screen.

You can save this figure in a variety of formats or to the clipboard, using the , and buttons (see Section 5.2 for further details). Figure 10.1 clearly shows that none of the sharp falls in consumption expenditure are explained by the simple ARDL(1,1) model in (10.1).

You can also compute static forecasts of $\Delta \log c_t$ over the period 1993(1) to 1994(4). Click CLOSE to leave Figure 10.1, then click OK. Choose option 8 in the Post Regression Menu to obtain forecasts of $\Delta \log c_t$ together with a number of summary statistics. You can also see a plot of actual and forecast values of $\Delta \log c_t$ by choosing option 9 in the Post Regression Menu and clicking OK when the dialog appears (see Figure 10.2).

Note that the forecasts generated in the present application are 'static' in the sense that for every quarter in the period 1993(1) to 1994(4) actual values of $\log c_{t-1}$ are used in forecasting $\log c_t$ (see Section 18.26.1 for further details).

Note that in the above example, although the estimation period is specified as 1955(1) to 1992(4), because of the missing initial values for the lagged variables $\log y_{t-1}$ and $\log c_{t-1}$, the program automatically adjusts the sample period to take account of these missing observations and selects 1955(2) to 1992(4) as the estimation period.

## 10.2 Lesson 10.2: Two alternative methods of testing linear restrictions

This lesson describes two different methods of testing the hypothesis of constant returns to scale in the context of a Cobb–Douglas (CD) production function.

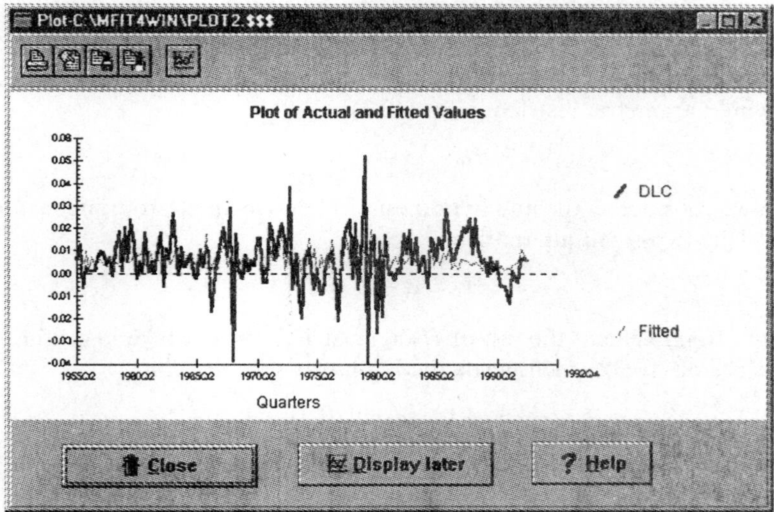


**Figure 10.1:** Plot of actual and fitted values of $\Delta \log c_t$

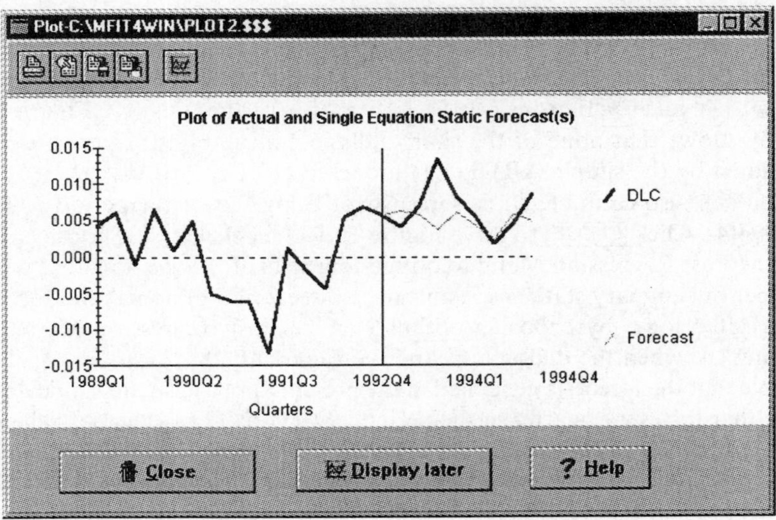


**Figure 10.2:** Plot of actual and single-equation static forecast(s)

Consider the CD production function

$$Y_t = AK_t^{\alpha} L_t^{\beta} e^{u_t}, \quad t = 1, 2, \ldots, n \tag{10.3}$$

where $Y_t$ = output, $K_t$ = capital stock, $L_t$ = employment.

The unknown parameters $A$, $\alpha$, and $\beta$ are fixed, and $u_t$s are serially uncorrelated disturbances with zero means and a constant variance. We also assume that $u_t$s are distributed independently of $K_t$ and $L_t$. Notice that for simplicity of exposition we have not allowed for technical progress in (10.3). The constant returns to scale hypothesis postulates that proportionate changes in inputs ($K_t$ and $L_t$) result in the *same* proportionate change in output. For example, doubling $K_t$ and $L_t$ should, under the constant returns to scale hypothesis, lead also to the doubling of $Y_t$. This imposes the following parametric restriction on (10.3):

$$H_0: \quad \alpha + \beta = 1$$

which we consider as the null hypothesis and derive an appropriate test of it against the two-sided alternative

$$H_1: \quad \alpha + \beta \neq 1$$

In order to implement the test of $H_0$ against $H_1$, we first take logarithms of both sides of (10.3) which yields the log-linear specification

$$LY_t = a + \alpha LK_t + \beta LL_t + u_t \tag{10.4}$$

where

$$LY_t = \log(Y_t), \quad LK_t = \log(K_t), \quad LL_t = \log(L_t)$$

and $a = \log A$.

It is now possible to obtain estimates of $\alpha$ and $\beta$ by running OLS regressions of $LY_t$ on $LK_t$ and $LL_t$ (for $t = 1, 2, \ldots, n$), including an intercept in the regression. Denote the OLS estimates of $\alpha$ and $\beta$ by $\hat{\alpha}$ and $\widehat{\beta}$, and define a new parameter, $\delta$, as

$$\delta = \alpha + \beta - 1 \tag{10.5}$$

The hypothesis $\alpha + \beta = 1$ against $\alpha + \beta \neq 1$ can now be written equivalently as

$$H_0: \quad \delta = 0,$$
$$H_1: \quad \delta \neq 0.$$

We now consider *two* alternative methods of testing $\delta = 0$: a *direct method* and a *regression method.*

**Direct method of testing $\delta = 0$**

This method directly focuses on the OLS estimates of $\delta$, namely $\hat{\delta} = \hat{\alpha} + \hat{\beta} - 1$, and examines whether this estimate is significantly different from zero. For this we need an estimate of the variance of $\hat{\delta}$. We have

$$V(\hat{\delta}) = V(\hat{\alpha}) + V(\hat{\beta}) + 2\text{Cov}(\hat{\alpha}, \hat{\beta})$$

where $V(\cdot)$ and $\text{Cov}(\cdot)$ stand for the variance and the covariance operators, respectively. The OLS estimator of $V(\hat{\delta})$ is given by

$$\hat{V}(\hat{\delta}) = \hat{V}(\hat{\alpha}) + \hat{V}(\hat{\beta}) + 2\widehat{\text{Cov}}(\hat{\alpha}, \hat{\beta})$$

where '^' stands for the estimate. The relevant test statistic for testing $\delta = 0$ against $\delta \neq 0$ is now given by

$$t_{\hat{\delta}} = \frac{\hat{\delta}}{\sqrt{\hat{V}(\hat{\delta})}} = \frac{\hat{\alpha} + \hat{\beta} - 1}{\sqrt{\hat{V}(\hat{\alpha}) + \hat{V}(\hat{\beta}) + 2\widehat{\text{Cov}}(\hat{\alpha}, \hat{\beta})}} \tag{10.6}$$

and under $\delta = 0$ has a $t$-distribution with $n - 3$ degrees of freedom.

**The regression method**

This method starts with (10.4) and replaces $\beta$ (or $\alpha$) in terms of $\delta$ and $\alpha$ (or $\beta$). Using (10.5) we have

$$\beta = \delta - \alpha + 1$$

Substituting this in (10.4) for $\beta$ now yields

$$LY_t - LL_t = a + \alpha(LK_t - LL_t) + \delta LL_t + u_t \tag{10.7}$$

or

$$Z_t = a + \alpha W_t + \delta LL_t + u_t \tag{10.8}$$

where $Z_t = \log(Y_t/L_t) = LY_t - LL_t$ and $W_t = \log(K_t/L_t) = LK_t - LL_t$. A test of $\delta = 0$ can now be carried out by first regressing $Z_t$ on $W_t$ and $LL_t$ (including an intercept term), and then carrying out the usual $t$-test on the coefficient of $LL_t$ in (10.8). The $t$-ratio of $\delta$ in (10.7) will be identical to $t_{\hat{\delta}}$ defined by (10.6).

We now apply the two methods discussed above to the historical data on

Y, K, and L used originally by Cobb–Douglas (1928). The relevant data is stored in the special *Microfit* file CD.FIT and covers the period 1899 to 1922. Load this file (using the [open] button), and in the Command Editor type

LY = log(Y); LL = log(L); INPT = 1;

Z = log(Y/L); W = log(K/L) [GO]

to generate the variables LY, LL, Z, and W defined above. Then open the Univariate Menu on the main menu bar and choose the Ordinary Least Squares option from the Linear Regression Menu. Type

LY INPT LK LL

Accept the full sample period (1899 to 1922) given in the Start and End fields, and click [START]. You should see the OLS estimates on the screen (see Table 10.2a). Click [CLOSE] to move to the Post Regression Menu and choose option 4 and then option 1 in the Standard, White and Newey–West Adjusted Variance Menu. The following estimates of the variance-covariance matrix of $(\hat{\alpha}, \widehat{\beta})'$ should appear on the screen:

$$\begin{bmatrix} \widehat{V}(\hat{\alpha}) & \widehat{\mathrm{Cov}}(\hat{\alpha},\widehat{\beta}) \\ \widehat{\mathrm{Cov}}(\hat{\alpha},\widehat{\beta}) & \widehat{V}(\widehat{\beta}) \end{bmatrix} = \begin{bmatrix} 0.004036 & -0.0083831 \\ -0.0083831 & 0.021047 \end{bmatrix}$$

Using the OLS estimates of $\alpha$ and $\beta$ given in Table 10.2a (namely $\hat{\alpha} = 0.23305$ and $\widehat{\beta} = 0.80728$ ) and the results in (10.6):

$$t_{\hat{\delta}} = \frac{0.23305 + 0.80728 - 1}{\sqrt{0.004036 + 0.021047 - 2(0.0083831)}} = 0.442 \qquad (10.9)$$

Comparing $t_{\hat{\delta}} = 0.442$ and the 5 per cent critical value of the $t$-distribution with $T - 3 = 24 - 3 = 21$ degrees of freedom (which is equal to 2.080), it is clear that since $t_{\hat{\delta}} = 0.442 < 2.080$, then the hypothesis $\delta = 0$ or $\alpha + \beta = 1$ cannot be rejected at the 5 per cent level.

To implement the regression approach, you need to move to the Linear Regression Backtracking Menu (click [CLOSE], choose option 0 to return to the Post Regression Menu, and there choose option 0), and choose option 4 to edit the regression equation. Click the [clear] button to clear the box editor and then type

Z INPT W LL [OK]

and when the menu appears click [OK]. You should see the results given in Table 10.2b on your screen. The $t$-ratio of the coefficient of the LL variable in this regression is equal to 0.442 which is identical to $t_{\hat{\delta}}$ as computed in (10.9).

It is worth noting that the above estimates of $\alpha$ and $\beta$, which have played a historically important role in the literature, are very 'fragile', in the sense that they are highly sensitive to the sample period chosen in estimating them. For example, estimating the model given in (10.4) over the period 1899 to 1920 (i.e.

**Table 10.2a:** Estimates of the log-linear Cobb–Douglas production function

| Ordinary Least Squares Estimation | | | |
|---|---|---|---|
| Dependent variable is LY<br>24 observations used for estimation from 1899 to 1922 | | | |
| Regressor | Coefficient | Standard Error | T-Ratio[Prob] |
| INPT | −.17731 | .43429 | −.40827[.687] |
| LK | .23305 | .063530 | 3.6684[.001] |
| LL | .80728 | .14508 | 5.5645[.000] |

| | | | |
|---|---|---|---|
| R-Squared | .95742 | R-Bar-Squared | .95337 |
| S.E. of Regression | .058138 | F-Stat. F( 2, 21) | 236.1219[.000] |
| Mean of Dependent Variable | 5.0773 | S.D. of Dependent Variable | .26923 |
| Residual Sum of Squares | .070982 | Equation Log-likelihood | 35.8261 |
| Akaike Info. Criterion | 32.8261 | Schwarz Bayesian Criterion | 31.0590 |
| DW-statistic | 1.5235 | | |

| Diagnostic Tests | | |
|---|---|---|
| Test Statistics | LM Version | F Version |
| A:Serial Correlation | CHSQ( 1)= .35950[.549] | F( 1, 20)= .30414[.587] |
| B:Functional Form | CHSQ( 1)= 2.1448[.143] | F( 1, 20)= 1.9627[.177] |
| C:Normality | CHSQ( 2)= 1.3613[.506] | Not applicable |
| D:Heteroscedasticity | CHSQ( 1)= 2.5774[.108] | F( 1, 22)= 2.6469[.118] |

A:Lagrange multiplier test of residual serial correlation
B:Ramsey's RESET test using the square of the fitted values
C:Based on a test of skewness and kurtosis of residuals
D:Based on the regression of squared residuals on squared fitted values

dropping the observations for the last two years) yields $\hat{\alpha} = 00807(0.1099)$ and $\widehat{\beta} = 1.0935(0.2241)$! The figures in brackets are standard errors.

## 10.3 Lesson 10.3: Estimation of long-run effects and mean lags

In this lesson we show how option 5 in the Post Regression Menu (see Section 6.21) can be used to estimate long-run effects, mean lags, and other functions of the underlying parameters of a regression model, together with their standard errors.

As an example, consider the following ARDL(1, 1) model relating capital expenditures in the US manufacturing sector ($Y_t$) to capital appropriations ($X_t$):

$$Y_t = \beta_0 + \beta_1 Y_{t-1} + \beta_2 X_t + \beta_3 X_{t-1} + u_t \tag{10.10}$$

Assuming that $|\beta_1| < 1$, we have

$$Y_t = \frac{\beta_0}{1-\beta_1} + \left(\frac{\beta_2 + \beta_3 L}{1-\beta_1 L}\right) X_t + \left(\frac{1}{1-\beta_1 L}\right) u_t$$

**Table 10.2b:** Log-linear estimates of the Cobb–Douglas production function in per capita terms

| Ordinary Least Squares Estimation | | | |
|---|---|---|---|
| Dependent variable is Z | | | |
| 24 observations used for estimation from 1899 to 1922 | | | |
| Regressor | Coefficient | Standard Error | T-Ratio[Prob] |
| INPT | −.17731 | .43429 | −.40827[.687] |
| W | .23305 | .063530 | 3.6684[.001] |
| LL | .040332 | .091197 | .44225[.663] |
| R-Squared | .63674 | R-Bar-Squared | .60215 |
| S.E. of Regression | .058138 | F-Stat. F( 2, 21) | 18.4052[.000] |
| Mean of Dependent Variable | .11461 | S.D. of Dependent Variable | .092173 |
| Residual Sum of Squares | .070982 | Equation Log-likelihood | 35.8261 |
| Akaike Info. Criterion | 32.8261 | Schwarz Bayesian Criterion | 31.0590 |
| DW-statistic | 1.5235 | | |

| Diagnostic Tests | | |
|---|---|---|
| Test Statistics | LM Version | F Version |
| A:Serial Correlation | CHSQ( 1)= .35950[.549] | F( 1, 20)= .30414[.587] |
| B:Functional Form | CHSQ( 1)= .2608E-5[.999] | F( 1, 20)= .2174E-5[.999] |
| C:Normality | CHSQ( 2)= 1.3613[.506] | Not applicable |
| D:Heteroscedasticity | CHSQ( 1)= 8.8809[.003] | F( 1, 22)= 12.9227[.002] |

A:Lagrange multiplier test of residual serial correlation
B:Ramsey's RESET test using the square of the fitted values
C:Based on a test of skewness and kurtosis of residuals
D:Based on the regression of squared residuals on squared fitted values
Z = log(Y/L), W = log(K/L) and LL = log(L)

or

$$Y_t = a_0 + \theta(L)X_t + (1 - \beta_1 L)^{-1} u_t$$

where $L$ is the lag-operator such that $LY_t = Y_{t-1}$; and $\theta(L)$ is the distributed lag function operating on $X_t$. The long-run response of $Y_t$ to a unit change in $X_t$ is given by

$$LR = \theta(1) = \frac{\beta_2 + \beta_3}{1 - \beta_1} \tag{10.11}$$

The mean lag of response of $Y_t$ to a unit change in $X_t$ is defined by

$$ML = \frac{1}{\theta(1)} \sum_{i=1}^{\infty} i\theta_i = \theta'(1)/\theta(1)$$

where $\theta'(1)$ denotes the first derivative of $\theta(L)$ with respect to $L$, evaluated at $L = 1$. It is now easily seen that[2]

$$ML = \frac{\theta'(1)}{\theta(1)} = \frac{\beta_1\beta_2 + \beta_3}{(1 - \beta_1)(\beta_2 + \beta_3)} \tag{10.12}$$

Suppose now that you wish to compute the estimates of $LR$ and $ML$ and

[2]For more details see Dhrymes (1971), Hendry *et al.* (1984); or Greene (1993, Chapter 18). Notice that the concept of mean lag is meaningful if all the lag coefficients, $\theta_i$, have the same sign.

their standard errors using observations in the special *Microfit* file ALMON.FIT. This file contains quarterly observations on $Y_t$ and $X_t$ over the period 1953(1) to 1967(4), which is an extended version of the data originally analysed by Almon (1965).

Choose option 1 in the Single Equation Estimation Menu (see Section 6.4) by selecting the Univariate Menu option and choosing Ordinary Least Squares from the Linear Regression Menu, and type

Y INPT Y(−1) X X(−1) [START]

You should now see the OLS results on the screen. Click [CLOSE] to move to the Post Regression Menu and choose option 5 in this menu. You will be presented with a box editor. Type the two functional relations (10.11) and (10.12) in the following manner:

LR = (A3 + A4)/(1 − A2);
ML = (A2 * A3 + A4)/((1 − A2) * (A3 + A4)) [OK]

Notice that *Microfit* assigns the coefficients *A*1, *A*2, *A*3, and *A*4 to the regressors *INPT*, *Y*(−1), *X*, and *X*(−1), respectively.

The results in Table 10.3 should now appear on the screen. According to these results, the hypothesis of a unit long-run coefficient on *X* cannot be rejected. The mean lag is also estimated with a reasonable degree of accuracy, and suggests a mean lag of 4.7 quarters between changes in capital appropriations and capital expenditures in US manufacturing.

If you now click [CLOSE], you will also see the covariance matrix of the estimates of LR and ML on the screen.

## 10.4 Lesson 10.4: The multicollinearity problem

Multicollinearity is commonly attributed to situations where there is a high degree of intercorrelations among the explanatory variables in a multivariate regression equation. Multicollinearity is particularly prevalent in the case of time

**Table 10.3:** Estimates of the long-run coefficient and the mean lag for the relationship between capital expenditures and capital appropriations in US manufacturing

Analysis of Function(s) of Parameter(s)

Based on OLS regression of Y on:
INPT Y(−1) X X(−1)
59 observations used for estimation from 1953Q2 to 1967Q4

Coefficients A1 to A4 are assigned to the above regressors respectively
List of specified functional relationship(s):
LR=(a3+a4)/(1−a2);ML=(a2*a3+a4)/((1−a2)*(a3+a4))

| Function | Estimate | Standard Error | T-Ratio[Prob] |
|---|---|---|---|
| LR | 1.0383 | .055739 | 18.6287[.000] |
| ML | 4.7030 | .52036 | 9.0381[.000] |

series data where there often exists the same common trend in two or more regressors in the regression equation. As a simple example, consider the model

$$y_t = \beta_1 x_{1t} + \beta_2 x_{2t} + u_t \tag{10.13}$$

and assume for simplicity that $(x_{1t}, x_{2t})$ have a bivariate distribution with the correlation coefficient, $\rho$. That is $\rho = Cov(x_{1t}, x_{2t})/\{V(x_{1t})V(x_{2t})\}^{\frac{1}{2}}$. It is clear that as $\rho$ approaches unity *separate* estimation of the slope coefficients $\beta_1$ and $\beta_2$ becomes more and more problematic. Multicollinearity will be a problem if the coefficients of $x_{1t}$ and $x_{2t}$ are jointly statistically significant but neither are statistically significant when tested individually. Put differently, multicollinearity will be a problem when the hypotheses $\beta_1 = 0$ and $\beta_2 = 0$ cannot be rejected when tested separately, while the hypothesis $\beta_1 = \beta_2 = 0$ is rejected when tested jointly. This clearly happens when $x_{1t}$ (or $x_{2t}$) is an exact linear function of $x_{2t}$ (or $x_{1t}$). In this case, $x_{2t} = \gamma x_{1t}$ and (10.13) reduce to the simple regression equation

$$y_t = \alpha + (\beta_1 + \beta_2\gamma)x_{1t} + u_t \tag{10.14}$$

and it is only possible to estimate $\beta_1 + \gamma\beta_2$. Neither $\beta_1$ nor $\beta_2$ can be estimated (or tested) separately. This is the case of 'perfect multicollinearity' and arises out of faulty specification of the regression equation. One such example occurs when four seasonal dummies are included in a quarterly regression model which already contains an intercept term.

The multicollinearity problem is also closely related to the problem of low power when separately testing hypotheses involving the regression coefficients. It is worth noting that no matter how large the correlation coefficient between $x_{1t}$ and $x_{2t}$, so long as it is not exactly equal to $\pm 1$, a test of $\beta_1 = 0$ (or $\beta_2 = 0$) will have the correct size (assuming that all the other classical normal assumptions are satisfied). The high degree of correlation between $x_{1t}$ and $x_{2t}$ causes the power of the test to be low and as a result we may end up not rejecting the null hypothesis that $\beta_1 = 0$ even if it is false.[3]

To demonstrate the multicollinearity problem and its relation to the problem of low power, consider the following (simulated) model

$$\begin{aligned}
x_1 &\sim N(0,1) \\
x_2 &= x_1 + 0.15v \\
v &\sim N(0,1) \\
y &= \alpha + \beta_1 x_1 + \beta_2 x_2 + u \\
u &\sim N(0,1)
\end{aligned}$$

with $\alpha = \beta_1 = \beta_2 = 1$, and where $x_1$, $v$ and $u$ are generated as independent standardized normal variates using respectively the 'seed' of 123, 321, and 4321 in the normal random generator (see the function NORMAL in Section 4.3.13). To generate $x_1, x_2$, and $y$, choose New... from the File Menu. In the New data set dialog choose Undated frequency, type 500 for the number of

[3]The power of a test is defined as the probability of rejecting the null hypothesis when it is false.

**Table 10.4:** An example of a multicollinear regression based on simulated data

Ordinary Least Squares Estimation

Dependent variable is Y
50 observations used for estimation from 1 to 50

| Regressor | Coefficient | Standard Error | TRatio[Prob] |
|---|---|---|---|
| INPT | .90469 | .12994 | 6.9625[.000] |
| X1 | 1.0950 | 1.0403 | 1.0526[.298] |
| X2 | .87191 | 1.0200 | .85483[.397] |

| | | | |
|---|---|---|---|
| R-Squared | .84982 | R-Bar-Squared | .84343 |
| S.E. of Regression | .88903 | F-Stat. F( 2, 47) | 132.9788[.000] |
| Mean of Dependent Variable | 1.4024 | S.D. of Dependent Variable | 2.2468 |
| Residual Sum of Squares | 37.1474 | Equation Log-likelihood | −63.5187 |
| Akaike Info. Criterion | −66.5187 | Schwarz Bayesian Criterion | −69.3868 |
| DW-statistic | 2.0705 | | |

Diagnostic Tests

| Test Statistics | LM Version | F Version |
|---|---|---|
| A:Serial Correlation | CHSQ( 1)= .37159[.542] | F( 1, 46)= .34442[.560] |
| B:Functional Form | CHSQ( 1)= .043743[.834] | F( 1, 46)= .040279[.842] |
| C:Normality | CHSQ( 2)= .21521[.898] | Not applicable |
| D:Heteroscedasticity | CHSQ( 1)= .85284[.356] | F( 1, 48)= .83293[.366] |
| E:Predictive Failure | CHSQ( 450)= 528.4668[.006] | F( 450, 47)= 1.1744[.253] |
| F:Chow Test | CHSQ( 3)= .44144[.932] | F( 3, 494)= .14715[.932] |

A:Lagrange multiplier test of residual serial correlation
B:Ramsey's RESET test using the square of the fitted values
C:Based on a test of skewness and kurtosis of residuals
D:Based on the regression of squared residuals on squared fitted values
E:A test of adequacy of predictions (Chow's second test)
F:Test of stability of the regression coefficients

observations and 0 for the number of variables and then click [OK]. Type the following formulae in the Command Editor to generate the variables Y, X1, and X2, each having 500 observations.[4]

**SAMPLE** 1 500;
X1 = normal(123); V = normal(321); U = normal(4321);
X2 = X1 + 0.15 * V; Y = 1 + X1 + X2 + U; INPT = 1 [GO]

Then move to the Single Equation Estimation Menu (the Univariate Menu on the main menu bar), choose option 1, and run the OLS regression of Y on INPT, X1, and X2 using only the first 50 observations. You should see the results in Table 10.4.

The value of F statistics F(2,47) for testing the joint hypothesis $H_0^J: \beta_1 = \beta_2 = 0$ against $H_1^J: \beta_1 \neq 0$, and/or $\beta_2 \neq 0$ is equal to 132.9788,

[4]Alternatively, you can retrieve the equation file MULTI.EQU into the box editor and then click [GO] to process.

which is well above the 95 per cent critical value of the F-distribution with 2 and 47 degrees of freedom and strongly rejects the joint hypothesis that $\beta_1 = \beta_2 = 0$. The $t$-statistics for the separate induced tests of $H_0^I{:}\beta_1 = 0$ against $H_1^I{:}\beta_1 \neq 0$; and of $H_0^{II}{:}\beta_2 = 0$ against $H_1^{II}{:}\beta_2 \neq 0$ are 1.0526 and 0.8548, respectively. Neither are statistically significant and do not lead to the rejection of $\beta_1 = 0$ and $\beta_2 = 0$ when these restrictions are considered separately. The joint hypothesis that $\beta_1$ and $\beta_2$ are both equal to zero is strongly rejected, but neither of the hypotheses that $\beta_1$ and $\beta_2$ are separately equal to zero can be rejected. Therefore there is clearly a multicollinearity problem. The sample correlation coefficient of $x_1$ and $x_2$ computed using the first 50 observations is equal to 0.99316, which is apparently too high, given the sample size and the fit of the underlying equation, for the $\beta_1$ and $\beta_2$ coefficients to be estimated separately with any degree of precision. In short, the separate induced tests lack the necessary power to allow rejection of $\beta_1 = 0$ and/or $\beta_2 = 0$ separately.

The relationship between the F statistic used to test the hypothesis $\beta_1 = \beta_2 = 0$ jointly and the $t$-statistics used to test $\beta_1 = 0$ and $\beta_2 = 0$ separately can also be obtained theoretically, and is given by:

$$F = \frac{t_1^2 + t_2^2 + 2\hat{\rho}\, t_1 t_2}{2(1 - \hat{\rho}^2)} \tag{10.15}$$

where $\hat{\rho}$ is the sample correlation coefficient between $x_{1t}$ and $x_{2t}$.[5] This relationship clearly shows that even for small values of $t_1$ and $t_2$ it is possible to get quite large values of F so long as $\hat{\rho}$ happens to be close enough to 1.

In the case of regression models with more than two regressors, the detection of the multicollinearity problem becomes even more complicated. An example occurs when there are three coefficients, tested separately: $\beta_1 = 0$, $\beta_2 = 0$, $\beta_3 = 0$ in pairs: $\beta_1 = \beta_2 = 0$, $\beta_2 = \beta_3 = 0$, $\beta_1 = \beta_3 = 0$; and jointly: $\beta_1 = \beta_2 = \beta_3 = 0$. Only in the case where the results of separate induced tests, the 'pairs' tests, and the joint tests are free from contradictions can we be confident that multicollinearity is not a problem.

There are a number of measures in the literature that purport to detect and measure the seriousness of the multicollinearity problem. These measures include the 'condition number' defined as the square root of the largest to the smallest eigenvalue of the matrix $\mathbf{X}'\mathbf{X}$, and the variance-inflation factor, defined as $(1 - R_i^2)$ for the $\beta_i$ coefficient where $R_i^2$ is the squared multiple correlation coefficient of the regression of $x_i$ on the other regressors in the regression equation. Both these measures only examine the intercorrelation between the regressors; at best they give a partial picture of the multicollinearity problem, and can often 'lead' to misleading conclusions.

To illustrate the main source of the multicollinearity problem in the present application, return to the simulation exercise, and use all the 500

---

[5] In the simulation exercise we obtained $t_1 = 1.0526$, $t_2 = 0.8548$, and $\hat{\rho} = 0.99316$. Using these estimates in (10.15) yields F = 132.9791 which is only slightly different from the F statistic reported in Table 10.4. The difference between the two values is due to rounding off errors.

observations (instead of the first 50 observations) in computing the regression of $y$ on $x_1$ and $x_2$. The results are

$$y_t = \underset{(0.0428)}{0.9307} + \underset{(0.28343)}{1.1045}\, x_{1t} + \underset{(0.27981)}{0.93138}\, x_{2t} + \hat{u}_t \qquad t = 1, 2, \ldots, 500$$

$$R^2 = 0.8333, \qquad \hat{\sigma} = 0.95664, \qquad F_{2,497} = 1242.3$$

As compared with the estimates based on the first 50 observations (see Table 10.4), these estimates have much smaller standard errors and, using the 95 per cent significance level, we arrive at the same conclusion whether we test $\beta_1 = 0$ and $\beta_2 = 0$ separately or jointly. Yet the sample correlation coefficient between $x_{1t}$ and $x_{2t}$ estimated over the 500 observations is equal to 0.9895 which is only marginally smaller than the estimate obtained for the first 50 observations. By increasing the sample size from 50 to 500 we have increased the precision with which $\beta_1$ and $\beta_2$ are estimated, and the power of testing $\beta_1 = 0$ and $\beta_2 = 0$, both separately and jointly.

The above illustration also points to the fact that the main cause of the multicollinearity problem is lack of adequate observations (or information), and hence the imprecision with which the parameters of interest are estimated. Assuming the regression model under consideration is correctly specified, the appropriate solution to the problem is to increase the information on the basis of which the regression is estimated. The new information could be either in the form of additional observations on $y$, $x_1$, and $x_2$, or it could be some a priori information concerning the parameters. The latter fits well with the Bayesian approach, but is difficult to accommodate within the classical framework. There are also other approaches suggested in the literature, such as ridge regression and principle component regression, to deal with the multicollinearity problem. A review of these approaches can be found in Judge *et al.* (1985).

## 10.5 Lesson 10.5: Testing common factor restrictions

Consider the following ARDL(1,1,1) model relating logarithm of real consumption expenditures ($\log c_t$) to the logarithm of the real disposable income ($\log y_t$) and the rate of inflation ($\Pi_t$) in the UK:

$$(1 - \beta_1 L)\log c_t = \beta_0 + (\beta_2 + \beta_3 L)\log y_t + (\beta_4 + \beta_5 L)\Pi_t + u_t \qquad (10.16)$$

where $L$ represents the backward lag operator. The idea of testing for common factor restrictions was originally proposed by Sargan (1964). The test explores the possibility of simplifying the dynamics of (10.16) by testing the hypothesis that the lag polynomials operating on $\log c_t$, $\log y_t$, and $\Pi_t$ have the same factor in common. The procedure can also be viewed as a method of testing the dynamics in the deterministic part of the regression model against the dynamics in the stochastic part (see Hendry *et al.* 1984, Section 2.6). In the case of the present example, the common factor restrictions are[6]

[6]To derive the restrictions in (10.17) note that for the lag polynomials $1 - \beta_1 L$ and $\beta_4 + \beta_5 L$ to have the same factor in common, it is necessary that $\beta_1^{-1}$, the root of $1 - \beta_1 L = 0$, should also be a root of $\beta_2 + \beta_3 L = 0$ and $\beta_4 + \beta_5 L = 0$.

| **Table 10.5:** Testing for common factor restrictions | | | | |
|---|---|---|---|---|
| Wald test of restriction(s) imposed on parameters | | | | |
| Based on OLS regression of LC on: | | | | |
| INPT | LC(−1) | LY | LY(−1) | PI |
| PI(−1) | | | | |
| 158 observations used for estimation from 1955Q3 to 1994Q4 | | | | |
| Coefficients A1 to A6 are assigned to the above regressors respectively | | | | |
| List of restriction(s) for the Wald test: | | | | |
| a2*a3+a4=0; a2*a5+a6=0 | | | | |
| Wald Statistic | | CHSQ( 2)= 22.0612[.000] | | |

$$\left.\begin{aligned}\beta_1\beta_2+\beta_3=0\\ \beta_1\beta_4+\beta_5=0\end{aligned}\right\} \tag{10.17}$$

A test of these restrictions can be carried out using *Microfit*. Here we assume that (10.16) is to be estimated by the OLS method, but the procedure outlined below is equally applicable if (10.16) is estimated by the IV method.

We use the quarterly observations in the special *Microfit* file UKCON.FIT to carry out the test. First read UKCON.FIT and make sure that the variables LC $= \log c_t$, LY $= \log y_t$, $P_t =$ CNOM/C and PI $= \log(P_t/P_{t-1})$ are in the variables list. To generate these variables in the Command Editor retrieve the file UKCON.EQU, or equivalently run the batch file UKCON.BAT (see also Lessons 9.1 and 9.2).

Choose option 1 in the Single Equation Estimation Menu (the Univariate Menu on the main menu bar: Section 6.4), make sure the OLS option is selected, and type

LC INPT LC(−1) LY LY(−1) PI PI(−1) [START]

You should see the OLS regression results on the screen. Move to the Post Regression Menu and choose option 2 (see Section 6.21). This takes you to the Hypothesis Testing Menu (see Section 6.24). Now choose option 7 in this menu to carry out a Wald test of the common factor restrictions in (10.17). In the box editor that appears on the screen type

A2 * A3 + A4 = 0;   A2 * A5 + A6 = 0 [OK]

You should now see the test results in Table 10.5 on the screen.

The Wald statistic for testing the two non-linear restrictions in (10.17) is equal to 22.06, which implies a strong rejection of the common factor restrictions. It is, however, important to note that the Wald statistic is sensitive to the way the non-linear restrictions are specified. See, for example, Gregory and Veall (1985, 1987). See also Exercise 10.3.

## 10.6 Lesson 10.6: Estimation of regression models with serially correlated errors

Suppose you wish to estimate the saving equation

$$s_t = \alpha_0 + \alpha_1 s_{t-1} + \alpha_2 \Delta \log y_t + \alpha_3(\Pi_t - \Pi_t^e) + u_t \tag{10.18}$$

using UK quarterly observations in the special *Microfit* file UKCON.FIT.

$s_t$ ≡ Saving rate (the variable S)
$\Delta \log y_t$ ≡ The rate of change of real disposable income (DLY)
$\Pi_t$ ≡ Actual rate of inflation (PI)
$\Pi_t^e$ ≡ Adaptive expectations of $\Pi_t$ as computed in Lesson 9.12

subject to the AR(1) error specification by the Cochrane–Orcutt method:

$$u_t = \rho_1 u_{t-1} + \epsilon_t \tag{10.19}$$

Equation (10.18) is a modified version of the saving function estimated by Deaton (1977).[7]

To carry out the computations for the above estimation problem, first go through the steps described in Lesson 9.12 to generate the variable PIE with $\lambda = 0.8$ on your workspace. Alternatively, read in UKCON.FIT and then retrieve the file UKCON.EQU into the Command Editor. If you now click GO, the variables S, DLY, PI, and INPT will be created. Click [icon] to clear the editor and then type

lambda = 0.8; **BATCH** PIE GO

to generate the inflation expectations variable PIE. Then create the unanticipated inflation variable $\Pi_t - \Pi_t^e$ by typing

DPIE = PI – PIE GO

Now move to the Single Equation Estimation Menu (the Univariate Menu), and choose option 4 from the Linear Regression Menu (see Section 6.9). Type

S INPT S(–1) DLY DPIE

and choose the start and end dates 1960Q1 and 1994Q4. Click START and, when prompted, type

1↵

You will now be presented with a menu for initializing the estimation process (see Section 6.13.1). Click OK or press the ↵ key to see the plot of the concentrated log-likelihood function, showing the log-likelihood profile for different values of $\rho_1$, in the range [–0.99, 0.99] (see Figure 10.3)

As you can see, the log-likelihood function is bimodal for a positive and a negative value of $\rho_1$. The global maximum of the log-likelihood is achieved

[7] However, note the saving function estimated by Deaton (1977) assumes that the inflation expectations $\Pi_t^e$ are time invariant.

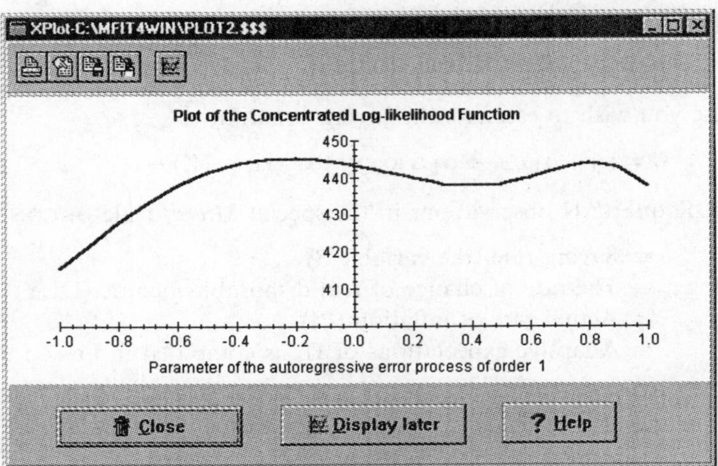


**Figure 10.3:** Log-likelihood profile for different values of $\rho_1$

for $\rho_1 < 0$. Bimodal log-likelihood functions frequently arise in estimation of models with lagged dependent variables estimated subject to a serially correlated error process, particularly in cases where the regressors show a relatively low degree of variability. The bimodal problem is *sure* to arise if apart from the lagged values of the dependent there are no other regressors in the regression equation.

To compute the ML estimates, click CLOSE to return to the menu for initialization of the unknown parameter, $\rho_1$. Choose option 2 and type −0.2 as the initial estimate for $\rho_1$ and click OK. The results in Table 10.6a should now appear on the screen. The iterative algorithm has converged to the correct estimate of $\rho_1$ (i.e. $\hat{\rho}_1 = -0.22838$) and refers to the global maximum of the log-likelihood function given by $LL(\hat{\rho}_1 = -0.22838) = 445.3720$. Notice also that the estimation results are reasonably robust to the choice of the initial estimates chosen for $\rho_1$, so long as negative or small positive values are chosen. However, if one starts the iterations from $\rho_1^{(0)} = 0.5$ or higher, the results in Table 10.6b will be obtained.

The iterative process has now converged to $\hat{\rho}_1 = 0.81487$ with the maximized value for the log-likelihood function given by $LL(\hat{\rho}_1 = 0.81487) = 444.3055$, which is a local maximum. (Recall from Table 10.6a that $LL(\hat{\rho}_1 = -0.22838) = 445.3720$.) This example clearly shows the importance of experimenting with different initial values where estimating regression models (particularly when they contain lagged dependent variables) with serially correlated errors. Suppose you now wish to estimate (10.18) subject to the following AR(4) error process with zero restrictions on two of its coefficients:

$$u_t = \rho_1 u_{t-1} + \rho_4 u_{t-4} + \epsilon_t$$

Return to the Single Equation Estimation window via the Backtracking Menu and choose option 5 in the Linear Regression Estimation Menu, run the same calculations, and when prompted, type:

1 4 ↩

**Table 10.6a:** Cochrane–Orcutt estimates of a UK saving function

Cochrane–Orcutt Method AR(1) converged after 3 iterations

Dependent variable is S
140 observations used for estimation from 1960Q1 to 1994Q4

| Regressor | Coefficient | Standard Error | T-Ratio[Prob] |
|---|---|---|---|
| INPT | −.0032323 | .0041204 | −.78448[.434] |
| S(−1) | .99250 | .040347 | 24.5989[.000] |
| DLY | .66156 | .060082 | 11.0111[.000] |
| DPIE | .31032 | .093382 | 3.3231[.001] |

| | | | |
|---|---|---|---|
| R-Squared | .76673 | R-Bar-Squared | .75977 |
| S.E. of Regression | .010004 | F-Stat. F( 4, 134) | 110.1102[.000] |
| Mean of Dependent Variable | .096441 | S.D. of Dependent Variable | .020696 |
| Residual Sum of Squares | .013412 | Equation Log-likelihood | 445.3720 |
| Akaike Info. Criterion | 440.3720 | Schwarz Bayesian Criterion | 433.0179 |
| DW-statistic | 1.9615 | | |

Parameters of the Autoregressive Error Specification

U= −.22838*U(−1)+E
( −2.5135)[.013]
T-ratio(s) based on asymptotic standard errors in brackets

Choose option 1 to use the initial estimate supplied by the program. The results in Table 10.6c should now appear on the screen. These estimates seem to be quite robust to the choice of the initial values for $\rho_1$ and $\rho_4$. For example, starting the iterations with $\rho_1^{(0)} = 0.8$ and $\rho_2^{(0)} = 0.0$ yields the same results as in Table 10.6c.

## 10.7 Lesson 10.7: Estimation of a 'surprise' consumption function: an example of two-step estimation

A simple version of the life cycle rational expectations theory of consumption predicts that changes in real consumption expenditures (or their logarithms) are only affected by innovations in real disposable income. Muellbauer (1983), building on the seminal work of Hall (1978), has estimated the following 'surprise' aggregate consumption function for the UK:

$$\Delta \log c_t = a_0 + a_1(\log y_t - \widehat{\log y_t}) + u_t \tag{10.20}$$

where $c_t$ = real consumption expenditures, $y_t$ = real disposable income, and $\widehat{\log y_t}$ is the predictor of $\log y_t$ based on information at time $t-1$.

In this lesson we use quarterly observations on $c_t$ and $y_t$ in the file UKCON.FIT to estimate (10.20). This is an example of the two-step estimation method for rational expectations discussed in Pagan (1984) and Pesaran (1987a, 1991).

In the first step, the predicted values of $\log y_t$ are obtained by running the

**Table 10.6b:** An example where the Cochrane–Orcutt method has converged to a local maximum

Cochrane–Orcutt Method AR(1) converged after 7 iterations

Dependent variable is S
140 observations used for estimation from 1960Q1 to 1994Q4

| Regressor | Coefficient | Standard Error | T-Ratio[Prob] |
|---|---|---|---|
| INPT | .075353 | .0098576 | 7.6441[.000] |
| S(−1) | .19990 | .084385 | 2.3689[.019] |
| DLY | .55758 | .052907 | 10.5388[.000] |
| DPIE | .45522 | .10271 | 4.4322[.000] |

| | | | |
|---|---|---|---|
| R-Squared | .76312 | R-Bar-Squared | .75605 |
| S.E. of Regression | .010081 | F-Stat. F( 4, 134) | 107.9234[.000] |
| Mean of Dependent Variable | .096441 | S.D. of Dependent Variable | .020696 |
| Residual Sum of Squares | .013619 | Equation Log-likelihood | 444.3055 |
| Akaike Info. Criterion | 439.3055 | Schwarz Bayesian Criterion | 431.9514 |
| DW-statistic | 2.2421 | | |

Parameters of the Autoregressive Error Specification

U= .81487*U(−1)+E
( 16.1214) [.000]
T-ratio(s) based on asymptotic standard errors in brackets
NOTE: The iterations has converged to a local optimum

**Table 10.6c:** ML estimates of a saving equation with restricted AR(4) error process

Maximum Likelihood Estimation: Fixed Initial Values of Disturbances
Error TERM : Restricted AR(4) converged after 7 iterations

Dependent variable is S
140 observations used for estimation from 1960Q1 to 1994Q4

| Regressor | Coefficient | Standard Error | T-Ratio[Prob] |
|---|---|---|---|
| INPT | −.0048180 | .0042275 | −1.1397[.256] |
| S(−1) | 1.0080 | .041256 | 24.4335[.000] |
| DLY | .65590 | .061110 | 10.7330[.000] |
| DPIE | .29880 | .093110 | 3.2091[.002] |

| | | | |
|---|---|---|---|
| R-Squared | .76567 | R-Bar-Squared | .75666 |
| S.E. of Regression | .010094 | F-Stat. F( 5, 130) | 84.9560[.000] |
| Mean of Dependent Variable | .096441 | S.D. of Dependent Variable | .020696 |
| Residual Sum of Squares | .013247 | Equation Log-likelihood | 435.1181 |
| Akaike Info. Criterion | 429.1181 | Schwarz Bayesian Criterion | 420.2932 |
| DW-statistic | 1.9598 | | |

Parameters of the Autoregressive Error Specification

U= −.25410*U(−1)+ −.014586*U(−4)+E
( −2.7908)[.006] ( −.16654)[.868]
T-ratio(s) based on asymptotic standard errors in brackets

OLS regression of $\log y_t$ on its past values, and possibly on lagged values of other variables. In what follows we estimate a second-order autoregressive process, AR(2), in $\log y_t$. In the second step, (10.20) is estimated by running the OLS regression of $\Delta \log c_t$ on a constant term and the residuals obtained from the regression in the first step.

To carry out the computations in the first step, read in the special *Microfit* file UKCON.FIT, generate the variables LC $= \log c_t$ and LY $= \log y_t$, and an intercept term, and then choose option 1 in the Single Equation Estimation Menu (Univariate Menu: see Section 6.4), make sure the OLS option is selected, and type:

LY INPT LY(−1) LY(−2) [START]

When the table appears, click [CLOSE], and from the Post Regression Menu choose option 3. You should now see the Display/Save Residuals and Fitted Values Menu on the screen. Choose option 6 and, when prompted type

DRLY Unanticipated change in log(Y)↵

The variable $DRLY(= \log y_t - \widehat{\log y_t})$ is now saved, and you can now carry out the computations in the second step.

Return to the Single Equation Estimation window (making sure the OLS option from the Linear Regression Menu is selected), click [ ] to clear the box editor, and then type

DLC INPT DRLY

You should now see the results in Table 10.7 on the screen. The $t$-ratio of the coefficient of $DRLY$ is 4.8269 which is much higher than the critical value of the $t$ distribution with $158 - 2 = 156$ degrees of freedom; thus suggesting that innovations in income growth have significant impact on consumption growth.[8]

Repeat the above exercise using USCON.FIT file. Also try additional regressors, such as $\Delta \log y_{t-1}$ and $\Delta \log c_{t-1}$ in (10.20). Are your results sensitive to the order of the AR process chosen to compute $\widehat{\log y_t}$?

## 10.8 Lesson 10.8: An example of non-nested hypothesis testing

Suppose you are faced with the following models:

$$M_1: \Delta \log c_t = \alpha_0 + \alpha_1 \log y_t + \alpha_2 \log c_{t-1} + \alpha_3 \log y_{t-1} + \alpha_4 \Pi_t + u_{t1}$$
$$M_2: \Delta \log c_t = \beta_0 + \beta_1 (\log y_t - \widehat{\log y_t}) + \beta_2 \Pi_t + u_{t2}$$

Model $M_1$ is an inflation-augmented version of the error correction model (10.1) in Lesson 10.1. The inflation rate, $\Pi_t$, is measured as the change in the logarithm of the implicit price deflator of consumption.

[8]Notice that

$$\begin{aligned} \log y_t - \widehat{\log y_t} &= (\log y_t - \log y_{t-1}) - (\widehat{\log y_t} - \log y_{t-1}) \\ &= \Delta \log y_t - \Delta \widehat{\log y_t} \end{aligned}$$

**Table 10.7:** Surprise consumption function for the UK

| Ordinary Least Squares Estimation | | | |
|---|---|---|---|
| Dependent variable is DLC<br>158 observations used for estimation from 1955Q3 to 1994Q4 | | | |
| Regressor | Coefficient | Standard Error | T-Ratio[Prob] |
| INPT | .0061568 | .8913E-3 | 6.9076[.000] |
| DRLY | .27395 | .056753 | 4.8269[.000] |

| | | | |
|---|---|---|---|
| R-Squared | .12995 | R-Bar-Squared | .12437 |
| S.E. of Regression | .011203 | F-Stat. F( 1, 156) | 23.2993[.000] |
| Mean of Dependent Variable | .0061568 | S.D. of Dependent Variable | .011973 |
| Residual Sum of Squares | .019581 | Equation Log-likelihood | 486.4768 |
| Akaike Info. Criterion | 484.4768 | Schwarz Bayesian Criterion | 481.4142 |
| DW-statistic | 2.4947 | | |

| Diagnostic Tests | | |
|---|---|---|
| Test Statistics | LM Version | F Version |
| A:Serial Correlation | CHSQ( 4)= 13.5373[.009] | F( 4, 152)= 3.5609[.008] |
| B:Functional Form | CHSQ( 1)= .19194[.661] | F( 1, 155)= .18852[.665] |
| C:Normality | CHSQ( 2)= 99.9521[.000] | Not applicable |
| D:Heteroscedasticity | CHSQ( 1)= 1.1184[.290] | F( 1, 156)= 1.1121[.293] |

A:Lagrange multiplier test of residual serial correlation
B:Ramsey's RESET test using the square of the fitted values
C:Based on a test of skewness and kurtosis of residuals
D:Based on the regression of squared residuals on squared fitted values

Model $M_2$ is the inflation-augmented 'surprise' consumption function and is estimated in Lesson 10.7. First load the special *Microfit* file UKCON.FIT and make sure that the following variables are in the variables list:

$$
\begin{aligned}
\text{DLC} &= \Delta \log c_t \\
\text{DLY} &= \Delta \log y_t \\
\text{PI} &= \log(p_t/p_{t-1}) \\
\text{P} &\equiv \text{Implicit price deflator of consumption expenditure} \\
\text{DRLY} &= \log y_t - \widehat{\log y_t} \\
&= \log y_t - \hat{\rho}_0 - \hat{\rho}_1 \log y_{t-1} - \hat{\rho}_2 \log y_{t-2} \\
\text{INPT} &\equiv \text{Intercept term}
\end{aligned}
$$

If one or more of these variables are not in your variables list, you need to consult the relevant lessons on how to generate them (see Lessons 10.6 and 10.7).

Suppose now that you wish to test model $M_1$ against $M_2$ and vice versa. Choose option 1 in the Single Equation Estimation Menu (Univariate Menu: see Section 6.4), make sure the OLS option is selected, and type

DLC INPT DLY LC(−1) LY(−1) PI [START]

[CLOSE]

↩

**Table 10.8:** Non-nested statistics for testing ARDL and surprise consumption functions

| Alternative Tests for Non-Nested Regression Models | | | | |
|---|---|---|---|---|
| Dependent variable is DLC | | 158 observations used from 1955Q3 to 1994Q4 | | |
| Regressors for model M1: | | | | |
| INPT | DLY | LC(−1) | LY(−1) | PI |
| Regressors for model M2: | | | | |
| INPT | DRLY | PI | | |
| Test Statistic | | M1 against M2 | | M2 against M1 |
| N-Test | | −3.6717[.000] | | −6.1894[.000] |
| NT-Test | | −3.4159[.001] | | −2.2548[.024] |
| W-Test | | −3.3767[.001] | | −2.2163[.027] |
| J-Test | | 3.3888[.001] | | 2.7843[.005] |
| JA-Test | | 3.3888[.001] | | −2.7045[.007] |
| Encompassing | F( 1, 152) | 11.4840[.001] | F( 3, 152) | 6.3517[.000] |
| Model M1: | DW 2.1543 | ;R-Bar-Squared .21629 | ;Log-likelihood 497.2737 | |
| Model M2: | DW 2.4300 | ;R-Bar-Squared .19057 | ;Log-likelihood 493.6973 | |
| Model M1+M2: | DW 2.2193 | ;R-Bar-Squared .26655 | ;Log-likelihood 503.0276 | |
| Akaike's Information Criterion of M1 versus M2= 1.5764 favours M1 | | | | |
| Schwarz's Bayesian Criterion of M1 versus M2= −1.4862 favours M2 | | | | |

You should now see the Hypothesis Testing Menu (see Section 6.24) on the screen. Choose option 8 and when prompted, first click to clear the box editor and then type the regressors of model $M_2$:

INPT DRLY PI [OK]

The results in Table 10.8 should now appear on the screen. All the non-nested tests suggest that both models should be rejected. There is also a conflict between the two model selection criteria, with the Akaike information criterion (AIC) favouring $M_2$, and the Schwarz Bayesian criterion (SBC) favouring $M_1$. The test results point to another model, possibly a combination of models $M_1$ and $M_2$, as providing a more satisfactory specification.

## 10.9 Lesson 10.9: Testing linear versus log-linear models

Suppose you are interested in testing the linear form of the inflation augmented ARDL(1,1) model

$$M_1: c_t = \alpha_0 + \alpha_1 c_{t-1} + \alpha_2 y_t + \alpha_3 y_{t-1} + \alpha_4 \Pi_t + u_{1t}$$

against its log-linear form

$$M_2: \log c_t = \beta_0 + \beta_1 \log c_{t-1} + \beta_2 \log y_t + \beta_3 \log y_{t-1} + \beta_4 \Pi_t + u_{2t}$$

where

$c_t \equiv$ Real non-durable consumption expenditure in the US

$y_t \equiv$ Real disposable income in the US
$\pi_t \equiv$ The inflation rate

First load the special *Microfit* file USCON.FIT, and generate the necessary variables for running the above regressions (for example, by using the [button] button to retrieve the file USCON.EQU into the box editor). Choose option 1 in the Single Equation Estimation Menu (Univariate Menu: see Section 6.4), make sure the OLS option is selected, and type

C INPT C(−1) Y Y(−1) PI [START]
[CLOSE]
↩

You should now see the Hypothesis Testing Menu (see Section 6.24) on the screen. Choose option 9 and, when prompted, type the regressors of model $M_2$, namely

INPT LC(−1) LY LY(−1) PI [OK]

You will now be asked to specify the nature of the transformation of the dependent variable in model $M_1$. Choose the linear option 1.

A similar menu concerning the nature of the transformation of the dependent variable in model $M_2$ now appears on the screen. Choose option 2. You will be prompted to specify the number of replications ($R$) to be used in the computations of the Cox statistic by simulation (see Section 18.8 and option 9 in Section 6.24). For most applications, values of $R$ in the range 100–250 will be adequate. Enter 100, and press ↩ or [OK] for the computations to start. Once the computations are completed, the results in Table 10.9 should appear on the screen. This table gives the parameter estimates under both models. The estimates of the parameters of $M_1$ computed under $M_1$ are the *OLS* estimates ($\hat{\alpha}$), while the estimates of the parameters of $M_1$ computed under $M_2$ are the pseudo-true estimators ($\hat{\alpha}_* = \hat{\alpha}_*(\hat{\beta})$). If model $M_1$ is correctly specified, one would expect $\hat{\alpha}$ and $\hat{\alpha}_*$ to be near to one another. The same also applies to the estimates of the parameters of model $M_2$ (i.e. $\beta$).

The bottom part of Table 10.9 gives a number of different statistics for testing the linear versus the log-linear model and vice versa. This table also gives the Sargan (1964) and Vuong (1989) likelihood function criteria for the choice between the two models. For other details and references to the literature, see Section 18.8.

In the present application all the tests reject the linear model against the log-linear model, and none reject the log-linear model against the linear one at the 5 per cent significance level; although the simulated Cox and the double-length tests also suggest rejection of the log-linear model at the 10 per cent significance level. Increasing the number of replications to 500 does not alter this conclusion. The two choice criteria also favour the log-linear specification over the linear one.

**Table 10.9:** Testing linear versus log-linear consumption functions

Non-Nested Tests by Simulation

Dependent variable in model M1 is C
Dependent variable in model M2 is LOG(C)
136 observations used from 1960Q2 to 1994Q1. Number of replications 100

| Estimates of parameters of M1 | Under M1 | Under M2 | Estimates of parameters of M2 | Under M2 | Under M1 |
|---|---|---|---|---|---|
| INPT | 20.1367 | 24.7609 | INPT | .14429 | .098439 |
| C(−1) | .93128 | .90987 | LC(−1) | .89781 | .94227 |
| Y | .092935 | .098593 | LY | .29526 | .27626 |
| Y(−1) | −.076891 | −.077510 | LY(−1) | −.22532 | −.23860 |
| PI | −160.9665 | −156.5597 | PI | −.23880 | −.23041 |
| Standard Error | 4.6528 | 4.8476 | Standard Error | .0057948 | .0061028 |
| Adjusted Log-L | −399.5709 | −404.4709 | Adjusted Log-L | −399.0233 | −405.2882 |

Non-Nested Test Statistics and Choice Criteria

| Test Statistic | M1 against M2 | M2 against M1 |
|---|---|---|
| S-Test 100 replications | −2.5592[.010] | −1.8879[.059] |
| PE-Test | 2.3021[.021] | −.26402[.792] |
| BM-Test | 2.0809[.037] | −.50743[.612] |
| DL-Test | 2.0006[.045] | 1.8004[.072] |

Sargan's Likelihood Criterion for M1 versus M2= −.54764 favours M2
Vuong's Likelihood Criterion for M1 versus M2= −1.7599[.078] favours M2

S-Test is the SC_c test proposed by Pesaran and Pesaran (1995) and is the simple version of the simulated Cox test statistic.
PE-Test is the PE test due to MacKinnon, White and Davidson.
BM-Test is due to Bera and McAleer.
DL-Test is the double-length regression test statistic due to Davidson and MacKinnon.

## 10.10 Lesson 10.10: Testing for exogeneity: computation of the Wu–Hausman statistic

In this lesson we show how the variable addition test option in the Hypothesis Testing Menu (see Section 6.24) can be used to compute Wu's (1973) $T_2$ statistic for testing the independence (or more precisely the lack of correlation) of the regressors, $\log y_t$ and $\Pi_t$, and the disturbance term, $u_t$ in the following regression equation estimated on UK data:[9]

$$\log c_t = \alpha_0 + \alpha_1 \log c_{t-1} + \alpha_2 \log y_t + \alpha_3 \log y_{t-1} + \alpha_4 \Pi_t + u_t \qquad (10.21)$$

We assume that you have read in the file UKCON.FIT and that the variables $\log c_t$, $\log y_t$, and $\Pi_t$ are in the variables list (these variables can be generated by running the batch file UKCON.BAT). We also assume that the variables $\log y_{t-1}$,

[9]Wu's $T_2$ statistic is also known as the Wu–Hausman statistic. For details see Wu (1973), Hausman (1978), Nakamura and Nakamura (1981), and Pesaran and Smith (1990).

$\log y_{t-2}$, $\log c_{t-1}$, $\log c_{t-2}$, $\Pi_{t-1}$, and $\Pi_{t-2}$ can be used as instruments for this test.[10]

Computation of the Wu–Hausman $T_2$ statistic can be carried out in the following manner:

1. Run OLS regressions of $LY$ (i.e. $\log y_t$) and PI (i.e. $\Pi_t$) on the variables INPT, LY(−1), LY(−2), LC(−1), LC(−2), PI(−1), and PI(−2), over the period 1960(1) to 1994(4), and save the residuals (using option 6 in the Display/Save Residuals and Fitted Values Menu) in the variables RLY and RPI, respectively (on how to do this, see Lesson 10.7). More specifically, choose option 1 in the Single Equation Estimation Menu (the Univariate Menu: see Section 6.4), make sure the OLS option is selected, choose the estimation period 1960Q1 to 1994Q4. Then enter

   LY INPT LY{1 − 2} LC{1 − 2} PI{1 − 2} [OK]

   When the table appears, click [CLOSE]. Choose option 3 from the Post Regression Menu and option 6 from the Display/Save Residuals and Fitted Values Menu. When prompted, enter

   RLY Residuals from LY regression ↩

   Press ↩ to return to the Post Regression Menu and select option 4 from the Backtracking Menu. Replace LY by PI in the screen editor box. Click [OK], press ↩, and when the table appears, click [CLOSE]. Choose option 3 from the Post Regression Menu and option 6 from the Display/Save Residuals and Fitted Values Menu. When prompted, enter the following string:

   RPI Residuals from PI regression ↩

   Press ↩ to move to the Post Regression Menu. Choose option 0 and then option 1 from the Backtracking Menu to return to the Single Equation Estimation window.

2. Make sure that the variables RLY and RPI are correctly saved (click the [Variables] button to check the list). Then choose option 1 in the Single Equation Estimation Menu (the Univariate Menu on the menu bar), and make sure the OLS option is selected. Click the [clear] button to clear the box editor and make sure the start and end dates are set to 1960Q1 and 1994Q4. Then type

   LC INPT LC(–1) LY{1–2} PI [START]

   Click the [OK] button and proceed. When the table appears, click [CLOSE]. In the Post Regression Menu, press ↩ and choose option 6 from the Hypothesis Testing Menu. Into the box editor enter

   RLY RPI [OK]

[10] The Wu–Hausman test is also asymptotically equivalent to testing the statistical significance of the difference between the OLS and the 2SLS estimates of the regression coefficients in (10.21). It is also advisable to carry out Sargan's general misspecification test given in the result table in the case of IV regressions.

**Table 10.10:** Wu–Hausman statistic for testing the exogeneity of LY and PI

Variable Addition Test (OLS case)

Dependent variable is LC
List of the variables added to the regression:
RLY RPI
140 observations used for estimation from 1960Q1 to 1994Q4

| Regressor | Coefficient | Standard Error | T-Ratio[Prob] |
|---|---|---|---|
| INPT | .017173 | .039516 | .43458[.665] |
| LC(−1) | 1.3181 | .15256 | 8.6400[.000] |
| LY | −1.2561 | .48159 | −2.6083[.010] |
| LY(−1) | .94106 | .34011 | 2.7669[.006] |
| PI | −.26192 | .094060 | −2.7846[.006] |
| RLY | 1.5019 | .48568 | 3.0923[.002] |
| RPI | −.21711 | .15261 | −1.4227[.157] |

Joint test of zero restrictions on the coefficients of additional variables:

| | | |
|---|---|---|
| Lagrange Multiplier Statistic | CHSQ( 2)= | 11.0589[.004] |
| Likelihood Ratio Statistic | CHSQ( 2)= | 11.5201[.003] |
| F Statistic | F( 2, 133)= | 5.7035[.004] |

F-Statistic is equal to the Wu–Hausman statistic

The results in Table 10.10 should now appear on the screen.

The Wu–Hausman statistic (i.e. Wu's $T_2$ statistic) is equal to the value of the F statistic in Table 10.10, which is computed as 5.70, and under the null hypothesis (of exogeneity) is distributed approximately as an F with 2 and 133 degrees of freedom. The exogeneity test can also be based on the Lagrange multiplier, or the likelihood ratio statistic reported in the above Table. All three tests are asymptotically equivalent and in the case of the present application, reject the null hypothesis that the income and inflation variables are exogenous in the inflation augmented ARDL(1,1) in (10.21). However, as can be seen from Table 10.10 the $t$-ratio of the inflation variable, RPI, is −1.4227 and suggests that the hypothesis that the inflation rate is exogenous cannot be rejected.

Also, the rejection of the exogeneity of $\log y_t$ in (24) crucially depends on the exclusion of $\log y_{t-2}$ from the ARDL specification. As an exercise, include $\log y_{t-2}$ among the regressors of (10.21) and try the above exogeneity test again.

## 10.11 Lesson 10.11: Recursive prediction of US monthly excess returns

The literature on the predictability of returns or excess returns on common stocks is quite extensive. It has been shown that a substantial part of variations in excess returns at different time intervals is predictable. See, for example, Campbell (1987), Fama and French (1989), Pesaran (1991), Breen, *et al.* (1990), Glosten *et al.* (1993), and Pesaran and Timmermann

(1994). In this lesson we replicate some of the excess return regressions reported in Pesaran and Timmermann (1994) at monthly frequencies and show how to use such regressions to generate recursive predictions of excess returns on standard and poor's 500 (SP500) portfolio using only *ex ante* dated variables.

The special *Microfit* file PTMONTH.FIT contains monthly observations on a number of financial and macroeconomic variables over the period 1948(1) to 1992(12) for the US economy. (Notice, however, that there are missing observations for most of the variables during the 1948 to 1951 period.) Load this file and run the batch file PTMONTH.BAT on it in the Command Editor. The following variables should now be in the variables list:

| | |
|---|---|
| DI11 | $i1 - i1(-1)$ |
| DIP12 | $\log(ip12/ip12(-12))$ |
| ERSP | $nrsp - ((1 + (i1(-1)/100)\hat{}(1/12)) + 1$ |
| INPT | 1 |
| PI12 | $\log(ppi12/ppi12(-12))$ |
| YSP | $divsp/psp$ |

where

| | |
|---|---|
| DIVSP | Twelve-month average of dividends on SP500 |
| I1 | One-month *t*-bill rate (Fama–Bliss) |
| IP | Index of industrial production |
| IP12 | $MAV(ip, 12)$ |
| NRSP | $(psp - psp(-1) + divsp)/psp(-1)$ |
| PPI | Producer price index |
| PPI12 | $MAV(ppi, 12)$ |
| PSP | SP500 price index (end of month) |

ERSP is the excess return on SP500 defined as the difference between the nominal return on SP500 (NRSP) minus the lagged one-month treasury bill (TB) rate converted from an annual rate to a monthly rate (allowing for compounding).

| | |
|---|---|
| DI11 | Change in the one-month *t*-bill rate |
| DIP12 | Rate of change of twelve-month moving-average of the index of industrial production |
| PI12 | Rate of change of the twelve-month moving-average of the producer price index |
| YSP | Dividend yield defined as the ratio of dividends to share prices |

Notice that in computing the twelve-month moving-averages of the industrial production and producer price indices we have made use of the 'moving-average' function MAV(·,·) described in Section 4.3.10.

The excess return regressions reported in Pesaran and Timmermann (1994) were initially estimated over the period 1954(1) to 1990(12), but were later extended to include the two years 1991 and 1992 (see Tables III and PIII in Pesaran and Timmermann, 1994). Here we consider estimating the following monthly excess return regression over the whole period 1954(1) to 1992(12):

$$\begin{aligned} \mathrm{ERSP_t} = \beta_0 + \beta_1 YSP_{t-1} + \beta_2 PI12_{t-2} + \beta_3 DI11_{t-1} \\ + \beta_{4t} DIP12_{t-2} + u_t \end{aligned} \tag{10.22}$$

Under the joint hypothesis of risk neutrality and market efficiency it should not be possible to predict the excess returns, $\mathrm{ERSP}_t$, using publicly available information. It is therefore important that observations on the regressors in (10.22) are available publicly at time $t-1$, when $\mathrm{ERSP}_t$ is being forecast. Such information is readily available for the interest rates, share prices, and dividends, but not for the production and the producers' price indices. Observations on these latter variables are released by the US government with a delay. In view of this, the variables PI12 and DIP12 are included in the excess return regression with a lag of two months.

To replicate the OLS results in table PIII in Pesaran and Timmermann (1994, p. 61), choose option 1 in the Single Equation Estimation Menu (the Univariate Menu) and make sure the OLS option is selected. When prompted, type[11]

ERSP INPT YSP(−1) PI12(−2) DI11(−1) DIP12(−2) START

The OLS results in Table 10.11 should appear on the screen. Check that these estimates are identical with those reported by Pesaran and Timmermann (1994, p. 61).

Now to estimate (10.22) recursively, choose option 2 in the Single Equation Estimation Menu (the Univariate Menu: see Section 6.4) and select the Recursive Least Squares option. The following variable lists should be in the box editor.

ERSP INPT YSP(−1) PI12(−2) DI11(−1) DIP12(−2)

Click START. The program now carries out the necessary computations and presents you with the Recursive OLS Regression Results Menu (see Section 6.15.1). You can use option 1 in this menu to plot the recursive estimates. For example, if you choose to see the recursive estimates of the coefficient of the dividend yield variable, YSP(−1), the plot in Figure 10.4 will appear on the screen.

To save recursive predictions of excess return, choose option 7 and when prompted type

ERHAT Recursive predictions of excess return on SP500 ↵

You will now be asked to supply the variable name for the standard errors of the recursive predictions, themselves computed recursively. Type[12]

[11]The relevant variable list is saved in the special *Microfit* file PTMONTH.LST and can be retrieved using the [icon] button.

[12]Notice that the descriptions that follow ERHAT and ERSE are optional.

**Table 10.11:** Regression of excess returns on Standard and Poor 500 portfolio

Ordinary Least Squares Estimation

Dependent variable is ERSP
468 observations used for estimation from 1954M1 to 1992M12

| Regressor | Coefficient | Standard Error | T-Ratio[Prob] |
|---|---|---|---|
| INPT | −.024013 | .0096634 | −2.4850[.013] |
| YSP(−1) | 14.2719 | 3.3204 | 4.2983[.000] |
| PI12(−2) | .27856 | .063504 | −4.3865[.000] |
| DI11(−1) | −.0068798 | .0024969 | −2.7554[.006] |
| DIP12(−2) | −.15856 | .040177 | −3.9465[.000] |

| | | | |
|---|---|---|---|
| R-Squared | .086960 | R-Bar-Squared | .079072 |
| S.E. of Regression | .040716 | F-Stat. F( 4, 463) | 11.0243[.000] |
| Mean of Dependent Variable | .0059055 | S.D. of Dependent Variable | .042428 |
| Residual Sum of Squares | .76758 | Equation Log-likelihood | 836.5758 |
| Akaike Info. Criterion | 831.5758 | Schwarz Bayesian Criterion | 821.2046 |
| DW-statistic | 1.9900 | | |

Diagnostic Tests

| Test Statistics | LM Version | F Version |
|---|---|---|
| A:Serial Correlation | CHSQ( 12)= 10.2137[.597] | F( 12, 451)= .83852[.611] |
| B:Functional Form | CHSQ( 1)= 1.4695[.225] | F( 1, 462)= 1.4552[.228] |
| C:Normality | CHSQ( 2)= 70.2152[.000] | Not applicable |
| D:Heteroscedasticity | CHSQ( 1)= .20274[.653] | F( 1, 466)= .20196[.653] |

A:Lagrange multiplier test of residual serial correlation
B:Ramsey's RESET test using the square of the fitted values
C:Based on a test of skewness and kurtosis of residuals
D:Based on the regression of squared residuals on squared fitted values

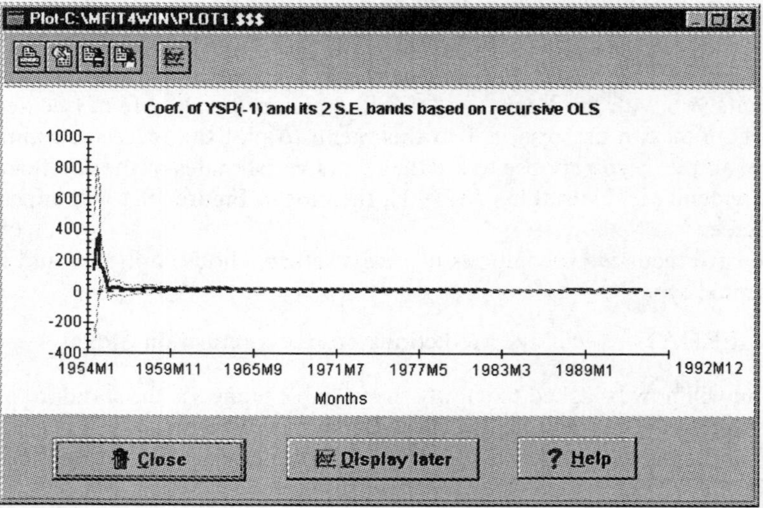


**Figure 10.4:** Recursive estimates of the coefficients of the dividend yield variable in (10.22)

ERSE standard errors of the recursive predictions of excess return on SP500
↩
↩

In the Backtracking Menu choose option 1. You should now see the variables ERHAT and ERSE in the variables list (click VARIABLES to display). To estimate the extent to which the recursive predictions of excess return (ERHAT) and the actual excess returns (ERSP) are correlated, you can either compute simple correlation coefficients between these variables, or use the function PTTEST(·,·) to compute the Pesaran and Timmermann predictive failure test statistic. To avoid uncertain initial estimates, we suggest computing these statistics over the period 1960(1) to 1992(12). You need to return to the Command Editor (click PROCESS), clear the editor, and type

**SAMPLE** 60m1 92m12; **COR** ERSP ERHAT;
STAT = PTTEST(ERSP, ERHAT); **LIST** STAT [GO]

The sample correlation between ERSP and ERHAT is 0.2066, and the coefficients of variations computed for these variables suggest that actual returns are three times more variable than recursively predicted returns. The Pesaran–Timmermann test statistic is 2.8308 which is well above 1.67, the 95 per cent critical value for a one-sided test. There is clearly significant evidence that monthly excess returns are predictable using *ex ante* dated variables.

## 10.12 Lesson 10.12: Rolling regressions and the Lucas critique

This lesson will illustrate the use of rolling regression to examine parameter variation. In an influential paper Lucas (1976) argued that estimated econometric parameters are unlikely to be stable since, as policy regimes change, people will change how they form their expectations, and this will alter the estimated decisions rules. The issue is discussed in more detail in Algoskoufis and Smith (1991a). Consider the simple expectations augmented Phillips curve:

$$\Delta w_t = f(u_t) + \beta E(\Delta p_t \mid \Omega_{t-1}) \tag{10.23}$$

where $w_t$ is the logarithm of money wages, $u_t$ the unemployment rate, $p_t$ the logarithm of a general price index, and $\Omega_{t-1}$ denotes the information set at $t-1$. We would expect $\beta = 1$, if workers lacked money illusion. Now suppose the evolution of inflation could be described by a first order autoregression, with time varying parameters:

$$E(\Delta p_t \mid \Omega_{t-1}) = \pi_t(1 - \rho_t) + \rho_t \Delta p_{t-1} \tag{10.24}$$

where $\pi_t$ is the steady state rate of inflation and $\rho_t$ measures the persistence of inflation. Algoskoufis and Smith (1991a) estimate the above equations using UK data over the period 1855 to 1987. Over this 130-year period, with its varying policy regimes—Gold Standard, the two World Wars, Bretton Woods, etc.—we would not expect either steady state inflation or its persistence to be constant. Substituting, the expectations equation (10.24) into the inflation-augmented Phillips curve (10.23) gives:

$$\Delta w_t = f(u_t) + \beta\pi_t(1 - \rho_t) + \beta\rho_t\Delta p_{t-1} \tag{10.25}$$

The coefficient on lagged inflation in the above Phillips curve, should move in line with the coefficient of lagged inflation in the inflation expectations equation (10.24). The two coefficients must be equal when $\beta = 1$. To determine whether this is the case, we need to obtain time-varying parameter estimates of the coefficients in the two equations and compare their movements. We do this using the rolling regression function in *Microfit*.

Load the special *Microfit* file PHILLIPS.FIT. This file contains annual observations over the period 1855 to 1987 on the following variables:

$e$ = Log employment
$n$ = Log labour force
$p$ = Log consumer prices
$w$ = Log earnings
$y$ = Log real GDP

In the Command Editor type

```
c = 1; dw = w – w(–1); dp = p – p(–1);
u = n – e; du = u – u(–1)        [GO]
```

to create a constant term in *c*, the rate of change of money wages in *dw*, the rate of price inflation in *dp*, the rate of unemployment in *u*, and the change in the rate of unemployment in *du*. Click the Univariate Menu option, choose Rolling Linear Regression Menu and then Rolling Least Squares. In the box editor specify the equation as:

```
DW C DU U   DP(–1)      [START]
```

This allows both the level and change in unemployment to influence the rate of growth of wages. In response to the question about window size, type 25. Whereas recursive regression extends the sample by one each time it re-estimates, rolling regression keeps the sample size the same; here at 25 years. Algoskoufis and Smith (1991a) keep the sample size fixed because they think that information about the persistence of inflation before World War I is probably not informative about the persistence of inflation after World War II. The program will now estimate the equation over all sub-samples of 25 years. When it has stopped calculating, choose to plot the rolling coefficients and standard errors. Choose DP(–1) to see the plot in Figure 10.5. You will see that the estimated coefficients of DP(–1) were not significantly different from zero on pre-World War I samples, shot upwards after 1914, tended to decline thereafter, and started rising towards the end of the period. You can examine the other coefficients as well. Since we wish to compare the coefficient on DP(–1) with that from another equation, click [CLOSE] to

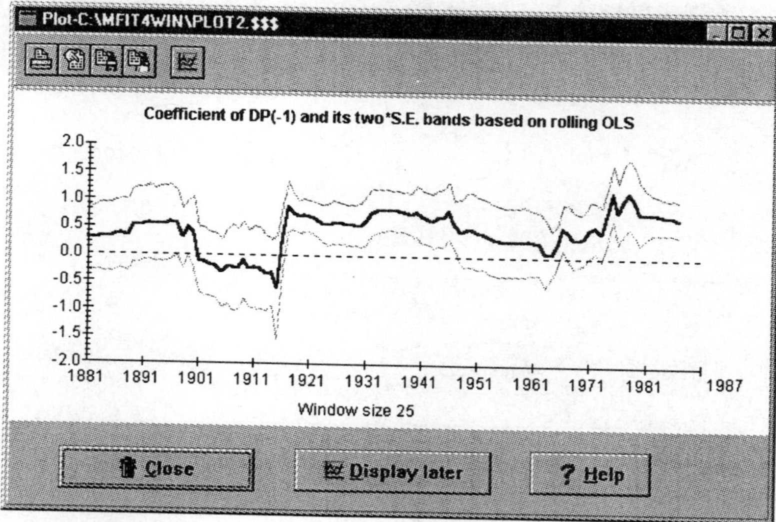


**Figure 10.5:** Rolling OLS estimates of the coefficient of the lagged inflation in the inflation equation

leave the graph, and choose option 3 in the Rolling Regression Results Menu to save the rolling coefficients. Once again, choose the regressor DP(−1) and, in response to the prompt, name it PCCOEF (Phillips curve coefficient). Backtrack and choose the option to edit the regression. In the editor, edit the regression to

DP C DP(−1) [OK]

Repeat the earlier process and save the OLS rolling coefficients on DP(−1) for this autoregression as ARCOEF. Backtrack to the Command Editor, clear the box editor, then type:

PLOT PCCOEF ARCOEF [GO]

You should see Figure 10.6 on the screen. As the theory suggests, this shows quite similar movements, though the match is less good before World War I. The correlation between the coefficients is 0.69.

## 10.13 Exercises in linear regression analysis

### 10.13.1 Exercise 10.1

Use the data in the file UKCON.FIT to estimate the equation (10.16) by the IV method, using 1, $\log y_{t-1}$, $\log y_{t-2}$, $\log c_{t-1}$, $\log c_{t-2}$, $\Pi_{t-1}$, and $\Pi_{t-2}$ as instruments. Compare these estimates with the corresponding OLS estimates. What is the interpretation of Sargan's misspecification test statistic given in the IV regression result table?

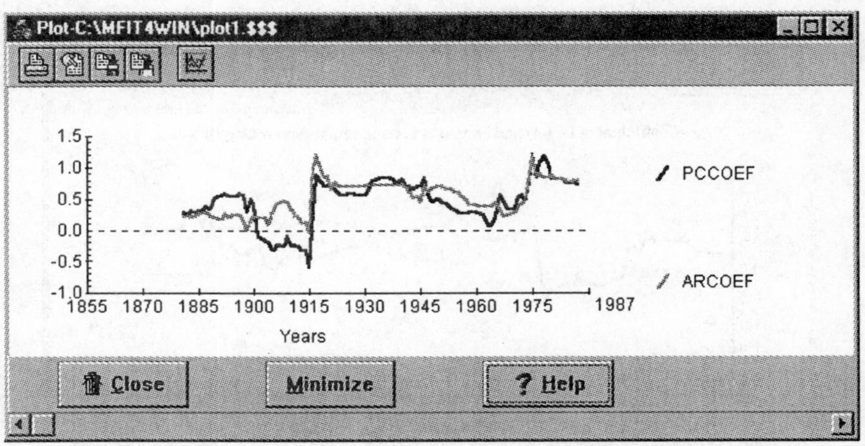


**Figure 10.6:** Rolling OLS coefficients of the lagged inflation rate in the Phillips and inflation equations

### 10.13.2 Exercise 10.2

Carry out the non-nested tests in Lesson 10.9 using the UK quarterly consumption data in UKCON.FIT.

### 10.13.3 Exercise 10.3

Check the sensitivity of the Wald test statistics to the way the non-linear restrictions in Lesson 10.5 are specified by computing the relevant statistics for testing the restrictions $\beta_1 + (\beta_3/\beta_2) = 0$ and $\beta_1 + (\beta_5/\beta_4) = 0$. Notice that when it is known *a priori* that $\beta_2 \neq 0$ and $\beta_4 \neq 0$, the above restrictions are algebraically equivalent to those in Lesson 10.5: see (10.17).

### 10.13.4 Exercise 10.4

Carry out the test of the common factor restrictions in Lesson 10.5 on the US data using the file USCON.FIT.

### 10.13.5 Exercise 10.5

Repeat the computations in Lesson 10.11 using the returns on the Dow Jones portfolio instead of the SP500 portfolio.

### 10.13.6 Exercise 10.6

Carry out the analysis in Lesson 10.12 using a larger window size (say 30), and discuss the robustness of your conclusions in relation to the choice of the observation window.

# 11

# Lessons in Univariate Time Series Analysis

The lessons in this chapter show you how to identify (select), estimate, and calculate dynamic forecasts using univariate ARMA$(p, q)$, and ARIMA$(p, d, q)$ models. Univariate ARMA and ARIMA processes have been used extensively in the time series literature and are particularly useful for short-term (one-step ahead) forecasting. Following the seminal work of Box and Jenkins (1970), a number of dedicated computer packages for the estimation of ARIMA models have been developed. In *Microfit*, the MA option in the Linear Regression Menu can be used to provide estimates of univariate ARIMA models containing up to 12 unknown parameters in their MA part.

The ARIMA$(p, d, q)$ model for the variable $x$ is given by

$$y_t = f(t) + \phi_1 y_{t-1} + \phi_2 y_{t-2} + \cdots + \phi_p y_{t-p} + \epsilon_t + \theta_1 \epsilon_{t-1} + \cdots + \theta_q \epsilon_{t-q} \tag{11.1}$$

where $y_t = \Delta^d x_t = (1 - L)^d x_t$, and $f(t)$ is the deterministic trend in $y_t$ (if any). In most economic applications either $d = 0$ and $f(t) = \alpha + \delta t$, or $d = 1$ and $f(t) = \mu$. The first step in univariate analysis concerns the selection of the orders $p, d$, and $q$. In Box–Jenkins' terminology, this is called the identification of the univariate model. The selection of these orders is often carried out in two stages: in the first stage, $d$, the order of integration of the process is determined using the augmented Dickey–Fuller (ADF) tests.[1] Once the order of integration of the process is established, the orders of the ARMA process, $p$, and $q$, are then selected either by plotting the correlogram of a time series and comparing it with the theoretical correlogram of a specific time series model (Box–Jenkins approach) or by specifying a relatively high order ARMA model, as the most general one, and then using likelihood ratio tests or one of the popular model selection criteria such as the Akaike information (AIC), or the Schwarz Bayesian (SBC) to select a more parsimonious model (see Section 18.6). The ADF test

[1] A process is said to be integrated in order $d$, if it must be differenced $d$ times before it is rendered stationary. An integrated process of order $d$ is often denoted by $I(d)$.

statistics and plots of the correlogram can be obtained automatically by using commands ADF and COR in the Command Editor: see Sections 4.4.2 and 4.4.4. Values of the AIC and SBC can be computed by estimating ARMA models of different orders using the MA option in the Linear Regression Estimation Menu: see Section 6.5. The model with the highest value for the information criteria is selected. Notice that the use of different information criteria can lead to different models. The use of the SBC tends to select a more parsimonious model as compared to the use of the AIC. See Section 18.6 for more details and relevant references to the literature.

## 11.1 Lesson 11.1: Using the ADF command to test for unit roots

In this lesson we shall consider the problem of testing for a unit root in the US real GNP using the command ADF in the Command Editor.

The file GDP95.FIT contains quarterly observations over the period 1960(1) to 1995(1) on USGNP (the US gross national product at 1987 prices, Source: Citibase), and quarterly observations over the period 1955(1) to 1995(1) on UKGDP (the UK gross domestic product at 1990 prices, Source: CSO95 Macroeconomic Variables). See also Lessons 9.8 and 9.9.

Use the the [open] button to load the file GDP95.FIT. In the Command Editor create the log of output, its first difference, constant, and time trend by typing

yus = log(USGNP); dyus = yus − yus(−1); inpt = 1; t = csum(1) [GO]

Before applying the ARMA methodology to the US output series, it is important to check if it is difference or trend stationary. If it is (trend) stationary, we use the ARMA model for YUS plus a deterministic trend, while if it is first-difference stationary, or integrated of order 1, $I(1)$, we use the ARIMA model for YUS.[2]

Consider the univariate AR(1) process

$$y_t = \alpha + (1 - \phi)\delta t + \phi y_{t-1} + \epsilon_t, \; t = 1, \ldots, n \qquad (11.2)$$

where $\epsilon_t$ is $iid(0, \sigma^2)$. If $|\phi| < 1$, it is trend stationary, while if $\phi = 1$, it is difference stationary with a non-zero drift $\alpha$. Attempts to distinguish the difference stationary process from the trend stationary series have generally taken the form of a (one-sided) test of the null hypothesis of a unit AR root against the alternative of stationarity:

$$H_0\colon \phi = 1 \text{ against } H_1\colon \phi < 1.$$

It is important to note that when using the $t$-statistic for testing $\phi = 1$, we

[2]See Box and Jenkins (1970).

should use the critical values of the non-standard Dickey–Fuller unit root distribution rather than the standard normal distribution.[3] In the more general case where the disturbances, $\epsilon_t, t = 1, 2, \ldots, n$ are serially correlated, we should use the augmented Dickey–Fuller (ADF) unit root test statistic,[4] which is proposed to accommodate error autocorrelation by adding lagged differences of $y_t$:[5]

$$y_t = \alpha + (1 - \phi)\delta t + \phi y_{t-1} + \sum_{i=1}^{p+1} \phi_i y_{t-i} + \epsilon_t, \; t = 1, \ldots, n \tag{11.3}$$

which can also be rewritten as

$$\Delta y_t = \alpha + \rho\delta t - \rho y_{t-1} + \sum_{i=1}^{p} \gamma_i \Delta y_{t-i} + \epsilon_t, \; t = 1, \ldots, n \tag{11.4}$$

where the null is now $H_0 : \rho = 1 - \phi = 0$. When using the ADF tests and interpreting the results, the following points are worth bearing in mind:

1. Although ADF has good power characteristics as compared to other unit root tests in the literature, it is nevertheless not very powerful in finite samples for alternatives $H_1 : \phi = \phi_0 < 1$, when $\phi_0$ is near unity.
2. There is a size–power trade-off depending on the order of augmentation used in dealing with the problem of residual serial correlation.[6] Therefore, it is often crucial that an appropriate value is chosen for $p$, the order of augmentation of the test.[7]

To test for the unit-root in log of USGNP, clear the Command Editor and type

---

[3]Critical values have been generated by Monte Carlo simulation for the cases (1) $\alpha = 0, \delta = 0$, (2) $\alpha \neq 0, \delta = 0$, and (3) $\alpha \neq 0, \delta \neq 0$. See Fuller (1976), Dickey and Fuller (1979), and Hamilton (1994, Chapter 17). For a comprehensive survey of the unit literature, see Stock (1994).

[4]There are other unit root test statistics such as the semi-parametric approach of Phillips and Perron (1988), and the tests of the stationarity hypothesis proposed in Kwiatkwoski *et al.* (1992). The Phillips–Perron test can be computed in *Microfit* as the ratio of the OLS estimate of $\rho$, in the simple DF regression $\Delta y_t = \alpha + \rho\delta t - \rho y_{t-1} + \epsilon_t$, to its Newey–West standard error obtained using options 4 to 6 in the standard, White and Newey–West Adjusted Variance Menu (see Section 6.23). The critical values for the Phillips–Perron test are the same as those for the Dickey–Fuller test, and depend on whether the DF regression contains an intercept term or a time trend. (see the previous footnote). For an application, see Lesson 16.1.

[5]Said and Dickey (1984) show that if the order $p$ is suitably chosen, the ADF test statistics have the same asymptotic distribution as the simple DF statistic under *iid* errors. If $\epsilon_t$ follows the AR($p$) process, the number of lagged differences in the ADF regression must be at least as large as $p$. If $\epsilon_t$ has an MA component, the order $p$ must be allowed to increase with the sample size, though at a slower rate (e.g. at the rate of $n^{1/3}$).

[6]In the case of autocorrelated disturbances, the size distortion of the uncorrected DF test is quite considerable. The ADF($p$) test performs better, and with a sufficiently high enough value for $p$. This happens, however, at the expense of power. ADF tests with a large value for $p$ relative to the sample size have almost no power.

[7]Since we do not know the true order of $p$, the two-step procedure might be used whereby model selection criteria such as the Akaike information criterion (AIC) or the Schwarz Bayesian criterion (SBC) are used to select the order of the ADF regression, and the test is then performed.

**ADF** YUS(5) [GO]

where we have chosen $p = 5$. The results in Table 11.1a should appear on the screen. This table has two parts: the first part computes the ADF statistics for models with an intercept term but no trends; the second part gives the ADF statistics for models with an intercept and a linear deterministic trend. Since USGNP is trended, only the latter half of the Table 11.1a is relevant. Before carrying out the unit root tests, the order of the ADF regression defined by (11.4) needs to be selected. The values reported in Table 11.1a for the different model selection criteria suggest that the correct order is likely to be between 1 and 2, with the Schwarz Bayesian criterion (SBC) selecting the lower order. The ADF statistics for $p = 1$ and 2 are equal to $-3.0616$ and $-3.2291$, respectively, which are both (in absolute value) below their (asymptotic) 95 per cent critical value given at the foot of the table ($-3.4435$). The same is also true if we consider higher values of $p$. It is therefore not possible to reject the null of a unit root ($H_0$: $\phi = 1$) in the log of USGNP at the 5 per cent significance level.

**Table 11.1a:** Unit root tests for variable YUS

The Dickey–Fuller regressions include an intercept but not a trend

135 observations used in the estimation of all ADF regressions
Sample period from 1961Q3 to 1995Q1

| | Test Statistic | LL | AIC | SBC | HQC |
|---|---|---|---|---|---|
| DF | −2.4732 | 448.1691 | 446.1691 | 443.2638 | 444.9885 |
| ADF(1) | −1.8788 | 454.0377 | 451.0377 | 446.6798 | 449.2667 |
| ADF(2) | −1.6595 | 455.3623 | 451.3623 | 445.5517 | 449.0010 |
| ADF(3) | −1.7318 | 455.8193 | 450.8193 | 443.5561 | 447.8678 |
| ADF(4) | −1.6948 | 455.8539 | 449.8539 | 441.1380 | 446.3120 |
| ADF(5) | −1.7756 | 456.4991 | 449.4991 | 439.3306 | 445.3669 |

95% critical value for the augmented Dickey–Fuller statistic = −2.8828
LL = Maximized log-likelihood AIC = Akaike Information Criterion
SBC = Schwarz Bayesian Criterion HQC = Hannan–Quinn Criterion

The Dickey–Fuller regressions include an intercept and a linear trend

135 observations used in the estimation of all ADF regressions
Sample period from 1961Q3 to 1995Q1

| | Test Statistic | LL | AIC | SBC | HQC |
|---|---|---|---|---|---|
| DF | −2.9715 | 451.6814 | 448.6814 | 444.3235 | 446.9105 |
| ADF(1) | −3.0616 | 458.0269 | 454.0269 | 448.2164 | 451.6657 |
| ADF(2) | −3.2291 | 459.9455 | 454.9455 | 447.6823 | 451.9939 |
| ADF(3) | −3.1084 | 460.0603 | 454.0603 | 445.3444 | 450.5184 |
| ADF(4) | −3.1760 | 460.3419 | 453.3419 | 443.1734 | 449.2097 |
| ADF(5) | −3.0175 | 460.5375 | 452.5375 | 440.9164 | 447.8150 |

95% critical value for the augmented Dickey–Fuller statistic = −3.4435
LL = Maximized log-likelihood AIC = Akaike Information Criterion
SBC = Schwarz Bayesian Criterion HQC = Hannan–Quinn Criterion

Next we test for a unit root in DYUS (the growth of USGNP) by typing

**ADF** DYUS(5) [GO]

Since the output growth is not trended, the relevant ADF statistics are given in the upper part of Table 11.1b. The model selection criteria suggest selecting either $p=0$ or 1. However, irrespective of the order of the augmentation chosen for the ADF test, the absolute values of the ADF statistics are all well above the 95 per cent critical value of the test given at the foot of the table ($-2.8830$) and hence the hypothesis that the growth rate of USGNP has a unit root is firmly rejected. The model selection criteria in the upper part of Table 11.1b also suggest that the process of US output growth can be approximated by a low order AR process, with the AIC selecting an AR(1) process and the SBC selecting an AR(0) process for the US output growth. Estimating an AR(1) process for US output growth over the period 1960(3) to 1995(1) gives:

**Table 11.1b:** Unit root tests for variable DYUS

The Dickey–Fuller regressions include an intercept but not a trend

134 observations used in the estimation of all ADF regressions
Sample period from 1961Q4 to 1995Q1

| | Test Statistic | LL | AIC | SBC | HQC |
|---|---|---|---|---|---|
| DF | −8.3346 | 448.5896 | 446.5896 | 443.6918 | 445.4120 |
| ADF(1) | −5.7556 | 450.2928 | 447.2928 | 442.9460 | 445.5264 |
| ADF(2) | −5.4562 | 450.5486 | 446.5486 | 440.7529 | 444.1934 |
| ADF(3) | −4.7231 | 450.6403 | 445.6403 | 438.3957 | 442.6964 |
| ADF(4) | −4.7182 | 451.0983 | 445.0983 | 436.4047 | 441.5655 |
| ADF(5) | −4.0889 | 451.3262 | 444.3262 | 434.1838 | 440.2047 |

95% critical value for the augmented Dickey–Fuller statistic = − 2.8830
LL = Maximized log-likelihood AIC = Akaike Information Criterion
SBC = Schwarz Bayesian Criterion HQC = Hannan–Quinn Criterion

The Dickey–Fuller regressions include an intercept and a linear trend

134 observations used in the estimation of all ADF regressions
Sample period from 1961Q4 to 1995Q1

| | Test Statistic | LL | AIC | SBC | HQC |
|---|---|---|---|---|---|
| DF | −8.4806 | 449.5871 | 446.5871 | 442.2403 | 444.8207 |
| ADF(1) | −5.8735 | 450.9750 | 446.9750 | 441.1794 | 444.6199 |
| ADF(2) | −5.6057 | 451.3615 | 446.3615 | 439.1169 | 443.4175 |
| ADF(3) | −4.8797 | 451.4015 | 445.4015 | 436.7080 | 441.8687 |
| ADF(4) | −4.9100 | 452.0155 | 445.0155 | 434.8730 | 440.8939 |
| ADF(5) | −4.2808 | 452.1493 | 444.1493 | 432.5579 | 439.4389 |

95% critical value for the augmented Dickey–Fuller statistic = − 3.4437
LL = Maximized log-likelihood AIC = Akaike Information Criterion
SBC = Schwarz Bayesian Criterion HQC = Hannan–Quinn Criterion

$$\text{DYUS}_t = \underset{(0.00927)}{0.00498} + \underset{(0.0806)}{0.31881}\ \text{DYUS}_{t-1} + \hat{u}_t$$

thus suggesting log(USGNP$_t$) is an $I(1)$ process with a non-zero drift, estimated as $0.00498/(1-0.31881) = 0.00732(0.0011)$, representing the quarterly average rate of growth of the US economy. The figure in brackets is the asymptotic standard error of the average growth rate and can be obtained using option 5 in the Post Regression Menu, once the OLS estimation of the AR(1) process in DYUS is completed.

## 11.2 Lesson 11.2: Spectral analysis of US output growth

The spectral approach enables us to investigate the properties of time series in the frequency domain. Let $\{x_t,\ t = -\infty, \ldots, \infty\}$ be a univariate covariance stationary process with mean $E(x_t) = \mu$ and the $k$th autocovariance function

$$E(x_t - \mu)(x_{t-k} - \mu) = \gamma_k = \gamma_{-k}, \quad k = 0, 1, 2, \ldots$$

The main goal of the spectral analysis is to determine how important cycles of different frequencies are in accounting for the behaviour of $x_t$.[8] Assuming that autocovariances are absolutely summable (i.e. $\sum_{k=0}^{\infty} \gamma_k$ is finite), the population spectrum can be written as[9]

$$f(\omega) = \frac{1}{\pi}\left\{\gamma_0 + 2\sum_{k=1}^{\infty} \gamma_k \cos(\omega k)\right\}, \qquad 0 \leqslant \omega < \pi$$

1. If $x_t$ is a white noise process (*i.e.* $\gamma_0 = \sigma^2$ and $\gamma_j = 0$ for $j \neq 0$), then $f(\omega)$ is flat at $\sigma^2/\pi$ for all $\omega \in [0, \pi]$.
2. If $x_t$ is a stationary AR(1) process, $x_t = \mu + \phi x_{t-1} + \epsilon_t$ with $|\phi| < 1$, and $\epsilon_t$ is a white noise process, then $f(\omega)$ is monotonically decreasing in $\omega$ for $\phi > 0$, and monotonically increasing function of $\omega$ for $\phi < 0$.

---

[8]Any covariance stationary process has both a time-domain and a frequency-domain representation, and any feature of the data that can be represented by one representation can equally be described by the other. For any introductory account of the spectral analysis see Chatfield (1989). A more advanced treatment can be found in Priestley (1981).

[9]Given the population spectrum, $f(\omega)$, then the $j$th autocovariance of the covariance stationary process $x_t$ can be written as

$$\int_{-\pi}^{\pi} f(\omega) \exp(i\omega j) d\omega = \gamma_j,\ j = 0, 1, \ldots,$$

For example, in the special case when $j = 0$, then the variance of $x_t$ can be obtained by

$$\int_{-\pi}^{\pi} f(\omega) d\omega = \gamma_0$$

In general, $\int_{-\omega_1}^{\omega_1} f(\omega) d\omega = 2\int_0^{\omega_1} f(\omega) d\omega$ represents the portion of the variance of $x_t$ that is attributable to the periodic random components with frequency less than or equal to $\omega_1$.

3. If $x_t$ is a stationary MA(1) process, $x_t = \mu + \epsilon_t + \theta\epsilon_{t-1}$ with $|\theta| < 1$, and $\epsilon_t$ is a white noise process, then $f(\omega)$ is monotonically decreasing (increasing) in $\omega$ for $\theta > 0$ (for $\theta < 0$).

The sample spectral density function (or the sample periodogram) can be estimated by

$$\hat{f}(\omega) = \frac{1}{\pi}\left\{\hat{\gamma}_0 + 2\sum_{k=1}^{\infty}\hat{\gamma}_k \cos(\omega k)\right\}, \; 0 \leqslant \omega < \pi$$

where $\hat{\gamma}_k$ is the sample autocovariances obtained by

$$\hat{\gamma}_k = n^{-1}\sum_{t=k+1}^{\infty}(x_t - \bar{x})(x_{t-k} - \bar{x}), \text{ for } k = 0, 1, \ldots, n-1$$

and $\bar{x}$ is the sample mean. However, one serious limitation of the use of the sample periodogram is that the estimator $\hat{f}(\omega)$ is not consistent, namely it is not getting any more accurate even as the sample size, $n$, increases. This is because in estimating it we have made use of as many parameter estimates ($\hat{\gamma}_k$, for $k = 0, 1, \ldots, n-1$) as we had observations ($x_1, \ldots, x_n$). Alternatively, the population spectrum can be estimated non-parametrically by use of *kernel* estimates given by

$$\hat{f}(\omega_j) = \sum_{i=-m}^{m}\lambda(\omega_{j+i}, \omega_j)\hat{f}_{xx}(\omega_{j+i})$$

where $\omega_j = j\pi/m$, $m$ is a *bandwidth* parameter[10] indicating how many frequencies $\{\omega_j, \omega_{j\pm 1}, \ldots, \omega_{j\pm m}\}$ are used in estimating the population spectrum, and the *kernel* $\lambda(\omega_{j+i}, \omega_j)$ indicates how much weight each frequency is to be given, where $\Sigma_{i=-m}^{m}\lambda(\omega_{j+i}, \omega_j) = 1$. Specification of *kernel* $\lambda(\omega_{j+i}, \omega_j)$ can equivalently be described in terms of a weighting sequence $\{\lambda_j, j = 1, \ldots, m\}$, so that

$$\hat{f}(\omega_j) = \frac{1}{\pi}\left\{\hat{\gamma}_0 + 2\sum_{k=1}^{m}\lambda_k\hat{\gamma}_k \cos(\omega_j k)\right\} \tag{11.5}$$

*Microfit* computes a scaled and standardized version of $\hat{f}(\omega_j)$ by multiplying it by $\pi/\hat{\gamma}_0$, and gives

$$\hat{f}_*(\omega_j) = 1 + 2\sum_{k=1}^{m}\lambda_k(\hat{\gamma}_k/\hat{\gamma}_0)\cos(k\omega_j) \tag{11.6}$$

and their estimated standard errors using Bartlett, Tukey, and Parzen lag

[10] One important problem is the choice of the bandwidth parameter, $m$. One practical guide is to plot an estimate of the spectrum using several different bandwidths and rely on subjective judgement to choose the bandwidth that produces the most plausible estimate. Another possibility often recommended in practice is to set $m = 2\sqrt{n}$. This is the default value chosen by *Microfit*. For more formal statistical procedures see, for example, Andrews (1991), and Andrews and Monahan (1992).

windows at the frequencies $\omega_j = j\pi/m$, $j = 0, 1, 2, \ldots, m$ (see Section 18.2). Each of these frequencies are associated with the *period* $= 2\pi/\omega_j = 2m/j$, $j = 0, 1, 2, \ldots, m$. For example, at zero frequency the periodicity of the series is infinity. The value of the standardized spectrum at zero frequency refers to the long-run properties of the series. The higher this value, the more persistent are the effects of deviations of $x_t$ from its trend. The spectrum of a unit root process at zero frequency is unbounded.

In this lesson we carry out the spectrum analysis of the detrended and first-differenced log of USGNP. The unit-root analysis of YUS (the logarithm of the USGNP) in the previous lesson suggests that we should first-difference the output series before doing any spectral analysis on it. Spectral analysis of trended or non-stationary processes can be very misleading. To illustrate this, we first consider the spectral analysis of output series, when it is de-trended using a simple regression of YUS on a linear trend.

Load the file GDP95.FIT, create the variables YUS etc. as described in Lesson 11.1, and then choose option 1 in the Single Equation Estimation Menu (the Univariate Menu), selecting the OLS option (see also Lesson 9.11). In the box editor, type

YUS INPT T [START]

which is a regression of YUS on a constant term (INPT) and a time trend (T). When the results table appears click [CLOSE], and in the Post Regression Menu choose option 3 (List/Plot/Save residuals), and then option 6. When prompted, type the name of the residual and its description as

RESYUS Residual obtained from the regression of YUS on a linear trend↵

Then, press the **Esc** key as many times as required to move back to the Command Editor, clear it, and type

**SPECTRUM** RESYUS [GO]

Since we have not specified any window size after the variable, RESYUS, the program uses the default value of $2\sqrt{n} = 2\sqrt{144} = 24$ for the window (bandwidth) size. (Notice that observations on US output are available only over the period 1960(1) to 1995(1), and hence $n = 144$.) You will be presented with three alternative estimates of the spectrum (click CLOSE) followed by their plots. To save the graphs, click [icon], [icon] or [icon] as appropriate (see Section 5.2 on details of how to print/save/retrieve graphs). The plots of the estimated standardized spectral density function of RESYUS using the Bartlett, Tukey, and Parzen lag windows are given in Figure 11.1.

One prominent feature of this plot is that the contribution to the sample variance of the lowest frequency component is much larger than the contributions of other frequencies (for example, at business cycle frequencies). This is due to the non-stationary nature of the de-trended

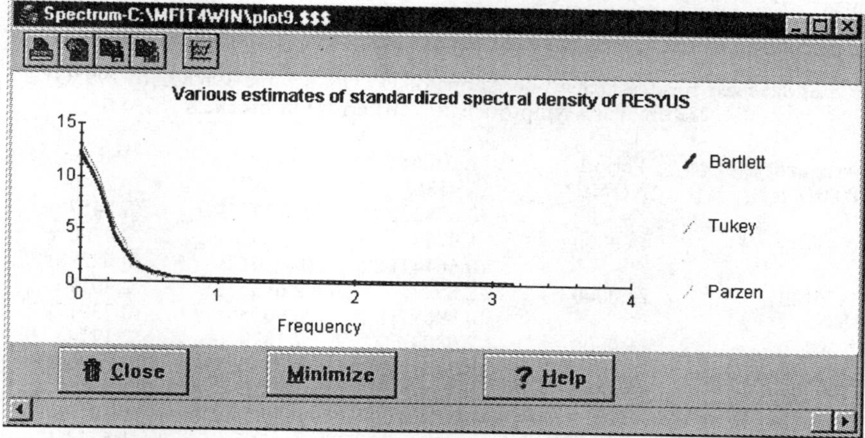


**Figure 11.1:** Alternative estimates of the spectrum of deviations of US output (in logs) from a linear trend

series, RESYUS. In general, if the process is non-stationary (e.g. has a unit root), then its spectral density becomes dominated by the value of the spectrum at the zero frequency, and drops dramatically immediately thereafter, thus hiding possible peaks at higher (business cycle) frequencies.

To avoid this problem, one could either try other de-trending procedures such as the Hodrick–Prescott method described in Sections 4.3.6 and 18.3 and Lesson 9.8, or apply the SPECTRUM command to DYUS, the first-difference of output series (in logarithms). Here we do the latter.

Move to the Command Editor, clear it, and type:

**SPECTRUM** DYUS(24) GO

The results in Table 11.2 should now appear on the screen followed by plots of the spectrum for three different windows: see Figure 11.2. In the case of output growths, we find that the spectral density function of DYUS, as

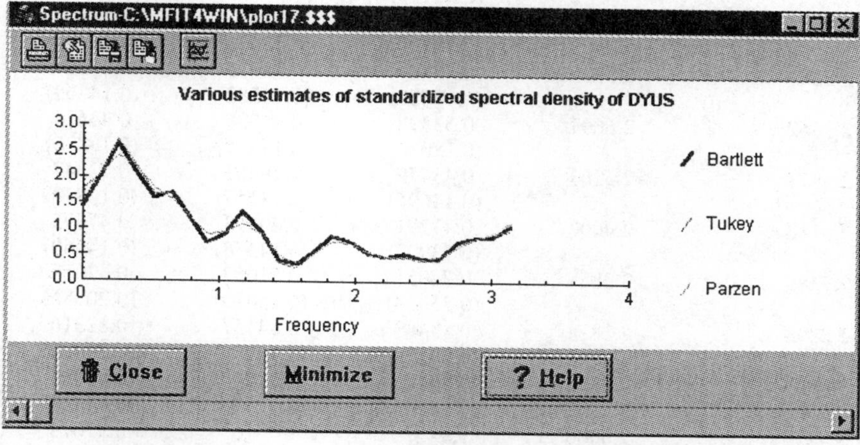


**Figure 11.2:** Alternative estimates of the spectrum of US output growth

**Table 11.2:** Estimates of the spectral density of US output growth

Standardized spectral density functions of DYUS, sample 1960Q2 to 1995Q1
Estimated asymptotic standard errors in brackets

| Frequency | Period | Bartlett | Tukey | Parzen |
|---|---|---|---|---|
| 0.00 | *NONE* | 1.4186 | 1.4387 | 1.7345 |
| | | (0.67822) | (0.72957) | (0.74570) |
| 0.13090 | 48.0000 | 1.9744 | 2.0362 | 2.0490 |
| | | (0.66747) | (0.73012) | (0.62288) |
| 0.26180 | 24.0000 | 2.6527 | 2.6935 | 2.4019 |
| | | (0.89677) | (0.96580) | (0.73017) |
| 0.39270 | 16.0000 | 2.0804 | 2.1879 | 2.1714 |
| | | (0.70332) | (0.78452) | (0.66009) |
| 0.52360 | 12.0000 | 1.5628 | 1.6517 | 1.7797 |
| | | (0.52834) | (0.59224) | (0.54104) |
| 0.65450 | 9.6000 | 1.6946 | 1.6545 | 1.5514 |
| | | (0.57286) | (0.59325) | (0.47163) |
| 0.78540 | 8.0000 | 1.2296 | 1.2257 | 1.2044 |
| | | (0.41569) | (0.43951) | (0.36614) |
| 0.91630 | 6.8571 | 0.73965 | 0.70097 | 0.88047 |
| | | (0.25005) | (0.25135) | (0.26766) |
| 1.0472 | 6.0000 | 0.88126 | 0.89154 | 0.94651 |
| | | (0.29792) | (0.31968) | (0.28774) |
| 1.1781 | 5.3333 | 1.3180 | 1.2947 | 1.1098 |
| | | (0.44557) | (0.46424) | (0.33737) |
| 1.3090 | 4.8000 | 0.93593 | 0.95044 | 0.88559 |
| | | (0.31640) | (0.34080) | (0.26922) |
| 1.4399 | 4.3636 | 0.39230 | 0.35453 | 0.47872 |
| | | (0.13262) | (0.12712) | (0.14553) |
| 1.5708 | 4.0000 | 0.32515 | 0.24582 | 0.35209 |
| | | (0.10992) | (0.088145) | (0.10704) |
| 1.7017 | 3.6923 | 0.54794 | 0.53500 | 0.54209 |
| | | (0.18524) | (0.19183) | (0.16479) |
| 1.8326 | 3.4286 | 0.86221 | 0.85046 | 0.75330 |
| | | (0.29148) | (0.30495) | (0.22900) |
| 1.9635 | 3.2000 | 0.76574 | 0.78221 | 0.73309 |
| | | (0.25887) | (0.28048) | (0.22286) |
| 2.0944 | 3.0000 | 0.53634 | 0.52077 | 0.56553 |
| | | (0.18131) | (0.18673) | (0.17192) |
| 2.2253 | 2.8235 | 0.45729 | 0.44015 | 0.47264 |
| | | (0.15459) | (0.15782) | (0.14368) |
| 2.3562 | 2.6667 | 0.53392 | 0.48736 | 0.45624 |
| | | (0.18050) | (0.17475) | (0.13870) |
| 2.4871 | 2.5263 | 0.43472 | 0.39481 | 0.42347 |
| | | (0.14696) | (0.14157) | (0.12873) |
| 2.6180 | 2.4000 | 0.41271 | 0.40593 | 0.47895 |
| | | (0.13952) | (0.14556) | (0.14560) |
| 2.7489 | 2.2857 | 0.74051 | 0.71057 | 0.67058 |
| | | (0.25034) | (0.25479) | (0.20386) |
| 2.8798 | 2.1818 | 0.83469 | 0.84157 | 0.82310 |
| | | (0.28218) | (0.30176) | (0.25022) |
| 3.0107 | 2.0870 | 0.85445 | 0.90842 | 0.91736 |
| | | (0.28886) | (0.32573) | (0.27888) |
| 3.1416 | 2.0000 | 1.0467 | 1.0316 | 0.97073 |
| | | (0.50040) | (0.52313) | (0.41733) |

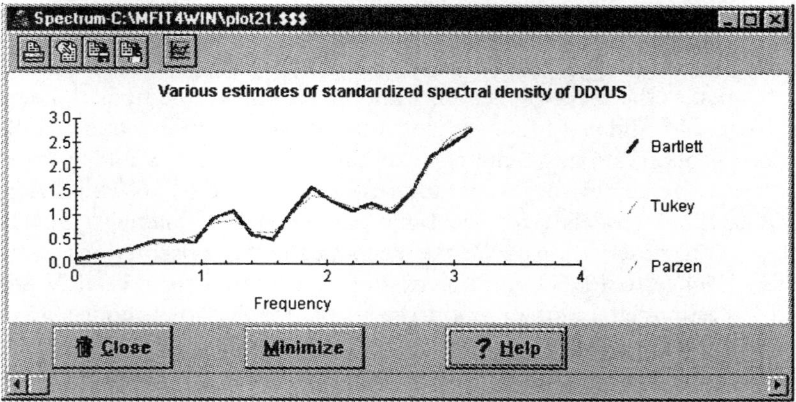


**Figure 11.3:** Alternative estimates of the spectrums of changes in US output growth

compared to that of RESYUS, is relatively flat, but decreases over the entire frequency. This may imply that DYUS is a stationary process with a positive autocorrelation coefficient.

The value of the scaled spectrum at zero frequency measures the long-run variance of DYUS, and is proposed by Cochrane (1988) as a measure of persistence of shocks to real output. In the case of the US, output growth it is estimated to be 1.4186 (0.6782), 1.4387 (0.7296), and 1.7345 (0.7457), for the Bartlett, Tukey, and Parzen windows, respectively. See the first row of Table 11.2 and Lesson 11.4.

If the process is over-differenced, then its spectral density at zero frequency becomes zero. For example, consider the spectrum of the second-difference of YUS. Clear the Command Editor and type:

DDYUS = DYUS − DYUS(−1); **SPECTRUM** DDYUS(20) [GO]

The plots of the estimated standardized spectral density function of DDYUS are given in Figure 11.3, from which we find that DDYUS is in fact over-differenced, since its spectral density at zero frequency is very close to zero.

The spectrum analysis in general supports our finding in Lesson 11.1 that YUS is an $I(1)$ process.

## 11.3 Lesson 11.3: Using an ARMA model for forecasting US output growth

In the previous two lessons we found that YUS (the logarithm of USGNP) is an integrated process of order 1 but DYUS (the growth of USGNP) is a persistent stationary process. In this lesson we consider the problem of selecting the orders $p$ and $q$ for an ARIMA($p, 1, q$) model of YUS, or the ARMA($p, q$) model of DYUS:

$$\phi(L)dyus_t = \mu + \theta(L)\epsilon_t \tag{11.7}$$

where $\phi(L) = 1 - \sum_{i=1}^{p} \phi_i L^i$ and $\theta(L) = 1 + \sum_{i=1}^{q} \theta_i L^i$. We assume that (11.7) satisfies the necessary stability and invertibility conditions.[11] To select the orders of $p$ and $q$, we first set them equal to a maximum value of 3. Since we lose 4 observations at the start of the sample when $p$ and $q$ take the maximum value of 3, we must estimate all the 16 ARMA($p, q$), $p, q = 0, 1, 2, 3$ models over the same sample period, namely 1961(1) to 1993(4) (132 observations). We are keeping the five observations over the period 1994(1) to 1995(1) for forecasting. We show how the ARMA(1, 1) model is estimated and then report the results for the other models. Choose option 1 Linear Regression Menu from the Single Equation Menu (the Univariate Menu), selecting option 7 MA Errors. In the editor, type

DYUS INPT DYUS(−1)

which implies that you specify the AR order to be 1. Then specify the sample period as

1961Q1 1993Q4

Click START and, when prompted, type

1↵

which means that you specify the MA order to be 1. Next, we see that there are two choices of initial estimates. When there is a convergence failure, use option 3 to look at the plot of the concentrated log-likelihood function (which shows that the maximum is found when the MA(1) parameter is around −0.20), and decide the initial estimate accordingly. For example, using 0.0 as the initial estimate, we obtain the estimation results for the ARMA(1, 1) specification in Table 11.3a.

The values of the Akaike information criterion (AIC) and Schwarz Bayesian criterion (SBC) for this model are 437.92 and 433.60, respectively. Repeat this procedure to estimate the other ARMA($p, q$) models for, $p, q = 0, 1, 2, 3$. Then, comparing the values of the AIC and/or the SBC, select the model specification with the highest value. When using the AIC, we have:

| $p\backslash q$ | 0 | 1 | 2 | 3 |
|---|---|---|---|---|
| 0 | 432.59 | 436.47 | 438.87 | 438.02 |
| 1 | 438.35 | 437.92 | 438.08 | 437.10 |
| 2 | 438.76 | 438.21 | 437.22 | 436.25 |
| 3 | 438.13 | 437.29 | 436.30 | 435.35 |

and therefore, the ARMA(0, 2) specification for DYUS is selected. When using SBC, we have:

[11] That is, the roots of $1 - \phi_1 z - \cdots - \phi_p z^p = 0$ and $1 + \theta_1 z + \cdots + \theta_q z^q = 0$ lie outside the unit circle.

**Table 11.3a:** An ARMA(1,1) model for US output growth

Exact Maximum Likelihood Estimation Method
Error TERM :MA(1) converged after 5 iterations

Dependent variable is DYUS
132 observations used for estimation from 1961Q1 to 1993Q4

| Regressor | Coefficient | Standard Error | T-Ratio[Prob] |
|---|---|---|---|
| INPT | 0.0036509 | 0.0014541 | 2.5108[.013] |
| DYUS(−1) | 0.511071 | 0.18049 | 2.8317[.005] |

| | | | |
|---|---|---|---|
| R-Squared | 0.10502 | R-Bar-Squared | 0.091142 |
| S.E. of Regression | 0.0086714 | F-Stat. F( 2, 129) | 7.5684[.001] |
| Mean of Dependent Variable | 0.0073650 | S.D. of Dependent Variable | 0.0090958 |
| Residual Sum of Squares | 0.0096999 | Equation Log-likelihood | 440.9237 |
| Akaike Info. Criterion | 437.9237 | Schwarz Bayesian Criterion | 433.5995 |
| DW-statistic | 2.0294 | | |

Parameters of the Moving Average Error Specification
U=E+ −.21465*E(−1)
( −1.1184) [.265]
T-ratio(s) based on asymptotic standard errors in brackets

| $p\backslash q$ | 0 | 1 | 2 | 3 |
|---|---|---|---|---|
| 0 | 431.15 | 433.59 | 434.55 | 432.25 |
| 1 | 435.46 | 433.60 | 432.32 | 429.89 |
| 2 | 434.43 | 432.44 | 430.02 | 427.60 |
| 3 | 432.37 | 430.08 | 427.65 | 425.26 |

and ARMA(1, 0) is selected. In what follows, we base the forecasts on the model selected by the SBC, namely the ARMA(1, 0) or simply the AR(1) specification.

To compute the forecasts for the growth rate of the US GNP for the period 1994(1) to 1995(1), now set the sample period to

1961Q1 1993Q4

and use the AR(1) specification for DYUS to estimate the parameters. In the Post Regression Menu, choose option 8 ('Forecast') and then press the ↩ key to compute dynamic forecasts of the US output growth over the period 1994(1) to 1995(1). The results in Table 11.3b should appear on the screen. The forecasts are very close to the actual values for the first two quarters, and then settle down to around 0.0074 which is only slightly above the average quarterly rate of growth of US real GNP. Option 9 also provides a plot of actual and forecasted values, which is presented in Figure 11.4.

**Table 11.3b:** Forecasts of US output growth based on an AR(1) model

Single Equation Dynamic Forecasts

Based on OLS regression of DYUS on:
INPT DYUS(−1)
132 observations used for estimation from 1961Q1 to 1993Q4

| Observation | Actual | Prediction | Error | S.D. of Error |
|---|---|---|---|---|
| 1994Q1 | 0.0083959 | 0.0093314 | −0.9355E-3 | 0.0087240 |
| 1994Q2 | 0.0090418 | 0.0080202 | 0.0010216 | 0.0091424 |
| 1994Q3 | 0.0092593 | 0.0076139 | 0.0016454 | 0.0091837 |
| 1994Q4 | 0.0104120 | 0.0074880 | 0.0029242 | 0.0091888 |
| 1995Q1 | 0.0077799 | 0.0074490 | 0.3309E-3 | 0.0091897 |

Summary statistics for single equation dynamic forecasts

Based on 5 observations from 1994Q1 to 1995Q1

| | | | |
|---|---|---|---|
| Mean Prediction Errors | 0.9973E-3 | Mean Sum Abs Pred Errors | 0.0013715 |
| Sum Squares Pred Errors | 0.2657E-5 | Root Mean Sumsq Pred Errors | 0.0016301 |

Predictive failure test F( 5, 130) = 0.027714[1.00]
Structural stability test F( 2, 133) = 0.050736[.951]

## 11.4 Lesson 11.4: Alternative measures of persistence of shocks to US real GNP

One of the important features of unit root processes lies in the fact that the effect of shocks on these series (or random deviations from their trend) do not die out. In the case of random walk models the long-run impact of the

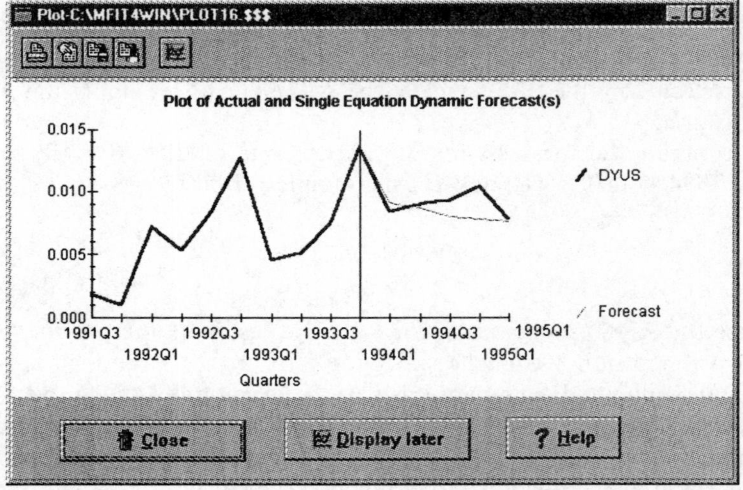


**Figure 11.4:** Dynamic forecasts of US output growth over the period 1994(1) to 1995(1)

shocks is unity. But for more general $I(1)$ processes this long-run impact could be more or less than unity. The most satisfactory overall measure of persistence is the value of the spectral density of the first-differences of the series evaluated at zero frequency, and then appropriately scaled. In the case of the ARIMA$(p, 1, q)$, process

$$\Delta x_t = \mu + \phi_1 \Delta x_{t-1} + \cdots + \phi_p \Delta x_{t-p} + \epsilon_t + \theta_1 \epsilon_{t-1} + \cdots + \theta_q \epsilon_{t-q} \qquad (11.8)$$

where $\epsilon_t \sim iid(0, \sigma^2)$. The spectral density of $\Delta x_t$ at zero frequency is given by

$$f_{\Delta x}(0) = \frac{\sigma^2}{\pi}\left(\frac{1 + \theta_1 + \theta_2 + \cdots + \theta_q}{1 - \phi_1 - \phi_2 - \cdots - \phi_q}\right)^2$$

The measure proposed by Campbell and Mankiw (1987) is given by

$$P_{cm} = \left\{\frac{\pi f_{\Delta x}(0)}{\sigma^2}\right\}^{\frac{1}{2}} = \frac{1 + \theta_1 + \theta_2 + \cdots + \theta_q}{1 - \phi_1 - \phi_2 - \cdots - \phi_q} \qquad (11.9)$$

Cochrane (1988) suggests, scaling $f_{\Delta x}(0)$ by the unconditional variance of $\Delta x_t$, namely

$$P_c = \left\{\frac{\pi f_{\Delta x}(0)}{V(\Delta x_t)}\right\}^{\frac{1}{2}} = \left\{\frac{\sigma^2}{V(\Delta x_t)}\right\}^{\frac{1}{2}} P_{cm} \qquad (11.10)$$

Notice, however, that $\sigma^2 / V(\Delta x_t) = 1 - R^2$, where $R^2$ is the squared multiple correlation coefficient of the ARIMA model (11.8). Hence

$$P_c = (1 - R^2)^{\frac{1}{2}} P_{cm} \qquad (11.11)$$

In practice, $f_{\Delta x}(0)$ can be estimated either using the non-parametric approach of spectral analysis (see Lesson 11.2), or by first estimating the ARIMA model (11.8) and then computing $P_{cm}$ by replacing the unknown parameters $\theta_1, \theta_2, \ldots, \theta_q, \phi_1, \phi_2, \ldots, \phi_q$ in (11.9) by their ML estimates. Cochrane (1988) favours the former while Campbell and Mankiw (1987) employ the latter approach. The two estimates can differ a great deal in practice. This is primarily because the estimates obtained using the ARIMA specification are conditional on the orders $p$ and $q$ being *correctly* selected. However, the estimates based on the spectral density estimation are less rigidly tied up to a given parametric model, and hence are often much less precisely estimated. In the case of both estimates, it is important that their standard errors are also computed.

Here we estimate the two persistent measures, $P_{cm}$, and $P_c$, for US real GNP using both the spectral density and the ARIMA modelling approaches. We use the data in the special *Microfit* file GDP95.FIT to

**Table 11.4a:** An MA(2) model for US output growth

Exact Maximum Likelihood Estimation Method
Error TERM :MA(2) converged after 5 iterations

Dependent variable is DYUS
140 observations used for estimation from 1960Q2 to 1995Q1

| Regressor | Coefficient | Standard Error | T-Ratio[Prob] |
|---|---|---|---|
| INPT | 0.0071916 | 0.0010445 | 6.8851[.000] |

| | | | |
|---|---|---|---|
| R-Squared | 0.12172 | R-Bar-Squared | 0.10889 |
| S.E. of Regression | 0.0084593 | F-Stat. F( 2, 137) | 9.4930[.000] |
| Mean of Dependent Variable | 0.0072140 | S.D. of Dependent Variable | 0.0089613 |
| Residual Sum of Squares | 0.0098037 | Equation Log-likelihood | 470.9812 |
| Akaike Info. Criterion | 467.9812 | Schwarz Bayesian Criterion | 463.5687 |
| DW-statistic | 1.9677 | | |

Parameters of the Moving Average Error Specification
U=E+ 0.27280*E(−1)+ 0.20932*E(−2)
( 3.2601)[.001] ( 2.8332)[.005]
T-ratio(s) based on asymptotic standard errors in brackets

estimate the following ARIMA(0, 1, 2) process for $y_t$ (the logarithm of the US real GNP) over the period 1960(2) to 1995(1):[12,13]

$$\Delta y_t = \mu + \theta_1 \epsilon_{t-3} + \theta_2 \epsilon_{t-2} + \epsilon_t$$

Load the file GDP95.FIT into *Microfit*. In the Command Editor create the variables

INPT = 1; DYUS = log(USGNP/USGNP(−1)) [GO]

Then choose option 1 in the Single Equation Estimation Menu (Univariate Menu), selecting option 7 MA Errors. Enter the start and end dates of 1960Q1 and 1995Q1, then type

DYUS INPT [START]

When prompted, type

1 2↩
↩

to obtain the results in Table 11.4a.

Both of the moving average coefficients, $\hat{\theta}_1 = 0.2728\{3.26\}$ and $\hat{\theta}_2 = 0.2093\{2.83\}$, are statistically significant. The figures in { } are

[12]Time series observations on US real GNP are analysed extensively in the recent literature on the measurement of the persistence of shocks to the US aggregate output. See, for example, Campbell and Mankiw (1987), Stock and Watson (1988a), Evans (1989), and Pesaran *et al.* (1993). The present data set extends the data used in these studies.

[13]The choice of the ARIMA(0, 1, 2) process for $y_t$ is based on the Schwarz Bayesian criterion: see Lesson 11.3.

| **Table 11.4b:** Estimates of Campbell and Mankiw persistence measure for US output growth based on an MA(2) specification | | | |
|---|---|---|---|
| Analysis of Function(s) of Parameter(s) | | | |
| Based on stochastic initial value(s) MA(2) regression of DYUS on:<br>INPT<br>140 observations used for estimation from 1960Q2 to 1995Q1 | | | |
| Coefficients A1 to A1 are assigned to the above regressors respectively<br>Coeffs. B1 to B2 are assigned to MA parameters respectively<br>List of specified functional relationship(s):<br>PCM = 1+B1+B2 | | | |
| Function | Estimate | Standard Error | T-Ratio[Prob] |
| PCM | 1.4821 | 0.11730 | 12.6348[.000] |

asymptotic $t$-ratios. The Campbell and Mankiw (1987) measure of persistence, $P_{cm}$, for the ARIMA(0,1,2) specification is given by

$$P_{cm} = 1 + \theta_1 + \theta_2$$

An estimate of $P_{cm}$, together with its (asymptotic) standard error, can be computed by first choosing option 5 in the Post Regression Menu and typing

PCM = (1 + B1 + B2) [OK]

to obtain the results shown in Table 11.4b.

This yields $\hat{P}_{cm} = 1.4821(0.1173)$, where the bracketed figure is the asymptotic standard error of $\hat{P}_{cm}$. This estimate is smaller than the one obtained by Campbell and Mankiw (1987), and it is still significantly larger than unity, which is the persistence measure for a pure random walk model. The $t$-statistic for this latter test is computed as

$$t_{P_{cm}=1} = \left(\hat{P}_{cm} - 1\right)/\sqrt{\hat{V}(\hat{P}_{cm})} = \frac{1.4821 - 1.0}{0.1173} = 4.11$$

Consider now the measure of persistence proposed by Cochrane (1988) in (11.10). The non-parametric estimate of this measure is given by the standardized spectral density function of DYUS at zero frequency. To obtain this estimate move to the Command Editor, clear it, and type

**SPECTRUM** DYUS [GO]

You should see the estimates of $P_c^2$ using the Bartlett, Tukey, and Parzen windows in the first row of the result table that appears on the screen: namely 1.4186(0.6782), 1.4387(0.7296), and 1.7345(0.7457), respectively. To make these estimates comparable to the estimates for the Campbell and Mankiw (1987) measure, $P_{cm}$, we need to divide their square root by $(1 - R^2)^{1/2}$, where $R^2$ is estimated to be 0.12 in the present application. Therefore, the point estimates of the persistence measures are rather similar, although not surprisingly the non-parametric estimates based on the spectrum are much less precisely estimated than the estimate based on the parametric approach.

## 11.5 Exercises in univariate time series analysis

### 11.5.1 Exercise 11.1

Detrend the logarithm of US real GNP using the Hodrick–Prescott filter, and then investigate the cyclical properties of the detrended series by using the SPECTRUM command. Show that the most likely periodic cycle in this series is 24 quarters. How robust is this conclusion to the choice of $\lambda$, the smoothing coefficient in the Hodrick–Prescott filter? Carry out this analysis on UKGDP and compare the results.

### 11.5.2 Exercise 11.2

Estimate the spectral density function of the UK output growth evaluated at zero frequency, using both parametric and non-parametric approaches. The relevant data is given in the file GDP95.FIT.

### 11.5.3 Exercise 11.3

Estimate a suitable ARIMA($p, d, q$) model for UK consumer prices over the period 1965 to 1990 and use it to forecast the inflation rate over the period 1991 to 1993. Compare the forecasting performance of the model with a 'naive' forecast based on a random walk model, possibly with a drift.

# 12
# Lessons in GARCH Modelling

Lessons in this section show how to estimate linear regression models under a variety of specifications for conditional error variances. The relevant estimation options, the underlying econometric methods, and computational algorithms are described in Sections 6.14 and 18.16. For a comprehensive review of the application of the GARCH modelling to financial data see Pagan (1996).

## 12.1 Lesson 12.1: Testing for ARCH effects in monthly dollar/sterling exchange rates

In this lesson we consider the following AR(1) model for the rate of change of the dollar/sterling exchange rate:

$$\Delta \log(USD_t) = \beta_0 + \beta_1 \Delta \log(USD_{t-1}) + u_t \qquad (12.1)$$

We also test for ARCH effects in the conditional variance of $u_t$, ($h_t^2 = Var(u_t|\Omega_{t-1})$). The ARCH($q$) specification for $h_t^2$ is given by

$$h_t^2 = \rho_0 + \rho_1 u_{t-1}^2 + \rho_2 u_{t-2}^2 + \cdots + \rho_q u_{t-q}^2 \qquad (12.2)$$

The null hypothesis of 'no ARCH effect' is

$$H_0{:}\rho_1 = \rho_2 = \cdots = \rho_q = 0$$

to be tested against the alternative hypothesis that

$$H_0{:}\rho_1 \neq 0, \quad \rho_2 \neq 0, \ldots, \quad \rho_q \neq 0$$

The test involves running a regression of squared OLS residuals from the regression (12.1) on lagged squared residuals (see Section 18.16.7). In what follows we apply the test to monthly observations on the US dollar/sterling rate available in the special *Microfit* file EXMONTH.FIT. This file contains monthly observations on the following exchange rates over the period 1973(1) to 1995(6):

CAN Canadian dollar to one British sterling
DM German Deutschmark to one British sterling
EP Spanish peseta to one British sterling
FF French franc to one British sterling

ITL Italian lira to one British sterling
SF Swiss franc to one British sterling
USD US dollar to one British sterling
YEN Japanese yen to one British sterling

Read this file into *Microfit*, and in the Command Editor type

DLUSD = log(USD/USD(−1)); ONE = 1 [GO]

to create the rate of change of dollar/sterling in the variable DLUSD. ONE is a vector of ones. To specify the regression equation (12.1) and test for ARCH effects, choose option 1 from the Single Equation Estimation Menu (Univariate Menu), selecting the OLS option. Type

DLUSD ONE DLUSD(−1)

For the estimation period enter

1973M1 1994M12

thus keeping the observations for the first six months of 1995 for volatility predictions (see Lesson 12.4). Click [START] and when the results appear, click [CLOSE] to move to the Post Regression Menu. Choose option 2 to move to the Hypothesis Testing Menu (see Section 6.24), and in that menu choose option 2 to carry out the ARCH test. You will be asked to specify the order (from 1 to 12) of the test. Type

1 ↩

The test results should now appear on the screen. The LM version of the test yields a statistic of 8.65 which is well above the 95 per cent critical value of $\chi_1^2$, and hence rejects the hypothesis that there are no ARCH effects in (12.1): see Table 12.1. The same conclusion is reached if one considers the F version of the test. Tests of higher order ARCH effects also yield similar results, although as the order of the test increases, the power of the test tends to decline. For example, the value of the ARCH(12) test statistic is 11.89 which is well below the 95 per cent critical value of $\chi_{12}^2$, and does not reject the hypothesis that $\rho_1 = \rho_2 = \cdots = \rho_{12} = 0$. In practice, it is prudent to carry out the test for different orders and then make an overall judgement.

**Table 12.1:** Testing for the ARCH effect in monthly dollar/sterling rate

Autoregressive Conditional Heteroscedasticity Test of Residuals (OLS Case)

Dependent variable is DLUSD
List of the variables in the regression:
ONE DLUSD(−1)
262 observations used for estimation from 1973M3 to 1994M12

| | |
|---|---|
| Lagrange Multiplier Statistic | CHSQ( 1) = 8.6475[.003] |
| F Statistic | F( 1, 259) = 8.8403[.003] |

As with all diagnostic tests, rejection of the null hypothesis that there are no ARCH effects, does not *necessarily* imply that conditional variance of $\Delta \log(\text{USD})$ is variable. This can happen particularly if the disturbances, $u_t$, in (12.1) are serially correlated. But in the present application, using option 1 in the Hypothesis Testing Menu, the hypothesis that $u_t$s are serially uncorrelated cannot be rejected, and therefore there may well be important ARCH effects in the data. We estimate various ARCH type models of exchange rate changes in Section 12.2.

## 12.2 Lesson 12.2: Estimating GARCH models for monthly dollar/sterling exchange rates

In the previous lesson we found some evidence of an ARCH effect in the rate of change of the dollar/sterling exchange rate, $\Delta \log(\text{USD}_t)$: see (12.1). Here we show how to use *Microfit* to estimate GARCH models for $h_t^2$, the conditional variance of $\Delta \log(\text{USD}_t)$. We assume that the mean equation for the exchange rate changes follows the AR(1) process,

$$x_t = \beta_0 + \beta_1 x_{t-1} + u_t$$

where $x_t = \Delta \log(\text{USD}_t)$, $u_t$ is a white noise process,

$$E(u_t) = 0;\ E(u_t u_{t-j}) = \left\{ \begin{array}{l} \sigma^2 \text{for } j = 0 \\ 0 \text{for } j \neq 0 \end{array} \right\}$$

and $|\beta_1| < 1$. Therefore, $x_t$ is a covariance-stationary process. In this case, the optimal linear forecast of $x_t$ is given by

$$E(x_t | x_{t-1}, x_{t-2}, \ldots) = \beta_0 + \beta_1 x_{t-1}$$

where $E(x_t | x_{t-1}, x_{t-2}, \ldots)$ denotes the linear projection of $x_t$ on constant and the past observations $(x_{t-1}, x_{t-2}, \ldots)$. While the conditional mean of $x_t$ changes over time, if the process is covariance stationary, the *unconditional* mean of $x_t$ is constant:

$$E(x_t) = \frac{\beta_0}{1 - \beta_1}$$

We may be interested in forecasting not only the level of $x_t$, but also its variance. Although the unconditional variance of $u_t$ is constant, $\sigma^2$, its conditional variance could be time varying. A simple example of such a process is the autoregressive conditional heteroscedastic process of order 1, denoted $u_t \sim \text{ARCH}(1)$ or GARCH(0, 1):

$$V(x_t | \Omega_{t-1}) = V(u_t | \Omega_{t-1}) = h_t^2 = \alpha_0 + \alpha_1 u_{t-1}^2$$

Further, if $\alpha_1 < 1$, then the unconditional variance of $u_t$ is given by

$$\sigma^2 = \frac{\alpha_0}{1 - \alpha_1}$$

which is constant. In general, if $h_t^2$ evolves according to

$$h_t^2 = \alpha_0 + \alpha_1 u_{t-1}^2 + \cdots + \alpha_q u_{t-q}^2 + \phi_1 h_{t-1}^2 + \cdots + \phi_p h_{t-p}^2$$

we have the generalized autoregressive conditional heteroscedastic model, denoted by $u_t \sim \text{GARCH}(p, q)$. For further details and other models of volatility, see Sections 6.14 and 18.16.

In this lesson we consider estimating the following GARCH(1, 1) models:

$$V(u_t|\Omega_{t-1}) = h_t^2 = \alpha_0 + \alpha_1 u_{t-1}^2 + \phi_1 h_{t-1}^2 \tag{12.3}$$

For a well defined GARCH(1, 1) process we must have $\alpha_0 > 0$, $|\phi_1| < 1$, and $1 - \alpha_1 - \phi_1 > 0$. These restrictions ensure that the unconditional variance of $u_t$ given by $V(u_t) = \alpha_0/(1 - \alpha_1 - \phi_1)$ is positive. In a number of econometric applications the coefficient $\alpha_1$ in (12.3) is also assumed to be positive. *Microfit* does not impose this restriction in estimation of the model, but if a large negative estimate of $\alpha_1$ is encountered, or if $\alpha_0/(1 - \alpha_1 - \phi_1)$ becomes negative in the course of the iterations, the program produces an error message.

To estimate the GARCH(1, 1) model (12.3) on the dollar/sterling exchange rate variable, $\Delta \log(\text{USD}_t)$, first follow the steps in Lesson 12.1, and specify the regression equation (12.1) to be estimated over the sample period 1973(1) to 1994(12). Move to the Linear Regression Estimation Menu and choose option 9. Choose option 1 in the GARCH Estimation Menu. You will be asked to choose between a normal and a *t*-distribution for the conditional distribution of the errors, $u_t$. Choose the normal distribution option by pressing the ↵ key. In the box editor that appears on the screen, type the orders of the GARCH($p, q$) model to be estimated as follows:

1; 1 [OK]

You will now be presented with another box editor to list any additional variables that you may wish to include in the model for the conditional variance, (12.3): see Section 6.14 for more details. In the present application there are no additional regressors in the GARCH model, so click [OK] to move to the next screen where you will be asked to give initial estimates for the parameters of the GARCH model, namely $\alpha_0, \alpha_1$, and $\phi_1$, respectively. *Microfit* automatically suggests using the OLS estimate of the unconditional variance, $\hat{\sigma}^2$, as the initial estimate for $\alpha_0$. You must, however, give initial estimates for $\alpha_1$ and $\phi_1$. For $\alpha_1$ (the 'MA lag 1' coefficient), type 0.1, and for $\phi_1$ (the 'AR lag 1' coefficient) type 0.4, and click [OK] to accept these initial estimates. For the damping factor, accept the default value of 0.01 by pressing the ↵ key. *Microfit* starts the computations which converge after 36 iterations. The results reproduced in Table 12.2a should now appear on the screen.

The ML estimates $\hat{\alpha}_1 = 0.19668(0.1138)$ and $\hat{\phi}_1 = 0.19894(0.2625)$ have the correct signs but neither are statistically significant at the 95 per cent level. The bracketed figures are asymptotic standard errors.

*Microfit* also allows you to test linear or non-linear restrictions on the coefficients of the GARCH model. Suppose you are interested in testing the joint hypothesis that

**Table 12.2a:** Modelling conditional heteroscedasticity of the dollar/sterling rate

GARCH(1,1) assuming a normal distribution
converged after 36 iterations

Dependent variable is DLUSD
262 observations used for estimation from 1973M3 to 1994M12

| Regressor | Coefficient | Standard Error | T-Ratio[Prob] |
|---|---|---|---|
| ONE | −.0010863 | .0019866 | −.54682[.585] |
| DLUSD(−1) | .073362 | .068313 | 1.0739[.284] |

| | | | |
|---|---|---|---|
| R-Squared | .0098745 | R-Bar-Squared | −.0016386 |
| S.E. of Regression | .033712 | F-Stat. F( 3, 258) | .85768[.464] |
| Mean of Dependent Variable | −.0016091 | S.D. of Dependent Variable | .033684 |
| Residual Sum of Squares | .29321 | Equation Log-likelihood | 520.8315 |
| Akaike Info. Criterion | 516.8315 | Schwarz Bayesian Criterion | 509.6948 |
| DW-statistic | 1.9360 | | |

Parameters of the Conditional Heteroscedastic Model
Explaining HSQ, the Conditional Variance of the Error Term

| | Coefficient | Asymptotic Standard Error |
|---|---|---|
| Constant | .6844E-3 | .2591E-3 |
| E-SQ(−1) | .19668 | .11384 |
| H-SQ(−1) | .19894 | .26253 |

H-SQ stands for the conditional variance of the error term
E-SQ stands for the square of the error term

$$H_0\colon \alpha_1 = \phi_1 = 0$$

against

$$H_1\colon \alpha_1 \neq 0, \phi_1 \neq 0$$

Choose option 2 in the Post Regression Menu (following the GARCH estimation) and type

$\hookleftarrow$

B2 = 0; B3 = 0 [OK]

The results in Table 12.2b should appear on the screen. The Wald statistic for testing the joint hypothesis that $\alpha_1 = \phi_1 = 0$ is equal to 4.93 which is significant at the 91.5 per cent level, but not at the conventional 95 per cent level.

Suppose you now wish to estimate the GARCH(1, 1) model (12.3) using the Student-*t* density distribution for the conditional distribution of the errors. Choose option 0 in the GARCH Post Regression Menu and then press $\hookleftarrow$. When asked to specify the underlying distribution, choose option 2. Click [OK] to accept the figure in the box editor and [OK] again when the second editor appears.

| **Table 12.2b:** Testing joint restrictions on the parameters of the GARCH model for dollar/sterling rate | |
|---|---|
| Wald test of restriction(s) imposed on parameters | |
| Based on GARCH regression of DLUSD on:<br>ONE DLUSD(−1)<br>262 observations used for estimation from 1973M3 to 1994M12 | |
| Coefficients A1 to A2 are assigned to the above regressors respectively<br>Coeffs. B1 to B3 are assigned to ARCH parameters respectively<br>List of restriction(s) for the Wald test:<br>b2 = 0;b3 = 0 | |
| Wald Statistic | CHSQ( 2) = 4.9302[.085] |

You will now be asked to give initial estimates for $\alpha_1$ and $\phi_1$. For the degrees of freedom of the $t$-distribution (denoted by $\nu$), the default initial value of 10 is suggested by *Microfit*. Type 0.1 and 0.4 for the 'MA lag 1' and 'AR lag 1' coefficients and click OK to accept. Then press the ↩ key to accept the default value given for the damping factor. *Microfit* starts the computations which converge after 31 iterations. The estimates in Table 12.2c should appear on the screen. The estimate of 9.896 obtained for $\nu$, the parameter of the $t$-distribution suggests only a mild departure from the normality. However, the ML estimate of $\phi_1$ given by 0.5598(0.1107) now suggests a significant GARCH effect. The Wald statistic for the test of the joint hypothesis $\alpha_1 = \phi_1 = 0$ is now 49.52 which is highly significant.

A comparison of the Akaike information and Schwarz Bayesian criteria across the above two specification of the conditional error distribution tends to favour the $t$-distribution, although, as is to be expected, the SBC heavily penalizes the $t$-distribution for the additional degrees of freedom parameter, $\nu$, which is estimated: see Tables 12.2a and 12.2c.

## 12.3 Lesson 12.3: Estimating EGARCH models for monthly dollar/sterling exchange rates

The exponential GARCH(1, 1), or EGARCH(1, 1), model is defined by

$$\log h_t^2 = \alpha_0 + \alpha_1\left(\frac{u_{t-1}}{h_{t-1}}\right) + \alpha_1^*\left(\left|\frac{u_{t-1}}{h_{t-1}}\right| - \mu\right) + \phi_1 \log h_{t-1}^2$$

where $\mu = E(|u_{t-1}/h_{t-1}|)$. Unlike the GARCH(1, 1) model estimated in Lesson 12.2, the above specification has a well-defined conditional variance, $h_t^2 = V(u_t|\Omega_{t-1})$, for all parameter values, $\alpha_0, \alpha_1, \alpha_1^*$. But for the process to be stable it is still required that $|\phi_1| < 1$. For further details and references to the literature, see Section 18.16.

**Table 12.2c:** Modelling conditional heteroscedasticity of the dollar/sterling rate

| GARCH(1,1) assuming a *t*-distribution converged after 31 iterations | | | |
|---|---|---|---|
| Dependent variable is DLUSD<br>262 observations used for estimation from 1973M3 to 1994M12 | | | |
| Regressor | Coefficient | Standard Error | T-Ratio[Prob] |
| ONE | −.0011082 | .0019593 | −.56564[.572] |
| DLUSD(−1) | .10873 | .066424 | 1.6369[.103] |
| R-Squared | .010930 | R-Bar-Squared | −.5707E-3 |
| S.E. of Regression | .033694 | F-Stat. F( 3, 258) | .95037[.417] |
| Mean of Dependent Variable | −.0016091 | S.D. of Dependent Variable | .033684 |
| Residual Sum of Squares | .29290 | Equation Log-likelihood | 523.8620 |
| Akaike Info. Criterion | 518.8620 | Schwarz Bayesian Criterion | 509.9412 |
| DW-statistic | 2.0098 | | |

| Parameters of the Conditional Heteroscedastic Model Explaining HSQ, the Conditional Variance of the Error Term | | |
|---|---|---|
| | Coefficient | Asymptotic Standard Error |
| Constant | .3441E-3 | .8618E-4 |
| E-SQ(−1) | .13418 | .088345 |
| H-SQ(−1) | .55978 | .11069 |
| D.F. of t-Dist. | 9.8960 | 5.0508 |

H-SQ stands for the conditional variance of the error term.
E-SQ stands for the square of the error term.

The exchange rate model to be estimated is the same as in Lessons 12.1 and 12.2. Load the *Microfit* file EXMONTH.FIT and specify the regression equation (12.1) to be estimated over the period 1973(1) to 1994(12), and then choose option 9 in the Linear Regression Menu. Click [START], then press ↩ to move to the GARCH Estimation Menu (see Section 6.14). Then choose option 5 and enter

↩

1; 1 [OK]

[OK]

For the initial estimate of $\alpha_1$ ('MA lag 1'), $\alpha_1^*$ ('ABS MA 1'), and $\phi_1$ ('AR lag 1'), type 0.1, 0.2, and 0.4, respectively. Click [OK] and then press ↩. The program starts the computations but after 19 iterations will present you with the error message

*Very large conditional variance/standard errors encountered!*

Click [OK] to continue. You will be presented with a number of likely reasons for the failure of the GARCH estimation procedure to converge. In the case of the present application, the problem can be resolved by choosing a different set of initial values. Click OK to return to the box editor and then click OK twice to return to the screen for giving initial parameter values. Now choose the values of −0.2, 0.1, and 0.3 for $\alpha_1$, $\alpha_1^*$, and $\phi_1$, respectively. This time the computations converge after 39 iterations, and you will be presented with the results in Table 12.3a. According to these estimates, only $\alpha_1^*$ is significantly different from zero at the 95 per cent level.

Consider now estimating the EGARCH(1, 1) model with a *t*-distribution for the conditional distribution of the errors. Move to the GARCH Estimation Menu and choose option 5, then choose option 2. Click OK twice. You should see the screen editor for the specification of the initial estimates. Choose the ML estimates of $\alpha_1$, $\alpha_1^*$, and $\phi_1$ in Table 12.3a as initial values (namely −0.13, 0.33, and 0.15) and start the computations. You should see the results in Table 12.3b on the screen. A comparison of the results in Tables 12.3a and 12.3b shows that according to the Akaike information criterion (AIC), there is a clear evidence in favour of the *t*-distribution, but the evidence is much less clear cut, if the Schwarz Bayesian criterion (SBC) is used.

**Table 12.3a:** Modelling conditional heteroscedasticity of the dollar/sterling rate

Exponential GARCH(1,1) assuming a normal distribution
converged after 39 iterations

Dependent variable is DLUSD
262 observations used for estimation from 1973M3 to 1994M12

| Regressor | Coefficient | Standard Error | T-Ratio[Prob] |
|---|---|---|---|
| ONE | −.0014268 | .0018710 | −.76258[.446] |
| DLUSD(−1) | .080850 | .066757 | 1.2111[.227] |

| | | | |
|---|---|---|---|
| R-Squared | .010448 | R-Bar-Squared | −.0049531 |
| S.E. of Regression | .033768 | F-Stat. F( 4, 257) | .67840[.607] |
| Mean of Dependent Variable | −.0016091 | S.D. of Dependent Variable | .033684 |
| Residual Sum of Squares | .29304 | Equation Log-likelihood | 522.6913 |
| Akaike Info. Criterion | 517.6913 | Schwarz Bayesian Criterion | 508.7705 |
| DW-statistic | 1.9519 | | |

Parameters of the Conditional Heteroscedastic Model
Explaining the Logarithm of HS-Q, the Conditional Variance of the Error Term

| | Coefficient | Asymptotic Standard Error |
|---|---|---|
| Constant | −5.8218 | 3.0708 |
| (E/H)(−1) | −.13235 | .094091 |
| ABS(E/H)(−1)-MEU | .33411 | .15825 |
| LOG(H-SQ(−1)) | .14800 | .44819 |

H stands for the conditional standard error of the error term.
E stands for the error term.
MEU stands for the expectation of the absolute value of the standardized disturbance term.
MEU = SQRT(2/3.14159) = .79788

**Table 12.3b:** Modelling conditional heteroscedasticity of the dollar/sterling rate

Exponential GARCH(1,1) assuming a $t$-distribution
converged after 34 iterations

Dependent variable is DLUSD
262 observations used for estimation from 1973M3 to 1994M12

| Regressor | Coefficient | Standard Error | T-Ratio[Prob] |
|---|---|---|---|
| ONE | −.0012210 | .0018677 | −.65371[.514] |
| DLUSD(−1) | .11649 | .065920 | 1.7671[.078] |

| | | | |
|---|---|---|---|
| R-Squared | .010881 | R-Bar-Squared | −.0045138 |
| S.E. of Regression | .033760 | F-Stat. F( 4, 257) | .70680[.588] |
| Mean of Dependent Variable | −.0016091 | S.D. of Dependent Variable | .033684 |
| Residual Sum of Squares | .29292 | Equation Log-likelihood | 525.2848 |
| Akaike Info. Criterion | 519.2848 | Schwarz Bayesian Criterion | 508.5797 |
| DWstatistic | 2.0260 | | |

Parameters of the Conditional Heteroscedastic Model
Explaining the Logarithm of H-SQ, the Conditional Variance of the Error Term

| | Coefficient | Asymptotic Standard Error |
|---|---|---|
| Constant | −2.6090 | 2.6181 |
| (E/H)(−1) | −.098597 | .10733 |
| ABS(E/H)(−1)-MEU | .29787 | .13413 |
| LOG(H-SQ(−1)) | .61877 | .38207 |
| D.F. of $t$-Dist. | 10.8349 | 5.8479 |

H stands for the conditional standard error of the error term.
E stands for the error term.
MEU stands for the expectation of the absolute value of the standardized disturbance term.
The maximum likelihood estimate of MEU = .77566

## 12.4 Lesson 12.4: Forecasting volatility

In this lesson we use the GARCH(1, 1) model estimated for the monthly observations on dollar/sterling exchange rate in Lesson 12.2 to compute the conditional standard errors, $h_t$, over the estimation period 1973(1) to 1994(12), and then obtain (multi)-step ahead forecasts of $h_t$ over the period 1995(1) to 1995(6). In Lesson 12.2 we found that the $t$-distribution performs slightly better than the normal. So in what follows we base our estimation on the exchange rate model

$$\Delta \log USD_t = \beta_0 + \beta_1 \Delta \log(USD_{t-1}) + u_t$$
$$V(u_t|\Omega_{t-1}) = h_t^2 = \alpha_0 + \alpha_1 u_{t-1}^2 + \phi_1 h_{t-1}^2$$

assuming that, conditional on $\Omega_{t-1}$, the errors have the standardized student $t$-distribution.

First follow the steps in Lesson 12.2 and choose option 1 in the GARCH Estimation Menu to estimate the above model. Once you have successfully estimated the model, choose option 8 in the Post Regression Menu following the GARCH result screen, to compute dynamic forecasts of $\Delta$ log USD$_t$ over

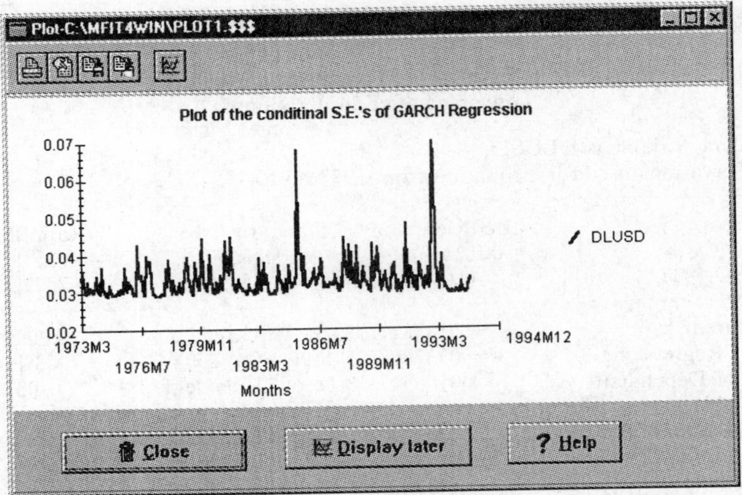


**Figure 12.1:** Estimated values of $\hat{h}_t$ for the dollar/sterling exchange rate

the six months from 1995(1) to 1995(6). The program presents you with the forecasts of $\Delta \log \text{USD}_t$, $t = 1995(1), \ldots, 1995(6)$. To obtain the forecasts of $h_t$, return to the Post Regression Menu, and choose option 3 to move to the Display/Save Residuals and Fitted Values Menu (see Section 6.22). Option 9 in this menu allows you to save the values of $\hat{h}_t$ over the estimation and the forecast period. You can see the plot of $\hat{h}_t$ over the sample period 1973(1) to 1994(12) if you choose option 8 in this menu: see Figure 12.1.

To list or plot the forecasts of $h_t$ over the period 1995(1) to 1995(6), choose option 9 in the Display/Save Residuals and Fitted Values Menu and type

HHAT Estimates of the Conditional Standard Errors ↩

Press ↩ to return to the Post Regression Menu, choose option 0, and in the GARCH Estimation Menu choose option 0 again. Return to the Single Equation Estimation window and click PROCESS to move to the Command Editor. Clear it and type

**SAMPLE** 1995M1 1995M6; **LIST** HHAT [GO]

The volatility forecasts in Table 12.4 should now appear on the screen. Note that these are multi-step ahead forecasts of $h_t$ computed using the formulae in Section 18.26.4.

## 12.5 Lesson 12.5: Modelling volatility in daily exchange rates

The degree of volatility tends to increase with the frequency with which observations are sampled. This can be seen clearly as one moves from monthly to daily observations on exchange rates. As an example, consider

**Table 12.4:** Volatility forecasts

| Month | Forecasts of $\hat{h}_t$ |
|---|---|
| 1995M1 | 0.034190 |
| 1995M2 | 0.033990 |
| 1995M3 | 0.033850 |
| 1995M4 | 0.033753 |
| 1995M5 | 0.033686 |
| 1995M6 | 0.033639 |

the daily dollar/sterling exchange rates in the file EXDAILY.FIT covering the period from January 2 1985 to July 18 1993. In total, this file contains 2,168 daily observations. Load this file into *Microfit* and in the Command Editor create the rate of change of the dollar/sterling exchange rate in the variable DEUS:

DEUS = log(EUS/EUS(−1));   INPT = 1   [GO]

Now choose option 1 in the Single Equation Estimation Menu (Univariate Menu), selecting option 9 GARCH-M Estimation. Specify the following AR(2) specification for the conditional mean of DEUS:

DEUS   INPT   DEUS(−1)   DEUS(−2)

Specify the start and end dates as

1265   2148

keeping the remaining 20 observations for forecast analysis. The estimation sample covers the period January 2 1990 to June 30 1993.[1]

To fit a GARCH(1, 2) model to the errors of this regression equation, click [START]. Choose option 1 in the GARCH Estimation Menu and then enter

↩
↩
1;   1   2   [OK]
[OK]

For the initial values, type 0.1 (for 'MA lag 1'), 0.2 (for 'MA lag 2'), and 0.6 (for 'AR lag 1'). Notice that the sum of these initial estimates cannot exceed unity. Click [OK] and press the ↩ key to start the computations. The process converges after 23 iterations and you will be presented with the results in Table 12.5a. The second part of this table clearly shows the importance of the AR component in the GARCH(1, 2) specification. However, the second order coefficient of the

[1]To check that these dates are correct, move to the data processing stage and type

**SAMPLE**   1265   2148;
**LIST**   Day   Month   Year   [GO]

**Table 12.5a:** Modelling conditional heteroscedasticity of daily dollar/sterling rate

GARCH(1, 2) assuming a normal distribution
converged after 26 iterations

Dependent variable is DEUS
884 observations used for estimation from 1265 to 2148

| Regressor | Coefficient | Standard Error | T-Ratio[Prob] |
|---|---|---|---|
| INPT | .3094E-3 | .2449E-3 | 1.2633[.207] |
| DEUS(−1) | .12093 | .037494 | 3.2254[.001] |
| DEUS(−2) | −.047882 | .036072 | −1.3273[.185] |

| | | | |
|---|---|---|---|
| R-Squared | .021039 | R-Bar-Squared | .015464 |
| S.E. of Regression | .0076251 | F-Stat. F( 5, 878) | 3.7738[.002] |
| Mean of Dependent Variable | −.8143E-4 | S.D. of Dependent Variable | .0076847 |
| Residual Sum of Squares | .051048 | Equation Log-likelihood | 3081.0 |
| Akaike Info. Criterion | 3075.0 | Schwarz Bayesian Criterion | 3060.7 |
| DW-statistic | 1.9178 | | |

Parameters of the Conditional Heteroscedastic Model
Explaining H-SQ, the Conditional Variance of the Error Term

| | Coefficient | Asymptotic Standard Error |
|---|---|---|
| Constant | .1640E-5 | .5549E-5 |
| E-SQ(−1) | .084428 | .041143 |
| E-SQ(−2) | −.031462 | .041740 |
| H-SQ(−1) | .91966 | .020599 |

H-SQ stands for the conditional variance of the error term.
E-SQ stands for the square of the error term.

MA part of the process is not statistically significant. Therefore, a GARCH(1, 1) model seems to fit the observations reasonably well once again. Re-estimating the exchange rate equation assuming a GARCH(1, 1) model yields the results in Table 12.5b. (To obtain these results we started the iterations with 0.8 and 0.1 for AR and MA coefficients.)

One hypothesis of interest involving the coefficients of the GARCH(1, 1) model concerns the question of whether the sum of the coefficients of this model is unity or not. When the coefficients add up to unity, the model is known as the integrated GARCH or IGARCH model, and this implies that the shocks to the conditional variance are persistent. From the results in Table 12.5b it is clear that the sum of the estimates $\hat{\alpha}_1 = 0.0560$ and $\hat{\phi}_1 = 0.9146$ is very close to unity. To test the hypothesis that $\alpha_1 + \phi_1 = 1$, choose option 7 in the Hypothesis Testing Menu and type in the box editor

$$B2 + B3 = 1 \quad \boxed{GO}$$

(Recall that in *Microfit* the coefficients of the GARCH model are denoted by B1, B2, . . . .) The Wald statistic, distributed asymptotically as a $\chi^2$ with

**Table 12.5b:** Modelling conditional heteroscedasticity of daily dollar/sterling rate

GARCH(1, 1) assuming a normal distribution
converged after 25 iterations

Dependent variable is DEUS
884 observations used for estimation from 1265 to 2148

| Regressor | Coefficient | Standard Error | T-Ratio[Prob] |
|---|---|---|---|
| INPT | .2933E-3 | .2454E-3 | 1.1952[.232] |
| DEUS(−1) | .12538 | .036192 | 3.4643[.001] |
| DEUS(−2) | −.046197 | .036108 | −1.2794[.201] |

| | | | |
|---|---|---|---|
| R-Squared | .021586 | R-Bar-Squared | .017133 |
| S.E. of Regression | .0076186 | F-Stat. F( 4, 879) | 4.8481[.001] |
| Mean of Dependent Variable | −.8143E-4 | S.D. of Dependent Variable | .0076847 |
| Residual Sum of Squares | .051020 | Equation Log-likelihood | 3084.8 |
| Akaike Info. Criterion | 3079.8 | Schwarz Bayesian Criterion | 3067.9 |
| DW-statistic | 1.9273 | | |

Parameters of the Conditional Heteroscedastic Model
Explaining H-SQ, the Conditional Variance of the Error Term

| | Coefficient | Asymptotic Standard Error |
|---|---|---|
| Constant | .1758E-5 | .5026E-5 |
| E-SQ(−1) | .056014 | .020252 |
| H-SQ(−1) | .91459 | .018823 |

H-SQ stands for the conditional variance of the error term.
E-SQ stands for the square of the error term.

one degree of freedom is equal to 42.74, and strongly rejects the hypothesis that the GARCH model is integrated.

## 12.6 Lesson 12.6: Estimation of GARCH-in-mean models of US excess returns

The regressions in Lesson 10.11 show that a statistically significant fraction of the variance of excess returns can be predicted by *ex ante* data variables, such as lagged dividend yields and lagged interest rates. This evidence (also replicated using other portfolios in other stock markets) rejects the joint hypothesis of market efficiency and risk neutrality. However, in situations where market participants are risk averse, standard efficient market models do not rule out the possibility that excess returns on stocks can be predicted. One important class of asset pricing models predicts a positive relationship between conditional expectations of excess returns and their conditional variances (see, for example, Merton, 1980). If $ERSP_t$ is the excess return on the SP500 defined in Lesson 10.11, then a generalized version of Merton's (1980) mean–variance model can be written as

$$\mathrm{ERSP}_t = \boldsymbol{\beta}'\mathbf{x}_{t-1} + \gamma V(\mathrm{ERSP}_t|\Omega_{t-1}) + u_t \tag{12.4}$$

where

$$V(\mathrm{ERSP}_t|\Omega_{t-1}) = V(u_t|\Omega_{t-1}) = h_t^2$$

$\Omega_{t-1}$ is the publicly available information at time $t-1$, and $\mathbf{x}_{t-1}$ is a vector of ex ante dated variables. In what follows, we assume $\mathbf{x}_{t-1}$ includes the variables $\mathrm{YSP}_{t-1}$, $\mathrm{PI12}_{t-2}$, $\mathrm{DI11}_{t-1}$, and $\mathrm{DIP12}_{t-2}$, defined in Lesson 10.11, and that $h_t^2$ has the GARCH(1, 1) specification:

$$h_t^2 = \alpha_0 + \alpha_1 u_{t-1}^2 + \phi_1 h_{t-1}^2 \tag{12.5}$$

This model can be readily estimated using the GARCH-in-mean option in *Microfit* (see Section 6.14). Load the special *Microfit* file PTMONTH.FIT and then run the batch file PTMONTH.BAT on it in the Command Editor. Choose option 1 in the Single Equation Estimation Menu (Univariate Menu), selecting option 9 GARCH-M Estimation. Retrieve the file PTMONTH.LST into the box editor, and click START to move to the GARCH Estimation Menu. Choose option 2 (the GARCH-in-mean), followed by the normal distribution option, and enter

1; 1 OK
OK

Choose the values of 0.5, 0.1, and 0.2 for the initial estimates of $\gamma$, $\alpha_1$, and $\phi_1$ in (12.4), respectively, and click OK, then press the ← key to start the computations. The iterative procedure converges after 34 iterations and the results in Table 12.6a should appear on the screen. According to these results, the ML estimate of $\gamma$ is 5.89 (6.74) and has the correct sign, but is not statistically significant. Therefore, there does not seem to be any evidence of a GARCH-in-mean effect in this model. Notice, however, that the other variables in the excess return regression continue to be highly significant. The evidence on the volatility of the conditional variance of $u_t$ (i.e. $h_t^2$) is rather mixed. The ML estimate of $\phi_1$ at 0.84898 (0.0325) is highly significant, but the ML estimate of $\alpha_1$ is near zero and is not statistically significant.

Consider now estimating the above GARCH-in-mean model (12.4) and (12.5), assuming the conditional distribution of the errors to be $t$-distributed. Return to the GARCH Estimation Menu, choose option 2, then select the $t$-distribution option. Click OK to accept the contents of the first box editor, then click OK again. For the initial estimates of $\gamma$, $\alpha_1$, and $\phi_1$, choose the values 0.1 ('in mean'), 0.2 ('MA lag 1'), and 0.4 ('AR lag 1'), respectively. Click OK to accept these initial estimates and press the ← key to accept the default value of 0.01 for the damping factor. The program starts the computations and yields the results in Table 12.6b after 25 iterations.

Comparing these results with those in Table 12.6a clearly suggests that the

**Table 12.6a:** Excess return regression for SP500 portfolio with GARCH-in-mean effect

GARCH(1,1)-in-mean assuming a normal distribution
converged after 34 iterations

Dependent variable is ERSP
468 observations used for estimation from 1954M1 to 1992M12

| Regressor | Coefficient | Standard Error | T-Ratio[Prob] |
|---|---|---|---|
| INPT | −.027861 | .014131 | −1.9716[.049] |
| YSP(−1) | 12.7056 | 3.2047 | 3.9647[.000] |
| PI12(−2) | −.29479 | .068527 | −4.3018[.000] |
| DI11(−1) | −.0067114 | .0027614 | −2.4304[.015] |
| DIP12(−2) | −.14717 | .038211 | −3.8514[.000] |
| H-Squared | 5.8897 | 6.7440 | .87333[.383] |

| | | | |
|---|---|---|---|
| R-Squared | .091374 | R-Bar-Squared | .077547 |
| S.E. of Regression | .040750 | F-Stat. F( 7, 460) | 6.6084[.000] |
| Mean of Dependent Variable | .0059055 | S.D. of Dependent Variable | .042428 |
| Residual Sum of Squares | .76386 | Equation Log-likelihood | 841.5218 |
| Akaike Info. Criterion | 833.5218 | Schwarz Bayesian Criterion | 816.9279 |
| DW-statistic | 2.0030 | | |

Parameters of the Conditional Heteroscedastic Model
Explaining H-SQ, the Conditional Variance of the Error Term

| | Coefficient | Asymptotic Standard Error |
|---|---|---|
| Constant | .1383E-3 | .1152E-4 |
| E-SQ(−1) | .067967 | .043356 |
| H-SQ(−1) | .84898 | .032462 |

H-SQ stands for the conditional variance of the error term.
E-SQ stands for the square of the error term.

$t$-distribution fits the data much better than the normal. Even the Schwarz Bayesian criterion (SBC) unambiguously selects the model with conditionally $t$-distributed errors. Nevertheless $\hat{\gamma} = 8.72$ (8.94) and hence the hypothesis that $\gamma = 0$ cannot be rejected. The same conclusion also applies to $\alpha_1$ (we have $\hat{\alpha}_1 = 0.0616$ (0.043)).

The extent to which the $t$-distribution has been successful in dealing with the non-normal errors can be assessed graphically. Click CLOSE to move to the Post Regression Menu, then choose option 3, followed by option 5 in the Display/Save Residuals and Fitted Values Menu. The histogram of the scaled residuals (defined by $\hat{u}_t/\hat{h}_t$) should now appear on the screen (see Figure 12.2).

Except for a possible 'outlier' to the left of the graph, the $t$-distribution seems to provide a reasonable fit for the distribution of the scaled residuals. A closer inspection of the results shows, perhaps not surprisingly, that the apparent outlier refers to the 1987 October crash.

**Table 12.6b:** Excess return regression for SP500 portfolio with GARCH-in-mean effect

GARCH(1,1)-in-mean assuming a *t*-distribution
converged after 25 iterations

Dependent variable is ERSP
468 observations used for estimation from 1954M1 to 1992M12

| Regressor | Coefficient | Standard Error | T-Ratio[Prob] |
|---|---|---|---|
| INPT | −.028471 | .016611 | −1.7140[.087] |
| YSP(−1) | 11.7721 | 3.1699 | 3.7137[.000] |
| PI12(−2) | −.30636 | .067573 | −4.5337[.000] |
| DI11(−1) | −.0045283 | .0026368 | −1.7174[.087] |
| DIP12(−2) | −.14492 | .037070 | −3.9094[.000] |
| H-Squared | 8.7211 | 8.9381 | .97573[.330] |

| | | | |
|---|---|---|---|
| R-Squared | .087992 | R-Bar-Squared | .074114 |
| S.E. of Regression | .040826 | F-Stat. F( 7, 460) | 6.3402[.000] |
| Mean of Dependent Variable | .0059055 | S.D. of Dependent Variable | .042428 |
| Residual Sum of Squares | .76671 | Equation Log-likelihood | 848.2294 |
| Akaike Info. Criterion | 839.2294 | Schwarz Bayesian Criterion | 820.5613 |
| DW-statistic | 2.0006 | | |

Parameters of the Conditional Heteroscedastic Model
Explaining H-SQ, the Conditional Variance of the Error Term

| | Coefficient | Asymptotic Standard Error |
|---|---|---|
| Constant | .1917E-3 | .2273E-4 |
| E-SQ(−1) | .061567 | .043319 |
| H-SQ(−1) | .82076 | .033397 |
| D.F. of t-Dist. | 8.6484 | 3.2140 |

H-SQ stands for the conditional variance of the error term.
E-SQ stands for the square of the error term.

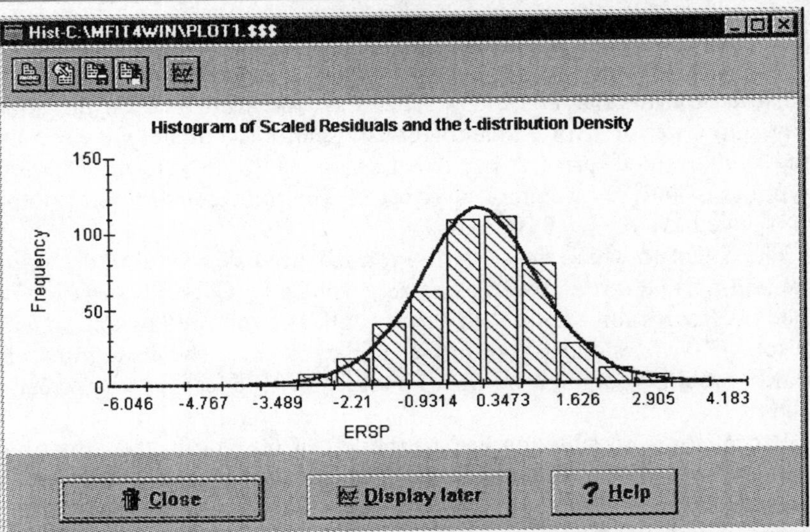


**Figure 12.2:** Histogram of the scaled residuals ($\hat{u}_t/\hat{h}_t$) for the SP500 excess return regression

## 12.7 Exercises in GARCH modelling

### 12.7.1 Exercise 12.1

Use the monthly observations in EXMONTH.FIT to estimate a first-order autoregressive model in the rate of change of the Deutschmark/sterling exchange rate. Is there any evidence of ARCH effects in this regression?

### 12.7.2 Exercise 12.2

Use the data in PTMONTH.FIT to estimate the GARCH-in-mean regression (12.4) assuming that $V(u_t|\Omega_{t-1})$ has the exponential specification. Compare your result with those obtained in Lesson 12.6.

# 13

# Lessons in Non-linear Estimation

In this chapter we show how the non-linear option in the Single Equation Estimation Menu can be used to estimate simple non-linear models such as the Cobb–Douglas production function, and the Phillips curve, Almon distributed lag functions, and parameters of the Euler equation that arise in intertemporal optimization models. For the relevant estimation menus, see Section 6.17, and for the underlying econometric and computational methods, see Section 18.21.

## 13.1 Lesson 13.1: Non-linear estimation of Cobb–Douglas production function

The non-linear estimation option in *Microfit* provides a powerful tool for the estimation of non-linear equations and/or the estimation of linear equations subject to linear or non-linear parametric restrictions. Suppose you are interested in estimating the following non-linear form of the Cobb–Douglas production function:

$$Y_t = AK_t^{\alpha} L_t^{1-\alpha} + u_t \tag{13.1}$$

Read into *Microfit* the file CD.FIT which contains the annual observations on US output (Y), capital stock (K), and labour input (L), in the period from 1899 to 1922 originally analysed by Cobb and Douglas (1928). Choose option 4 in the Single Equation Estimation Menu (Univariate Menu: see Section 6.4), selecting option 1 Non-linear Least Squares. In the box editor, type

Y = A0 * (K ^ A1) * (L ^ (1 − A1)) [START]

You will now be prompted to specify the initial estimates for the parameters A0 and A1 (see Section 6.17.2). The initial choice of A0 and A1 is often critical for the convergence of the iterative process. For example, the iterative process is unlikely to converge if the iterations are started with very small values of A0 and A1. Starting the iterations with A0 = A1 = 0, will result in the message

*An invalid operation has been carried out or a very large number has been calculated.*

*Either initial values of parameters are not appropriate or variables need to be scaled! Try again.*

There are no general rules concerning the choice of the initial estimates for the unknown parameters, but in most applications a preliminary linear regression based on a Taylor series expansion of the non-linear equation can be very helpful in providing a reasonable set of initial estimates for the unknown parameters. In the case of the present example, one can obtain initial estimates for these parameters by running the constrained linear regression of $\log Y_t - \log L_t$ on an intercept term and $(\log K_t - \log L_t)$. This yields the initial estimates of 0.0145 and 0.2541 for the parameters log A0 and A1, respectively. Therefore, using 1.0147(= exp(0.0145)) and

**Table 13.1a:** Non-linear estimates of the Cobb–Douglas production function

Non-Linear Least Squares Estimation
The estimation method converged after 2 iterations

Nonlinear regression formula:
Y = a0*(K^a1)*(L^(1 − a1))
24 observations used for estimation from 1899 to 1922

| Parameter | Estimate | Standard Error | T-Ratio[Prob] |
|---|---|---|---|
| A0 | 1.0182 | .028085 | 36.2551[.000] |
| A1 | .24962 | .048076 | 5.1921[.000] |

| | | | |
|---|---|---|---|
| R-Squared | .94175 | R-Bar-Squared | .93910 |
| S.E. of Regression | 10.7970 | F-Stat. F( 1, 22) | 355.6956[.000] |
| Mean of Dependent Variable | 165.9167 | S.D. of Dependent Variable | 43.7532 |
| Residual Sum of Squares | 2564.6 | Equation Log-likelihood | −90.1128 |
| Akaike Info. Criterion | −92.1128 | Schwarz Bayesian Criterion | −93.2909 |
| DW-statistic | 1.5256 | | |

Diagnostic Tests

| Test Statistics | LM Version | F Version |
|---|---|---|
| A:Serial Correlation | CHSQ( 1)= .14424[.704] | F( 1, 21)= .12697[.725] |
| B:Functional Form | CHSQ( 1)= .55738[.455] | F( 1, 21)= .49931[.488] |
| C:Normality | CHSQ( 2)= 3.9850[.136] | Not applicable |
| D:Heteroscedasticity | CHSQ( 1)= 4.1286[.042] | F( 1, 22)= 4.5708[.044] |

A:Lagrange multiplier test of residual serial correlation
B:Ramsey's RESET test using the square of the fitted values
C:Based on a test of skewness and kurtosis of residuals
D:Based on the regression of squared residuals on squared fitted values

0.25 as initial estimates for A0 and A1, we obtain the results shown in Table 13.1a.

It is generally advisable to carry out the iterations from different initial estimates to guard against the possibility of local optima. For the present application, we retried the computations using the initial values (1, 0.8), (3, 0.75), (5, 0.01), and (10, 0.95), and arrived at exactly the same estimates as above.

Suppose now that you are interested in estimating (13.1) by the non-linear 2-stage least squares (2SLS or NLS-IV) method, using $\{1, \log K_{t-1}, \log K_{t-2}, \log L_{t-1}$, and $\log L_{t-2}\}$ as instruments. First specify the non-linear equation using option 4 in the Single Equation Estimation Menu (Univariate Menu), and selecting the Nonlinear 2-stage Least Squares option. Use the NLS estimates of A0 and A1, namely 1.02 and 0.25, as initial estimates and, when prompted, type

INPT LK(−1), LK(−2) LL(−1) LL(−2) [OK]

**Table 13.1b:** Non-linear estimates of the Cobb–Douglas production function

Non-Linear Two-Stage Least Squares Estimation
The estimation method converged after 3 iterations

Non-linear regression formula:
Y = a0*(K^a1)*(L^(1−a1))
List of instruments:
INPT LK(−1) LK(−2) LL(−1) LL(−2)
22 observations used for estimation from 1901 to 1922

| Parameter | Estimate | Standard Error | T-Ratio[Prob] |
|---|---|---|---|
| A0 | 1.0114 | .033088 | 30.5684[.000] |
| A1 | .26253 | .056247 | 4.6674[.000] |

| | | | |
|---|---|---|---|
| R-Squared | .92682 | R-Bar-Squared | .92316 |
| GR-Squared | .36254 | GR-Bar-Squared | .33067 |
| S.E. of Regression | 11.2670 | F-Stat. F( 1, 20) | 253.2878[.000] |
| Mean of Dependent Variable | 171.8636 | S.D. of Dependent Variable | 40.6451 |
| Residual Sum of Squares | 2538.9 | Value of IV Minimand | 1454.7 |
| DW-statistic | 1.5378 | Sargan's CHSQ( 3) | 11.4596[.009] |

Diagnostic Tests

| Test Statistics | LM Version | F Version |
|---|---|---|
| A:Serial Correlation | CHSQ( 1)= .17498[.676] | Not applicable |
| B:Functional Form | CHSQ( 1)= .36454[.546] | Not applicable |
| C:Normality | CHSQ( 2)= 1.2578[.533] | Not applicable |
| D:Heteroscedasticity | CHSQ( 1)= 4.0354[.045] | Not applicable |

A:Lagrange multiplier test of residual serial correlation
B:Ramsey's RESET test using the square of the fitted values
C:Based on a test of skewness and kurtosis of residuals
D:Based on the regression of squared residuals on squared fitted values

You should see the results in Table 13.1b on the screen. In this example the NLS estimates in Table 13.1a, and the NLS-IV estimates in Table 13.1b are very similar.

## 13.2 Lesson 13.2: Estimation of Euler equations by the NLS-IV method

The non-linear instrumental variable option in *Microfit* can also be used to estimate the parameters of Euler equations obtained as first-order conditions of a representative agent's utility maximization problem under uncertainty. Typically, a Euler equation takes the form of

$$E\{H(\mathbf{x}_t, \gamma)|\boldsymbol{\Omega}_{t-1}\} = 0 \tag{13.2}$$

where $E(\cdot|\boldsymbol{\Omega}_{t-1})$. stands for conditional expectations, $\gamma$ is a $k \times 1$ vector of unknown parameters to be estimated, $\mathbf{x}_t$ is a vector of observable variables, and $\boldsymbol{\Omega}_{t-1}$ is the information known to the agent (but not necessarily to the econometrician) at time $t-1$ (see, for example, Hansen and Singleton 1983). As an example, consider the optimization problem of a representative consumer with a constant relative risk averse utility function who faces a consumption/investment decision in an uncertain environment. Assuming that only investment in stocks is being considered, the Euler equation for this optimization problem will be given by

$$u_t = \beta(\mathbf{x}_{1t})^{\sigma}\mathbf{x}_{2t} - 1 \tag{13.3}$$

where $E(u_t|\boldsymbol{\Omega}_{t-1}) = 0$, $\beta$ is the discount factor, $\sigma$ is the constant relative risk aversion parameter, $\mathbf{x}_{1t} = (c_{t-1}/c_t)$, and $\mathbf{x}_{2t}$ is the one-period real return on stocks (see, for example, Grossman and Shiller 1981, Hansen and Singleton 1983, and Pesaran 1991). On the assumption that the parameters of (13.2) are identified, the NLS-IV option in *Microfit* can be used to obtain consistent estimates of $\beta$ and $\sigma$ by defining $u_t$ to be a vector with all its elements set equal to zero, using $E(E(u_t|\Omega_{t-1})) = 0$ and then running the non-linear regression of $u_t$ on $\mathbf{x}_{1t}$ and $\mathbf{x}_{2t}$ as in (13.3). To implement this procedure proceed in the following manner:

1. First load the file HS.FIT into *Microfit*. This file covers monthly observations over the period 1959(3) to 1978(12) on the following variables:

   X1 = the ratio of consumption in time period t − 1 to consumption in time period *t*
   X2 = the one-period real return on stocks

   This is the corrected version of the data set used by Hansen and Singleton (1983).
2. In the Command Editor generate the variables

   INPT = 1;  U = 0  GO

3. From the Single Equation Estimation Menu (Univariate Menu) choose option 4, selecting Nonlinear 2-stage Least Squares. Type

$$U = b * (X1\hat{\ }s) * X2 - 1 \quad \boxed{\text{START}}$$

You will now be asked to give initial estimates for the unknown parameters $b$ and $s$. These correspond to the discount factor, $\beta$, and the risk aversion coefficient, $\sigma$. Try the initial values of 0.8 and 1 for these two parameters, respectively, and click [OK]. You need to list at least two instruments. You can try different lagged values of X1 and X2, and the unit vector (namely INPT in the variables list) as your instruments. If you choose the variables

INPT X1(−1) X2(−1) [OK]

as instruments, the results given in Table 13.2a should appear on the screen. The results seem to be robust to the choice of the initial parameter

**Table 13.2a:** Euler equation estimates of the Hansen–Singleton consumption-based asset pricing model

Non-Linear Two-Stage Least Squares Estimation
The estimation method converged after 4 iterations

Nonlinear regression formula:
u=b*(x1^s)*x2−1
List of instruments:
INPT X1(−1) X2(−1)
237 observations used for estimation from 1959M4 to 1978M12

| Parameter | Estimate | Standard Error | T-Ratio[Prob] |
|---|---|---|---|
| B | .99895 | .0049466 | 201.9465[.000] |
| S | .86474 | 2.0461 | .42263[.673] |

| | | | |
|---|---|---|---|
| R-Squared | *NONE* | R-Bar-Squared | *NONE* |
| GR-Squared | *NONE* | GR-Bar-Squared | *NONE* |
| S.E. of Regression | .041545 | F-Stat. F( 1, 235) | *NONE* |
| Mean of Dependent Variable | 0.00 | S.D. of Dependent Variable | 0.00 |
| Residual Sum of Squares | .40561 | Value of IV Minimand | .0027813 |
| DW-statistic | 1.8293 | Sargan's CHSQ( 1) | 1.6114[.204] |

Diagnostic Tests

| Test Statistics | LM Version | F Version |
|---|---|---|
| A:Serial Correlation | CHSQ( 12)= 14.5944[.264] | Not applicable |
| B:Functional Form | CHSQ( 1)= .049064[.825] | Not applicable |
| C:Normality | CHSQ( 2)= 10.6268[.005] | Not applicable |
| D:Heteroscedasticity | CHSQ( 1)= 237.0000[.000] | Not applicable |

A:Lagrange multiplier test of residual serial correlation
B:Ramsey's RESET test using the square of the fitted values
C:Based on a test of skewness and kurtosis of residuals
D:Based on the regression of squared residuals on squared fitted values

estimates, and yield the estimate 0.865 (2.046) for the risk aversion coefficient, which is very poorly estimated. In contrast, the discount factor, $\beta$, is estimated much more precisely.

*Notes*

1. The diagnostic and other summary statistics that follow the NLS-IV results for the estimation of the the Euler equation should be treated with caution. Given the way the non-linear regression (13.3) is set up, the functional form and the heteroscedasticity test statistics are not appropriate and should be ignored.
2. In the context of non-linear rational expectation models, the disturbances, $u_t$, need not be homoscedastic and are likely to be serially correlated if the observation horizon exceeds the decision horizon of the economic agent (see, for example, Chapter 7 in Pesaran 1987a). In these circumstances, the appropriate standard errors for the parameter estimates are given by White's or Newey and West's adjusted estimates. To compute these standard errors, first choose option 4 in the Post Regression menu (see Section 6.21), and then choose option 4 (Newey–West adjusted with Bartlett weights) in the Standard, White and Newey–West Adjusted Variance Menu that follows. When asked to specify the truncation point (or horizon) for the Bartlett window, type 12 and press ↵. The Newey–West adjusted variance matrix of ($\hat{\beta}$ and $\hat{\sigma}$) should appear on the screen. Click CLOSE and press ↵ to obtain the estimation results in Table 13.2b giving the GMM (generalized method of moments) estimates with Newey–West adjusted standard error using the Bartlett weights. The results in Table 13.2b are only marginally different from the estimates based on the unadjusted standard errors given in Table 13.2a.
3. The NLS-IV procedure applied to Euler equations also provides a simple method of implementing the GMM due to Hansen (1982). The possible effects of serial correlation and heteroscedasticity in $u_t$s on the standard

**Table 13.2b:** Euler equation estimates of the Hansen–Singleton consumption based asset pricing model

Non-Linear Two-Stage Least Squares Estimation
The estimation method converged after 1 iterations
Based on Newey–West adjusted S.E.'s Bartlett weights, truncation lag = 12

Nonlinear regression formula:
u = b*(x1^s)*x2 − 1
List of instruments:
INPT X1(−1) X2(−1)
237 observations used for estimation from 1959M4 to 1978M12

| Parameter | Estimate | Standard Error | T-Ratio[Prob] |
|---|---|---|---|
| B | .99895 | .0041580 | 240.2460[.000] |
| S | .86474 | 1.6366 | .52839[.598] |

errors can be dealt with using option 4 in the Post Regression Menu (see Note 2 above).

4. Sargan's general misspecification test statistic, described in Section 18.9.3, can also be computed for the present application and is given by $0.0027813/0.041545^2 = 1.61$, which should be compared with the critical value of a chi-squared variate with one degree of freedom (the difference between the number of instruments and the number of unknown parameters).

## 13.3 Lesson 13.3: Estimation of Almon distributed lag models

Suppose you are interested in estimating the following polynomial distributed lag model:

$$Y_t = \sigma + \sum_{i=0}^{m} w_i X_{t-i} + u_t \tag{13.4}$$

where the weights, $w_i$, are determined by polynomials of order $r$:

$$w_i = b_0 + b_1 i + b_2 i^2 + \cdots + b_r i^r \tag{13.5}$$

for $i = 0, 1, \ldots, m$. The above model is also known as the Almon distributed lag model, ALMON$(m, r)$ and in the case where $r < m$, it imposes $m - r$ restrictions on the lag coefficient $w_i$ (see for example Greene 1993, Chapter 18, and the original paper by Almon 1965). Here we show how to estimate such a model using *Microfit*.

There are two different ways of estimating the polynomial distributed lag model (13.5).

**Method A: using the BATCH command**

One possibility would be to construct the following weighted averages:

$$Z_{tj} = \sum_{i=0}^{m} i^j X_{t-i}, \quad j = 0, 1, \ldots, r \tag{13.6}$$

and then regress $Y_t$ on an intercept term and the variables $Z_{t0}$, $Z_{t1}$,, . . ., $Z_{tr}$. This would then yield the estimates of $a$, $b_0$, $b_1$, . . ., $b_r$. The construction of the Zs can be carried out in the Command Editor, preferably using the BATCH command on a previously prepared batch file.

**Method B: using the non-linear option**

Alternatively, one can estimate the Almon distributed lag model directly using the non-linear least squares option. You simply need to type the formula for the distributed lag model (13.4) in the screen editor box for the non-linear estimation option, substituting (13.5) for the weights $w_i$.

As an example, consider the estimation of a polynomial distributed lag model with $m = 8$ and $r = 3$, ALMON(8, 3), between appropriations (X), and capital expenditures (Y) for the US manufacturing sector. The relevant data are in the special *Microfit* file ALMON.FIT, and contain observations on Y and X over the period 1953(1) to 1967(4). This is an extended version of the data analysed originally by Almon (1965). The special *Microfit* file ALMON.FIT, and two other related files, namely ALMON83.BAT and ALMON83.EQU, should all be in the TUTORIAL directory.

**Method A**

First load the file ALMON.FIT into *Microfit*. To implement method A, in the Command Editor run the batch file ALMON83.BAT by typing

**BATCH** ALMON83 [GO]

This creates the variables Z0, Z1, Z2, and Z3 defined by (13.6). Now run a linear regression of Y on an intercept term and the variables Z0, Z1, Z2, and

**Table 13.3a:** Estimation of the Almon distributed lag model using constructed variables (method A)

Ordinary Least Squares Estimation

Dependent variable is Y
52 observations used for estimation from 1955Q1 to 1967Q4

| Regressor | Coefficient | Standard Error | T-Ratio[Prob] |
|---|---|---|---|
| INPT | 62.3626 | 57.4400 | 1.0857[.283] |
| Z0 | .051777 | .030495 | 1.6979[.096] |
| Z1 | .11843 | .051512 | 2.2991[.026] |
| Z2 | −.033676 | .016538 | −2.0363[.047] |
| Z3 | .0023995 | .0013856 | 1.7318[.090] |

| | | | |
|---|---|---|---|
| R-Squared | .98924 | R-Bar-Squared | .98832 |
| S.E. of Regression | 124.8792 | F-Stat. F( 4, 47) | 1080.1[.000] |
| Mean of Dependent Variable | 3253.9 | S.D. of Dependent Variable | 1155.6 |
| Residual Sum of Squares | 732955.9 | Equation Log-likelihood | −322.1783 |
| Akaike Info. Criterion | −327.1783 | Schwarz Bayesian Criterion | −332.0564 |
| DW-statistic | .45710 | | |

Diagnostic Tests

| Test Statistics | LM Version | F Version |
|---|---|---|
| A:Serial Correlation | CHSQ( 4)= 32.8237[.000] | F( 4, 43)= 18.4005[.000] |
| B:Functional Form | CHSQ( 1)= .031975[.858] | F( 1, 46)= .028303[.867] |
| C:Normality | CHSQ( 2)= 8.7992[.012] | Not applicable |
| D:Heteroscedasticity | CHSQ( 1)= .011755[.914] | F( 1, 50)= .011305[.916] |

A:Lagrange multiplier test of residual serial correlation
B:Ramsey's RESET test using the square of the fitted values
C:Based on a test of skewness and kurtosis of residuals
D:Based on the regression of squared residuals on squared fitted values

Z3. To do this, you need to select option 1 from the Single Equation Estimation Menu (Univariate Menu), choosing the OLS option. Type

Y INPT Z0 Z1 Z2 Z3 [START]

The results in Table 13.3a should now appear on the screen. The estimates of $b_0$, $b_1$, $b_2$, and $b_3$ are given by the coefficients of Z0, Z1, Z2, and Z3, respectively. Notice, however, that the very low value obtained for the DW static suggests the possibility of a serious dynamic misspecification.

**Method B**

The same results can be obtained using the non-linear option. Choose option 4 in the Single Equation Estimation Menu (Univariate Menu), selecting the Nonlinear Least Squares option. In the box editor, retrieve the equation file ALMON83.EQU using the button, and then selecting the file. This gives the equation for the estimation of the Almon distributed lag model between X and Y with $m = 8$ and $r = 3$. Click [START] to accept the equation. You will now be prompted to specify the initial parameter estimates. Since the equation is inherently linear in the unknown parameters, click [OK] to accept the default values of zeros for the initial estimates. The results of the non-linear estimation are reproduced in Table 13.3b.

## 13.4 Lesson 13.4: Estimation of a non-linear Phillips curve

Phillips (1958) estimated his famous curve, a non-linear relationship between the rate of growth of wages and unemployment, graphically from pre-World War I UK data. In this lesson we estimate the same curve on the same data using econometric methods.

The file PHILLIPS.FIT contains annual aggregate UK data for the years 1855 to 1987 (inclusive) on the following five variables:[1]

E = Logarithm of employment
N = Logarithm of labour force
Y = Logarithm of real GDP
P = Logarithm of a price index
W = Logarithm of a nominal wage index

Load this file and in the Command Editor create an intercept, C, the rate of growth of money wages, DW, and the (log) unemployment rate, U, and then graphically examine the pre-World War I Phillips Curve by typing:

C = 1; DW = W − W(−1); U = N − E;

**SAMPLE** 1861 1913; **SCATTER** DW U [GO]

[1]The background to the estimation of the Phillips curve is discussed in Alogoskoufis and Smith (1991b). It should also be remembered that there are likely to be substantial measurement errors in such historical data.

**Table 13.3b:** Estimation of the Almon distributed lag model by non-linear estimation (method B)

Non-Linear Least Squares Estimation
The estimation method converged after 2 iterations

Nonlinear regression formula:
Y = a + b0*x + (b0 + b1 + b2 + b3)*x(−1) + (b0 + 2*b1 + 4*b2 + 8*b3)*x(−2) + (b0 + 3*b1 + 9*b2 + 27*b3)*x(−3) + (b0 + 4*b1 + 16*b2 + 64*b3)*x(−4) + (b0 + 5*b1 + 25*b2 + 125*b3)*x(−5) + (b0 + 6*b1 + 36*b2 + 26*b3)*x(−6) + (b0 + 7*b1 + 49*b2 + 343*b3)*x(−7) + (b0 + 8*b1 + 64*b2 + 512*b3)*x(−8)
52 observations used for estimation from 1955Q1 to 1967Q4

| Parameter | Estimate | Standard Error | T-Ratio[Prob] |
|---|---|---|---|
| A | 62.3626 | 57.4400 | 1.0857[.283] |
| B0 | .051777 | .030495 | 1.6979[.096] |
| B1 | .11843 | .051512 | 2.2991[.026] |
| B2 | −.033676 | .016538 | −2.0363[.047] |
| B3 | .0023995 | .0013856 | 1.7318[.090] |

| | | | |
|---|---|---|---|
| R-Squared | .98924 | R-Bar-Squared | .98832 |
| S.E. of Regression | 124.8792 | F-Stat. F( 4, 47) | 1080.1[.000] |
| Mean of Dependent Variable | 3253.9 | S.D. of Dependent Variable | 1155.6 |
| Residual Sum of Squares | 732955.9 | Equation Log-likelihood | −322.1783 |
| Akaike Info. Criterion | −327.1783 | Schwarz Bayesian Criterion | −332.0564 |
| DW-statistic | .45710 | | |

Diagnostic Tests

| Test Statistics | LM Version | F Version |
|---|---|---|
| A:Serial Correlation | CHSQ( 4) = 32.8237[.000] | F( 4, 43) = 18.4005[.000] |
| B:Functional Form | CHSQ( 1) = .031975[.858] | F( 1, 46) = .028303[.867] |
| C:Normality | CHSQ( 2) = 8.7992[.012] | Not applicable |
| D:Heteroscedasticity | CHSQ( 1) = .011755[.914] | F( 1, 50) = .011305[.916] |

A:Lagrange multiplier test of residual serial correlation
B:Ramsey's RESET test using the square of the fitted values
C:Based on a test of skewness and kurtosis of residuals
D:Based on the regression of squared residuals on squared fitted values

The scatter diagram associated with the original Phillips curve is given in Figure 13.1. Although the fit is not very close, there is clearly a negative relationship between DW and U, with some evidence of non-linearity: at high rates of unemployment the effect on wage growth is much smaller than at low rates of unemployment. Using averages of data for 1861 to 1913, Phillips obtained estimates of a curve of the form:

$$DW_t = a_1 + a_2 U_t^{a_3} + \xi_t \tag{13.7}$$

where $\xi_t$ represents an error term. His estimate of $a_3$ was $-1.4$, close to a linear relationship between wage growth and the *reciprocal* of the unemployment rate.

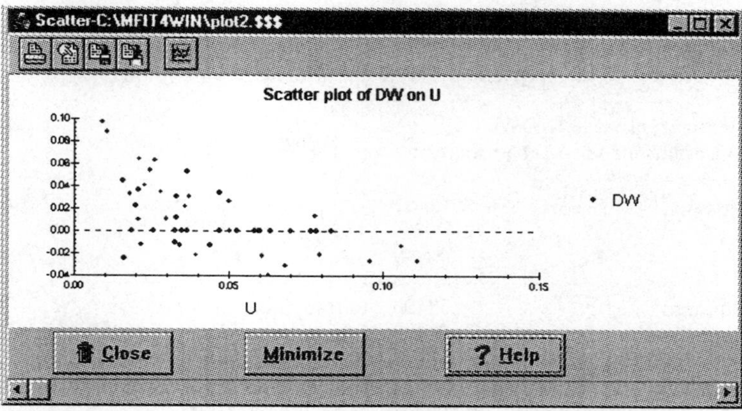


**Figure 13.1:** Scatter of changes in money wages against the unemployment rate 1861 to 1913

To evaluate the importance of non-linearity in the Phillips curve, we first estimate two linear relationships: one between the wage growth and the level of the unemployment variable, and the other between the wage growth and the reciprocal of the unemployment variable. We can use these estimates to obtain initial values for the non-linear estimation of (13.7) which we shall be carrying out subsequently. Close the scatter plot and click [icon] to clear the content of the Command Editor and type

**SAMPLE** 1855 1987; RU = 1/U [GO]

This creates the inverse of the unemployment rate in RU. Choose option 1 from the Single Equation Estimation Menu (Univariate Menu), making sure that the OLS option is selected. Specify the equation as: DW C U and click [START]. Set the sample from 1861 to 1913. You should get the results in Table 13.4a. The unemployment rate is statistically highly significant with a negative coefficient, but the failure of the functional form and heteroscedasticity tests suggests that there may be important non-linearities in the relationship. For a comparison of this linear specification with the non-linear ones to be estimated below, also note that $\bar{R}^2$, AIC, and SBC for this regression are given by 0.321, 121.35, and 119.38, respectively.

Click [CLOSE] to move to the Post Regression Menu, and then backtrack and edit the regression equation to

DW C RU [START]

Estimating this equation by the OLS method over the same sample period (1861 to 1913) yields the results in Table 13.4b.

Note that the functional form and heteroscedasticity tests are now acceptable and the equation is preferred on the basis of all the three model selection criteria. The values of $\bar{R}^2$, AIC, and SBC, for this specification are 0.449, 126.88, and 124.91, respectively.

Now backtrack to the Single Equation Estimation Menu and choose the

**Table 13.4a:** OLS estimates of a linear Phillips curve

Ordinary Least Squares Estimation

Dependent variable is DW
53 observations used for estimation from 1861 to 1913

| Regressor | Coefficient | Standard Error | T-Ratio[Prob] |
|---|---|---|---|
| C | .041152 | .0069416 | 5.9284[.000] |
| U | −.68564 | .13556 | −5.0580[.000] |

| | | | |
|---|---|---|---|
| R-Squared | .33406 | R-Bar-Squared | .32100 |
| S.E. of Regression | .024063 | F-Stat. F( 1, 51) | 25.5831[.000] |
| Mean of Dependent Variable | .010278 | S.D. of Dependent Variable | .029202 |
| Residual Sum of Squares | .029531 | Equation Log-likelihood | 123.3507 |
| Akaike Info. Criterion | 121.3507 | Schwarz Bayesian Criterion | 119.3804 |
| DW-statistic | 1.5404 | | |

Diagnostic Tests

| Test Statistics | LM Version | F Version |
|---|---|---|
| A:Serial Correlation | CHSQ( 1)= 2.6976[.101] | F( 1, 50)= 2.6814[.108] |
| B:Functional Form | CHSQ( 1)= 4.0615[.044] | F( 1, 50)= 4.1496[.047] |
| C:Normality | CHSQ( 2)= .59581[.742] | Not applicable |
| D:Heteroscedasticity | CHSQ( 1)= 11.6186[.001] | F( 1, 51)= 14.3193[.000] |
| E:Predictive Failure | CHSQ( 74)= 766.3090[.000] | F( 74, 51)= 10.3555[.000] |
| F:Chow Test | CHSQ( 2)= 38.0303[.000] | F( 2, 123)= 19.0151[.000] |

A:Lagrange multiplier test of residual serial correlation
B:Ramsey's RESET test using the square of the fitted values
C:Based on a test of skewness and kurtosis of residuals
D:Based on the regression of squared residuals on squared fitted values
E:A test of adequacy of predictions (Chow's second test)
F:Test of stability of the regression coefficients

Non-linear Regression option 4, selecting the Nonlinear Least Squares option. Type

DW = A1 + A2 * U ^ A3

and set the sample from 1861 to 1913. Click START. For the initial values of A1, A2, and, A3, choose 0.1, 0.1, and −1, respectively. Click OK. You should get the results in Table 13.4c.

The estimate of $a_3$ is very close to, and not significantly different from, −1, though $a_2$ is not significantly different from zero. Such mixed results do arise in non-linear estimation and special care needs to be taken in interpreting them. First, if $a_2 = 0$, then $a_3$ is not identified. We would also expect a high covariance between the two estimates. For instance, given the negative relationship between DW and U, if $a_3$ is positive, $a_2$ will be negative and vice versa. Comparing the results to the regression using RU above, where $a_3$ is set to −1, we see that the reciprocal formulation is preferred by all the three model selection criteria, and has a much sharper estimate of $a_2$.

**Table 13.4b:** OLS estimates of a non-linear Phillips curve

Ordinary Least Squares Estimation

Dependent variable is DW
53 observations used for estimation from 1861 to 1913

| Regressor | Coefficient | Standard Error | T-Ratio[Prob] |
|---|---|---|---|
| C | −.020083 | .0054899 | −3.6582[.001] |
| RU | .9873E-3 | .1500E-3 | 6.5831[.000] |

| | | | |
|---|---|---|---|
| R-Squared | .45939 | R-Bar-Squared | .44879 |
| S.E. of Regression | .021681 | F-Stat. F( 1, 51) | 43.3377[.000] |
| Mean of Dependent Variable | .010278 | S.D. of Dependent Variable | .029202 |
| Residual Sum of Squares | .023973 | Equation Log-likelihood | 128.8761 |
| Akaike Info. Criterion | 126.8761 | Schwarz Bayesian Criterion | 124.9058 |
| DW-statistic | 1.7224 | | |

Diagnostic Tests

| Test Statistics | LM Version | F Version |
|---|---|---|
| A:Serial Correlation | CHSQ( 1)= .96053[.327] | F( 1, 50)= .92289[.341] |
| B:Functional Form | CHSQ( 1)= .10424[.747] | F( 1, 50)= .098535[.755] |
| C:Normality | CHSQ( 2)= 1.2645[.531] | Not applicable |
| D:Heteroscedasticity | CHSQ( 1)= .14444[.704] | F( 1, 51)= .13937[.710] |
| E:Predictive Failure | CHSQ( 74)= 986.3012[.000] | F( 74, 51)= 13.3284[.000] |
| F:Chow Test | CHSQ( 2)= 24.9302[.000] | F( 2, 123)= 12.4651[.000] |

A:Lagrange multiplier test of residual serial correlation
B:Ramsey's RESET test using the square of the fitted values
C:Based on a test of skewness and kurtosis of residuals
D:Based on the regression of squared residuals on squared fitted values
E:A test of adequacy of predictions (Chow's second test)
F:Test of stability of the regression coefficients

## 13.5 Lesson 13.5: Estimation of a non-linear Phillips curve with serially correlated errors

The non-linear option is very flexible and can be used to estimate linear regression models subject to linear and/or non-linear parametric restrictions, or to estimate non-linear models with serially correlated errors. Suppose that we wished to estimate the Phillips equation defined by (13.7) subject to a first-order autoregressive error process

$$DW_t = a_1 + a_2 U_t^{a_3} + \xi_t$$

where

$$\xi_t = \rho\xi_{t-1} + \epsilon_t, \qquad \epsilon_t \sim iid(0, \sigma^2)$$

We first note that the above relations can also be written as

**Table 13.4c:** Phillips curve estimated by non-linear least squares

Non-Linear Least Squares Estimation
The estimation method converged after 6 iterations

Nonlinear regression formula:
DW=A1+A2*U^A3
53 observations used for estimation from 1861 to 1913

| Parameter | Estimate | Standard Error | T-Ratio[Prob] |
|---|---|---|---|
| A1 | −.020325 | .016049 | −1.2665[.211] |
| A2 | .0010202 | .0020655 | .49391[.624] |
| A3 | −.99311 | .47045 | −2.1110[.040] |

| | | | |
|---|---|---|---|
| R-Squared | .45939 | R-Bar-Squared | .43777 |
| S.E. of Regression | .021896 | F-Stat. F( 2, 50) | 21.2441[.000] |
| Mean of Dependent Variable | .010278 | S.D. of Dependent Variable | .029202 |
| Residual Sum of Squares | .023973 | Equation Log-likelihood | 128.8762 |
| Akaike Info. Criterion | 125.8762 | Schwarz Bayesian Criterion | 122.9207 |
| DW-statistic | 1.7227 | | |

Diagnostic Tests

| Test Statistics | LM Version | F Version |
|---|---|---|
| A:Serial Correlation | CHSQ( 1)= .96172[.327] | F( 1, 49)= .90557[.346] |
| B:Functional Form | CHSQ( 1)= 3.5802[.058] | F( 1, 49)= 3.5498[.065] |
| C:Normality | CHSQ( 2)= 1.2727[.529] | Not applicable |
| D:Heteroscedasticity | CHSQ( 1)= .15415[.695] | F( 1, 51)= .14876[.701] |

A:Lagrange multiplier test of residual serial correlation
B:Ramsey's RESET test using the square of the fitted values
C:Based on a test of skewness and kurtosis of residuals
D:Based on the regression of squared residuals on squared fitted values

$$DW_t = a_1 + a_2 U_t^{a_3} + \rho(DW_{t-1} - a_1 - a_2 U_{t-1}^{a_3}) + \epsilon_t$$

which is another, albeit more complicated, non-linear equation. To estimate this model using Phillips' original data set, first read the file PHILLIPS.FIT. Then follow the steps in Lesson 13.4 to create the rate of growth of money wages in DW and the logarithm of the rate of unemployment in U. Choose option 4 in the Single Equation Estimation Menu (Univariate Menu), selecting Nonlinear Least Squares, and type

DW = A1 + A2 * U ^ A3 + A4 * (DW(−1) − A1 − A2 * U(−1) ^ A3)

Select 1861 to 1913 as the sample period and click START. For the initial values of A1, A2, A3, and A4, choose 0.1, 0.1, −1.0, and 0.0, respectively, then click OK. You should see the results in Table 13.5 on the screen. The estimate of $\rho$, denoted by A4 in Table 13.5, is not significantly different from zero, and is in line with the diagnostic test results obtained in Lesson 13.4.

**Table 13.5:** Estimates of Phillips curve with AR(1) serially correlated residuals

Non-Linear Least Squares Estimation
The estimation method converged after 9 iterations

Nonlinear regression formula:
DW=A1+A2*U^A3+A4*(DW(-1)-A1-A2*U(-1)^A3)
53 observations used for estimation from 1861 to 1913

| Parameter | Estimate | Standard Error | T-Ratio[Prob] |
|---|---|---|---|
| A1 | -.018585 | .015696 | -1.1841[.242] |
| A2 | .7996E-3 | .0017130 | .46680[.643] |
| A3 | -1.0444 | .51522 | -2.0271[.048] |
| A4 | .11842 | .14609 | .81062[.422] |

| | | | |
|---|---|---|---|
| R-Squared | .46940 | R-Bar-Squared | .43691 |
| S.E. of Regression | .021913 | F-Stat. F( 3, 49) | 14.4494[.000] |
| Mean of Dependent Variable | .010278 | S.D. of Dependent Variable | .029202 |
| Residual Sum of Squares | .023529 | Equation Log-likelihood | 129.3714 |
| Akaike Info. Criterion | 125.3714 | Schwarz Bayesian Criterion | 121.4308 |
| DW-statistic | 1.9403 | | |

Diagnostic Tests

| Test Statistics | LM Version | F Version |
|---|---|---|
| A:Serial Correlation | CHSQ( 1)= .87106[.351] | F( 1, 48)= .80206[.375] |
| B:Functional Form | CHSQ( 1)= .4156E-4[.995] | F( 1, 48)= .3764E-4[.995] |
| C:Normality | CHSQ( 2)= 1.9032[.386] | Not applicable |
| D:Heteroscedasticity | CHSQ( 1)= .16699[.683] | F( 1, 51)= .16119[.690] |

A:Lagrange multiplier test of residual serial correlation
B:Ramsey's RESET test using the square of the fitted values
C:Based on a test of skewness and kurtosis of residuals
D:Based on the regression of squared residuals on squared fitted values

## 13.6 Exercises in non-linear estimation

### 13.6.1 Exercise 13.1

Use the data in the special *Microfit* file CD.FIT to estimate the Cobb–Douglas production function

$$Y_t = AK_t^{\alpha} L_t^{\beta} + u_t$$

Use option 7 in the Hypothesis Testing Menu (see Section 6.24) to test the constant returns to scale restriction $\alpha + \beta = 1$. Compare your results with those in Table 13.1a.

### 13.6.2 Exercise 13.2

Estimate the Euler equation (13.3) in Lesson 13.2 by the non-linear least squares method and compare your results with those in Table 13.2a.

### 13.6.3 Exercise 13.3

Re-estimate the Phillips curve in Lesson 13.4 over the entire sample period and the sub-periods 1954 to 1969 and 1970 to 1987, allowing for the possible effects of current and past changes in inflation and unemployment on changes in money wages. Compare your results with those obtained by Phillips (1958).

### 13.6.4 Exercise 13.4

Use the quarterly observations on US real GNP (USGNP) in the file GDP95.FIT to estimate the following non-linear autoregressive model, known as the threshold autoregressive (TAR) model

$$\begin{aligned} y_t = a_{01} + a_{01} * I(y_{t-2} - b) + \\ a_{11} * y_{t-1} + a_{11} * y_{t-1} * I(y_{t-2} - b) \end{aligned} \quad (1)$$

where $y_t = \log(\text{USGNP}/\text{USGNP}(-1))$ and $I(y_{t-2} - b)$ represent the indicator (or sign) function such that it is equal to unity when $y_{t-2} > b$ and zero otherwise. You may find it easier to estimate the model for different values of the threshold parameter, $b$. Note that the sample mean of $y_t$ is 0.0072, which corresponds to an annual average growth rate of 2.9 per cent.

For a discussion of this class of models, see Tong (1990). For an application to US output, see Potter (1995).

# 14

# Lessons in Logit and Probit Estimation

The lessons in this section demonstrate the Logit/Probit options described in Section 6.20.

## 14.1 Lesson 14.1: Modelling the choice of fertilizer use by Philippine farmers

The file PHIL.FIT contains observations on fertilizer use by 491 small farmers in the Philippines together with five explanatory variables. The dependent variable to be explained is FERUSE, a binary variable equal to one if fertilizer is used, and equal to zero otherwise. The explanatory variables are:

| | |
|---|---|
| CREDIT | The amount of credit (per hectares) held by the farmer |
| DMARKET | The distance of the farm from the nearest market |
| HOURMEET | Number of hours the farmer spent with an agricultural 'expert' |
| IRSTAT | A binary variable equal to 1 if irrigation is used, 0 otherwise |
| OWNER | A binary variable equal to 1 if the farmer owns the land, 0 otherwise |
| ONE | 1 |

The appropriate probability model for explaining the binary choice variable FERUSE is defined by

$$\Pr(\text{FERUSE}_i = 1) = F(\beta' \mathbf{x}_i), \quad i = 1, 2, \ldots, 491$$

where $\mathbf{x}_i$ is a $6 \times 1$ vector of the regressors for the $i$-th farmer. The program allows you to compute ML estimates of $\beta$ both when $F(\cdot)$ is the cumulative distribution function of the standard normal (the Probit model) and when it has the logistic form (the Logit model): see Sections 6.20 and 18.20 for further details.

Load the *Microfit* file PHIL.FIT and choose option 7 in the Single Equation Estimation Menu (Univariate Menu: see Section 6.4). List the dependent variable FERUSE followed by the explanatory variables in the editor:

FERUSE ONE CREDIT DMARKET HOURMEET IRSTAT OWNER

**Table 14.1a** Probability of fertilizer use by Philippine farmers Logit maximum likelihood estimation

The estimation method converged after 6 iterations

Dependent variable is FERUSE
450 observations used for estimation from 1 to 450

| Regressor | Coefficient | Standard Error | T-Ratio [Prob] |
|---|---|---|---|
| ONE | −1.5111 | .23152 | −6.5270[.000] |
| CREDIT | .2720E−3 | .1330E−3 | 2.0453[.041] |
| DMARKET | −.026518 | .021826 | −1.2149[.225] |
| HOURMEET | .033875 | .016509 | 2.0519[.041] |
| IRSTAT | 1.7645 | .2230 | 7.9021[.000] |
| OWNER | .48739 | .22475 | 2.1686[.031] |

Factor for the calculation of marginal effects = .24416
Maximized value of the log-likelihood function = −252.5396
Akaike Information Criterion = −258.5396
Schwarz Bayesian Criterion = −270.8673
Hannan–Quinn Criterion = −263.3984
Mean of FERUSE = .42889
Mean of fitted FERUSE = .50667
Goodness of fit = .71778
Pesaran–Timmermann test statistic = −7.3977[.000]
Pseudo-R-Squared = .17833

For the estimation sample enter 1 and 450 into the start and end fields, thus keeping the remaining 41 observations for forecasting. Click START. You should now see the Logit/Probit Estimation Menu on the screen. Choose option 1; the Logit option. The results in Table 14.1a should appear on the screen.

Similar results are also obtained using the Probit option. See Table 14.1b. Although the maximized value of the log-likelihood function is slightly larger for the Logit model, the two models fit the data equally well. The goodness of fit measure, computed as the proportion of observations with correctly predicted values of FERUSE, and the associated Pesaran–Timmermann test statistic are the same for both models. In what follows we focus on the Logit estimates.

The estimated coefficients have the expected signs, with the variables CREDIT, HOURMEET, IRSTAT, and OWNER having a positive effect, and the DMARKET variable (the distance of the farm from the nearest market) having a negative effect on the probability of the fertilizer use.[1]

To estimate the marginal effect of a unit change in, say, the CREDIT variable, computed at sample means on the probability of the fertilizer use, you must multiply the factor 0.24416 given in the second part of Table 14.1a

[1] Notice that the magnitudes of the coefficients reported for the Logit and the Probit models in Tables 14.1a and 14.1b, respectively are not comparable. To make them comparable, the coefficients estimated under the Probit option must be multiplied by 1.814.

**Table 14.1b:** Probability of fertilizer use by Philippine farmers Probit maximum likelihood estimation

The estimation method converged after 6 iterations

Dependent variable is FERUSE
450 observations used for estimation from 1 to 450

| Regressor | Coefficient | Standard Error | T-Ratio [Prob] |
|---|---|---|---|
| ONE | −.91034 | .13245 | −6.8733[.000] |
| CREDIT | .1522E−3 | .7652E−4 | 1.9893[.047] |
| DMARKET | −.014658 | .012261 | −1.1955[.233] |
| HOURMEET | .018227 | .0089651 | 2.0332[.043] |
| IRSTAT | 1.0770 | .13225 | 8.1440[.000] |
| OWNER | .28423 | .13323 | 2.1334[.033] |

Factor for the calculation of marginal effects = .39184
Maximized value of the log-likelihood function = −252.8353
Akaike Information Criterion = −258.8353
Schwarz Bayesian Criterion = −271.1631
Hannan–Quinn Criterion = −263.6942
Mean of FERUSE = .42889
Mean of fitted FERUSE = .50667
Goodness of fit = .71778
Pesaran–Timmermann test statistic = −7.3977[.000]
Pseudo-R-Squared = .17737

by the coefficient of CREDIT, using $0.24416 \times 0.00272 = 0.00066$ (see Section 6.20.2). Similarly, the marginal effect of the DMARKET variable on the probability of fertilizer use (evaluated at sample means) is given by $0.24416 \times (-0.026518) = -0.0065$.

The standard errors reported in Tables 14.1a and 14.1b allow you to carry out tests on the individual coefficients in $\beta$. To implement joint linear/nonlinear tests on these coefficients, you need to choose option 5 (Wald test of linear/nonlinear restrictions) in the Post Estimation Menu (Logit model). Suppose you wish to test the joint hypothesis that coefficients of the CREDIT and DMARKET variables are zero. Type

A2 = 0;   A3 = 0   [OK]

The result of the test is given in Table 14.1c, and the value of the Wald statistic for this test is equal to 5.1871, which is below the critical value of the $\chi^2$ distribution with two degrees of freedom at the 95 percent level.

A plot of actual values and fitted probabilities for the Logit specification is given in Figure 14.1.

### 14.1.1 Forecasting with Logit/Probit models

Forecasts of the probability of fertilizer use for the remaining 41 farmers in the sample can be computed using option 7 in the Logit Post Estimation

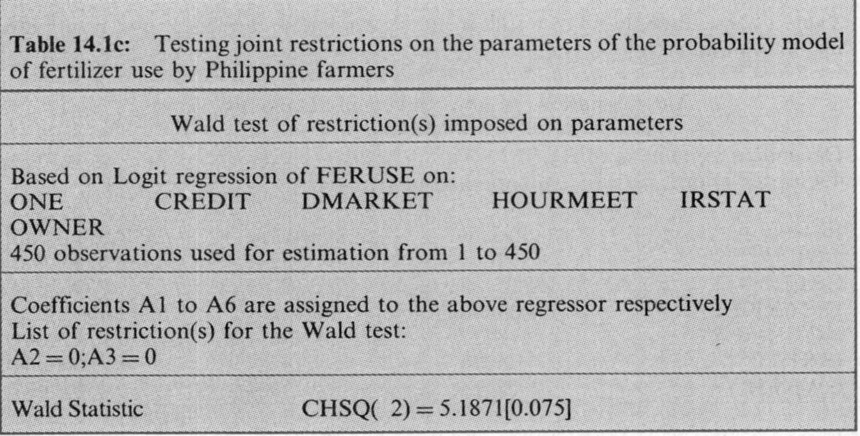

**Table 14.1c:** Testing joint restrictions on the parameters of the probability model of fertilizer use by Philippine farmers

Wald test of restriction(s) imposed on parameters

Based on Logit regression of FERUSE on:
ONE CREDIT DMARKET HOURMEET IRSTAT
OWNER
450 observations used for estimation from 1 to 450

Coefficients A1 to A6 are assigned to the above regressor respectively
List of restriction(s) for the Wald test:
A2 = 0;A3 = 0

| Wald Statistic | CHSQ( 2) = 5.1871[0.075] |
|---|---|

Menu (see Section 6.20.4). When you choose this option you will be asked to choose the forecast sample. Press ↵ to select all the remaining farmers in the sample. You will now be presented with the results in Table 14.1d.

The second part of this table gives a number of summary statistics for the estimation and the prediction samples. As is to be expected, the fitted values match the actual observations much better over the estimation sample as compared to the prediction sample. The Pesaran–Timmermann statistic is equal to −2.20 over the forecast sample which is still statistically significant, but much less so than over the estimation sample.

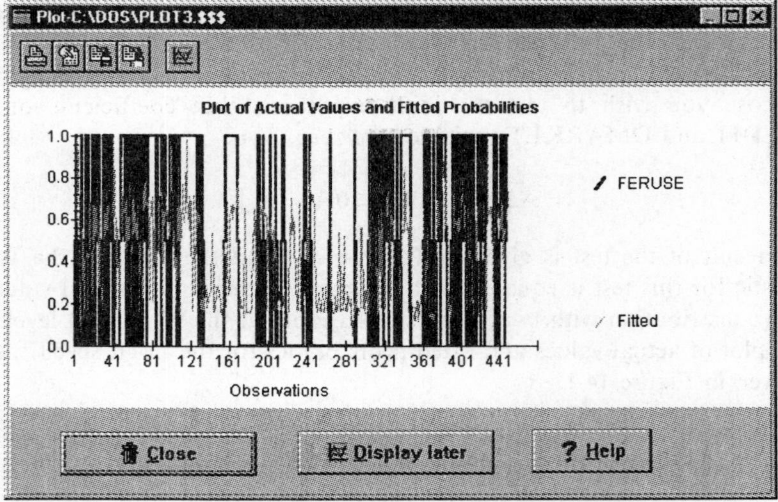


**Figure 14.1** Actual values of FERUSE and the fitted probabilities for the Logit specification

**Table 14.1d** Forecasting the probability of fertilizer use by Philippine farmers

Actual and Forecast Values of Regression

Based on Logit regression of FERUSE on:
ONE CREDIT DMARKET HOURMEET IRSTAT OWNER
450 observations used for estimation from 1 to 450

| Observation | Actual | Predicted Probability | Predicted |
|---|---|---|---|
| 451 | 1.0000 | .67313 | 1.0000 |
| 452 | 1.0000 | .79683 | 1.0000 |
| 453 | 1.0000 | .92595 | 1.0000 |
| 454 | 1.0000 | .17116 | 0.00 |
| 455 | 0.00 | .27194 | 0.00 |
| 456 | 1.0000 | .66279 | 1.0000 |
| 457 | 1.0000 | .59973 | 1.0000 |
| 458 | 1.0000 | .92810 | 1.0000 |
| 459 | 1.0000 | .76485 | 1.0000 |
| 460 | 0.00 | .57036 | 1.0000 |
| 461 | 0.00 | .16929 | 0.00 |
| 462 | 1.0000 | .63879 | 1.0000 |
| 463 | 1.0000 | .27300 | 0.00 |
| 464 | 1.0000 | .73589 | 1.0000 |
| 465 | 1.0000 | .63212 | 1.0000 |
| 466 | 0.00 | .59318 | 1.0000 |
| 467 | 0.00 | .70850 | 1.0000 |
| 468 | 1.0000 | .71838 | 1.0000 |
| 469 | 1.0000 | .56605 | 1.0000 |
| 470 | 0.00 | .55321 | 1.0000 |
| 471 | 1.0000 | .67297 | 1.0000 |
| 472 | 0.00 | .65805 | 1.0000 |
| 473 | 1.0000 | .25842 | 0.00 |
| 474 | 1.0000 | .17180 | 0.00 |
| 475 | 1.0000 | .26025 | 0.00 |
| 476 | 1.0000 | .28074 | 0.00 |
| 477 | 1.0000 | .40079 | 0.00 |
| 478 | 1.0000 | .34445 | 0.00 |
| 479 | 1.0000 | .64146 | 1.0000 |
| 480 | 1.0000 | .25012 | 0.00 |
| 481 | 1.0000 | .63523 | 1.0000 |
| 482 | 1.0000 | .25162 | 0.00 |
| 483 | 1.0000 | .18879 | 0.00 |
| 484 | 1.0000 | .17630 | 0.00 |
| 485 | 1.0000 | .19336 | 0.00 |
| 486 | 1.0000 | .22671 | 0.00 |
| 487 | 1.0000 | .19940 | 0.00 |
| 488 | 0.00 | .60793 | 1.0000 |
| 489 | 1.0000 | .23203 | 0.00 |
| 490 | 1.0000 | .19978 | 0.00 |
| 491 | 0.00 | .18909 | 0.00 |

Summary Statistics for Residuals and Prediction Errors

| | Estimation Period 1 to 450 | Forecast Period 451 to 491 |
|---|---|---|
| Mean of FERUSE | .42889 | .78049 |
| Mean of predicted FERUSE | .50667 | .51220 |
| Goodness of fit | .71778 | .43902 |
| Pesaran–Timmermann Stat. | −7.3977[.000] | −2.2088[0.027] |

## 14.2 Lesson14.2: Fertilizer use model estimated over a sub-sample of farmers

*Microfit* allows you to estimate regression or Logit/Probit models over a sub-sample of observations selected according to a particular set of criteria. For example, suppose you wish to estimate the probability of fertilizer use only over the sample of farmers who use irrigation and own their own farms. Move to the Command Editor and generate the variable

$$X = 1 - \text{sign(IRSTAT)} * \text{sign(OWNER)} \quad \boxed{\text{GO}}$$

It is clear that

X = 0 if IRSTAT = 1 and OWNER = 1

X = 1 if either IRSTAT or OWNER is equal to zero

Now reorder the observations so that all farmers who own their farms and use irrigation are put at the top of the variables list. This can be done using the REORDER command (see Section 4.4.11):

**REORDER** X; N = Sum(1 − X) [GO]

The number of farmers who own their farms and use irrigation is given by N. (In the present example N=96.) The first 96 observations of the reordered data set represent the observations on farmers who own their land and use irrigation. To see that this is in fact the case use the LIST (see Section 4.4.9) command to list the observations.[2]

To estimate the Logit model for this sub-sample of farmers, move to the Single Equation Estimation window, making sure option 7 is selected from the Univariate Menu, and type

feruse one credit dmarket hourmeet

Enter 1 and 96 into the start and end fields, and click [START]. Press ↩ or [OK] to choose the Logit model. The results in Table 14.2 should now appear on the screen.

For this sub-sample only the credit variable is significant. However, the Pesaran–Timmermann statistic is equal to 0.55 and does not reject the hypothesis that the fitted and actual values for this sub-sample are not related.

---

[2] Note that you can use the RESTORE command to restore the original ordering of your observations: see Section 4.4.12

**Table 14.2** Probability of fertilizer use by a sub-sample of Philippine farmers owning their farms and using irrigation

Logit Maximum Likelihood Estimation
The estimation method converged after 6 iterations

Dependent variable is FERUSE
96 observations used for estimation from 1 to 96

| Regressor | Coefficient | Standard Error | T-Ratio[Prob] |
|---|---|---|---|
| ONE | .86021 | .38301 | 2.2459[.027] |
| CREDIT | .0020980 | .9248E−3 | 2.2686[.026] |
| DMARKET | −.077630 | .066965 | −1.1593[.249] |
| HOURMEET | .015895 | .022009 | .72222[.472] |

Factor for the calculation of marginal effects = .15999
Maximized value of the log-likelihood function = −49.8423
Akaike Information Criterion = −53.8423
Schwarz Bayesian Criterion = −58.9710
Hannan–Quinn Criterion = −55.9154
Mean of FERUSE = .73958
Mean of fitted FERUSE = .98958
Goodness of fit = .75000
Pesaran–Timmermann test statistic = .55167[.581]
Pseudo-R-Squared = .094685

## 14.3 Exercises in Logit/Probit estimation

### 14.3.1 Exercise 14.1

Use the observations in the file PHIL.FIT to estimate a Probit model of the probability of fertilizer use for the sub-sample of farmers who reside within a two-mile radius of market (see Lessons 14.1 and 14.2).

### 14.3.2 Exercise 14.2

Read the special *Microfit* file PTMONTH.FIT and run the batch file on it to generate the variables INPT, ERSP, YSP, DI11, DIP12, and PI12. See Lesson 10.11 for more details. Use the SIGN(.) function to construct a dummy variable that takes the value of unity if ERSP (the excess returns on SP500) is positive and zero otherwise. Then estimate Logit and Probit regressions of this (1,0) variable on INPT, YSP(-1), PI12(-2), DI11(-1), and DIP12(-2) over the period 1954(1)-1992(12). Compare these results with the OLS estimates in Table 10.11. Comment on the relative merits of the two estimation approaches.

Re-estimate the Probit/Logit regressions over the period 1954(1) to 1992(11), and forecast the probability of a negative excess return in 1992(12).

[illegible]

## 14.3.1 Exercise 14.1

[illegible]

## 14.3.2 Exercise 14.2

[illegible]

# 15

# Lessons in VAR Modelling

The lessons in this chapter demonstrate some of the main features of the unrestricted VAR options in *Microfit*. The relevant menus and options for these lessons are described in Section 7.4, and the related econometric methods are briefly reviewed in Section 19.3.

The lessons are based on a trivariate VAR model in output growths of the USA, Japan, and Germany. These series have already been analysed in some detail in Canova (1995, Section 8), where he provides some empirical justification for modelling output growths rather than output levels. Canova's study, however, covers the period 1955(1) to 1986(4), while the data that we will be using covers the period 1963(1) to 1993(4).

The file G7GDP.FIT contains quarterly observations on GDP (GNP) at constant 1990 prices for the G7 countries, namely Canada, France, Germany, Italy, Japan, the USA, and the UK. This file also contains data on patents granted by the US Patent Office to all the G7 countries.[1]

## 15.1 Lesson 15.1: Selecting the order of the VAR

In this lesson we consider the problem of selecting the order of the trivariate VAR model in the output growths of USA, Japan and Germany.

The special *Microfit* file G7GDP.FIT contains quarterly observations on 83 different variables over the period 1963(1) to 1993(4). Read this file into *Microfit*. Check that the following variables are in the variables list (click VARIABLES):

DLYUSA ≡ US output growth
DLYJAP ≡ Japan's output growth
DLYGER ≡ Germany's output growth
CONST ≡ A vector of ones

[1] The source of output data is the International Financial Statistics (IMF). The output series for Japan and Germany refer to GNP at constant 1990 prices. The quarterly patent data has been compiled by Silvia Fabiani from primary sources (the file PATSIC supplied by the US Patent Office). We are grateful to her for providing us with this data set. For more details, see Fabiani (1995) and the file G7READ.ME in the TUTOR directory.

Open the System Estimation Menu (the Multivariate Menu on the main menu bar) and choose option 1 (see Section 7.3). In the box editor type

DLYUSA DLYJAP DLYGER & CONST

This specifies an unrestricted VAR model in the output growths of the USA, Japan and Germany, and includes a vector of intercepts in the model. For the estimation period enter

1963Q1 1992Q4

and keep the quarterly observations in 1993 for forecasting purposes. You now need to specify the order of the VAR. Since the aim is to select an 'optimal' order for the VAR, it is important that at this stage you select an order high enough to be reasonably confident that the optimal order will not exceed it. In the case of the present application we recommend using 6 as the maximum order for the VAR. Therefore, enter 6 into the Order of VAR field. Click START. You will now be presented with the Unrestricted VAR Post Estimation Menu (see Section 7.4.1). Choose option 4 to move to the VAR Hypothesis Testing Menu (see Section 7.4.3). Choosing option 1 in this menu presents you with the results in Table 15.1a.

All the seven VAR($p$), $p = 0, 1, 2, \ldots, 6$, models are estimated over the same sample period, namely 1964(3) to 1992(4) and, as to be expected, the maximized values of the log-likelihood function given under the column headed LL increase with $p$. However, the Akaike (AIC) and the Schwarz (SBC) criteria select the orders 1 and 0, respectively. The log-likelihood ratio statistics (whether adjusted for small samples or not) reject order 0, but do not reject a VAR of order 1. In the light of these we choose the VAR(1) model. Notice that it is quite usual for the SBC to select a lower order VAR as compared with the AIC.

**Table 15.1a:** Selecting the order of a trivariate VAR model in output growths

Test Statistics and Choice Criteria for Selecting the Order of the VAR Model

Based on 114 observations from 1964Q3 to 1992Q4. Order of VAR = 6
List of variables included in the unrestricted VAR:
DLYUSA DLYJAP DLYGER
List of deterministic and/or exogenous variables:
CONST

| Order | LL | AIC | SBC | LR test | Adjusted LR test |
|---|---|---|---|---|---|
| 6 | 1128.4 | 1071.4 | 993.3935 | — | — |
| 5 | 1125.2 | 1077.2 | 1011.5 | CHSQ( 9) = 6.4277[.696] | 5.3564[.802] |
| 4 | 1120.4 | 1081.4 | 1028.1 | CHSQ(18) = 15.8583[.602] | 13.2152[.779] |
| 3 | 1112.8 | 1082.8 | 1041.8 | CHSQ(27) = 31.1322[.266] | 25.9435[.522] |
| 2 | 1108.1 | 1087.1 | 1058.4 | CHSQ(36) = 40.5268[.277] | 33.7724[.575] |
| 1 | 1101.5 | 1089.5 | 1073.1 | CHSQ(45) = 53.7352[.175] | 44.7793[.481] |
| 0 | 1084.2 | 1081.2 | 1077.1 | CHSQ(54) = 88.2988[.002] | 73.5824[.039] |

AIC = Akaike Information Criterion SBC = Schwarz Bayesian Criterion

**Table 15.1b:** US output growth equation

OLS estimation of a single equation in the Unrestricted VAR

Dependent variable is DLYUSA
114 observations used for estimation from 1964Q3 to 1992Q4

| Regressor | Coefficient | Standard Error | T-Ratio[Prob] |
|---|---|---|---|
| DLYUSA(−1) | .28865 | .095475 | 3.0233[.003] |
| DLYJAP(−1) | .029389 | .080403 | .36552[.715] |
| DLYGER(−1) | .072501 | .085957 | .84346[.401] |
| CONST | .0039865 | .0014390 | 2.7704[.007] |

| | | | |
|---|---|---|---|
| R-Squared | .10155 | R-Bar-Squared | .077044 |
| S.E. of Regression | .0092075 | F-Stat. F(3,110) | 4.1442[.008] |
| Mean of Dependent Variable | .0068049 | S.D. of Dependent Variable | .0095841 |
| Residual Sum of Squares | .0093256 | Equation Log-likelihood | 374.6786 |
| Akaike Info. Criterion | 370.6786 | Schwarz Bayesian Criterion | 365.2062 |
| DW-statistic | 2.0058 | System Log-likelihood | 1101.5 |

Diagnostic Tests

| Test Statistics | LM Version | F Version |
|---|---|---|
| A: Serial Correlation | CHSQ(4) = 2.5571[.634] | F(4,106) = .60806[.658] |
| B: Functional Form | CHSQ(1) = .28508[.593] | F(1,109) = .27326[.602] |
| C: Normality | CHSQ(2) = 9.0063[.011] | Not applicable |
| D: Heteroscedasticity | CHSQ(1) = 2.1578[.142] | F(1,112) = 2.1609[.144] |

A: Lagrange multiplier test of residual serial correlation
B: Ramsey's RESET test using the square of the fitted values
C: Based on a test of skewness and kurtosis of residuals
D: Based on the regression of squared residuals on squared fitted values

Having chosen the order of the VAR, it is prudent to examine the residuals of individual equations for serial correlation. Click CLOSE, return via the VAR Post Estimation Menu to the Backtracking Menu for Unrestricted VAR, choose option 3, and estimate a VAR(1) model over the period 1964Q3 to 1992Q4. Then choose option 1 in the Unrestricted VAR Post Estimation Menu to inspect the results on individual equations in the VAR. Tables 15.1b–15.1d give the regression results for the US, Japan, and Germany, respectively. There is no evidence of residual serial correlation in the case of the US and Germany's output equations, but there is a statistically significant evidence of residual serial correlation in the case of the Japan's output equation. There are also important evidence of departures from normality in the case of output equations for the USA and Japan. A closer examination of the residuals of these equations suggest considerable volatility during the early 1970s as a result of the abandonment of the Bretton Wood system and the quadrupling increase in oil prices. Therefore, it is likely that the remaining serial correlation in the residuals of Japan's output equation may be due to these unusual events. Such a possibility can be handled by introducing a dummy variable for the oil shock in the VAR model (see Lesson 15.2).

**Table 15.1c:** Japanese output growth equation

OLS estimation of a single equation in the Unrestricted VAR

Dependent variable is DLYJAP
114 observations used for estimation from 1964Q3 to 1992Q4

| Regressor | Coefficient | Standard Error | T-Ratio[Prob] |
|---|---|---|---|
| DLYUSA(−1) | .065140 | .10992 | .59262[.555] |
| DLYJAP(−1) | .21958 | .092566 | 2.3721[.019] |
| DLYGER(−1) | .23394 | .098960 | 2.3640[.020] |
| CONST | .0081150 | .0016567 | 4.8984[.000] |

| | | | |
|---|---|---|---|
| R-Squared | .12935 | R-Bar-Squared | .10560 |
| S.E. of Regression | .010600 | F-Stat. F(3,110) | 5.4473[.002] |
| Mean of Dependent Variable | .013128 | S.D. of Dependent Variable | .011209 |
| Residual Sum of Squares | .012361 | Equation Log-likelihood | 358.6189 |
| Akaike Info. Criterion | 354.6189 | Schwarz Bayesian Criterion | 349.1465 |
| DW-statistic | 2.1004 | System Log-likelihood | 1101.5 |

Diagnostic Tests

| Test Statistics | LM Version | F Version |
|---|---|---|
| A: Serial Correlation | CHSQ(4) = 13.5014[.009] | F(4,106) = 3.5601[.009] |
| B: Functional Form | CHSQ(1) = 1.3036[.254] | F(1,109) = .2608[.264] |
| C: Normality | CHSQ(2) = 39.9038[.000] | Not applicable |
| D: Heteroscedasticity | CHSQ(1) = 2.8502[.091] | F(1,112) = 2.8720[.093] |

A: Lagrange multiplier test of residual serial correlation
B: Ramsey's RESET test using the square of the fitted values
C: Based on a test of skewness and kurtosis of residuals
D: Based on the regression of squared residuals on squared fitted values

## 15.2 Lesson 15.2: Testing for the presence of oil shock dummies in output equations

Consider the VAR model of output growths of the US, Germany, and Japan in Lesson 15.1. Suppose we are interested in testing the significance of an oil shock dummy variable, which takes the value of unity in the first quarter of 1974 and zeros elsewhere, in that model.

Load the file G7GDP.FIT, and in the Command Editor type

D74 = 0; **SAMPLE** 74Q1 74Q4; D74 = 1;
**SAMPLE** 63Q1 93Q4 [GO]

You should now see the dummy variable D74 among the variables in the variables list (click [Variables] to view it). Choose the unrestricted VAR option

**Table 15.1d:** Germany's output growth equation

OLS estimation of a single equation in the Unrestricted VAR

Dependent variable is DLYGER
114 observations used for estimation from 1964Q3 to 1992Q4

| Regressor | Coefficient | Standard Error | T-Ratio[Prob] |
|---|---|---|---|
| DLYUSA(−1) | .19307 | .10327 | 1.8695[.064] |
| DLYJAP(−1) | .23045 | .086968 | 2.6499[.009] |
| DLYGER(−1) | −.031787 | .092975 | −.34188[.733] |
| CONST | .0025928 | .0015565 | 1.6658[.099] |

| | | | |
|---|---|---|---|
| R-Squared | .10562 | R-Bar-Squared | .081232 |
| S.E. of Regression | .0099594 | F-Stat. F(3,110) | 4.3303[.006] |
| Mean of Dependent Variable | .0067337 | S.D. of Dependent Variable | .010390 |
| Residual Sum of Squares | .010911 | Equation Log-likelihood | 365.7306 |
| Akaike Info. Criterion | 361.7306 | Schwarz Bayesian Criterion | 356.2582 |
| DW-statistic | 2.0799 | System Log-likelihood | 1101.5 |

Diagnostic Tests

| Test Statistics | LM Version | F Version |
|---|---|---|
| A: Serial Correlation | CHSQ(4) = 7.1440[.128] | F(4,106) = 1.7717[.140] |
| B: Functional Form | CHSQ(1) = .30999[.578] | F(1,109) = .29721[.587] |
| C: Normality | CHSQ(2) = .56351[.754] | Not applicable |
| D: Heteroscedasticity | CHSQ(1) = .52835[.467] | F(1,112) = .52150[.472] |

A: Lagrange multiplier test of residual serial correlation
B: Ramsey's RESET test using the square of the fitted values
C: Based on a test of skewness and kurtosis of residuals
D: Based on the regression of squared residuals on squared fitted values

in the System Estimation Menu (Multivariate Menu), and specify the following augmented VAR model:

DLYUSA DLYJAP DLYGER & CONST D74

For the sample period choose

1964Q1 1992Q4

For the order of the VAR enter 1. Click START and move to the VAR Hypothesis Testing Menu (see section 7.4.3). Select option 2 and type

D74 OK

The results in Table 15.2 appear on the screen.

As can be seen from this table, the log-likelihood ratio statistic for testing the deletion of the oil shock dummy from *all* the three output equations is 8.61 which is statistically significant at the 3.5 per cent level.

To check the significance of the oil shock dummy in individual output equations, you need to choose option 1 in the Unrestricted VAR Post Estimation Menu. The dummy variable is significant in Japan's output

**Table 15.2:** Testing for the effect of the oil shock in the VAR model

| LR Test of Deterministic/Exogenous Variables in the VAR | | |
|---|---|---|
| Based on 116 observations from 1964Q1 to 1992Q4. Order of VAR = 1 | | |
| List of variables included in the unrestricted VAR: | | |
| DLYUSA | DLYJAP | DLYGER |
| List of deterministic and/or exogenous variables: | | |
| CONST | D74 | |
| Maximized value of log-likelihood = 1124.0 | | |
| List of variables included in the restricted VAR: | | |
| DLYUSA | DLYJAP | DLYGER |
| List of deterministic and/or exogenous variables: | | |
| CONST | | |
| Maximized value of log-likelihood = 1119.7 | | |
| LR test of restrictions, CHSQ(3) = 8.6083[0.035] | | |

growth equation, marginally significant in the US output growth equation, and not statistically significant in Germany's equation. Also note that the inclusion of the dummy has reduced the significance of the residual serial correlation in Japan's output equation, but has not eliminated the problem. Therefore, there may be other factors (such as non-linear effects) that should be taken into account. Another possibility is to try a higher order for the VAR model—although this course is not recommended by the model selection criteria or the likelihood ratio test statistics.

## 15.3 Lesson 15.3: International transmission of output shocks

One important issue in the analysis of the international business cycle is the extent to which output shocks are transmitted from one country to another. In this lesson we examine this issue by Granger non-causality tests applied to the trivariate VAR in the US, Japanese, and German output growths.

Load the file G7GDP.FIT into *Microfit*, go through the steps in Lesson 15.2, and specify the augmented VAR(1) model

DLYUSA DLYJAP DLYGER & CONST D74

to be estimated over the period 1964Q1 to 1992Q4. For the order of the VAR choose 1, then click START. Choose option 3 in the VAR Hypothesis Testing Menu (see Section 7.4.3). You will be asked to list the sub-set of variables with respect to which you wish to carry out the block non-causality tests. Type

DLYJAP DLYGER OK

to test for the non-causality of the Japanese and German output growths in

**Table 15.3:** Granger non-causality test of the US output growth with respect to the output growths of Germany and Japan

LR Test of Block Granger Non-Causality in the VAR

Based on 116 observations from 1964Q1 to 1992Q4. Order of VAR = 1
List of variables included in the unrestricted VAR:
DLYUSA DLYJAP DLYGER
List of deterministic and/or exogenous variables:
CONST D74
Maximized value of log-likelihood = 1124.0

List of variable(s) assumed to be 'non-causal' under the null hypothesis:
DLYJAP DLYGER
Maximized value of log-likelihood = 1123.7
LR test of block non-causality, CHSQ(2) = .50437[.777]
The above statistic is for testing the null hypothesis that the coefficients of the lagged values of:

DLYJAP DLYGER
in the block of equations explaining the variable(s):
DLYUSA
are zero. The maximum order of the lag(s) is 1.

the US output equation. You should now see the test results on the screen, reproduced in Table 15.3.

The log-likelihood ratio statistic for this test is equal to 0.50 which is asymptotically distributed as a $\chi^2$ variate with 2 degrees of freedom, and is clearly not significant statistically. Carrying out a similar exercise for the other output equations we obtain the LR statistic of 4.93 [0.085] when testing for the non-causality of the US and Germany's output growth in the Japanese output equation, and the LR statistic of 11.975 [0.003] for testing the non-causality of the US and Japanese output growth in Germany's output equation. The figures in square brackets refer to rejection probabilities. Therefore, if there is any transmission of output shocks between these three countries, it seems that it goes from the US to the other two countries rather than the reverse.

## 15.4 Lesson 15.4: Contemporaneous correlation of output shocks

Another aspect of the international transmission of output shocks is the extent to which shocks in different output equations are contemporaneously correlated. Again using the augmented VAR(1) model of the output growths of the US, Japan, and Germany, in this lesson we test the hypothesis that

$$H_0 : \sigma_{12} = \sigma_{13} = \sigma_{23} = 0$$

against the alternative that

$$H_1 : \sigma_{12} \neq 0, \quad \sigma_{13} \neq 0, \quad \sigma_{23} \neq 0$$

where $\sigma_{ij}$ stands for the contemporaneous covariance between the shocks in the output equations of countries $i$ and $j$.

One possible method of testing the above hypothesis is to compute the log-likelihood ratio statistic

$$\mathcal{LR}(H_0|H_1) = 2(LL_U - LL_R)$$

where $LL_U$ and $LL_R$ are the maximized values of the log-likelihood function under $H_1$ (the unrestricted model) and under $H_0$ (the restricted model), respectively. See also Section 19.1.3.

To compute $LL_U$ for the present application, follow the steps in Lesson 15.2 and estimate the augmented VAR(1) model in

$$\mathbf{x}_t = (DLYUSA, DLYJAP, DLYGER)$$

augmented with the variables $\mathbf{w}_t = (CONST, D74)$, over the period 1964(1) to 1992(4). Choose option 1 in the Unrestricted VAR Post Estimation Menu and press ↩ to see the regression results for the US output equation. The value of $LL_U$ is the value of the 'system log-likelihood' given in the bottom right-hand corner of the result table, namely

$$LL_U = 1124.0$$

To compute the restricted log-likelihood value, $LL_R$, we first note that under $H_0$ :

$$LL_R = LL_{US} + LL_{GER} + LL_{JAP}$$

where $LL_{US}$, $LL_{GER}$ and $LL_{JAP}$ are the single equation log-likelihood values of the output equations for the US, Germany and Japan, respectively. They are readily computed using the OLS option. For example, to compute $LL_{US}$, choose option 1 in the Single Equation Estimation Menu (Univariate Menu: see Section 6.4), selecting the OLS option. Click [icon] to clear the box editor, and then type

DLYUSA CONST D74 DLYUSA(−1) DLYJAP(−1) DLYGER(−1)

Enter the start and end dates 1964Q1 and 1992Q4, and click START. You should see the OLS regression results on the screen. $LL_{US}$ is given by the value of the 'equation log-likelihood' in this result table, that is $LL_{US} = 381.95$. Now click CLOSE and return to the Backtracking Menu for the linear regression options and choose option 4 in this menu. Change the dependent variable from DLYUSA to DLYGER and run the regression by the OLS to obtain $LL_{GER} = 373.31$. Similarly we have $LL_{JAP} = 367.02$. Therefore,

$$\begin{aligned} LR(H_0 : H_1) &= 2(1124 - 381.95 - 373.31 - 367.02)(1) \\ &= 3.44 \end{aligned}$$

which is asymptotically distributed as a $\chi^2$ variate with 3 degrees of

**Table 15.4:** Estimated system covariance matrix of errors for a trivariate VAR model of output growths

| | DLYUSA | DLYJAP | DLYGER |
|---|---|---|---|
| DLYUSA | .8447E-4 | .1014E-4 | .6001E-5 |
| DLYJAP | .1014E-4 | .1093E-3 | .1282E-4 |
| DLYGER | .6001E-5 | .1282E-4 | .9803E-4 |

freedom. The 95 per cent critical value of the $\chi^2$ distribution with 3 degrees of freedom is 7.81. Therefore, the null hypothesis that the shocks in different output equations are contemporaneously uncorrelated cannot be rejected.

The estimates of $\sigma_{ij}$, obtainable using option 2 in the Unrestricted VAR Post Estimation Menu, also corroborate this finding. These estimates are reproduced in Table 15.4, which shows that the estimates $\hat{\sigma}_{12} = 0.1014 \times 10^{-4}$, $\hat{\sigma}_{13} = 0.6001 \times 10^{-5}$, and $\hat{\sigma}_{23} = 0.1282 \times 10^{-4}$ are about 1/10 of the estimated error variances, given by the diagonal elements of the 3 × 3 matrix in Table 15.4.

## 15.5 Lesson 15.5: Forecasting output growths using the VAR

Here we use the augmented VAR(1) model estimated in the previous lessons to compute multivariate, multi-step ahead forecasts of output growths.

Load the file G7GDP.FIT and follow the steps in Lesson 15.2 to estimate the VAR(1) model of output growths of the US, Japan, and Germany over the period 1964Q1 to 1992Q4. Then choose option 5 in the Unrestricted VAR Post Estimation Menu and, when prompted, press ↩ to select 1993Q4 as the final quarter of the forecast period. You will then be asked to choose the growth rate that you wish to forecast. Press ↩ to choose the US output growth, and then select 'Level of DLYUSA' rather than 'Change in DLYUSA' to see the forecasts of the levels of output growth. You should now see the Multivariate Forecast Menu on the screen (see Section 7.4.4). Press ↩ to see the forecasts and the forecast errors for the four quarters of 1993 on the screen. These forecast results are reproduced in Table 15.5.

As can be seen from the summary statistics, the size of the forecast errors and the in-sample residuals are very similar. A similar picture also emerges by plotting in-sample fitted values and out of sample forecasts (see Figure 15.1).

It is, however, important to note that the US growth experience in 1993 may not have been a stringent enough test of the forecast performance of the VAR, as the US output growths were positive in all the four quarters. A good test of forecast performance is to see whether the VAR model predicts the turning points of the output movements.

Similarly, forecasts of output growths for Japan and Germany can also be computed. For Japan the root mean sum of squares of the forecast errors over the 1993(1) to 1993(4) period turned out to be 1.48 per cent, which is slightly higher than the value of 1.02 per cent obtained for the root mean

**Table 15.5:** Multivariate dynamic forecasts for the US output growth (DLYUSA)

Unrestricted Vector Autoregressive Model

Based on 116 observations from 1964Q1 to 1992Q4. Order of VAR = 1
List of variables included in the unrestricted VAR:
DLYUSA DLYJAP DLYGER
List of deterministic and/or exogenous variables:
CONST D74

| Observation | Actual | Prediction | Error |
|---|---|---|---|
| 1993Q1 | .0019499 | .011379 | −.0094288 |
| 1993Q2 | .0047025 | .0084160 | −.0037135 |
| 1993Q3 | .0070727 | .0076889 | −.6162E-3 |
| 1993Q4 | .016841 | .0075384 | .0093022 |

Summary Statistics for Residuals and Forecast Errors

| | Estimation Period 1964Q1 to 1992Q4 | Forecast Period 1993Q1 to 1993Q4 |
|---|---|---|
| Mean | .0000 | −.0011141 |
| Mean Absolute | .0067166 | .0057652 |
| Mean Sum Squares | .8082E-4 | .4740E-4 |
| Root Mean Sum Squares | .0089902 | .0068848 |

sum of squares of residuals over the estimation period. It is also worth noting that the growth forecasts for Japan miss the two negative quarterly output growths that occurred in the second and the fourth quarters of 1993.

A similar conclusion is also reached in the case of output growth forecasts for Germany.

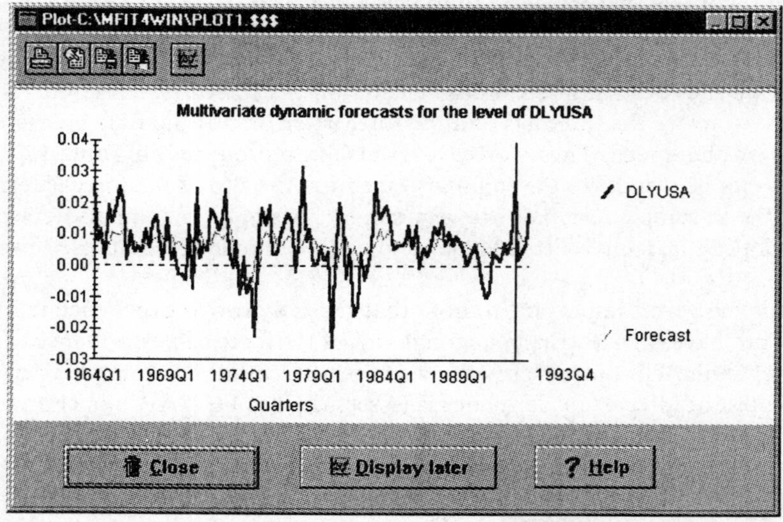


**Figure 15.1:** Multivariate dynamic forecasts of US output growth (DLYUSA)

## 15.6 Lesson 15.6: Impulse responses of the effects of output growth shocks

In this lesson we show how to use *Microfit* to compute/plot impulse responses (and forecast error variance decomposition) for the effect of unit shocks (equal to one standard error) to the US output growth equation on the growth of outputs in Germany and Japan within the trivariate VAR model analysed in earlier lessons. Since in Lesson 15.4 we could not reject the hypothesis that the variance matrix of the errors in the VAR model is diagonal, we do not expect the orthogonalized and the generalized impulse responses (and the associated forecast error variance decompositions) to be very different. Also in view of the results of Lesson 15.3, we estimate the model with the US output growth as the first variable in the VAR.

Load the file G7GDP.FIT and choose the unrestricted VAR option in the System Estimation Menu (Multiavariate Menu) and set up the VAR model in the box editor by typing:

DLYUSA DLYGER DLYJAP & CONST D74

Select the sample period 1964Q1 to 1993Q4 and a VAR of order 1, then click START. *Microfit* carries out the necessary computations and presents you with the Unrestricted VAR Post Estimation Menu (see Section 7.4.1). Choose option 3 to move to the Unrestricted VAR Dynamic Response Analysis Menu (see Section 7.4.2). Initially, choose option 1 to compute orthogonalized impulse responses, and then select the variable/equation DLYUSA to shock. Since there is little persistence in output growth shocks, it is advisable to select a short horizon for the impulse responses. We recommend choosing 25 when you are asked to specify the 'horizon for impulse responses'. The results are reproduced in Table 15.6. As you can see the effect of a unit shock to the US output growth has only a small impact on the output growths of Germany and Japan, and this effect dies out very quickly with the forecast horizon.

To see the plot of impulse responses, click CLOSE to move to the Impulse Response Results Menu, and choose the graph option. You will be presented with a list of the jointly determined variables in the VAR. Select all three variables, DLYUSA, DLYGER, and DLYJAP, and click OK. Figure 15.2 should now appear on the screen. As you can see the impact of US output growth shocks on Germany and Japan is small on impact and they generally tend to die out very quickly.

Consider now the generalized impulse responses of the effect of unit shocks to DLYUSA, the US output growth. Since DLYUSA is the first variable in the VAR, the orthogonalized and generalized impulse responses will be identical. To see that this is in fact the case, choose option 2 in the Unrestricted VAR Dynamic Response Analysis Menu (see Section 7.4.2), select DLYUSA to shock and 25 for the forecast horizon, and compare the results that appear on the screen with those in Table 15.6. This is not, however, the case if you choose to shock Japan's output growth equation. For example, in the case of the orthogonalized responses, the effects of

**Table 15.6:** Orthogonalized impulse responses to one SE shock in the equation for US output growth (DLYUSA) using an unrestricted vector autoregressive model

Based on 120 observations from 1964Q1 to 1993Q4. Order of VAR = 1
List of variables included in the unrestricted VAR:
DLYUSA DLYGER DLYJAP
List of deterministic and/or exogenous variables:
CONST D74

| Horizon | DLYUSA | DLYGER | DLYJAP |
|---|---|---|---|
| 0 | .0091174 | .8103E-3 | .9367E-3 |
| 1 | .0022248 | .0015059 | .8355E-3 |
| 2 | .6358E-3 | .4971E-3 | .6469E-3 |
| 3 | .1960E-3 | .2403E-3 | .2981E-3 |
| 4 | .6809E-4 | .9687E-4 | .1354E-3 |
| 5 | .2525E-4 | .4121E-4 | .5773E-4 |
| 6 | .9870E-5 | .1704E-4 | .2441E-4 |
| 7 | .3960E-5 | .7096E-5 | .1020E-4 |
| 8 | .1614E-5 | .2941E-5 | .4248E-5 |
| 9 | .6632E-6 | .1220E-5 | .1764E-5 |
| 10 | .2737E-6 | .5059E-6 | .7322E-6 |
| 11 | .1132E-6 | .2097E-6 | .3037E-6 |
| 12 | .4686E-7 | .8693E-7 | .1259E-6 |
| 13 | .1941E-7 | .3604E-7 | .5220E-7 |
| 14 | .8043E-8 | .1494E-7 | .2164E-7 |
| 15 | .3333E-8 | .6191E-8 | .8969E-8 |
| 16 | .1382E-8 | .2566E-8 | .3718E-8 |
| 17 | .5726E-9 | .1064E-8 | .1541E-8 |
| 18 | .2373E-9 | .4409E-9 | .6387E-9 |
| 19 | .0000 | .1827E-9 | .2647E-9 |
| 20 | .0000 | .0000 | .1097E-9 |
| 21 | .0000 | .0000 | .0000 |
| 22 | .0000 | .0000 | .0000 |
| 23 | .0000 | .0000 | .0000 |
| 24 | .0000 | .0000 | .0000 |
| 25 | .0000 | .0000 | .0000 |

shocking Japan's output growth on the US and Germany's output growths on *impact* (at zero horizon) are zero (by construction) but the corresponding generalized impulse responses are 0.08 and 0.12 per cent, respectively. However, due to the almost diagonal nature of the variance matrix of the shocks, the two impulse responses are not significantly different from one another in this particular application.

## 15.7 Exercises in VAR modelling

### 15.7.1 Exercise 15.1

Carry out the Lessons 15.1 to 15.5 using a VAR model in output levels, and compare your findings with those obtained using the VAR model in growth rates.

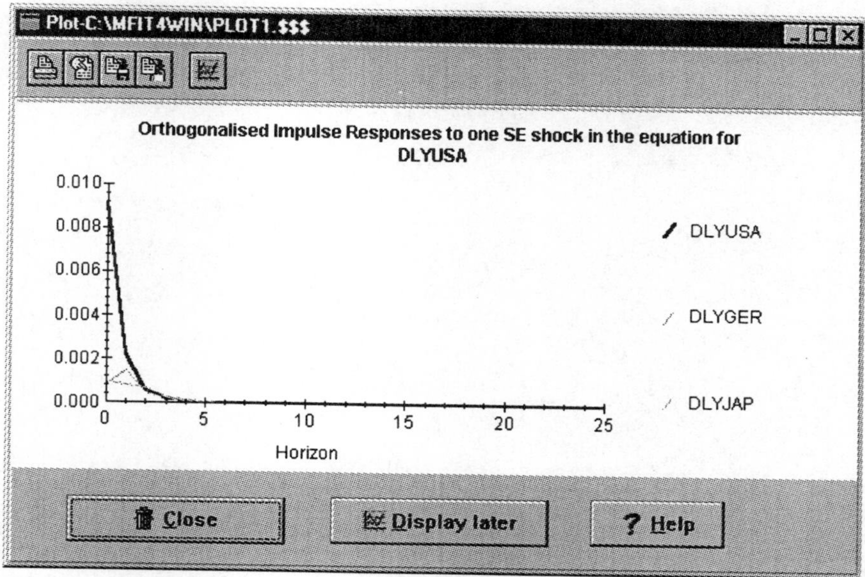


**Figure 15.2:** Orthogonalised impulse responses to one SE shock in the equation for DLYUSA

### 15.7.2 Exercise 15.2

The file G7GDP.FIT (in the TUTOR directory) also contains patent data for the G7 countries. Repeat the Lessons 15.1 to 15.5 using rates of change of patents granted by the US Patent Office to the US, Japan, and Germany instead of the output growth rates. Discuss the similarity and the differences between the two sets of results.

### 15.7.3 Exercise 15.3

Again using the file G7GDP.FIT, estimate an augmented VAR model in output growths and rates of change of patents granted in the case of the US, Japan, and Germany.

- Select an optimal order for this six-variable VAR model
- Test the statistical significance of the D74 oil shock dummy variable in this combined VAR model.
- Test the Granger non-causality of output growths with respect to the rates of change of the number of patents granted and vice versa.

# 16

# Lessons in Cointegration Analysis

The lessons in this chapter are concerned with single-equation and multiple-equation approaches to cointegration analysis. They show how *Microfit* can be used to test for cointegration under a variety of circumstances, how to estimate long-run relations using both single-equation approaches, such as the Phillips–Hansen (1990) fully-modified OLS estimators, and the autoregressive distributed lag (ARDL) estimators discussed in Pesaran and Shin (1995a) and the system approaches such as the full maximum likelihood procedure applied to the underlying VAR model. The lessons in this chapter also demonstrate *Microfit*'s capabilities in the areas of impulse response analysis and forecasting using cointegrating VAR models.

The literature on cointegrating VAR is vast and growing. Excellent accounts of the early developments can be found in Watson (1994) and Hamilton (1994, Chapter 19). The basic cointegrating VAR model underlying most of the lessons in this chapter is set out in Chapter 19, where further references to the literature can also be found. The ARDL approach is described in Section 18.19.

These lessons deal with the problem of testing for cointegration, and cover both the residual-based methods proposed by Engle and Granger (1987), and a generalization of Johansen's (1988, 1991, 1995) full information maximum likelihood (FIML) approach. Two main procedures are currently used to test for cointegration. One is the residual-based ADF method proposed by Engle and Granger (1987), and the other is Johansen's (1988, 1991) maximum likelihood approach. There are also other procedures such as the common stochastic trends approach of Stock and Watson (1988), the auxiliary regression procedure of Park (1992), and variants of the residual-based approach proposed by Phillips and Ouliaris (1990), and extended by Hansen (1992). For a review of these tests see Watson (1994) and Hamilton (1994, Chapter 19). We shall also consider a new approach to testing for the existence of long run relations when it is not known whether the underlying regressors are $I(1)$ or $I(0)$. This testing method is developed in Pesaran *et al.* (1996b). For reasons that will become clear from Lesson 16.5, we shall refer to this as the *bounds test*.

With the exception of the ARDL approach to cointegration analysis and the related bounds test, the cointegrating options in *Microfit* presume that the variables under consideration are first-difference stationary (or are integrated of order 1). On the problem of how to test for the order of integration of the variables, see the ADF command (Section 4.4.2), and Lessons 11.1 and 11.2.

## 16.1 Lesson 16.1: Testing for cointegration when the cointegrating coefficients are known

Economic theory often suggests certain variables are cointegrated with a *known* cointegrating vector. Examples are the 'great ratios' and the 'purchasing power parity' (PPP) relations. In this lesson we use the long historical data analysed by Alogoskoufis and Smith (1991b) to test the hypothesis that wages (W), prices (P), output (Y), and employment (E), all measured in logarithms, are cointegrated with coefficients (+1, −1, − 1, + 1). Such a cointegrating relation implies that the logarithm of the share of wages in output has been mean-reverting to a constant value over time. Similarly, real wages, WP = W − P, and labour productivity, YE = Y − E, should cointegrate with coefficients (1, − 1). In this lesson we test this hypothesis using univariate procedures.

The file PHILLIPS.FIT contains UK data on the logarithms of employment, labour force, prices, wages, and real GDP over the period 1855 to 1987 (for more details see Lesson 13.4). Load this file, and in the Command Editor type

C = 1; WP = W − P; YE = Y − E; WPYE = WP − YE;
DWPYE = WPYE − WPYE(−1) [GO]

to create an intercept term (C = 1), the logarithm of the real wage, WP, the logarithm of labour productivity, YE, and the logarithm of the share of wages in output, WPYE.

In the case of most tests of cointegration, the hypothesis being tested is the null of 'non-cointegration'.[1] In the present application the relevant hypothesis is that WPYE = W − P − Y + E is not a cointegrating relation, or equivalently that WPYE contains a unit root. Any one of the unit root tests can be used for this purpose. Initially, we use a standard ADF test; later we consider the application of the Phillips–Perron (1988) semi-parametric test procedure (see footnote 4 to Lesson 11.1).

Use the [clear] button to clear the box editor and type

ADF WPYE(4) [GO]

The ADF test results, reproduced in Table 16.1a, should appear on the screen.

[1]The exception is the test of the stationarity hypothesis proposed by Kwiatkowski *et al.* (1992).

**Table 16.1a:** Part I: Unit root tests for variable WPYE

The Dickey–Fuller regressions include an intercept but not a trend

128 observations used in the estimation of all ADF regressions.
Sample period from 1860 to 1987

| | Test Statistic | LL | AIC | SBC | HQC |
|---|---|---|---|---|---|
| DF | −1.6854 | 267.2550 | 265.2550 | 262.4030 | 264.0962 |
| ADF(1) | −2.4481 | 272.5111 | 269.5111 | 265.2331 | 267.7729 |
| ADF(2) | −1.9485 | 273.8123 | 269.8123 | 264.1083 | 267.4947 |
| ADF(3) | −1.5082 | 275.4135 | 270.4135 | 263.2834 | 267.5165 |
| ADF(4) | −1.3525 | 275.6501 | 269.6501 | 261.0940 | 266.1738 |

95% critical value for the augmented Dickey–Fuller statistic = −2.8840
LL = Maximized log-likelihood AIC = Akaike Information Criterion
SBC = Schwarz Bayesian Criterion HQC = Hannan-Quinn Criterion

Part II: Unit root tests for variable WPYE

The DickeyFuller regressions include an intercept and a linear trend

128 observations used in the estimation of all ADF regressions.
Sample period from 1860 to 1987

| | Test Statistic | LL | AIC | SBC | HQC |
|---|---|---|---|---|---|
| DF | −2.9562 | 270.7909 | 267.7909 | 263.5129 | 266.0527 |
| ADF(1) | −3.8079 | 277.0338 | 273.0338 | 267.3298 | 270.7163 |
| ADF(2) | −3.3022 | 277.9466 | 272.9466 | 265.8165 | 270.0496 |
| ADF(3) | −2.8785 | 279.3377 | 273.3377 | 264.7816 | 269.8613 |
| ADF(4) | −2.7328 | 279.5868 | 272.5868 | 262.6047 | 268.5310 |

95% critical value for the augmented Dickey–Fuller statistic = −3.4452
LL = Maximized log-likelihood AIC = Akaike Information Criterion
SBC = Schwarz Bayesian Criterion HQC = Hannan–Quinn Criterion

The Akaike information (AIC) and Schwarz Bayesian criteria (SBC) suggest selecting ADF regressions of orders 3 and 1, respectively. But if all the ADF($p$) statistics reported in Table 16.1a are considered, the null of a unit root is only rejected by an ADF(1) with trend. Since we would not expect the share to be trended, it is worth trying to determine what is happening. Plotting WPYE indicates that the share seemed to have moved to a higher level and become somewhat more stable after World War II (see Figure 16.1). However, formally to allow for a shift in the mean of WPYE requires a different set of critical values, and will be subject to the uncertainty associated with the point at which such a shift in the mean share of wages may have occurred (see Perron 1989).

A similar conclusion also follows from the Phillips–Perron (1988) test. To compute this test statistic, choose the linear regression option from the Single Equation Estimation Menu (Univariate Menu), choosing the OLS option, and specify the following simple Dickey–Fuller regression:

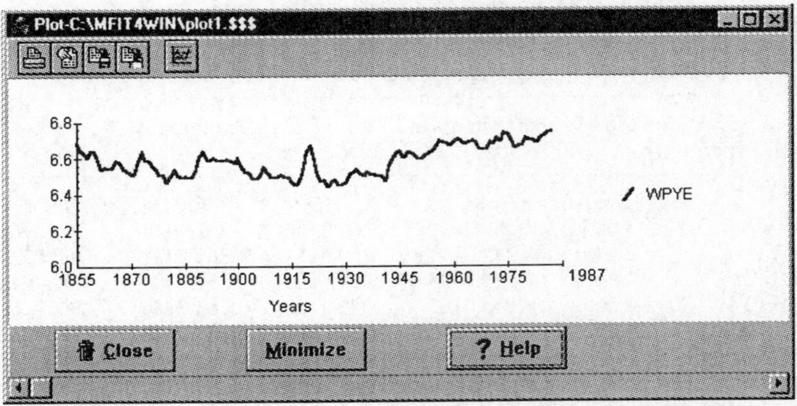


**Figure 16.1:** Logarithm of the share of wages in output in the UK

DWPYE C WPYE(−1) START

where DWPYE = WPYE − WPYE(−1). This regression is estimated over the whole sample period. The *t*-ratio of the coefficient of WPYE(−1), namely −1.86, is the simple ADF statistic. To carry out the non-parametric correction to this statistic proposed by Phillips–Perron, choose option 4 (Standard, White and Newey–West adjusted variance matrices) in the Post Regression Menu, choose the Newey–West adjusted variances with Bartlett weights, and when asked use a window size of 12 (say). Similar results are obtained with other window sizes in the range (4, 20). Now click OK to leave the estimation results for the adjusted variance matrices, and choose option 1 (Display regression results for the adjusted covariance matrix). The *t*-ratio of WPYE(−1) in this result screen (namely −2.368) is a Phillips–Perron type statistic (see Table 16.1b). The critical values for this test are the same as those for the ADF test. Once again the hypothesis that WPYE contains a unit root cannot be rejected at the 95 per cent level. There is clear evidence that the share of wages in output has changed over the 1855 to 1987 period. This is easily confirmed by adding a dummy variable, say D46, which takes the value of zero before World War II, and unity thereafter to the ADF

**Table 16.1b:** Simple Dickey–Fuller regression with Newey–West adjusted standard errors

Ordinary Least Squares Estimation
Based on Newey–West adjusted S.E.'s Bartlett weights, truncation lag = 12

Dependent variable is DWPYE
132 observations used for estimation from 1856 to 1987

| Regressor | Coefficient | Standard Error | T-Ratio[Prob] |
|---|---|---|---|
| C | .39937 | .16752 | 2.3840[.019] |
| WPYE(−1) | −.060596 | .025591 | −2.3679[.019] |

regression. However, the inclusion of such a dummy variable alters the critical values for the unit root tests. On this see Perron (1989).

## 16.2 Lesson 16.2: A residual-based approach to testing for cointegration

This lesson is concerned with the residual-based augmented Dickey–Fuller (ADF) test of cointegration. Engle and Granger (1987) consider seven, asymptotically valid, residual-based test statistics for testing the null hypothesis of non-cointegration against the alternative of cointegration, but pointed out that in most applications the ADF test is preferable to the other six tests. More recently, other residual-based type tests have also been proposed by Phillips and Ouliaris (1990), and extended by Hansen (1992) to allow for the possibility of a deterministic trend in the cointegrating relation. The ADF residual-based tests and the Phillips–Ouliaris–Hansen tests are asymptotically equivalent and only differ in the way in which they deal with the problem of residual serial correlation in the simple ADF regression.

Here we show how the residual-based approach can be applied to test the stability of the share of wages in output analysed in Lesson 16.1. Load the file PHILLIPS.FIT and make sure that the variables YE (log of output per man) and WP (log of real wages), and the intercept term (C) are in the list of variables. You also need to satisfy yourself that the time series WP and YE are integrated processes of order 1.

Choose the linear regression option in the Single Equation Estimation Menu (Univariate Menu: see Section 6.4), selecting the OLS option. Then enter

WP C YE [START]

to set up the cointegrating equation (under the alternative hypothesis of cointegration).[2] This regression is estimated using the whole sample period, 1855 to 1987. Then move to the Hypothesis Testing Menu (see Section 6.24) and choose option 3 to compute ADF statistics of different orders (up to a maximum order of 12) based on the residuals of the cointegration regression. The ADF($p$) statistics are computed as the $t$-ratios of the estimated coefficient of R(−1) in the following OLS regressions:

$$DR = -\lambda R(-1) + \sum_{i=1}^{p} \delta_i R(-i) + \text{error}$$

for $p = 0, 1, \ldots, P$, where R represents the residual of the OLS regression of WP on an intercept and YE, and DR = R − R(−1). Now choose 4 for the

[2]We could have equally considered the regression of YE on WP. Asymptotically the results should not depend on whether the ADF test is applied to the residuals from the regression of WP on YE or the reverse regression. This may not, however, be the case in small samples. It is, therefore, important that the above computations are also carried out using the residuals from the regression of YE on WP. See Section 16.8.2.

**Table 16.2a:** Residual-based statistics for testing cointegration between real wages and labour productivity

Unit root tests for residuals

Based on OLS regression of WP on:
C YE
133 observations used for estimation from 1855 to 1987

| | Test Statistic | LL | AIC | SBC | HQC |
|---|---|---|---|---|---|
| DF | −3.2833 | 263.5320 | 262.5320 | 261.1060 | 261.9526 |
| ADF(1) | −4.2689 | 270.3642 | 268.3642 | 265.5122 | 267.2054 |
| ADF(2) | −3.7199 | 271.0256 | 268.0256 | 263.7475 | 266.2874 |
| ADF(3) | −3.3064 | 271.8257 | 267.8257 | 262.1216 | 265.5081 |
| ADF(4) | −3.1371 | 272.0243 | 267.0243 | 259.8942 | 264.1273 |

95% critical value for the Dickey–Fuller statistic = −3.3849
LL = Maximized log-likelihood AIC = Akaike Information Criterion
SBC = Schwarz Bayesian Criterion HQC = Hannan–Quinn Criterion

maximum order of the ADF statistics, to obtain the results in Table 16.2a on the screen. The different model selection criteria in Table 16.2a favour a relatively low order for the ADF test, with the Akaike information criterion (AIC) selecting the order 2, and the Schwarz Bayesian criterion (SBC) selecting the order 1. For these orders the hypothesis of a unit root in the residuals is rejected. But the evidence is less convincing when higher order ADF statistics are considered. This is very similar to our finding in the previous lesson.

Consider now adding a dummy variable, say D46, which takes the value of zero before World War II, and unity thereafter to the cointegrating relation. First return to the Command Editor and create the dummy variable D46 by typing

D46 = 0; **SAMPLE** 1946 1987; D46 = 1 [GO]

Then choose the linear regression option in the Single Equation Estimation Menu (Univariate Menu), with the OLS option selected, add the variable D46 to the list of the regressors, and estimate the new regression equation over the whole sample period. If you now choose option 3 in the Hypothesis Testing Menu (see Section 6.24), with 4 as the maximum order for the ADF test, you should get the results reproduced in Table 16.2b.

The residual-based ADF statistics are now much higher (in absolute value) than those given in Table 16.2a, but due to the presence of the shift dummy variable, D46, in the regression, the critical value given at the foot of Table 16.2b is not appropriate. The correct critical value for the test is also higher (in absolute value) than 3.3849. Overall, the tests in Lessons 16.1 and 16.2 suggest a reasonably stable share of wages in output, with an important shift in this share in the aftermath of World War II.

**Table 16.2b:** Residual-based statistics for testing cointegration between real wages and labour productivity allowing for a World War II dummy

Unit root tests for residuals

Based on OLS regression of WP on:
C YE D46
133 observations used for estimation from 1855 to 1987

| | Test Statistic | LL | AIC | SBC | HQC |
|---|---|---|---|---|---|
| DF | −4.1359 | 258.3337 | 257.3337 | 255.9077 | 256.7543 |
| ADF(1) | −5.3074 | 264.4931 | 262.4931 | 259.6410 | 261.3343 |
| ADF(2) | −5.0510 | 264.6720 | 261.6720 | 257.3940 | 259.9339 |
| ADF(3) | −4.3891 | 264.8753 | 260.8753 | 255.1713 | 258.5578 |
| ADF(4) | −4.0394 | 264.9369 | 259.9369 | 252.8068 | 257.0399 |

95% critical value for the Dickey–Fuller statistic = −3.8090
LL = Maximized log-likelihood AIC = Akaike Information Criterion
SBC = Schwarz Bayesian Criterion HQC = Hannan–Quinn Criterion

*Notes*

1. The critical values for the ADF residual-based tests are computed using the response surface estimates given in MacKinnon (1991), and differ from the critical values reported when the ADF command is utilized in the Command Editor (see Section 4.4.2).
2. While it is possible to save the residuals and then apply the ADF command to the saved residuals in the Command Editor, it is important to note that in this case the reported critical values are not valid and can therefore result in misleading inferences. Therefore, it is important that residual-based ADF tests are carried out using option 3 in the Hypothesis Testing Menu (see Section 6.24).

## 16.3 Lesson 16.3: Testing for cointegration: Johansen ML approach

The residual-based cointegration tests described in the previous lesson are inefficient and can lead to contradictory results, especially when there are more than two $I(1)$ variables under consideration. A more satisfactory approach would be to employ Johansen's *ML* procedure. This provides a unified framework for estimation and testing of cointegrating relations in the context of vector autoregressive (VAR) error correction models (see Section 7.5). Here we show how to use the cointegrating VAR options in *Microfit* to carry out FIML cointegration tests.

In Lesson 13.3 we estimated a distributed lag relationship between capital expenditures (Y) and appropriations (X) for the US manufacturing sector employing Almon's (1965) polynomial distributed lag approach. However, we found that the estimated model suffered from a significant degree of residual serial correlation. In this lesson we re-examine the relationship

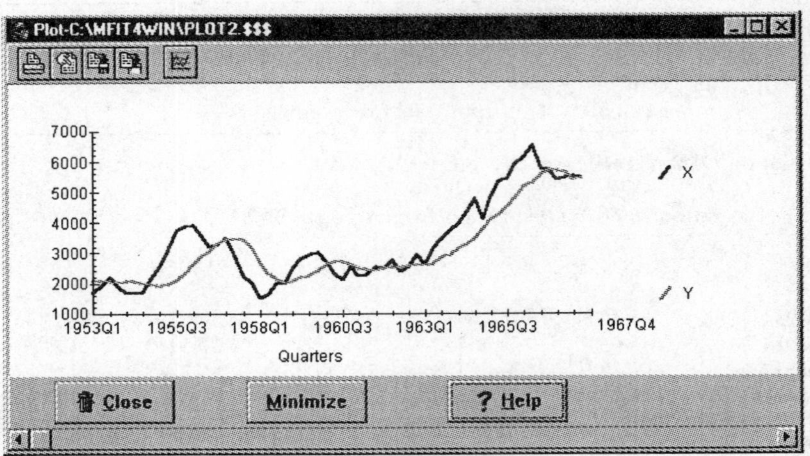


**Figure 16.2:** Capital expenditures (Y) and appropriations (X) in US manufacturing

between Y and X using cointegration techniques. The relevant data are in the special *Microfit* file ALMON.FIT, which contains observations on Y and X over the period 1953(1) to 1967(4) (see Lesson 13.3 for more details). Load this file and plot the variables Y and X in the Command Editor. As can be seen from Figure 16.2, the two series are trended and generally move with one another, but from just looking at the graph it is not possible to say whether they are cointegrated.

Before using the cointegrating VAR options we need to make sure that the variables Y and X are in fact $I(1)$, ascertain the nature of the intercept/trend in the underlying VAR model, and choose the order for the VAR. Clear the Command Editor and type

DY = Y − Y(−1); DX = X − X(−1); ADF Y; ADF X;
ADF DY; ADF DX [GO]

You should see the various ADF statistics needed for testing the unit root hypothesis on the screen. From these results it seems reasonable to conclude that Y and X are $I(1)$.

To select the order of the VAR in these variables, select the Unrestricted VAR option from the System Estimation Menu (Multivariate Menu). In the box editor type

Y X & INPT

to specify a bivariate VAR model in Y and X, containing an intercept term (INPT) as its deterministic component.

Choose the whole sample and set the maximum order of the VAR to 4, then click [START]. In the Post Estimation Menu, choose the hypothesis testing option 4, and then choose to test/select the lag length, option 1 in the VAR Hypothesis Testing Menu. The results in Table 16.3a should now appear on the screen.

The Schwarz Bayesian criterion (SBC) suggests a VAR of order 2, the

**Table 16.3a:** Selecting the order of the VAR model in capital expenditures (Y) and appropriations (X) for US manufacturing

Test Statistics and Choice Criteria for Selecting the Order of the VAR Model

Based on 56 observations from 1954Q1 to 1967Q4. Order of VAR = 4
List of variables included in the unrestricted VAR:
Y X
List of deterministic and/or exogenous variables:
INPT

| Order | LL | AIC | SBC | LR test | Adjusted LR test |
|---|---|---|---|---|---|
| 4 | −720.3923 | −738.3923 | −756.6205 | ... | ... |
| 3 | −720.8494 | −734.8494 | −749.0269 | CHSQ(4) = .91413[.923] | .76722[.943] |
| 2 | −725.2045 | −735.2045 | −745.3313 | CHSQ(8) = 9.6244[.292] | 8.0776[.426] |
| 1 | −738.3078 | −744.3078 | −750.3839 | CHSQ(12) = 35.8310[.000] | 30.0724[.003] |
| 0 | −916.7598 | −918.7598 | −920.7852 | CHSQ(16) = 392.7350[.000] | 329.6168[.000] |

AIC = Akaike Information Criterion SBC = Schwarz Bayesian Criterion

Akaike information criterion (AIC) of order 3. Since we have a short time-series (60 observations), we cannot take the risk of over-parameterization and therefore choose 2 as the order of the VAR. In such situations it is, however, important to check the residuals of the individual equations in the VAR for possible serial correlation. An inspection of the results suggests that this is not a problem in the present application.

Backtrack to the System Estimation window and from the System Estimation Menu (Multivariate Menu) choose the cointegrating VAR option, selecting the Restricted Intercepts option 2. In the box editor delete the intercept term (INPT) so that the content of the box editor is

Y X

In the case of the cointegrating VAR option, specification of intercept and (linear) trend terms is done at a later stage. Use the whole period for estimation and set the order of the VAR to 2. The choice of intercepts/trends is very important in testing for cointegration. In the present application, although the underlying variables are trended, they move together, and it seems unlikely that there will be a trend in the cointegrating relation between Y and X. The results in Table 16.3b should now appear on the screen. Both the maximum and trace eigenvalue statistics strongly reject the null hypothesis that there is no cointegration between Y and X (namely that $r = 0$), but do not reject the hypothesis that there is one cointegrating relation between these variables (i.e. $r = 1$).

A similar result also follows from the values of the various model selection criteria reported in panel C of Table 16.3b. This complete agreement between the three procedures for testing/selecting the number of cointegrating relations is very rare, however. In practice, these three methods often result in conflicting conclusions, and the decision concerning

**Table 16.3b:** Testing for cointegration between capital expenditures (Y) and appropriations (X) in US manufacturing

Panel A

Cointegration with restricted intercepts and no trends in the VAR
Cointegration LR Test Based on Maximal Eigenvalue of the Stochastic Matrix

58 observations from 1953Q3 to 1967Q4. Order of VAR = 2.
List of variables included in the cointegrating vector:
Y X Intercept
List of eigenvalues in descending order:
.52365 .038066 0.00

| Null | Alternative | Statistic | 95% Critical Value | 90% Critical Value |
|---|---|---|---|---|
| r = 0 | r = 1 | 43.0135 | 15.8700 | 13.8100 |
| r <= 1 | r = 2 | 2.2510 | 9.1600 | 7.5300 |

Use the above table to determine r (the number of cointegrating vectors).

Panel B

Cointegration with restricted intercepts and no trends in the VAR
Cointegration LR Test Based on Trace of the Stochastic Matrix

58 observations from 1953Q3 to 1967Q4. Order of VAR = 2.
List of variables included in the cointegrating vector:
Y X Intercept
List of eigenvalues in descending order:
.52365 .038066 0.00

| Null | Alternative | Statistic | 95% Critical Value | 90% Critical Value |
|---|---|---|---|---|
| r = 0 | r >= 1 | 45.2645 | 20.1800 | 17.8800 |
| r <= 1 | r = 2 | 2.2510 | 9.1600 | 7.5300 |

Use the above table to determine r (the number of cointegrating vectors).

Panel C

Cointegration with restricted intercepts and no trends in the VAR Choice of the Number of Cointegrating Relations Using Model Selection Criteria

58 observations from 1953Q3 to 1967Q4. Order of VAR = 2.
List of variables included in the cointegrating vector:
Y X Intercept
List of eigenvalues in descending order:
.52365 .038066 0.00

| Rank | Maximized LL | AIC | SBC | HQC |
|---|---|---|---|---|
| r = 0 | −772.7598 | −776.7598 | −780.8807 | −778.3649 |
| r = 1 | −751.2530 | −759.2530 | −767.4948 | −762.4633 |
| r = 2 | −750.1275 | −760.1275 | −770.4297 | −764.1404 |

AIC = Akaike Information Criterion SBC = Schwarz Bayesian Criterion
HQC = Hannan–Quinn Criterion

the choice of $r$, the number of cointegrating relations, must be made in view of other information, perhaps from economic theory.

As an example, consider the application of the cointegrating VAR option to the problem of testing the purchasing power parity (PPP) hypothesis studied in Johansen and Juselius (1992), and Pesaran and Shin (1996). The relevant data is in the special *Microfit* file PPP.FIT and contains the following variables:

| | |
|---|---|
| P | ≡ Logarithm of UK wholesale prices |
| PF | ≡ Logarithm of foreign prices |
| E | ≡ Logarithm of the UK effective exchange rate |
| R | ≡ Domestic interest rate |
| RF | ≡ Foreign interest rate |
| DPO | ≡ Changes in real oil prices |
| S1, S2, S3 | ≡ Quarterly seasonal dummies |
| INPT | ≡ An intercept term |

Load this file into *Microfit* and make sure that the above variables are in the variables list. Using the ADF command in the Command Editor, it is easy to see that we cannot reject the hypothesis that the variables P, PF, E, R, and RF are $I(1)$, and that DPO is $I(0)$. The second stage in the cointegration analysis is to decide on the order of the underlying VAR model and the nature of the intercepts/trends in the model. Using the unrestricted VAR option in the System Estimation Menu (Multivariate Menu), and choosing 4 as the maximum order for the following specification,

P E PF R RF & INPT S1 S2 S3 DPO DPO(−1) START

the AIC and SBC select orders 3 and 1, respectively. Johansen and Juselius (JJ) (1992) select the order 2. Given the fact that the sample is relatively small (only 62 quarters) we follow JJ and select 2 for the order of the VAR.[3] As far as the specification of the intercept and trend in the VAR is concerned, we also follow JJ and assume that the underlying VAR model does not contain deterministic trends, but contains unrestricted intercepts. However, recall from the discussion in Sections 19.6 and 7.5 that such specifications will generate deterministic trends in the level of the variables (P, PF, E, R, and RF) when the long-run multiplier matrix is rank deficient, which will be the case in this application if one accepts the conclusion that variables P, PF, E, R, and RF are $I(1)$.

With the above considerations in mind, choose the cointegrating VAR option 2 in the System Estimation Menu (Multivariate Menu), selecting the Unrestricted intercepts, no trends option 3, and type

P E PF R RF & S1 S2 S3 DPO DPO(−1)

Select the whole period for estimation, choose 2 for the order of the VAR,

---

[3]However, an inspection of the regression results for the individual equations in the VAR(2) model suggest important evidence of residual serial correlation for the RF equation. In fact, this equation decisively fails all four diagnostic tests (residual serial correlation, functional form, normality, and heteroscedasticity) automatically supplied by *Microfit*.

**Table 16.3c:** Testing for cointegration between prices, interest rates, and the exchange rate in the UK economy

Cointegration with unrestricted intercepts and no trends in the VAR
Cointegration LR Test Based on Maximal Eigenvalue of the Stochastic Matrix

60 observations from 1972Q3 to 1987Q2. Order of VAR = 2.
List of variables included in the cointegrating vector:
P E PF R RF
List of I(0) variables included in the VAR:
DPO DPO(−1) S1 S2 S3
List of eigenvalues in descending order:
.40680 .28525 .25423 .10228 .082827

| Null | Alternative | Statistic | 95% Critical Value | 90% Critical Value |
|---|---|---|---|---|
| r=0 | r=1 | 31.3337 | 33.6400 | 31.0200 |
| r<=1 | r=2 | 20.1497 | 27.4200 | 24.9900 |
| r<=2 | r=3 | 17.6006 | 21.1200 | 19.0200 |
| r<=3 | r=4 | 6.4739 | 14.8800 | 12.9800 |
| r<=4 | r=5 | 5.1875 | 8.0700 | 6.5000 |

Use the above table to determine r (the number of cointegrating vectors).

Cointegration with unrestricted intercepts and no trends in the VAR
Cointegration LR Test Based on Trace of the Stochastic Matrix

60 observations from 1972Q3 to 1987Q2. Order of VAR = 2.
List of variables included in the cointegrating vector:
P E PF R RF
List of I(0) variables included in the VAR:
DPO DPO(−1) S1 S2 S3
List of eigenvalues in descending order:
.40680 .28525 .25423 .10228 .082827

| Null | Alternative | Statistic | 95% Critical Value | 90% Critical Value |
|---|---|---|---|---|
| r=0 | r>=1 | 80.7454 | 70.4900 | 66.2300 |
| r<=1 | r>=2 | 49.4117 | 48.8800 | 45.7000 |
| r<=2 | r>=3 | 29.2620 | 31.5400 | 28.7800 |
| r<=3 | r>=4 | 11.6614 | 17.8600 | 15.7500 |
| r<=4 | r=5 | 5.1875 | 8.0700 | 6.5000 |

Use the above table to determine r (the number of cointegrating vectors).

Cointegration with unrestricted intercepts and no trends in the VAR
Choice of the Number of Cointegrating Relations Using Model Selection Criteria

60 observations from 1972Q3 to 1987Q2. Order of VAR = 2.
List of variables included in the cointegrating vector:
P E PF R RF
List of I(0) variables included in the VAR:
DPO DPO(−1) S1 S2 S3
List of eigenvalues in descending order:
.40680 .28525 .25423 .10228 .082827

| Rank | Maximized LL | AIC | SBC | HQC |
|---|---|---|---|---|
| r=0 | 900.3650 | 845.3650 | 787.7705 | 822.8367 |
| r=1 | 916.0319 | 852.0319 | 785.0128 | 825.8170 |
| r=2 | 926.1067 | 855.1067 | 780.7575 | 826.0247 |
| r=3 | 934.9070 | 858.9070 | 779.3219 | 827.7769 |
| r=4 | 938.1440 | 859.1440 | 776.4174 | 826.7850 |
| r=5 | 940.7377 | 860.7377 | 776.9639 | 827.9692 |

AIC = Akaike Information Criterion SBC = Schwarz Bayesian Criterion
HQC = Hannan–Quinn Criterion

and click START. The results in Table 16.3c should now appear on the screen.

The maximum eigenvalue and the trace statistics in this table are almost identical with those reported in Johansen and Juselius (1992, Table 2). However, there are important differences between the critical values used by *Microfit* and those reported in JJ (1992) and also by Osterwald-Lenum (1992). The reasons for these differences are explained in Pesaran *et al.* (1996b). Irrespective of which sets of critical values one uses, there is a clear conflict between the test results based on the maximum eigenvalue statistic and the trace statistic. Taken literally, the maximum eigenvalue statistic does not reject $r = 0$ (no cointegration), while the trace statistic does not reject $r = 2$ at the 95 per cent significant level. Changing the significance level of the two tests to 90 per cent results in the maximum eigenvalue value statistic selecting $r = 1$, and in the trace statistic selecting $r = 3$. Turning to the model selection criteria (given in panel C of the table), we find that the AIC and SBC choose $r = 5$ and zero, the two opposite extremes; while the Hannan–Quinn criterion chooses $r = 5$. The data in this application seems hopelessly uninformative on the choice of $r$. Turning to long-run economic theory based on arbitrage in the product and capital markets we would expect *two* cointegrating relations: the PPP relation

$$P - E - PF \sim I(0)$$

and the interest-rate arbitrage relation (which is a long-run implication of the uncovered interest parity hypothesis)

$$R - RF \sim I(0).$$

Combining this theoretical insight with the mixed test results (based on a very short sample), it seems reasonable to set $r = 2$.

## 16.4 Lesson 16.4: Testing for cointegration in models with $I(1)$ exogenous variables

In certain applications, particularly in the context of small open economies, it is reasonable to assume that one or more of the $I(1)$ variables in the cointegrating VAR model are 'long-run forcing' variables, in the sense that in the long run they are not 'caused' by the other variables in the model. This does not, of course, rule out contemporaneous or short-run interactions between the $I(1)$ variables. (For a more formal discussion see Section 19.6.) For example, in the case of the five-variable VAR model in (P, E, R, PF and RF) analysed in Lesson 16.3, it seems a priori plausible to assume that in the long run there are no feedbacks from UK prices, interest rates, and exchange rates into foreign prices and interest rates; that is PF and RF are the 'long-run forcing' variables of the system. To test the purchasing power parity (PPP) hypothesis under these assumptions, first read the file PPP.FIT and choose option 2 in the System Estimation Menu (Multivariate Menu) – see Lesson 16.3 and Johansen and Juselius (1992) for further details – selecting the Unrestricted intercepts, no trends option 3. This is the intercept/trend specification chosen by Johansen and Juselius (JJ) (1992) which we also adopt in order to make our analysis comparable with theirs. To set up the VAR model with PF and RF as 'long-run forcing' variables, changes in real oil prices (DPO), and seasonal dummies (S1, S2, and S3) as exogenous I(0) variables in the box editor, you need to type:

P E R; RF PF & DPO DPO(−1) S1 S2 S3

The semicolon separates the $I(1)$ variables of the model into the set of jointly determined variables, P, E, and R, and the long-run forcing variables PF and RF. Select the whole sample period and for the order of the VAR choose 2 (as in JJ's analysis). Then click START. You should now get the results in Table 16.4a on the screen.

Both the maximum eigenvalue and the trace statistic suggest $r = 1$. The hypothesis that $r = 0$ is rejected against $r = 1$, but the hypothesis that $r = 1$ cannot be rejected against $r = 2$, etc. The Schwarz Bayesian (SBC) and the Hannan–Quinn (HQC) also favour $r = 1$, but the same is not true of Akaike information criterion (AIC), which selects $r = 3$! In what follows we assume $r = 1$ and present the estimates of the cointegrating coefficients normalized on the coefficient of $P$.

Click CLOSE to move to the Cointegrating VAR Post Estimation Menu (see Section 7.5.2), choose option 2 and, when prompted, type 1 to specify $r = 1$. To obtain estimates of the cointegrating coefficients (together with their asymptotic standard errors), choose option 6 (Long Run Structural Modelling, IR Analysis and Forecasting), and then choose option 4 by pressing the ↵ key. You will be asked to specify exactly one restriction to identify the cointegrating relation. In the present application where $r = 1$, this can be achieved by normalizing on one of the coefficients. In the box editor type

A1 = 1 OK

to normalize on the coefficient of P, the first variable in the cointegrating VAR. You should now see the estimates of the cointegrating coefficients and their asymptotic standard errors on the screen: see Table 16.4b.

Notice that the maximized value of the log-likelihood function $LL(r = 1) = 536.1264$, which is identical to the value 'maximized LL' for $r = 1$ in the bottom panel of Table 16.4a. Also, only the coefficient of RF, estimated at $-0.77615(0.8925)$, with its asymptotic standard error in brackets, is not statistically significant. It is therefore reasonable to re-estimate the cointegrating relation, imposing the over-identifying restriction A4 = 0, where A4 stands for the coefficient of RF. To impose this restriction, click CLOSE to move to the IR Analysis and Forecasting Menu, choose option 0, and then click YES to return to the box editor for the specification of the coefficient restrictions. You should see the normalizing (or exactly identifying) restriction A1 = 1 on the screen. *Add* the restriction A4 = 0 to it. The box editor should now contain the two restrictions

A1 = 1;   A4 = 0

**Table 16.4a:** Testing for cointegration between prices, interest rates, and the exchange rate in the UK economy–treating foreign prices and interest rates as exogenous

Cointegration with unrestricted intercepts and no trends in the VAR
Cointegration LR Test Based on Maximal Eigenvalue of the Stochastic Matrix

60 observations from 1972Q3 to 1987Q2. Order of VAR = 2, chosen r = 1.
List of variables included in the cointegrating vector:
P E R RF PF
List of I(1) exogenous variables included in the VAR:
RF PF
List of I(0) variables included in the VAR:
S1 S2 S3 DPO DPO(−1)
List of eigenvalues in descending order:
.38501 .18433 .12159 0.0 0.0

| Null | Alternative | Statistic | 95% Critical Value | 90% Critical Value |
|---|---|---|---|---|
| r=0 | r=1 | 29.1690 | 27.7500 | 25.2100 |
| r<=1 | r=2 | 12.2249 | 21.0700 | 18.7800 |
| r<=2 | r=3 | 7.7788 | 14.3500 | 12.2700 |

Use the above table to determine r (the number of cointegrating vectors).

Cointegration with unrestricted intercepts and no trends in the VAR
Cointegration LR Test Based on Trace of the Stochastic Matrix

60 observations from 1972Q3 to 1987Q2. Order of VAR = 2, chosen r = 1.
List of variables included in the cointegrating vector:
P E R RF PF
List of I(1) exogenous variables included in the VAR:
RF PF
List of I(0) variables included in the VAR:
S1 S2 S3 DPO DPO(−1)
List of eigenvalues in descending order:
.38501 .18433 .12159 0.0 0.0

| Null | Alternative | Statistic | 95% Critical Value | 90% Critical Value |
|---|---|---|---|---|
| r=0 | r>=1 | 49.1728 | 46.4400 | 42.6700 |
| r<=1 | r>=2 | 20.0037 | 28.4200 | 25.6300 |
| r<=2 | r=3 | 7.7788 | 14.3500 | 12.2700 |

Use the above table to determine r (the number of cointegrating vectors).

Cointegration with unrestricted intercepts and no trends in the VAR
Choice of the Number of Cointegrating Relations Using Model Selection Criteria

60 observations from 1972Q3 to 1987Q2. Order of VAR = 2, chosen r = 1.
List of variables included in the cointegrating vector:
P E R RF PF
List of I(1) exogenous variables included in the VAR:
RF PF
List of I(0) variables included in the VAR:
S1 S2 S3 DPO DPO(−1)
List of eigenvalues in descending order:
.38501 .18433 .12159 0.0 0.0

| Rank | Maximized LL | AIC | SBC | HQC |
|---|---|---|---|---|
| r=0 | 521.5419 | 488.5419 | 453.9852 | 475.0249 |
| r=1 | 536.1264 | 496.1264 | 454.2395 | 479.7421 |
| r=2 | 542.2389 | 497.2389 | 450.1161 | 478.8066 |
| r=3 | 546.1283 | 498.1283 | 447.8640 | 478.4672 |

AIC = Akaike Information Criterion SBC = Schwarz Bayesian Criterion
HQC = Hannan–Quinn Criterion

| **Table 16.4b:** ML estimates subject to exactly identifying restriction(s)–estimates of restricted cointegrating relations (SEs in brackets) | | | | |
|---|---|---|---|---|
| Converged after 2 iterations<br>Cointegration with unrestricted intercepts and no trends in the VAR | | | | |
| 60 observations from 1972Q3 to 1987Q2. Order of VAR = 2, chosen r = 1. | | | | |
| List of variables included in the cointegrating vector: | | | | |
| P | E | R | RF | PF |
| List of I(1) exogenous variables included in the VAR: | | | | |
| RF | PF | | | |
| List of I(0) variables included in the VAR: | | | | |
| S1 | S2 | S3 | DPO | DPO(−1) |
| List of imposed restriction(s) on cointegrating vectors:<br>A1 = 1 | | | | |
| | Vector 1 | | | |
| P | 1.0000<br>(*NONE*) | | | |
| E | −.94623<br>(.33076) | | | |
| R | −4.7556<br>(1.4337) | | | |
| RF | −.77615<br>(.89249) | | | |
| PF | −.90197<br>(.19997) | | | |
| LL subject to exactly identifying restrictions = 536.1264 | | | | |

Click OK to estimate the cointegrating relations subject to these restrictions. You will be asked to specify/edit initial values for the cointegrating coefficients. Click OK to accept the initial values supplied by the program, press ↩ to choose the modified Newton–Raphson iterative algorithm, and then accept the default value of the damping vector (set at 0.01). *Microfit* carries out the computations and converges after 19 iterations. The results are reproduced in Table 16.4c.

The log-likelihood ratio statistic for testing the restriction A4 = 0, is given by CHSQ(1) = 0.74, which is not statistically significant and hence suggests that the restriction A4 = 0 cannot be rejected. The PPP hypothesis, however, postulates that the coefficients of E and PF should also both be equal to −1. To impose (and then test) this restriction, you can now click CLOSE to move to the IR Analysis and Forecasting Menu (see Section 7.5.5), from where you can return to the box editor to specify the additional restrictions A2 = −1 and A5 = −1 (choose option 0). Once computations are completed, you should obtain the results in Table 16.4d.

The LR statistic for the three over-identifying restrictions (A2 = −1, A4 = 0, A5 = −1) is equal to 3.61 which is distributed asymptotically as a

**Table 16.4c:** ML estimates subject to over-identifying restriction(s)–estimates of restricted cointegrating relations (SEs in brackets)

Converged after 19 iterations
Cointegration with unrestricted intercepts and no trends in the VAR

60 observations from 1972Q3 to 1987Q2. Order of VAR = 2, chosen r = 1.
List of variables included in the cointegrating vector:

| P | E | R | RF | PF |
|---|---|---|---|---|

List of I(1) exogenous variables included in the VAR:

| RF | PF |
|---|---|

List of I(0) variables included in the VAR:

| S1 | S2 | S3 | DPO | DPO(−1) |
|---|---|---|---|---|

List of imposed restriction(s) on cointegrating vectors:
A1 = 1; A4 = 0

| | Vector 1 |
|---|---|
| P | 1.0000 |
| | ( *NONE*) |
| E | −.79464 |
| | (.26577) |
| R | −5.2257 |
| | (1.4960) |
| RF | .0000 |
| | ( *NONE*) |
| PF | −.98320 |
| | (.16874) |

LR Test of Restrictions CHSQ(1) = 0.74335[0.389]
DF = Total no of restrictions (2) − no of just-identifying restrictions (1)
LL subject to exactly identifying restrictions = 536.1264
LL subject to overidentifying restrictions = 535.7547

$\chi^2$ variate with 3 degrees of freedom, and hence is not statistically significant. Therefore, the restricted cointegrating relation is estimated as

$$\underset{}{P_t - E_t - PF_t - \underset{(0.8754)}{5.3198}\ R_t \sim I(0)}$$

What is striking about this result is the significant positive long-run effect of the domestic interest rate on the PPP relation, defined by $P_t - E_t - PF_t$. This provides evidence against the validity of the PPP (in the case of the present data set), but also pinpoints the reason for the departure from PPP, namely the effect of the nominal interest rate.

Finally, to see the error correction form of the relations in the cointegrating VAR model, you can choose option 7 in the IR Analysis and Forecasting Menu (see Section 7.5.5). The number of error-correction equations in the present application is 3, corresponding to the jointly determined variables of the model, namely P, E, and R. The EC equation for P is given in Table 16.4e.

The coefficient of the error-correction term, −0.0423 (0.0136), has the correct sign and is statistically significant, but rather small, suggesting that it

**Table 16.4d:** ML estimates subject to over-identifying restriction(s)—estimates of restricted cointegrating relations (SEs in brackets)

Converged after 19 iterations
Cointegration with unrestricted intercepts and no trends in the VAR

60 observations from 1972Q3 to 1987Q2. Order of VAR = 2, chosen r = 1.
List of variables included in the cointegrating vector:

| P | E | R | RF | PF |
|---|---|---|---|---|

List of I(1) exogenous variables included in the VAR:

| RF | PF |
|---|---|

List of I(0) variables included in the VAR:

| S1 | S2 | S3 | DPO | DPO(−1) |
|---|---|---|---|---|

List of imposed restriction(s) on cointegrating vectors:
A1 = 1; A4 = 0; A2 = −1; A5 = −1

| | Vector 1 |
|---|---|
| P | 1.0000 |
| | (*NONE*) |
| E | −1.0000 |
| | (*NONE*) |
| R | −5.3198 |
| | (.87543) |
| RF | .0000 |
| | (*NONE*) |
| PF | −1.0000 |
| | (*NONE*) |

LR Test of Restrictions CHSQ(3) = 3.6052[.307]
DF = Total no of restrictions (4) − no of justidentifying restrictions (1)
LL subject to exactly identifying restrictions = 536.1264
LL subject to overidentifying restrictions = 534.3238

would take a long time for the equation to return to its equilibrium once it has been shocked. The error correction terms in the exchange rate and the domestic interest rate equations are also statistically significant, but only just. Notice that the positive coefficients obtained for the error correction terms in these two equations are correct. This is because E and R enter the error correction terms with negative coefficients.

## 16.5 Lesson 16.5: Long-run analysis of consumption, income, and inflation – ARDL approach

In this lesson we employ the testing and estimation procedure advanced in Pesaran *et al.* (1996a), and Pesaran and Shin (1995a) to examine the relationship between the logarithm of non-durable consumption expenditures (LC), the logarithm of real disposable income (LY), and the inflation rate (DP) in the US, using quarterly observations over the period 1960(1) to 1994(1). The main advantage of this testing and estimation strategy (which

**Table 16.4e** ECM for variable P estimated by OLS based on cointegrating VAR(2)

Dependent variable is dP
60 observations used for estimation from 1972Q3 to 1987Q2

| Regressor | Coefficient | Standard Error | T-Ratio[Prob] |
|---|---|---|---|
| Intercept | .17444 | .055071 | 3.1676[.003] |
| dP1 | .43577 | .11238 | 3.8777[.000] |
| dE1 | .040618 | .034748 | 1.1689[.248] |
| dR1 | −.070052 | .11897 | −.58880[.559] |
| dPF1 | .12503 | .11915 | 1.0494[.299] |
| ecm1(−1) | −.042265 | .013610 | −3.1053[.003] |
| S1 | .0056492 | .0031539 | 1.7912[.080] |
| S2 | .8278E-3 | .0032346 | .25593[.799] |
| S3 | .5328E-3 | .0032104 | .16597[.869] |
| DPO | .024890 | .0077761 | 3.2009[.002] |
| DPO(−1) | .0012268 | .012356 | .099290[.921] |

List of additional temporary variables created:
dP = P − P( − 1)
dP1 = P( − 1) − P( − 2)
dE1 = E( − 1) − E( − 2)
dR1 = R( − 1) − R( − 2)
dRF1 = RF( − 1) − RF( − 2)
dPF1 = PF( − 1) − PF( − 2)
ecm1 = 1.0000*P − 1.0000*E − 5.3198*R − .0000*RF − 1.0000*PF

| | | | |
|---|---|---|---|
| R-Squared | .81889 | R-Bar-Squared | .77739 |
| S.E. of Regression | .0083111 | F-Stat. F(11, 48) | 19.7307[.000] |
| Mean of Dependent Variable | .026359 | S.D. of Dependent Variable | .017615 |
| Residual Sum of Squares | .0033156 | Equation Log-likelihood | 208.9679 |
| Akaike Info. Criterion | 196.9679 | Schwarz Bayesian Criterion | 184.4018 |
| DWstatistic | 1.7786 | System Log-likelihood | 534.3238 |

Diagnostic Tests

| Test Statistics | LM Version | F Version |
|---|---|---|
| A:Serial Correlation | CHSQ(4) = 3.2948[.510] | F(4, 44) = .63914[.637] |
| B:Functional Form | CHSQ(1) = 3.0856[.079] | F(1, 47) = 2.5481[.117] |
| C:Normality | CHSQ(2) = 2.0421[.360] | Not applicable |
| D:Heteroscedasticity | CHSQ(1) = .4119E-3[.984] | F(1, 58) = .3982E-3[.984] |

A:Lagrange multiplier test of residual serial correlation
B:Ramsey's RESET test using the square of the fitted values
C:Based on a test of skewness and kurtosis of residuals
D:Based on the regression of squared residuals on squared fitted values

we refer to as the ARDL procedure) lies in the fact that it can be applied irrespective of whether the regressors are $I(0)$ or $I(1)$, and this avoids the pre-testing problems associated with standard cointegration analysis which requires the classification of the variables into $I(1)$ and $I(0)$.

The ARDL procedure involves two stages. At the first stage the existence of the long-run relation between the variables under investigation is tested by computing the F-statistic for testing the significance of the lagged levels of the variables in the error correction form of the underlying ARDL model. However, the (asymptotic) distribution of this F-statistic is non-standard, irrespective of whether the regressors (in the present application LY and DP) are $I(0)$ or $I(1)$. Pesaran *et al.* (1996a) have tabulated the appropriate critical values for different numbers of regressors ($k$), and whether the ARDL model contains an intercept and/or trend. They give two sets of critical values. One set assuming that *all* the variables in the ARDL model are $I(1)$, and another computed assuming all the variables are $I(0)$. For each application, this provides a band covering all the possible classifications of the variables into $I(0)$ and $I(1)$, or even fractionally integrated ones. If the computed F-statistic falls outside this band, a conclusive decision can be made without needing to know whether the underlying variables are $I(0)$ or $I(1)$, or fractionally integrated. If the computed statistic falls within the critical value band, the result of the inference is inconclusive and depends on whether the underlying variables are $I(0)$ or $I(1)$. It is at this stage in the analysis that the investigator may have to carry out unit root tests on the variables.

The second stage of the analysis is to estimate the coefficients of the long-run relations and make inferences about their values using the ARDL option (see Section 6.19). Note that it is only appropriate to embark on this stage if you are satisfied that the long-run relationship between the variables to be estimated is not in fact spurious.

To apply the above approach to the US consumption data, first load the special *Microfit* file USCON.FIT and then run the transformations in the equation file USCON.EQU on this data in the Command Editor. You should have the following variables in the variables list:

LC = Log of non-durable real consumption expenditures
DLC = LC − LC(−1)
LY = Log of real disposable income
DLY = LY − LY(−1)
PI = The rate of inflation
DPI = PI − PI(−1)
INPT = A vector of ones

Since the observations are quarterly, for the maximum order of the lags in the ARDL model we choose 4 and carry out the estimation over the period 1960(1) to 1992(4), retaining the remaining five observations, 1993(1) to 1994(1) for predictions.

The error correction version of the ARDL(4, 4, 4) model in the variables LC, LY, and DP is given by:

$$DLC_t = a_0 + \sum_{i=1}^{4} b_i DLC_{t-i} + \sum_{i=1}^{4} d_i DLY_{t-i} + \sum_{i=1}^{4} e_i DPI_{t-i} + \delta_1 LC_{t-1} + \delta_2 LY_{t-1} + \delta_3 PI_{t-1} + u_t \qquad (16.1)$$

Due to the high levels of cross-sectional and temporal aggregations involved, it is not possible to know a priori whether LY and DP are the 'long-run forcing' variables for aggregate consumption (LC), so we have excluded the current values of DLY and DPI from (16.1). We shall reconsider this issue once we have completed our *stability* tests, namely whether there exists a long-run relationship between LC, LY and PI.

The hypothesis that we will be testing is the null of 'non-existence of the long-run relationship' defined by

$$H_0\colon \delta_1 = \delta_2 = \delta_3 = 0$$

against

$$H_1\colon \delta_1 \neq 0, \quad \delta_2 \neq 0, \quad \delta_3 \neq 0$$

The relevant statistic is the familiar F-statistic for the joint significance of $\delta_1$,$\delta_2$, and $\delta_3$. To compute this statistic, choose option 1 in the Single Equation Estimation Menu (Univariate Menu: see Section 6.4), selecting the OLS option, and in the box editor type

DLC INPT DLC{1 – 4} DLY{1 – 4} DPI{1 – 4}

Choose the sample 1960(1) to 1992(4) for estimation, click START and then OK to see the OLS results for the regression in first differences. This regression is of no direct interest. Click CLOSE and then press the ↩ key to move to the Hypothesis Testing Menu and choose option 6 (variable addition test). Now list the lagged values of the level variables by typing:

LC(–1) LY(–1) PI(–1) OK

The F-statistic for testing the joint null hypothesis that the coefficients of these level variables are zero (i.e. there exists no long-run relationship between them) is given in the last row of the result table that appears on the screen. We denote it by F(LC|LY, PI) = 5.43. As we have already noted under $H_0$: $\delta_1 = \delta_2 = \delta_3 = 0$ this statistic has a non-standard distribution irrespective of whether LC, LY, and PI are $I(0)$ or $I(1)$. The critical value bounds for this test are computed by Pesaran *et al.* (1996a), and are reproduced as Tables F and W in Appendix C. Table W gives the bounds for the W-statistic for three cases depending on whether the underlying regression contains an intercept or trend. Table F gives the critical value bounds for the F-statistic version of the test. The relevant critical value bounds for the present application are given in the middle panel of Table W, and at the 95 per cent level are given by 3.793 to 4.855. Since F(LC|LY, PI) = 5.43 exceeds the upper bound of the critical value band, we can reject the null of no long-run relationship between LC, LY, and PI, irrespective of the order of their integration.

Consider now the significance of the lagged level variables in the error correction models explaining $DLY_t$ and $DPI_t$. Backtrack and choose option 4 in the Backtracking Menu to edit the regression equation, and change DLC (the dependent variable) to DLY and then follow the same steps as above to compute the F-statistic for the joint significance of LC(–1),

LY(−1), and PI(−1) in this new regression. You should obtain F(LY|LC, PI) = 2.631: similarly for the PI equation F(PI|LC, LY) = 1.359. Both these statistics fall well below the lower bound of the critical value band (which is 3.793–4.855), and hence the null hypothesis that the level variables do not enter significantly in the equations for DLY and DPI cannot be rejected. Once again this conclusion holds irrespective of whether the underlying variables are $I(0)$ and $I(1)$.

The above test results suggest that there exists a long-run relationship between LC, LY, and PI, and that the variables LY and PI can be treated as the 'long-run forcing' variables for the explanation of LC.

The estimation of the long-run coefficients and the associated error-correction model can now be accomplished using the ARDL option in *Microfit* (see Section 6.19). Move to the Single Equation Estimation window, and choose the ARDL option 6 in the Univariate Menu. Click to clear the box editor and type

LC LY PI & INPT

Choose the sample 1960(1) to 1992(4) for estimation, enter 4 for the maximum lag to be used in the model selection that follows, and click START. *Microfit* estimates 125 regressions and presents you with the ARDL Order Selection Menu (see Section 6.19.2). This offers a choice between different model selection criteria. The Schwarz Bayesian (SBC) and the Akaike information (AIC) criteria select the ARDL(1, 2, 0) and ARDL(2, 2, 3) specifications, respectively. The estimates of the long-run coefficients based on these models are summarized in Table 16.5a.

The point estimates are very similar but, as is to be expected, the estimated standard errors obtained using the model selected by the AIC are considerably smaller given the much higher order ARDL model selected by the AIC as compared to the SBC.

To obtain the estimates of the error correction model associated with these long-run estimates, you need to choose option 3 in the Post ARDL Model Selection Menu (see Section 6.19.3). The estimated error correction model selected using the AIC is given in Table 16.5b. With the exception of the coefficient of $DLC_{t-1}$, all the other coefficients are statistically

**Table 16.5a:** Estimates of the long-run coefficients based on ARDL models selected by AIC and SBC

| | Model Selection Criteria | |
|---|---|---|
| Long-Run Coefficients | *SBC*-ARDL(1, 2, 0) | *AIC*-ARDL(2, 2, 3) |
| INPT | 1.336 | 1.269 |
| | (.167) | (.112) |
| LY | .693 | .700 |
| | (.021) | (.014) |
| PI | −2.595 | −2.288 |
| | (1.171) | (.754) |

**Table 16.5b:** A log-linear error correction model of US consumption

Error Correction Representation for the Selected ARDL Model
ARDL(2, 2, 3) selected based on Akaike Information Criterion

Dependent variable is dLC
127 observations used for estimation from 1961Q2 to 1992Q4

| Regressor | Coefficient | Standard Error | T-Ratio[Prob] |
|---|---|---|---|
| dLC1 | .11651 | .085463 | 1.3633[.175] |
| dLY | .26694 | .056676 | 4.7098[.000] |
| dLY1 | .16621 | .060825 | 2.7326[.007] |
| dPI | −.18461 | .080063 | −2.3058[.023] |
| dPI1 | .18936 | .087764 | 2.1576[.033] |
| dPI2 | .25269 | .078663 | 3.2123[.002] |
| dINPT | .15989 | .047712 | 3.3511[.001] |
| ecm(1) | −.12599 | .036172 | −3.4832[.001] |

List of additional temporary variables created:
dLC = LC − LC(−1)
dLC1 = LC(−1) − LC(−2)
dLY = LY − LY(−1)
dLY1 = LY(−1) − LY(−2)
dPI = PI − PI(−1)
dPI1 = PI(−1) − PI(−2)
dPI2 = PI(−2) − PI(−3)
dINPT = INPT − INPT(−1)
ecm = LC − .70016*LY + 2.2877*PI − 1.2690*INPT

| | | | |
|---|---|---|---|
| R-Squared | .46234 | R-Bar-Squared | .42098 |
| S.E. of Regression | .0054148 | F-Stat. F(7, 119) | 14.3727[.000] |
| Mean of Dependent Variable | .0055870 | S.D. of Dependent Variable | .0071160 |
| Residual Sum of Squares | .0034305 | Equation Log-likelihood | 487.7664 |
| Akaike Info. Criterion | 477.7664 | Schwarz Bayesian Criterion | 463.5455 |
| DW-statistic | 1.9835 | | |

significant. The underlying ARDL equation also passes all the diagnostic tests that are automatically computed by *Microfit*.

The error correction coefficient, estimated at −0.12599(0.036172) is statistically highly significant, has the correct sign, and suggests a moderate speed of convergence to equilibrium. The larger the error correction coefficient (in absolute value) the faster is the economy's return to its equilibrium, once shocked.

The above error correction model can also be used in forecasting the rate of change of consumption conditional on current and past changes in real disposable income and inflation. Proceed to the Post ARDL Model Selection Menu and choose option 4. Now press the ↩ key four times to forecast DLC over the period 1993(1) to 1994(1). You should get the results in Table 16.5c.

The root mean squares of forecast errors of around 0.45 per cent per

**Table 16.5c:** Dynamic forecasts for the change in LC

ARDL Regression Estimation

Based on 127 observations from 1961Q2 to 1992Q4.
ARDL(2,2,3) based on Akaike Information Criterion.
Dependent variable in the ARDL model is LC included with a lag of 2.
List of other regressors in the ARDL model:

| | | | | |
|---|---|---|---|---|
| LY | LY(−1) | LY(−2) | PI | PI(−1) |
| PI(−2) | PI(−3) | INPT | | |

| Observation | Actual | Prediction | Error |
|---|---|---|---|
| 1993Q1 | −.0053759 | .0034962 | −.0088721 |
| 1993Q2 | .0065768 | .0026170 | .0039599 |
| 1993Q3 | .0090587 | .0078788 | .0011798 |
| 1993Q4 | .0066042 | .0048395 | .0017647 |
| 1994Q1 | .0101880 | .0078575 | .0023304 |

Summary Statistics for Residuals and Forecast Errors

| | Estimation Period 1961Q2 to 1992Q4 | Forecast Period 1993Q1 to 1994Q1 |
|---|---|---|
| Mean | −.6546E-9 | .7253E-4 |
| Mean Absolute | .0040512 | .0036214 |
| Mean Sum Squares | .2701E-4 | .2087E-4 |
| Root Mean Sum Squares | .0051973 | .0045679 |

quarter compares favourably with the value of the same criterion computed over the estimation period. However, the model fails to forecast the extent of the fall in the non-durable consumption expenditures in the first quarter of 1993.

## 16.6 Lesson 16.6: Great ratios and long-run money demand in the US

In their paper King, Plosser, Stock and Watson (1991), (KPSW) examine long-run relations between (private) output (Y), consumption (C), investment (I), real money balances (M − P), the interest rate (R), and the rate of inflation (DP = P − P(−1)). With the exception of the interest rate, all the other variables are in logarithms. Output, consumption, investment, and money balances are measured on a per capita basis using civilian non-institutional population as the deflator.[4] KPSW estimate two sets of cointegrated VAR models: a three-variable model containing the real variables, C, I, and Y; and a six-variable model containing the real as well as

[4]For further details of the variables and their sources, see King *et al.* (1991). We are grateful to Mark Watson for providing us with their data set.

the nominal variables. For the three-variable model, they estimate restricted and unrestricted VARs over the 1949(1) to 1988(4) period, but for the six-variable model they choose the shorter estimation period of 1954(1)–1988(4), to avoid dealing with the possible effects of the Korean War, and other rather special developments in the US economy on nominal variables. They also experimented with VARs of different orders and settled on the order $p = 6$.

In this lesson we re-consider the cointegrating VAR models analysed by KPSW, and show how to analyse these models and their long-run properties using the cointegrating VAR options available in *Microfit*. The cointegrating VAR analysis involves a number of important steps, namely (1) ensuring that the jointly determined variables of the model are $I(1)$, (2) deciding the order of the VAR model, (3) identifying the nature of the deterministic variables such as intercepts and trends in the underlying VAR, (4) resolving the identification problem of the long-run relations that arises when the number of the cointegrating relations is larger than unity, (5) testing over-identifying restrictions on the long-run relations (if any). This analysis should also be supplemented by an examination of the short-run dynamic properties of the model, by considering the effect of variable-specific and system-wide shocks on the cointegrating (long-run relations) with the help of impulse response analysis and persistence profiles. See also Section 7.5.5.

With the above considerations in mind, load the file KPSW.FIT (containing quarterly observations over the period 1947(1) to 1988(4) for the US economy) and ensure that the following variables are in the list:

C Real per capita consumption (GC82, in logs).
DP Inflation (rate of change of GNP deflator)
I Investment per capital (GIE82, in logs)
MP Real money balance M2 defined as log of M2/P, P = GNP deflator
R Interest rate (FYGM3/100)
Y Real private output per capita (GNP82–GGE82, in logs)

The first stage in the analysis is to ascertain the order of the integration of the variables. The simplest way to achieve this in *Microfit* is to use the ADF command, although as we pointed out earlier the test results can be subject to a considerable margin of uncertainty.[5] To compute the ADF statistics for the six variables in the KPSW.FIT file, type in the Command Editor

**ADF** c(6); **ADF** i(6); **ADF** mp(6);
**ADF** y(6); **ADF** r(6); **ADF** dp(6) [GO]

The test results will appear on the screen. From the results for the ADF regression with both intercept and trend, we find that the null of a unit root is not rejected for C, MP, Y, and R, but may be rejected for the inflation rate, DP and investment I. To check if any of these variables are $I(2)$, create their first-differences and apply the ADF command to them:

[5] For more details on the *ADF* tests, see Lesson 11.1.

dc = c − c(−1); di = i − i(−1); dmp = mp − mp(−1);
dy = y − y(−1); dr = r − r(−1); ddp = dp − dp(−1);

**ADF** dc(5); **ADF** di(5); **ADF** dmp(5);
**ADF** dy(5); **ADF** dr(5); **ADF** ddp(5) GO

From the ADF statistics based on the regressions with an intercept term but no trend, we find that the null hypothesis that the first-differences of these variables have a unit root is strongly rejected in the case of all the six variables. Hence, we conclude that C, MP, Y, and R could be $I(1)$ but that the evidence on DP and I is less certain and they could be $I(0)$. In view of this uncertainty over the order of integration of DP, in what follows we shall focus on the remaining five $I(1)$ variables, namely C, I, MP, Y, and R. The analysis of the cointegrating VAR models when the orders of integration of the variables are unknown or are uncertain is beyond the scope of the present lesson. For later use we create a constant and a linear time trend by typing

inpt = 1; t = csum(1) GO

To decide on the order of the VAR, choose option 1 in the System Estimation Menu, and in the box editor type

C I MP Y R & INPT T

where the intercept and time trend are included in each equation of the VAR system since all variables seem to have a linear trend. Specify the sample period

1954Q1 1988Q4

This is the same sample period as used by KPSW in their analysis of the six-variable VAR model. Set the maximum order of the VAR to 6 and click START. Choose option 4 in the Unrestricted VAR Post Estimation Menu (see Section 7.4.1) and then option 1. The results in Table 16.6a should now appear on the screen.

On the basis of these results, the Akaike information criterion (AIC) selects order 3, and the Schwarz Bayesian criterion (SBC) selects the order 2. You can now inspect the estimates of the individual equations in the VAR for these orders. Since the values of AIC for the VAR(2) and VAR(3) specifications differ by a decimal point, and the sample size is small relative to the number of variables in the VAR, we choose the order 2 in the cointegrating VAR analysis that follows. Once again, the choice of the order of the VAR is subject to an important degree of uncertainty.

We now employ the cointegrating VAR option to test the null hypothesis that the five variables in the VAR are not cointegrated. If this hypothesis is rejected, we can then move to the next stage and, on the assumption that there exists a cointegrating relation among the five variables, test the hypothesis that there are no more cointegrating relations among them, and so on. In this way we should get some idea as to the number of the cointegrating relations that may exist among these variables. Given the complicated nature of this testing procedure, the overall size of the cointegration test is not known, even

**Table 16.6a:** Selecting the order of the VAR model–King *et al.* (1991) data set

Test Statistics and Choice Criteria for Selecting the Order of the VAR Model

Based on 140 observations from 1954Q1 to 1988Q4. Order of VAR = 6
List of variables included in the unrestricted VAR:
C I MP Y R
List of deterministic and/or exogenous variables:
INPT T

| Order | LL | AIC | SBC | LR Test | Adjusted LR Test |
|---|---|---|---|---|---|
| 6 | 2475.0 | 2315.0 | 2079.7 | | |
| 5 | 2449.4 | 2314.4 | 2115.9 | CHSQ( 25) = 51.1425[.002] | 39.4528[.033] |
| 4 | 2435.0 | 2325.0 | 2163.2 | CHSQ( 50) = 80.0707[.004] | 61.7688[.123] |
| 3 | 2422.1 | 2337.1 | 2212.0 | CHSQ( 75) = 105.9165[.011] | 81.7070[.279] |
| 2 | 2397.0 | 2337.0 | 2248.8 | CHSQ(100) = 156.0384[.000] | 120.3724[.081] |
| 1 | 2327.5 | 2292.5 | 2241.0 | CHSQ(125) = 294.9906[.000] | 227.5642[.000] |
| 0 | 1618.5 | 1608.5 | 1593.8 | CHSQ(150) = 1712.9[.000] | 1321.4[.000] |

AIC = Akaike Information Criterion SBC = Schwarz Bayesian Criterion

in large samples, and hence special care needs to be exercised when interpreting the test results.

Return to the System Estimation window, and this time choose option 2 from the System Estimation Menu (Multivariate Menu), selecting the Unrestricted intercepts, restricted trends option 4, since data are trended and we wish to avoid the possibility of quadratic trends in some of the variables.[6] Delete the intercept and the trend terms so that the box editor contains the following variables

C I MP Y R

For the sample size, enter

1954Q1 1988Q4

For the order of the VAR, enter 2, then click START. The test results in Table 16.6b should now appear on the screen.

According to the maximum eigenvalue and the trace statistics in this table, the null hypothesis of 'no cointegration' (namely $r = 0$) is rejected, but the null hypothesis that there exists one cointegrating relation (namely $r = 1$) cannot be rejected. So, we find only one statistically significant cointegrating relation among the five $I(1)$ variables. From economic theory, however, we expect three long-run relations among these variables, given by

$$z_1 = C - Y \tag{16.2}$$

$$z_2 = I - Y \tag{16.3}$$

$$z_3 = MP - c_4 Y - c_5 R \tag{16.4}$$

with $c_4 > 0$, and $c_5 < 0$. The $z_1$ and $z_2$ relations are known as the 'great

[6]See Section 7.5 for the rationale behind the different options in this menu.

**Table 16.6b:** Cointegration properties of the King *et al.* (1991) model

Cointegration with unrestricted intercepts and restricted trends in the VAR
Cointegration LR Test Based on Maximal Eigenvalue of the Stochastic Matrix

140 observations from 1954Q1 to 1988Q4. Order of VAR = 2.
List of variables included in the cointegrating vector:
C I MP Y R
Trend
List of eigenvalues in descending order:
.25832 .14277 .12331 .040600 .013589

| Null | Alternative | Statistic | 95% Critical Value | 90% Critical Value |
|---|---|---|---|---|
| r = 0 | r = 1 | 41.8376 | 37.8600 | 35.0400 |
| r<= 1 | r = 2 | 21.5670 | 31.7900 | 29.1300 |
| r<= 2 | r = 3 | 18.4237 | 25.4200 | 23.1000 |
| r<= 3 | r = 4 | 5.8027 | 19.2200 | 17.1800 |
| r<= 4 | r = 5 | 1.9155 | 12.3900 | 10.5500 |

Use the above table to determine r (the number of cointegrating vectors).

Cointegration with unrestricted intercepts and restricted trends in the VAR
Cointegration LR Test Based on Trace of the Stochastic Matrix

140 observations from 1954Q1 to 1988Q4. Order of VAR = 2.
List of variables included in the cointegrating vector:
C I MP Y R
Trend
List of eigenvalues in descending order:
.25832 .14277 .12331 .040600 .013589

| Null | Alternative | Statistic | 95% Critical Value | 90% Critical Value |
|---|---|---|---|---|
| r = 0 | r>= 1 | 89.5464 | 87.1700 | 82.8800 |
| r<= 1 | r>= 2 | 47.7088 | 63.0000 | 59.1600 |
| r<= 2 | r>= 3 | 26.1418 | 42.3400 | 39.3400 |
| r<= 3 | r>= 4 | 7.7182 | 25.7700 | 23.0800 |
| r<= 4 | r = 5 | 1.9155 | 12.3900 | 10.5500 |

Use the above table to determine r (the number of cointegrating vectors).

Cointegration with unrestricted intercepts and restricted trends in the VAR
Choice of the Number of Cointegrating Relations Using Model Selection Criteria

140 observations from 1954Q1 to 1988Q4. Order of VAR = 2.
List of variables included in the cointegrating vector:
C I MP Y R
Trend
List of eigenvalues in descending order:
.25832 .14277 .12331 .040600 .013589

| Rank | Maximized LL | AIC | SBC | HQC |
|---|---|---|---|---|
| r = 0 | 2352.2 | 2322.2 | 2278.1 | 2304.3 |
| r = 1 | 2373.1 | 2333.1 | 2274.3 | 2309.2 |
| r = 2 | 2383.9 | 2335.9 | 2265.3 | 2307.2 |
| r = 3 | 2393.1 | 2339.1 | 2259.7 | 2306.9 |
| r = 4 | 2396.0 | 2338.0 | 2252.7 | 2303.4 |
| r = 5 | 2397.0 | 2337.0 | 2248.8 | 2301.1 |

AIC = Akaike Information Criterion SBC = Schwarz Bayesian Criterion
HQC = Hannan–Quinn Criterion

ratios'. The balanced growth literature, and the more recent real business cycle literature both predict $C-Y$ and $I-Y$ as the two cointegrating relations. The relation defined by $z_3$ is the long-run money demand equation. The test results seem to be in conflict with economic theory. Notice, however, that the finite sample performance of Johansen's log-likelihood ratio statistics are not known, and also tends to be quite sensitive to the order of the VAR chosen. Hence, we will continue our analysis assuming that there are three cointegrating relations among C, I, MP, Y, and R. Under this assumption we need 3 independent a priori restrictions on each of the three cointegrating relations to identify them exactly.[7]

In view of the theory-based restrictions implicit in the relations (16.2)–(16.4), we start the long-run structural analysis with the following just-identifying restrictions:

$$\begin{array}{lll} \beta_{11}=1, & \beta_{12}=0, & \beta_{13}=0 \\ \beta_{21}=0, & \beta_{22}=1, & \beta_{23}=0 \\ \beta_{31}=0, & \beta_{32}=0, & \beta_{33}=1 \end{array}$$

where we have denoted the three cointegrating vectors by $\beta_1=(\beta_{11}, \beta_{12}, \beta_{13}, \beta_{14}, \beta_{15}, \beta_{16})'$, $\beta_2=(\beta_{21}, \beta_{22}, \beta_{23}, \beta_{24}, \beta_{25}, \beta_{26})'$, and $\beta_3'=(\beta_{31}, \beta_{32}, \beta_{33}, \beta_{34}, \beta_{35}, \beta_{36})'$. Notice that there are six elements in each of these three vectors. The first five elements are the coefficients of the $I(1)$ variables C, I, MP, Y, and R, respectively, and the last element (i.e. $\beta_{i6}$, $i=1, 2, 3$) refers to the time trend. Recall that under case 4 where the underlying VAR model contains linear deterministic trends with restricted coefficients, the trend term is automatically included as a part of the cointegrating relation: see Section 7.5.3. The above exactly identifying restrictions do not impose any testable restrictions on the cointegrating VAR model.

To estimate the VAR model subject to the above restrictions, click CLOSE to leave the cointegration test results in Table 16.6b, and move to the Cointegrating VAR Post Estimation Menu (see Section 7.5.2). Choose option 2 and set the number of cointegrating relations to 3 by typing

3 ↩

This returns you to the Cointegrating VAR Post Estimation Menu to start your long-run structural analysis. Choose option 6 and in the Long-Run Structural Modelling Menu choose option 4. Type the exactly identifying restrictions in the box editor that appears on the screen:[8]

A1 = 1; A2 = 0; A3 = 0;
B1 = 0; B2 = 1; B3 = 0;
C1 = 0; C2 = 0; C3 = 1 OK

[7]In principle, it seems more appropriate to select the order of the VAR and the number of the cointegrating relations simultaneously. This could be clearly achieved by means of the familiar model selection criteria, such as AIC or SBC. But as yet little is known about their small sample performance.

[8]Alternatively, you can retrieve the contents of the file CO3.EQU, in the TUTOR directory, into the box editor by clicking [icon].

**Table 16.6c:** An exactly identified structural long-run model for the US economy–King *et al.* (1991) data set

ML estimates subject to exactly identifying restriction(s)
Estimates of Restricted Cointegrating Relations (SE's in Brackets)
Converged after 2 iterations
Cointegration with unrestricted intercepts and restricted trends in the VAR

140 observations from 1954Q1 to 1988Q4. Order of VAR = 2, chosen r = 3.
List of variables included in the cointegrating vector:
C I MP Y R
Trend

List of imposed restriction(s) on cointegrating vectors:
a1 = 1; a2 = 0; a3 = 0;
b1 = 0; b2 = 1; b3 = 0;
c1 = 0; c2 = 0; c3 = 1;

| | Vector 1 | Vector 2 | Vector 3 |
|---|---|---|---|
| C | 1.0000 | 0.00 | 0.00 |
| | (*NONE*) | (*NONE*) | (*NONE*) |
| I | 0.00 | 1.0000 | 0.00 |
| | (*NONE*) | (*NONE*) | (*NONE*) |
| MP | 0.00 | 0.00 | 1.0000 |
| | (*NONE*) | (*NONE*) | (*NONE*) |
| Y | −.88600 | −1.2278 | −1.4465 |
| | (.095419) | (.25405) | (.14934) |
| R | .81756 | 1.2052 | .61093 |
| | (.27519) | (.73451) | (.40651) |
| Trend | −.0010563 | .1643E3 | .0013923 |
| | (.4350E-3) | (.0011584) | (.6775E-3) |

LL subject to exactly identifying restrictions = 2393.1

The exactly identified ML estimates of the three cointegrating vectors, $\beta_1$, $\beta_2$, and $\beta_3$, should appear on the screen together with their asymptotic estimated standard errors in brackets. These results are reproduced in Table 16.6c.

The estimates in the first two columns (under Vector 1 and Vector 2) refer to the 'great ratios', and those under Vector 3 refer to the money demand equation. Notice that the maximized value of the log-likelihood function given in this table (namely 2393.1) is the same as the log-likelihood value reported in the third panel of Table 16.6b for *rank* = 3. Since we do not expect these long-run relations to include a linear trend we first test the following over-identifying restrictions:

$$\beta_{16} = \beta_{26} = \beta_{36} = 0$$

Click CLOSE to leave the screen with the exactly identified estimates and then choose option 0 in the IR Analysis and Forecasting Menu (see Section 7.5.5). You will be asked whether you wish to test over-identifying restrictions on the cointegrating vectors (CVs). Press ↵ to say 'yes'. The box editor appears on the screen containing the exactly identified restrictions. *Do not* delete these restrictions. Simply *add* the following over-identifying restrictions to them:

$$A6 = 0; \quad B6 = 0; \quad C6 = 0$$

You can add these restrictions anywhere in the box editor so long as all the restrictions are separated by semicolons (;). If you add these restrictions at the end of each row, your window will look like Screen 16.1.

Now click [OK] to process. Accept the initial estimates suggested by the program by clicking [OK] again, and choose the modified Newton–Raphson algorithm. Our experience suggests that in general this algorithm converges more often and faster than the back substitution algorithm. For the damping factor choose the default value of 0.01. You only need to alter the default value if you encounter convergence problems. The program now starts the computations and presents you with the ML estimates obtained subject to the over-identifying restrictions (see Table 16.6d). The LR statistic for testing the three over-identifying restrictions is computed to be 6.48 which is below the 95 critical value of the $\chi^2$ distribution with 3 degrees of freedom. We therefore do not reject the hypothesis that there are no linear trends in the cointegrating relations, although there was a linear trend in the underlying VAR model. Hence the cointegrating relations are also 'co-trending'.

We can now consider imposing further over-identifying restrictions. In the context of the present model there are two sets of restrictions implied by the 'great ratios' (16.2) and (16.3); namely that the interest rates do not enter these relationships and that Y enters with a coefficient of −1. To impose these

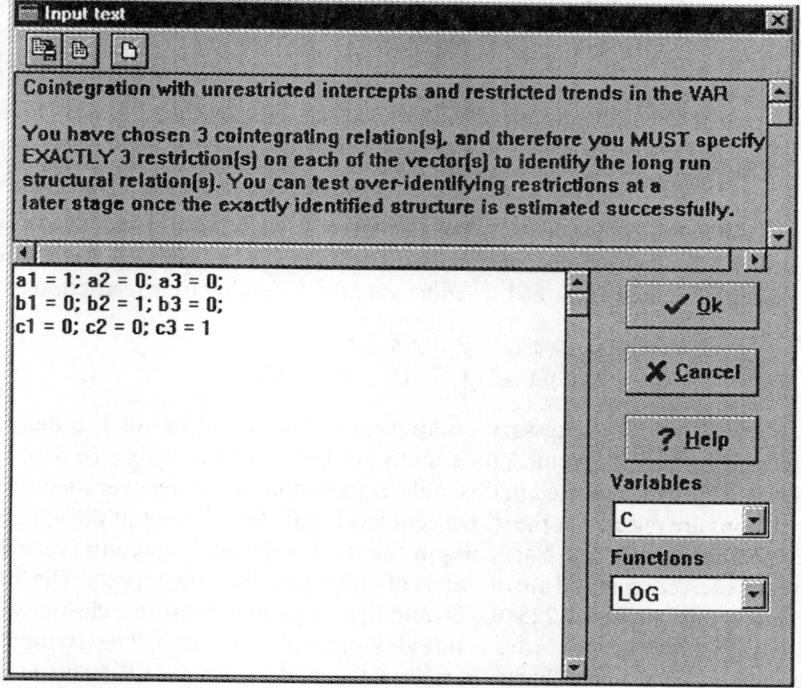


Screen16.1

**Table 16.6d:** A structural long-run model for the US economy subject to three over-identifying restrictions—King *et al.* (1991) data set

ML estimates subject to over identifying restriction(s)
Estimates of Restricted Cointegrating Relations (SE's in Brackets)
Converged after 22 iterations
Cointegration with unrestricted intercepts and restricted trends in the VAR

140 observations from 1954Q1 to 1988Q4. Order of VAR = 2, chosen r = 3.
List of variables included in the cointegrating vector:

| C | I | MP | Y | R |
|---|---|---|---|---|
| Trend | | | | |

List of imposed restriction(s) on cointegrating vectors:
a1 = 1; a2 = 0; a3 = 0; a6 = 0;
b1 = 0; b2 = 1; b3 = 0; b6 = 0;
c1 = 0; c2 = 0; c3 = 1; c6 = 0

| | Vector 1 | Vector 2 | Vector 3 |
|---|---|---|---|
| C | 1.0000 | −.0000 | .0000 |
| | (*NONE*) | (*NONE*) | (*NONE*) |
| I | .0000 | 1.0000 | −.0000 |
| | (*NONE*) | (*NONE*) | (*NONE*) |
| MP | −.0000 | .0000 | 1.0000 |
| | (*NONE*) | (*NONE*) | (*NONE*) |
| Y | −1.1521 | −1.1881 | −1.0999 |
| | (.074887) | (.10617) | (.084412) |
| R | .99689 | 1.1903 | .40383 |
| | (.60976) | (.84901) | (.67990) |
| Trend | .0000 | .0000 | −.0000 |
| | (*NONE*) | (*NONE*) | (*NONE*) |

LR Test of Restrictions CHSQ(3) = 6.4807[.090]
DF = Total no of restrictions (12) − no of just-identifying restrictions (9)
LL subject to exactly identifying restrictions = 2393.1
LL subject to over-identifying restrictions = 2389.9

restrictions, choose option 0 in the IR Analysis and Forecasting Menu (see Section 7.5.5), say that you wish to test (further) over-identifying restrictions, and when presented with the box editor *add* the following four restrictions:

$$A4 = -1; \quad A5 = 0;$$
$$B4 = -1; \quad B5 = 0 \qquad \boxed{\text{OK}}$$

Then carry out the necessary computations by accepting all the defaults suggested by the program. You should get the results in Table 16.6e.

The LR statistic reported in this table suggests that the seven over-identifying restrictions are rejected at the 95 per cent level. But the estimates of the long-run income and interest rate elasticities in the money demand equation (vector 3) have the correct signs and are of orders of magnitude that one expects. The long-run income elasticity is 1.225 (0.079) and the long-run interest rate elasticity is −1.26 (0.45), although the latter is not very precisely estimated. The asymptotic standard errors are in brackets. In view of the tendency of the LR tests to over-reject the null hypothesis, and the strong theoretical underpinning of the three

**Table 16.6e:** A structural long-run model for the US economy subject to seven over-identifying restrictions — King *et al.* (1991) data set

ML estimates subject to over identifying restriction(s)
Estimates of Restricted Cointegrating Relations (SE's in Brackets)
Converged after 18 iterations
Cointegration with unrestricted intercepts and restricted trends in the VAR

140 observations from 1954Q1 to 1988Q4. Order of VAR = 2, chosen r = 3.
List of variables included in the cointegrating vector:
C I MP Y R
Trend

List of imposed restriction(s) on cointegrating vectors:
a1 = 1; a2 = 0; a3 = 0; a4 = −1; a5 = 0; a6 = 0;
b1 = 0; b2 = 1; b3 = 0; b4 = − 1; b5 = 0; b6 = 0;
c1 = 0; c2 = 0; c3 = 1; c6 = 0

| | Vector 1 | Vector 2 | Vector 3 |
|---|---|---|---|
| C | 1.0000 | −.0000 | −.0000 |
| | (*NONE*) | (*NONE*) | (*NONE*) |
| I | −.0000 | 1.0000 | −.0000 |
| | (*NONE*) | (*NONE*) | (*NONE*) |
| MP | −.0000 | −.0000 | 1.0000 |
| | (*NONE*) | (*NONE*) | (*NONE*) |
| Y | −1.0000 | −1.0000 | −1.2252 |
| | (*NONE*) | (*NONE*) | (.079379) |
| R | .0000 | −.0000 | 1.2622 |
| | (*NONE*) | (*NONE*) | (.44882) |
| Trend | .0000 | .0000 | −.0000 |
| | (*NONE*) | (*NONE*) | (*NONE*) |

LR Test of Restrictions CHSQ( 7) = 17.3821[.015]
DF = Total no of restrictions (16) − no of just-identifying restrictions (9)
LL subject to exactly identifying restrictions = 2393.1
LL subject to over-identifying restrictions = 2384.4

relations, we shall now adopt the cointegrating vectors in Table 16.6e and analyse the short-run dynamic properties of the model.

We shall first examine the effect of system-wide shocks on the cointegrating (or long-run) relations, by plotting the 'persistence profiles' of these relations. Choose option 4 in the IR Analysis and Forecasting Menu (see Section 7.5.5), and accept the default horizon of 50 quarters for the persistence profiles. You should see the estimates listed on the screen. To obtain a plot of these estimates click CLOSE to move to the Impulse Response Results Menu, and choose option 2 to graph the profiles. Figure 16.3 gives the plots of the persistence profiles for all the three long-run relations. These profiles clearly show that while all the three relations have a strong tendency to converge to their respective equilibria, the speed of convergence of the money demand equation (vector CV3) to its equilibrium is noticeably faster than those of the two great ratios, CV1 = C − Y and CV2 = I − Y, with the consumption output ratio equilibrating faster than the investment–output ratio. These profiles also show a marked overshooting effect for the consumption–output and investment–output ratios.

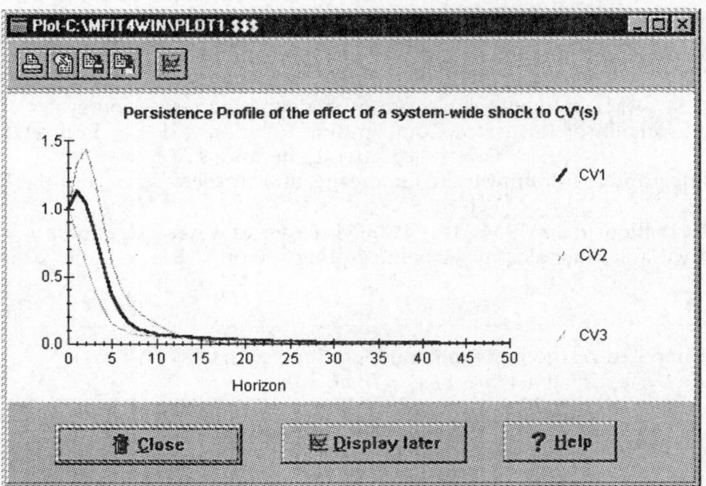


**Figure 16.3:** Persistence profile of the effect of a system-wide shock to CV(s)

To see the effect of variable- (or equation-) specific shocks on the cointegrating vectors you need to choose option 3 in the IR Analysis and Forecasting Menu. In this case, you can either use the orthogonalized or the generalized impulse responses. If you choose the orthogonalized IR option and choose to consider the effect of shocking the nominal interest on the cointegrating vectors, you should obtain Figures 16.4. Choosing the generalized IR option provides you with Figure 16.5. In both cases the effect of the shocks on the cointegrating relations dies out, although the profiles have very different shapes. The two sets of profiles would have been, however, identical if we had decided to shock the first variable in the VAR, namely consumption (see Section 7.5.5).

Consider now the dynamic effects of a shock to the output equation on all the variables in the cointegrating VAR model. Choose option 1 in the IR Analysis and Forecasting Menu, select the orthogonalized IR option, and then choose the Y equation to shock. The orthogonalized impulse responses should now appear on the screen. Notice that the impact effect of shocking Y on the variables that have been entered in the VAR before it (namely C, I, and MP) are zero by *construction*. Also note that the impact effect of a unit shock in output (measured as one standard error) on the nominal interest rate is positive, but relatively small. To see the plots of these impulse responses, press the **Esc** key and then choose to plot the orthogonalized impulse responses for C, I, MP, and Y. You should see Figure 16.6 on the screen. A similar graph can also be obtained using the generalized IR option. This option is more satisfactory and, unlike the orthogonalized IR option, does not impose zero impact effects on C, I, and MP when Y is shocked. For example, using the generalized IR option the impact effect of a unit shock to output on investment is quite large, and is in fact slightly larger than the effect on output itself. The result is given in Figure 16.7, and suggests an important cyclical effect of an output shock on investment, with

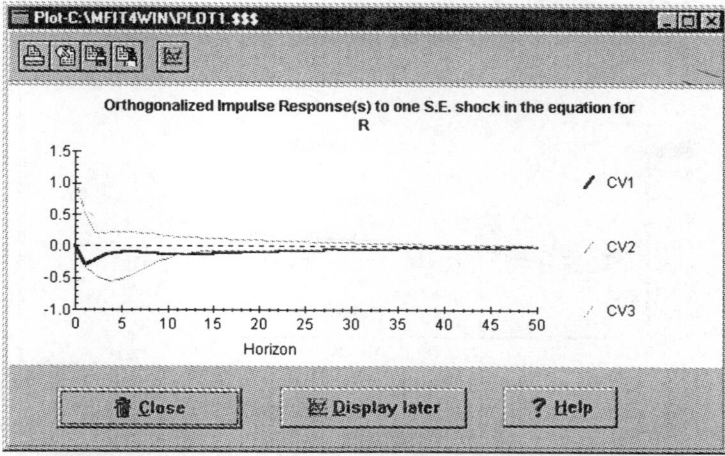


**Figure 16.4:** Orthogonalized impulse responses to one SE shock in the equation for R

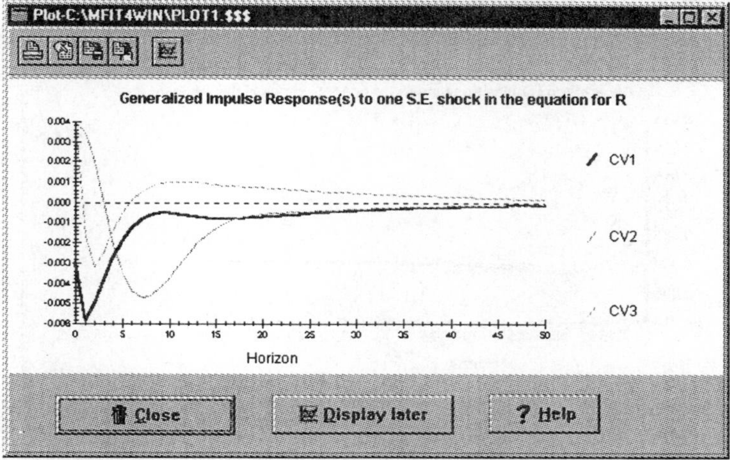


**Figure 16.5:** Generalized impulse responses to one SE shock in the equation for R

investment responding very strongly to an output shock and then declining very sharply.

Other options in the IR Analysis and Forecasting Menu can also be used to compute multivariate dynamic forecasts, based on the cointegrating VAR model subject to the over-identifying restrictions. See Lesson 16.7. You can also obtain error correction relations for all the variables in the VAR. Suppose you are interested in the error correction equation for consumption. Choose option 7 in this menu and, when asked for the choice of the variable, press return to choose consumption. The results in Table 16.6f should now appear on the screen.

In the case of this equation, only the error correction term associated with the long-run money demand equation has a significant impact on

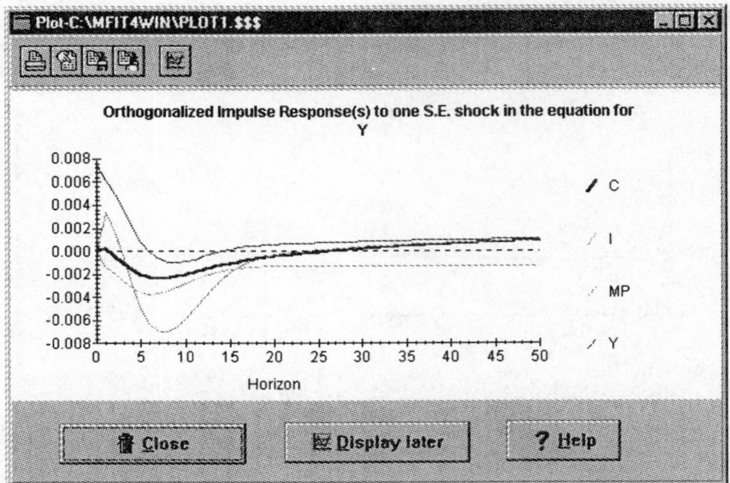


**Figure 16.6:** Orthogonalized impulse response(s) to one SE shock in the equation for Y

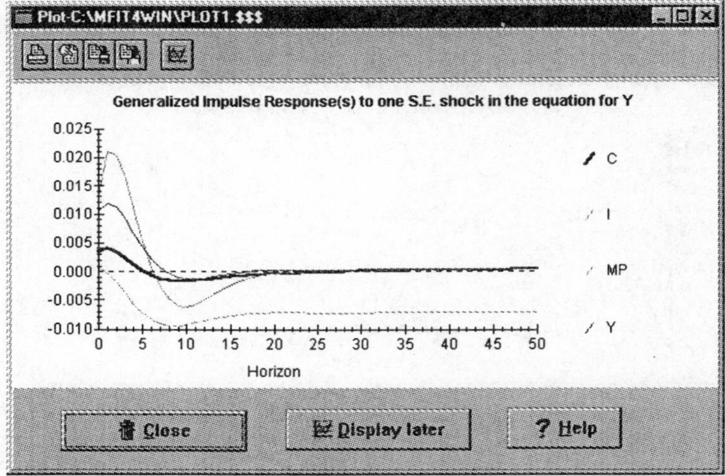


**Figure 16.7:** Generalized impulse response(s) to one SE shock in the equation for Y

consumption growth. The equation also suffers from residual serial correlation, reflecting the fact that the order 2 chosen for the underlying VAR is not high enough to deal with the problem of the residual serial correlation. This is in line with the LR test statistics reported in Table 16.6a.

## 16.7 Lesson 16.7: Application of the cointegrating VAR analysis to the UK term structure of interest rates

Let $R(k, t)$ be the rate of interest with a maturity of $k$ periods as observed at the beginning of time $t$. The expectations theory of the term structure of interest rates postulates that:

$$R(k, t) = \frac{1}{k}[E_t R(1, t) + E_t R(1, t + 1) + \ldots + E_t R(1, t + k - 1)] + L(k, t) \tag{16.5}$$

where $L(k, t)$ is the risk/liquidity premium. Notice that $E_t R(1, t) = R(1, t)$ which is known at the beginning of period $t$, and that equation (16.5) simply states that the average expected rate of return of investing a certain sum of money in $k$ successive time periods should be equal to the rate of return of investing this sum of money for $k$ periods with the fixed rate of return $R(k, t)$—after allowing for a risk/liquidity premium. Equation (16.5) can be rearranged to give

$$R(k, t) - R(1, t) = \frac{1}{k}\left[\sum_{i=1}^{k-1}\sum_{j=1}^{i} E_t\{\Delta R(1, t + j)\}\right] + L(k, t) \tag{16.6}$$

Assuming that $R(k, t)$ is $I(1)$ and $L(k, t)$ is stationary, it can be seen that the right-hand side of (16.6) is stationary and hence the left-hand side of (16.6), which represents the spread between two interest rates $R(k, t)$ and $R(1, t)$, should also be stationary.

The above analysis shows that we should expect to find $(n - 1)$ cointegrating relations between a set of $n$ interest rates with different maturities. These can be represented by

$$R(k, t) = R(1, t) + a_k; \quad k = 2, n \tag{16.7}$$

Hall *et al.* (1992) have applied the above model to analysis of the US term structure of interest rates and have found strong support for the existence of $(n - 1)$ cointegrating vectors of the form (16.7) amongst a set of $n$ interest rates with different maturities. We should point out that we expect $a_k$ to be positive and rise with maturity.

In what follows we apply the cointegrating VAR techniques to the UK term structure, in the case of London interbank offer rates (LIBORs) at different maturities. (For further details see Pesaran and Wright 1995.)

The special *Microfit* file TERMUK.FIT contains monthly observations on LIBORs with one month, three month, six month and twelve month-maturities, which we denote by R1, R3, R6, and R12, respectively. This file also contains the UK effective exchange rate, EER.

In order to apply the cointegrating VAR technique to the above data set we need to make a number of decisions regarding:

1. The variables to be included as $I(1)$ endogenous (jointly determined) variables.
2. The variables to be included as $I(1)$ exogenous variables.
3. The variables to be included as additional $I(0)$ variables in the VAR.
4. The inclusion and nature (restricted or unrestricted) of the intercept and/or time trend in the VAR.
5. The selection of the order of the VAR.

We obviously should include R1, R3, R6, and R12 as endogenous $I(1)$ variables. As an exercise you should convince yourself that all these four

**Table 16.6f:** ECM for variable C estimated by OLS based on cointegrating VAR(2)

Dependent variable is dC
140 observations used for estimation from 1954Q1 to 1988Q4

| Regressor | Coefficient | Standard Error | T-Ratio[Prob] |
|---|---|---|---|
| Intercept | −.048594 | .029784 | −1.6315[.105] |
| dC1 | −.032789 | .10213 | −.32104[.749] |
| dI1 | .034235 | .032717 | 1.0464[.297] |
| dMP1 | .14640 | .072354 | 2.0233[.045 ] |
| dY1 | .12490 | .069410 | 1.7995[.074] |
| dR1 | −.23200 | .073506 | −3.1561[.002] |
| ecm1(−1) | −.0038103 | .030946 | −.12313[.902] |
| ecm2(−1) | −.0054789 | .014163 | −.38684[.700] |
| ecm3(−1) | .055074 | .019651 | 2.8027[.006] |

List of additional temporary variables created:
dC = C − C(−1)
dC1 = C(−1) − C(−2)
dI1 = I(−1) − I(−2)
dMP1 = MP(−1) − MP(−2)
dY1 = Y(−1) − Y(−2)
dR1 = R(−1) − R(−2)
ecm1 = 1.0000*C − .0000*I − .0000*MP − 1.0000*Y + .0000*R + .00
00*Trend; ecm2 = − .0000*C + 1.0000*I − .0000*MP − 1.0000*Y − .0000*R
+ .0000*Trend; ecm3 = − .0000*C − .0000*I + 1.0000*MP − 1.2252*Y +
1.2622*R − .0000*Trend

| | | | |
|---|---|---|---|
| R-Squared | .27311 | R-Bar-Squared | .22872 |
| S.E. of Regression | .0063724 | F-Stat. F( 8, 131) | 6.1526[.000] |
| Mean of Dependent Variable | .0045623 | S.D. of Dependent Variable | .0072560 |
| Residual Sum of Squares | .0053195 | Equation Log-likelihood | 513.8094 |
| Akaike Info. Criterion | 504.8094 | Schwarz Bayesian Criterion | 491.5720 |
| DW-statistic | 2.1860 | System Log-likelihood | 2384.4 |

Diagnostic Tests

| Test Statistics | LM Version | F Version |
|---|---|---|
| A:Serial Correlation | CHSQ( 4) = 11.3399[.023] | F( 4, 127) = 2.7984[.029] |
| B:Functional Form | CHSQ( 1) = 2.0946[.148] | F( 1, 130) = 1.9745[.162] |
| C:Normality | CHSQ( 2) = 16.7897[.000] | Not applicable |
| D:Heteroscedasticity | CHSQ( 1) = 1.0879[.297] | F( 1, 138) = 1.0808[.300] |

A:Lagrange multiplier test of residual serial correlation
B:Ramsey's RESET test using the square of the fitted values
C:Based on a test of skewness and kurtosis of residuals
D:Based on the regression of squared residuals on squared fitted values

variables are $I(1)$ before including them in the cointegrating VAR analysis. In this application there are no $I(1)$ exogenous variables.

The additional $I(0)$ variables included in the VAR allow for the short-run movements in the $I(1)$ variables which moves them away from their long-run equilibrium. We propose to include the lag of the per centage change of

EER as well as three dummy variables which take the value of 1 in 1984(8), 1985(2), and 1992(10), and zeros elsewhere. The inclusion of the last dummy variable is intended to capture the effect of UK exit from the ERM, and the first two dummy variables are included because on each occasion the interest rates were raised by 2 per cent by the Bank of England, and could be regarded as outliers for our purposes (namely identification of the long-run relations). Since interest rates are not trended, we should not include a trend in the VAR and, given the relationships in (16.7), we expect each cointegrating vector to include an intercept term; moreover, the intercept term should be restricted.

In order to determine the order of the VAR, we first run an unrestricted VAR of a relatively high order (12 let's say). We also include an intercept term, $\Delta \log \text{EER}(-1)$ and the above three dummy variables as additional $I(0)$ deterministic/exogenous variables.

We therefore load the file TERMUK.FIT into *Microfit*, click [icon], and retrieve the file TERMUK.EQU which contains the necessary transformations. Click [GO] to create the above three dummy variables. The following variables should now be in the variables list (click [Variables] to check):

R1 R3 R6 R12 EER INPT DLEER
D84M8 D85M2 D92M10

Now move to the System Estimation Menu and choose option 1 (the unrestricted VAR) and type the following in the box editor:

R1 R3 R6 R12 & INPT DLEER(−1)
D84M8 D85M2 D92M10

Select the maximum order of the VAR to be 12, and click [START]. In order to decide whether it is justifiable to consider a VAR model with an order of less than 12, choose option 4 in the VAR Post Estimation Menu, move to the Unrestricted VAR Hypothesis Testing Menu, and then choose option 1. You will be presented with Table 16.7a.

We can see that according to the Akaike information criterion (AIC) the order of the VAR should be 2, whilst the Schwarz Bayesian criterion (SBC) indicates choosing 1 as the order of the VAR. Since we have a reasonable number of observations we choose the order of VAR to be 2, bearing in mind that choosing the higher order is less damaging than choosing the lower order when the sample size is reasonably large. Also, we notice that if we choose option 2 in the VAR Hypothesis Testing Menu to test for the significance of deletion of DLEER(−1) in the VAR and enter

DLEER(−1) [OK]

we will be presented with Table 16.7b with a $\chi^2(4) = 23.0018$ which is highly significant, justifying the inclusion of DLEER(−1) in each equation of the VAR.

We are now in a position to estimate a cointegrating VAR. Return to the System Estimation window. Choose option 2 in the System Estimation

**Table 16.7a:** Selecting the order of the VAR for the analysis of the UK term structure of interest rates

Test Statistics and Choice Criteria for Selecting the Order of the VAR Model

Based on 165 observations from 1981M1 to 1994M9 . Order of VAR = 12
List of variables included in the unrestricted VAR:
R1 R3 R6 R12
List of deterministic and/or exogenous variables:
INPT DLEER(−1) D84M8 D85M2 D92M10

| Order | LL | AIC | SBC | LR Test | Adjusted LR Test |
|---|---|---|---|---|---|
| 12 | 223.7027 | 11.7027 | −317.5275 | — | — |
| 11 | 213.2903 | 17.2903 | −287.0924 | CHSQ( 16)= 20.8248[.185] | 14.1357[.589] |
| 10 | 201.6576 | 21.6576 | −257.8775 | CHSQ( 32)= 44.0902[.076] | 29.9279[.572] |
| 9 | 197.4085 | 33.4085 | −221.2791 | CHSQ( 48)= 52.5885[.301] | 35.6964[.905] |
| 8 | 189.1103 | 41.1103 | −188.7296 | CHSQ( 64)= 69.1847[.307] | 46.9618[.946] |
| 7 | 179.1601 | 47.1601 | −157.8323 | CHSQ( 80)= 89.0853[.228] | 60.4700[.949] |
| 6 | 155.9621 | 39.9621 | −140.1827 | CHSQ( 96)=135.4811[.005] | 91.9629[.598] |
| 5 | 145.1763 | 45.1763 | −110.1210 | CHSQ(112)=157.0529[.003] | 106.6056[.626] |
| 4 | 134.5754 | 50.5754 | −79.8743 | CHSQ(128)=178.2546[.002] | 120.9970[.657] |
| 3 | 121.0112 | 53.0112 | −52.5909 | CHSQ(144)=205.3830[.001] | 139.4115[.592] |
| 2 | 110.4686 | 58.4686 | −22.2859 | CHSQ(160)=226.4681[.000] | 153.7238[.625] |
| 1 | 93.9668 | 57.9668 | 2.0598 | CHSQ(176)=259.4719[.000] | 176.1264[.483] |
| 0 | −312.1241 | −332.1241 | −363.1836 | CHSQ(192)= 1071.7[.000] | 727.4255[.000] |

AIC = Akaike Information Criterion SBC = Schwarz Bayesian Criterion

Menu (Multivariate Menu), selecting the Restricted intercepts, no trends option 2, and type

R1 R3 R6 R12 & DLEER(−1)
D84M8 D85M2 D92M10

in the box editor. Remember not to include INPT amongst the above. Choose all available observations, select the order of the VAR to be 2, and click START. You will now be presented with Table 16.7c and, as expected, we find support for the existence of three cointegrating vectors amongst these four interest rates.

In order to identify and test relationships of the form (16.7), choose option 2 in the Cointegrating VAR Post Estimation Menu, then choose the number of cointegrating vectors to be 3. Then choose option 6 in the Cointegrating VAR Post Estimation Menu to move to the Long-Run Structural Modelling Menu. In this menu choose option 4 for carrying out an LR test of imposing general restrictions on the cointegrating vectors. You will be asked to specify exactly three identifying restrictions for each of the three cointegrating vectors. In the box editor you should type the following:

$$A2 = -1; \quad A3 = 0; \quad A4 = 0;$$
$$B2 = 0; \quad B3 = -1; \quad B4 = 0;$$
$$C2 = 0; \quad C3 = 0; \quad C4 = -1$$

OK

**Table 16.7b:** Testing for the deletion of DLEER(−1) from the VAR

| LR Test of Deletion of Deterministic/Exogenous Variables in the VAR | | | | |
|---|---|---|---|---|
| Based on 165 observations from 1981M1 to 1994M9 . Order of VAR = 12 | | | | |
| List of variables included in the unrestricted VAR: | | | | |
| R1 | R3 | R6 | R12 | |
| List of deterministic and/or exogenous variables: | | | | |
| INPT | DLEER(−1) | D84M8 | D85M2 | D92M10 |
| Maximized value of log-likelihood = 223.7027 | | | | |
| List of variables included in the restricted VAR: | | | | |
| R1 | R3 | R6 | R12 | |
| List of deterministic and/or exogenous variables: | | | | |
| INPT | D84M8 | D85M2 | D92M10 | |
| Maximized value of log-likelihood = 212.2018 | | | | |
| LR test of restrictions, CHSQ( 4) = 23.0018[.000] | | | | |

You should see Table 16.7d.

In order to impose and test the three over-identifying restrictions by restricting the coefficient of R1 to be unity in each of the three cointegrating vectors, choose option 0 of the IR Analysis and Forecasting Menu and answer 'yes' to the question which follows. You should add the restrictions gradually one by one. Therefore, first add the restriction A1 = 1 to the existing set of restrictions and carry out the test. Then repeat the procedure for each of the extra restrictions, B1 = 1 and C1 = 1. At each stage you should choose the initial values suggested by *Microfit* and also choose the default modified Newton–Raphson algorithm. Choose the damping factor to be 0.01 at each stage. The final result is presented in Table 16.7e, which gives the LR statistic for testing the three over-identifying restrictions given by $\chi^2(3) = 8.782$. This is significant at the 3.3 per cent level, thus suggesting that the theory restrictions are rejected at the conventional 95 per cent significance level.

It is also possible to estimate the generalized impulse responses of all interest rates to a unit shock in equation for R1 (say). To do this, choose option 1 in the IR Analysis and Forecasting Menu for these restricted CVs. Select option 2 to choose the generalized impulse response and then choose R1 to be shocked. Choose the horizon for the impulse responses to be 50 months. You can inspect the results that follow or, more instructively, you can choose option 2 in the following Impulse Response Results Menu to obtain a graphic display of these impulse responses. Choose all four variables to be included in the graph by checking all the boxes, and then click OK. You will be presented with Figure 16.8. As you can see, all interest rates converge to the same level after the effect of the shock dies away.

You can also compute forecasts from this cointegrating VAR model using these restricted CVs. Choose option 5 in the IR Analysis and Forecasting Menu and press ↵ to forecast all the remaining data periods. Choose to view the forecasts for the change in R1. You will be presented with the results in Table 16.7f.

**Table 16.7c:** Sequence of log-likelihood ratio statistics for testing the rank of the long-run multiplier matrix

Cointegration with restricted intercepts and no trends in the VAR
Cointegration LR Test Based on Maximal Eigenvalue of the Stochastic Matrix

175 observations from 1980M3 to 1994M9 . Order of VAR = 2.
List of variables included in the cointegrating vector:
R1 R3 R6 R12 Intercept
List of I(0) variables included in the VAR:
DLEER(−1) D84M8 D85M2 D92M10
List of eigenvalues in descending order:
.39641 .31188 .11064 .022479

| Null | Alternative | Statistic | 95% Critical Value | 90% Critical Value |
|---|---|---|---|---|
| r = 0 | r = 1 | 88.3497 | 28.2700 | 25.8000 |
| r < = 1 | r = 2 | 65.4148 | 22.0400 | 19.8600 |
| r < = 2 | r = 3 | 20.5200 | 15.8700 | 13.8100 |
| r < = 3 | r = 4 | 3.9787 | 9.1600 | 7.5300 |

Use the above table to determine r (the number of cointegrating vectors).

Cointegration with restricted intercepts and no trends in the VAR
Cointegration LR Test Based on Trace of the Stochastic Matrix

175 observations from 1980M3 to 1994M9 . Order of VAR = 2.
List of variables included in the cointegrating vector:
R1 R3 R6 R12 Intercept
List of I(0) variables included in the VAR:
DLEER(−1) D84M8 D85M2 D92M10
List of eigenvalues in descending order:
.39641 .31188 .11064 .022479

| Null | Alternative | Statistic | 95% Critical Value | 90% Critical Value |
|---|---|---|---|---|
| r = 0 | r > = 1 | 178.2633 | 53.4800 | 49.9500 |
| r < = 1 | r > = 2 | 89.9136 | 34.8700 | 31.9300 |
| r < = 2 | r > = 3 | 24.4987 | 20.1800 | 17.8800 |
| r < = 3 | r = 4 | 3.9787 | 9.1600 | 7.5300 |

Use the above table to determine r (the number of cointegrating vectors).

Cointegration with restricted intercepts and no trends in the VAR
Choice of the Number of Cointegrating Relations Using Model Selection Criteria

175 observations from 1980M3 to 1994M9. Order of VAR = 2.
List of variables included in the cointegrating vector:
R1 R3 R6 R12 Intercept
List of I(0) variables included in the VAR:
DLEER(−1) D84M8 D85M2 D92M10
List of eigenvalues in descending order:
.39641 .31188 .11064 .022479

| Rank | Maximized LL | AIC | SBC | HQC |
|---|---|---|---|---|
| r = 0 | −19.2767 | −51.2767 | −101.9133 | −71.8163 |
| r = 1 | 24.8982 | −15.1018 | −78.3975 | −40.7764 |
| r = 2 | 57.6056 | 11.6056 | −61.1845 | −17.9201 |
| r = 3 | 67.8656 | 17.8656 | −61.2541 | −14.2276 |
| r = 4 | 69.8550 | 17.8550 | −64.4295 | −15.5220 |

AIC = Akaike Information Criterion SBC = Schwarz Bayesian Criterion
HQC = Hannan–Quinn Criterion

**Table 16.7d:** The exact identification of the cointegrating vectors for the UK term structure of interest rates

ML estimates subject to exactly identifying restriction(s)
Estimates of Restricted Cointegrating Relations (SE's in Brackets)
Converged after 2 iterations
Cointegration with restricted intercepts and no trends in the VAR

175 observations from 1980M3 to 1994M9 . Order of VAR = 2, chosen r = 3.
List of variables included in the cointegrating vector:
R1 R3 R6 R12 Intercept
List of I(0) variables included in the VAR:
DLEER(−1) D84M8 D85M2 D92M10
List of imposed restriction(s) on cointegrating vectors:
a2 = −1; a3 = 0; a4 = 0;
b2 = 0; b3 = −1; b4 = 0;
c2 = 0; c3 = 0; c4 = −1

| | Vector 1 | Vector 2 | Vector 3 |
|---|---|---|---|
| R1 | .98321 | .93871 | .86499 |
| | ( .011437) | ( .028626) | ( .050086) |
| R3 | −1.0000 | 0.00 | 0.00 |
| | (*NONE*) | (*NONE*) | (*NONE*) |
| R6 | 0.00 | −1.0000 | 0.00 |
| | (*NONE*) | (*NONE*) | (*NONE*) |
| R12 | 0.00 | 0.00 | −1.0000 |
| | (*NONE*) | (*NONE*) | (*NONE*) |
| Intercept | .29809 | .85018 | 1.7407 |
| | ( .13362) | ( .33287) | ( .58088) |

LL subject to exactly identifying restrictions = 67.8656

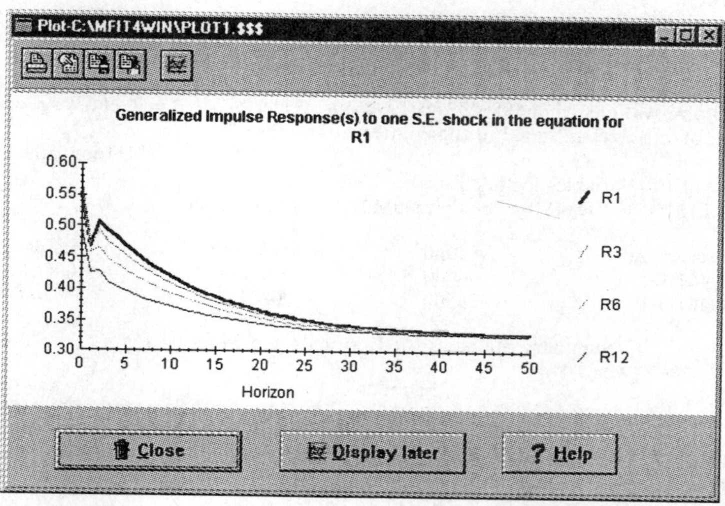


**Figure 16.8:** Generalized impulse response(s) to one SE shock in the equation for R1

**Table 16.7e:** Test of over-identifying restrictions for the UK term structure of interest rates

ML estimates subject to over identifying restriction(s)
Estimates of Restricted Cointegrating Relations (SE's in Brackets)
Converged after 19 iterations
Cointegration with restricted intercepts and no trends in the VAR

175 observations from 1980M3 to 1994M9 . Order of VAR = 2, chosen r = 3.
List of variables included in the cointegrating vector:

| R1 | R3 | R6 | R12 | Intercept |
|---|---|---|---|---|

List of I(0) variables included in the VAR:

| DLEER(−1) | D84M8 | D85M2 | D92M10 |
|---|---|---|---|

List of imposed restriction(s) on cointegrating vectors:
a2 = −1; a3 = 0; a4 = 0; a1 = 1;
b1 = 1; b2 = 0; b3 = −1; b4 = 0;
c1 = 1; c2 = 0; c3 = 0; c4 = −1;

| | Vector 1 | Vector 2 | Vector 3 |
|---|---|---|---|
| R1 | 1.0000 | 1.0000 | 1.0000 |
| | (*NONE*) | (*NONE*) | (*NONE*) |
| R3 | −1.0000 | .0000 | .0000 |
| | (*NONE*) | (*NONE*) | (*NONE*) |
| R6 | −.0000 | −1.0000 | −.0000 |
| | (*NONE*) | (*NONE*) | (*NONE*) |
| R12 | −.0000 | −.0000 | −1.0000 |
| | (*NONE*) | (*NONE*) | (*NONE*) |
| Intercept | .13974 | .26894 | .45696 |
| | (.058229) | (.16604) | (.32054) |

LR Test of Restrictions CHSQ( 3) = 8.7382[.033]
DF = Total no of restrictions (12) − no of justidentifying restrictions (9)
LL subject to exactly identifying restrictions = 67.8656
LL subject to over-identifying restrictions = 63.4965

**Table 16.7f:** Multivariate dynamic forecasts of the change in the one-month LIBOR

Multivariate dynamic forecasts for the change in R1
Cointegration with restricted intercepts and no trends in the VAR

175 observations from 1980M3 to 1994M9 . Order of VAR = 2, chosen r = 3.
List of variables included in the cointegrating vector:

| R1 | R3 | R6 | R12 | Intercept |
|---|---|---|---|---|

List of I(0) variables included in the VAR:

| DLEER(−1) | D84M8 | D85M2 | D92M10 |
|---|---|---|---|

| Observation | Actual | Prediction | Error |
|---|---|---|---|
| 1994M10 | .44000 | .44561 | −.0056107 |
| 1994M11 | .29500 | .088422 | .20658 |

Summary Statistics for Residuals and Forecast Errors

| | Estimation Period 1980M3 to 1994M9 | Forecast Period 1994M10 to 1994M11 |
|---|---|---|
| Mean | −.0056588 | .10048 |
| Mean Absolute | .37963 | .10609 |
| Mean Sum Squares | .28092 | .021353 |
| Root Mean Sum Squares | .53002 | .14613 |

## 16.8 Exercises in cointegration analysis

### 16.8.1 Exercise 16.1

Recompute the residual-based ADF statistic for testing cointegration between real wages (WP) and labour productivity (YE) in Lesson 16.2 by running the reverse regression of YE on WP. Comment on your results.

### 16.8.2 Exercise 16.2

Use the time series observations in the file PHILLIPS.FIT to test the hypothesis that WP = W − P, and YE = Y − E are cointegrated using the cointegrating VAR approach discussed in Lesson 16.3. Compare your results to the univariate approaches applied to the same problem in Lessons 16.1 and 16.2.

### 16.8.3 Exercise 16.3

In the first part of Lesson 16.3 we estimated a bivariate cointegrating VAR model in Y (capital expenditures) and X (appropriations) for US manufacturing. Check the robustness of the results by carrying out the exercise using logs of these variables instead of their levels. Which specification is preferable?

### 16.8.4 Exercise 16.4

Carry out tests of the purchasing power parity (PPP) hypothesis for the UK and the USA using the quarterly observations contained in the file G7EXCH.FIT. See Lesson 9.14 for details of the variables in this file and the batch file needed to construct the effective exchange rate and the foreign price indices.

### 16.8.5 Exercise 16.5

The file TERMUS.FIT contains monthly observations on 11 interest rates analysed by Hall *et al.* (1992). Denote these interest rates by Y1, Y2, . . ., Y11.

1. Analyse the cointegrating properties of the four interest rates Y1, Y2, Y3, and Y4.
2. Test the hypothesis that there are three cointegrating vectors among these four interest rates, and interpret the resultant cointegrating relations from the viewpoint of economic theory.
3. Test the hypothesis that Y1 − Y2, Y2 − Y3, and Y1 − Y4 are the long-run relations linking these interest rates together. Initially you need three

restrictions on each of the three cointegrating vectors in order to just identify them. You should then impose the over-identifying restrictions (one by one and gradually) and test to see if these over-identifying restrictions are supported by the data.

Compare your results with those in Lesson 16.7. Graph the persistence profile of the three restricted cointegrating vectors and comment on your findings.

# 17

# Lessons in SURE Estimation

The lessons in this chapter are concerned with the options in *Microfit* for the maximum likelihood (ML) estimation of seemingly unrelated regression equations (SURE) models. They can be used for estimation of VAR (or vector error correction) models subject to restrictions on their short-run parameters, or can be used to estimate systems of equations. The restricted SURE option can also be used to estimate systems of equations subject to general linear restrictions, including linear cross-equation restrictions. This option is particularly useful for estimation of systems of budget shares, and factor demand share equations subject to homogeneity and/or symmetry restrictions. Another important use of the restricted SURE option is in pooling time series across a relatively small number of groups (countries, firms, etc.). For an account of the SURE options and how they can be used, see Sections 7.6.1 and 7.6.2. The econometrics that underlie the analysis of SURE models and the numerical algorithms used to compute them can be found in Section 19.1.

## 17.1 Lesson 17.1: A restricted bivariate VAR model of patents and output growth in the US

In this lesson we show how to use the SURE option to estimate restricted VAR models. For this purpose we consider the following bivariate model in the rates of change of US GDP output (DLYUSA) and patents (DLQUSA) granted to US firms by the US Patent Office:

$$DLYUSA_t = a_1 + \sum_{j=1}^{2} b_{1j} DLYUSA_{t-j} + \sum_{j=9}^{10} c_{1j} DLQUSA_{t-j} + d_1 D74_t + u_{1t},$$

$$DLQUSA_t = a_2 + \sum_{j=1}^{2} b_{2j} DLYUSA_{t-j} + \sum_{j=1}^{2} c_{2j} DLQUSA_{t-j} + u_{2t}$$

where D74 is an oil shock dummy variable which takes the value of 1 in the four quarters of 1974 and zero elsewhere. This model assumes that changes in patents (intended to proxy technological innovations) only start to affect output growth after at least two years. It also assumes that only output growth was immediately affected by the oil crisis. This model is a restricted version of a VAR(10) model in $DLYUSA_t$ and $DLQUSA_t$, and needs to be estimated using the SURE option.

The relevant data is available in the special *Microfit* file, G7GDP.FIT, and is described in detail in Chapter 15, and in particular in Lesson 15.1. Read this file into *Microfit* and choose the unrestricted SURE option 3, in the System Estimation Menu (Multivariate Menu: see Section 7.3). Specify the restricted VAR model set out above by typing:

```
dlyusa   const   dlyusa{1 – 2}   dlqusa{9 – 10}   d74;
dlqusa   const   dlyusa{1 – 2}   dlqusa{1 – 2}
```

Choose the whole sample for estimation and click START to carry out the computations. You will be presented with the SURE Post Estimation Menu. To see the estimates of the output growth equation, choose option 2 and then select the variable DLYUSA. You should get the results in Table 17.1. The lagged patent variables are marginally significant. A test of the joint hypothesis that $c_{1,9} = 0$ and $c_{1,10} = 0$ can be carried out using option 4 in the SURE Post Estimation Menu. Click CLOSE, then click CANCEL twice to reach this menu, choose option 4, and then type:

$$A4 = 0; \quad A5 = 0 \quad \boxed{\text{OK}}$$

The test results should appear on the screen. The Wald statistic for testing the joint hypothesis that lagged patent growths have no impact on output growth is rejected at the 5.1 per cent level. Other hypotheses of interest, such as the Granger non-causality of output growth, can also be tested using option 4 in the SURE Post Estimation Menu.

**Table 17.1:** Relationship between US output growth and patents

Seemingly Unrelated Regressions Estimation
The estimation method converged after 1 iterations

Dependent variable is DLYUSA
113 observations used for estimation from 1965Q4 to 1993Q4

| Regressor | Coefficient | Standard Error | T-Ratio[Prob] |
|---|---|---|---|
| CONST | .004545 | .0011482 | 3.9584[.000] |
| DLYUSA(−1) | 0.22006 | .093828 | 2.3443[.021] |
| DLYUSA(−2) | .12922 | .093318 | 1.3847[.169] |
| DLQUSA(−9) | .011251 | .0061970 | 1.8156[.072] |
| DLQUSA(−10) | .012663 | .0062412 | 2.0289[.045] |
| D74 | −.0094370 | .0046040 | −2.0497[.043] |

| | | | |
|---|---|---|---|
| R-Squared | .17183 | R-Bar-Squared | .13313 |
| S.E. of Regression | .0088589 | F-Stat. F( 5, 107) | 4.4400[.001] |
| Mean of Dependent Variable | .0065667 | S.D. of Dependent Variable | .0095149 |
| Residual Sum of Squares | .0083974 | Equation Log-likelihood | 376.8179 |
| DW-statistic | 2.0114 | System Log-likelihood | 450.6296 |
| System AIC | 439.6412 | System SBC | 424.6406 |

In an important study of investment demand, Grunfeld (1958) and Grunfeld and Griliches (1960) estimated investment equations for ten firms in the US economy over the period 1935 to 1954. In this lesson we estimate investment equations for five of these firms by the SURE method. This smaller data set is also analysed in Greene's (1993) textbook. The *Microfit* file GGSURE.FIT contains annual observations over the period 1935 to 1954 (inclusive) on the variables

$I_{it}$ = Gross investment
$F_{it}$ = Market value of the firm at the end of the previous year
$C_{it}$ = Value of the stock of plant and equipment at the end of the previous year.

The five firms indexed by $i$ are General Motors (GM), Chrysler (CH), General Electric (GE), Westinghouse (WE), and US Steel (USS). In the file, these variables are denoted by adding the prefixes GM, CH, GE, WE, and USS to the variable names. For example, GMI refers to General Motors' gross investment, and WEF to the market value of Westinghouse.

The SURE model to be estimated is given by

$$I_{it} = \beta_{i1} + \beta_{i2}F_{it} + \beta_{i3}C_{it} + u_{it} \tag{17.1}$$

for $i$ = GM, CH, GE, WE, and USS, and $t = 1935, 1936, \ldots, 1954$. Load the file GGSURE.FIT and choose option 3 (unrestricted SURE method) in the System Estimation Menu (Multivariate Menu). You will now need to specify all the equations in the SURE model, separating them by semicolons (;). In the box editor type

```
GMI   const  gmf   gmc;
CHI   const  chf   chc;
GEI   const  gef   gec;
WEI   const  wef   wec;
USSI  const  ussf  ussc
```

Notice that upper- and lower-case letters are treated identically in *Microfit*; here we have used upper-case letters for the left-hand-side variables simply for expositional convenience. It is often much simpler to specify the different equations in the model one after another without starting on a new line. For an example, see Screen 17.1. (The equations are saved in the file GGSURE.EQU and can be retrieved using the button.) Estimate the model over the whole sample period and click START to begin the calculations. The program carries out the computations and then presents you with the SURE Post Estimation Menu. You can use the various options in this menu to see the SURE estimates, test restrictions on the coefficients, and compute forecasts. For example, if you wish to see the results for Chrysler, choose option 2 and, when prompted, select the variable CHI. The results in Table 17.2a should now appear on the screen.

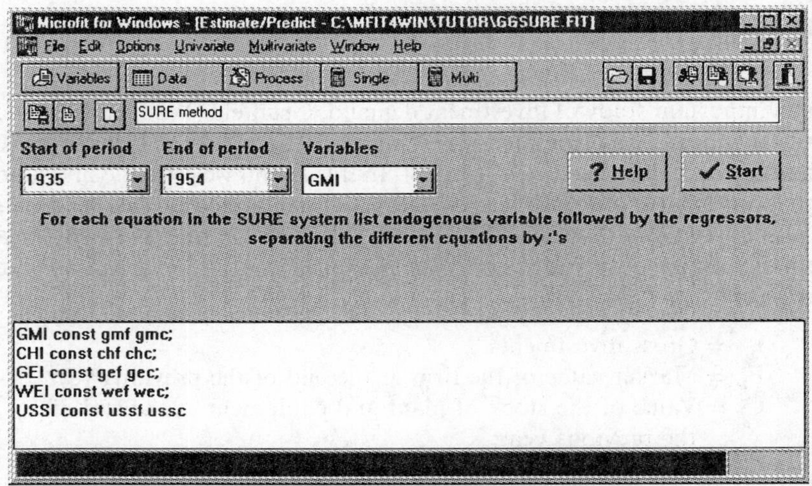


Screen 17.1

Except for the intercept term, the results in this table are comparable with the SURE estimates for the same equations reported in Table 17.6 in Greene (1993). Similarly, the estimates for the other investment equations in the model can be inspected.

Since the SURE estimation is appropriate under a non-diagonal error covariance matrix, it may now be of interest to test this hypothesis. For this purpose we need to estimate all the five individual equations separately by the OLS method, and then employ the log-likelihood ratio procedure discussed in Section 19.1.3 (see also Lesson 15.4). The

**Table 17.2a:** SURE estimates of the investment equation for Chrysler company

Seemingly Unrelated Regressions Estimation
The estimation method converged after 18 iterations

Dependent variable is CHI
20 observations used for estimation from 1935 to 1954

| Regressor | Coefficient | Standard Error | T-Ratio[Prob] |
|---|---|---|---|
| CONST | 2.3783 | 12.6160 | .18852[.853] |
| CHF | .067451 | .018550 | 3.6362[.002] |
| CHC | .30507 | .028274 | 10.7898[.000] |

| | | | |
|---|---|---|---|
| R-Squared | .91057 | R-Bar-Squared | .90004 |
| S.E. of Regression | 13.5081 | F-Stat. F( 2, 17) | 86.5413[.000] |
| Mean of Dependent Variable | 86.1235 | S.D. of Dependent Variable | 42.7256 |
| Residual Sum of Squares | 3102.0 | Equation Log-likelihood | −78.8193 |
| DW-statistic | 1.8851 | System Log-likelihood | −459.0922 |
| System AIC | −474.0922 | System SBC | −481.5602 |

**Table 17.2b:** Estimated system covariance matrix of errors for Grunfeld–Griliches investment equations

| | GMI | CHI | GEI | WEI | USSI |
|---|---|---|---|---|---|
| GMI | 8600.8 | −389.2322 | 644.4398 | 139.1155 | −3394.4 |
| CHI | −389.2322 | 182.4680 | 13.6558 | 22.1336 | 544.8885 |
| GEI | 644.4398 | 13.6558 | 873.1736 | 259.9662 | 1663.1 |
| WEI | 139.1155 | 22.1336 | 259.9662 | 121.7357 | 868.3544 |
| USSI | −3394.4 | 544.8885 | 1663.1 | 868.3544 | 11401.0 |

maximized log-likelihood values for the five equations estimated separately are for General Motors (−117.1418), Chrysler (−78.4766), General Electric (−93.3137), Westinghouse (−73.2271) and US Steel (−119.3128), respectively, yielding the restricted log-likelihood value of −481.472 (≡ −117.1418 − 78.4766 − 93.3137 − 73.2271 − 119.3128). The maximized log-likelihood value for the unrestricted system (i.e. when the error covariance matrix is *not* restricted) is given at the bottom right-hand corner of Table 17.2a, under 'System Log-likelihood' (≡ −459.0922). Therefore, the log-likelihood ratio statistic for testing the diagonality of the error covariance matrix is given by $LR = 2(-459.0922 + 481.472) = 44.76$ which is asymptotically distributed as a chi-squared variate with $5(5-1)/2 = 10$ degrees of freedom. The 95 per cent critical value of the chi-squared distribution with 10 degrees of freedom is 18.31. Hence, we reject the hypothesis that the error covariance matrix of the five investment equations is diagonal, which provides support for the application of the SURE technique to this problem. To see the magnitude of the off-diagonal elements of the estimated error covariance matrix, you need to choose option 3 in the SURE Post Estimation Menu. If you choose this option, you should get the results in Table 17.2b. As you can see the covariance estimates on the off-diagonal elements are quite large relative to the respective diagonal elements.

## 17.3 Lesson 17.3: Testing cross-equation restrictions after SURE estimation

In the previous lesson we estimated investment equations for five US firms and found that the SURE procedure was an appropriate estimation method to apply. Suppose you are now interested in testing the hypothesis that the coefficients of $F_{it}$, the market value of the firms, are the same across all the five companies. In terms of the coefficients of the equations in (17.1), the relevant null hypothesis is

$$H_0\colon \beta_{i2} = \beta_2, \quad \text{for} \quad i = GM, CH, GE, WE, USS$$

These four restrictions clearly involve coefficients from all the five equations. To implement this test, load the file GGSURE.FIT and then

| **Table 17.3:** Testing the slope homogeneity hypothesis |
|---|
| Wald test of restriction(s) imposed on parameters |
| The underlying estimated SURE model is:<br>GMI const gmf gmc; CHI const chf chc; GEI const gef gec ; WEI const wef wec;<br>USSI const ussf ussc<br>20 observations used for estimation from 1935 to 1954 |
| List of restriction(s) for the Wald test:<br>a2 = b2;b2 = c2;c2 = d2;d2 = e2 |
| Wald Statistic CHSQ( 4)= 20.4580[.000] |

choose the unrestricted SURE option (option 3) in the System Estimation Menu (Multivariate Menu). Retrieve the file GGSURE.EQU into the box editor by using the [icon] button. Estimate the equations over the whole sample period and choose option 4 in the SURE Post Estimation Menu. Type the following *four* restrictions in the box editor which appears on the screen

A2 = B2;   B2 = C2;   C2 = D2;   D2 = E2   [OK]

You should now get the test results in Table 17.3 on the screen. The LR statistic for testing these restrictions is 20.45, which is well above the 95 per cent critical value of the chi-squared distribution with 4 degrees of freedom, and we therefore strongly reject the slope homogeneity hypothesis.

## 17.4 Lesson 17.4: Estimation of a static almost ideal demand system

In this lesson we show how to use the restricted SURE option to estimate a system of demand equations subject to homogeneity and symmetry restrictions. For this purpose we consider the static version of the almost ideal demand model of Deaton and Muellbauer (1980), which postulates that the expenditure share of the $i$th commodity group, $w_{it}$, $i = 1,2, \ldots, m$, is determined by

$$w_{it} = \alpha_i + \sum_{j=1}^{m} \gamma_{ij} \log P_{jt} + \delta_i \log(Y_t/P_t) + u_{it} \tag{17.2}$$

where $P_{jt}$ is the price deflator of the commodity group $j$; $Y_t$ is the per capita expenditure on all the goods; and $P_t$ is the general price index, approximated using the Stone formula

$$\log P_t = \sum_{j=1}^{m} w_{j0} \log P_{jt} \tag{17.3}$$

The weights $w_{j0}$ refer to the budget shares in the base year, which is taken to be 1990. Consumer theory imposes the following restrictions on the parameters of the share equation:

$$\textit{Homogeneity restrictions:} \quad \sum_{j=1}^{m} \gamma_{ij} = 0, \qquad i = 1,2, \ldots, m \qquad (17.4)$$

$$\textit{Symmetry restrictions:} \quad \gamma_{ij} = \gamma_{ji}, \qquad \text{for all} \quad i,j \qquad (17.5)$$

We also have $\Sigma_{i=1}^{m} w_{it} = 1$, and hence only $m-1$ of the shares can be independently explained/estimated.

The share equations in (17.2) are unlikely to hold in each and every period, and are best incorporated within a dynamic framework which freely allows for *short-run* departures from the 'equilibrium' budget share equations given by (17.2). Such an exercise is carried out in Pesaran and Shin (1995b). Here we consider the above static formulation both to demonstrate how the restricted SURE option in *Microfit* can be used, and to highlight the importance of appropriately allowing for dynamics in estimation of demand equations.

We estimate a three-commodity system on the UK quarterly seasonally adjusted data over the period 1956(1) to 1993(2). The three commodity groups are:

1. Food, drink, and tobacco
2. Services (including rents and rates)
3. Energy and other non-durables

The relevant data is in the special *Microfit* file CONG3.FIT and is comprised of the following variables:[1]

INPT = Intercept term
LP1 = Log of implicit price deflator for the food, drink, and tobacco group
LP2 = Log of implicit price deflator for the services group
LP3 = Log of implicit price deflator for the energy group
LRY = Log of per capita real total expenditure
W1 = Share of expenditure on food, drink, and tobacco group
W2 = Share of expenditure on the services group
W3 = Share of expenditure on the energy group

Load this file and move to the System Estimation window. Initially choose option 3 from the System Estimation (Multivariate) Menu to estimate the unrestricted version of the equations in (17.2), and type

```
W1 INPT LP1 LP2 LP3 LRY;
W2 INPT LP1 LP2 LP3 LRY
```

Notice that we have decided to work with the budget shares W1 and W2,

[1]For the source of this data set and other details, see Pesaran and Shin (1995b).

but that we could equally have considered any one of the pairs: W2, W3 or W1, W3. The results are invariant to this choice.

For the estimation period enter

1956Q1 1993Q2

Click START. You can now inspect the estimation results by choosing option 2 in the SURE Post Estimation Menu. The results seem quite satisfactory, except for the low value of the Durbin–Watson statistics obtained for both of the share equations, thus highlighting the importance of the missing dynamics.

To test the homogeneity restrictions given in (17.4), return to the SURE Post Estimation Menu, choose option 4, and type

A2 + A3 + A4 = 0;
B2 + B3 + B4 = 0 OK

The Wald statistic, 4.0755, for testing these restrictions should now appear on the screen, and this statistic suggests that the homogeneity restrictions cannot be rejected.

We now re-estimate the share equations subject to the homogeneity restrictions. For this purpose, return to the System Estimation window and choose the restricted SURE option 4. Click START to accept the (unrestricted) specification of the share equations, still retained in the box editor. You now need to specify your parameter restrictions. Type

A2 + A3 + A4 = 0;
B2 + B3 + B4 = 0 OK

The program now carries out the necessary computations and presents you

**Table 17.4a:** SURE estimates of the budget share equation for food subject to the homogeneity restrictions

Restricted Seemingly Unrelated Regressions
The estimation method converged after 0 iterations

Dependent variable is W1
150 observations used for estimation from 1956Q1 to 1993Q2

| Regressor | Coefficient | Standard Error | T-Ratio[Prob] |
|---|---|---|---|
| INPT | .29913 | .0013826 | 216.3456[.000] |
| LP1 | .24282 | .010707 | 22.6792[.000] |
| LP2 | −.13966 | .012037 | −11.6027[.000] |
| LP3 | −.10315 | .012448 | −8.2866[.000] |
| LRY | −.23062 | .0097290 | −23.7049[.000] |

| | | | |
|---|---|---|---|
| R-Squared | .99391 | R-Bar-Squared | .99378 |
| S.E. of Regression | .0059733 | F-Stat. F( 4, 145) | 5955.8[.000] |
| Mean of Dependent Variable | .41741 | S.D. of Dependent Variable | .075761 |
| Residual Sum of Squares | .0052093 | Equation Log-likelihood | 557.2548 |
| DW-statistic | .41831 | System Log-likelihood | 1140.5 |
| System AIC | 1132.5 | System SBC | 1120.5 |

| **Table 17.4b:** Wald test of the symmetry restriction |
|---|
| Wald test of restriction(s) imposed on parameters |
| The underlying estimated restricted SURE model is:<br>w1 inpt lp1 lp2 lp3 lry; w2 inpt lp1 lp2 lp3 lry<br>List of restrictions imposed on the SURE model:<br>a2 + a3 + a4 = 0;b2 + b3 + b4 = 0<br>150 observations used for estimation from 1956Q1 to 1993Q2 |
| List of restriction(s) for the Wald test:<br>a3 = b2 |
| Wald Statistic CHSQ( 1) = 21.9498[.000] |

with the restricted SURE estimates. For example, to see the estimates for the W1 equation (the share of food, drink, and tobacco) choose option 2 in the SURE Post Estimation Menu and select W1. The results in Table 17.4a should appear on the screen. Notice that the sum of the estimated coefficients on the price variables do in fact add up to zero, as required by the homogeneity hypothesis.

Consider now testing the symmetry restriction. In the present case where $m = 2$, there is only one restriction implied by the symmetry hypothesis, namely $\gamma_{12} = \gamma_{21}$. Return to the SURE Post Estimation Menu, and choose the Wald test option (4). Click to clear the box editor and type

A3 = B2 [OK]

to get the test results reproduced in Table 17.4b. The Wald statistic for testing the symmetry restriction is equal to 21.95, which is well in excess of 3.84, the 95 critical value of the chi-squared distribution with one degree of freedom. Therefore, in the present static formulation, the symmetry hypothesis is decisively rejected. But in view of the very low DW statistics of the estimated equations and the problem of dynamic misspecifications that surround these share equations, this may not be a valid conclusion. In fact, using the long-run structural modelling approach where the share equations are embodied within an unrestricted VAR model, Pesaran and Shin (1995b) cannot reject the homogeneity or the symmetry restrictions using the same data set.

## 17.5 Exercises in SURE estimation

### 17.5.1 Exercise 17.1

In Lesson 17.1 we assumed that growth of patents only influences output growth with a lag of two years. Estimate similar bivariate models for Japan and Germany, and comment on your results. The relevant data can be found in the special *Microfit* file G7GDP.FIT.

### 17.5.2 Exercise 17.2

Test the hypothesis that the error covariance matrix of the restricted bivariate model estimated in Lesson 17.1 is diagonal.

### 17.5.3 Exercise 17.3

Re-estimate the Grunfeld–Griliches investment equations using a log-linear specification. Compute the values of the Akaike and Schwarz criteria to discriminate between the linear and the log-linear specifications.

### 17.5.4 Exercise 17.4

Estimate a simple dynamic version of the Grunfeld–Griliches investment equations by including a first-order lag of the investments variable among the regressors.

### 17.5.5 Exercise 17.5

Repeat the estimation and testing exercises in Lesson 17.4 with (W1, W3) and (W2, W3) as the budget shares to be explained. Check that you do in fact obtain identical estimation results and make the same inferences.

### 17.5.6 Exercise 17.6

Use the data in CONG3.FIT to estimate the following dynamic version of the share equations given by (17.2) over the period 1956(1) to 1993(2):

$$w_{1t} = \alpha_1 + \lambda_{11} w_{1,t-1} + \lambda_{12} w_{2,t-1} + \sum_{j=1}^{3} \gamma_{1j} \log P_{jt} + \delta_1 \log(Y_t/P_t) + u_{1t}$$

$$w_{2t} = \alpha_2 + \lambda_{21} w_{1,t-1} + \lambda_{22} w_{2,t-1} + \sum_{j=1}^{3} \gamma_{2j} \log P_{jt} + \delta_2 \log(Y_t/P_t) + u_{2t}$$

Derive the parameter restrictions for testing the *long-run* homogeneity and the symmetry restrictions. Test the validity of these restrictions and compare your results with those obtained in Lesson 17.4.

# Part V
# Econometric Methods

# 18

# Econometrics of Single-Equation Models

This chapter provides the technical details of the econometric methods and the algorithms that underlie the computation of the various estimators and test statistics in the case of single equation models. It complements Chapter 6 which describes the estimation options in *Microfit* for single-equation models. Textbook treatments of some of the topics covered here can be found in Harvey (1981), Amemiya (1985), Judge *et al.* (1985), Godfrey (1988), Maddala (1988), Chatfield (1989), Greene (1993), Davidson and MacKinnon (1993), and Hamilton (1994).

## 18.1 Summary statistics and autocorrelation coefficients

The COR command applied to the observation $x_t$, $t = 1, 2, \ldots, n$ computes the following statistics:

$$\text{Sample mean} = \bar{x} = \sum_{t=1}^{n} x_t / n$$

$$\text{Standard Deviation} = S_x = \sqrt{\left( \sum_{t=1}^{n} (x_t - \bar{x})^2 / (n-1) \right)}$$

$$\text{Coefficient of Variation} = \text{Absolute value of } (S_x / \bar{x})$$

$$\text{Skewness} = \sqrt{b_1} = m_3 / m_2^{3/2}$$

$$\text{Kurtosis} = m_4 / m_2^2$$

where

$$m_k = \sum_{t=1}^{n} (x_t - \bar{x})^k / n, \qquad k = 2, 3, 4$$

The program displays $\sqrt{b_1}$ and $b_2 - 3$. These estimates can be used to construct different tests of departures from normality. A non-normal distribution which is asymmetrical has a value of $\sqrt{\beta_1}$ (the population value of $\sqrt{b_1}$) which is non-zero. $\sqrt{\beta_1} > 0$ indicates skewness to the right, and $\sqrt{\beta_1} < 0$ indicates skewness to the left. The measure of kurtosis (or curvature), usually denoted by $\beta_2$, is equal to 3 for the normal distribution. For unimodal non-normal distributions with thicker tails than normal, we have $\beta_2 - 3 > 0$, and for distributions with thinner tails than normal, we have $\beta_2 - 3 < 0$. (See, for example, D'Agostin *et al.* (1990) for further details.)

The Jarque–Bera (1980) test of the normality of regression residuals in Section 18.5.2 can also be computed using the COR command, and is given by

$$\chi_N^2(2) = n\{\tfrac{1}{6}b_1 + \tfrac{1}{24}(b_2 - 3)^2\}$$

where $\sqrt{b_1}$ and $b_2$ are computed by applying the COR command to the OLS residuals. (The above expression assumes that an intercept term is included in the regression.)

The $l$th order autocorrelation coefficient $= R_l = C_l/C_0$, $l = 1, 2, \ldots, [n/3]$,

$$C_l = n^{-1} \sum_{t=l+1}^{n} (x_t - \bar{x})(x_{t-l} - \bar{x})$$

The program also computes an approximate estimate of the standard error of $R_l$, using Bartlett's (1946) approximation reported in Kendall *et al.* (1983, Chapter 48, p. 549):

$$\text{Standard error of } R_l = \sqrt{\left[\frac{1}{n}\left(1 + 2\sum_{j=1}^{l-1} R_j^2\right)\right]}, \qquad l = 1, 2, \ldots, [n/3]$$

The Box–Pierce (1970), $Q$-statistic (of order $p$):

$$Q = n \sum_{j=1}^{p} R_j^2 \overset{a}{\sim} \chi_p^2$$

The Ljung–Box (1978) statistic (of order $p$):[1]

$$Q^* = n(n+2) \sum_{j=1}^{p} R_j^2/(n-j) \overset{a}{\sim} \chi_p^2$$

## 18.1.1 Box–Pierce and Ljung–Box tests

Under the assumption that $x_t$ are serially uncorrelated, the Box–Pierce and the Ljung–Box statistics are both distributed asymptotically as chi-squared

[1]The symbol $\overset{a}{\sim}$ stands for 'approximately distributed as', and $\chi_p^2$ denotes the chi-squared variate with $p$ degrees of freedom.

variates with $p$ degrees of freedom. The two tests are asymptotically equivalent, although the Ljung–Box statistic is likely to perform better in small samples. See, for example, Harvey (1981, p. 211), and Chapters 48 and 50 in Kendall *et al.* (1983), for more details.

When the COR command is followed by more than one variable, say $x_{1t}, x_{2t}, \ldots, x_{kt}$, $t = 1, 2, \ldots, n$, the program computes the correlation matrix of these variables over the specified sample period using the formula

$$\begin{aligned}\hat{\rho}_{ij} &= \text{estimated (or sample) correlation coefficient of } x_i \text{ and } x_j \\ &= \textstyle\sum_{t=1}^{n}(x_{it} - \bar{x}_i)(x_{jt} - \bar{x}_j)/(n-1)S_iS_j, \qquad i,j = 1, 2, \ldots, k\end{aligned}$$

where $\bar{x}_i$ and $S_i$ are the mean and the standard deviation of $x_{it}$, $t = 1, 2, \ldots, n$, respectively.

## 18.2 Estimation of spectral density

The SPECTRUM command computes the estimates of the standardized spectrum of $x_t$ multiplied by $\pi$, for the $n$ observations $x_1, x_2, \ldots, x_n$, using the formula

$$\hat{f}(\omega_j) = \left(\lambda_0 + 2\sum_{k=1}^{m} \lambda_k R_k \cos(k\omega_j)\right)$$

where $\omega_j = j\pi/m, j = 0, 1, \ldots, m$; $m$ is the 'window size'; $R_k$ is the autocorrelation coefficient of order $k$ defined by

$$R_k = \left(\sum_{t=k+1}^{n}(x_t - \bar{x})(x_{t-k} - \bar{x})\right) \bigg/ \left(\sum_{t=1}^{n}(x_t - \bar{x})^2\right)$$

and $\{\lambda_k\}$ are a set of weights called the 'lag window'. The program computes estimates of $\hat{f}(\omega_j), j = 0, 1, \ldots, m$ for the following lag windows:

$$\begin{aligned}&\text{Bartlett window:} \quad \lambda_k = 1 - k/m, \qquad 0 \leqslant k \leqslant m \\ &\text{Tukey window:} \quad \lambda_k = \tfrac{1}{2}\{1 + \cos(\pi k/m)\}, \qquad 0 \leqslant k \leqslant m \\ &\text{Parzen window:} \quad \lambda_k = \left\{\begin{array}{l} 1 - 6(k/m)^2 + 6(k/m)^3, \ 0 \leqslant k \leqslant \frac{m}{2} \\ 2(1 - k/m)^3, \ \frac{m}{2} \leqslant k \leqslant m \end{array}\right\}\end{aligned}$$

The default value for $m$ is set equal to $2\sqrt{n}$.

The standard errors reported for the estimates of the standardized spectrum are calculated according to the following formulae, which are valid asymptotically:

$$\begin{aligned}\widehat{S.E.}(\hat{f}(\omega_j)) &= \sqrt{\tfrac{2}{v}}\,\hat{f}(\omega_j), \qquad \text{for } j = 1, 2, \ldots, m-1 \\ &= \sqrt{\tfrac{4}{v}}\,\hat{f}(\omega_j), \qquad \text{for } j = 0, m\end{aligned}$$

where $v = 2n/\sum_{k=-m}^{m}(\lambda_k^2)$. For the three different windows, $v$ is given by:

Bartlett window: $v = 3n/m$

Tukey window: $v = 8n/3m$

Parzen window: $v = 3.71n/m$

The spectrum for the residuals is estimated using the Parzen window and does not display the standard error bands for the estimates.

For an introductory text on the estimation of the spectrum, see Chatfield (1989, Chapter 7). For more advanced treatments of the subject, see Priestly (1981, Chapter 6), and Brockwell and Davis (1987, Chapter 10).

## 18.3 Hodrick–Prescott (HP) filter

The HP filter is a curve fitting procedure proposed by Hodrick and Prescott (1980) to estimate the trend path $\{y_t^*,\ t = 1, 2, \ldots, n\}$ of a series $\{y_t,\ t = 1, 2, \ldots, n\}$ subject to the constraint that the sum of the squared second differences of the trend series is not too large. More specifically, $\{y_t^*,\ t = 1, 2, \ldots, n\}$ is computed from $\{y_t,\ t = 1, 2, \ldots, n\}$ by solving the following optimization problem:

$$\min_{y_1^*, y_2^*, \ldots, y_n^*} \left\{ \sum_{t=1}^{n} (y_t - y_t^*)^2 + \lambda \sum_{t=2}^{n-1} (\Delta^2 y_{t+1}^*)^2 \right\}$$

The 'smoothing' parameter $\lambda$ is usually chosen by trial and error, and for quarterly observations is set to 1,600. For a discussion of the statistical properties of the HP filter, see, for example, Cogley (1995), Harvey and Jaeger (1993), and Söderlind (1994). In particular, Harvey and Jaeger (1993) show that the use of HP filter can generate spurious cyclical patterns.

## 18.4 Pesaran–Timmermann non-parametric test of predictive performance

Let $x_t = \hat{E}(y_t|\Omega_{t-1})$ be the predictor of $y_t$ found with respect to the information set, $\Omega_{t-1}$, and suppose that the observations $(y_1, x_1)$, $(y_2, x_2)$, . . ., $(y_n, x_n)$ are available on these variables. The test proposed by Pesaran and Timmermann (1992, 1994) is based on the proportion of times that the direction of change in $y_t$ is correctly predicted by $x_t$. The test statistic is computed as

$$S_n = \frac{\hat{P} - \hat{P}_*}{\{\hat{V}(\hat{P}) - \hat{V}(\hat{P}_*)\}^{\frac{1}{2}}} \overset{a}{\sim} N(0, 1)$$

where

$$\hat{P} = n^{-1}\sum_{t=1}^{n}\text{Sign}(y_t x_t),\ \hat{P}_* = \hat{P}_y\hat{P}_x + (1-\hat{P}_y)(1-\hat{P}_x)$$
$$\hat{V}(\hat{P}) = n^{-1}\hat{P}_*(1-\hat{P}_*)$$
$$\hat{V}(\hat{P}_*) = n^{-1}(2\hat{P}_y - 1)^2\hat{P}_x(1-\hat{P}_x) + n^{-1}(2\hat{P}_x - 1)^2\hat{P}_y(1-\hat{P}_y) + 4n^{-2}\hat{P}_y\hat{P}_x(1-\hat{P}_y)(1-\hat{P}_x)$$
$$\hat{P}_y = n^{-1}\sum_{t=1}^{n}\text{Sign}(y_t),\ \hat{P}_x = n^{-1}\sum_{t=1}^{n}\text{Sign}(x_t)$$

and Sign($A$) is the sign (or the indicator) function that takes the value of unity if $A > 0$ and zero otherwise.

Under the null hypothesis that $y_t$ and $x_t$ are distributed independently (namely $x_t$ has no power in prediction $y_t$), $S_n$ is asymptotically distributed as a standard normal. This test does not require quantitative information on $y$ and uses only information on the signs of $y_t$ and $x_t$. The test statistic is undefined when $\hat{P}_y$ or $\hat{P}_x$ take the extreme values of zero or unity.

## 18.5 Ordinary least squares estimates

The estimates computed using the OLS option are based on the following linear regression model

$$y_t = \boldsymbol{\beta}'\mathbf{x}_t + u_t,\ t = 1, 2, \ldots, n \tag{18.1}$$

where $y_t$ is the dependent variable; $\boldsymbol{\beta}$ is a $k \times 1$ vector of unknown coefficients; $\mathbf{x}_t$ is the $k \times 1$ vector of regressors; and $u_t$ is a disturbance term, assumed here to satisfy the classical normal assumptions (**A1** to **A5**), set out in Section 6.1. Writing the $n$ relations in (18.1) in vector and matrix notations we have:

$$\mathbf{y} = \mathbf{X}\boldsymbol{\beta} + \mathbf{u} \tag{18.2}$$

where $\mathbf{y}$ is the $n \times 1$ vector of observations on the dependent variable; $\mathbf{X}$ is the $n \times k$ matrix of observations on the regressors (usually including an intercept term); and $\mathbf{u}$ is the $n \times 1$ vector of disturbances (errors). We shall also assume that $\mathbf{X}$ has a full column rank, and therefore that $\mathbf{X}'\mathbf{X}$ has an inverse.

### 18.5.1 Regression results

The program computes the OLS estimates using the following formulae:

$$\hat{\boldsymbol{\beta}}_{OLS} = (\mathbf{X}'\mathbf{X})^{-1}\mathbf{X}'\mathbf{y} \tag{18.3}$$

$$\hat{V}(\hat{\boldsymbol{\beta}}_{OLS}) = \hat{\sigma}^2_{OLS}(\mathbf{X}'\mathbf{X})^{-1} \tag{18.4}$$

where $\hat{\sigma}_{OLS}$ is the standard error (SE) of the regression given by

$$\hat{\sigma}^2_{OLS} = (y - \mathbf{X}\hat{\beta}_{OLS})'(\mathbf{y} - \mathbf{X}\hat{\beta}_{OLS})/(n-k) \tag{18.5}$$

$$\text{Fitted values} = \hat{\mathbf{y}} = \mathbf{X}\hat{\beta}_{OLS} \tag{18.6}$$

$$\text{Residuals} = \mathbf{e}_{OLS} = \mathbf{y} - \hat{\mathbf{y}} \tag{18.7}$$

A typical element of $\mathbf{e}_{OLS}$ is given by

$$e_t = y_t - \mathbf{x}_t'\hat{\beta}_{OLS}, \qquad t = 1, 2, \ldots, n \tag{18.8}$$

where $\mathbf{x}_t$ is the $k \times 1$ vector of the regressors observed at time $t$.

$$RSS = \text{residual sum of squares} = \sum_{t=1}^{n} e_t^2 = \mathbf{e}'_{OLS}\mathbf{e}_{OLS}$$

$$\text{Mean of the dependent variable} = \bar{y} = \sum_{t=1}^{n} y_t/n$$

$$TSS = \text{total sum of squares} = S_{yy} = \sum_{t=1}^{n}(y_t - \bar{y})^2$$

$$\text{Standard deviation (SD) of the dependent variable} = \hat{\sigma}_y = \sqrt{S_{yy}/(n-1)} \tag{18.9}$$

$$R\text{-squared} = R^2 = 1 - (RSS/TSS) \tag{18.10}$$

$$R\text{-bar-squared} = \bar{R}^2 = 1 - (\hat{\sigma}_{OLS}/\hat{\sigma}_y)^2 \tag{18.11}$$

Notice also that we have the following relationship between $R^2$ and $\bar{R}^2$:

$$1 - \bar{R}^2 = \left(\frac{n-1}{n-k}\right)(1 - R^2)$$

$$\text{Maximized value of the log-likelihood function} = LL_{OLS} = \frac{-n}{2}\{1 + \log(2\pi\tilde{\sigma}^2)\} \tag{18.12}$$

where $\tilde{\sigma}^2 = \mathbf{e}'\mathbf{e}/n$, is the maximum likelihood (ML) estimator of $\sigma^2$. Notice that unlike $\hat{\sigma}^2_{OLS}$, which is an unbiased estimator of $\sigma^2$ under the classical assumptions, $\tilde{\sigma}^2$ is biased. However, for large enough sample sizes, the two estimators ($\hat{\sigma}^2_{OLS}$ and $\tilde{\sigma}^2$) are equivalent.

In addition to the above statistics, the regression results also include the following test statistics and model selection criteria:

$$\text{F statistic} = \left(\frac{R^2}{1-R^2}\right)\left(\frac{n-k}{k-1}\right) \sim F(k-1, n-k) \tag{18.13}$$

which is appropriate only when the regression equation includes an intercept (or a constant) term. Under classical assumptions the F statistic can be used to test the statistical significance of the included regressors other than the intercept term. The F statistic is distributed as F with $k-1$ and $n-k$ degrees of freedom under the null hypothesis that all the regression coefficients, except for the intercept terms are zero.

$$DW \text{ statistic} = DW = \sum_{t=2}^{n}(e_t - e_{t-1})^2 \Big/ \sum_{t=1}^{n} e_t^2 \tag{18.14}$$

This is the familiar Durbin–Watson (1950, 1951) statistic for testing residual serial correlation. It is valid only when lagged values of the dependent variable are *not* included amongst the regressors.

In the case where the regressors include a single one-period lag of the dependent variable (i.e. $y_{t-1}$), and this is specified explicitly at the estimation stage, we have

$$y_t = \lambda y_{t-1} + \boldsymbol{\beta}'\mathbf{x}_t + u_t \tag{18.15}$$

the program also reports Durbin's (1970) $h$-statistic

$$h\text{-statistic} = h = \left(1 - \frac{DW}{2}\right)\sqrt{\{n/[1 - n\hat{V}(\hat{\lambda})]\}} \tag{18.16}$$

where $\hat{V}(\hat{\lambda})$ is the estimated variance of the OLS estimator of the coefficient of the lagged dependent variable, $\lambda$.[2] In situations where $n\hat{V}(\hat{\lambda}) \geqslant 1$, the $h$-statistic is not defined, and it will be set equal to *NONE* by the program. Under the null hypothesis of non-autocorrelated disturbances, the $h$-statistic is asymptotically distributed as a standardized normal variate. For a two-sided test, a value of $h$, exceeding 1.96 (the 5 per cent critical value of the standard normal distribution) in absolute value indicates rejection of the null hypothesis that the disturbances $u_t$ in (18.15) are serially uncorrelated.

## 18.5.2 Diagnostic test statistics (the OLS case)

In the case of the OLS option the diagnostic statistics are computed according to the following formulae:

**Godfrey's test of residual serial correlation**

The Lagrange multiplier ($LM$) version of the test statistic is computed using the following formula (see Godfrey 1978a, 1978b)

$$\chi^2_{SC}(p) = n\left(\frac{\mathbf{e}'_{OLS}\mathbf{W}(\mathbf{W}'\mathbf{M}_x\mathbf{W})^{-1}\mathbf{W}'\mathbf{e}_{OLS}}{\mathbf{e}'_{OLS}\mathbf{e}_{OLS}}\right) \overset{a}{\sim} \chi^2_p \tag{18.17}$$

[2] Notice also that $1-(DW/2) \approx r_1$, where $r_1$ is the first order autocorrelation of the OLS residuals. For more detail, see, for example, Harvey (1981, pp. 274–5).

where

$$\mathbf{M}_x = \mathbf{I}_n - \mathbf{X}(\mathbf{X}'\mathbf{X})^{-1}\mathbf{X}'$$

$$\mathbf{e}_{OLS} = \mathbf{y} - \mathbf{X}\hat{\beta}_{OLS} = (e_1, e_2, \ldots, e_n)'$$

$$\mathbf{W} = \begin{bmatrix} 0 & 0 & \cdots & 0 \\ e_1 & 0 & \cdots & 0 \\ e_2 & e_1 & \cdots & 0 \\ \vdots & e_2 & & \vdots \\ \vdots & \vdots & & e_{n-p-1} \\ e_{n-1} & e_{n-2} & \cdots & e_{n-p} \end{bmatrix} \tag{18.18}$$

and $p$ is the order of the error process.

The F-version of (18.17) is given by[3]

$$F_{SC}(p) = \left(\frac{n-k-p}{p}\right)\left(\frac{\chi^2_{SC}(p)}{n - \chi^2_{SC}(p)}\right) \overset{a}{\sim} F_{p,n-k-p} \tag{18.19}$$

The expression for $\chi^2_{SC}(p)$ is already given by (18.17). The above statistic can also be computed as the F statistic for the (joint) test of zero restrictions on the coefficients of $\mathbf{W}$ in the auxiliary regression

$$\mathbf{y} = \mathbf{X}\alpha + \mathbf{W}\delta + \mathbf{v}$$

Harvey (1981, p. 173) refers to the F-version of the LM statistic (18.17) as a 'modified LM' statistic. The two versions of the test of residual serial correlation, namely $\chi^2_{SC}(p)$ and $F_{SC}(p)$, are asymptotically equivalent.

**Ramsey's RESET test of functional form**

The form of Ramsey's RESET test statistic is the same as those given by (18.17) and (18.19), for the LM and the F-versions, respectively (Anscombe 1961 and Ramsey 1969, 1970). In the case of the RESET test, the columns of $\mathbf{W}$ are set equal to the powers of fitted values, $\hat{\mathbf{y}} = \mathbf{X}\hat{\beta}_{OLS}$. In the diagnostic tests table, the statistics reported for the RESET test are computed for the simple case where the elements of $\mathbf{W}$ are specified to be equal to the square of fitted values. That is

$$\mathbf{W} = (\hat{y}_1^2, \hat{y}_2^2, \ldots, \hat{y}_n^2)'$$

Higher order RESET tests can be computed using the variable addition test in the Hypothesis Testing Menu, with $\hat{y}_t^2, \hat{y}_t^3, \ldots, \hat{y}_t^p$ as the additional variables.

**Jarque–Bera's test of the normality of regression residuals**

The LM version of the statistic for the normality test is given by

---

[3]For a derivation of the relationship between the LM version, and the F-version of the test statistics see, for example, Pesaran (1981, pp. 78–80).

$$\chi_N^2(2) = n\{\mu_3^2/(6\mu_2^3) + (1/24)(\mu_4/\mu_2^2 - 3)^2\} \\ +n\{3\mu_1^2/(2\mu_2) - \mu_3\mu_1/\mu_2^2\} \overset{a}{\sim} \chi^2(2) \tag{18.20}$$

where

$$\mu_j = \sum_{t=1}^{n} e_t^j/n, \qquad j = 1, 2, \ldots$$

Notice that in situations where an intercept term is included in the regression, $\mu_1 = 0$. (See Jarque and Bera 1980, and Bera and Jarque 1981).

**Test of homoscedasticity**

The statistics reported for this test (the equality of error-variances) are based on the auxiliary regression

$$e_t^2 = \text{constant} + \alpha\hat{y}_t^2 \tag{18.21}$$

and give the LM and the F statistics for the test of $\alpha = 0$, against $\alpha \neq 0$.

**Predictive failure test**

Consider the following linear regression models specified for each of two sample periods:

$$\mathbf{y}_1 = \mathbf{X}_1\beta_1 + \mathbf{u}_1; \qquad \mathbf{u}_1 \sim N(0, \sigma_1^2\mathbf{I}_{n1}) \tag{18.22}$$

$$\mathbf{y}_2 = \mathbf{X}_2\beta_2 + \mathbf{u}_2; \qquad \mathbf{u}_2 \sim N(0, \sigma_2^2\mathbf{I}_{n2}) \tag{18.23}$$

where $\mathbf{y}_i, \mathbf{X}_i, i = 1, 2$, are $n_i \times 1$ and $n_i \times k$ observation matrices on the dependent variable and the regressors for the two sample periods; and $\mathbf{I}_{n_1}$ and $\mathbf{I}_{n_2}$ are identity matrices of order $n_1$ and $n_2$, respectively. Combining (18.22) and (18.23) by stacking the observations on the two sample periods now yields

$$\begin{bmatrix} \mathbf{y}_1 \\ \mathbf{y}_2 \end{bmatrix} = \begin{bmatrix} \mathbf{X}_1 & \mathbf{0} \\ \mathbf{X}_2 & \mathbf{I}_{n2} \end{bmatrix} \begin{bmatrix} \beta_1 \\ \delta \end{bmatrix} + \begin{bmatrix} \mathbf{u}_1 \\ \mathbf{u}_2 \end{bmatrix}$$

The above system of equations may also be written more compactly as

$$\mathbf{y}_0 = \mathbf{X}_0\beta_1 + \mathbf{S}_2\delta + \mathbf{u}_0 \tag{18.24}$$

where $\mathbf{y}_0 = (\mathbf{y}_1', \mathbf{y}_2')', \mathbf{X}_0 = (\mathbf{X}_1', \mathbf{X}_2')'$, and $\mathbf{S}_2$ represents the $(n_1 + n_2) \times n_2$ matrix of $n_2$ dummy variables, one dummy variable for each observation in the second period. The predictive failure test can now be carried out by testing the hypothesis of $\delta = 0$ against $\delta \neq 0$ in (18.24). This yields the following F statistic:

$$F_{PF} = \frac{(\mathbf{e}_0'\mathbf{e}_0 - \mathbf{e}_1'\mathbf{e}_1)/n_2}{\mathbf{e}_1'\mathbf{e}_1/(n_1 - k)} \sim F(n_2, n_1 - k), \tag{18.25}$$

where

$\mathbf{e}_0$ is the OLS residual vector of the regression of $\mathbf{y}_0$ on $\mathbf{X}_0$ (i.e. based on the first and the second sample periods together).

$\mathbf{e}_1$ is the OLS residual vector of the regression of $\mathbf{y}_1$ on $\mathbf{X}_1$ (i.e. based on the first sample period).

Under the classical normal assumptions, the predictive failure test statistic, $F_{PF}$, has an exact F-distribution with $n_2$ and $n_1 - k$ degrees of freedom.

The LM version of the above statistic is computed as

$$\chi^2_{PF} = n_2 F_{PF} \overset{a}{\sim} \chi^2(n_2) \tag{18.26}$$

which is distributed as a chi-squared with $n_2$ degrees of freedom for large $n_1$. (See Chow 1960, Salkever 1976, Dufour 1980 and Pesaran *et al.* 1985, Section III.)

**A test of the stability of the regression coefficients: the Chow test**

This is the first test proposed by Chow (1960) and is aimed at testing the hypothesis that in (18.22) and (18.23) $\beta_1 = \beta_2$, conditional on equality of variances, i.e. $\sigma_1^2 = \sigma_2^2$. The Chow test is also known as the analysis of covariance test (see Scheffe 1959). The F-version of the Chow test statistic is defined by

$$F_{SS} = \frac{(\mathbf{e}_0'\mathbf{e}_0 - \mathbf{e}_1'\mathbf{e}_1 - \mathbf{e}_2'\mathbf{e}_2)/k}{(\mathbf{e}_1'\mathbf{e}_1 + \mathbf{e}_2'\mathbf{e}_2)/(n_1 + n_2 - 2k)} \sim F(k, n_1 + n_2 - 2k) \tag{18.27}$$

where

$\mathbf{e}_0$ is the OLS residual vector for the first two sample periods together.

$\mathbf{e}_1$ is the OLS residual vector for the first sample period.

$\mathbf{e}_2$ is the OLS residual vector for the second sample period.

The LM version of this test statistic is computed as

$$\chi^2_{SS} = kF_{SS} \overset{a}{\sim} \chi^2(k) \tag{18.28}$$

For more details see, for example, Pesaran *et al.* (1985, p. 285).

## 18.6 Statistical model selection criteria

Model selection in econometric analysis involves both statistical and non-statistical considerations. It depends on the objective(s) of the analysis, the nature and the extent of economic theory used, and the statistical adequacy of the model under consideration compared with other econometric models. (For a discussion of the general principles involved in model selection, see Pesaran and Smith 1985.) The various choice criteria reported by *Microfit* are only concerned with the issue of 'statistical fit' and provide different approaches to trading off 'fit' and 'parsimony' of a given econometric model.

The program automatically computes Theil's (1971) $\bar{R}^2$ criterion for choosing between linear (and non-linear) regression models estimated by least squares, and the $GR^2$ criterion proposed by Pesaran and Smith (1994) for choosing between linear and non-linear single equation regression models estimated by the instrumental variables method. (See Sections 18.5.1 and 18.9.2 for details.)

In addition, *Microfit* computes the values of the criteria functions proposed by Akaike (1973, 1974), Schwarz (1978), and Hannan and Quinn (1979), both for single- and multi-equation models. All these model selection criteria measure the 'fit' of a given model by its maximised value of the log-likelihood function, and then use different penalty functions to take account of the fact that different numbers of unknown parameters may have been estimated for different models under consideration.

### 18.6.1 Akaike information criterion (AIC)

Let $\ell_n(\tilde{\boldsymbol{\theta}})$ be the maximized value of the log-likelihood function of an econometric model, where $\tilde{\boldsymbol{\theta}}$ is the maximum likelihood estimator of $\tilde{\boldsymbol{\theta}}$, based on a sample of size $n$. The Akaike information criterion (AIC) for this model is defined as

$$AIC_\ell = \ell_n(\tilde{\boldsymbol{\theta}}) - p \tag{18.29}$$

where

$$p \equiv \text{Dimension } (\boldsymbol{\theta}) \equiv \text{The number of freely estimated parameters}$$

In the case of single-equation linear (or non-linear) regression models, the $AIC_\ell$ can also be written equivalently as

$$AIC_\sigma = \log(\tilde{\sigma}^2) + \frac{2p}{n} \tag{18.30}$$

where $\tilde{\sigma}^2$ is the ML estimator of the variance of regression disturbances, $u_t$, given by $\tilde{\sigma}^2 = \mathbf{e}'\mathbf{e}/n$ in the case of linear regression models (see Section 18.5.1). The two versions of the AIC in (18.29) and (18.30) yield identical results. When using (18.29), the model with the highest value of $AIC_\ell$ is chosen. But when using the criterion based on the estimated standard errors (18.30), the model with the lowest value for $AIC_\sigma$ is chosen.[4]

---

[4]For linear regression models, the equivalence of (18.29) and (18.30) follows by substituting for $\ell_n(\hat{\theta})$ given by (18.12) in (18.29):

$$AIC_\ell = -\frac{n}{2}(1 + \log 2\pi) - \frac{n}{2}\log \tilde{\sigma}^2 - p$$

hence using (18.30)

$$AIC_\ell = -\frac{n}{2}(1 + \log 2\pi) - \frac{n}{2}AIC_\sigma$$

Therefore, in the case of regression models estimated over the same sample period, the same preference ordering across models will result irrespective of whether the $AIC_\ell$ or $AIC_\sigma$ criterion is used.

### 18.6.2 Schwarz Bayesian criterion (SBC)

The SBC provides a large sample approximation to the posterior odds ratio of models under consideration. It is defined by

$$SBC_\ell = \ell_n(\tilde{\theta}) - \tfrac{1}{2} p \log n \tag{18.31}$$

In application of the SBC across models, the model with the highest SBC value is chosen. For regression models an alternative version of (18.31), based on the estimated standard error of the regression, $\tilde{\sigma}$, is given by

$$SBC_\sigma = \log(\tilde{\sigma}^2) + \left(\frac{\log n}{n}\right) p$$

According to this criterion, a model is chosen if it has the lowest $SBC_\sigma$ value.

### 18.6.3 Hannan–Quinn criterion (HQC)

This criterion has been primarily proposed for selection of the order of autoregressive moving average or vector autoregressive models, and is defined by

$$HQC_\ell = \ell_n(\tilde{\theta}) - (\log \log n) p$$

or equivalently (in the case of regression models)

$$HQC_\sigma = \log \tilde{\sigma} + \left(\frac{2 \log \log n}{n}\right) p$$

### 18.6.4 Consistency properties of the different model selection criteria

Among the above three model selection criteria, the SBC selects the most parsimonious model (a model with the least number of freely estimated parameters) if $n \geqslant 8$, and the AIC selects the least parsimonious model. The HQC lies somewhere between the other two criteria. Useful discussion of these and other model selection criteria can be found in Amemiya (1980), Judge *et al.* (1985, Chapter 21), and Lütkepohl (1991, Section 4.3). The latter reference is particularly useful for selecting the order of the vector autoregressive models and contains some discussion of the consistency property of the above three model selection criteria. Under certain regularity conditions it can be shown that the SBC and the HQC are consistent, in the sense that for large enough samples they lead to the correct model choice, assuming of course that the 'true' model does in fact belong to the set of models over which one is searching. The same is not true of the AIC or Theil's (1971) $\bar{R}^2$ criterion. This does not, however, mean that the SBC (or HQC) is necessarily preferable to the AIC or the $\bar{R}^2$ criterion, bearing in mind that one is rarely sure that the 'true' model is one of the models under consideration.

## 18.7 Non-nested tests for linear regression models

Consider the following two linear regression models:

$$M_1: \quad \mathbf{y} = \mathbf{X}\boldsymbol{\beta}_1 + \mathbf{u}_1, \qquad \mathbf{u}_1 \sim N(0, \sigma^2 \mathbf{I}_n) \tag{18.32}$$

$$M_2: \quad \mathbf{y} = \mathbf{Z}\boldsymbol{\beta}_2 + \mathbf{u}_2, \qquad \mathbf{u}_2 \sim N(0, \omega^2 \mathbf{I}_n) \tag{18.33}$$

where $\mathbf{y}$ is the $n \times 1$ vector of observations on the dependent variable; $\mathbf{X}$ and $\mathbf{Z}$ are $n \times k_1$ and $n \times k_2$ observation matrices for the regressors of models $M_1$ and $M_2$; $\boldsymbol{\beta}_1$ and $\boldsymbol{\beta}_2$ are the $k_1 \times 1$ and $k_2 \times 1$ unknown regression coefficient vectors; and $\mathbf{u}_1$ and $\mathbf{u}_2$ are the $n \times 1$ disturbance vectors.

Broadly speaking, models $M_1$ and $M_2$ are said to be non-nested if the regressors of $M_1$ (respectively $M_2$) cannot be expressed as an exact linear combination of the regressors of $M_2$ (respectively $M_1$). For a formal definition of the concepts of nested and non-nested models, see Pesaran (1987b). A review of the literature of non-nested hypothesis testing can be found in McAleer and Pesaran (1986).

The program computes the following statistics for the test of $M_1$ against $M_2$ and vice versa:

### The N-test

This is the Cox (1961, 1962) test originally derived in Pesaran (1974, pp. 157–8). The Cox statistic for the test of $M_1$ against $M_2$ is computed as

$$N_1 = \left\{ \frac{n}{2} \log \left( \hat{\omega}^2 / \hat{\omega}_*^2 \right) \right\} \Big/ \hat{V}_1 \tag{18.34}$$

where

$$\hat{\omega}^2 = \mathbf{e}_2'\mathbf{e}_2/n$$
$$\hat{\omega}_*^2 = (\mathbf{e}_1'\mathbf{e}_1 + \hat{\boldsymbol{\beta}}_1'\mathbf{X}'\mathbf{M}_2\mathbf{X}\hat{\boldsymbol{\beta}}_1)/n$$
$$\hat{V}_1^2 = (\hat{\sigma}^2/\hat{\omega}_*^4)\hat{\boldsymbol{\beta}}_1'\mathbf{X}'\mathbf{M}_2\mathbf{M}_1\mathbf{M}_2\mathbf{X}\hat{\boldsymbol{\beta}}_1$$
$$\hat{\sigma}^2 = \mathbf{e}_1'\mathbf{e}_1/n, \quad \hat{\boldsymbol{\beta}}_1 = (\mathbf{X}'\mathbf{X})^{-1}\mathbf{X}'y$$
$$\mathbf{M}_1 = \mathbf{I}_n - \mathbf{X}(\mathbf{X}'\mathbf{X})^{-1}\mathbf{X}'; \qquad \mathbf{M}_2 = \mathbf{I}_n - \mathbf{Z}(\mathbf{Z}'\mathbf{Z})^{-1}\mathbf{Z}'$$

Similarly, the Cox statistic, $N_2$, is also computed for the test of $M_2$ against $M_1$.

### The NT-test

This is the *adjusted* Cox test derived in Godfrey and Pesaran (1983 p. 138), which is referred to as the Ñ-test (or the NT-test). The NT statistic for the test of $M_1$ against $M_2$ (see equations (20) and (21) in Godfrey and Pesaran 1983) is given by

$$\tilde{N}_1 = \tilde{T}_1 \Big/ \sqrt{\{\tilde{V}_1(\tilde{T}_1)\}} \tag{18.35}$$

where

$$\begin{aligned}
\tilde{T}_1 &= \tfrac{1}{2}(n-k_2)\log(\tilde{\omega}^2/\tilde{\omega}_*^2) \\
\tilde{\omega}^2 &= \mathbf{e}_2'\mathbf{e}_2/(n-k_2), \quad \tilde{\sigma}^2 = \mathbf{e}_1'\mathbf{e}_1/(n-k_1) \\
\tilde{\omega}_*^2 &= \{\tilde{\sigma}^2 Tr(\mathbf{M}_1\mathbf{M}_2) + \hat{\beta}_1'\mathbf{X}'\mathbf{M}_2\mathbf{X}\hat{\beta}_1\}/(n-k_2) \\
\tilde{V}_1(\tilde{T}_1) &= (\tilde{\sigma}^2/\tilde{\omega}_*^4)\{\hat{\beta}_1'\mathbf{X}'\mathbf{M}_2\mathbf{M}_1\mathbf{M}_2\mathbf{X}\hat{\beta}_1 + \tfrac{1}{2}\tilde{\sigma}^2 Tr(\mathbf{B}^2)\} \\
Tr(\mathbf{B}^2) &= k_2 - Tr(\mathbf{A}_1\mathbf{A}_2)^2 - \frac{\{k_2 - Tr(\mathbf{A}_1\mathbf{A}_2)\}^2}{n-k_1} \\
\mathbf{A}_1 &= \mathbf{X}(\mathbf{X}'\mathbf{X})^{-1}\mathbf{X}', \qquad \mathbf{A}_2 = \mathbf{Z}(\mathbf{Z}'\mathbf{Z})^{-1}\mathbf{Z}'
\end{aligned} \tag{18.36}$$

Similarly, the Ñ-test statistic, $\tilde{N}_2$, is also computed for the test of $M_2$ against $M_1$.

### The W-test

This is the Wald-type test of $M_1$ against $M_2$ proposed in Godfrey and Pesaran (1983), and based on the statistic

$$W_1 = \frac{(n-k_2)(\tilde{\omega}^2 - \tilde{\omega}_*^2)}{\{2\tilde{\sigma}^4 Tr(\mathbf{B}^2) + 4\tilde{\sigma}^2\hat{\beta}_1'\mathbf{X}'\mathbf{M}_2\mathbf{M}_1\mathbf{M}_2\mathbf{X}\hat{\beta}_1\}^{1/2}}. \tag{18.37}$$

All the notations are as above. The program also computes a similar statistic, $W_2$, for the test of $M_2$ against $M_1$.

### The J-test

This test is due to Davidson and MacKinnon (1981), and for the test of $M_1$ against $M_2$ is based on the $t$-ratio of $\lambda$ in the 'artificial' OLS regression

$$\mathbf{y} = \mathbf{X}\beta_1 + \lambda(\mathbf{Z}\hat{\beta}_2) + \mathbf{u}$$

The relevant statistic for the J-test of $M_2$ against $M_1$ is the $t$-ratio of $\mu$ in the OLS regression

$$\mathbf{y} = \mathbf{Z}\beta_2 + \mu(\mathbf{X}\hat{\beta}_1) + \mathbf{v}$$

where $\hat{\beta}_1 = (\mathbf{X}'\mathbf{X})^{-1}\mathbf{X}'\mathbf{y}$, and $\hat{\beta}_2 = (\mathbf{Z}'\mathbf{Z})^{-1}\mathbf{Z}'\mathbf{y}$. The J-test is asymptotically equivalent to the above non-nested tests but, as demonstrated by extensive Monte Carlo experiments in Godfrey and Pesaran (1983), in small samples the Ñ-test, and the W-test defined above, are preferable to it.

### The JA-test

This test is due to Fisher and McAleer (1981), and for the test of $M_1$ against $M_2$ is based on the $t$-ratio of $\lambda$ in the OLS regression

$$\mathbf{y} = \mathbf{X}\beta_1 + \lambda(\mathbf{A}_2\mathbf{X}\hat{\beta}_1) + \mathbf{u}$$

The relevant statistic for the JA-test of $M_2$ against $M_1$ is the $t$-ratio of $\mu$ in the OLS regression

$$\mathbf{y} = \mathbf{Z}\beta_2 + \mu(\mathbf{A}_1\mathbf{Z}\hat{\beta}_2) + \mathbf{v}$$

The matrices $\mathbf{A}_1$ and $\mathbf{A}_2$ are already defined by (18.36).

**The encompassing test**

This test has been proposed in the literature by Deaton (1982), Dastoor (1983), Gourierous *et al.* (1983), and Mizon and Richard (1986). In the case of testing $M_1$ against $M_2$, the encompassing test is the same as the classical F test and is computed as the F statistic for testing $\delta = 0$ in the combined OLS regression

$$\mathbf{y} = \mathbf{X}\mathbf{a}_0 + \mathbf{Z}^*\delta + \mathbf{u}$$

where $\mathbf{Z}^*$ denotes the variables in $M_2$ that cannot be expressed as exact linear combinations of the regressors of $M_1$. Similarly, the program computes the F statistic for the test of $M_2$ against $M_1$. The encompassing test is asymptotically equivalent to the above non-nested tests under the null hypothesis, but in general it is less powerful than these for a large class of alternative non-nested models (see Pesaran 1982b).

A Monte Carlo study of the relative performance of the above non-nested tests in small samples can be found in Godfrey and Pesaran (1983).

**Choice criteria**

Let the maximized log-likelihood functions of models $M_1$ and $M_2$ be $LL_1$ and $LL_2$ respectively.

The Akaike information criterion (AIC) for the choice between models $M_1$ and $M_2$ (Akaike 1973, 1974) is computed as

$$AIC(M_1{:}M_2) = LL_1 - LL_2 - (k_1 - k_2)$$

Model $M_1$ is preferred to $M_2$ if $AIC(M_1{:}M_2) > 0$, otherwise, $M_2$ is preferred to $M_1$.

The Schwarz Bayesian criterion (SBC) for the choice between models $M_1$ and $M_2$ is computed as (Schwarz 1978)

$$SBC(M_1{:}M_2) = LL_1 - LL_2 - \tfrac{1}{2}(k_1 - k_2)\log(n)$$

Model $M_1$ is preferred to $M_2$ if $SBC(M_1{:}M_2) > 0$, otherwise $M_2$ is preferred to $M_1$ (see also Section 18.6).

## 18.8 Non-nested tests for models with different transformations of the dependent variable

The program computes four non-nested test statistics and two choice criteria for pairwise testing and choice between non-nested models, where their left-hand-side variables are *different* known functions of a given underlying dependent variable. More specifically, *Microfit* enables you to consider the following non-nested models:

$$M_f\colon \mathbf{f(y)} = \mathbf{X}\boldsymbol{\beta}_1 + \mathbf{u}_1, \qquad \mathbf{u}_1 \sim N(0, \sigma^2\mathbf{I}_n) \tag{18.38}$$

$$M_g\colon \mathbf{g(y)} = \mathbf{Z}\boldsymbol{\beta}_2 + \mathbf{u}_2, \qquad \mathbf{u}_2 \sim N(0, \omega^2\mathbf{I}_n) \tag{18.39}$$

where $\mathbf{f(y)}$ and $\mathbf{g(y)}$ are known transformations of the $n \times 1$ vector of observations on the underlying dependent variable of interest, $\mathbf{y}$. You can either specify your particular choice for the functions $\mathbf{f(y)}$ and $\mathbf{g(y)}$, or you can select one of the following specifications:

1. Linear form $\mathbf{f(y)} = \mathbf{y}$
2. Logarithmic form $\mathbf{f(y)} = \log(\mathbf{y})$
3. Ratio form $\mathbf{f(y)} = \mathbf{y}/\mathbf{z}$
4. Difference form $\mathbf{f(y)} = \mathbf{y} - \mathbf{y}(-1)$
5. Log-difference form $\mathbf{f(y)} = \log \mathbf{y} - \log \mathbf{y}(-1)$

where $\mathbf{z}$ is a variable in the variables list. Notice that log(**y**) refers to a vector of observations with elements equal to $\log(y_t)$, $t = 1, 2, \ldots, n$. Also $\mathbf{y} - \mathbf{y}(-1)$ refers to a vector with a typical element equal to $y_t - y_{t-1}$, $t = 1, 2, \ldots, n$.

### 18.8.1 The $P_E$ test statistic

This statistic is proposed by MacKinnon *et al.* (1983) and, in the case of testing $M_f$ against $M_g$, is given by the $t$-ratio of $\alpha_f$ in the auxiliary regression

$$\mathbf{f(y)} = \mathbf{Xb} + \alpha_f[\mathbf{Z}\hat{\boldsymbol{\beta}}_2 - \mathbf{g}\{\mathbf{f}^{-1}(\mathbf{X}\hat{\boldsymbol{\beta}}_1)\}] + \text{Error} \tag{18.40}$$

Similarly, the $P_E$ statistic for testing $M_g$ against $M_f$ is given by the $t$-ratio of $\alpha_g$ in the auxiliary regression

$$\mathbf{g(y)} = \mathbf{Zd} + \alpha_g[\mathbf{X}\hat{\boldsymbol{\beta}}_1 - \mathbf{f}\{\mathbf{g}^{-1}(\mathbf{Z}\hat{\boldsymbol{\beta}}_2)\}] + \text{Error} \tag{18.41}$$

Functions $f^{-1}(\cdot)$ and $g^{-1}(\cdot)$ represent the inverse functions for $f(\cdot)$ and $g(\cdot)$, respectively, such that $f(f^{-1}(y)) = y$, and $g(g^{-1}(y)) = y$. For example, in the case where $M_f$ is linear (i.e., $f(y) = y$) and $M_g$ is log-linear (i.e. $g(y) = \log y$), we have

$$f^{-1}(y_t) = y_t$$
$$g^{-1}(y_t) = \exp(y_t)$$

In the case where $M_f$ is in first-differences (i.e. $f(y_t) = y_t - y_{t-1}$) and $M_g$ is in log-differences (i.e. $g(y_t) = \log(y_t/y_{t-1})$), we have

$$f^{-1}(y_t) = f(y_t) + y_{t-1}$$
$$g^{-1}(y_t) = y_{t-1} \exp\{g(y_t)\}$$

$\hat{\beta}_1$ and $\hat{\beta}_2$ are the OLS estimators of $\beta_1$ and $\beta_2$ under $M_f$ and $M_g$, respectively.

### 18.8.2 The Bera–McAleer test statistic (BM)

The statistic proposed by Bera and McAleer (1989) is for testing linear versus log-linear models, but can be readily extended to general known one-to-one transformations of the dependent variable of interest, namely $y_t$. To compute the Bera–McAleer (BM) statistic to test $M_f$ against $M_g$, the program first computes the residuals $\hat{\eta}_g$ from the regression of $\mathbf{g}[\mathbf{f}^{-1}(\mathbf{X}\hat{\beta}_1)]$ on $\mathbf{Z}$. It then computes the BM statistic for the test of $M_f$ against $M_g$ as the $t$-ratio of $\theta_f$ in the auxiliary regression

$$\mathbf{f}(\mathbf{y}) = \mathbf{X}\mathbf{b} + \theta_f \hat{\eta}_g + \text{Error} \tag{18.42}$$

The BM statistic for the test of $M_g$ against $M_f$ is given by the $t$-ratio of $\theta_g$ in the auxiliary regression

$$\mathbf{g}(\mathbf{y}) = \mathbf{Z}\mathbf{d} + \theta_g \hat{\eta}_f + \text{Error} \tag{18.43}$$

where $\hat{\eta}_f$ is the residual vector of the regression of $\mathbf{f}\{\mathbf{g}^{-1}(\mathbf{Z}\hat{\beta}_2)\}$ on $\mathbf{X}$.

### 18.8.3 The double-length regression test statistic (DL)

The double-length (DL) regression statistic is proposed by Davidson and MacKinnon (1984) and, for the test of $M_f$ against $M_g$, is given by

$$DL_f = 2n - SSR_f \tag{18.44}$$

where $SSR_f$ denotes the sums of squares of residuals from the DL regression

$$\begin{bmatrix} \mathbf{e}_1/\hat{\sigma} \\ \boldsymbol{\tau} \end{bmatrix} = \begin{bmatrix} -\mathbf{X} \\ \mathbf{0} \end{bmatrix} \mathbf{b} + \begin{bmatrix} \mathbf{e}_1/\hat{\sigma} \\ -\boldsymbol{\tau} \end{bmatrix} \mathbf{c} + \begin{bmatrix} -\mathbf{e}_2 \\ \hat{\sigma}\hat{\mathbf{v}} \end{bmatrix} \mathbf{d} + \text{Error} \tag{18.45}$$

where

$$\mathbf{e}_1 = \mathbf{f}(\mathbf{y}) - \mathbf{X}\hat{\beta}_1, \qquad \hat{\sigma}^2 = \mathbf{e}_1'\mathbf{e}_1/(n - k_1)$$
$$\mathbf{e}_2 = \mathbf{g}(\mathbf{y}) - \mathbf{Z}\hat{\beta}_2, \qquad \hat{\omega}^2 = \mathbf{e}_2'\mathbf{e}_2/(n - k_2)$$
$$\hat{\mathbf{v}} = (\hat{v}_1, \hat{v}_2, \ldots, \hat{v}_n)', \quad \hat{v}_t = g'(y_t)/f'(y_t)$$

and $\boldsymbol{\tau} = (1, 1, \ldots, 1)'$ is an $n \times 1$ vector of ones, and $g'(y_t)$ and $f'(y_t)$ stand for the derivatives of $g(y_t)$ and $f(y_t)$ with respect to $y_t$.

To compute the $SSR_f$ statistic, we first note that

$$SSR_f = \tilde{\mathbf{y}}'\tilde{\mathbf{y}} - \tilde{\mathbf{y}}'\tilde{\mathbf{X}}(\tilde{\mathbf{X}}'\tilde{\mathbf{X}})^{-1}\tilde{\mathbf{X}}'\tilde{\mathbf{y}}$$

where

$$\tilde{\mathbf{y}} = \begin{bmatrix} \mathbf{e}_1/\hat{\sigma} \\ \boldsymbol{\tau} \end{bmatrix}, \qquad \tilde{\mathbf{X}} = \begin{bmatrix} -\mathbf{X} & \mathbf{e}_1/\hat{\sigma} & -\mathbf{e}_2 \\ \mathbf{0} & -\boldsymbol{\tau} & \hat{\sigma}\hat{\mathbf{v}} \end{bmatrix}$$

But $\tilde{\mathbf{y}}'\tilde{\mathbf{y}} = \mathbf{e}_1'\mathbf{e}_2/\hat{\sigma}^2 + n = 2n - k_1$,

$$\tilde{\mathbf{y}}'\tilde{\mathbf{X}} = \left[0, -k_1, \hat{\sigma}\boldsymbol{\tau}'\hat{\mathbf{v}} - \frac{\mathbf{e}_1\mathbf{e}_2}{\hat{\sigma}}\right]$$

and

$$\tilde{\mathbf{X}}'\tilde{\mathbf{X}} = \begin{bmatrix} \mathbf{X}'\mathbf{X} & \mathbf{0} & \mathbf{X}'\mathbf{e}_2 \\ \mathbf{0} & 2n-k_1 & \dfrac{-\mathbf{e}_1'\mathbf{e}_2}{\hat{\sigma}} - \hat{\sigma}(\boldsymbol{\tau}'\hat{\mathbf{v}}) \\ \mathbf{e}_2'\mathbf{X} & \dfrac{-\mathbf{e}_1'\mathbf{e}_2}{\hat{\sigma}} - \hat{\sigma}(\boldsymbol{\tau}'\hat{\mathbf{v}}) & \mathbf{e}_2'\mathbf{e}_2 + \hat{\sigma}^2\hat{v}'\hat{v} \end{bmatrix}$$

Using these results, and after some algebra, we obtain:[5]

$$DL_f = \frac{1}{D}(k_1^2 R_1 + (2n - k_1)R_3^2 - 2k_1 R_2 R_3) \tag{18.46}$$

where

$$\begin{aligned} R_1 &= (\mathbf{e}_2'\mathbf{M}_1\mathbf{e}_2)/\hat{\sigma}^2 + \hat{\mathbf{v}}'\hat{\mathbf{v}} \\ R_2 &= (\boldsymbol{\tau}'\hat{\mathbf{v}}) + (\mathbf{e}_1'\mathbf{e}_2)/\hat{\sigma}^2 \\ R_3 &= (\boldsymbol{\tau}'\hat{\mathbf{v}}) - (\mathbf{e}_1'\mathbf{e}_2)/\hat{\sigma}^2 \\ D &= (2n - k_1)R_1 - R_2^2 \end{aligned}$$

A similar statistic is also computed for the test of $M_g$ against $M_f$.

### 18.8.4 Cox's non-nested statistics computed by simulation

The simulated Cox test statistics were introduced in Pesaran and Pesaran (1993) and subsequently applied to tests of linear versus log-linear models, and first-difference versus log-difference stationary models in Pesaran and Pesaran (1995) (or PP(95)).

Three versions of the simulated Cox statistic are considered by PP(95). All the three test statistics have the same numerator and differ by the choice of the estimator of the variance used to standardize the Cox statistic. In *Microfit* 4.0 we have only programmed the $SC_c$ statistic which seems to have much better small sample properties than the other two test statistics (namely $SC_a$ and $SC_b$) considered by PP(95).[6] (In the program this is referred as the SC_c test statistic.) The numerator of the $SC_c$ statistic for testing $M_f$ against $M_g$ is computed as

[5] The expression for $DL_f$ given in the manual for *Microfit* 3.0 (Pesaran and Pesaran 1991) is incorrect, but the DL statistics computed by *Microfit* 3.23 are correct, and use the expression in (18.46).

[6] The Monte Carlo results reported in PP(95) also clearly show that the $SC_c$ and the DL tests are more powerful than the PE or BM tests discussed in Section 18.8.1 and 18.8.2 above.

$$n^{1/2}T_f(R) = -\tfrac{1}{2}n^{1/2}\log(\hat{\sigma}^2/\hat{\omega}^2) + n^{-1/2}\sum_{t=1}^{n}\log(|f'(y_t)/g'(y_t)|)$$
$$+\tfrac{1}{2}n^{-1/2}(k_1 - k_2) - n^{1/2}C_R(\hat{\boldsymbol{\theta}}, \hat{\gamma}_*(R)) \tag{18.47}$$

where

$$\hat{\boldsymbol{\theta}} = (\hat{\beta}_1', \hat{\sigma}^2)'$$

$R$ is the number of replications and, $\hat{\gamma}_*(R)$ is the simulated pseudo-ML estimator of $\gamma = (\beta_2', \omega^2)'$ under $M_f$:

$$\hat{\gamma}_*(R) = R^{-1}\sum_{j=1}^{R}\hat{\gamma}_j, \tag{18.48}$$

where $\hat{\gamma}_j$ is the ML estimator of $\gamma$ computed using the artificially simulated independent observations $\mathbf{Y}_j = (\mathbf{Y}_{j1}, \mathbf{Y}_{j2}, \ldots, \mathbf{Y}_{jn})$ obtained under $M_f$ with $\boldsymbol{\theta} = \hat{\boldsymbol{\theta}}$. $C_R(\hat{\boldsymbol{\theta}}, \hat{\gamma}_*(R))$ is the simulated estimator of the 'closeness' measure of $M_f$ with respect to $M_g$ (see Pesaran 1987b):

$$C_R(\hat{\boldsymbol{\theta}}, \hat{\gamma}_*(R)) = R^{-1}\sum_{j=1}^{R}[L_f(\mathbf{Y}_j, \hat{\boldsymbol{\theta}}) - L_g\{\mathbf{Y}_j, \hat{\gamma}_*(R)\}] \tag{18.49}$$

where $L_f(\mathbf{Y}, \boldsymbol{\theta})$ and $L_g(\mathbf{Y}, \gamma)$ are the average log-likelihood functions under $M_f$ and $M_g$, respectively:

$$L_f(\mathbf{Y}, \boldsymbol{\theta}) = -\tfrac{1}{2}\log(2\pi\sigma^2) - \frac{1}{2\sigma^2}\left[\sum_{t=1}^{n}\{f(y_t) - \beta_1'\mathbf{x}_t\}^2/n\right]$$
$$+n^{-1}\sum_{t=1}^{n}\log|f'(y_t)| \tag{18.50}$$

$$L_g(\mathbf{Y}, \gamma) = -\tfrac{1}{2}\log(2\pi\omega^2) - \frac{1}{2\omega^2}\left[\sum_{t=1}^{n}\{g(y_t) - \beta_2'z_t\}^2/n\right]$$
$$+n^{-1}\sum_{t=1}^{n}\log|g'(y_t)| \tag{18.51}$$

The denominator of the $SC_c$ statistic is computed as

$$V_{*d}^2(R) = (n-1)^{-1}\sum_{t=1}^{n}(d_{*t} - \bar{d}_*)^2 \tag{18.52}$$

where

$$\bar{d}_* = n^{-1}\sum_{t=1}^{n}d_{*t}$$

and

$$d_{*t} = -\tfrac{1}{2}\log(\hat{\sigma}^2/\hat{\omega}_*^2(R)) - \frac{1}{2\hat{\sigma}^2}e_{t1}^2$$
$$+\frac{1}{2\hat{\omega}_*^2(R)}\left[g(y_t) - \mathbf{z}_t'\hat{\beta}_{*2}(R)\right]^2 + \log(|f'(y_t)/g'(y_t)|)$$

and

$$e_{t1} = f(y_t) - \mathbf{x}_t'\hat{\beta}_1.$$

Recall also that $\hat{\beta}_{*2}(R)$ and $\hat{\omega}_*^2(R)$ are given by (18.48), where $\hat{\gamma}_*(R) = (\hat{\beta}_{*2}'(R), \hat{\omega}_*^2(R))'$.

The standardized Cox statistic reported by *Microfit* 4.0 for the test of $M_f$ against $M_g$ is given by

$$SC_c(R) = n^{\frac{1}{2}}T_f(R)/V_{*d}(R)$$

where $n^{\frac{1}{2}}T_f(R)$ is defined by (18.47) and $V_{*d}(R)$ by (18.52). A similar statistic is also computed for the test of $M_g$ against $M_f$.

### 18.8.5 Sargan and Vuong's likelihood criteria

Sargan's (1964) likelihood criterion simply compares the maximized values of the log-likelihood functions under $M_f$ and $M_g$:[7]

$$LL_{fg} = n\{L_f(\mathbf{Y}, \hat{\theta}) - L_g(\mathbf{Y}, \hat{\gamma})\}$$

or using (18.50) and (18.51)

$$LL_{fg} = -\frac{n}{2}\log(\hat{\sigma}^2/\hat{\omega}^2) + \sum_{t=1}^{n}\log|f'(y_t)/g'(y_t)| + \tfrac{1}{2}(k_1 - k_2) \qquad (18.53)$$

One could also apply the known model selection criteria such as the Akaike information criterion (AIC) and the Schwarz Bayesian criterion (SBC) to the models $M_f$ and $M_g$ (see Section 18.6). For example, in the case of the AIC we have

$$AIC(M_f{:}M_g) = LL_{fg} - (k_1 - k_2)$$

Vuong's (1989) criterion is motivated in the context of testing the hypothesis that $M_f$ and $M_g$ are equivalent, using the Kullback–Leibler (1951) information criterion as a measure of goodness of fit. Vuong's (1989) test criterion for the comparison of $M_f$ and $M_g$ is computed as

$$V_{fg} = \frac{\sum_{t=1}^{n} d_t}{\left(\sum_{t=1}^{n}(d_t - \bar{d})^2\right)^{1/2}} \qquad (18.54)$$

[7]Notice that throughout $\hat{\sigma}^2 = \mathbf{e}_1'\mathbf{e}_1/(n-k_1)$ and $\hat{\omega}^2 = \mathbf{e}_2'\mathbf{e}_2/(n-k_2)$ are used as estimators of $\sigma^2$ and $\omega^2$, respectively.

where

$$\bar{d} = n^{-1}\sum_{t=1}^{n} d_t$$

and

$$d_t = -\tfrac{1}{2}\log(\hat{\sigma}^2/\hat{\omega}^2) - \tfrac{1}{2}\left(\frac{e_{t1}^2}{\hat{\sigma}^2} - \frac{e_{t2}^2}{\hat{\omega}^2}\right) + \log(|f'(y_t)/g'(y_t)|)$$

$$e_{t1} = f(y_t) - \hat{\beta}_1'\mathbf{x}_t, \qquad e_{t2} = g(y_t) - \hat{\beta}_2'\mathbf{z}_t$$

Under the null hypothesis that '$M_f$ and $M_g$ are equivalent', $V_{fg}$ is approximately distributed as a standard normal variate.

## 18.9 The generalized instrumental variable method (GIVE)

Consider the linear regression model

$$\underset{n\times 1}{\mathbf{y}} = \underset{n\times k}{\mathbf{X}}\ \underset{k\times 1}{\beta} + \underset{n\times 1}{\mathbf{u}}$$

and suppose that there exists an $n \times s$ matrix $\mathbf{Z}$ containing observations on $s$ instrumental variables ($s \geqslant k$). Then the GIVE[8] of $\beta$ is given by

$$\hat{\beta}_{IV} = (\mathbf{X}'\mathbf{P}_z\mathbf{X})^{-1}\mathbf{X}'\mathbf{P}_z\mathbf{y} \tag{18.55}$$

where $\mathbf{P}_z$ is the $n \times n$ projection matrix

$$\mathbf{P}_z = \mathbf{Z}(\mathbf{Z}'\mathbf{Z})^{-1}\mathbf{Z}' \tag{18.56}$$

The estimator of the variance matrix of $\hat{\beta}_{IV}$ is given by

$$\hat{V}(\hat{\beta}_{IV}) = \hat{\sigma}_{IV}^2(\mathbf{X}'\mathbf{P}_z\mathbf{X})^{-1} \tag{18.57}$$

where $\hat{\sigma}_{IV}^2$ is the IV estimator of $\sigma^2$ (the variance of $u_t$):

$$\hat{\sigma}_{IV}^2 = (n-k)^{-1}\hat{\mathbf{e}}_{IV}'\hat{\mathbf{e}}_{IV} \tag{18.58}$$

where $\hat{\mathbf{e}}_{IV}$ is the IV residuals given by

$$\hat{\mathbf{e}}_{IV} = \mathbf{y} - \mathbf{X}\hat{\beta}_{IV} \tag{18.59}$$

The estimator $\hat{\beta}_{IV}$ can also be derived by minimizing the weighted quadratic for

$$Q(\beta) = (\mathbf{y} - \mathbf{X}\beta)'\mathbf{P}_z(\mathbf{y} - \mathbf{X}\beta) \tag{18.60}$$

with respect to $\beta$. The program reports the minimized value of $Q(\beta)$ (namely $Q(\hat{\beta}_{IV})$) under the heading 'value of IV minimand'. Notice that $Q(\hat{\beta}_{IV})$ will

[8]The idea of the generalized IV estimator is due to Sargan (1958).

be identically equal to zero when the number of instruments is exactly equal to the number of the regressors (i.e. when $s = k$).

### 18.9.1 Two-stage least squares (2SLS)

The IV estimator, $\hat{\beta}_{IV}$, can also be computed using a two-step procedure, known as the two-stage least squares (2SLS), where in the first step, the fitted values of the OLS regression of $\mathbf{X}$ on $\mathbf{Z}$, $\hat{\mathbf{X}} = \mathbf{P}_z\mathbf{X}$ are computed. Then $\hat{\beta}_{IV}$ is obtained by the OLS regression of $\mathbf{y}$ on $\hat{\mathbf{X}}$. Notice, however, that such a two-step procedure does not, in general, give a correct estimator of $\sigma^2$, and hence of $\hat{V}(\hat{\beta}_{IV})$. This is because the *IV* residuals, $\hat{\mathbf{e}}_{IV}$, defined by (18.59), used in the estimation of $\hat{\sigma}^2_{IV}$ are not the same as the residuals obtained at the second stage of the 2SLS method. To see this, denote the 2SLS residuals by $\mathbf{e}_{2SLS}$ and note that

$$\begin{aligned} \mathbf{e}_{2SLS} &= \mathbf{y} - \hat{\mathbf{X}}\hat{\beta}_{IV} \\ &= (\mathbf{y} - \mathbf{X}\hat{\beta}_{IV}) + (\mathbf{X} - \hat{\mathbf{X}})\hat{\beta}_{IV} \\ &= \mathbf{e}_{IV} + (\mathbf{X} - \hat{\mathbf{X}})\hat{\beta}_{IV} \end{aligned} \tag{18.61}$$

where $\mathbf{X} - \hat{\mathbf{X}}$ are the residual matrix ($n \times k$) of the regressions of $\mathbf{X}$ on $\mathbf{Z}$. Only in the case where $\mathbf{Z}$ is an exact predictor of $\mathbf{X}$, will the two sets of residuals be the same.

### 18.9.2 Generalized $R^2$ for IV Regressions ($GR^2$)

The use of $R^2$ and $\bar{R}^2$ as measures of goodness of fit in the case of *IV* regressions is not valid. As it is well known, there is no guarantee that the $R^2$ of a regression model estimated by the *IV* method is positive, and this result does not depend on whether or not an intercept term is included in the regression (see, for example, Maddala 1988, p. 309). An appropriate measure of fit for *IV* regressions is the generalized $R^2$, or $GR^2$, measure proposed by Pesaran and Smith (1994). In the case of *IV* regressions, *Microfit* reports this measure along with the other summary statistics. The $GR^2$ is computed as

$$GR^2 = 1 - (\mathbf{e}'_{2SLS}\mathbf{e}_{2SLS}) \Big/ \left( \sum_{t=1}^{n} (y_t - \bar{y})^2 \right) \tag{18.62}$$

where $\mathbf{e}_{2SLS}$, given by (18.61), is the vector of residuals from the second stage in the 2SLS procedure (described in Section 18.9.1). Notice also that

$$\mathbf{e}_{2SLS} = \mathbf{e}_{IV} + (\mathbf{X} - \hat{\mathbf{X}})\hat{\beta}_{IV} \tag{18.63}$$

A degrees-of-freedom adjusted $GR^2$ measure is given by

$$\overline{GR}^2 = 1 - \left( \frac{n-1}{n-k} \right)(1 - GR^2) \tag{18.64}$$

Pesaran and Smith (1994) show that under reasonable assumptions the use of $GR^2$ is a valid discriminator for models estimated by the *IV* method, asymptotically.

### 18.9.3 Sargan's general misspecification test

This test is proposed in Sargan (1964, pp. 28–9), as a general test of misspecification in the case of IV estimation, and is based on the statistic $(s > k)$

$$\chi^2_{SM} = Q(\hat{\beta}_{IV})/\hat{\sigma}^2_{IV} \overset{a}{\sim} \chi^2(s-k) \tag{18.65}$$

where $Q(\hat{\beta}_{IV})$ is the value of IV minimand given by

$$\begin{aligned} Q(\hat{\beta}_{IV}) &= (\mathbf{y} - \mathbf{X}\hat{\beta}_{IV})'\mathbf{P}_z(\mathbf{y} - \mathbf{X}\hat{\beta}_{IV}) \\ &= \mathbf{y}'[\mathbf{P}_z - \mathbf{P}_z\mathbf{X}(\mathbf{X}'\mathbf{P}_z\mathbf{X})^{-1}\mathbf{X}'\mathbf{P}_z]\mathbf{y} \\ &= \hat{\mathbf{y}}'[\mathbf{I} - \hat{\mathbf{X}}(\hat{\mathbf{X}}'\hat{\mathbf{X}})^{-1}\mathbf{X}']\hat{\mathbf{y}} \end{aligned} \tag{18.66}$$

Under the null hypothesis that the regression equation (18.2) is correctly specified, and that the $s\,(s > k)$ instrumental variables $\mathbf{Z}$ are valid instruments, Sargan's misspecification statistic, $\chi^2_{SM}$, is asymptotically distributed as a chi-squared variate with $s - k$ degrees of freedom. The J-statistic proposed by Hansen (1982) is a generalization of Sargan's misspecification statistic.

### 18.9.4 Sargan's test of residual serial correlation for IV regressions

The statistic underlying this test is given in Appendix B of Breusch and Godfrey (1981), and can be written as

$$\chi^2_{SC}(p) = n\mathbf{e}'_{IV}\mathbf{W}(\mathbf{W}'\mathbf{H}\mathbf{W})^{-1}\mathbf{W}'\mathbf{e}_{IV}/\mathbf{e}'_{IV}\mathbf{e}_{IV} \overset{a}{\sim} \chi^2(p) \tag{18.67}$$

where $\mathbf{e}_{IV}$ is the vector of IV residuals defined by (18.59):

$$\mathbf{e}_{IV} = \mathbf{y} - \mathbf{X}\hat{\beta}_{IV} = (e_{1,IV}, e_{2,IV}, \ldots, e_{n,IV})'$$

$\mathbf{W}$ is the $n \times p$ matrix consisting of the $p$ lagged valued of $\mathbf{e}_{IV}$, namely

$$\mathbf{W} = \begin{bmatrix} 0 & 0 & \cdots & 0 \\ e_{1,IV} & 0 & \cdots & 0 \\ e_{2,IV} & e_{1,IV} & \cdots & 0 \\ \vdots & \vdots & & \vdots \\ & & & e_{n-p-1,IV} \\ e_{n-1,IV} & e_{n-2,IV} & \cdots & e_{n-p,IV} \end{bmatrix} \tag{18.68}$$

and

$$\mathbf{H} = \mathbf{I}_n - \mathbf{X}(\hat{\mathbf{X}}'\hat{\mathbf{X}})^{-1}\hat{\mathbf{X}}' - \hat{\mathbf{X}}(\hat{\mathbf{X}}'\hat{\mathbf{X}})^{-1}\mathbf{X}' + \mathbf{X}(\hat{\mathbf{X}}'\hat{\mathbf{X}})^{-1}\mathbf{X}'$$

in which $\hat{\mathbf{X}} = \mathbf{P}_z\mathbf{X}$.[9] Notice that when $\mathbf{Z}$ includes $\mathbf{X}$, then $\hat{\mathbf{X}} = \mathbf{X}$, and (18.67) reduces to (18.17). Under the null hypothesis that the disturbances in (18.2) are serially uncorrelated, $\chi^2_{SC}(p)$ in (18.67) is asymptotically distributed as a chi-squared variate with $p$ degrees of freedom. See Pesaran and Taylor (1997) for details of other diagnostic test statistics for IV regressions.

## 18.10 Exact ML/AR estimators

This estimation method (option 3 in the Linear Regression Menu, described in Section 6.5), provides exact maximum likelihood (ML) estimates of the parameters of (18.1) under the assumption that the disturbances, $u_t$, follow stationary

$$AR(1)\text{: } u_t = \rho u_{t-1} + \epsilon_t, \qquad \epsilon_t \sim N(0, \sigma^2_\epsilon), \quad t = 1, 2, \ldots, n \tag{18.69}$$

or

$$AR(2)\text{: } u_t = \rho_1 u_{t-1} + \rho_2 u_{t-2} + \epsilon_t, \qquad \epsilon_t \sim N(0, \sigma^2_\epsilon), \quad t = 1, 2, \ldots, n \tag{18.70}$$

processes with 'stochastic initial values'. This estimation procedure assumes that the underlying AR error processes are started a long time prior to the first observation date (i.e. $t = 1$) and are stationary. This implies that the initial values ($u_1$ for the AR(1) process, and $u_1$ and $u_2$ for the AR(2) process) are normally distributed with zero means and a constant variance given by

$$\text{AR(1) Case:} \quad V(u_1) = \frac{\sigma^2_\epsilon}{1 - \rho^2}$$

$$\text{AR(2) Case:} \quad \begin{cases} V(u_1) = V(u_2) = \dfrac{\sigma^2_\epsilon(1 - \rho_2)}{(1 + \rho_2)^3 - \rho_1^2(1 + \rho_2)} \\[2ex] Cov(u_1, u_2) = \dfrac{\sigma^2_\epsilon \rho_1}{(1 + \rho_2)^3 - \rho_1^2(1 + \rho_2)} \end{cases}$$

The exact ML estimation procedure then allows for the effect of initial values on the parameter estimates by adding the logarithm of the density function of the initial values to the log-density function of the remaining observations obtained conditional on the initial values. For example, in the case of the AR(1) model, the log-density function of $(u_2, u_3, \ldots, u_n)$ conditional on the initial value, $u_1$, is given by

$$\log\{f(u_2, u_3, \ldots, u_n | u_1)\} = -\frac{(n-1)}{2}\log(2\pi\sigma^2_\epsilon) - \frac{1}{2\sigma^2_\epsilon}\left(\sum_{t=2}^{n} \sigma^2_t\right) \tag{18.71}$$

[9] See Breusch and Godfrey (1981, p. 101) for further details. The statistic in (18.67) is derived from the results in Sargan (1976).

and

$$\log\{f(u_1)\} = -\frac{1}{2}\log(2\pi\sigma_\epsilon^2) + \frac{1}{2}\log(1-\rho^2) - \frac{(1-\rho^2)}{2\sigma_\epsilon^2}u_1^2$$

Combining the above log densities yields the full (unconditional) log-density function of $(u_1, u_2, \ldots, u_n)$.

$$\begin{aligned}\log\{f(u_1, u_2, \ldots, u_n)\} = &-\frac{n}{2}\log(2\pi\sigma_\epsilon^2) + \frac{1}{2}\log(1-\rho^2) \\ &- \frac{1}{2\sigma_\epsilon^2}\left(\sum_{t=2}^{n}(u_t - \rho u_{t-1})^2 + (1-\rho^2)u_1^2\right)\end{aligned} \tag{18.72}$$

Asymptotically, the effect of the distribution of the initial values on the ML estimators is negligible, but it could be important in small samples where $\mathbf{x}_t$s are trended and $\rho$ is suspected to be near but *not* equal to unity. See Pesaran (1972), and Pesaran and Slater (1980, Chapters 2–3) for further details. Also see Judge *et al.* (1985, Section 8.2), Davidson and MacKinnon (1993, Section 10.6), and the papers by Hildreth and Dent (1974), and Beach and MacKinnon (1978). Strictly speaking, the ML estimation will be exact if lagged values of $y_t$ are not included amongst the regressors. For a discussion of the exact ML estimation of models with lagged dependent variable and serially correlated errors, see Pesaran (1981).

### 18.10.1 The AR(1) case

For this case, the ML estimators are computed by maximizing the log-likelihood function[10]

$$\begin{aligned}LL_{AR1}(\boldsymbol{\theta}) = &-\frac{n}{2}\log(2\pi\sigma_\epsilon^2) + \tfrac{1}{2}\log(1-\rho^2) \\ &- \frac{1}{2\sigma_\epsilon^2}(\mathbf{y} - \mathbf{X}\boldsymbol{\beta})'\mathbf{R}(\rho)(\mathbf{y} - \mathbf{X}\boldsymbol{\beta})\end{aligned} \tag{18.73}$$

with respect to the unknown parameters $\boldsymbol{\theta} = (\boldsymbol{\beta}', \sigma_\epsilon^2, \rho)'$, where $\mathbf{R}(\rho)$ is the $n \times n$ matrix

$$R(\rho) = \begin{bmatrix} 1 & -\rho & 0 & 0 & & \cdots & 0 \\ -\rho & 1+\rho^2 & -\rho & 0 & & \cdots & 0 \\ \vdots & & & & & & \vdots \\ 0 & 0 & \cdots & \cdots & -\rho & 1+\rho^2 & -\rho \\ 0 & 0 & \cdots & \cdots & 0 & -\rho & 1 \end{bmatrix} \tag{18.74}$$

and $|\rho| < 1$.

The computations are carried out by the 'inverse interpolation' method

[10]This result follows readily from (18.72) and can be obtained by substituting $u_t = y_t - \boldsymbol{\beta}'\mathbf{x}_t$ in (18.72).

which is *certain to converge*. See Pesaran and Slater (1980, pp. 36–8) for further details.

The concentrated log-likelihood function in this case is given by

$$LL_{AR1}(\rho) = -\frac{n}{2}[1 + \log(2\pi)] + \tfrac{1}{2}\log(1 - \rho^2) - \frac{n}{2}\log\{\tilde{\mathbf{u}}' R(\rho)\tilde{\mathbf{u}}/n\}, \qquad |\rho| < 1 \tag{18.75}$$

where $\tilde{\mathbf{u}}$ is the $n \times 1$ vector of ML residuals

$$\tilde{\mathbf{u}} = \mathbf{y} - \mathbf{X}[\mathbf{X}'\mathbf{R}(\rho)\mathbf{X}]^{-1}\mathbf{X}'\mathbf{R}(\rho)\mathbf{y}$$

## 18.10.2 The AR(2) case

For this case, the ML estimators are obtained by maximizing the log-likelihood function

$$LL_{AR2}(\boldsymbol{\theta}) = -\frac{n}{2}\log(2\pi\sigma_\epsilon^2) + \log(1 + \rho_2) + \tfrac{1}{2}\log\left[(1 - \rho_2)^2 - \rho_1^2\right] - \frac{1}{2\sigma_\epsilon^2}(\mathbf{y} - \mathbf{X}\boldsymbol{\beta})'\mathbf{R}(\boldsymbol{\rho})(\mathbf{y} - \mathbf{X}\boldsymbol{\beta}) \tag{18.76}$$

with respect to $\boldsymbol{\theta} = (\boldsymbol{\beta}', \sigma_\epsilon^2, \boldsymbol{\rho})'$, where $\boldsymbol{\rho} = (\rho_1, \rho_2)'$

$$R(\rho) = \begin{bmatrix} 1 & -\rho_1 & -\rho_2 & 0 & 0 & \dots & 0 & 0 \\ -\rho_1 & 1+\rho_1^2 & -\rho_1+\rho_1\rho_2 & -\rho_2 & 0 & \dots & 0 & 0 \\ -\rho_2 & -\rho_1+\rho_1\rho_2 & 1+\rho_1^2+\rho_2^2 & -\rho_1+\rho_1\rho_2 & -\rho_2 & \dots & 0 & 0 \\ 0 & -\rho_2 & -\rho_1+\rho_1\rho_2 & 1+\rho_1^2+\rho_2^2 & \dots & & 0 & 0 \\ \vdots & \vdots & \vdots & \vdots & & & \vdots & \vdots \\ 0 & 0 & 0 & 0 & & \dots & 1+\rho_1^2 & -\rho_1 \\ 0 & 0 & 0 & 0 & & \dots & -\rho_1 & 1 \end{bmatrix} \tag{18.77}$$

The estimation procedure imposes the restrictions

$$\left.\begin{array}{l} 1 + \rho_2 > 0 \\ 1 - \rho_2 + \rho_1 > 0 \\ 1 - \rho_2 - \rho_1 > 0 \end{array}\right\} \tag{18.78}$$

needed if the AR(2) process (18.70), is to be stationary.

## 18.10.3 Covariance matrix of the exact ML estimators for the AR(1) and AR(2) options

The estimates of the covariance matrix of the exact ML estimators defined in the above sub-sections are computed on the assumption that the regressors, $\mathbf{x}_t$, do not include lagged values of the dependent variable.[11]

For the AR(1) case we have

$$\tilde{V}(\tilde{\beta}) = \hat{\sigma}_\epsilon^2[\mathbf{X}'\mathbf{R}(\tilde{\rho})\mathbf{X}]^{-1} \tag{18.79}$$

$$\tilde{V}(\tilde{\rho}) = n^{-1}(1 - \tilde{\rho}^2) \tag{18.80}$$

where $\mathbf{R}(\tilde{\rho})$ is already defined by (18.74), and $\hat{\sigma}_\epsilon^2$ is given below by (18.89).

For the AR(2) case we have

$$\tilde{V}(\tilde{\beta}) = \hat{\sigma}_\epsilon^2[\mathbf{X}'\mathbf{R}(\tilde{\rho}_1, \tilde{\rho}_2)\mathbf{X}]^{-1} \tag{18.81}$$

$$\tilde{V}(\tilde{\rho}_1) = \tilde{V}(\tilde{\rho}_2) = n^{-1}(1 - \tilde{\rho}_2^2) \tag{18.82}$$

$$\widetilde{Cov}(\tilde{\rho}_1, \tilde{\rho}_2) = -n^{-1}\tilde{\rho}_1(1 + \tilde{\rho}_2) \tag{18.83}$$

where $\mathbf{R}(\tilde{\rho}_1, \tilde{\rho}_2)$ is defined by (18.77). Here the ML estimators are designated by $\sim$.

### 18.10.4 Adjusted residuals, $R^2$, $\bar{R}^2$, and other statistics

In the case of the exact ML estimators, the 'adjusted' residuals are computed as follows (see Pesaran and Slater 1980, pp. 49, 136)

$$\tilde{\epsilon}_1 = \tilde{u}_1\sqrt{\{[(1 - \tilde{\rho}_2)^2 - \tilde{\rho}_1^2](1 + \tilde{\rho}_2)/(1 - \tilde{\rho}_2)\}} \tag{18.84}$$

$$\tilde{\epsilon}_2 = \tilde{u}_2\sqrt{(1 - \tilde{\rho}_2^2)} - \tilde{u}_1\,\tilde{\rho}_1\sqrt{[(1 + \tilde{\rho}_2)/(1 - \tilde{\rho}_2)]} \tag{18.85}$$

$$\tilde{\epsilon}_t = \tilde{u}_t - \tilde{\rho}_1\tilde{u}_{t-1} - \tilde{\rho}_2\tilde{u}_{t-2}, \qquad t = 3, 4, \ldots, n \tag{18.86}$$

where

$$\tilde{u}_t = y_t - \mathbf{x}_t'\tilde{\beta}, \qquad t = 1, 2, \ldots, n$$

are the 'unadjusted' residuals, and

$$\tilde{\beta} = (\mathbf{X}'\mathbf{R}(\tilde{\rho})\mathbf{X})^{-1}\mathbf{X}'\mathbf{R}(\tilde{\rho})\mathbf{y} \tag{18.87}$$

Recall that $\tilde{\boldsymbol{\rho}} = (\tilde{\rho}_1, \tilde{\rho}_2)'$. The program also takes account of the specification of the AR-error process in computations of the fitted values. Denoting these adjusted (or conditional) fitted values by $\tilde{y}_t$, we have

$$\tilde{y}_t = \tilde{E}(y_t|y_{t-1}, y_{t-2}, \ldots; \mathbf{x}_t, \mathbf{x}_{t-1}, \ldots) = y_t - \tilde{\epsilon}_t, \quad t = 1, 2, \ldots, n \tag{18.88}$$

[11] When the regression contains lagged values of the dependent variable, the Cochrane–Orcutt or the Gauss–Newton options (4 or 5) in the Linear Regression Menu should be used (see Sections 18.11 and 18.12).

The standard error of the regression is computed using the formula

$$\hat{\sigma}_\epsilon^2 = \tilde{\mathbf{u}}'\mathbf{R}(\tilde{\rho})\tilde{\mathbf{u}}/(n-k-m) \tag{18.89}$$

where $m = 1$, for the AR(1) case, and $m = 2$ for the AR(2) case. Given the way the adjusted residuals, $\tilde{\epsilon}_t$, are defined above, we also have

$$\hat{\sigma}_\epsilon^2 = \tilde{\mathbf{u}}'\mathbf{R}(\tilde{\rho})\tilde{\mathbf{u}}/(n-k-m) = \sum_{t=1}^{n} \tilde{\epsilon}_t^2/(n-k-m) \tag{18.90}$$

Notice that this estimator of $\sigma_\epsilon^2$ differs from the ML estimator given by

$$\tilde{\sigma}_\epsilon^2 = \sum_{t=1}^{n} \tilde{\epsilon}_t^2/n$$

and the estimator adopted in Pesaran and Slater (1980). The difference lies in the way the sum of the squares of residuals, $\sum \tilde{\epsilon}_t^2$, is corrected for the loss in degrees of freedom arising from the estimation of the regression coefficients, $\beta$, and the parameters of the error process, $\boldsymbol{\rho} = (\rho_1, \rho_2)'$.

The $R^2$, $\bar{R}^2$, and the F statistic are computed from the adjusted residuals:

$$\begin{aligned} R^2 &= 1 - \left( \sum_{t=1}^{n} \tilde{\epsilon}_t^2 \Big/ \sum_{t=1}^{n} (y_t - \bar{y})^2 \right) \\ \bar{R}^2 &= 1 - (\hat{\sigma}_\epsilon^2/\hat{\sigma}_y^2) \end{aligned} \tag{18.91}$$

where $\hat{\sigma}_y$ is the standard deviation of the dependent variable, defined as before by $\hat{\sigma}_y^2 = \sum_{t=1}^{n}(y_t - \bar{y})^2/(n-1)$.

The Durbin–Watson statistic is also computed using the adjusted residuals, $\tilde{\epsilon}_t$:

$$\widetilde{DW} = \frac{\sum_{t=2}^{n} (\tilde{\epsilon}_t - \tilde{\epsilon}_{t-1})^2}{\sum_{t=1}^{n} \tilde{\epsilon}_t^2}$$

The F statistics reported following the regression results are computed according to the formula

$$\text{F statistic} = \left( \frac{R^2}{1-R^2} \right) \left( \frac{n-k-m}{k+m-1} \right) \overset{a}{\sim} F(k+m-1,\ n-k-m) \tag{18.92}$$

with $m = 1$ under AR(1) error specification and $m = 2$ under AR(2) error specification.

Notice that $R^2$ in (18.92) is given by (18.91). The above F statistic can be used to test the joint hypothesis that except for the intercept term, all the other regression coefficients *and* the parameters of the AR-error process are zero. Under this hypothesis the F statistic is distributed *approximately* as F with $k + m - 1$ and $n - k - m$ degrees of freedom. The chi-squared version of this test can be based on $nR^2/(1 - R^2)$, which, under the null hypothesis of zero slope and AR coefficients, is asymptotically distributed as a chi-squared variate with $k + m - 1$ degrees of freedom.

### 18.10.5 Log-likelihood ratio statistics for tests of residual serial correlation

The log-likelihood ratio statistic for the test of AR(1) against the non-autocorrelated error specification is given by

$$\chi^2_{AR1,OLS} = 2(LL_{AR1} - LL_{OLS}) \overset{a}{\sim} \chi^2_1$$

The log-likelihood ratio statistic for the test of the AR(2) error specification against the AR(1) error specification is given by

$$\chi^2_{AR1,OLS} = 2(LL_{AR2} - LL_{AR1}) \overset{a}{\sim} \chi^2_1$$

Both of the above statistics are asymptotically distributed, under the null hypothesis, as a chi-squared variate with one degree of freedom.

The log-likelihood values, $LL_{OLS}$, $LL_{AR1}$, and $LL_{AR2}$, represent the maximized values of the log-likelihood functions defined by (18.12), (18.73), and (18.76), respectively.

## 18.11 Cochrane–Orcutt iterative method

This estimation method employs the Cochrane–Orcutt (1949) iterative procedure to compute ML estimators of (18.2) under the assumption that the disturbances, $u_t$, follow the AR($m$) process

$$u_t = \sum_{i=1}^{m} \rho_i u_{t-i} + \epsilon_t, \qquad \epsilon_t \sim N(0, \sigma^2_\epsilon), \quad t = 1, 2, \ldots, n \tag{18.93}$$

with 'fixed initial' values. The fixed initial value assumption is the same as treating the values $y_1, y_2, \ldots, y_m$ as given or non-stochastic. This procedure in effect ignores the possible contribution of the distribution of the initial values to the overall log-likelihood function of the model. Once again, the primary justification of treating initial values as fixed is asymptotic, and is plausible only when (18.93) is stationary and $n$ is reasonably large. (See Pesaran and Slater 1980, Section 3.2, and Judge *et al.* 1985, Section 8.2.1c for further discussion.)

The log-likelihood function for this case is defined by

$$LL_{CO}(\theta) = -\frac{(n-m)}{2}\log(2\pi\sigma^2_\epsilon) - \frac{1}{2\sigma^2_\epsilon}\sum_{t=m+1}^{n} \epsilon^2_t + c \tag{18.94}$$

where $\theta = (\beta', \sigma^2_\epsilon, \rho')'$ with $\rho = (\rho_1, \rho_2, \ldots, \rho_m)'$. Notice that the constant term, $c$, in (18.94) is undefined, and is usually set equal to zero. The Cochrane–Orcutt (CO) method maximizes $LL_{CO}(\theta)$, or equivalently minimizes $\Sigma^n_{t=m+1}\epsilon^2_t$ with respect to $\theta$ by the iterative method of 'successive substitution'. Each iteration involves two steps. In the first step, $LL_{CO}$ is maximized with respect to $\beta$, taking $\rho$ as given. In the second step, $\beta$ is taken as given and the log-likelihood function is maximized with respect to $\rho$. In each of these steps the optimization problem is solved by running OLS regressions. To start the iterations, $\boldsymbol{\rho}$ is initially set equal to zero. The iterations are terminated if

$$\sum_{i=1}^{m} |\tilde{\rho}_{i,(j)} - \tilde{\rho}_{i,(j-1)}| < m/1000 \tag{18.95}$$

where $\boldsymbol{\rho}_{(j)} = (\tilde{\rho}_{1,(j)}, \tilde{\rho}_{2,(j)}, \ldots, \tilde{\rho}_{m(j)})'$, and $\boldsymbol{\rho}_{(j-1)}$ stand for estimators of $\boldsymbol{\rho}$ in the $j$th and $(j-1)$th iterations, respectively. The estimator of $\sigma_\epsilon^2$ is computed as

$$\hat{\sigma}_\epsilon^2 = \sum_{t=m+1}^{n} \tilde{\epsilon}_t^2/(n - 2m - k) \tag{18.96}$$

where $\tilde{\epsilon}_t$, the adjusted residuals, are given by

$$\tilde{\epsilon}_t = \tilde{u}_t - \sum_{i=1}^{m} \tilde{\rho}_i \tilde{u}_{t-i}, \qquad t = m+1, m+2, \ldots, n \tag{18.97}$$

where

$$\tilde{u}_t = y_t - \sum_{i=1}^{k} \tilde{\beta}_i x_{it}, \qquad t = 1, 2, \ldots, n \tag{18.98}$$

As before, the symbol $\sim$ above an unknown parameter stands for ML estimators (now under fixed initial values). The estimator of $\sigma_\epsilon^2$ in (18.96) differs from the ML estimator, given by $\tilde{\sigma}_\epsilon^2 = \sum_{t=m+1}^{n} \tilde{\epsilon}_t^2/(n-m)$. The estimator, $\hat{\sigma}_\epsilon^2$, allows for the loss of the degrees of freedom associated with the estimation of the unknown coefficients, $\boldsymbol{\beta}$, and the parameters of the AR process, $\boldsymbol{\rho}$. Notice also that the estimator of $\sigma_\epsilon^2$ is based on $n - m$ adjusted residuals, since the initial values $y_1, y_2, \ldots, y_m$ are treated as fixed.

The adjusted fitted values, $\tilde{y}_t$, in the case of this option are computed as

$$\tilde{y}_t = \hat{E}(y_t | y_{t-1}, y_{t-2}, \ldots; \mathbf{x}_t, \mathbf{x}_{t-1}, \ldots) = y_t - \tilde{\epsilon}_t \tag{18.99}$$

for $t = m+1, m+2, \ldots, n$. Notice that the initial values, $\tilde{y}_1, \tilde{y}_2, \ldots, \tilde{y}_m$, are not defined.

In the case where $m = 1$, the program also provides a plot of the concentrated log-likelihood function in terms of $\rho_1$, defined by

$$LL_{CO}(\tilde{\rho}_1) = -\frac{(n-1)}{2}[1 + \log(2\pi\tilde{\sigma}_\epsilon^2)] \tag{18.100}$$

where

$$\tilde{\sigma}_\epsilon^2 = \sum_{t=2}^{n} \tilde{\epsilon}_t^2/(n-1)$$

and $\tilde{\epsilon}_t = \tilde{u}_t - \tilde{\rho}_1 \tilde{u}_{t-1}$.

### 18.11.1 Covariance matrix of the CO estimators

The estimator of the asymptotic variance matrix of $\tilde{\phi} = (\tilde{\beta}', \tilde{\rho}')'$ is computed as

$$\hat{V}(\tilde{\phi}) = \hat{\sigma}_\epsilon^2 \begin{bmatrix} \tilde{\mathbf{X}}_*'\tilde{\mathbf{X}}_* & \tilde{\mathbf{X}}_*'\mathbf{S} \\ \mathbf{S}'\tilde{\mathbf{X}}_* & \mathbf{S}'\mathbf{S} \end{bmatrix}^{-1} \tag{18.101}$$

where $\tilde{X}_*$ is the $(n-m) \times k$ matrix of transformed regressors[12]

$$\tilde{\mathbf{X}}_* = \sum_{i=1}^{m} \tilde{\rho}_i \mathbf{X}_{-i} \tag{18.102}$$

and $\mathbf{S}$ is an $(n-m) \times m$ matrix containing the $m$ lagged values of the CO residuals, $\tilde{u}_t$, namely

$$\mathbf{S} = \begin{bmatrix} \tilde{u}_m & \tilde{u}_{m-1} & \cdots & \tilde{u}_1 \\ \tilde{u}_{m+1} & \tilde{u}_m & \cdots & \tilde{u}_2 \\ \vdots & \vdots & & \vdots \\ \tilde{u}_{n-1} & \tilde{u}_{n-2} & \cdots & \tilde{u}_{n-m} \end{bmatrix} \tag{18.103}$$

The unadjusted residuals, $\tilde{u}_t$, are already defined by (18.98). The above estimator of the variance matrix of $\tilde{\beta}$ and $\tilde{\rho}$ is asymptotically valid even if the regression model (18.2) contains lagged dependent variables.

## 18.12 ML/AR estimators by the Gauss–Newton method

This method provides an alternative numerical procedure for the maximization of the log-likelihood function (18.94). In cases where this log-likelihood function has a unique maximum, the Gauss–Newton and the CO iterative methods should converge to nearly identical results. But in general this need not be the case. However, the Gauss–Newton method is likely to perform better than the CO method when the regression equation contains lagged dependent variables.

The computations for the Gauss–Newton procedure are based on the following iterative relations:

$$\begin{pmatrix} \tilde{\beta} \\ \tilde{\rho} \end{pmatrix}_j = \begin{pmatrix} \tilde{\beta} \\ \tilde{\rho} \end{pmatrix}_{j-1} + \begin{bmatrix} \tilde{\mathbf{X}}_*'\tilde{\mathbf{X}}_* & \tilde{\mathbf{X}}_*'\mathbf{S} \\ \mathbf{S}'\tilde{\mathbf{X}}_* & \mathbf{S}'\mathbf{S} \end{bmatrix}_{j-1}^{-1} \begin{bmatrix} \tilde{\mathbf{X}}_*'\tilde{\epsilon} \\ \mathbf{S}'\tilde{\epsilon} \end{bmatrix}_{j-1} \tag{18.104}$$

where the subscripts $j$ and $j-1$ refer to the $j$th and the $(j-1)$th iterations; and $\tilde{\epsilon} = (\tilde{\epsilon}_{m+1}, \tilde{\epsilon}_{m+2}, \ldots, \tilde{\epsilon}_n)'$, $\tilde{\mathbf{X}}_*$, and $\mathbf{S}$ have the same expressions as those already defined by (18.97), (18.102), and (18.103), respectively. The program starts the iterations with

[12] A typical element of $\tilde{\mathbf{X}}_*$ is given by

$$\tilde{x}_{jt}^* = x_{jt} - \sum_{i=1}^{m} \tilde{\rho}_i x_{j,t-i} \quad t = m+1, m+2, \ldots, n, \quad j = 1, 2, \ldots, k$$

$$\tilde{\beta}_{(0)} = \tilde{\beta}_{OLS} = (\mathbf{X}'\mathbf{X})^{-1}\mathbf{X}'\mathbf{y}$$
$$\tilde{\rho}_{(0)} = 0$$

and ends them either if the number of iterations exceeds 20 or if the condition (18.95) is satisfied.

On exit from the iterations the program computes a number of statistics including estimates of $\sigma_\epsilon^2$, the variance matrices of $\tilde{\beta}$ and $\tilde{\rho}$, $R^2$, $\bar{R}^2$, etc. using the results already set out in Sections 18.11.1 and 18.10.4.

### 18.12.1 AR(m) error process with zero restrictions

The program applies the Gauss–Newton iterative method to compute estimates of the regression equation when the AR($m$) error process (18.93) is subject to zero restrictions (see option 5 in the Linear Regression Menu and Section 6.10). Notice that in the restricted case the estimator of the standard error of the regression is given by

$$\hat{\sigma}_\epsilon^2 = \sum_{t=m+1}^{n} \tilde{\epsilon}_t^2/(n-m-r-k), \qquad n > m+r+k \tag{18.105}$$

where $r$ represents the number of non-zero parameters of the AR($m$) process.

Similarly, the appropriate formula for the F statistic (18.13) is now given by

$$F = \left(\frac{R^2}{1-R^2}\right)\left(\frac{n-m-k-r}{k+r-1}\right) \overset{a}{\sim} F(k+r-1, n-m-k-r) \tag{18.106}$$

The chi-squared version of this statistic can, as before, be computed by $nR^2/(1-R^2)$, which is asymptotically distributed (under the null hypothesis) as a chi-squared variate with $k+r-1$ degrees of freedom.

## 18.13 The IV/AR estimation method

This procedure provides estimates of the following linear regression model with AR(m) errors by the instrumental variable method.

$$y_t = \mathbf{x}_t'\boldsymbol{\beta} + u_t, \qquad t = 1, 2, \ldots, n$$
$$u_t = \sum_{i=1}^{m} \rho_i u_{t-i} + \epsilon_t, \qquad t = m+1, m+2, \ldots, n$$

The method assumes that there exists an $n \times s$ matrix $Z$ containing observations on the $s$ instrumental variables, $\mathbf{z}_t$ ($s \geqslant k+m$). Then the IV/AR estimators of $\boldsymbol{\beta}$ and $\boldsymbol{\rho}$ are computed by minimizing the criterion function (see Sargan 1959)

$$Q(\boldsymbol{\beta}, \boldsymbol{\rho}) = \boldsymbol{\epsilon}'\mathbf{P}_z\boldsymbol{\epsilon} \tag{18.107}$$

with respect to $\boldsymbol{\beta}$ and $\boldsymbol{\rho}$, where $\mathbf{P}_z$ is the projection matrix defined by (18.56);

and $\epsilon = (\epsilon_{m+1}, \epsilon_{m+1}, \ldots, \epsilon_n)'$ is the $(n-m)\times 1$ vector of 'adjusted' residuals.

Application of the Gauss–Newton method to solve the above minimization problem yields the following iterative relations which are a generalization of (18.104):

$$\begin{pmatrix}\tilde{\beta}\\ \tilde{\rho}\end{pmatrix}_j = \begin{pmatrix}\tilde{\beta}\\ \tilde{\rho}\end{pmatrix}_{j-1} + \begin{bmatrix}\tilde{\mathbf{X}}_*'\mathbf{P}_z\tilde{\mathbf{X}}_* & \tilde{\mathbf{X}}_*'\mathbf{P}_z\mathbf{S}\\ \mathbf{S}'\mathbf{P}_z\tilde{\mathbf{X}}_* & \mathbf{S}'\mathbf{P}_z\mathbf{S}\end{bmatrix}_{j-1}^{-1}\begin{bmatrix}\tilde{\mathbf{X}}_*'\mathbf{P}_z\tilde{\epsilon}\\ \mathbf{S}'\mathbf{P}_z\tilde{\epsilon}\end{bmatrix}_{j-1} \tag{18.108}$$

The notations are as before (see Section 18.11).

The program starts the iterations with

$$\tilde{\beta}_{(0)} = \tilde{\beta}_{IV} = (\mathbf{X}'\mathbf{P}_z\mathbf{X})^{-1}\mathbf{X}'\mathbf{P}_z\mathbf{y}$$

and

$$\tilde{\rho}_{(0)} = 0$$

See Section 18.12 for details of the iterative process.

In addition to the usual summary statistics, the program also reports the minimized value of $Q(\beta, \rho)$, namely $Q(\tilde{\beta}, \tilde{\rho})$, where $\tilde{\beta}$ and $\tilde{\rho}$ represent the IV/AR estimators of $\beta$ and $\rho$, respectively. The program reports $Q(\tilde{\beta}, \tilde{\rho})$ as the 'value of the IV minimand'.

### 18.13.1 Sargan's general misspecification test in the case of the IV/AR option

This is the generalization of Sargan's (1964) test, described in Section 18.9.3, and is based on the statistic

$$\chi^2_{SM} = Q(\tilde{\beta}, \tilde{\rho})/\tilde{\sigma}^2_\epsilon \overset{a}{\sim} \chi^2(s-k-r) \tag{18.109}$$

where, as before,

$$\tilde{\sigma}^2_\epsilon = \sum_{t=m+1}^{n} \tilde{\epsilon}_t^2/(n-m-r-k),$$

and $Q(\tilde{\beta}, \tilde{\rho})$ is the minimized value of the IV minimand (18.107).[13] Under the null hypothesis that the regression equation (18.2) and the AR-error process (18.93) are correctly specified, and that the $s(s > k+r)$ instrumental variables $\mathbf{z}_t$ are valid instruments, Sargan's misspecification statistic $\chi^2_{SM}$ in (18.109) is asymptotically distributed as a chi-squared variate with $s-k-r$ degrees of freedom.

[13]Recall that $r$ is the number of non-zero coefficients of (18.93).

### 18.13.2 $R^2$, $\bar{R}^2$, $GR^2$, $\overline{GR}^2$, and other statistics—AR options

The summary statistics reported in the case of the AR and IV/AR options are computed using the adjusted residuals, $\tilde{\epsilon}_t$, defined by (18.97). The $R^2$ of the regression is computed as

$$R^2 = 1 - \left\{ \sum_{t=m+1}^{n} \tilde{\epsilon}_t^2 \Big/ \sum_{t=m+1}^{n} (y_t - \bar{y}_m)^2 \right\} \tag{18.110}$$

where

$$\bar{y}_m = \sum_{t=m+1}^{n} y_t/(n-m) \tag{18.111}$$

Notice that in the case of the CO and IV/AR options the initial values $y_1, y_2, \ldots, y_m$ are assumed fixed.

The $\bar{R}^2$ is computed as

$$\bar{R}^2 = 1 - \left( \frac{n-m-1}{n-m-r-k} \right)(1 - R^2) \tag{18.112}$$

The F statistic in the case of the AR options is computed as

$$\text{F statistic} = \left( \frac{R^2}{1-R^2} \right)\left( \frac{n-m-r-k}{k+r-1} \right) \overset{a}{\sim} F(k+r-1, n-m-k-r) \tag{18.113}$$

On the null hypothesis that all the regression coefficients other than the intercept term are zero, and that $\rho = 0$, the above F statistic is approximately distributed as F with $k+r-1$, and $n-m-k-r$ degrees of freedom. Notice that in the case of the CO option $r = m$. Also asymptotically,

$$nR^2/(1-R^2) \overset{a}{\sim} \chi^2_{k+r-1}$$

The DW statistic is computed for this option using the adjusted residuals, $\tilde{\epsilon}_t$, namely

$$DW = \frac{\sum_{t=m+2}^{n} (\tilde{\epsilon}_t - \tilde{\epsilon}_{t-1})^2}{\sum_{t=m+1}^{n} \tilde{\epsilon}_t^2}$$

The computation of the $GR^2$ and $\overline{GR}^2$ statistics is based on the one-step ahead (in-sample) prediction errors defined by

$$\tilde{\xi}_t = \tilde{\epsilon}_t + \tilde{\boldsymbol{\beta}}'(\mathbf{x}_t - \hat{\mathbf{x}}_t),\ t = m+1, m+2, \ldots, n \tag{18.114}$$

where $\hat{\mathbf{x}}_t$, $t = 1, 2, \ldots, n$ are the fitted values from the regression of $\mathbf{x}_t$ on the instrumental variables $\mathbf{z}_t$. Relation (18.114) is a generalization of (18.63) to the case of serially correlated errors. More specifically, we have

$$GR^2 = 1 - \left(\sum_{t=m+1}^{n} \tilde{\xi}_t^2\right) \Big/ \left(\sum_{t=m+1}^{n} (y_t - \bar{y}_m)^2\right)$$

$$\overline{GR}^2 = 1 - \left(\frac{n-m-1}{n-m-r-k}\right)(1 - GR^2) \tag{18.115}$$

where $\bar{y}_m$ is defined by (18.111). Clearly, these measures reduce to the corresponding least squares measures in (18.110) and (18.112) when $\mathbf{z}_t$ is a subset of $\mathbf{x}_t$. (See also Section 18.9.2.)

## 18.14 Exact ML/MA estimators

The moving-average (MA) estimation option in the Linear Regression Menu (see Section 6.5) computes estimates of the parameters of the regression model

$$y_t = \mathbf{x}_t'\beta + u_t, \qquad t = 1, 2, \ldots, n \tag{18.116}$$

where

$$u_t = \sum_{i=0}^{q} \gamma_i \epsilon_{t-i}, \qquad \epsilon_t \sim N(0, \sigma_\epsilon^2), \qquad \gamma_0 \equiv 1 \tag{18.117}$$

by maximizing the log-likelihood function

$$LL_{MA}(\theta) = -\frac{n}{2}(2\pi\sigma_\epsilon^2) - \tfrac{1}{2}\log|\Omega| - \frac{1}{2\sigma_\epsilon^2}(\mathbf{y} - \mathbf{X}\beta)'\Omega^{-1}(\mathbf{y} - \mathbf{X}\beta) \tag{18.118}$$

where $\mathbf{u} = \mathbf{y} - \mathbf{X}\beta$, and $E(\mathbf{uu}') = \sigma_\epsilon^2\Omega$. This yields *exact* ML estimates of the unknown parameters $\theta = (\beta', \gamma_1, \gamma_2, \ldots, \gamma_q, \sigma_\epsilon^2)'$ when the regressors, $\mathbf{x}_t$, do not include lagged values of $y_t$.

The numerical method used to carry out the above maximization problem is similar to the Kalman filter procedure and is described in B. Pesaran (1988).[14]

The method involves a Cholesky decomposition of the variance–covariance matrix $\Omega$. For the MA(1) error specification we have

$$\Omega = \begin{bmatrix} 1+\gamma_1^2 & \gamma_1 & 0 & \ldots & 0 & 0 \\ \gamma_1 & 1+\gamma_1^2 & \gamma_1 & \ldots & 0 & 0 \\ \vdots & \vdots & \vdots & & \vdots & \vdots \\ & & & & 1+\gamma_1^2 & \gamma_1 \\ 0 & 0 & 0 & \ldots & \gamma_1 & 1+\gamma_1^2 \end{bmatrix} = \mathbf{HWH}' \tag{18.119}$$

where $\mathbf{W}$ is a diagonal matrix with elements $w_t$, $t = 1, 2, \ldots, n$, and $\mathbf{H}$ is the upper triangular matrix

[14]For a description of the Kalman filter algorithm and its use in the estimation of MA processes, see, for example, Harvey (1989).

$$H = \begin{bmatrix} 1 & h_1 & 0 & \cdots & & 0 \\ & 1 & h_2 & \cdots & & 0 \\ & & \cdot & & & \vdots \\ & & & \cdot & & \\ & 0 & & & \cdot & 0 \\ & & & & 1 & h_{n-1} \\ & & & & & 1 \end{bmatrix} \tag{18.120}$$

The elements $w_t$ and $h_t$ satisfy the following *forward* recursions:[15]

$$h_t = \gamma_1 / w_{t+1}, \qquad \text{for} \quad t = n-1, n-2, \ldots, 1$$
$$w_t = 1 + \gamma_1^2 - w_{t+1} h_t^2, \qquad \text{for} \quad t = n-1, n-2, \ldots, 1$$

starting with the terminal value of $w_n = 1 + \gamma_1^2$.

Using (18.119) in (18.118) now yields (notice that $\mathbf{\Omega}^{-1} = \mathbf{H}'^{-1}\mathbf{W}^{-1}\mathbf{H}^{-1}$ and $|\mathbf{\Omega}| = |\mathbf{W}| = w_1, w_2, \ldots, w_n$)

$$LL_{MA}(\boldsymbol{\theta}) = -\tfrac{n}{2}\log(2\pi\sigma_\epsilon^2) - \tfrac{1}{2}\sum_{t=1}^{n} \log w_t - \frac{1}{2\sigma_\epsilon^2}(\mathbf{y}^* - \mathbf{X}^*\boldsymbol{\beta})'(\mathbf{y}^* - \mathbf{X}^*\boldsymbol{\beta}) \tag{18.121}$$

where

$$y_t^* = w_t^{-1/2} y_t^f$$
$$\mathbf{x}_t^* = w_t^{-1/2} \mathbf{x}_t^f$$

and $y_t^f$ and $\mathbf{x}_t^f$ represent the forward filtered values of $y_t$ and $\mathbf{x}_t$ defined by

$$y_t^f = y_t - h_t y_{t+1}^f, \qquad \text{for} \quad t = n-1, n-2, \ldots, 1$$
$$\mathbf{x}_t^f = \mathbf{x}_t - h_t \mathbf{x}_{t+1}^f, \qquad \text{for} \quad t = n-1, n-2, \ldots, 1$$

with the terminal values $y_n^f = y_n$, $\mathbf{x}_n^f = \mathbf{x}_n$. The ML estimators of $\boldsymbol{\beta}$ and $\sigma_\epsilon^2$ are given by

$$\tilde{\boldsymbol{\beta}} = (\mathbf{X}^{*\prime}\mathbf{X}^*)^{-1}\mathbf{X}^{*\prime}\mathbf{y}^*$$
$$\tilde{\sigma}_\epsilon^2 = (\mathbf{y}^* - \mathbf{X}^*\tilde{\boldsymbol{\beta}})'(\mathbf{y}^* - \mathbf{X}^*\tilde{\boldsymbol{\beta}})/n$$

The estimation of $\gamma_1$ is carried out iteratively using the modified Powell conjugate direction algorithm that does not require derivatives (see below for further details and references).

The above procedure can be readily extended to higher order MA processes. For a general MA($q$) process, the generalization of (18.120) is given by

---

[15]In B. Pesaran (1988) **H** is chosen to be a lower triangular matrix, and the resultant recursions are consequently backward in $w_t$ and $h_t$. In the case of the MA option, both the backward and the forward recursion methods yield identical results, but forward recursion is the appropriate method to use for estimation of certain classes of rational expectations models. (See Section 18.15.)

$$\mathbf{H} = \begin{bmatrix} 1 & h_{11} & h_{21} & \dots & h_{q1} & \dots & & 0 \\ & 1 & h_{12} & h_{22} & \dots & h_{q2} & & 0 \\ & & \cdot & \cdot & \cdot & & \ddots & \vdots \\ & & & \cdot & \cdot & \cdot & & h_{q,n-q} \\ & & & & \cdot & \cdot & & \vdots \\ & & \mathbf{0} & & & \cdot & \cdot & h_{2,n-2} \\ & & & & & & 1 & h_{1,n-1} \\ & & & & & & & 1 \end{bmatrix}$$

$$w_t = \delta_0 - \sum_{i=1}^{q} h_{it}^2 w_{t+i}, \qquad t = n-1, n-2, \dots, 1$$

$$h_{jt} = w_{t+j}^{-1}\left(\delta_j - \sum_{i=j+1}^{q} h_{it} h_{i-j,t+j} w_{t+i}\right), \qquad \begin{matrix} t = n-j, n-j-1, \dots, 1 \\ j = q-1, q-2, \dots, 1 \end{matrix}$$

$$h_{qt} = w_{t+q}^{-1}\delta_q$$

$$\delta_s = \begin{cases} \sum_{i=1}^{q} \gamma_i\gamma_{i-s} & 0 \leqslant s \leqslant q \\ 0 & s > q \end{cases}$$

The forward filters on $y_t$ and $\mathbf{x}_t$ are given by

$$y_t^f = y_t - \sum_{i=1}^{q} h_{it} y_{t+i}^f, \qquad \text{for} \quad t = n-1, n-2, \dots, 1$$

$$\mathbf{x}_t^f = \mathbf{x}_t - \sum_{i=1}^{q} h_{it} \mathbf{x}_{t+i}^f, \qquad \text{for} \quad t = n-1, n-2, \dots, 1$$

and as before $y_t^* = w_t^{-1/2} y_t^f, \mathbf{x}_t^* = w_t^{-1/2}\mathbf{x}_t^f$, The terminal values for the above recursions are given by

$$w_n = \delta_0 = 1 + \gamma_1^2 + \gamma_2^2 + \dots + \gamma_q^2$$
$$h_{jn} = h_{j,n-1} = \dots = h_{j,n-j+1} = 0$$
$$y_n^f = y_n$$
$$\mathbf{x}_n^f = \mathbf{x}_n$$

For a given value of $\gamma = (\gamma_1, \gamma_2, \dots, \gamma_q)'$, the estimator of $\beta$ is computed by the OLS regression of $y_t^*$ on $\mathbf{x}_t^*$. The estimation of $\gamma$ is carried out iteratively by Powell's modified method of conjugate directions which *does not* require derivatives of the log-likelihood function. (See Powell 1964, Brent 1973, Chapter 7, and Press *et al.* 1989, Section 10.5.) The application of the Gauss–Newton method to the present problem requires derivatives of the log-likelihood function which are analytically intractable and can be very time-consuming if they are to be computed numerically.

### 18.14.1 Covariance matrix of the unknown parameters in the MA option

In the case of the MA option, the covariance matrix of $\tilde{\psi} = (\tilde{\beta}, \tilde{\gamma})$ is computed as

$$\left[\frac{-\partial^2 LL_{MA}(\theta)}{\partial\psi\partial\psi'}\right]^{-1}_{\psi=\tilde{\psi}}$$

where the Hessian matrix, $-\partial^2 LL_{MA}(\theta)/\partial\psi\partial\psi'$, is computed by taking second numerical derivatives of the log-likelihood function defined by (18.121) at the ML estimators, $\tilde{\psi} = (\tilde{\beta}, \tilde{\gamma})$. Notice that this estimator of the variance matrix of $\tilde{\beta}$ and $\tilde{\gamma}$ is asymptotically valid even if the regression model (18.116) contains lagged values of the dependent variable.[16]

## 18.15 The IV/MA estimators

Consider the regression model (18.116) with the moving average errors (18.117) and suppose that there exists an $n \times s$ matrix, $\mathbf{Z}$, containing observations on the $s$ instrumental variables, $\mathbf{z}_t$. Then the IV/MA estimators of $\beta$ and $\gamma$ are computed by minimizing the criterion function

$$S(\beta, \gamma) = (n/2)\mathbf{u}^{*'}\mathbf{P}_z\mathbf{u}^* + \tfrac{1}{2}\log|\boldsymbol{\Omega}| \qquad (18.122)$$

where $\mathbf{u}^*$ are the forward filtered values of $\mathbf{u} = \mathbf{y} - \mathbf{X}\beta$, $E(\mathbf{uu}') = \sigma_\epsilon^2\boldsymbol{\Omega}$ and $\mathbf{P}_z$ is the projection matrix defined by (18.56). The forward filter procedure applied to the $u_t$s is the same as that described in Section 18.14. The term $\mathbf{u}^{*'}\mathbf{P}_z\mathbf{u}^*$ is the same as the IV criterion used in the Hayashi and Sims (1983) estimation procedure. Notice that only $y_t$ and $x_{it}$s are forward filtered, and not the instruments. The second term in (18.122) is asymptotically negligible when the MA process in (18.117) is invertible but, as argued in B. Pesaran (1990), its inclusion in the criterion function helps ensure that in small samples $S(\beta, \gamma)$ achieves a minimum when the roots of the MA process are close to the unit circle.

For given values of $\gamma_i$, $i = 1, 2, \ldots, q$, the regression coefficients, $\beta$, are estimated by the IV regression of the forward filtered variables, $\mathbf{y}^*$ on $X^*$ (see Section 18.14 for the relevant expressions for the forward filtering procedure). The estimation of $\gamma$ is carried out iteratively by Powell's modified conjugate direction algorithm which does not require derivatives of the IV minimand defined in (18.122) (see Section 18.14 and B. Pesaran

[16]The program reports standard errors and probability values for the MA parameters only when none of the roots of

$$\sum_{i=0}^{q} \gamma_i \mathbf{z}^i = 0, \qquad \gamma_0 \equiv 1$$

fall on the unit circle. The Lahmer–Schur algorithm is used to check whether any of the roots of the above polynomial equation falls on the unit circle. See, for example, Acton (1970, Chapter 7).

(1990) for further details). The computation of the variance–covariance matrix of the parameter estimates, and the various summary statistics reported by the program for this option are also carried out along the lines set out in Sections 18.14.1 and 18.15.1.

### 18.15.1 $R^2$, $\bar{R}^2$, $GR^2$, $\overline{GR}^2$, and other statistics – MA options

The summary statistics reported in the case of the MA and the MA/IV options are computed using the adjusted residuals, $\tilde{\epsilon}_t$, defined by

$$\tilde{\epsilon}_t = -\sum_{i=1}^{q} \gamma_i \tilde{\epsilon}_{t-i} + \tilde{u}_t, \qquad t = 1, 2, \ldots, n$$

where the initial values $\tilde{\epsilon}_0, \tilde{\epsilon}_{-1}, \ldots, \tilde{\epsilon}_{-q+1}$ are set equal to zero, and

$$\tilde{u}_t = y_t - \sum_{i=1}^{k} \tilde{\beta}_i \mathbf{x}_{it}, \qquad t = 1, 2, \ldots, n$$

Assuming that the MA($q$) process (18.117) is estimated with $q - r$ zero restrictions, $\sigma^2_\epsilon$, the variance of $\epsilon_t$ is estimated by ($\gamma_q \neq 0$)

$$\tilde{\sigma}^2_\epsilon = \sum_{t=1}^{n} \tilde{\epsilon}^2_t / (n - r - k), \qquad n > r + k$$

The other statistics included in the result table are computed as

$$R^2 = 1 - \left(\sum_{t=1}^{n} \tilde{\epsilon}^2_t\right) \Big/ \left(\sum_{t=1}^{n} (y_t - \bar{y})^2\right)$$

$$\bar{R}^2 = 1 - \left(\frac{n-1}{n-r-k}\right)(1 - R^2) \qquad (18.123)$$

$$F = \left(\frac{R^2}{1-R^2}\right)\left(\frac{n-k-r}{k+r-1}\right) \overset{a}{\sim} F(k+r-1, n-k-r) \qquad (18.124)$$

and

$$DW = \sum_{t=2}^{n} (\tilde{\epsilon}_t - \tilde{\epsilon}_{t-1})^2 \Big/ \sum_{t=1}^{n} \tilde{\epsilon}^2_t \qquad (18.125)$$

Under the null hypothesis that all the regression coefficients other than the intercept term are zero and $\gamma = 0$, the F statistic (18.124) is approximately distributed as F with $k + r - 1$ and $n - k - r$ degrees of freedom.

As in the case of the IV/AR option, the computation of the $GR^2$ and $\overline{GR}^2$ statistics is based on the one-step ahead (in-sample) prediction errors defined by

$$\tilde{\xi}_t = \tilde{\epsilon}_t + \tilde{\beta}'(\mathbf{x}_t - \hat{\mathbf{x}}_t), \; t = 1, 2, \ldots, n \qquad (18.126)$$

where $\hat{\mathbf{x}}_t$, $t = 1, 2, \ldots, n$ are the fitted values from the regression of $\mathbf{x}_t$ on the instrumental variables, $\mathbf{z}_t$. More specifically, we have

$$GR^2 = 1 - \left(\sum_{t=1}^{n} \tilde{\xi}_t^2\right) \Big/ \left(\sum_{t=1}^{n} (y_t - \bar{y})^2\right)$$

$$\overline{GR}^2 = 1 - \left(\frac{n-1}{n-r-k}\right)(1 - GR^2) \tag{18.127}$$

## 18.16 Conditionally heteroscedastic models

Under the classical assumptions, the disturbances, $u_t$, in the regression model (18.2) have a constant variance both *unconditionally* and *conditionally*. In many applications in macroeconomics and finance the assumption that the conditional variance of $u_t$ is constant over time is not valid. The class of regression models that allow the conditional variance of $u_t$ to vary over time as a function of past errors is known as the class of autoregressive conditional heteroscedastic (ARCH) models.

### 18.16.1 GARCH-in-mean models

The ARCH model was introduced into econometric literature by Engle (1982) and was subsequently generalized by Bollerslev (1986) who proposed the generalized ARCH (or GARCH) models. Other related models where the conditional variance of $u_t$ is used as one of the regressors explaining the conditional mean of $y_t$ have also been suggested in the literature and are known as ARCH-in-mean and GARCH-in-mean (or GARCH-M, for short) models (see, for example, Engle *et al.* 1987). For a useful survey of the literature on ARCH modelling, see Bollerslev *et al.* (1992).

The various members of the GARCH and GARCH-M class of models can be written compactly as

$$y_t = \boldsymbol{\beta}'\mathbf{x}_t + \gamma h_t^2 + u_t \tag{18.128}$$

where

$$\begin{aligned} h_t^2 &= V(u_t|\Omega_{t-1}) = E(u_t^2|\Omega_{t-1}) \\ &= \alpha_0 + \sum_{i=1}^{q} \alpha_i u_{t-i}^2 + \sum_{i=1}^{p} \phi_i h_{t-i}^2 \end{aligned} \tag{18.129}$$

and $\Omega_{t-1}$ is the information set at time $t-1$, containing at least observations on $\mathbf{x}_t$ and on lagged values of $y_t$ and $\mathbf{x}_t$; namely $\Omega_{t-1} = (\mathbf{x}_t, \mathbf{x}_{t-1}, \mathbf{x}_{t-2}, \ldots, y_{t-1}, y_{t-2}, \ldots)$. The unconditional variance of $u_t$ is constant and is given by[17]

[17]Notice that $V(u_t) = \lim_{s\to\infty} E(u_{t+s}^2|\Omega_{t-1})$.

$$V(u_t) = \sigma^2 = \frac{\alpha_0}{1 - \sum_{i=1}^{q} \alpha_i - \sum_{i=1}^{p} \phi_i} > 0 \qquad (18.130)$$

and the necessary condition for (18.128) to be covariance stationary is given by

$$\sum_{i=1}^{q} \alpha_i + \sum_{i=1}^{p} \phi_i < 1 \qquad (18.131)$$

In addition to the restrictions (18.130) and (18.131), Bollerslev (1986) also assumes that $\alpha_i \geqslant 0$, $i = 1, 2, \ldots, q$, and $\phi_i \geqslant 0$, $i = 1, 2, \ldots, q$. Although these additional restrictions are sufficient for the conditional variance to be positive, they are not necessary (see Nelson and Cao 1992).

*Microfit* computes approximate maximum likelihood estimates of the parameters of a generalization of the GARCH-M model where, in addition to the past disturbances, other variables could also influence $h_t^2$:

$$h_t^2 = \alpha_0 + \sum_{i=1}^{q} \alpha_i u_{t-i}^2 + \sum_{i=1}^{p} \phi_i h_{t-i}^2 + \delta' \mathbf{w}_t \qquad (18.132)$$

where $\mathbf{w}_t$ is a vector of covariance stationary variables in $\Omega_{t-1}$. The unconditional variance of $u_t$ in this case is given by

$$\sigma^2 = \frac{\alpha_0 + \delta' \mu_w}{1 - \sum_{i=1}^{q} \alpha_i - \sum_{i=1}^{p} \phi_i} > 0 \qquad (18.133)$$

where $\mu_\omega = E(\mathbf{w}_t)$.

The ML estimation of the above augmented GARCH-M model can be carried out in *Microfit* under two different assumptions concerning the conditional distribution of the disturbances, namely Gaussian and standardized $t$-distribution. In both cases, the *exact* log-likelihood function depends on the joint density function of the initial observations, $f(y_1, y_2, \ldots, y_q)$, which is non-Gaussian and intractable analytically. In most applications where the sample size is large (as is the case with most financial time series) the effect of the distribution of the initial observations is relatively small and can be ignored.[18]

## 18.16.2 ML estimation with Gaussian errors

The log-likelihood function used in computation of the ML estimators for the Gaussian case is given by

[18]Diebold and Schuermann (1992) examine the quantitative importance of the distribution of the initial observations in the case of simple ARCH models, and find their effect to be negligible.

$$\ell(\boldsymbol{\theta}) = -\frac{(n-q)}{2}\log(2\pi) - \tfrac{1}{2}\sum_{t=q+1}^{n}\log h_t^2 - \tfrac{1}{2}\sum_{t=q+1}^{n} h_t^{-2}u_t^2 \tag{18.134}$$

where $\boldsymbol{\theta} = (\boldsymbol{\beta}', \gamma, \alpha_0, \alpha_1, \alpha_2, \ldots, \alpha_q, \phi_1, \phi_2, \ldots, \phi_p, \boldsymbol{\delta}')'$, and $u_t$ and $h_t^2$ are given by (18.128) and (18.132), respectively.

### 18.16.3 ML estimation with student *t*-distributed errors

Under the assumption that conditional on $\Omega_{t-1}$, the disturbances are distributed as a student $t$-distribution with $v$ degrees of freedom ($v > 2$), the log-likelihood function is given by

$$\ell(\boldsymbol{\theta}, v) = \sum_{t=q+1}^{n} \ell_t(\boldsymbol{\theta}, v) \tag{18.135}$$

where

$$\ell_t(\boldsymbol{\theta}, v) = -\log\left\{B\left(\tfrac{v}{2}, \tfrac{1}{2}\right)\right\} - \tfrac{1}{2}\log(v-2) - \tfrac{1}{2}\log h_t^2 - \left(\frac{v+1}{2}\right)\log\left(1 + \frac{u_t^2}{h_t^2(v-2)}\right) \tag{18.136}$$

and $B\left(\frac{v}{2}, \frac{1}{2}\right)$ is the complete beta function.[19]

The degrees of freedom of the underlying $t$-distribution, $v$, is then estimated along with the other parameters. The Gaussian log-likelihood function (18.134) is a special case of (18.136) and can be obtained from it for large values of $v$. In most applications the two log-likelihood functions give very similar results for values of $v$ around 20. The $t$-distribution is particularly appropriate for the analysis of stock returns where the distribution of the standardized residuals, $\hat{u}_t/\hat{h}_t$, are often found to have fatter tails than the normal distribution.

### 18.16.4 Exponential GARCH-in-mean models

It is often the case that the conditional variance, $h_t^2$ is not an even function of the past disturbances, $u_{t-1}, u_{t-2}, \ldots$ The Exponential GARCH (or EGARCH) model proposed by Nelson (1991) aims at capturing this important feature, often observed when analysing stock market returns. *Microfit* provides ML estimates of the following augmented version of the EGARCH-M model

[19]Notice that $B\left(\frac{v}{2}, \frac{1}{2}\right) = \Gamma\left(\frac{v+1}{2}\right)/\Gamma\left(\frac{v}{2}\right)\Gamma\left(\frac{1}{2}\right)$. The constant term $\Gamma\left(\frac{1}{2}\right) = \sqrt{\pi}$ is omitted from the expression used by Bollerslev (1987). See his equation (1).

$$y_t = \beta' \mathbf{x}_t + \gamma h_t^2 + u_t \tag{18.137}$$

where, as before, $h_t^2 = V(u_t|\Omega_{t-1}) = E(u_t^2|\Omega_{t-1})$. However, for $h_t^2$, Nelson (1991) uses an exponential functional form, which can be written as

$$\log h_t^2 = \alpha_0 + \sum_{i=1}^{q} \alpha_i \left(\frac{u_{t-i}}{h_{t-i}}\right) + \sum_{i=1}^{q} \alpha_i^* \left(\left|\frac{u_{t-i}}{h_{t-i}}\right| - \mu\right) + \sum_{i=1}^{p} \phi_i \log h_{t-i}^2 + \delta' \mathbf{w}_t \tag{18.138}$$

where

$$\mu = E\left(\left|\frac{u_t}{h_t}\right|\right)$$

The value of $\mu$ depends on the density function assumed for the standardized disturbances, $\varepsilon_t = u_t/h_t$. We have

$$\mu = \sqrt{\frac{2}{\pi}}, \qquad \text{if} \quad \varepsilon_t \sim N(0, 1) \tag{18.139}$$

and

$$\mu = \frac{2(v-2)^{\frac{1}{2}}}{(v-1)B\left(\frac{v}{2}, \frac{1}{2}\right)} \tag{18.140}$$

if $\varepsilon_t$ has a standardized $t$-distribution with $v$ degrees of freedom.[20]

The (approximate) log-likelihood function for the EGARCH model has the same form as in (18.134) and (18.135) for the Gaussian and student $t$-distributions, respectively. Unlike the GARCH-M class of models, the EGARCH-M model always yields a positive conditional variance, $h_t^2$, for any choice of the unknown parameters; it is only required that the roots of $1 - \sum_{i=1}^{p} \phi_i z^i = 0$ should all fall outside the unit circle. The unconditional variance of $u_t$ in the case of the EGARCH model does not have a simple analytical form.

### 18.16.5 Absolute GARCH-in-mean models

This is the third class of conditionally heteroscedastic models that can be estimated in *Microfit* and has the following specification:[21]

$$y_t = \beta' \mathbf{x}_t + \gamma h_t^2 + u_t \tag{18.141}$$

where $h_t$ is given by

[20] Notice that in this case $E(|u_t/h_t|) = \frac{2}{\sqrt{v}B(v/2, 1/2)} \int_0^{\infty} a(1 + \frac{a^2}{v})^{-(v+1)/2} da$.

[21] The AGARCH model has been proposed in the literature by Heutschel (1991).

$$h_t = \alpha_0 + \sum_{i=1}^{q} \alpha_i |u_{t-i}| + \sum_{i=1}^{p} \phi_i h_{t-i} + \delta' \mathbf{w}_t \tag{18.142}$$

The AGARCH model can also be estimated for different error distributions. The log-likelihood functions for the cases where $\varepsilon_t = u_t/h_t$ has a standard normal distribution and when it has a standardized Student-$t$ distribution are given by (18.134) and (18.135), where $u_t$ and $h_t$ are now specified by (18.141) and (18.142), respectively.

### 18.16.6 Computational considerations

The computation of the ML estimators for the above models are carried out by the Newton–Raphson algorithm using numerical derivatives, after appropriate scaling of the parameters. We also use a 'damping factor' to control for the step-size in the iterations. The value of this damping factor can be changed by the user in the range [0.01, 2.0].[22] The convergence of the iterations often depends on the nature of the conditional heteroscedasticity in the data and the choice of the initial values for the parameters.

Once the ML estimates are computed, *Microfit* then computes their asymptotic standard errors using the inverse of the Hessian matrix (the second partial derivatives of the log-likelihood function).

### 18.16.7 Testing for ARCH (or GARCH) effects

The simplest way to test for ARCH(p) effects is to use the Lagrange multiplier procedure proposed by Engle (1982, p. 1000). The test involves two steps. In the first step, the OLS residuals, $\hat{u}_{t,OLS}$, from the regression of $y_t$ on $\mathbf{x}_t$ are obtained, and in the second step $\hat{u}^2_{t,OLS}$ is regressed on a constant and $p$ of its own lagged values:

$$\hat{u}^2_{t,OLS} = a_0 + b_1 \hat{u}^2_{t-1,OLS} + \ \ldots \ + b_q \hat{u}^2_{t-q,OLS} + e_t$$

for $t = q+1, q+2, \ldots, n$. A test of the ARCH($q$) effect can now be carried out by testing the statistical significance of the slope coefficients, $b_1 = b_2 = \ \ldots \ = b_q = 0$. This statistic is automatically computed by *Microfit* using option 2 in the Hypothesis Testing Menu (after the OLS regression).

### 18.16.8 Residuals, DW, R$^2$, and other statistics

*Microfit* reports the values of the unscaled residuals, $\hat{u}_t$, computed as

[22] The unobserved initial values of $h_t$ are set equal to $\tilde{\sigma}$, the OLS estimator of the unconditional variance of $u_t$.

$$\hat{u}_t = y_t - \hat{\beta}'\mathbf{x}_t - \hat{\gamma}\hat{h}_t^2,\ t = 1, 2, \ldots, n$$

and the conditional standard errors, $\hat{h}_t$, (namely the ML estimates of $h_t$) using the relations (18.132), (18.138), and (18.142). The scaled residuals, $\hat{u}_t/\hat{h}_t$, are used in the histogram plots. The program also reports the maximized value of the log-likelihood function, AIC, SBC, DW, and $R^2$ using formulae similar to those for the other estimation procedures.

The summary statistics are computed using the unscaled residuals. Users interested in computing these statistics using the scaled residuals can do so by first saving the values of $\hat{u}_t$ and $\hat{h}_t$ in the Post Regression Menu of the GARCH option, and then carrying out the necessary computations in the Command Editor.

## 18.17 Recursive regressions

The econometric model underlying the recursive regressions is given by

$$\underset{1\times 1}{\mathbf{y}_t} = \underset{1\times k}{\mathbf{x}_t'}\ \underset{k\times 1}{\beta_t} + \underset{1\times 1}{\mathbf{u}_t},\quad t = 1, 2, \ldots, n \tag{18.143}$$

where the coefficients, $\beta_t$, and the variances of the disturbance terms, $\sigma_t^2$, are now allowed to vary with $t$, typically a time subscript. (Notice that for this option it is necessary that the observations are ordered.)

### 18.17.1 The CUSUM test

The cumulative sum (CUSUM) test is described in Brown *et al.* (1975) and is based on the CUSUM of recursive residuals defined by

$$W_r = \frac{1}{\hat{\sigma}_{OLS}} \sum_{j=k+1}^{r} v_j,\qquad r = k+1, k+2, \ldots, n \tag{18.144}$$

where $v_t$ is the recursive residual based on the first $j$ observations given below by (18.149), and $\hat{\sigma}_{OLS}$ is already defined by (18.5).

The test employs a graphic technique and involves plotting $W_r$ and a pair of straight lines for values of $r = k+1, k+2, \ldots, n$. The straight lines are drawn assuming a five per cent significance level.

The equations of the lines are given by

$$W = \pm\{0.948\sqrt{(n-k)} + 1.896(r-k)\sqrt{(n-k)}\} \tag{18.145}$$

for $r = k+1, k+2, \ldots, n$.

For further details, see Brown *et al.* (1975, Section 2.3) and Harvey (1981, pp. 151–4).

### 18.17.2 The CUSUM of squares test

This test is described fully in Brown *et al.* (1975), and employs the squared recursive residuals, $v_j^2$. It is based on the quantities

$$WW_r = \sum_{j=k+1}^{r} v_j^2 \Big/ \sum_{j=k+1}^{n} v_j^2, \qquad r = k+1, k+2, \ldots, n \tag{18.146}$$

and involves plotting $WW_r$ and a pair of lines whose equations are given by

$$WW = \pm c_0 + (r-k)/(n-k), \qquad r = k+1, k+2, \ldots, n \tag{18.147}$$

where $c_0$ is determined by the significance level chosen for the test. The program uses the values of $c_0$ appropriate for a five per cent significance level. These are based on the critical values in Harvey (1981, Table C, pp. 364–5).

### 18.17.3 Recursive coefficients: the OLS option

Let

$$\begin{aligned}\mathbf{X}_r &= (\mathbf{x}_1, \mathbf{x}_2, \ldots, \mathbf{x}_r)' \\ \mathbf{y}_r &= (y_1, y_2, \ldots, y_r)'\end{aligned}$$

Then the recursive coefficients are defined by

$$\hat{\beta}_r = (\mathbf{X}_r'\mathbf{X}_r)^{-1}\mathbf{X}_r'\mathbf{y}_r, \qquad r = k+1, k+2, \ldots, n \tag{18.148}$$

The program computes $\hat{\beta}_r$ recursively, using the results (3) and (4) in Brown *et al.* (1975, p. 152).

### 18.17.4 Standardized recursive residuals: the OLS option

The standardized recursive residuals based on the first $r$ observations are defined by[23]

$$v_r = (y_r - \mathbf{x}_r'\hat{\beta}_{r-1})/d_r, \qquad r = k+1, k+2, \ldots, n \tag{18.149}$$

where $\hat{\beta}_r$ are defined by (18.148), and

$$d_r = \sqrt{\{1 + \mathbf{x}_r'(\mathbf{X}_{r-1}'\mathbf{X}_{r-1})^{-1}\mathbf{x}_r\}}. \tag{18.150}$$

---

[23]Notice that under

$$H_0: \begin{cases} \beta_1 = \beta_2 = \cdots = \beta_n = \beta \\ \sigma_1^2 = \sigma_2^2 = \cdots = \sigma_n^2 = \sigma^2 \end{cases}$$

the recursive residuals $v_r$, $r = k+1, \ldots, n$ are independent, $N(0, \sigma^2)$. See Lemma 1 in Brown *et al.* (1975).

### 18.17.5 Recursive standard errors: the OLS option

Denoting the estimator of $\sigma_t^2$ based on the first $r$ observations by $\hat{\sigma}_r^2$, we have

$$\hat{\sigma}_r^2 = S_r/(r-k), \qquad r = k+1, k+2, \ldots, n \tag{18.151}$$

where

$$S_r = S_{r-1} + v_r^2, \qquad r = k+1, k+2, \ldots, n$$

with $S_k = 0$. Equivalently, $S_r = (\mathbf{y}_r - \mathbf{X}_r\hat{\beta}_r)'(\mathbf{y}_r - \mathbf{X}_r\hat{\beta}_r)$.

### 18.17.6 Recursive estimation: the IV option

**Recursive coefficients**

In the IV case the recursive coefficients are computed using the relations

$$\hat{\beta}_{r,IV} = (\mathbf{X}_r'\mathbf{P}_r\mathbf{X}_r)^{-1}\mathbf{X}_r'\mathbf{P}_r\mathbf{y}_r \tag{18.152}$$

$$\hat{V}(\hat{\beta}_{r,IV}) = \hat{\sigma}_{r,IV}^2(\mathbf{X}_r'\mathbf{P}_r\mathbf{X}_r)^{-1} \tag{18.153}$$

for $r = k+1, k+2, \ldots, n$, where

$$\mathbf{P}_r = \mathbf{Z}_r(\mathbf{Z}_r'\mathbf{Z}_r)^{-1}\mathbf{Z}_r'$$
$$\mathbf{Z}_r = (\mathbf{z}_1, \mathbf{z}_2, \ldots, \mathbf{z}_r)'$$

$\hat{\sigma}_{r,IV}^2$ is defined by (18.156) below and $\mathbf{z}_t$, $t = 1, 2, \ldots, n$ are the $s \times 1$ vectors of observations on the $s$ instrumental variables.

**Standardized recursive residuals**

$$v_{r,IV} = (y_r - \mathbf{x}_r'\hat{\beta}_{r-1,IV})/d_{r,IV}, \qquad r = k+1, k+2, \ldots, n \tag{18.154}$$

where $\hat{\beta}_{r,IV}$ is defined by (18.152) and

$$d_{r,IV} = \{1 + \mathbf{x}_r'(\mathbf{X}_{r-1}'\mathbf{P}_{r-1}\mathbf{X}_{r-1})^{-1}\mathbf{x}_r\}^{1/2} \tag{18.155}$$

**Recursive standard errors**

$$\hat{\sigma}_{r,IV}^2 = (\mathbf{y}_r - \mathbf{X}_r\hat{\beta}_{r,IV})'(\mathbf{y}_r - \mathbf{X}_r\hat{\beta}_{r,IV})/(r-k) \tag{18.156}$$

for $r = k+1, k+2, \ldots, n$.

### 18.17.7 Adaptive coefficients in expectations formation models under incomplete learning

Starting with the parameter varying model (18.143), as shown in Pesaran (1987a, Section 9.3.2), the augmented adaptive learning model under incomplete information can be written as

$$ {}_t y^*_{t+1} - {}_{t-1} y^*_t = \mu_t (y_t - {}_{t-1} y^*_t) + (\Delta \mathbf{x}_t)' \hat{\beta}_{t-1} + \text{error} $$

where ${}_t y^*_{t+1}$ denotes the expectations of $y_{t+1}$ formed at time $t$. The adaptive coefficients in this model are computed as

$$ \mu_t = \mathbf{x}'_t \left( \sum_{j=1}^{t} \mathbf{x}_t \mathbf{x}'_j \right)^{-1} \mathbf{x}_t = \mathbf{x}'_t (\mathbf{X}'_t \mathbf{X}_t)^{-1} \mathbf{x}_t, \qquad t = k+1, k+2, \ldots, n \tag{18.157} $$

## 18.17.8 Recursive predictions

Two sets of recursive predictions are computed by the program:

1. Conditional on the actual values of $\mathbf{x}_t$
2. Conditional on the $k$ variables $\mathbf{w}_t$ (typically predictors of $\mathbf{x}_t$).

In case 1, recursive predictions of $y_t$ are computed as

$$ \hat{y}_{Rt} = \mathbf{x}'_t \hat{\beta}_{t-1}, \qquad t = k+1, k+2, \ldots, n \tag{18.158} $$

In case 2, predictions of $y_t$ are computed as

$$ \hat{y}_{Rt} = \mathbf{w}'_t \hat{\beta}_{t-1}, \qquad t = k+1, k+2, \ldots, n \tag{18.159} $$

where $\hat{\beta}_t$ are defined by (18.148) in the case of the OLS option, and by (18.152) in the case of the IV option.

The standard errors of the recursive forecasts are computed using the following results:

$$ \text{OLS option:} \qquad \hat{V}(\hat{y}_{Rt}) = \hat{\sigma}^2_{t-1} \mathbf{w}'_t (\mathbf{X}'_{t-1} \mathbf{X}_{t-1})^{-1} \mathbf{w}_t \tag{18.160} $$

where $\hat{\sigma}^2_{t-1}$ are defined by (18.151), and

$$ \text{IV option:} \qquad \hat{V}(\hat{y}_{Rt}) = \hat{\sigma}^2_{t-1} \mathbf{w}'_t (\mathbf{X}'_{t-1} \mathbf{P}_{t-1} \mathbf{X}_{t-1})^{-1} \mathbf{w}_t \tag{18.161} $$

where $\hat{\sigma}^2_{t-1}$ are defined by (18.156).

In the case where the forecasts are based on the actual values of the regressors, in the above formula $\mathbf{w}_t$ is replaced by $\mathbf{x}_t$. The matrices $\mathbf{X}_t$ and $\mathbf{P}_t$ are already defined in Sections 18.17.3 and 18.17.6.

## 18.18 Phillips–Hansen's fully modified OLS estimators

This estimator is proposed by Phillips and Hansen (1990) and is appropriate for estimation and inference when there exists a *single* cointegrating relation between a set of $I(1)$ variables. Consider the following linear regression model:

$$ y_t = \beta_0 + \beta'_1 \mathbf{x}_t + u_t, \; t = 1, 2, \ldots, n \tag{18.162} $$

where the $k \times 1$ vector of $I(1)$ regressors are not themselves cointegrated. Therefore, $\mathbf{x}_t$ has a first-difference stationary process given by

$$\Delta \mathbf{x}_t = \boldsymbol{\mu} + \mathbf{v}_t, \quad t = 2, 3, \ldots, n \tag{18.163}$$

in which $\boldsymbol{\mu}$ is a $k \times 1$ vector of drift parameters and $\mathbf{v}_t$ is a $k \times 1$ vector of $I(0)$, or stationary variables. It is also assumed that $\boldsymbol{\xi}_t = (u_t, \mathbf{v}_t')'$ is strictly stationary with zero mean and a finite positive-definite covariance matrix, $\Sigma$.

The computation of the FM-OLS estimator of $\boldsymbol{\beta}$ is carried out in two stages. In the first stage, $y_t$ is corrected for the long-run inter-dependence of $u_t$ and $\mathbf{v}_t$. For this purpose, let $\hat{u}_t$ be the OLS residual vector in (18.162), and write

$$\hat{\boldsymbol{\xi}}_t = \begin{pmatrix} \hat{u}_t \\ \hat{\mathbf{v}}_t \end{pmatrix}, \quad t = 2, 3, \ldots, n \tag{18.164}$$

where $\hat{\mathbf{v}}_t = \Delta \mathbf{x}_t - \hat{\boldsymbol{\mu}}$, for $t = 2, 3, \ldots, n$, and $\hat{\boldsymbol{\mu}} = (n-1)^{-1} \sum_{t=2}^{n} \Delta \mathbf{x}_t$.

A consistent estimator of the long-run variance of $\boldsymbol{\xi}_t$ is given by

$$\hat{\boldsymbol{\Omega}} = \hat{\boldsymbol{\Sigma}} + \hat{\boldsymbol{\Lambda}} + \hat{\boldsymbol{\Lambda}}' = \begin{bmatrix} \underset{1 \times 1}{\hat{\Omega}_{11}} & \underset{1 \times k}{\hat{\Omega}_{12}} \\ \underset{k \times 1}{\hat{\Omega}_{21}} & \underset{k \times k}{\hat{\Omega}_{22}} \end{bmatrix} \tag{18.165}$$

where

$$\hat{\boldsymbol{\Sigma}} = \frac{1}{n-1} \sum_{t=2}^{n} \hat{\boldsymbol{\xi}}_t \hat{\boldsymbol{\xi}}_t' \tag{18.166}$$

and

$$\hat{\boldsymbol{\Lambda}} = \sum_{s=1}^{m} \omega(s, m) \hat{\boldsymbol{\Gamma}}_s \tag{18.167}$$

$$\hat{\boldsymbol{\Gamma}}_s = n^{-1} \sum_{t=1}^{n-s} \hat{\boldsymbol{\xi}}_t \hat{\boldsymbol{\xi}}_{t+s}' \tag{18.168}$$

and $\omega(s, m)$ is the lag-window with horizon (or truncation) $m$.

Now let

$$\hat{\boldsymbol{\Delta}} = \hat{\boldsymbol{\Sigma}} + \hat{\boldsymbol{\Lambda}} = \begin{bmatrix} \hat{\boldsymbol{\Delta}}_{11} & \hat{\boldsymbol{\Delta}}_{12} \\ \hat{\boldsymbol{\Delta}}_{21} & \hat{\boldsymbol{\Delta}}_{22} \end{bmatrix} \tag{18.169}$$

$$\hat{\mathbf{Z}} = \hat{\boldsymbol{\Delta}}_{21} - \hat{\boldsymbol{\Delta}}_{22} \hat{\boldsymbol{\Omega}}_{22}^{-1} \hat{\boldsymbol{\Omega}}_{21} \tag{18.170}$$

$$\hat{y}_t^* = y_t - \hat{\boldsymbol{\Omega}}_{12} \hat{\boldsymbol{\Omega}}_{22}^{-1} \hat{\mathbf{v}}_t \tag{18.171}$$

$$\underset{(k+1)\times k}{\mathbf{D}} = \begin{bmatrix} \underset{1\times k}{\mathbf{0}} \\ \underset{k\times k}{\mathbf{I}_k} \end{bmatrix} \tag{18.172}$$

In the second stage the FM-OLS estimator of $\beta$ is given by

$$\hat{\beta}_* = (\mathbf{W}'\mathbf{W})^{-1}(\mathbf{W}'\hat{\mathbf{y}}^* - n\mathbf{D}\hat{Z}) \tag{18.173}$$

where $\hat{\mathbf{y}}^* = (\hat{y}_1^*, \hat{y}_2^*, \ldots, \hat{y}_n^*)'$, $\mathbf{W} = (\tau_n, \mathbf{X})$, and $\tau_n = (1, 1, \ldots, 1)'$.

### 18.18.1 Choice of lag windows: $\omega$(s, m)

The computation of the FM-OLS estimators can be carried out in *Microfit* for the following four choices of lag windows:

**Uniform window**

$$\omega(s, m) = 1, \qquad 0 \leqslant s \leqslant m$$

**Bartlett window**

$$\omega(s, m) = 1 - s/m, \qquad 0 \leqslant s \leqslant m$$

**Tukey window**

$$\omega(s, m) = \tfrac{1}{2}\{1 + \cos(\pi s/m)\}, \qquad 0 \leqslant s \leqslant \tfrac{m}{2}$$

**Parzen window**

$$\omega(s, m) = \begin{cases} 1 - 6(s/m)^2 + 6(s/m)^3, & 0 \leqslant s \leqslant \frac{m}{2}, \\ 2(1 - s/m)^3, & \frac{m}{2} < s \leqslant m \end{cases}$$

Notice, however, that the use of the uniform window may lead to an estimate of $\hat{\Omega}$ which is not a positive-definite matrix. The other three lag windows generally result in estimates of $\Omega$ that are positive definite.

### 18.18.2 Estimation of the variance matrix of the FM-OLS estimator

A consistent estimator of the variance matrix of $\hat{\beta}_*$ defined in (18.173) is given by

$$\hat{\mathbf{V}}(\hat{\beta}_*) = \hat{\omega}_{11.2}(\mathbf{W}'\mathbf{W})^{-1} \tag{18.174}$$

where

$$\hat{\omega}_{11.2} = \hat{\Omega}_{11} - \hat{\mathbf{\Omega}}_{12}\hat{\mathbf{\Omega}}_{22}^{-1}\hat{\mathbf{\Omega}}_{21} \tag{18.175}$$

The $t$-ratios of the FM-OLS estimators reported by *Microfit* are computed as the ratio of $\hat{\beta}_{*i}$ to the square root of the $i$th diagonal element of the matrix defined by (18.174).

The program also computes FM-OLS fitted values, $\hat{\mathbf{y}}_{FM\text{-}OLS} = \mathbf{W}\hat{\boldsymbol{\beta}}_*$; FM-OLS residuals, $\mathbf{e}_{FM\text{-}OLS} = \mathbf{y} - \mathbf{W}\hat{\boldsymbol{\beta}}_*$; autocorrelation coefficients of the FM-OLS residuals; and enables the user to estimate and test linear and/or non-linear functions of the coefficients, $\boldsymbol{\beta}$. The relevant formulae are as in Sections 18.24 and 18.25 with $\hat{\boldsymbol{\theta}} = \hat{\boldsymbol{\beta}}_*$ and $\hat{\sigma}^2\hat{\mathbf{V}}(\hat{\boldsymbol{\theta}}) = \hat{\mathbf{V}}(\hat{\boldsymbol{\beta}}_*)$ given by (18.173) and (18.174), respectively.

## 18.19 Autoregressive distributed lag models

Consider the following augmented autoregressive distributed lag ARDL$(p, q_1, q_2, \ldots, q_k)$ model:[24]

$$\phi(L, p)y_t = \sum_{i=1}^{k} \beta_i(L, q_i)x_{it} + \delta'\mathbf{w}_t + u_t \tag{18.176}$$

where

$$\phi(L, p) = 1 - \phi_1 L - \phi_2 L^2 - \ldots - \phi_p L^p \tag{18.177}$$

$$\beta_i(L, q_i) = \beta_{i0} + \beta_{i1} L + \ldots + \beta_{iq_i} L^{q_i}, \quad i = 1, 2, \ldots, k, \tag{18.178}$$

$L$ is a lag operator such that $Ly_t = y_{t-1}$, and $\mathbf{w}_t$ is a $s \times 1$ vector of deterministic variables such as the intercept term, seasonal dummies, time trends, or exogenous variables with fixed lags.

The ARDL option in *Microfit* (option 6 in the Single Equation Estimation Menu) first estimates (18.176) by the OLS method for *all* possible values of $p = 0, 1, 2, \ldots, m$, $q_i = 0, 1, 2, \ldots, m$, $i = 1, 2, \ldots, k$; namely a total of $(m+1)^{k+1}$ different ARDL models. The maximum lag, $m$, is chosen by the user, and all the models are estimated on the same sample period, namely $t = m+1, m+2, \ldots, n$.

In the second stage, the user is given the option of selecting one of the $(m+1)^{k+1}$ estimated models using one of the following four model selection criteria: the $\bar{R}^2$ criterion, the Akaike information criterion (AIC), Schwarz Bayesian criterion (SBC), or the Hannan–Quinn criterion (HQC).[25] The program then computes the long-run coefficients and their asymptotic standard errors for the selected ARDL model. It also provides estimates of the error correction model (ECM) that corresponds to the selected ARDL model. The long-run coefficients for the response of $y_t$ to a unit change in $x_{it}$ are estimated by

$$\hat{\theta}_i = \frac{\hat{\beta}_i(1, \hat{q}_i)}{\hat{\phi}(1, \hat{p})} = \frac{\hat{\beta}_{i0} + \hat{\beta}_{i1} + \ldots + \hat{\beta}_{i\hat{q}_i}}{1 - \hat{\phi}_1 - \hat{\phi}_2 - \ldots - \hat{\phi}_{\hat{p}}}, \quad i = 1, 2, \ldots, k \tag{18.179}$$

---

[24]For a comprehensive early review of the ARDL model, see Hendry *et al.* (1984).
[25]These model selection criteria are described in Section 18.6.

where $\hat{p}$ and $\hat{q}_i$, $i = 1, 2, \ldots, k$ are the selected (estimated) values of $p$ and $q_i$, $i = 1, 2, \ldots, k$. Similarly, the long-run coefficients associated with the deterministic/exogenous variables with fixed lags are estimated by

$$\hat{\psi} = \frac{\hat{\delta}(\hat{p}, \hat{q}_1, \hat{q}_2, \ldots, \hat{q}_k)}{1 - \hat{\phi}_1 - \hat{\phi}_2 - \ \ldots \ - \hat{\phi}_{\hat{p}}} \tag{18.180}$$

where $\hat{\delta}(\hat{p}, \hat{q}_1, \hat{q}_2, \ldots, \hat{q}_k)$ denotes the OLS estimate of $\boldsymbol{\delta}$ in (18.176) for the selected ARDL model. The estimates of the asymptotic standard errors of $\hat{\theta}_1, \hat{\theta}_2, \ldots, \hat{\theta}_k$, and $\hat{\psi}$ are computed using Bewley's (1979) regression approach, which yields the same result as applying the $\Delta$-method described in Section 18.24 to (18.179) and (18.180).

The error correction model associated with the ARDL$(\hat{p}, \hat{q}_1, \hat{q}_2, \ldots, \hat{q}_k)$ model can be obtained by writing (18.176) in terms of the lagged levels and the first differences of $y_t, x_{1t}, x_{2t}, \ldots, x_{kt}$, and $\mathbf{w}_t$. First note that

$$\begin{aligned} y_t &= \Delta y_t + y_{t-1} \\ y_{t-s} &= y_{t-1} - \sum_{j=1}^{s-1} \Delta y_{t-j}, \qquad s = 1, 2, \ldots, p \end{aligned}$$

and similarly

$$\begin{aligned} \mathbf{w}_t &= \Delta \mathbf{w}_t + \mathbf{w}_{t-1} \\ x_{it} &= \Delta x_{it} + x_{i,t-1} \\ x_{i,t-s} &= x_{i,t-1} - \sum_{j=1}^{s-1} \Delta x_{i,t-j}, \qquad s = 1, 2, \ldots, q_i \end{aligned}$$

Substituting these relations into (18.176) and after some rearrangements, we have

$$\begin{aligned} \Delta y_t = &- \phi(1, \hat{p}) EC_{t-1} + \sum_{i=1}^{k} \beta_{i0} \Delta x_{it} + \boldsymbol{\delta}' \Delta \mathbf{w}_t \\ &- \sum_{j=1}^{\hat{p}-1} \phi_j^* \Delta y_{t-j} - \sum_{i=1}^{k} \sum_{j=1}^{\hat{q}_i - 1} \beta_{ij}^* \Delta x_{i,t-j} + u_t \end{aligned} \tag{18.181}$$

where $EC_t$ is the correction term defined by

$$EC_t = y_t - \sum_{i=1}^{k} \hat{\theta}_i x_{it} - \hat{\psi}' \mathbf{w}_t$$

Recall that $\phi(1, \hat{p}) = 1 - \hat{\phi}_1 - \hat{\phi}_2 - \ \ldots \ - \hat{\phi}_{\hat{p}}$, which measures the quantitative importance of the error correction term. The remaining coefficients, $\phi_j^*$ and $\beta_{ij}^*$, relate to the short-run dynamics of the model's convergence to equilibrium. These are given by

$$\begin{array}{lcl} \phi_1^* & = & \phi_{\hat{p}} + \phi_{\hat{p}-1} + \ldots + \phi_3 + \phi_2 \\ \phi_2^* & = & \phi_{\hat{p}} + \phi_{\hat{p}-1} + \ldots + \phi_3 \\ \vdots & & \vdots \qquad \qquad \qquad \quad \iddots \\ \phi_{\hat{p}-1}^* & = & \phi_{\hat{p}} \end{array}$$

and similarly,

$$\begin{array}{lcl} \beta_{i1}^* & = & \beta_{i,\hat{q}_i} + \beta_{i,\hat{q}_i-1} + \ldots + \beta_{i,3} + \beta_{i,2} \\ \beta_{i2}^* & = & \beta_{i,\hat{q}_i} + \beta_{i,\hat{q}_i-1} + \ldots + \beta_{i,3} \\ \vdots & & \vdots \qquad \qquad \qquad \quad \iddots \\ \beta_{i,\hat{q}_i-1}^* & = & \beta_{i,\hat{q}_i} \end{array}$$

The estimates $\hat{\theta}_i$ and $\hat{\psi}$ are already computed using relations (18.179) and (18.180).

The estimates of the parameters of the error correction model (ECM) (18.181) are obtained from the coefficient estimates of the ARDL model using the above relations. The standard errors of these estimates are also obtained using the variance formula (18.209), and allow for possible non-zero covariances between the estimates of the short-run and the long-run coefficients. Notice that the covariances of the short-run and the long-run coefficients are asymptotically uncorrelated only in the case where it is known that the regressors are $I(1)$ and that they are not cointegrated among themselves.

Dynamic forecasts can also be generated using the error correction formulation (18.181). The relevant formulae and other details are the same as those described in Section 18.26.2 on the computation of univariate dynamic forecasts.

## 18.20 Logit and Probit models

Logit and Probit models represent particular formulations of the univariate binary quantitative response models defined by

$$Pr(y_i = 1) = F(\boldsymbol{\beta}'\mathbf{x}_i), \qquad i = 1, 2, \ldots, n \tag{18.182}$$

where $y_i$, $i = 1, 2, \ldots, n$ are independently distributed binary random variables taking the value of 1 or 0; $\mathbf{x}_i$ is a $k \times 1$ vector of explanatory variables; $\boldsymbol{\beta}$ is a $k \times 1$ vector of unknown coefficients; and $F(\cdot)$ is a known function. Under the Probit model, $F(\boldsymbol{\beta}'\mathbf{x}_i)$ is specified as

$$F(\boldsymbol{\beta}'\mathbf{x}_i) = \Phi(\boldsymbol{\beta}'\mathbf{x}_i) = \int_{-\infty}^{\boldsymbol{\beta}'\mathbf{x}_i} \frac{1}{\sqrt{2\pi}} \exp\{-\tfrac{1}{2}t^2\}dt \tag{18.183}$$

which is the cumulative distribution function of the standard normal. Under the Logit model, $F(\boldsymbol{\beta}'\mathbf{x}_i)$ is specified as

$$F(\boldsymbol{\beta}'\mathbf{x}_i) = \Lambda(\boldsymbol{\beta}'\mathbf{x}_i) = \frac{e^{\boldsymbol{\beta}'\mathbf{x}_i}}{1 + e^{\boldsymbol{\beta}'\mathbf{x}_i}} \tag{18.184}$$

The maximum likelihood estimator (ML) of $\boldsymbol{\beta}$ is obtained by maximizing the following log-likelihood function:

$$\ell(\boldsymbol{\beta}) = \sum_{i=1}^{n} y_i \log[F(\boldsymbol{\beta}'\mathbf{x}_i)] + \sum_{i=1}^{n}(1 - y_i)\log[1 - F(\boldsymbol{\beta}'\mathbf{x}_i)] \tag{18.185}$$

using the Newton–Raphson iterative algorithm. The first and the second derivatives of the log-likelihood function are given by

$$\frac{\partial \ell(\boldsymbol{\beta})}{\partial \boldsymbol{\beta}} = \sum_{i=1}^{n} \frac{(y_i - F_i)f_i\mathbf{x}_i}{F_i(1 - F_i)} \tag{18.186}$$

and

$$\frac{\partial^2 \ell(\boldsymbol{\beta})}{\partial \boldsymbol{\beta}\partial \boldsymbol{\beta}'} = -\sum_{i=1}^{n} \frac{(y_i - F_i)^2}{F_i(1 - F_i)} f_i^2 \mathbf{x}_i\mathbf{x}_i' + \sum_{i=1}^{n}\left[\frac{y_i - F_i}{F_i(1 - F_i)}\right] f_i\mathbf{x}_i\mathbf{x}_i' \tag{18.187}$$

where $f_i = f(\boldsymbol{\beta}'\mathbf{x}_i)$, and $F_i = F(\boldsymbol{\beta}'\mathbf{x}_i)$. These derivative functions simplify when $F(\cdot)$ takes the logistic form and are given by

$$\frac{\partial \ell(\boldsymbol{\beta})}{\partial \boldsymbol{\beta}} = \sum_{i=1}^{n}(y_i - \Lambda_i)\mathbf{x}_i \tag{18.188}$$

and

$$\frac{\partial^2 \ell(\boldsymbol{\beta})}{\partial \boldsymbol{\beta}\partial \boldsymbol{\beta}'} = -\sum_{i=1}^{n} \Lambda_i(1 - \Lambda_i)\mathbf{x}_i\mathbf{x}_i' \tag{18.189}$$

where $\Lambda_i = \Lambda(\boldsymbol{\beta}'\mathbf{x}_i)$.

For the Probit model, we have

$$\frac{\partial \ell(\boldsymbol{\beta})}{\partial \boldsymbol{\beta}} = \sum_{i=1}^{n} \lambda_i\mathbf{x}_i \tag{18.190}$$

and

$$\frac{\partial^2 \ell(\boldsymbol{\beta})}{\partial \boldsymbol{\beta}\partial \boldsymbol{\beta}'} = -\sum_{i=1}^{n} \lambda_i(\lambda_i + \boldsymbol{\beta}'\mathbf{x}_i)\mathbf{x}_i\mathbf{x}_i' \tag{18.191}$$

where

$$\lambda_i = \begin{cases} \dfrac{-\phi_i}{1 - \Phi_i}, & \textit{if } y_i = 0 \\ \dfrac{\phi_i}{\Phi_i}, & \textit{if } y_i = 1 \end{cases} \tag{18.192}$$

$$\phi_i = (2\pi)^{-\frac{1}{2}} \exp[-\tfrac{1}{2}(\boldsymbol{\beta}'\mathbf{x}_i)^2] \tag{18.193}$$

and

$$\Phi_i = \Phi(\boldsymbol{\beta}'\mathbf{x}_i) \tag{18.194}$$

It is easy to see that the matrix of the second derivatives, $\partial^2 \ell(\boldsymbol{\beta})/\partial\boldsymbol{\beta}\partial\boldsymbol{\beta}'$, is negative definite under both models, and therefore that the ML estimator of $\boldsymbol{\beta}$ (when it exists) is unique.[26]

The numerical computation of $\hat{\boldsymbol{\beta}}$ (the ML estimator of $\boldsymbol{\beta}$) is carried out by the scoring method using the following iterations:

$$\boldsymbol{\beta}_{(j)} = \boldsymbol{\beta}_{(j-1)} - \left[E\left(\frac{\partial^2 \ell(\boldsymbol{\beta})}{\partial\boldsymbol{\beta}\partial\boldsymbol{\beta}'}\right)\right]^{-1}_{\boldsymbol{\beta}=\boldsymbol{\beta}_{(j-1)}} \left[\frac{\partial \ell(\boldsymbol{\beta})}{\partial\boldsymbol{\beta}}\right]_{\boldsymbol{\beta}=\boldsymbol{\beta}_{(j-1)}}, \quad j = 0, 1, 2, \ldots \tag{18.195}$$

where $\boldsymbol{\beta}_{(j-1)}$ is the estimator of $\boldsymbol{\beta}$ at the $(j-1)$ iteration, and

$$E\left(\frac{\partial^2 \ell(\boldsymbol{\beta})}{\partial\boldsymbol{\beta}\partial\boldsymbol{\beta}'}\right) = -\sum_{i=1}^{n}\left[\frac{f_i^2}{F_i(1-F_i)}\right]\mathbf{x}_i\mathbf{x}_i' \tag{18.196}$$

Due to the global concavity of the log-likelihood function, in cases where the ML estimator of $\boldsymbol{\beta}$ exists, this iterative procedure is sure to converge, and in practice often converges in less than 10 iterations.[27]

The estimator of the variance matrix of $\hat{\boldsymbol{\beta}}$ is computed as

$$\hat{V}(\hat{\boldsymbol{\beta}}) = \left[-E\left(\frac{\partial^2 \ell(\boldsymbol{\beta})}{\partial\boldsymbol{\beta}\partial\boldsymbol{\beta}'}\right)\right]^{-1}_{\boldsymbol{\beta}=\hat{\boldsymbol{\beta}}} = \sum_{i=1}^{n}\left[\frac{f_i^2}{F_i(1-F_i)}\right]\mathbf{x}_i\mathbf{x}_i' \tag{18.197}$$

where

$F_i = \Lambda(\boldsymbol{\beta}'\mathbf{x}_i) = \Lambda_i$, and $f_i = \Lambda_i(1-\Lambda_i)$, in the case of the Logit model
$F_i = \Phi(\boldsymbol{\beta}'\mathbf{x}_i) = \Phi_i$, and $f_i = \phi_i$, in the case of the Probit model.

Comprehensive surveys of the literature on binary choice models and their various extensions can be found in Amemiya (1981), Maddala (1983), and Cramer (1991). See also Judge *et al.* (1985, Chapter 18) and Greene (1993, Chapter 21).

### 18.20.1 Estimating and testing vector functions of $\boldsymbol{\beta}$

To estimate linear/non-linear vector functions of $\boldsymbol{\beta}$, or test linear/non-linear restrictions on elements of $\boldsymbol{\beta}$, the variance formula (18.197) can be used in the relations (18.209) and (18.211) given below. The necessary computations can be carried out using options 5 and 6 in the Logit/Probit Post Estimation Menu.

---

[26] See, for example, Maddala (1983) and Amemiya (1985).

[27] For an example where $\hat{\boldsymbol{\beta}}$ does not exist, see the example by Albert and Anderson (1984), discussed in Amemiya (1985, pp. 271–2).

### 18.20.2 Fitted probability and fitted discrete values

*Microfit* reports fitted probability values, $\Phi(\hat{\beta}'\mathbf{x}_i)$ and $\Lambda(\hat{\beta}'\mathbf{x}_i)$ for the Probit and Logit models, respectively. The estimates under the column 'fitted' values refer to

$$\begin{aligned} \hat{y}_i &= 1, \quad \text{if} \quad F(\hat{\beta}'\mathbf{x}_i) \geqslant 0.5, \\ &= 0, \quad \text{if} \quad F(\hat{\beta}'\mathbf{x}_i) < 0.5, \end{aligned} \tag{18.198}$$

where $F(\cdot)$ could be either the Probit or the Logit specification.

### 18.20.3 Measures of goodness of fit and related test statistics

The following statistics are reported after Logit or Probit estimation:

| | |
|---|---|
| Maximized value of the log-likelihood function | $= \ell(\hat{\beta})$ |
| Akaike information criterion | $= \ell(\hat{\beta}) - k$ |
| Schwarz Bayesian Criterion | $= \ell(\hat{\beta}) - \frac{k}{2}\log(n)$ |
| Hannan–Quinn criterion | $= \ell(\hat{\beta}) - k \log\log n$ |
| Mean of $y$ | $= \sum_{i=1}^{n} y_i/n$ |
| Mean of predicted (fitted) $y$ | $= \sum_{i=1}^{n} \hat{y}_i/n$ |
| Goodness of fit | $= \sum_{i=1}^{n} sign(y_i\hat{y}_i)/n$ |
| Pseudo-$R^2$ | $= 1 - (\ell(\hat{\beta})/\ell(\beta_0))$ |
| Chi-squared statistic | $= 2(\ell(\hat{\beta}) - \ell(\beta_0))$ |

where $\hat{y}_i$ is defined by (18.198), and the goodness of fit statistic measures the proportion of observations with correctly predicted (fitted) values of $y$.

The Pesaran–Timmermann test statistic is computed by applying the PTTEST function to $y_i$ (actual) and $\hat{y}_i$ (fitted) values. Under the null hypothesis that $y_i$ and $\hat{y}_i$ are independently distributed, the PTTEST statistic is asymptotically distributed as a standard normal variate. See Section 18.4 for more details.

Pseudo-$R^2$ is a popular measure of the model's performance in the binary choice literature and compares the fit of the model (as measured by the maximized log-likelihood value, $\ell(\hat{\beta})$), relative to the maximized value of the log-likelihood function, when all the coefficients except the intercept term (if any) in $\beta'\mathbf{x}_i$ are set equal to zero. In the case where $\beta'\mathbf{x}_i$ contains an intercept term

$$\ell(\beta_0) = m \log\left(\frac{m}{n}\right) + (n - m)\log\left(\frac{n-m}{n}\right)$$

where $m = \sum_{i=1}^{n} y_i/n$. See, for example, Judge *et al.* (1985, pp. 766–8). When $\beta'\mathbf{x}_i$ does not contain an intercept term, we have $\ell(\beta_0) = n\log(1/2)$.

The Chi-Squared Statistic, $2(\ell(\hat{\beta}) - \ell(\beta_0))$, is asymptotically distributed as a $\chi^2$ variate with $k - 1$ degrees of freedom when $\beta'\mathbf{x}_i$ contains an intercept term, and will be asymptotically distributed as a $\chi^2$ variate with $k$ degrees of freedom when $\beta'\mathbf{x}_i$ does not contain an intercept term.

### 18.20.4 Forecasting with Logit/Probit models

The forecasts of $y$ are obtained by first computing the probability values $\Phi(\hat{\beta}'\mathbf{x}_{n+j})$ or $\Lambda(\hat{\beta}'\mathbf{x}_{n+j})$, and then setting

$$\begin{aligned}\hat{y}^*_{n+j} &= 1 \quad \text{if} \quad \Phi(\hat{\beta}'\mathbf{x}_{n+j}) \geqslant 0.5\\ &= 0 \quad \text{if} \quad \Phi(\hat{\beta}'\mathbf{x}_{n+j}) < 0.5\end{aligned}$$

for the Probit model, and

$$\begin{aligned}\hat{y}^*_{n+j} &= 1 \quad \text{if} \quad \Lambda(\hat{\beta}'\mathbf{x}_{n+j}) \geqslant 0.5\\ &= 0 \quad \text{if} \quad \Lambda(\hat{\beta}'\mathbf{x}_{n+j}) < 0.5\end{aligned}$$

for the Logit model. The index for $j = 1, 2, \ldots, p$, where $p$ is the forecast horizon. It is assumed that $\mathbf{x}_i$s do not include lagged values of $y_i$.

The following summary statistics are computed for the estimation and forecast periods:

| | Estimation Period | Forecast Period |
|---|---|---|
| Mean of $y$ | $\sum_{i=1}^{n} y_i/n$ | $\sum_{j=1}^{p} y_{n+j}/p$ |
| Mean of Predicted $y$ | $\sum_{i=1}^{n} \hat{y}_i/n$ | $\sum_{j=1}^{p} \hat{y}^*_{n+j}/p$ |
| Goodness of Fit | $\sum_{i=1}^{n} sign(y_i\hat{y}_i)/n$ | $\sum_{j=1} sign(y_{n+j}\hat{y}^*_{j+j})$ |
| Pesaran–Timmermann Statistic | PTTEST($\mathbf{y}$,$\hat{\mathbf{y}}$) | PTTEST($\mathbf{y}^*$, $\hat{\mathbf{y}}^*$) |

where $\mathbf{y} = (y_1, y_2, \ldots, y_n)'$, $\hat{\mathbf{y}} = (\hat{y}_1, \hat{y}_2, \ldots, \hat{y}_n)'$, $\mathbf{y}^* = (y_{n+1}, y_{n+2}, \ldots, y_{n+p})'$, and $\hat{\mathbf{y}}^* = (\hat{y}^*_{n+1}, \hat{y}^*_{n+2}, \ldots, \hat{y}^*_{n+p})$.

## 18.21 Non-linear estimation

Consider the non-linear regression equation with additive errors

$$y_t = f(\mathbf{x}_t, \beta) + u_t, \qquad u_t \sim i.i.d(0, \sigma^2) \tag{18.199}$$

where $\mathbf{x}_t$ is a $k \times 1$ vector of explanatory variables, and $\beta$ is a $p$-dimensional vector of unknown parameters. It is assumed that the $u_t$s are serially uncorrelated with mean zero and variance $\sigma^2$. The case where $\{u_t\}$ follows an AR process can be easily dealt with by first transforming the regression equation to remove the residual serial correlation and then applying the nonlinear estimation method to the resultant regression. For example, suppose the $u_t$s have the AR(1) specification

$$u_t = \rho u_{t-1} + \epsilon_t$$

where the $\epsilon_t$s are serially uncorrelated. Then (18.199) may be transformed to yield the following non-linear equation:

$$y_t = \psi(\mathbf{x}_t, \mathbf{x}_{t-1}, \mathbf{y}_{t-1}, \boldsymbol{\theta}) + \epsilon_t$$

with serially uncorrelated residuals, where

$$\psi(\mathbf{x}_t, \mathbf{x}_{t-1}, \mathbf{y}_{t-1}, \boldsymbol{\theta}) = f(\mathbf{x}_t, \boldsymbol{\beta}) - \rho f(\mathbf{x}_{t-1}, \boldsymbol{\beta}) + \rho y_{t-1}$$

and $\boldsymbol{\theta} = (\boldsymbol{\beta}', \rho)'$. This method does not work if the error process, $u_t$, has an MA representation.

### 18.21.1 The Non-linear least squares (NLS) method

The NLS estimates of $\boldsymbol{\beta}$ are computed by finding a $p \times 1$ vector, $\hat{\boldsymbol{\beta}}_{NLS}$, which minimizes

$$Q_{LS}(\boldsymbol{\beta}) = \{\mathbf{y} - \mathbf{f}(\mathbf{X}, \boldsymbol{\beta})\}'\{\mathbf{y} - \mathbf{f}(\mathbf{X}, \boldsymbol{\beta})\} \tag{18.200}$$

where $\mathbf{y}$ is the $n \times 1$ vector of observations on the dependent variable $y_t$, and $\mathbf{X}$ is the $n \times k$ matrix of observations on $\mathbf{x}_t$. The computation of $\hat{\boldsymbol{\beta}}_{NLS}$ is achieved by means of the Gauss–Newton method. Let $\boldsymbol{\beta}_{(j)}$ be the estimate of $\boldsymbol{\beta}$ in the $j$th iteration, and denote the $n \times p$ matrix of the first derivatives of $\mathbf{f}(\mathbf{X}, \boldsymbol{\beta})$ evaluated at $\boldsymbol{\beta}_{(j)}$ by

$$\mathbf{F}_{(j)} = \partial \mathbf{f}(\mathbf{X}, \boldsymbol{\beta})/\partial \boldsymbol{\beta} | \boldsymbol{\beta} = \boldsymbol{\beta}_{(j)} \tag{18.201}$$

Then the iterations

$$\boldsymbol{\beta}_{(j+1)} = \boldsymbol{\beta}_{(j)} + (\mathbf{F}'_{(j)}\mathbf{F}_{(j)})^{-1}\mathbf{F}'_{(j)}\{\mathbf{y} - \mathbf{f}(\mathbf{X}, \boldsymbol{\beta}_{(j)})\} \tag{18.202}$$

are carried out until convergence is achieved. It is worth noting that the second term on the right-hand side of (18.202) can be computed as the coefficient estimates in the regression of the residual vector $\mathbf{u}_{(j)} = \mathbf{y} - \mathbf{f}(\mathbf{X}, \boldsymbol{\beta}_{(j)})$ on $\mathbf{F}_{(j)}$.

The convergence criterion used is

$$\sum_{i=1}^{p} |\hat{\beta}_{i(j)} - \hat{\beta}_{i(j-1)}| < 0.00001p$$

where $\hat{\beta}_{i(j)}$ is the estimate of the $i$th element of $\boldsymbol{\beta}$ in the $j$th iteration, and $p$ is the number of parameters. The derivatives, $F_{(j)}$, are computed numerically.

The estimate of $\sigma^2$ is computed as

$$\hat{\sigma}^2 = \hat{\mathbf{u}}'\hat{\mathbf{u}}/(n-p)$$

and the asymptotic variance–covariance matrix of $\hat{\boldsymbol{\beta}}_{OLS}$ as

$$\hat{V}(\hat{\boldsymbol{\beta}}_{NLS}) = \hat{\sigma}^2(\hat{\mathbf{F}}'\hat{\mathbf{F}})^{-1}$$

where $\hat{\mathbf{F}}$ is the value of $\partial \mathbf{f}(\mathbf{X}, \boldsymbol{\beta})/\partial \boldsymbol{\beta}$ evaluated at the NLS estimates, $\hat{\boldsymbol{\beta}}_{NLS}$. The diagnostic statistics reported for the non-linear least squares option are computed using the formulae in Section 18.5.2 with

$$e_t = \hat{u}_t = y_t - f(\mathbf{x}_t, \hat{\boldsymbol{\beta}}_{NLS})$$

and $\mathbf{X}$ replaced by $\hat{\mathbf{F}}$.

### 18.21.2 The Non-linear instrumental variables (NL/IV) method

The NL/IV estimates of $\beta$ in (18.199) are computed by finding a $p \times 1$ vector, $\hat{\beta}_{IV}$, which minimizes

$$Q_{IV}(\beta) = \{\mathbf{y} - \mathbf{f}(\mathbf{X}, \beta)\}'\mathbf{P}_z\{\mathbf{y} - \mathbf{f}(\mathbf{X}, \beta)\} \tag{18.203}$$

where $\mathbf{P}_z$ is the $n \times n$ projection matrix $\mathbf{Z}(\mathbf{Z}'\mathbf{Z})^{-1}\mathbf{Z}'$, and $\mathbf{Z}$ is the $n \times s$ matrix of observations on $s(\geqslant p)$ instruments.

The numerical procedure followed is similar to the one used for the computation of NLS estimates (see Section 18.21.1) and utilizes the following iterative algorithm:

$$\beta_{(j+1)} = \beta_{(j)} + (\mathbf{F}'_{(j)}\mathbf{P}_z\mathbf{F}_{(j)})^{-1}\mathbf{F}'_{(j)}\mathbf{P}_z\{\mathbf{y} - \mathbf{f}(\mathbf{X}, \beta_{(j)})\}$$

where $F_{(j)}$ is defined by (18.201). The convergence criterion and other details are as in Section 18.21.1.

The other estimates and statistics reported by *Microfit* are computed as in Section 18.9, with $\mathbf{X}$ replaced by

$$\hat{\mathbf{F}} = \partial\mathbf{f}(\mathbf{X}, \beta)/\partial\beta|_{\beta=\hat{\beta}_{IV}}$$

where $\hat{\beta}_{IV}$ is the NL/IV estimator.

For a comprehensive discussion of nonlinear least squares and nonlinear instrumental variables methods, see Amemiya (1974) and Gallant (1987).

## 18.22 Heteroscedasticity-consistent variance estimators

In situations where the homoscedasticity assumption A2 does not apply (see Section 6.1), the estimator of the covariance matrices of the OLS and the IV estimators given, respectively, by (18.4) and (18.57) are not generally valid, and can result in misleading inferences. Consistent estimators of the covariance matrix of the OLS and the IV estimators when the form of heteroscedasticity is unknown have been suggested by Eicker (1963, 1967), Rao (1970), and White (1980, 1982). In the case of the OLS option, the program computes a degrees of freedom corrected version of White's (1980) estimator using the following formula:[28]

$$\widehat{HCV}(\hat{\beta}_{OLS}) = \left(\frac{n}{n-k}\right)(\mathbf{X}'\mathbf{X})^{-1}\left(\sum_{t=1}^{n} e_t^2\mathbf{x}_t\mathbf{x}'_t\right)(\mathbf{X}'\mathbf{X})^{-1} \tag{18.204}$$

where $e_t = y_t - \mathbf{x}'_t\hat{\beta}_{OLS}$ are the OLS residuals (see Section 18.5 for the computational details of the OLS option).

In the case of the IV option, the heteroscedasticity-consistent estimator of

[28]The correction for the degrees of freedom is suggested in, amongst others, MacKinnon and White (1985).

the covariance matrix of $\hat{\beta}_{IV}$ is computed as follows according to White (1982, p. 489):

$$\widehat{HCV}(\hat{\beta}_{IV}) = \left(\frac{n}{n-k}\right)\mathbf{Q}_n^{-1}\mathbf{P}_n'\hat{\mathbf{V}}_n\mathbf{P}_n\mathbf{Q}_n^{-1} \tag{18.205}$$

where

$$\mathbf{Q}_n = \mathbf{X}'\mathbf{P}_z\mathbf{X}, \qquad \mathbf{P}_z = \mathbf{Z}(\mathbf{Z}'\mathbf{Z})^{-1}\mathbf{Z}'$$

$$\mathbf{P}_n = (\mathbf{Z}'\mathbf{Z})^{-1}\mathbf{Z}'\mathbf{X}, \qquad \hat{\mathbf{V}}_n = \sum_{t=1}^{n} e_{t,IV}^2\mathbf{z}_t\mathbf{z}_t'$$

As before, $\mathbf{Z} = (\mathbf{z}_1, \mathbf{z}_2, \ldots, \mathbf{z}_n)'$ is the $n \times s$ matrix of instrumental variables, and $e_{t,IV}, t = 1, 2, \ldots, n$ are the IV residuals. (For more details of the computations in the case of the IV option, see Section 18.9.)

Notice that (18.205) can also be written as

$$\widehat{HCV}(\hat{\beta}_{IV}) = \left(\frac{n}{n-k}\right)(\hat{\mathbf{X}}'\hat{\mathbf{X}})^{-1}\left(\sum_{t=1}^{n} e_{t,IV}^2\hat{\mathbf{x}}_t\hat{\mathbf{x}}_t'\right)(\hat{\mathbf{X}}'\hat{\mathbf{X}})^{-1} \tag{18.206}$$

where

$$\hat{\mathbf{X}} = \mathbf{P}_z\mathbf{X}$$

$$\hat{\mathbf{x}}_t = \mathbf{X}'\mathbf{Z}(\mathbf{Z}'\mathbf{Z})^{-1}\mathbf{z}_t$$

Hence, it follows that if $\mathbf{Z}$ is specified to include $\mathbf{X}$, then $\hat{\mathbf{X}} = \mathbf{X}$, $\hat{\mathbf{x}}_t = \mathbf{x}_t$, $e_t = e_{t,IV}$, and $\widehat{HCV}(\hat{\beta}_{OLS}) = \widehat{HCV}(\hat{\beta}_{IV})$.

The relevant expressions for the heteroscedasticity-consistent estimators in the case of the non-linear least squares and the non-linear IV options discussed in Section 18.21 are given by (18.204) and (18.205), respectively, with $\mathbf{X}$ replaced by the matrix of the first derivatives of the non-linear function, namely $\hat{\mathbf{F}}$ defined in Section 18.21.

## 18.23 Newey–West variance estimators

The Newey and West (1987) heteroscedasticity and autocorrelation consistent variance matrix is a direct generalization of White's estimators described in Section 18.22. In the general case where the non-linear regression model (18.199) is estimated by the IV method, the Newey–West variance matrix is computed according to the following formula:

$$\hat{V}(\hat{\beta}_{IV}) = \left(\frac{n}{n-k}\right)\mathbf{Q}_n^{-1}\mathbf{P}_n'\hat{\mathbf{S}}_n\mathbf{P}_n\mathbf{Q}_n^{-1} \tag{18.207}$$

where

$$\mathbf{Q}_n = \hat{\mathbf{F}}'\mathbf{P}_z\hat{\mathbf{F}}, \qquad \mathbf{P}_z = \mathbf{Z}(\mathbf{Z}'\mathbf{Z})^{-1}\mathbf{Z}'$$

$$\mathbf{P}_n = (\mathbf{Z}'\mathbf{Z})^{-1}\mathbf{Z}'\hat{\mathbf{F}}, \qquad \hat{\mathbf{F}} = \left.\frac{\partial \mathbf{f}(\mathbf{X},\beta)}{\partial \beta}\right|_{\beta=\hat{\beta}_{IV}}$$

and

$$\hat{\mathbf{S}}_n = \hat{\mathbf{\Omega}}_0 + \sum_{j=1}^{m} w(j,m)(\hat{\mathbf{\Omega}}_j + \hat{\mathbf{\Omega}}_j')$$

in which

$$\hat{\mathbf{\Omega}}_j = \sum_{t=j+1}^{m} \hat{\mathbf{u}}_t\hat{\mathbf{u}}_{t-j}\mathbf{z}_t\mathbf{z}_{t-j}'$$

$$\hat{u}_t = y_t - f(\mathbf{x}_t, \hat{\beta}_{IV})$$

$\mathbf{z}_t$ is the $s \times 1$ vector of instruments, and $w(j, m)$ is the 'lag window' used. *Microfit* allows three choices for the lag window:

**Uniform (or rectangular) window**

$$w(j,m) = 1, \qquad \text{for} \quad j = 1, 2, \ldots, m$$

**Bartlett window**

$$w(j,m) = 1 - \frac{j}{m+1}, \qquad j = 1, 2, \ldots, m$$

**Parzen window**

$$w(j,m) = 1 - 6\left(\frac{j}{m+1}\right)^2 + 6\left(\frac{j}{m+1}\right)^3, \qquad 1 \leqslant j \leqslant \frac{m+1}{2}$$

$$= 2\left(1 - \frac{j}{m+1}\right)^2 \qquad \frac{m+1}{2} < j \leqslant m$$

The 'window size' or the 'truncation point', $m$, is specified by the user.

Newey and West (1987) use the Bartlett window and do not make the small sample correction proposed by MacKinnon and White (1985). Users interested in exactly replicating the Newey–West adjusted standard errors should therefore choose the Bartlett window and multiply the standard errors computed by *Microfit* by $\{(n-k)/n\}^{1/2}$. Also note that White's heteroscedasticity-consistent estimators outlined in Section 18.22 can be computed using the Newey–West option by setting the window size, $m$, equal to zero.

The equal weight (or the uniform) window option is appropriate when estimating a regression model with moving average errors of known order. This type of model arises in testing the market efficiency hypothesis where the forecast horizon exceeds the sampling interval (see, for example, Pesaran 1987a, Section 7.6). In other situations a Parzen window is generally preferable to the other two windows. Notice that the positive semi-definiteness of the Newey–West variance matrix is only ensured in the case of the Bartlett and Parzen windows. The choice of the uniform window can result in a negative-definite variance matrix especially if a large value for $m$ is chosen relative to the number of available observations, $n$. Also see the discussion in Andrews (1991), and Andrews and Monahan (1992).

## 18.24 Variance of vector function of estimators

Let $\boldsymbol{\phi} = \boldsymbol{\phi}(\boldsymbol{\theta})$ be an $r \times 1$ first-order differentiable function of the $k \times 1$ parameter vector, $\boldsymbol{\theta}$, of a given econometric model. Suppose also that $\boldsymbol{\Phi}(\boldsymbol{\theta}) = \partial\boldsymbol{\phi}(\boldsymbol{\theta})/\partial\boldsymbol{\theta}'$ is an $r \times k$ matrix of rank $r(\leqslant k)$. Then the estimator of $\boldsymbol{\phi}$ and the estimator of its asymptotic variance are given by

$$\hat{\boldsymbol{\phi}} = \boldsymbol{\phi}(\hat{\boldsymbol{\theta}}) \tag{18.208}$$

and

$$\hat{V}(\boldsymbol{\phi}) = \hat{\sigma}^2 \left[\frac{\partial\boldsymbol{\phi}(\boldsymbol{\theta})}{\partial\boldsymbol{\theta}'}\right]_{\boldsymbol{\theta}=\hat{\boldsymbol{\theta}}} \hat{\mathbf{V}}(\hat{\boldsymbol{\theta}}) \left[\frac{\partial\boldsymbol{\phi}(\boldsymbol{\theta})}{\partial\boldsymbol{\theta}'}\right]'_{\boldsymbol{\theta}=\hat{\boldsymbol{\theta}}} \tag{18.209}$$

where $\hat{\boldsymbol{\theta}}$ represents the estimator of $\boldsymbol{\theta}$ and $\hat{\sigma}^2\hat{V}(\hat{\boldsymbol{\theta}})$ is the estimator of the variance matrix of $\hat{\boldsymbol{\theta}}$. The above procedure for estimation of the variance of $\hat{\boldsymbol{\phi}}$ is also known as the $\Delta$-method. See, for example, Serfling (1980).

## 18.25 Wald statistic for testing linear and non-linear restrictions

Option 7 in the Hypothesis Testing Menu (see Section 6.24) allows the user to compute Wald statistics for testing $r$ independent linear or non-linear restrictions on the parameters of the regression model, $\boldsymbol{\theta}$. Let the $r$ restrictions on $\boldsymbol{\theta}$ be given by

$$\boldsymbol{\phi}(\boldsymbol{\theta}) = \mathbf{0} \tag{18.210}$$

where $\boldsymbol{\phi}(\cdot)$ is an $r \times 1$ first-order differentiable function of the unknown parameters of the regression model. Denote the estimator of the (asymptotic) variance matrix of $\hat{\boldsymbol{\theta}}$ by $\hat{\sigma}^2\hat{\mathbf{V}}(\hat{\boldsymbol{\theta}})$, where $\hat{\boldsymbol{\theta}}$ stands for the estimator of $\boldsymbol{\theta}$. Then the Wald (W) statistic for testing the $r$ restrictions in (18.210) is given by

$$W = \hat{\boldsymbol{\phi}}'[\hat{\boldsymbol{\Phi}}\hat{\mathbf{V}}(\theta)\hat{\boldsymbol{\Phi}}']^{-1}\hat{\boldsymbol{\phi}}/\hat{\sigma}^2 \overset{a}{\sim} \chi^2(r) \tag{18.211}$$

where

$$\hat{\boldsymbol{\phi}} = \boldsymbol{\phi}(\hat{\boldsymbol{\theta}}), \qquad \hat{\boldsymbol{\Phi}} = (\partial\boldsymbol{\phi}(\boldsymbol{\theta})/\partial\boldsymbol{\theta})'_{\boldsymbol{\theta}=\hat{\boldsymbol{\theta}}} \tag{18.212}$$

Before calculating the W statistic, the program first checks the rank condition on $\hat{\boldsymbol{\Phi}}$, and proceeds with the computations only if $\hat{\boldsymbol{\Phi}}$ is of full rank, namely when $Rank[\hat{\boldsymbol{\Phi}}] = r$.

## 18.26 Univariate forecasts in regression models

This section considers the problem of forecasting with single equation linear and non-linear regression models. Forecasting with Probit and Logit models is discussed in Section 18.20.

The following general dynamic regression model underlies the forecasts computed by the program for the linear regression model:

$$y_t = \sum_{i=1}^{l} \lambda_i y_{t-i} + \mathbf{g}_t'\alpha + u_t \tag{18.213}$$

$$= \mathbf{x}_t'\beta + u_t, \qquad \mathbf{x}_t = (y_{t-1}, y_{t-2}, \ldots, y_{t-l}, \mathbf{g}_t')' \tag{18.214}$$

where for the AR options

$$u_t = \sum_{i=1}^{m} \rho_i u_{t-i} + \epsilon_t \tag{18.215}$$

and for the MA options

$$u_t = \epsilon_t + \sum_{i=1}^{q} \gamma_i \epsilon_{t-i} \tag{18.216}$$

and $\epsilon_t$ are serially uncorrelated random disturbances with zero means. The program computes univariate dynamic forecasts if the regression equation is specified *explicitly* to include lagged values of the dependent variable, namely $\ell \geqslant 1$. Otherwise, it will generate static forecasts.

### 18.26.1 Univariate static forecasts

The static forecasts are computed taking as given the values of the regressors, $\mathbf{x}_{t+j}$. The values of $y_{t+j}$, $j = 1, 2, \ldots, p$ are forecast by

$$\hat{y}^*_{t+j} = \mathbf{x}'_{t+j}\hat{\beta} + \hat{u}^*_{t+j} \tag{18.217}$$

For the OLS and the IV options, $\hat{u}^*_{t+j} = 0$ and the estimators of $\hat{y}^*_{t+j}$ are given by

$$\hat{y}^*_{t+j,OLS} = \mathbf{x}'_{t+j}\hat{\beta}_{OLS}$$

and

$$\hat{y}^*_{t+j,IV} = \mathbf{x}'_{t+j}\hat{\beta}_{IV}$$

respectively. The forecasts for the nonlinear options are given by

$$\hat{y}^*_{t+j} = f(\mathbf{x}_{t+j}, \hat{\beta})$$

For the AR options, $\hat{u}^*_{t+j}$, $j = 1, 2, \ldots, p$ in (18.217) are computed recursively according to the following relations:

$$
\begin{aligned}
\hat{u}^*_{t+1} &= \sum_{i=1}^{m} \hat{\rho}_i \hat{u}_{t+1-i} \\
\hat{u}^*_{t+2} &= \hat{\rho}_1 \hat{u}^*_{t+1} + \sum_{i=2}^{m} \hat{\rho}_i \hat{u}_{t+2-i} \\
\hat{u}^*_{t+3} &= \hat{\rho}_1 \hat{u}^*_{t+2} + \hat{\rho}_2 \hat{u}^*_{t+1} \sum_{i=3}^{m} \hat{\rho}_i \hat{u}_{t+3-i} \\
&\vdots \\
\hat{u}^*_{t+m} &= \sum_{i=1}^{m-1} \hat{\rho}_i \hat{u}^*_{t+m-i} + \hat{\rho}_m \hat{u}_t
\end{aligned}
$$

and

$$
\hat{u}^*_{t+j} = \sum_{i=1}^{m} \hat{\rho}_i \hat{u}^*_{t+j-i}, \qquad \text{for} \quad j = m+1, m+2, \ldots, p
$$

For the MA options, $\hat{u}^*_{t+j}$ in (18.217) are computed as

$$
\begin{aligned}
\hat{u}^*_{t+j} &= \hat{\gamma}_j \hat{\epsilon}_t + \hat{\gamma}_{j+1} \hat{\epsilon}_{t-1} + \ldots + \hat{\gamma}_q \hat{\epsilon}_{t+j-q}, \quad && \text{for } j \leqslant q \\
&= 0, && \text{for } j > q
\end{aligned}
$$

and the $\hat{\epsilon}_t$s are obtained recursively:

$$
\hat{\epsilon}_t = -\sum_{i=1}^{q} \hat{\gamma}_i \hat{\epsilon}_{t-i} + \hat{u}_t, \qquad t = 1, 2, \ldots
$$

with the initial values $\hat{\epsilon}_0 = \hat{\epsilon}_{-1} = \hat{\epsilon}_{-2} = \ldots = \hat{\epsilon}_{q+1} = 0$.

### 18.26.2 Univariate dynamic forecasts

In computing dynamic forecasts the program takes the values of $\mathbf{g}_{t+j}, j = 1, 2, \ldots, p$ in (18.213) as given, and computes $y_{t+j}, j = 1, 2, \ldots, p$ as $j$-step ahead forecasts using the following recursive relations:

$$
\begin{aligned}
y^*_{t+1} &= \sum_{i=1}^{l} \lambda_i y_{t+1-i} + \mathbf{g}'_{t+1} \boldsymbol{\alpha} + u^*_{t+1} \\
y^*_{t+2} &= \lambda_1 y^*_{t+1} + \sum_{i=2}^{l} \lambda_i y_{t+1-i} + \mathbf{g}'_{t+2} \boldsymbol{\alpha} + u^*_{t+2} \\
&\vdots \\
y^*_{t+l} &= \sum_{i=1}^{l-1} \lambda_i y^*_{t+\ell-i} + \lambda_l y_t + \mathbf{g}'_{t+l} \boldsymbol{\alpha} + u^*_{t+l}
\end{aligned}
$$

and

$$
y^*_{t+j} = \sum_{i=1}^{l} \lambda_i y^*_{t+j-i} + \mathbf{g}'_{t+j} \boldsymbol{\alpha} + u^*_{t+j}, \qquad \text{for} \quad j = l+1, l+2, \ldots, p
$$

where, as before, estimates of $u^*_{t+j}$ are obtained by means of the recursive relations given in Section 18.26.1 above. The program computes estimates of $y^*_{t+j}$ by replacing the unknown parameters $\lambda_1, \ldots, \lambda_q, \alpha, \rho_1, \ldots, \rho_m, \gamma_1, \gamma_2, \ldots, \gamma_q$ by their appropriate ML estimators, defined in Sections 18.5 to 18.15.

### 18.26.3 Standard errors of univariate forecast errors: the OLS and IV options

The program computes standard errors of the forecast errors

$$e^*_{t+j} = y_{t+j} - \hat{y}^*_{t+j}, \qquad j = 1, 2, \ldots, p$$

for the OLS and the IV options only.

Let $\mathbf{e}^* = (e^*_{n+1}, e^*_{n+2}, \ldots, e^*_{n+p})'$ be the $p \times 1$ vector of forecast errors. For the static forecasts given in Section 18.26.1, we have

OLS option: $$\hat{\mathbf{V}}(\mathbf{e}^*) = \hat{\sigma}^2_{OLS}\{\mathbf{I}_p + \mathbf{X}^*(\mathbf{X}'\mathbf{X})^{-1}\mathbf{X}^{*'}\} \qquad (18.218)$$

IV option: $$\hat{\mathbf{V}}(\mathbf{e}^*) = \hat{\sigma}^2_{IV}\{\mathbf{I}_p + \mathbf{X}^*(\mathbf{X}'\mathbf{P}_z\mathbf{X})^{-1}\mathbf{X}^{*'}\} \qquad (18.219)$$

where $\mathbf{I}_p$ is an identity matrix of order $p$; $\mathbf{X}^*$ is the $p \times k$ matrix of observations on $\mathbf{x}_t$ over the forecast period; $\mathbf{X}$ is the $n \times k$ matrix of observations on $\mathbf{x}_t$ over the estimation period; and $\mathbf{P}_z$ is the projection matrix defined by (18.56).

The variance matrix of the dynamic forecast errors is computed according to the following formula due to Pagan and Nicholls (1984):

OLS option: $$\hat{\mathbf{V}}(\mathbf{e}^*) = \hat{\sigma}^2_{OLS}\mathbf{D}^{-1}\{\mathbf{I}_p + \mathbf{X}^*(\mathbf{X}'\mathbf{X})^{-1}\mathbf{X}^{*'}\}\mathbf{D}'^{-1} \qquad (18.220)$$

IV option: $$\hat{\mathbf{V}}(\mathbf{e}^*) = \hat{\sigma}^2_{IV}\mathbf{D}^{-1}\{\mathbf{I}_p + \mathbf{X}^*(\mathbf{X}'\mathbf{P}_z\mathbf{X})^{-1}\mathbf{X}^{*'}\}\mathbf{D}'^{-1} \qquad (18.221)$$

where

$$\mathbf{D} = \begin{bmatrix} -1 & 0 & \cdot & \cdot & \cdot & 0 & \cdot & \cdot & \cdot & 0 & 0 \\ \hat{\lambda}_1 & -1 & \cdot & \cdot & \cdot & 0 & \cdot & \cdot & \cdot & 0 & 0 \\ \hat{\lambda}_2 & \hat{\lambda}_1 & & -1 & & 0 & \cdot & \cdot & \cdot & 0 & 0 \\ \cdot & \cdot & & \cdot & & \cdot & & & & \cdot & \cdot \\ \cdot & \cdot & & \cdot & & \cdot & & & & \cdot & \cdot \\ \cdot & \cdot & & \cdot & & \cdot & & & & \cdot & \cdot \\ \hat{\lambda}_l & \hat{\lambda}_{l-1} & \cdot & \cdot & \cdot & -1 & & 0 & & 0 & 0 \\ \cdot & \cdot & & & & \cdot & & & & \cdot & \cdot \\ \cdot & \cdot & & & & \cdot & & & & \cdot & \cdot \\ \cdot & \cdot & & & & \cdot & & & & \cdot & 0 \\ 0 & \ldots & & 0 & & \hat{\lambda}_l & \cdot & \cdot & \hat{\lambda}_2 & \hat{\lambda}_1 & -1 \end{bmatrix}$$

and $\hat{\lambda}_1, \hat{\lambda}_2, \ldots, \hat{\lambda}_l$ are the estimates of $\lambda_i$ in (18.213). The $p \times k$ matrix of observations on $\mathbf{x}_t$ in the case of dynamic forecasts is given by

$$\mathbf{X}^* = \begin{bmatrix} y_n & y_{n-1} & \cdots & y_{n-l} & \mathbf{g}_{n+1} \\ y_{n+1} & y_n & \cdots & y_{n+1-l} & \mathbf{g}_{n+2} \\ \vdots & \vdots & & \vdots & \vdots \\ \hat{y}_{n+p-1} & \hat{y}_{n+p-2} & \cdots & \hat{y}_{n+p-l} & \mathbf{g}_{n+p} \end{bmatrix}$$

### 18.26.4 Forecasting with conditionally heteroscedastic models

There are two components in GARCH or GARCH-M models that require forecasting: the conditional mean and the conditional variance. The forecasts of the former are given by

$$\hat{y}^*_{t+j} = \hat{\boldsymbol{\beta}}' \, {}_t\hat{\mathbf{x}}_{t+j} + \hat{\gamma} \, {}_t\hat{h}^2_{t+j}, \; j = 1, 2, \ldots, p$$

where $\hat{\boldsymbol{\beta}}$, and $\hat{\gamma}$ are ML estimators of the regression coefficients; ${}_t\hat{\mathbf{x}}_{t+j}$ is the $j$-step ahead forecast of $\mathbf{x}_t$; and ${}_t\hat{h}^2_{t+j}$ is the $j$-step ahead forecast of the conditional variance, namely $E(u^2_{t+j} \mid \Omega_t)$, $j = 1, 2, \ldots, p$. The computation of ${}_t\hat{\mathbf{x}}_{t+j}$ is carried out along the lines set out in Section 18.26.2, and depends on whether $\mathbf{x}_t$ contains lagged values of the dependent variable or not.

The computation of ${}_t\hat{h}^2_{t+j}$ varies depending on the conditional heteroscedasticity model under consideration. For the GARCH specification defined by (18.132), the one-step ahead forecast of the conditional volatility is given by

$${}_t\hat{h}^2_{t+1} = \hat{\alpha}_0 + \sum_{i=1}^{q} \hat{\alpha}_i \hat{u}^2_{t+1-i} + \sum_{i=1}^{p} \hat{\phi}_i \hat{h}^2_{t+1-i} + \hat{\boldsymbol{\delta}}' \, {}_t\hat{\mathbf{w}}_{t+1}$$

where ${}_t\hat{\mathbf{w}}_{t+1}$ is the one-step ahead predictor of $\mathbf{w}_t$,

$$\hat{u}_{t-i} = y_{t-i} - \hat{\boldsymbol{\beta}}' \mathbf{x}_{t-i} - \gamma \hat{h}^2_{t-i}, \; i = 0, 1, 2, \ldots \tag{18.222}$$

and

$$\hat{h}^2_{t-j} = \hat{\alpha}_0 + \sum_{i=1}^{q} \hat{\alpha}_i \hat{u}^2_{t-j-i} + \sum_{i=1}^{p} \hat{\phi}_i \hat{h}^2_{t-j-i} + \hat{\boldsymbol{\delta}}' \mathbf{w}_{t-j}, \text{ for } j = 0, 1, 2, \ldots$$

with the unobserved initial values of $\hat{h}^2$ set equal to the estimate of the unconditional variance of $u_t$. Similarly, two- and three-step ahead forecasts are given by

$${}_t\hat{h}^2_{t+2} = \hat{\alpha}_0 + (\hat{\alpha}_1 + \hat{\phi}_1) \, {}_t\hat{h}^2_{t+1} + \sum_{i=2}^{q} \hat{\alpha}_i \hat{u}^2_{t+2-i} + \sum_{i=2}^{p} \hat{\phi}_i \hat{h}^2_{t+2-i} + \hat{\boldsymbol{\delta}}' \, {}_t\hat{\mathbf{w}}_{t+2}$$

$${}_t\hat{h}^2_{t+3} = \hat{\alpha}_0 + (\hat{\alpha}_1 + \hat{\phi}_1) \, {}_t\hat{h}^2_{t+2} + (\hat{\alpha}_2 + \hat{\phi}_2) \, {}_t\hat{h}^2_{t+1} + \sum_{i=3}^{q} \hat{\alpha}_i \hat{u}^2_{t+3-i} + \sum_{i=3}^{p} \hat{\phi}_i \hat{h}^2_{t+3-i} + \hat{\boldsymbol{\delta}}' \, {}_t\hat{\mathbf{w}}_{t+3}$$

and so on.

For the EGARCH model defined by (18.138), the one-step ahead forecast of conditional volatility is given by

$$\widehat{\log {}_t h^2_{t+1}} = \hat{\alpha}_0 + \sum_{i=1}^{p} \hat{\phi}_i \log \hat{h}^2_{t+1-i} + \hat{\boldsymbol{\delta}}' \, {}_t\hat{\mathbf{w}}_{t+1} \tag{18.223}$$

where

$$\log \hat{h}^2_{t-j} = \hat{\alpha}_0 + \sum_{i=1}^{q} \hat{\alpha}_i \left( \frac{\hat{u}_{t-i-j}}{\hat{h}_{t-i-j}} \right) + \sum_{i=1}^{q} \hat{\alpha}^*_i \left( \left| \frac{\hat{u}_{t-i-j}}{\hat{h}_{t-i-j}} \right| - \hat{\mu} \right)$$
$$+ \sum_{i=1}^{p} \hat{\phi}_i \log \hat{h}^2_{t-j-i} + \hat{\boldsymbol{\delta}}' \mathbf{w}_{t-j}, \text{ for } j = 0, 1, 2, \ldots$$

and $\hat{u}_t$ is already defined by (18.222). For higher-step ahead forecasts, we have[29]

$$\widehat{\log {}_t h^2_{t+2}} = \hat{\alpha}_0 + \hat{\phi}_1 \widehat{\log {}_t h^2_{t+1}} + \sum_{i=2}^{p} \hat{\phi}_i \log \hat{h}^2_{t+2-i} + \hat{\boldsymbol{\delta}}' \, {}_t\hat{\mathbf{w}}_{t+2}$$

$$\widehat{\log {}_t h^2_{t+3}} = \hat{\alpha}_0 + \hat{\phi}_1 \widehat{\log {}_t h^2_{t+2}} + \hat{\phi}_2 \widehat{\log {}_t h^2_{t+1}} + \sum_{i=3}^{p} \hat{\phi}_i \log \hat{h}^2_{t+3-i} + \hat{\boldsymbol{\delta}}' \, {}_t\hat{\mathbf{w}}_{t+3}$$

and so on.

For the absolute GARCH model defined by (18.142), we have

$${}_t\hat{h}_{t+1} = \hat{\alpha}_0 + \sum_{i=1}^{q} \hat{\alpha}_i |\hat{u}_{t+1-i}| + \sum_{i=1}^{p} \hat{\phi}_i \hat{h}_{t+1-i} + \hat{\boldsymbol{\delta}}' \, {}_t\hat{\mathbf{w}}_{t+1}$$

where

$$\hat{h}_{t-j} = \hat{\alpha}_0 + \sum_{i=1}^{q} \hat{\alpha}_i |\hat{u}_{t-j-i}| + \sum_{i=1}^{p} \hat{\phi}_i \hat{h}_{t-j-i} + \hat{\boldsymbol{\delta}}' \mathbf{w}'_{t-j}{}' \text{ for } j = 0, 1, 2, \ldots$$

and $\hat{u}_{t-j}$, $j = 0, 1, 2, \ldots$ are defined by (18.222). For higher-step ahead forecasts we have[30]

$${}_t\hat{h}_{t+2} = \hat{\alpha}_0 + (\hat{\alpha}_1 + \hat{\phi}_1) \, {}_t\hat{h}_{t+1} + \sum_{i=2}^{q} \hat{\alpha}_i |\hat{u}_{t+1-i}| + \sum_{i=2}^{p} \hat{\phi}_i \hat{h}_{t+1-i} + \hat{\boldsymbol{\delta}}' \, {}_t\hat{\mathbf{w}}_{t+2}$$

$${}_t\hat{h}_{t+3} = \hat{\alpha}_0 + (\hat{\alpha}_1 + \hat{\phi}_1) \, {}_t\hat{h}_{t+2} + (\hat{\alpha}_2 + \hat{\phi}_2) \, {}_t\hat{h}_{t+1} + \sum_{i=3}^{q} \hat{\alpha}_i |\hat{u}_{t+1-i}|$$
$$+ \sum_{i=3}^{p} \hat{\phi}_i \hat{h}_{t+1-i} + \hat{\boldsymbol{\delta}}' \, {}_t\hat{\mathbf{w}}_{t+3}$$

and so on.

[29]The volatility forecasts for more than one-step ahead are computed assuming that $\exp(\widehat{\log {}_t h^2_{t+1}})$ is approximately equal to ${}_t\hat{h}^2_{t+1}$. Exact computation of ${}_t\hat{h}^2_{t+1}$ involves computing integrals by stochastic simulation techniques. The same point also applies to volatility forecasts based on the absolute GARCH model.

[30]Here we are making use of the approximation $E(|u_{t+j}| \mid \Omega_t) \simeq {}_t h_{t+j}$.

In all the above formulae the forecasts of $\mathbf{w}_{t+j}$ are obtained recursively if $\mathbf{w}_t$ contains lagged values of $y_t$. Otherwise, actual values of $\mathbf{w}_{t+j}$ will be used. Forecasts will not be computed if future values of $\mathbf{w}_t$ are not available or cannot be computed using recursive forecasts of $y_t$.

### 18.26.5 Forecasts based on non-linear models

Dynamic forecasts are computed for the non-linear least squares and the non-linear IV options, when the non-linear equation is specified to contain lagged values of $y_t$. For example, in the case of the non-linear equation

$$y_t = f(y_{t-1}, \mathbf{g}_t, \beta) + u_t$$

dynamic forecasts are computed recursively:[31]

$$\hat{y}^*_{t+1} = f(y_t, \mathbf{g}_{t+1}, \hat{\beta})$$

and

$$\hat{y}^*_{t+j} = f(\hat{y}^*_{t+j-1}, \mathbf{g}_{t+j}, \hat{\beta}), \qquad \text{for} \qquad j = 2, 3, \ldots, p$$

### 18.26.6 Measures of forecast accuracy

The program also computes the following summary statistics for the forecast values $(\hat{y}^*_{t+j}, j = 1, 2, \ldots, p)$:

$$\text{Mean Prediction Errors} = \left(\sum_{j=1}^{p} e^*_{t+j}\right)/p \tag{18.224}$$

where

$$e^*_{t+j} = y_{t+j} - \hat{y}^*_{t+j}, \qquad j = 1, 2, \ldots, p \tag{18.225}$$

$$\begin{array}{l}\text{Sum of Squares of}\\ \text{Prediction Errors}\end{array} = \sum_{j=1}^{p} (e^*_{t+j})^2 \tag{18.226}$$

$$\begin{array}{l}\text{Root Mean Sum of}\\ \text{Squares of Prediction}\\ \text{Errors}\end{array} = \sqrt{\left(\sum_{j=1}^{p} (e^*_{t+j})^2/p\right)} \tag{18.227}$$

$$\begin{array}{l}\text{Mean Sum of Absolute}\\ \text{Prediction Errors}\end{array} = \sum_{j=1}^{p} |e^*_{t+j}|/p \tag{18.228}$$

---

[31] Notice that the dynamic forecasts in the non-linear case are not necessarily equal to the conditional expectations of $y_{t+j}$, for $j > 1$, and can therefore be viewed as a 'certainty equivalent' approximation to $E(y_{t+j}|\Omega_t)$, for $j > 1$.

In the table giving the above summary statistics for the OLS option, the program also reports the F statistics for the predictive failure, and the structural stability tests, defined by relations (18.25) and (18.27) respectively. The latter test statistic is reported only if $p > k$.

# 19

# Econometrics of Multiple-Equation Models

This chapter complements Chapter 7 and provides the technical details of the econometric methods and algorithms used in *Microfit* for the analysis of multiple time series models. It covers a number of recent developments in the areas of impulse response analysis and long-run structural modelling. The chapter starts with Section 19.1 and a review of the seemingly unrelated regression equations (SURE), originally analysed by Zellner (1962). Section 19.2 deals with estimation of SURE models subject to general linear restrictions, possibly involving cross-equation restrictions. Section 3 reviews the estimation and hypothesis testing in augmented vector autoregressive models. Impulse response analysis, and forecast error variance decomposition of unrestricted VAR models are set out in Sections 19.4 and 19.5. The remaining sections deal with the long-run structural modelling approach; reviewing the literature on testing for cointegration, identification, and maximum likelihood estimation of long-run (or cointegrating) relations; and impulse response and persistence profile analysis in cointegrating VAR models.

Recent detailed treatments of multivariate time series analysis can be found in Lütkepohl (1991) and Hamilton (1994). More general textbook accounts of SURE estimation and VAR modelling are available in Judge *et al.* (1985, Chapter 16) and Greene (1993, Chapters 16–17). The more recent developments in the areas of impulse response analysis (including generalized impulse response functions and persistence profiles) are covered in Pesaran *et al.* (1993), Lee and Pesaran (1993), Koop *et al.* (1996), and Pesaran and Shin (1996). An excellent survey of the early developments in the literature on cointegration can be found in Bannerjee *et al.* (1993) and Watson (1994). For more recent developments and further references to the literature on long-run structural modelling, see Pesaran and Shin (1995a, 1995b), Pesaran *et al.* (1996a, 1996b), and Pesaran (1997).

## 19.1 Seemingly unrelated regression equations (SURE)

Consider the following $m$ 'seemingly' separate linear regression equations:

$$\mathbf{y}_i = \mathbf{X}_i\beta_i + \mathbf{u}_i, \quad i = 1, 2,, \ldots, m \tag{19.1}$$

where $\mathbf{y}_i$ is an $n \times 1$ vector of observations on the dependent variable $y_{it}$, $i = 1, 2,, \ldots, m$; $t = 1, 2,, \ldots, n$; $\mathbf{X}_i$ is an $n \times k_i$ matrix of observations on the $k_i$ vector of regressors explaining $y_{it}$; $\beta_i$ is a $k_i \times 1$ vector of unknown coefficients; and $\mathbf{u}_i$ is an $n \times 1$ vector of disturbances or errors, for $i = 1, 2,, \ldots, m$. It is further assumed that for each $i$ the regressors, $\mathbf{X}_i$, and the disturbance, $\mathbf{u}_i$, satisfy the classical assumptions A1 to A5, set out in Section 6.1.

In econometric analysis of the system of equations in (19.1), three cases can be distinguished:

1. Contemporaneously uncorrelated disturbances, namely $E(\mathbf{u}_i\mathbf{u}_j') = \mathbf{0}$, for $i \neq j$.
2. Contemporaneously correlated disturbances, with identical regressors across all the equations, namely

   $$E(\mathbf{u}_i\mathbf{u}_j') = \sigma_{ij}\mathbf{I}_n \neq \mathbf{0}$$

   where $\mathbf{I}_n$ is an identity matrix of order $n$ and

   $$\mathbf{X}_i = \mathbf{X}_j, \text{ for all } i, j$$

3. Contemporaneously correlated disturbances, with different regressors across the equations, namely

   $$E(\mathbf{u}_i\mathbf{u}_j') = \sigma_{ij}\mathbf{I}_n \neq \mathbf{0}$$

   and

   $$\mathbf{X}_i \neq \mathbf{X}_j, \text{ at least for some } i, \text{ and } j$$

In the first case where $E(\mathbf{u}_i\mathbf{u}_j') = \mathbf{0}$, for $i \neq j$, there is nothing to be gained by considering the equations in (19.1) as a system and the application of single equation methods to the individual relations in (19.1) will be valid. There is also no efficiency gain in estimating the equations in (19.1) as a system under case (2) where $\mathbf{X}_i = \mathbf{X}_j$, for all $i$ and $j$. Once again application of single equation methods to each of the equations in the system will be valid (see Zellner 1962).

It is therefore only under case (3) where there is likely to be some efficiency gain in large samples by estimating the equations in (19.1) as a system in large samples.

### 19.1.1 Maximum likelihood estimation

In order to compute the maximum likelihood (ML) estimators of the parameters of (19.1), namely $\boldsymbol{\theta} = (\beta_1', \beta_2', \ldots, \beta_m', \sigma_{11}, \sigma_{12}, \ldots, \sigma_{1m}; \sigma_{22},$

$\sigma_{23}, \ldots, \sigma_{2m}; \ldots, \sigma_{mm})'$, it is convenient to stack the different equations in the system in the following manner:

$$\begin{pmatrix} \mathbf{y}_1 \\ \mathbf{y}_2 \\ \vdots \\ \mathbf{y}_m \end{pmatrix} = \begin{pmatrix} \mathbf{X}_1 & & & 0 \\ & \mathbf{X}_2 & & \\ & & \ddots & \\ 0 & & & \mathbf{X}_m \end{pmatrix} \begin{pmatrix} \beta_1 \\ \beta_2 \\ \vdots \\ \beta_m \end{pmatrix} + \begin{pmatrix} \mathbf{u}_1 \\ \mathbf{u}_2 \\ \vdots \\ \mathbf{u}_m \end{pmatrix} \tag{19.2}$$

or more compactly

$$\mathbf{y} = \mathbf{X}\beta + \mathbf{u} \tag{19.3}$$

where $\mathbf{y}$, $\mathbf{X}$, $\beta$, and $\mathbf{u}$ have the dimensions $mn \times 1$, $mn \times k$, $k \times 1$ and $mn \times 1$, respectively, where $k = \sum_{i=1}^{m} k_i$. Under the classical assumptions where $E(\mathbf{u}_i) = 0$, $E(\mathbf{u}_i\mathbf{u}_j') = \sigma_{ij}\mathbf{I}_n$, we have

$$E(\mathbf{uu}') = \boldsymbol{\Omega} = \boldsymbol{\Sigma} \otimes \mathbf{I}_n$$

where $\boldsymbol{\Sigma}$ is the $m \times m$ matrix of covariances with its $(i, j)$ elements equal to $\sigma_{ij}$, and $\otimes$ stands for Kronecker products.[1] More specifically, we have

$$\boldsymbol{\Omega} = \boldsymbol{\Sigma} \otimes \mathbf{I}_n = \begin{pmatrix} \sigma_{11} & \mathbf{I}_n\sigma_{12}\mathbf{I}_n & \cdots & \sigma_{1m}\mathbf{I}_n \\ \sigma_{21}\mathbf{I}_n & \sigma_{22}\mathbf{I}_n & \cdots & \sigma_{2m}\mathbf{I}_n \\ \vdots & & & \\ \sigma_{m1}\mathbf{I}_n & \sigma_{m2}\mathbf{I}_n & \cdots & \sigma_{mm}\mathbf{I}_n \end{pmatrix} \tag{19.4}$$

If we now assume that $\mathbf{u}$ has a Gaussian distribution, the log-likelihood function of the stacked system (19.3) can be written as

$$\ell(\boldsymbol{\theta}) = -\frac{nm}{2}\log(2\pi) - \frac{1}{2}\log|\Omega| - \frac{1}{2}(\mathbf{y} - \mathbf{X}\beta)'\boldsymbol{\Omega}^{-1}(\mathbf{y} - \mathbf{X}\beta)$$

Since

$$\boldsymbol{\Omega} = \boldsymbol{\Sigma} \otimes \mathbf{I}_n, \ |\boldsymbol{\Omega}| = |\boldsymbol{\Sigma} \otimes \mathbf{I}_n| = |\boldsymbol{\Sigma}|^n|\mathbf{I}_n|^m = |\boldsymbol{\Sigma}|^n$$

hence

$$\ell(\boldsymbol{\theta}) = -\frac{nm}{2}\log(2\pi) - \frac{n}{2}\log|\boldsymbol{\Sigma}| - \frac{1}{2}(\mathbf{y} - \mathbf{X}\beta)'(\boldsymbol{\Sigma}^{-1} \otimes \mathbf{I}_n)(\mathbf{y} - \mathbf{X}\beta) \tag{19.5}$$

Denoting the ML estimators by $\tilde{\theta} = (\tilde{\beta}_1', \tilde{\beta}_2', \ldots, \tilde{\beta}_m', \tilde{\sigma}_{11}, \tilde{\sigma}_{12}, \ldots)'$, it is easily seen that

$$\tilde{\sigma}_{ij} = \frac{(\mathbf{y}_i - \mathbf{X}_i\tilde{\beta}_i)'(\mathbf{y}_j - \mathbf{X}_j\tilde{\beta}_j)}{n} \tag{19.6}$$

and

$$\tilde{\beta} = (\mathbf{X}'(\tilde{\boldsymbol{\Sigma}}^{-1} \otimes \mathbf{I}_n)\mathbf{X})^{-1}\mathbf{X}'(\tilde{\boldsymbol{\Sigma}}^{-1} \otimes \mathbf{I}_n)\mathbf{y} \tag{19.7}$$

[1]For the definition of Kronecker productus, the *vec*(·) operators and the rules of their operations see, for example, Magnus and Neudecker (1988).

The computation of the ML estimators $\tilde{\beta} = (\tilde{\beta}'_1, \tilde{\beta}'_2 \cdots \tilde{\beta}'_m)'$, and $\tilde{\sigma}_{ij}$, $i,j = 1,2, \ldots, m$ are carried out in *Microfit* by iterating between (19.6) and (19.7) starting from the OLS estimators of $\beta_i$, namely $\hat{\beta}_{i,OLS} = (\mathbf{X}'_i\mathbf{X}_i)^{-1}\mathbf{X}'_i\mathbf{y}_i$. This iterative procedure is continued until the following convergence criteria are met:

$$\sum_{\ell=1}^{k_i} |\beta_{i\ell}^{(r)} - \beta_{i\ell}^{(r-1)}| < 0.00001 k_i, \quad i = 1, 2, \ldots, m \tag{19.8}$$

where $\beta_{i\ell}^{(r)}$ stands for the estimate of the $\ell$th element of $\beta_i$ at the $r$th iteration. On convergence, *Microfit* reports $\tilde{\beta}_i$, $i = 1,2, \ldots, m$ and the estimates of their covariances computed as

$$\widehat{Cov}(\tilde{\beta}) = (\mathbf{X}'(\hat{\Sigma}^{-1} \otimes \mathbf{I}_n)\mathbf{X})^{-1} \tag{19.9}$$

where $\hat{\Sigma} = (\hat{\sigma}_{ij})$ is a degrees-of-freedom adjusted version of $\widetilde{\sum}$ whose $(i, j)$ element is given by

$$\hat{\sigma}_{ij} = \frac{\tilde{\mathbf{u}}'_i\tilde{\mathbf{u}}_j}{\sqrt{(n - k_i)(n - k_j)}}, \quad i,j = 1,2, \ldots, m \tag{19.10}$$

For further details see, for example, Judge *et al.* (1985, Chapter 12).

The fitted values, residuals, and other statistics such as DW, $R^2$, $\bar{R}^2$, and the maximized log-likelihood values for each equation in the system are computed as in Section (18.5.1). The maximized value of the system log-likelihood function is given by

$$\ell(\tilde{\theta}) = -\frac{nm}{2}\log(2\pi) - \frac{n}{2}\log|\tilde{\Sigma}| \tag{19.11}$$

The system's Akaike (AIC) and Schwarz (SBC) criteria are computed as

$$\text{System AIC} = \ell(\tilde{\theta}) - k \tag{19.12}$$

$$\text{System SBC} = \ell(\tilde{\theta}) - \frac{k}{2}\log(n) \tag{19.13}$$

where $k = \sum_{i=1}^{m} k_i$.

### 19.1.2 Testing linear/non-linear restrictions

Under fairly general conditions the ML estimators, $\tilde{\beta} = (\tilde{\beta}'_1, \tilde{\beta}'_2, \ldots, \tilde{\beta}'_m)'$, are asymptotically normally distributed with mean $\beta$ and the covariance matrix given by (19.9). It is therefore possible to test linear or non-linear restrictions on the elements of $\beta$ using the Wald procedure. (see Section 18.25). Notice that the restrictions to be tested could involve coefficients from different equations (i.e. they could be cross-equation restrictions). To be more precise, suppose you are interested in testing the following $r \times 1$ general non-linear restrictions on $\beta$:

$$H_0 : \mathbf{h}(\beta) = \mathbf{0}$$
$$H_1 : \mathbf{h}(\beta) \neq \mathbf{0}$$

where $\mathbf{h}(\beta)$ is a known $r \times 1$ vector function of $\beta$, with continuous partial derivatives. The Wald statistic for testing $\mathbf{h}(\beta) = 0$ against $\mathbf{h}(\beta) \neq \mathbf{0}$ is given by

$$W = \mathbf{h}(\tilde{\beta})'[\mathbf{H}(\tilde{\beta})\widehat{Cov}(\tilde{\beta})\mathbf{H}'(\tilde{\beta})]^{-1}\mathbf{h}(\tilde{\beta}) \tag{19.14}$$

where $\mathbf{H}(\tilde{\beta})$ is given by $\partial\mathbf{h}(\beta)/\partial\beta'$ at $\beta = \tilde{\beta}$. It is assumed that $Rank(\mathbf{H}(\beta)) = r$.

### 19.1.3 LR statistic for testing whether $\Sigma$ is diagonal

Suppose it is of interest to test the hypothesis

$$\begin{aligned} H_0 : \sigma_{12} = \quad & \sigma_{13} = \cdots = \sigma_{1m} = 0 \\ & \sigma_{23} = \cdots = \sigma_{2m} = 0 \\ & \ddots \\ & \sigma_{mm} = 0 \end{aligned}$$

against the alternative that one or more of the off-diagonal elements of $\Sigma$ are non-zero. The relevant log-likelihood ratio statistic for testing this hypothesis can be computed in *Microfit* as

$$LR = 2\left[\ell(\tilde{\theta}) - \sum_{i=1}^{m} \ell_i(\hat{\theta}_{i,OLS})\right] \tag{19.15}$$

where $\ell(\tilde{\theta})$ is given by (19.11) and $\ell_i(\hat{\theta}_{i,OLS})$ is the log-likelihood function of the $i$th equation computed at the OLS estimators. Equivalently, we have

$$LR = T\left[\sum_{i=1}^{m} \log\tilde{\sigma}_i^2 - \log|\tilde{\Sigma}|\right] \tag{19.16}$$

where

$$\tilde{\sigma}_{ii} = n^{-1}(\mathbf{y}_i - \mathbf{X}_i\hat{\beta}_{i,OLS})'(\mathbf{y}_i - \mathbf{X}_i\hat{\beta}_{i,OLS})$$

Under $H_0$, LR is asymptotically distributed as a $\chi^2$ with $m(m-1)/2$ degrees of freedom.[2] See Lesson 17.2 for an implementation of this test.

[2]An alternative LM test statistic is proposed by Breusch and Pagan (1980), which is given by

$$LM = n\sum_{i=2}^{m}\sum_{j=1}^{i-1} s_{ij}^2$$

where $s_{ij}^2 = \tilde{\sigma}_{ij,OLS}/\{\tilde{\sigma}_{ii,OLS}\tilde{\sigma}_{jj,OLS}\}^{\frac{1}{2}}$. This statistic is also asymptotically distributed as a $\chi^2$ with $m(m-1)/2$ degrees of freedom.

## 19.2 System estimation subject to linear restrictions

Consider now the problem of estimating the system of equations (19.1) where the coefficient vectors $\boldsymbol{\beta}_i$, $i = 1, 2, \ldots, m$ are subject to the following $r \times 1$ linear restrictions:

$$\mathbf{R}\boldsymbol{\beta} = \mathbf{b} \tag{19.17}$$

where $\mathbf{R}$ and $\mathbf{b}$ are the $r \times k$ matrix and the $r \times 1$ vector of known constants, and as in Section 19.1, $\boldsymbol{\beta} = (\boldsymbol{\beta}_1', \boldsymbol{\beta}_2', \ldots, \boldsymbol{\beta}_m')'$ is a $k \times 1$ vector of unknown coefficients, $k = \sum_{i=1}^{m} k_i$.

In what follows we distinguish between the cases where the restrictions are applicable to the coefficients, $\boldsymbol{\beta}_i$, in each equation separately, and where there are cross-equation restrictions. In the former case the matrix $\mathbf{R}$ is block diagonal, namely

$$\mathbf{R} = \begin{pmatrix} \mathbf{R}_1 & & & \mathbf{0} \\ & \mathbf{R}_2 & & \\ & & \ddots & \\ \mathbf{0} & & & \mathbf{R}_m \end{pmatrix} \tag{19.18}$$

where $\mathbf{R}_i$ is the $r_i \times k_i$ matrix of known constants applicable to $\boldsymbol{\beta}_i$ only. In the more general case where the restrictions involve coefficients from different equations, $\mathbf{R}$ is not block-diagonal.

The computations of the ML estimators of $\boldsymbol{\beta}$ in (19.1), subject to the restrictions in (19.17), can be carried out in the following manner. Initially, suppose $\boldsymbol{\Sigma}$ is known and define the $mn \times mn$ matrix, $\mathbf{P}$, such that

$$\mathbf{P}(\boldsymbol{\Sigma} \otimes \mathbf{I}_n)\mathbf{P}' = \mathbf{I}_{mn} \tag{19.19}$$

where $\mathbf{I}_{mn}$ is an identity matrix of order $mn$. Such a matrix always exists since $\boldsymbol{\Sigma}$ is a symmetric positive definite matrix. Then compute the transformations:

$$\mathbf{X}_* = \mathbf{P}\mathbf{X}, \quad \mathbf{y}_* = \mathbf{P}\mathbf{y} \tag{19.20}$$

Now using familiar results from the estimation of linear regression models subject to linear restrictions (see, for example, Amemiya 1985, Section 1.4) we have:

$$\tilde{\boldsymbol{\beta}} = (\mathbf{X}_*'\mathbf{X}_*)^{-1}\mathbf{X}_*'\mathbf{y}_* - (\mathbf{X}_*'\mathbf{X}_*)^{-1}\mathbf{R}'\tilde{\mathbf{q}} \tag{19.21}$$

where

$$\tilde{\mathbf{q}} = (\mathbf{R}(\mathbf{X}_*'\mathbf{X}_*)^{-1}\mathbf{R}')\{\mathbf{R}(\mathbf{X}_*'\mathbf{X}_*)^{-1}\mathbf{X}_*'\mathbf{y}_* - \mathbf{b}\} \tag{19.22}$$

In practice, since $\boldsymbol{\Sigma}$ is not known we need to estimate it. Starting with unrestricted SURE or other initial estimates of $\boldsymbol{\beta}_i$ (say $\hat{\boldsymbol{\beta}}_{i,OLS}$), an initial estimate of $\boldsymbol{\Sigma} = (\sigma_{ij})$ can be obtained. Using the OLS estimates of $\boldsymbol{\beta}_i$, the initial estimates of $\sigma_{ij}$ are given by

$$\hat{\sigma}_{ij,OLS} = \frac{\hat{\mathbf{u}}'_{i,OLS}\hat{\mathbf{u}}_{j,OLS}}{n}, \quad i,j = 1,2, \ldots, m$$

where

$$\hat{\mathbf{u}}_{i,OLS} = \mathbf{y}_i - \mathbf{X}_i\hat{\beta}_{i,OLS}, \quad i,j = 1,2, \ldots, m$$

With the help of these initial estimates, constrained estimates of $\beta_i$ can be computed using (19.21). Starting from these new estimates of $\beta_i$, another set of estimates for $\sigma_{ij}$ can then be computed. This process can be repeated until the convergence criteria in (19.8) are met.

The covariance matrix of $\tilde{\beta}$ in this case is given by

$$\widehat{\text{Cov}}(\tilde{\beta}) = (\hat{\mathbf{X}}'_*\hat{\mathbf{X}}_*)^{-1} - (\hat{\mathbf{X}}'_*\hat{\mathbf{X}}_*)^{-1}\mathbf{R}'(\mathbf{R}(\hat{\mathbf{X}}'_*\hat{\mathbf{X}}_*)^{-1}\mathbf{R}')^{-1}\mathbf{R}(\hat{\mathbf{X}}'_*\hat{\mathbf{X}}_*)^{-1}$$

Notice that

$$\hat{\mathbf{X}}'_*\hat{\mathbf{X}}_* = \mathbf{X}'\hat{\mathbf{P}}'\hat{\mathbf{P}}\mathbf{X} = \mathbf{X}'(\hat{\Sigma}^{-1} \otimes \mathbf{I}_n)\mathbf{X}$$

The $(i, j)$ element of $\hat{\Sigma}$ is computed differently depending on whether matrix $\mathbf{R}$ in (19.18) is block diagonal or not. When $\mathbf{R}$ is block diagonal, $\sigma_{ij}$ is estimated by

$$\hat{\sigma}_{ij} = \frac{\mathbf{u}'_i\mathbf{u}_j}{\sqrt{(n-s_i)(n-s_j)}}, \qquad i,j = 1,2, \ldots, m \tag{19.23}$$

where $s_i = k_i - Rank(\mathbf{R}_i) = k_i - r_i$. When $\mathbf{R}$ is not block diagonal $\sigma_{ij}$ is estimated by

$$\tilde{\sigma}_{ij} = \frac{\mathbf{u}'_i\mathbf{u}_j}{n}, \qquad i,j = 1,2, \ldots, m \tag{19.24}$$

The divisor in (19.23) ensures that the results from the unrestricted and the restricted SURE options in *Microfit* are compatible when there are no cross-equation restrictions. In the case where $\mathbf{R}$ is not block diagonal, an appropriate degrees of freedom correction is not available, and hence the ML estimator of $\sigma_{ij}$ is used in the computation of the covariance matrix of the ML estimators of $\beta$.

The maximum value of the log-likelihood function is computed as in (19.11), and the system Akaike (AIC) and Schwarz (SBC) criteria are computed as

$$AIC = \ell(\tilde{\theta}) - (k - r)$$

and

$$SBC = \ell(\tilde{\theta}) - \frac{1}{2}(k - r)\log n$$

where $k = \sum_{i=1}^{m} k_i$ and $r = Rank(\mathbf{R})$. When $\mathbf{R}$ is block diagonal, $r = \sum_{i=1}^{m} r_i$.

Wald statistics for testing linear and/or non-linear restrictions on the elements of $\beta$ can also be computed after the restricted SURE option. The relevant formula is given by (19.14).

## 19.3 Augmented vector autoregressive models

*Microfit* allows estimation of the following augmented vector autoregressive model:[3]

$$\mathbf{z}_t = \mathbf{a}_0 + \mathbf{a}_1 t + \sum_{i=1}^{p} \mathbf{\Phi}_i \mathbf{z}_{t-i} + \mathbf{\Psi} \mathbf{w}_t + \mathbf{u}_t, \qquad t = 1,2, \ldots, n \tag{19.25}$$
$$= \mathbf{A}'\mathbf{g}_t + \mathbf{u}_t$$

where $\mathbf{z}_t$ is an $m \times 1$ vector of jointly determined dependent variables and $\mathbf{w}_t$ is a $q \times 1$ vector of deterministic or exogenous variables. For example, $\mathbf{w}_t$ could include seasonal dummies or exogenously given variables such as oil prices, foreign interest rates, and prices in the case of small open economies. The $m \times 1$ vector of disturbances satisfies the following assumptions:

**B1**: $E(\mathbf{u}_t) = \mathbf{0}$
**B2**: $E(\mathbf{u}_t \mathbf{u}_t') = \mathbf{\Sigma}$ for all $t$
**B3**: $E(\mathbf{u}_t \mathbf{u}_{t'}') = \mathbf{0}$ for all $t \neq t'$

where $\mathbf{\Sigma}$ is an $m \times m$ positive-definite matrix.

**B4**: $E(\mathbf{u}_t | \mathbf{w}_t) = 0$
**B5**: The augmented VAR(p) model, (19.25), is stable; that is, all the roots of the determinantal equation

$$|\mathbf{I}_m - \mathbf{\Phi}_1 \lambda - \mathbf{\Phi}_2 \lambda^2 - \cdots - \mathbf{\Phi}_p \lambda^p| = 0, \tag{19.26}$$

fall outside the unit circle.[4]

**B6**: The $m \times 1$ vector of disturbances have a multivariate normal distribution
**B7**: The observations $\mathbf{g}_t = (1, t, \mathbf{z}_{t-1}, \mathbf{z}_{t-2}, \ldots, \mathbf{z}_{t-p}, \mathbf{w}_t)$, for $t = 1,2, \ldots, n$ are not perfectly collinear.

Since the system of equations (19.25) is in the form of a SURE model with all the equations having the same set of regressors, $\mathbf{g}_t = (1, t, \mathbf{z}_{t-1}, \mathbf{z}_{t-2}, \ldots, \mathbf{z}_{t-p}, \mathbf{w}_t)$, in common, it follows that when $\mathbf{u}_t$s are Gaussian the ML estimators of the unknown coefficients can be computed by OLS regressions of $\mathbf{z}_t$ on $\mathbf{g}_t$. Writing (19.25) in matrix notation we have

$$\underset{n \times m}{\mathbf{Z}} = \underset{n \times s}{\mathbf{G}} \; \underset{s \times m}{\mathbf{A}} + \underset{n \times m}{\mathbf{U}} \tag{19.27}$$

where $s = mp + q + 2$,

[3]In the analysis of trend-stationary VAR models, without any loss of generality, the intercept and the trend terms, $\iota_n$ and $t_n$ can be subsumed in $\mathbf{w}_t$. However, as it should become clear later, an explicit modelling of intercepts and trends is required in the case of cointegrating VAR models. See section 19.6.

[4]The case where one or more roots of (19.26) fall on the unit circle will be discussed in Section 19.6.

$$\underset{n \times m}{\mathbf{Z}} = (\mathbf{z}_1, \mathbf{z}_2, \ldots \mathbf{z}_n)'$$

$$\underset{m \times s}{\mathbf{A}'} = (\mathbf{a}_0, \mathbf{a}_1, \mathbf{\Phi}_1, \mathbf{\Phi}_2, \ldots, \mathbf{\Phi}_p, \mathbf{\Psi})$$

$$\underset{n \times (mp+q+2)}{\mathbf{G}} = (\iota_n, \mathbf{t}_n, \mathbf{Z}_{-1}, \mathbf{Z}_{-2}, \ldots, \mathbf{Z}_{-p}, \mathbf{W})$$

where $\iota_n$ and $\mathbf{t}_n$ are the $n$-dimensional vectors $(1, 1, \ldots, 1)'$ and $(1, 2, \ldots, n)'$, respectively, and

$$\underset{n \times q}{\mathbf{W}} = (\mathbf{w}_1, \mathbf{w}_2, \ldots, \mathbf{w}_n)'$$

The ML estimators of $\mathbf{A}$ and $\mathbf{\Sigma}$ are given by

$$\hat{\mathbf{A}} = (\mathbf{G}'\mathbf{G})^{-1}\mathbf{G}'\mathbf{Z} \tag{19.28}$$

and

$$\tilde{\mathbf{\Sigma}} = n^{-1}(\mathbf{Z} - \mathbf{G}\hat{\mathbf{A}})'(\mathbf{Z} - \mathbf{G}\hat{\mathbf{A}}) \tag{19.29}$$

The maximized value of the system's log-likelihood function is given by

$$\ell(\hat{\mathbf{A}}, \tilde{\mathbf{\Sigma}}) = -\frac{nm}{2}(1 + \log 2\pi) - \frac{n}{2}\log|\tilde{\mathbf{\Sigma}}| \tag{19.30}$$

The covariance matrix of the coefficients of the individual equations in the VAR model are computed using the standard least squares formula given in Section 18.5.1, making the usual degrees of freedom corrections; namely $\mathbf{\Sigma}$ is estimated by

$$\hat{\mathbf{\Sigma}} = (n - s)^{-1}(\mathbf{Z} - \mathbf{G}\hat{\mathbf{A}})'(\mathbf{Z} - \mathbf{G}\hat{\mathbf{A}}) \tag{19.31}$$

The individual equation log-likelihood function, $\mathrm{R}^2$, $\bar{\mathrm{R}}^2$, and other summary and diagnostic statistics for individual equations are also computed using the formulae in Section 18.5.1.

### 19.3.1 VAR order selection

The order of the augmented VAR model (19.25), $p$, can be selected either with the help of model selection criteria, such as the Akaike information criterion (AIC) or the Schwarz Bayesian criterion (SBC), or by means of a sequence of log-likelihood ratio tests. The values of the AIC and SBC for model (19.25) are given by

$$AIC_p = \frac{-nm}{2}(1 + \log 2\pi) - \frac{n}{2}\log|\tilde{\mathbf{\Sigma}}_p| - ms \tag{19.32}$$

and

$$SBC_p = \frac{-nm}{2}(1 + \log 2\pi) - \frac{n}{2}\log|\tilde{\mathbf{\Sigma}}_p| - \frac{ms}{2}\log(n) \tag{19.33}$$

where $s = mp + q + 2$, and $\tilde{\mathbf{\Sigma}}_p$ is defined by (19.29). *Microfit* reports $AIC_p$

and $SBC_p$ for values of $p = 0,1,2, \ldots, P$, where $P$ is the maximum order of the $VAR$ model chosen by the user. The same augmenting set of variables, $\boldsymbol{\iota}_n$, $\mathbf{t}_n$, and $\mathbf{w}_t$ (if any) are used in the computations as the order of VAR is changed.

The log-likelihood ratio statistic for testing the hypothesis that the order of the VAR is $p$ against the alternative that it is $P(P > p)$ are given by

$$LR_{P,p} = n(\log|\tilde{\Sigma}_p| - \log|\tilde{\Sigma}_P|) \tag{19.34}$$

for $p = 0,1,2, \ldots, P-1$, where $P$ is the maximum order for the VAR model selected by the user; $\tilde{\Sigma}_p$ is defined by (19.29); and $\tilde{\Sigma}_0$ refers to the ML estimator of the system covariance matrix in the regression of $\mathbf{z}_t$ on $\boldsymbol{\iota}_n$, $\mathbf{t}_n$, and $\mathbf{w}_t$.

Under the null hypothesis, the LR statistic in (19.34) is asymptotically distributed as a chi-squared variate with $m^2(P-p)$ degrees of freedom.

In small samples, the use of the LR statistic, (19.34), tends to result in over-rejection of the null hypothesis. In an attempt to take some account of this small sample problem, in practice the following degrees of freedom adjusted LR statistics are also computed:

$$LR^*_{P,p} = (n - q - 2 - mP)(\log|\tilde{\Sigma}_p| - \log|\tilde{\Sigma}_P|) \tag{19.35}$$

for $p = 0, 1, 2 \cdots, \mathrm{P} - 1$. These adjusted LR statistics have the same asymptotic distribution as the unadjusted statistics given by (19.34).

## 19.3.2 Testing the deletion of deterministic/exogenous variables

*Microfit* computes log-likelihood ratio statistics for testing the deletion of $\boldsymbol{\iota}_n$, $\mathbf{t}_n$, and $\mathbf{w}_t$ or a subset of these variables from the VAR(p) model (19.25). For notational convenience from here onwards until notice to the contrary we shall be subsuming the intercept and the trend terms, $\boldsymbol{\iota}_n$ and $\mathbf{t}_n$ under $\mathbf{w}_t$. Let

$$\underset{q\times 1}{\mathbf{w}_t} = \begin{pmatrix} \mathbf{w}_{1t}, & q_1 \times 1 \\ \mathbf{w}_{2t}, & q_2 \times 1 \end{pmatrix} \quad \text{and} \quad \underset{m\times q}{\boldsymbol{\Psi}} = \begin{pmatrix} \underset{m\times q_1}{\boldsymbol{\Psi}_1,} & \underset{m\times q_2}{\boldsymbol{\Psi}_2} \end{pmatrix} \tag{19.36}$$

where $q = q_1 + q_2$. The log-likelihood ratio statistic for testing the null hypothesis

$$H_0 : \boldsymbol{\Psi}_1 = \mathbf{0}, \quad \text{against} \quad H_1 : \boldsymbol{\Psi}_1 \neq \mathbf{0}$$

is computed as

$$LR(\boldsymbol{\Psi}_1 = \mathbf{0}) = 2\{LL_U - LL(\boldsymbol{\Psi}_1 = \mathbf{0})\} \tag{19.37}$$

where $LL_U$ is the unrestricted maximized value of the log-likelihood function given by (19.30), and $LL(\boldsymbol{\Psi}_1 = \mathbf{0})$ is the maximized value of the log-likelihood function obtained under $\boldsymbol{\Psi}_1 = \mathbf{0}$. Asymptotically $LR(\boldsymbol{\Psi}_1 = \mathbf{0})$ is distributed as a chi-squared variate with $mq_1$ degrees of freedom.

### 19.3.3 Testing for block Granger non-causality

Let $\mathbf{z}_t = (\mathbf{z}'_{1t}, \mathbf{z}'_{2t})'$, where $\mathbf{z}_{1t}$ and $\mathbf{z}_{2t}$ are $m_1 \times 1$ and $m_2 \times 1$, $(m_1 + m_2 = m)$ variables, and partition the system of equations (19.25), or equivalently, (19.27), into the two sub-systems:

$$\mathbf{Z}_1 = \mathbf{Y}_1\mathbf{A}_{11} + \mathbf{Y}_2\mathbf{A}_{12} + \mathbf{W}\mathbf{A}_{13} + \mathbf{U}_1 \tag{19.38}$$

$$\mathbf{Z}_2 = \mathbf{Y}_1\mathbf{A}_{21} + \mathbf{Y}_2\mathbf{A}_{22} + \mathbf{W}\mathbf{A}_{23} + \mathbf{U}_2 \tag{19.39}$$

where $\mathbf{Z}_1$ and $\mathbf{Z}_2$ are $n \times m_1$ and $n \times m_2$ matrices of observations on $\mathbf{z}_{1t}$ and $\mathbf{z}_{2t}$, respectively; $\mathbf{Y}_1$ and $\mathbf{Y}_2$ are $n \times pm_1$ and $n \times pm_2$ matrices of observations on the $p$ lagged values of $\mathbf{z}_{1,t-\ell}$ and $\mathbf{z}_{2,t-\ell}$ for $t = 1, 2, \ldots, n$, $\ell = 1, 2, \ldots, p$, respectively. The hypothesis that '$\mathbf{z}_{2t}$ do not Granger cause $\mathbf{z}_{1t}$' is defined by the $m_1 m_2 p$ restrictions $\mathbf{A}_{12} = \mathbf{0}$.

The log-likelihood ratio statistic for the test of these restrictions is computed as

$$LR_G(\mathbf{A}_{12} = \mathbf{0}) = 2(\log|\tilde{\boldsymbol{\Sigma}}_R| - \log|\tilde{\boldsymbol{\Sigma}}|)$$

where $\tilde{\boldsymbol{\Sigma}}$ is ML estimator of $\boldsymbol{\Sigma}$ for the unrestricted (full) system (19.29), and $\tilde{\boldsymbol{\Sigma}}_R$ is the ML estimator of $\boldsymbol{\Sigma}$ when the restrictions $\mathbf{A}_{12} = \mathbf{0}$ are imposed. Under the null hypothesis that $\mathbf{A}_{12} = \mathbf{0}$, $LR_G$ is asymptotically distributed as a chi-squared variate with $m_1 m_2 p$ degrees of freedom.

Since under $\mathbf{A}_{12} = \mathbf{0}$, the system of equations (19.38) and (19.39) are block recursive, $\tilde{\boldsymbol{\Sigma}}_R$ can be computed in the following manner:

1. Run OLS regressions of $\mathbf{Z}_1$ on $\mathbf{Y}_1$ and $\mathbf{W}$, and compute the $n \times m_1$ matrix of residuals, $\hat{\mathbf{U}}_1$
2. Run the OLS regressions

$$\mathbf{Z}_2 = \mathbf{Y}_1\mathbf{A}^*_{21} + \mathbf{Y}_2\mathbf{A}^*_{22} + \mathbf{W}\mathbf{A}^*_{23} + \hat{\mathbf{U}}_1\mathbf{A}^*_{24} + \mathbf{V}_2 \tag{19.40}$$

and compute the $n \times m_2$ matrix of residuals

$$\hat{\mathbf{U}}_2 = \mathbf{Z}_2 - \mathbf{Y}_1\hat{\mathbf{A}}^*_{21} - \mathbf{Y}_2\hat{\mathbf{A}}^*_{22} - \mathbf{W}\hat{\mathbf{A}}^*_{23}$$

where $\hat{\mathbf{A}}^*_{21}$, $\hat{\mathbf{A}}^*_{22}$ and $\hat{\mathbf{A}}^*_{23}$ are the OLS estimators of $\mathbf{A}^*_{21}$, $\mathbf{A}^*_{22}$, and $\mathbf{A}^*_{23}$, in (19.40). Define

$$\hat{\mathbf{U}} = (\hat{\mathbf{U}}_1 : \hat{\mathbf{U}}_2)$$

Then

$$\tilde{\boldsymbol{\Sigma}}_R = n^{-1}(\hat{\mathbf{U}}'\hat{\mathbf{U}}) \tag{19.41}$$

## 19.4 Impulse response analysis

The impulse response function measures the time profile of the effect of shocks on the future states of a dynamical system. In the case of the VAR(p) model (19.25), two different impulse response functions can be computed using *Microfit*:

1. The orthogonalized impulse response (IR) function advanced by Sims (1980, 1981).
2. The Generalized IR function recently proposed by Koop *et al.* (1996) and Pesaran and Shin (1997).

Both impulse response functions work with the $m \times m$ coefficient matrices, $\mathbf{A}_i$, in the infinite moving average representation of (19.25)[5]

$$\mathbf{z}_t = \sum_{j=0}^{\infty} \mathbf{A}_j \mathbf{u}_{t-j} + \sum_{j=0}^{\infty} \mathbf{B}_j \mathbf{w}_{t-j} \tag{19.42}$$

where the matrices, $\mathbf{A}_j$, are computed using the recursive relations

$$\mathbf{A}_j = \mathbf{\Phi}_1 \mathbf{A}_{j-1} + \mathbf{\Phi}_2 \mathbf{A}_{j-2} + \ \ldots\ + \mathbf{\Phi}_p \mathbf{A}_{j-p}, \quad j = 1, 2, \ldots \tag{19.43}$$

with $\mathbf{A}_0 = \mathbf{I}_m$, and $\mathbf{A}_j = \mathbf{0}$, for $j < 0$, and $\mathbf{B}_j = \mathbf{A}_j \mathbf{\Psi}$, for $j = 1,2, \ldots$

## 19.4.1 Orthogonalized impulse responses

Sims' approach employs the following Cholesky decomposition of $\mathbf{\Sigma}$ (i.e. the covariance matrix of the shocks, $\mathbf{u}_t$):

$$\mathbf{\Sigma} = \mathbf{T}\mathbf{T}' \tag{19.44}$$

where $\mathbf{T}$ is a lower triangular matrix. Sims then rewrites the moving average representation (19.42) as

$$\begin{aligned} \mathbf{z}_t &= \sum_{j=0}^{\infty} (\mathbf{A}_j \mathbf{T})(\mathbf{T}^{-1} \mathbf{u}_{t-j}) + \sum_{j=0}^{\infty} \mathbf{B}_j \mathbf{w}_{t-j} \\ &= \sum_{j=0}^{\infty} \mathbf{A}_j^* \epsilon_{t-j} + \sum_{j=0}^{\infty} \mathbf{B}_j \mathbf{w}_{t-j} \end{aligned} \tag{19.45}$$

where

$$\mathbf{A}_j^* = \mathbf{A}_j \mathbf{T}, \text{ and } \ \epsilon_t = \mathbf{T}^{-1} \mathbf{u}_t$$

It is now easily seen that

$$E(\epsilon_t \epsilon_t') = \mathbf{T}^{-1} E(\mathbf{u}_t \mathbf{u}_t') \mathbf{T}'^{-1} = \mathbf{T}^{-1}\ \mathbf{\Sigma} \mathbf{T}'^{-1} = \mathbf{I}_m,$$

and the new errors, $\epsilon_t$, obtained using the transformation matrix, $\mathbf{T}$, are now contemporaneously uncorrelated and have unit standard errors. In other words, the shocks $\epsilon_t = (\epsilon_{1t}, \epsilon_{2t} \cdots \epsilon_{mt})'$ are orthogonal to each other.

The 'orthogonalized IR' function of a 'unit shock' (equal to one standard error) at time $t$ to the $i$th orthogonalized error, namely $\epsilon_{it}$, on the $j$th variable at time $t + N$ is given by the $j$th element of

[5]Notice that the existence of such an infinite MA representation is ensured by condition **B5.**

$$\text{Orthogonalized IR function to the } i\text{th variable (equation)} = \mathbf{A}_N^*\mathbf{e}_i = \mathbf{A}_N\mathbf{T}\mathbf{e}_i \tag{19.46}$$

where $\mathbf{e}_i$ is the $m \times 1$ selection vector,

$$\mathbf{e}_i = (0, 0, \ldots 0, \underset{\substack{\uparrow \\ i\text{th element}}}{1}, 0, \ldots 0)' \tag{19.47}$$

Or, written more compactly,

$$OI_{ij,N} = \mathbf{e}_j'\mathbf{A}_N\mathbf{T}\mathbf{e}_i, \quad i,j, = 1,2, \ldots, m \tag{19.48}$$

These orthogonalized impulse responses are not unique and in general depend on the particular ordering of the variables in the VAR. The orthogonalized responses are invariant to the ordering of the variables only if $\mathbf{\Sigma}$ is diagonal (or almost diagonal).[6] The non-uniqueness of the orthogonalized impulse responses is also related to the non-uniqueness of the matrix $\mathbf{T}$ in the Cholesky decomposition of $\mathbf{\Sigma}$ in (19.44). For more details, see Lütkepohl (1991, Section 2.3.2).

### 19.4.2 Generalized impulse responses

The main idea behind the generalized IR function is to circumvent the problem of the dependence of the orthogonalized impulse responses on the ordering of the variables in the VAR. The concept of the generalized impulse response function, advanced in Koop *et al.* (1996) was originally intended to deal with the problem of impulse response analysis in the case of non-linear dynamical systems, but can also be readily applied to multivariate time series models such as the VAR.

Generalized IR analysis deals explicitly with the three main issues that arise in impulse response analysis:

1. How was the dynamical system hit by shocks at time $t$? Was it hit by a variable-specific shock or system-wide shocks?
2. What was the state of the system at time $t-1$, before the system was hit by shock(s)? Was the trajectory of the system in an upward or in a downward phase?
3. How would one expect the system to be shocked in the future, namely over the interim period from $t+1$ to $t+N$?

In the context of the VAR model (19.25), the generalized impulse response function for a system-wide shock, $\mathbf{u}_t^0$, is defined by

$$GI_{\mathbf{z}}(N,\mathbf{u}_t^0,\Omega_{t-1}^0) = E(\mathbf{z}_{t+N}|\mathbf{u}_t = \mathbf{u}_t^0,\Omega_{t-1}^0) - E(\mathbf{z}_{t+N}|\Omega_{t-1}^0) \tag{19.49}$$

[6] Tests of the diagonality of $\Sigma$ are discussed in Section 19.1.3.

where $E(\cdot|\cdot)$ is the conditional mathematical expectation taken with respect to the VAR model (19.25), and $\Omega_{t-1}^0$ is a particular historical realization of the process at time $t-1$. In the case of the VAR model having the infinite moving-average representation (19.42), we have

$$GI_{\mathbf{z}}(N,\mathbf{u}_t^0,\Omega_{t-1}^0) = \mathbf{A}_N\mathbf{u}_t^0, \tag{19.50}$$

which is independent of the 'history' of the process. This history invariance property of the impulse response function (also shared by the traditional methods of impulse response analysis) is, however, specific to linear systems and does not carry over to non-linear dynamic models.

In practice, the choice of the vector of shocks, $\mathbf{u}_t^0$, is arbitrary; one possibility would be to consider a large number of likely shocks and then examine the empirical distribution function of $\mathbf{A}_N\mathbf{u}_t^0$ for all these shocks. In the case where $\mathbf{u}_t^0$ is drawn from the same distribution as $\mathbf{u}_t$, namely a multivariate normal with zero means and a constant covariance matrix $\mathbf{\Sigma}$, we have the analytical result that

$$GI_{\mathbf{z}}(N,\mathbf{u}_t^0,\Omega_{t-1}^0) \sim N(0,\mathbf{A}_N\mathbf{\Sigma}\mathbf{A}_N') \tag{19.51}$$

The diagonal elements of $\mathbf{A}_N\mathbf{\Sigma}\mathbf{A}_N'$, when appropriately scaled, are the 'persistence profiles' proposed in Lee and Pesaran (1993), and applied in Pesaran and Shin (1996) to analyse the speed of convergence to equilibrium in cointegrated systems (see Section 19.8.5). It is also worth noting that when the underlying VAR model is stable (i.e. condition **B5** is met), the limit of the persistence profile as $N \to \infty$ tends to the spectral density function of $\mathbf{z}_t$ (without the $\mathbf{w}_t$s) at zero frequency (apart from a multiple of $\pi$).

Consider now the effect of a variable-specific shock on the evolution of $\mathbf{z}_{t+1}, \mathbf{z}_{t+2}, \ldots, \mathbf{z}_{t+N}$, and suppose that for a given $\mathbf{w}_t$, the VAR model is perturbed by a shock of size $\delta_i = \sqrt{\sigma_{ii}}$ to its $i$th equation at time $t$. By the definition of the generalized IR function we have

$$GI_{\mathbf{z}}(N,\delta_i,\Omega_{t-1}^0) = E(\mathbf{z}_t|u_{it} = \delta_i,\Omega_{t-1}^0) - E(\mathbf{z}_t|\Omega_{t-1}^0) \tag{19.52}$$

Once again using the infinite moving-average representation (19.42), we obtain

$$GI_{\mathbf{z}}(N,\delta_i,\Omega_{t-1}^0) \sim \mathbf{A}_N E(\mathbf{u}_t|u_{it} = \delta_i) \tag{19.53}$$

which is history invariant (i.e. does not depend on $\Omega_{t-1}^0$). The computation of the conditional expectations, $E(\mathbf{u}_t|u_{it} = \delta_i)$, depends on the nature of the multivariate distribution assumed for the disturbances, $\mathbf{u}_t$. In the case where $\mathbf{u}_t \sim N(0,\mathbf{\Sigma})$, we have

$$E(\mathbf{u}_t|u_{it} = \delta_i) = \begin{pmatrix} \sigma_{1i}/\sigma_{ii} \\ \sigma_{2i}/\sigma_{ii} \\ \vdots \\ \sigma_{mi}/\sigma_{ii} \end{pmatrix} \delta_i \tag{19.54}$$

where as before $(\mathbf{\Sigma} = \sigma_{ij})$. Hence for a 'unit shock' defined by $\delta_i = \sqrt{\sigma_{ii}}$, we have

$$GI_{\mathbf{z}}(N,\delta_i = \sqrt{\sigma_{ii}},\ \Omega^0_{t-1}) = \frac{\mathbf{A}_N \boldsymbol{\Sigma} \mathbf{e}_i}{\sqrt{\sigma_{ii}}}, \quad i,j, = 1,2 \cdots m \tag{19.55}$$

where $\mathbf{e}_i$ is a selection vector given by (19.47). The generalized impulse response function of a unit shock to the $i$th equation in the VAR model (19.25) on the $j$th variable at horizon $N$ is given by the $j$th element of (19.55), or expressed more compactly as

$$GI_{ij,N} = \frac{\mathbf{e}_j' \mathbf{A}_N \boldsymbol{\Sigma} \mathbf{e}_i}{\sqrt{\sigma_{ii}}}, \quad i,j, = 1,2, \ldots, m \tag{19.56}$$

Unlike the orthogonalized impulse responses in (19.46), the generalized impulse responses in (19.55) are invariant to the ordering of the variables in the VAR. It is also interesting to note that the two impulse responses coincide only for the first variable in the VAR, or when $\boldsymbol{\Sigma}$ is a diagonal matrix. See Pesaran and Shin (1997).

## 19.5 Forecast error variance decompositions

The forecast error variance decomposition provides a decomposition of the variance of the forecast errors of the variables in the VAR at different horizons.

### 19.5.1 Orthogonalized forecast error variance decomposition

In the context of the orthogonalized moving-average representation of the VAR model given by (19.45), the forecast error variance decomposition for the $i$th variable in the VAR is given by

$$\theta_{ij,N} = \frac{\sum_{\ell=0}^{N} (\mathbf{e}_i' \mathbf{A}_\ell \mathbf{T} \mathbf{e}_j)^2}{\sum_{\ell=0}^{N} \mathbf{e}_i' \mathbf{A}_\ell \boldsymbol{\Sigma} \mathbf{A}_\ell' \mathbf{e}_i}, \quad i,j = 1,2, \ldots, m \tag{19.57}$$

where $\mathbf{T}$ is defined by the Cholesky decomposition of $\boldsymbol{\Sigma}$, (19.44); $\mathbf{e}_i$ is the selection vector defined by (19.47); and $\mathbf{A}_\ell$, $\ell = 0, 1, 2, \ldots$ are the coefficient matrices in the moving-average representation, (19.42). Notice that $\mathbf{e}_i' \mathbf{A}_\ell \boldsymbol{\Sigma} \mathbf{A}_\ell' \mathbf{e}_i$ is simply the $i$th diagonal element of the matrix $\mathbf{A}_\ell \boldsymbol{\Sigma} \mathbf{A}_\ell'$, which also enters the persistence profile analysis (see Lee and Pesaran 1993).

$\theta_{ij,N}$ measures the proportion of the $N$-step ahead forecast error variance of variable $i$, which is accounted for by the orthogonalized innovations in variable $j$. For further details, see, for example, Lütkepohl (1991, Section 2.3.3).[7] As with the orthogonalized impulse response function, the orthogonalized forecast error variance decompositions in (19.57) are not invariant to the ordering of the variables in the VAR.

[7]Notice also that $\sum_{j=1}^{m} \theta_{ij,N} = 1$.

### 19.5.2 Generalized forecast error variance decomposition

An alternative procedure to the orthogonalized forecast error variance decomposition would be to consider the proportion of the variance of the $N$-step forecast errors of $\mathbf{z}_t$ which is explained by conditioning on the non-orthogonalized shocks, $u_{it}, u_{i,t+1}, \ldots, u_{i,t+N}$, but explicitly to allow for the contemporaneous correlations between these shocks and the shocks to the other equations in the system.

Using the MA representation (19.42),[8] the forecast error of predicting $\mathbf{z}_{t+N}$ conditional on the information at time $t-1$ is given by

$$\underset{m\times 1}{\boldsymbol{\xi}_t(N)} = \sum_{\ell=0}^{N} \mathbf{A}_\ell \mathbf{u}_{t+N-\ell} \tag{19.58}$$

with the *total* forecast error covariance matrix

$$\mathrm{Cov}(\boldsymbol{\xi}_t(N)) = \sum_{\ell=0}^{N} \mathbf{A}_\ell \boldsymbol{\Sigma} \mathbf{A}'_\ell \tag{19.59}$$

Consider now the forecast error covariance matrix of predicting $\mathbf{z}_{t+N}$ conditional on the information at time $t-1$, *and* the given values of the shocks to the $i$th equation, $u_{it}, u_{i,t+1}, \ldots, u_{i,t+N}$. Using (19.42), we have[9]

$$\underset{m\times 1}{\boldsymbol{\xi}_t^{(i)}(N)} = \sum_{\ell=0}^{N} \mathbf{A}_\ell(\mathbf{u}_{t+N-\ell} - E(\mathbf{u}_{t+N-\ell}|u_{i,t+N-\ell})) \tag{19.60}$$

As in the case of the generalized impulse responses, assuming $\mathbf{u}_t \sim N(0,\boldsymbol{\Sigma})$, we have

$$E(\mathbf{u}_{t+N-\ell}|u_{i,t+N-\ell}) = (\sigma_{ii}^{-1}\boldsymbol{\Sigma}\mathbf{e}_i)u_{i,t+N-\ell} \quad \text{for} \quad \begin{matrix} \ell = 0,1,2,\ldots, N \\ i = 1,2,\ldots, m \end{matrix}$$

Substituting this result back in (19.60),

$$\boldsymbol{\xi}_t^{(i)}(N) = \sum_{\ell=0}^{N} \mathbf{A}_\ell(\mathbf{u}_{t+N-\ell} - \sigma_{ii}^{-1}\boldsymbol{\Sigma}\mathbf{e}_i u_{i,t+N-\ell})$$

and taking unconditional expectations, yields

$$\mathrm{Cov}(\boldsymbol{\xi}_t^{(i)}(N)) = \sum_{\ell=0}^{N} \mathbf{A}_\ell \boldsymbol{\Sigma} \mathbf{A}'_\ell - \sigma_{ii}^{-1}\left(\sum_{\ell=0}^{N} \mathbf{A}_\ell \boldsymbol{\Sigma} \mathbf{e}_i \mathbf{e}'_i \boldsymbol{\Sigma} \mathbf{A}'_\ell\right) \tag{19.61}$$

Therefore, using (19.59) and (19.61), it follows that the decline in the $N$-step forecast error variance of $\mathbf{z}_t$ obtained as a result of conditioning on the future shocks to the $i$th equation is given by

---

[8] We continue to assume that $\mathbf{w}_t$s are given.

[9] Notice that since $\mathbf{u}_t$s are serially uncorrelated, $E(\mathbf{u}_{t+n-\ell}|u_{it}, u_{i,t+1}, \ldots, u_{i,t+n}) = E(\mathbf{u}_{t+N-\ell}| u_{i,t+n-\ell})$, $\ell = 0,1,2,\ldots, N$.

$$\begin{aligned}\boldsymbol{\Delta}_{iN} &= \text{Cov}[\boldsymbol{\xi}_t(N)] - \text{Cov}[\boldsymbol{\xi}_t^{(i)}(N)] \\ &= \sigma_{ii}^{-1} \sum_{\ell=0}^{N} \mathbf{A}_\ell \boldsymbol{\Sigma} \mathbf{e}_i \mathbf{e}_i' \boldsymbol{\Sigma} \mathbf{A}_\ell'\end{aligned} \tag{19.62}$$

Scaling the $j$th diagonal element of $\boldsymbol{\Delta}_{iN}$, namely $\mathbf{e}_j'\boldsymbol{\Delta}_{iN}\mathbf{e}_j$, by the $N$-step ahead forecast error variance of the $i$th variable in $\mathbf{z}_t$, we have the following generalized forecast error variance decomposition:

$$\Psi_{ij,N} = \frac{\sigma_{ii}^{-1} \sum_{\ell=0}^{N} (\mathbf{e}_j' \mathbf{A}_\ell \boldsymbol{\Sigma} \mathbf{e}_i)^2}{\sum_{\ell=0}^{N} \mathbf{e}_i' \mathbf{A}_\ell \boldsymbol{\Sigma} \mathbf{A}_\ell' \mathbf{e}_i} \tag{19.63}$$

Note that the denominator of this measure is the $i$th diagonal element of the total forecast error variance formula in (19.59) and is the same as the denominator of the orthogonalized forecast error variance decomposition formula, (19.57). Also, $\theta_{ij,N} = \Psi_{ij,N}$ when $z_{it}$ is the first variable in the VAR, and/or $\boldsymbol{\Sigma}$ is diagonal. However, in general the two decompositions differ.

For computational purposes it is worth noting that the numerator of (19.63) can also be written as the sum of squares of the generalized responses of the shocks to the $i$th equation on the $j$th variable in the model, namely $\sum_{\ell=0}^{N}(GI_{ij,\ell})^2$, where $GI_{ij,\ell}$ is given by (19.56).

## 19.6 Cointegrating VAR

The statistical framework for the cointegrating VAR options in *Microfit* is the following general vector error correction model (VECM):

$$\Delta \mathbf{y}_t = \mathbf{a}_{0y} + \mathbf{a}_{1y}t - \boldsymbol{\Pi}_y \mathbf{z}_{t-1} + \sum_{i=1}^{p-1} \boldsymbol{\Gamma}_{iy} \Delta \mathbf{z}_{t-i} + \boldsymbol{\Psi}_y \mathbf{w}_t + \boldsymbol{\epsilon}_t,\ t = 1,2, \ldots, n \tag{19.64}$$

where

- $\mathbf{z}_t = (\mathbf{y}_t', \mathbf{x}_t')'$, $\mathbf{y}_t$ is an $m_y \times 1$ vector of jointly determined (endogenous) $I(1)$ variables,
- $\mathbf{x}_t$ is an $m_x \times 1$ vector of exogenous $I(1)$ variables[10]

$$\Delta \mathbf{x}_t = \mathbf{a}_{0x} + \sum_{i=1}^{p-1} \boldsymbol{\Gamma}_{ix} \Delta \mathbf{z}_{t-i} + \boldsymbol{\Psi}_x \mathbf{w}_t + \mathbf{v}_t \tag{19.65}$$

- $\mathbf{w}_t$ is a $q \times 1$ vector of exogenous/deterministic $I(0)$ variables, excluding the intercepts and/or trends
- the disturbance vectors $\boldsymbol{\epsilon}_t$ and $\mathbf{v}_t$ satisfy the following assumptions:

[10]Notice that (19.65) allows for feedbacks from $\Delta y$ to $\Delta x$, but does not allow for level feedbacks, and hence assumes that $x_t$s are not themselves cointegrated.

$$\mathbf{u}_t = \begin{pmatrix} \epsilon_t \\ \mathbf{v}_t \end{pmatrix} \sim iid(\mathbf{0}, \mathbf{\Sigma}) \tag{19.66}$$

where $\mathbf{\Sigma}$ is a symmetric positive-definite matrix

- the disturbances in the combined model, $\mathbf{u}_t$, are distributed independently of $\mathbf{w}_t$:

$$E(\mathbf{u}_t|\mathbf{w}_t) = \mathbf{0} \tag{19.67}$$

The intercept and the trend coefficients, $\mathbf{a}_{0y}$ and $\mathbf{a}_{1y}$, are $m_y \times 1$ vectors; $\mathbf{\Pi}_y$ is the long-run multiplier matrix of order $m_y \times m$, where $m = m_x + m_y$; $\mathbf{\Gamma}_{1y}, \mathbf{\Gamma}_{2y}, \ldots, \mathbf{\Gamma}_{p-1,y}$ are $m_y \times m$ coefficient matrices capturing the short-run dynamic effects; and $\mathbf{\Psi}_y$ is the $m_y \times q$ matrix of coefficients on the $I(0)$ exogenous variables.

The VECM in (19.64) differs in a number of important respects from the usual VAR formulation for the VECM analysed inter alia by Johansen (1991). Firstly, (19.64) allows for a sub-system approach in which the $m_x$-vector of random variables, $\mathbf{x}_t$, is the forcing variables, or common 'stochastic trends', in the sense that the error correction terms do not enter in the sub-system for $\mathbf{x}_t$ (given by (19.65)). Therefore, cointegrating analysis in *Microfit* allows for contemporaneous and short-term feedbacks from $y_t$ to $\mathbf{x}_t$, but requires that no such feedbacks are possible in the long run. We refer to $\mathbf{x}_t$ as the 'long-run forcing' variables of the system. Secondly, the cointegration analysis critically depends on whether the underlying VECM contains intercepts and/or time trends, and whether the intercepts, $\mathbf{a}_{0y}$, and the trend coefficients, $\mathbf{a}_{1y}$, are restricted. Accordingly, the cointegration analysis in *Microfit* distinguishes between five cases of interest ordered according to the importance of the trends:

**Case I:** $\mathbf{a}_{0y} = \mathbf{a}_{1y} = \mathbf{0}$ (no intercepts and no trends)
**Case II:** $\mathbf{a}_{1y} = \mathbf{0}$, and $\mathbf{a}_{0y} = \mathbf{\Pi}_y \boldsymbol{\mu}_y$ (restricted intercepts and no trends)
**Case III:** $\mathbf{a}_{1y} = \mathbf{0}$, and $\mathbf{a}_{0y} \neq \mathbf{0}$ (unrestricted intercepts and no trends)
**Case IV:** $\mathbf{a}_{0y} \neq \mathbf{0}$ and $\mathbf{a}_{1y} = \mathbf{\Pi}_y \boldsymbol{\gamma}_y$ (unrestricted intercepts and restricted trends)
**Case V:** $\mathbf{a}_{0y} \neq \mathbf{0}$, and $\mathbf{a}_{1y} \neq \mathbf{0}$ (unrestricted intercepts and trends)

The rationale behind the restricted intercepts and the restricted trend cases is discussed below.

## 19.6.1 Cointegrating relations

The cointegrating VAR analysis is concerned with the estimation of (19.64) when the rank of the long-run multiplier matrix, $\mathbf{\Pi}$, could at most be equal to $m_y$. Therefore, rank deficiency of $\mathbf{\Pi}$ can be represented as

$$H_r : \text{Rank}(\mathbf{\Pi}_y) = r < m_y$$

In this case we can write

$$\mathbf{\Pi}_y = \boldsymbol{\alpha}_y \boldsymbol{\beta}'$$

where $\boldsymbol{\alpha}_y$ and $\boldsymbol{\beta}$ are $m_y \times r$ and $m \times r$ matrices, each with full column rank, $r$. In the case where $\mathbf{\Pi}_y$ is rank deficient, we have $\mathbf{y}_t \sim I(1)$, $\Delta\mathbf{y}_t \sim I(0)$, and $\boldsymbol{\beta}'\mathbf{z}_t \sim I(0)$. The $r \times 1$ trend-stationary relations, $\boldsymbol{\beta}'\mathbf{z}_t$, are referred to as the cointegrating relations, and characterize the long-run equilibrium (steady state) of the VECM, (19.64).

It is, however, important to recognize that in the case where the VECM, (19.64), contains deterministic trends (i.e. $\mathbf{a}_{1y} \neq \mathbf{0}$), in general there will also be a linear trend in the cointegrating relations. To see this, combining the equation systems (19.64) and (19.65), we have

$$\Delta\mathbf{z}_t = \mathbf{a}_0 + \mathbf{a}_1 t - \mathbf{\Pi}\mathbf{z}_{t-1} + \sum_{i=1}^{p-1} \mathbf{\Gamma}_i \Delta\mathbf{z}_{t-i} + \mathbf{\Psi}\mathbf{w}_t + \mathbf{u}_t \tag{19.68}$$

for $t = 1,2, \ldots, n$, where

$$\mathbf{z}_t = \begin{pmatrix} \mathbf{y}_t \\ \mathbf{x}_t \end{pmatrix}, \quad \mathbf{u}_t = \begin{pmatrix} \mathbf{u}_{yt} \\ \mathbf{v}_t \end{pmatrix}, \quad \mathbf{a}_0 = \begin{pmatrix} \mathbf{a}_{0y} \\ \mathbf{a}_{0x} \end{pmatrix}, \quad \mathbf{a}_1 = \begin{pmatrix} \mathbf{a}_{1y} \\ \mathbf{0} \end{pmatrix}$$

$$\mathbf{\Pi} = \begin{pmatrix} \mathbf{\Pi}_y \\ \mathbf{0} \end{pmatrix}, \quad \mathbf{\Gamma}_i = \begin{pmatrix} \mathbf{\Gamma}_{iy} \\ \mathbf{\Gamma}_{ix} \end{pmatrix}, \quad \mathbf{\Psi} = \begin{pmatrix} \mathbf{\Psi}_y \\ \mathbf{\Psi}_x \end{pmatrix}$$

which is the vector error correction form of (19.25).

In the case where $\mathbf{\Pi}$ is rank deficient the solution of (19.68) involves common stochastic trends, and is given by[11]

$$\mathbf{z}_t = \mathbf{z}_0 + \mathbf{b}_0 t + \mathbf{b}_1 \left\{ \frac{t(t+1)}{2} \right\} + \mathbf{C}(1)\mathbf{S}_t + \mathbf{C}^*(L)(\mathbf{h}_t - \mathbf{h}_0) \tag{19.69}$$

where

$$\mathbf{h}_t = \mathbf{\Psi}\mathbf{w}_t + \mathbf{u}_t \tag{19.70}$$

$$\mathbf{S}_t = \sum_{i=1}^{t} \mathbf{u}_i, \quad t = 1,2, \ldots \tag{19.71}$$

$$\mathbf{b}_0 = \mathbf{C}(1)\mathbf{a}_0 + \mathbf{C}^*(1)\mathbf{a}_1 \tag{19.72}$$

$$\mathbf{b}_1 = \mathbf{C}(1)\mathbf{a}_1 \tag{19.73}$$

$$\mathbf{C}(L) = \mathbf{C}(1) + (1 - L)\mathbf{C}^*(L) \tag{19.74}$$

$$\mathbf{C}^*(L) = \sum_{i=0}^{\infty} \mathbf{C}_i^* L^i$$

where $L$ is the one-period lag operator and the $m \times m$ matrices, $\mathbf{C}_i^*$, are obtained recursively from

$$\mathbf{C}_i^* = \mathbf{C}_{i-1}^* \mathbf{\Phi}_1 + \cdots + \mathbf{C}_{i-p}^* \mathbf{\Phi}_p \tag{19.75}$$

$i = 1, 2, \ldots$, with $\mathbf{C}_0^* = \mathbf{I}_m - \mathbf{C}(1)$, $\mathbf{C}_i^* = \mathbf{0}$, $i < 0$, and

---

[11]See, for example, Pesaran and Shin (1995b), and Pesaran *et al.* (1996b).

$$\mathbf{\Pi C}(1) = \mathbf{0} = \mathbf{C}(1)\mathbf{\Pi} \tag{19.76}$$

The matrices, $\mathbf{\Phi}_1, \mathbf{\Phi}_2, \ldots, \mathbf{\Phi}_p$ are the coefficient matrices in the VAR form of (19.68), and in terms of $\mathbf{\Pi}, \mathbf{\Gamma}_1, \mathbf{\Gamma}_2, \ldots,$ and $\mathbf{\Gamma}_{p-1}$ are given by

$$\mathbf{\Phi}_1 = \mathbf{I}_m - \mathbf{\Pi} + \mathbf{\Gamma}_1$$
$$\mathbf{\Phi}_i = \mathbf{\Gamma}_i - \mathbf{\Gamma}_{i-1}, \qquad i = 2,3 \cdots, p-1$$
$$\mathbf{\Phi}_p = -\mathbf{\Gamma}_{p-1}$$

From solution (19.69) it is clear that, in general, $\mathbf{z}_t$ will contain a quadratic trend. When $\mathbf{a}_1 \neq \mathbf{0}$, the quadratic trend disappears only if $\mathbf{C}(1)\mathbf{a}_1 = \mathbf{0}$, otherwise the number of independent quadratic trend terms in the solution of $\mathbf{z}_t$ will be equal to the rank of $\mathbf{C}(1)$, and hence depends on the number of cointegrating relations. Note that rank $[\mathbf{C}(1)] = m - r$. Therefore, without some restrictions on the trend coefficients, $\mathbf{a}_1$, the solution (19.69) has the unsatisfactory property that the nature of the trend in $\mathbf{z}_t$ varies with the assumed number of the cointegrating relations. This outcome can be avoided by restricting the trend coefficients as in case IV, namely by setting $\mathbf{a}_1 = \mathbf{\Pi}\boldsymbol{\gamma}$. Under these restrictions, using (19.73) and (19.76), we have

$$\mathbf{b}_1 = \mathbf{C}(1)\mathbf{a}_1 = \mathbf{C}(1)\mathbf{\Pi}\boldsymbol{\gamma} = \mathbf{0}$$

and the VECM in (19.68) becomes

$$\Delta\mathbf{z}_t = \mathbf{a}_0 - \mathbf{\Pi}(\mathbf{z}_{t-1} - \boldsymbol{\gamma}t) + \sum_{i=1}^{p-1} \mathbf{\Gamma}_i \Delta\mathbf{z}_{t-i} + \mathbf{\Psi}\mathbf{w}_t + \mathbf{u}_t \tag{19.77}$$

A similar consideration also applies where the VECM contains intercepts but no trends. In this case, unless the intercepts are appropriately restricted (as in case II), the nature of the trend in $\mathbf{z}_t$ will vary with the number of the cointegrating relations.

Using (19.69), the cointegrating relations, $\boldsymbol{\beta}'\mathbf{z}_t$, can also be derived in terms of the shocks $\mathbf{u}_{t-i}$, $i = 0,1,2, \ldots,$ and the current and past values of the $I(0)$ exogenous values. Pre-multiplying (19.69) by $\boldsymbol{\beta}'$ and bearing in mind the cointegration restrictions $\boldsymbol{\beta}'\mathbf{C}(1) = \mathbf{0}$, we obtain[12]

$$\boldsymbol{\beta}'\mathbf{z}_t = \boldsymbol{\beta}'\mathbf{z}_0 + (\boldsymbol{\beta}'\mathbf{b}_0)t + \boldsymbol{\beta}'\mathbf{C}^*(L)(\mathbf{h}_t - \mathbf{h}_0) \tag{19.78}$$

Using (19.72) we also have

$$\boldsymbol{\beta}'\mathbf{b}_0 = \boldsymbol{\beta}'\mathbf{C}^*(1)\mathbf{a}_1 \tag{19.79}$$

and hence when $\mathbf{a}_1 \neq \mathbf{0}$, the cointegrating relations, $\boldsymbol{\beta}'\mathbf{z}_t$, in general, contain deterministic trends, which do not disappear even if $\mathbf{a}_1$ is restricted as in case IV. When $\mathbf{a}_1 = \mathbf{\Pi}\boldsymbol{\gamma}$, the coefficients of the deterministic trend in the cointegrating relations are given by

---

[12]Notice that $\boldsymbol{\beta}'\mathbf{b}_1 = \boldsymbol{\beta}'\mathbf{C}(1)\mathbf{a}_1 = 0$, irrespective of whether the trend coefficients, $\mathbf{a}_1$, are restricted or not.

$$\beta' \mathbf{b}_0 = \beta' \mathbf{C}^*(1)\mathbf{\Pi}\gamma$$

But, as shown in Pesaran and Shin (1995b), $\mathbf{C}^*(1)\mathbf{\Pi} = \mathbf{I}_m$ and $\beta'\mathbf{b}_0 = \beta'\gamma \neq \mathbf{0}$. Using this result in (19.78), we have

$$\beta'\mathbf{z}_t = \beta'\mathbf{z}_0 + (\beta'\gamma)t + \beta'\mathbf{C}^*(L)(\mathbf{h}_t - \mathbf{h}_0) \qquad (19.80)$$

A test of whether the cointegrating relations are trended can be carried out by testing the following $r$ restrictions:

$$\beta'\gamma = \mathbf{0} \qquad (19.81)$$

We shall refer to these as the 'co-trending' restrictions.[13]

## 19.7 ML estimation and tests of cointegration

Suppose the $n$ observations $\mathbf{z}_1,\mathbf{z}_2, \ldots, \mathbf{z}_n$ and $\mathbf{w}_1,\mathbf{w}_2, \ldots, \mathbf{w}_n$ are available on the variables $\mathbf{z}_t = (\mathbf{y}_t',\mathbf{x}_t')'$ and $\mathbf{w}_t$. Then, stacking the VECM in (19.64) we have

$$\Delta\mathbf{Y} = \iota_n\mathbf{a}_{0y}' + \mathbf{t}_n\mathbf{a}_{1y}' - \mathbf{Z}_{-1}\mathbf{\Pi}_y' + \Delta\mathbf{Z}_p\mathbf{\Gamma}_y' + \mathbf{W}\mathbf{\Psi}_y' + \mathbf{E} \qquad (19.82)$$

where

$$\Delta\mathbf{Y} = (\Delta\mathbf{y}_1,\Delta\mathbf{y}_2, \ldots, \Delta\mathbf{y}_n)'$$

$$\mathbf{E} = (\epsilon_1,\epsilon_2, \ldots, \epsilon_n)'$$

$$\tau_n = (1,1, \ldots, 1)', \; \mathbf{t}_n = (1, 2, \ldots, n)'$$

$$\mathbf{\Gamma}_y = (\mathbf{\Gamma}_{1y},\mathbf{\Gamma}_{2y}, \ldots, \mathbf{\Gamma}_{p-1,y})$$

$$\Delta\mathbf{Z}_p = (\Delta\mathbf{Z}_{-1},\Delta\mathbf{Z}_{-2}, \ldots, \Delta\mathbf{Z}_{1-p})$$

$$\Delta\mathbf{Z}_{-i} = (\Delta\mathbf{z}_{1-i},\Delta\mathbf{z}_{2-i}, \ldots, \Delta\mathbf{z}_{n-i})', \; i = 1,2, \ldots, p-1$$

The log-likelihood function of (19.82) is given by

$$\ell_n(\varphi; r) = \frac{-nm_y}{2}\log 2\pi - \frac{n}{2}|\mathbf{\Sigma}_y| - \frac{1}{2}Tr(\mathbf{\Sigma}_y^{-1}\mathbf{E}'\mathbf{E}) \qquad (19.83)$$

where $\varphi$ stands for the vector of the unknown parameters of the model, and $r$ is the assumed rank of $\mathbf{\Pi}_y$. Writing $\mathbf{\Pi}_y = \alpha_y\beta'$ and maximizing the log-likelihood function with respect to the elements of $\mathbf{\Sigma}_y$, $\mathbf{a}_{0y}$, $\mathbf{a}_{1y}$, $\mathbf{\Gamma}_{iy}$, $i = 1,2, \ldots, p-1$, $\alpha_y$, and $\mathbf{\Psi}_y$, we have the following concentrated log-likelihood function:

$$\ell_n^c(\beta; r) = \frac{-nm_y}{2}(1 + \log 2\pi) - \frac{n}{2}\log|\widetilde{\mathbf{\Sigma}}_y(\beta)| \qquad (19.84)$$

---

[13]Also see Park (1992) and Ogaki (1992).

where

$$|\tilde{\boldsymbol{\Sigma}}_y(\boldsymbol{\beta})| = \frac{|\mathbf{S}_{00}||\boldsymbol{\beta}'\mathbf{A}_n\boldsymbol{\beta}|}{|\boldsymbol{\beta}'\mathbf{B}_n\boldsymbol{\beta}|} \tag{19.85}$$

$$\mathbf{A}_n = \mathbf{S}_{11} - \mathbf{S}_{10}\mathbf{S}_{00}^{-1}\mathbf{S}_{01}, \text{ and } \mathbf{B}_n = \mathbf{S}_{11} \tag{19.86}$$

$$\mathbf{S}_{ij} = n^{-1}\sum_{t=1}^{n} \mathbf{r}_{it}\mathbf{r}'_{jt}, \quad i,j = 0,1 \tag{19.87}$$

$\mathbf{r}_{0t}$ and $\mathbf{r}_{1t}$ for $t = 1,2, \ldots, n$ are the residual vectors obtainable from the following regressions:

**Case I: $(\mathbf{a}_{0y} = \mathbf{a}_{1y} = \mathbf{0})$**

$\mathbf{r}_{0t}$ is the residual vector from the OLS regressions of $\Delta\mathbf{y}_t$ on $(\Delta\mathbf{z}_{t-1}, \Delta\mathbf{z}_{t-2}, \ldots, \Delta\mathbf{z}_{t-p+1}, \mathbf{w}_t)$, and

$\mathbf{r}_{1t}$ is the residual vector from the OLS regressions of $\mathbf{z}_{t-1}$ on $(\Delta\mathbf{z}_{t-1}, \Delta\mathbf{z}_{t-2}, \ldots, \Delta\mathbf{z}_{t-p+1}, \mathbf{w}_t)$

**Case II: $(\mathbf{a}_{1y} = \mathbf{0}, \mathbf{a}_{0y} = \boldsymbol{\Pi}_y\boldsymbol{\mu}_y)$**

$\mathbf{r}_{0t}$ is the residual vector from the OLS regressions of $\Delta\mathbf{y}_t$ on $(\Delta\mathbf{z}_{t-1}, \Delta\mathbf{z}_{t-2}, \ldots, \Delta\mathbf{z}_{t-p+1}, \mathbf{w}_t)$, and

$\mathbf{r}_{1t}$ is the residual vector from the OLS regressions of $\binom{1}{\mathbf{z}_{t-1}}$ on $(\Delta\mathbf{z}_{t-1}, \Delta\mathbf{z}_{t-2}, \ldots, \Delta\mathbf{z}_{t-p+1}, \mathbf{w}_t)$

**Case III: $(\mathbf{a}_{1y} = \mathbf{0}, \mathbf{a}_{0y} \neq \mathbf{0})$**

$\mathbf{r}_{0t}$ is the residual vector from the OLS regressions of $\Delta\mathbf{y}_t$ on $(1, \Delta\mathbf{z}_{t-1}, \Delta\mathbf{z}_{t-2}, \ldots, \Delta\mathbf{z}_{t-p+1}, \mathbf{w}_t)$, and

$\mathbf{r}_{1t}$ is the residual vector from the OLS regressions of $\mathbf{z}_{t-1}$ on $(1, \Delta\mathbf{z}_{t-1}, \Delta\mathbf{z}_{t-2}, \ldots, \Delta\mathbf{z}_{t-p+1}, \mathbf{w}_t)$

**Case IV: $(\mathbf{a}_{0y} \neq \mathbf{0}, \mathbf{a}_{1y} = \boldsymbol{\Pi}_y\boldsymbol{\gamma}_y)$**

$\mathbf{r}_{0t}$ is the residual vector from the OLS regressions of $\Delta\mathbf{y}_t$ on $(1, \Delta\mathbf{z}_{t-1}, \Delta\mathbf{z}_{t-2}, \ldots, \Delta\mathbf{z}_{t-p+1}, \mathbf{w}_t)$, and

$\mathbf{r}_{1t}$ is the residual vector from the OLS regressions of $\binom{t}{\mathbf{z}_{t-1}}$ on $(1, \Delta\mathbf{z}_{t-1}, \Delta\mathbf{z}_{t-2}, \ldots, \Delta\mathbf{z}_{t-p+1}, \mathbf{w}_t)$

**Case V: $(\mathbf{a}_{0y} \neq \mathbf{0}, \mathbf{a}_{1y} \neq \mathbf{0})$**

$\mathbf{r}_{0t}$ is the residual vector from the OLS regressions of $\Delta\mathbf{y}_t$ on $(1, t, \Delta\mathbf{z}_{t-1}, \Delta\mathbf{z}_{t-2}, \ldots, \Delta\mathbf{z}_{t-p+1}, \mathbf{w}_t)$, and

$\mathbf{r}_{1t}$ is the residual vector from the OLS regressions of $\mathbf{z}_{t-1}$ on $(1, t, \Delta\mathbf{z}_{t-1}, \Delta\mathbf{z}_{t-2}, \ldots, \Delta\mathbf{z}_{t-p+1}, \mathbf{w}_t)$

Substituting (19.85) in (19.84) yields

$$\ell_n^c(\beta; r) = \frac{-nm_y}{2}(1 + \log 2\pi) - \frac{n}{2}\log|\mathbf{S}_{00}| - \frac{n}{2}\{\log|\beta'\mathbf{A}_n\beta| - \log|\beta'\mathbf{B}_n\beta|\} \tag{19.88}$$

The dimension of $\beta$ depends on whether the intercepts, $\mathbf{a}_{0y}$, and/or the trend coefficients, $\mathbf{a}_{1y}$, are restricted or not. For example, in case IV where $\mathbf{a}_{0y} \neq \mathbf{0}$ and $\mathbf{a}_{1y} = \mathbf{\Pi}_y\gamma_y$, the term $\mathbf{t}_n\mathbf{a}'_{1y} - \mathbf{Z}_{-1}\mathbf{\Pi}'_y$ in (19.82) can be written as

$$\mathbf{t}_n\mathbf{a}'_{1y} - \mathbf{Z}_{-1}\mathbf{\Pi}'_y = -\mathbf{Z}^*_{-1}\mathbf{\Pi}^{*\prime}_y,$$

where

$$\mathbf{\Pi}^*_y = \mathbf{\Pi}_y(-\gamma_y, \mathbf{I}_m)$$

$$\mathbf{Z}^*_{-1} = (\mathbf{z}^*_0, \mathbf{z}^*_1, \ldots, \mathbf{z}^*_{n-1})$$

and $\mathbf{z}^*_t = \begin{pmatrix} \mathbf{t} \\ \mathbf{z}_{t-1} \end{pmatrix}$. In this case the cointegrating vectors are defined by

$$\mathbf{\Pi}^*_y = \alpha_y\beta'_*$$

and $\beta$ in (19.88) should be replaced by the $(m + 1) \times r$ matrix, $\beta_*$.

The unconstrained maximization of $\ell_n^c(\beta; r)$ will not lead to unique estimates of $\beta$ (or $\beta_*$), and $\beta$ can only be identified up to post-multiplication by an $r \times r$ non-singular matrix. It is easily seen that

$$\ell_n^c(\beta; r) = \ell_n^c(\beta\mathbf{Q}; r)$$

where $\mathbf{Q}$ is any non-singular $r \times r$ matrix. Therefore, $r^2$ just-identifying restrictions on $\beta$ (or $\beta_*$) are required for exact identification. The resultant maximized concentrated log-likelihood function, $\ell_n^c(\beta; r)$, at the ML estimator of $\beta$ does not, however, depend on $\mathbf{Q}$ and is given by

$$\ell_n^c(r) = \frac{-nm_y}{2}(1 + \log 2\pi) - \frac{n}{2}\log|\mathbf{S}_{00}| - \frac{n}{2}\sum_{i=1}^{r}\log(1 - \hat{\lambda}_i) \tag{19.89}$$

for all exactly identified choices of $\beta$, where $\hat{\lambda}_1 > \hat{\lambda}_2 > \cdots \hat{\lambda}_r > 0$ are the $r$ largest eigenvalues of $\mathbf{S}_{00}^{-1}\mathbf{S}_{01}\mathbf{S}_{11}^{-1}\mathbf{S}_{10}$ (or equivalently the eigenvalues of $\mathbf{S}_{11}^{-1}\mathbf{S}_{10}\mathbf{S}_{00}^{-1}\mathbf{S}_{01}$).

### 19.7.1 Maximum eigenvalue statistic

Suppose the interest is in testing the null hypothesis of $r$ cointegrating relations

$$H_r : \text{Rank}(\mathbf{\Pi}_y) = r \tag{19.90}$$

against the alternative hypothesis

$$H_{r+1} : \text{Rank}(\mathbf{\Pi}_y) = r + 1 \tag{19.91}$$

$r = 0, 1, 2, \ldots, m_y - 1$, in the VECM (19.64). The appropriate test statistic is given by the log-likelihood ratio statistic

$$\mathcal{LR}(H_r|H_{r+1}) = -n\log(1 - \hat{\lambda}_{r+1}) \tag{19.92}$$

where $\hat{\lambda}_r$ is the $r$th largest eigenvalue of $\mathbf{S}_{00}^{-1}\mathbf{S}_{01}\mathbf{S}_{11}^{-1}\mathbf{S}_{10}$, and the matrices $\mathbf{S}_{00}$, $\mathbf{S}_{01}$, and $\mathbf{S}_{11}$ are defined by (19.87).

### 19.7.2 Trace statistic

Suppose the interest is in testing the null hypothesis $H(r)$ defined in (19.90) against the alternative of trend-stationarity, that is

$$H_{m_y}:\ \text{Rank}(\mathbf{\Pi}_y) = m_y \tag{19.93}$$

for $r = 0, 1, 2, \ldots, m_y - 1$. The log-likelihood ratio statistic for this test is given by

$$\mathcal{LR}(H_r|H_{m_y}) = -n \sum_{i=r+1}^{m_y} \log(1 - \hat{\lambda}_{r+1}) \tag{19.94}$$

where $\hat{\lambda}_{r+1}, \hat{\lambda}_{r+1}, \ldots, \hat{\lambda}_{m_y}$ are the largest eigenvalues of $\mathbf{S}_{00}^{-1}\mathbf{S}_{01}\mathbf{S}_{11}^{-1}\mathbf{S}_{10}$, where the matrices $\mathbf{S}_{00}$, $\mathbf{S}_{01}$, and $\mathbf{S}_{11}$ are defined by (19.87).

The critical values for the maximum eigenvalue and the trace statistics defined by (19.92) and (19.94), respectively, depend on $m_y - r$, $m_x$, whether the VECM (19.64) contains intercepts and/or trends, and whether these are restricted, i.e. which one of the five cases (set out above) is applicable. They are computed in Pesaran *et al.* (1996b) using stochastic simulation techniques. Pesaran *et al.* cover all the five cases allowing for up to 12 endogenous $I(1)$ variables and up to five exogenous $I(1)$ variables in the VECM (19.64). The critical values do not, however, depend on the order of the VAR, $p$, and the stochastic properties of the $I(0)$ exogenous variables, $\mathbf{w}_t$, at least in large samples.

Following Johansen's (1991) approach, Osterwald-Lenum (1992) also provide the critical values of both the trace and the Maximum eigenvalue statistics only in the case where up to 11 endogenous variables and no $I(1)$ exogenous variables are considered in the system. There are also differences between his critical values and the critical values tabulated by Pesaran *et al.* (1996b) for cases III and V, because Johansen does not restrict the intercept coefficient in case III or the trend coefficients in case V.

### 19.7.3 Model selection criteria for choosing the number of cointegrating relations

The model selection criteria AIC, SBC, and HQC, defined in Section 18.6, are also computed for different values of $r$, the rank of the long-run matrix $\mathbf{\Pi}_y$ in (19.64). We have

$$AIC = \ell_n^c(r) - \varsigma \tag{19.95}$$

$$SBC = \ell_n^c(r) - \left(\frac{\varsigma}{2}\right) \log n \tag{19.96}$$

$$HQC = \ell_n^c(r) - \left(\frac{\varsigma}{2}\right) \log \log n \tag{19.97}$$

where $\ell_n^c(r)$ is given by (19.89), and $\varsigma$ is the total number of coefficients estimated. The value of $\varsigma$ depends on whether the intercepts and the trend coefficients in (19.64) are restricted. The values of $\varsigma$ for the five cases distinguished in *Microfit* are as follows:[14]

**Case I: ($\mathbf{a}_{0y} = \mathbf{a}_{1y} = \mathbf{0}$)**

$$\varsigma = mm_y(p-1) + (m + m_y)r - r^2 + qm_y$$

**Case II: ($\mathbf{a}_{1y} = \mathbf{0}, \mathbf{a}_{0y} = \mathbf{\Pi}_y \boldsymbol{\mu}_y$)**

$$\varsigma = mm_y(p-1) + (m + m_y + 1)r - r^2 + qm_y$$

**Case III: ($\mathbf{a}_{1y} = \mathbf{0}, \mathbf{a}_{0y} \neq \mathbf{0}$)**

$$\varsigma = mm_y(p-1) + (m + m_y)r - r^2 + (q+1)m_y$$

**Case IV: ($\mathbf{a}_{0y} \neq \mathbf{0}, \mathbf{a}_{1y} = \mathbf{\Pi}_y \boldsymbol{\gamma}_y$)**

$$\varsigma = mm_y(p-1) + (m + m_y + 1)r - r^2 + (q+1)m_y$$

**Case V: ($\mathbf{a}_{0y} \neq \mathbf{0}, \mathbf{a}_{1y} \neq \mathbf{0}$)**

$$\varsigma = mm_y(p-1) + (m + m_y)r - r^2 + (q+2)m_y$$

Recall also that $m = m_x + m_y$.

## 19.8 Long-run structural modelling

As we have seen already, the estimation of the VECM, (19.64), subject to deficient rank restrictions on the long-run multiplier matrix, $\mathbf{\Pi}_y$, does not generally lead to a unique choice for the cointegrating relations. The identification of $\boldsymbol{\beta}$ (in $\mathbf{\Pi}_y = \boldsymbol{\alpha}_y \boldsymbol{\beta}'$) requires at least $r$ restrictions per each of the $r$ cointegrating relations.[15] In the simple case where $r = 1$, the one restriction needed to identify the cointegrating relation can be viewed as a 'normalizing' restriction which could be applied to the coefficient of any one of the integrated variables which enter the cointegrating relation. However, in the more general case where $r > 1$, the number of such 'normalizing'

[14] The number of free parameters in the $m_y \times m$ long-run matrix $\Pi_y$ depends on its rank. When rank$(\mathbf{\Pi}_y) = r$, $\mathbf{\Pi}_y$ contains $(m_y + m)r - r^2$ free parameters (or equivalently $\mathbf{\Pi}_y$ will be subject to $(m - r)(m_y - r)$ restrictions). This result follows from the so-called 'UDV' decomposition of $\mathbf{\Pi}_y = \mathbf{UDV}$, where $\mathbf{U}$, $\mathbf{D}$, and $\mathbf{V}$ are $m_y \times r$, $r \times r$ and $r \times m$ matrices such that $\mathbf{U}'\mathbf{U} = \mathbf{I}_r$, $\mathbf{V}'\mathbf{V} = \mathbf{I}_r$, and $\mathbf{D}$ is a diagonal matrix of rank $r$.

[15] Readers interested in more details should consult Pesaran and Shin (1995b).

restrictions is just equal to $r$ which needs to be supplemented with further $r^2 - r$ a priori restrictions, preferably obtained from a suitable economic theory.[16]

### 19.8.1 Identification of the cointegrating relations

The structural estimation of the cointegrating relations requires maximization of the concentrated log-likelihood function, (19.88), subject to appropriate just-identifying or over-identifying restrictions on $\boldsymbol{\beta}$. The just-identifying restrictions utilized in Johansen's (1988, 1991) estimation procedure involve the observation matrices $\mathbf{A}_n$ and $\mathbf{B}_n$ defined by (19.86) and are often referred to as 'empirical' or 'statistical' identifying restrictions, as compared to a priori restrictions on $\boldsymbol{\beta}$ which are independent of particular values of $\mathbf{A}_n$ and $\mathbf{B}_n$. Johansen's estimates of $\boldsymbol{\beta}$, which we denote by $\hat{\boldsymbol{\beta}}_J$, are obtained as the first $r$ eigenvectors of $\mathbf{B}_n - \mathbf{A}_n$ with respect to $\mathbf{B}_n$, satisfying the following 'normalization' and 'orthogonalization' restrictions:

$$\hat{\boldsymbol{\beta}}'_J \mathbf{B}_n \hat{\boldsymbol{\beta}}_J = \mathbf{I}_r \tag{19.98}$$

and

$$\hat{\boldsymbol{\beta}}'_{iJ}(\mathbf{B}_n - \mathbf{A}_n)\hat{\boldsymbol{\beta}}_{jJ} = 0, \qquad i \neq j, \quad i,j = 1, 2, \ldots, r \tag{19.99}$$

where $\hat{\boldsymbol{\beta}}_{iJ}$ represents the $i$th column of $\hat{\boldsymbol{\beta}}_J$. The conditions (19.98) and (19.99) together exactly impose $r^2$ just-identifying restrictions on $\boldsymbol{\beta}$. It is, however, clear that the $r^2$ restrictions in (19.98) and (19.99) are adopted for their mathematical convenience and not because they are meaningful from the perspectives of any long-run economic theory.

A more satisfactorily procedure would be directly to estimate the concentrated log-likelihood function (19.89) subject to exact or over-identifying a priori restrictions obtained from the long-run equilibrium properties of a suitable underlying economic model (on this see Pesaran 1997). *Microfit* enables you to compute ML estimates of $\boldsymbol{\beta}$, and hence the other parameters in the VECM (19.64), when the elements of $\boldsymbol{\beta}$ are subject to the following general linear restrictions

$$\mathbf{R}\mathrm{vec}(\boldsymbol{\beta}) = \mathbf{b} \tag{19.100}$$

where $\mathbf{R}$ and $\mathbf{b}$ are the $k \times rm$ matrix and $k \times 1$ vector of known constants (with $\mathrm{Rank}(\mathbf{R}) = k$); and $\mathrm{vec}(\boldsymbol{\beta})$ is the $rm \times 1$ vector of long-run coefficients, which stacks the $r$ columns of $\boldsymbol{\beta}$ into a vector. As in Section 19.2, we can distinguish between the cases where the restrictions are applicable to columns of $\boldsymbol{\beta}$ separately, and where they involve parameters from two or more cointegrating vectors. In the former case, the matrix $\mathbf{R}$ is block diagonal and (19.100) can be written as

[16] The role of economic theory in providing suitable identifying restrictions on the cointegrating vectors is discussed in Pesaran (1997).

$$\mathbf{R}_i\boldsymbol{\beta}_i = \mathbf{b}_i,\ i = 1,2, \ldots, r \tag{19.101}$$

where $\boldsymbol{\beta}_i$ is the $i$th cointegrating vector; $\mathbf{R}_i$ is the $i$th block in matrix $\mathbf{R}$ and $\mathbf{b}_i$ is defined by $\mathbf{b}' = (\mathbf{b}_1', \mathbf{b}_2', \ldots, \mathbf{b}_r')$. In this case the necessary and sufficient conditions for identification of the cointegrating vectors are given by

$$\text{Rank}(\mathbf{R}_i\boldsymbol{\beta}_i) = r, \qquad i = 1,2, \ldots, r \tag{19.102}$$

This result also implies that *there must be at least r independent restrictions on each of the r cointegrating vectors.*

The identification condition in the case where $\mathbf{R}$ is not block diagonal is given by

$$\text{Rank}\{\mathbf{R}(\mathbf{I}_r \otimes \boldsymbol{\beta})\} = r^2 \tag{19.103}$$

A necessary condition for (19.103) to hold is given by the order condition $k \geq r^2$. As with the Cowles Commission approach, three cases of interest can be distinguished:

1. $k < r^2$, the under-identified case.
2. $k = r^2$, the exactly identified case.
3. $k > r^2$, the over-identified case.

### 19.8.2 Estimation of the cointegrating relations under general linear restrictions

Here we distinguish between two cases: when the long-run restrictions are exactly identified (i.e. $k = r^2$), and when there are over-identifying restrictions on the cointegrating vectors (i.e. $k > r^2$).

**Exactly identified case** ($k = r^2$)
In this case, the ML estimators of $\boldsymbol{\beta}$ that satisfy the restrictions (19.100) are readily computed using Johansen's estimates, $\hat{\boldsymbol{\beta}}_J$. We have:

$$\text{vec}(\hat{\boldsymbol{\beta}}) = (\mathbf{I}_r \otimes \hat{\boldsymbol{\beta}}_J)[\mathbf{R}(I_r \otimes \hat{\boldsymbol{\beta}}_J)]^{-1}\mathbf{b} \tag{19.104}$$

where $\otimes$ stands for Kronecker product. It is easily verified that this estimator satisfies the restriction (19.100), and is invariant to non-singular transformations of the cointegrating space spanned by columns of $\hat{\boldsymbol{\beta}}$.[17]

**Over-identified case** ($k > r^2$)
In this case there are $k - r^2$ additional restrictions that need to be taken into account at the estimation stage. This can be done by maximization of the concentrated log-likelihood function given by (19.88), subject to the restrictions given by (19.100). We assume that the normalization restrictions on each of the $r$ cointegrating vectors is also included in $\mathbf{R}\text{vec}(\boldsymbol{\beta}) = \mathbf{b}$. The advantage of working with (19.88) lies in the fact that the data matrices, $\mathbf{A}_n$

[17]For a derivation of this result, see Pesaran and Shin (1995b).

and $\mathbf{B}_n$, defined by (19.86), need to be computed only once, and the speed of convergence of the proposed algorithm does not depend on the sample size, $T$. The Lagrangian function for this problem is given by

$$\Lambda(\boldsymbol{\theta}, \boldsymbol{\lambda}) = \frac{1}{n}\ell_n^c(\boldsymbol{\theta}; r) - \frac{1}{2}\boldsymbol{\lambda}'(\mathbf{R}\boldsymbol{\theta} - \mathbf{b})$$

$$= \text{constant} - \frac{1}{2}\{\log|\boldsymbol{\beta}'\mathbf{A}_n\boldsymbol{\beta}| - \log|\boldsymbol{\beta}'\mathbf{B}_n\boldsymbol{\beta}|\} - \frac{1}{2}\boldsymbol{\lambda}'(\mathbf{R}\boldsymbol{\theta} - \mathbf{b}) \tag{19.105}$$

where $\boldsymbol{\theta} = \text{vec}(\boldsymbol{\beta})$, $\boldsymbol{\lambda}$ is a $k \times 1$ vector of Lagrange multipliers, and $\mathbf{A}_n$ and $\mathbf{B}_n$ are defined in (19.86). Then, first order conditions are given by

$$\mathbf{d}_n(\tilde{\boldsymbol{\theta}}) = \mathbf{R}'\tilde{\boldsymbol{\lambda}} \tag{19.106}$$

$$\mathbf{R}\tilde{\boldsymbol{\theta}} = \mathbf{b} \tag{19.107}$$

where $\tilde{\boldsymbol{\theta}}$ and $\tilde{\boldsymbol{\lambda}}$ stand for the restricted ML estimators, and $\mathbf{d}_n(\tilde{\boldsymbol{\theta}})$ is the score function defined by

$$\mathbf{d}_n(\tilde{\boldsymbol{\theta}}) = \{[(\tilde{\boldsymbol{\beta}}'\mathbf{A}_n\tilde{\boldsymbol{\beta}})^{-1} \otimes \mathbf{A}_n] - [(\tilde{\boldsymbol{\beta}}'\mathbf{B}_n\tilde{\boldsymbol{\beta}})^{-1} \otimes \mathbf{B}_n]\}\tilde{\boldsymbol{\theta}} \tag{19.108}$$

Here we propose two different but related numerical procedures for the computation of $\tilde{\boldsymbol{\theta}}$. The first procedure is a 'back-substitution' type algorithm and uses only the information on the first derivatives. It involves solving the system of equations (19.106) and (19.107) numerically for $\tilde{\boldsymbol{\theta}}$ $(= \text{vec}(\tilde{\boldsymbol{\beta}}))$, after eliminating $\tilde{\boldsymbol{\lambda}}$. Define

$$\mathbf{P}_n = (\tilde{\boldsymbol{\beta}}'\mathbf{A}_n\tilde{\boldsymbol{\beta}}) \otimes \mathbf{A}_n^{-1}, \quad \text{and} \quad \mathbf{F}_n = (\tilde{\boldsymbol{\beta}}'\mathbf{A}_n\tilde{\boldsymbol{\beta}})(\tilde{\boldsymbol{\beta}}'\mathbf{B}_n\tilde{\boldsymbol{\beta}})^{-1} \otimes \mathbf{A}_n^{-1}\mathbf{B}_n \tag{19.109}$$

and pre-multiply (19.106) by $\mathbf{P}_n$ to obtain[18]

$$\tilde{\boldsymbol{\theta}} = \mathbf{F}_n\tilde{\boldsymbol{\theta}} + \mathbf{P}_n\mathbf{R}'\tilde{\boldsymbol{\lambda}} \tag{19.110}$$

Now multiplying both sides of this relation by $\mathbf{R}$ we have

$$\mathbf{R}\tilde{\boldsymbol{\theta}} = \mathbf{R}\mathbf{F}_n\tilde{\boldsymbol{\theta}} + (\mathbf{R}\mathbf{P}_n\mathbf{R}')\tilde{\boldsymbol{\lambda}} = \mathbf{b} \tag{19.111}$$

Since by assumption $\mathbf{P}_n$ is non-singular, then $\text{Rank}(\mathbf{R}\mathbf{P}_n\mathbf{R}') = \text{Rank}(\mathbf{R}) = k$, which means that $\mathbf{R}\mathbf{P}_n\mathbf{R}'$ is also non-singular, and $\tilde{\boldsymbol{\lambda}}$ is given by

$$\tilde{\boldsymbol{\lambda}} = (\mathbf{R}\mathbf{P}_n\mathbf{R}')^{-1}(\mathbf{b} - \mathbf{R}\mathbf{F}_n\tilde{\boldsymbol{\theta}}) \tag{19.112}$$

Next, eliminating $\tilde{\boldsymbol{\lambda}}$ from (19.110) using (19.112), we have

$$\tilde{\boldsymbol{\theta}} = \mathbf{f}(\tilde{\boldsymbol{\theta}}) \tag{19.113}$$

where

$$\mathbf{f}(\tilde{\boldsymbol{\theta}}) = \mathbf{S}_n^{-1}\mathbf{P}_n\mathbf{R}'(\mathbf{R}\mathbf{P}_n\mathbf{R}')^{-1}\mathbf{b} \tag{19.114}$$

$$\mathbf{S}_n = \mathbf{I}_{mr} - \mathbf{F}_n + \mathbf{P}_n\mathbf{R}'(\mathbf{R}\mathbf{P}_n\mathbf{R}')^{-1}\mathbf{R}\mathbf{F}_n \tag{19.115}$$

[18] The computations are carried out assuming that $r$, the number of cointegrating vectors, is known and hence that $\boldsymbol{\beta}'\mathbf{A}_T\boldsymbol{\beta}$ and $\boldsymbol{\beta}'\mathbf{B}_T\boldsymbol{\beta}$ are of full rank. Notice that the data matrices, $\mathbf{A}_T$ and $\mathbf{B}_T$, are assumed to be non-singular.

The $mr \times 1$ vector function $\mathbf{f}(\cdot)$ depends on $\tilde{\theta}$ through the positive definite matrices $\tilde{\beta}'\mathbf{A}_T\tilde{\beta}$ and $\tilde{\beta}'\mathbf{B}_T\tilde{\beta}$. The numerical problem to be solved is then to find the fixed point of

$$\tilde{\theta} = \mathbf{f}(\tilde{\theta})$$

This can be achieved by starting with an initial estimate of $\theta$, say $\tilde{\theta}^{(0)}$, and using (19.113) to compute a new estimate of $\theta$, namely

$$\tilde{\theta}^{(1)} = \mathbf{f}(\tilde{\theta}^{(0)})$$

and so on until convergence.

The second procedure (which we shall refer to as the generalized Newton–Raphson procedure) makes use of both the first and second derivatives of the concentrated log-likelihood function to solve numerically for $\tilde{\theta}$.

Let $\tilde{\theta}^{(0)}$ and $\tilde{\lambda}^{(0)}$ be the initial estimates of the ML estimators of $\theta$ and $\lambda$. Taking the Taylor series expansion of (19.106) around $\tilde{\theta}^{(0)}$ and $\tilde{\lambda}^{(0)}$, and using (19.107), we obtain

$$\begin{bmatrix} \mathbf{G}_n(\tilde{\theta}^{(0)}) & \mathbf{R}' \\ \mathbf{R} & 0 \end{bmatrix} \begin{bmatrix} n(\tilde{\theta} - \tilde{\theta}^{(0)}) \\ \tilde{\lambda} - \tilde{\lambda}^{(0)} \end{bmatrix} = \begin{bmatrix} \mathbf{d}_n(\tilde{\theta}^{(0)}) - \mathbf{R}'\tilde{\lambda}^{(0)} \\ -n(\mathbf{R}\tilde{\theta}^{(0)} - \mathbf{b}) \end{bmatrix} + o_p(1) \qquad (19.116)$$

where $\mathbf{G}_n(\tilde{\theta})$ is given by

$$\begin{aligned} \mathbf{G}_n(\tilde{\theta}) = & -n^{-1}(\tilde{\beta}'\mathbf{A}_n\tilde{\beta})^{-1} \otimes [(\mathbf{A}_n\tilde{\beta})(\tilde{\beta}'\mathbf{A}_n\tilde{\beta})^{-1}(\tilde{\beta}'\mathbf{A}_n)] \\ & + n^{-1}(\tilde{\beta}'\mathbf{B}_n\tilde{\beta})^{-1} \otimes [(\mathbf{B}_n\tilde{\beta})(\tilde{\beta}'\mathbf{B}_n\tilde{\beta})^{-1}(\tilde{\beta}'\mathbf{B}_n)] \\ & - n^{-1}\mathbf{C}_{rm}\{[(\mathbf{A}_n\tilde{\beta})(\tilde{\beta}'\mathbf{A}_n\tilde{\beta})^{-1}] \otimes [(\tilde{\beta}'\mathbf{A}_n\tilde{\beta})^{-1}(\tilde{\beta}'\mathbf{A}_n)] \\ & + n^{-1}\mathbf{C}_{rm}\{[(\mathbf{B}_n\tilde{\beta})(\tilde{\beta}'\mathbf{B}_n\tilde{\beta})^{-1}] \otimes [(\tilde{\beta}'\mathbf{B}_n\tilde{\beta})^{-1}(\tilde{\beta}'\mathbf{B}_n)] \\ & + n^{-1}(\tilde{\beta}'\mathbf{A}_n\tilde{\beta})^{-1} \otimes \mathbf{A}_n - n^{-1}(\tilde{\beta}'\mathbf{B}_n\tilde{\beta})^{-1} \otimes \mathbf{B}_n \end{aligned}$$

and $\mathbf{C}_{rm}$ is the $rm \times rm$ commutation matrix (see section 3.7 in Magnus and Neudecker 1988). To deal with the singularity of $\mathbf{G}_n(\theta)$, partition $\mathbf{R} = (\mathbf{R}'_A, \mathbf{R}_B)'$, where $\mathbf{R}_A$ and $\mathbf{R}_B$ are matrices of order $r^2 \times rm$ and $(k - r^2) \times rm$, representing the $r^2$ just-identifying restrictions, and the $(k - r^2)$, over-identifying restrictions respectively; and let $\mathbf{J}_n(\tilde{\theta}) = \mathbf{G}_n(\tilde{\theta}) + \mathbf{R}'_A\mathbf{R}_A$. Then, the solution of (19.116) using a generalized inverse based on $\mathbf{J}_n(\tilde{\theta})$ is given by[19]

$$\begin{bmatrix} n(\tilde{\theta} - \tilde{\theta}^{(0)}) \\ \tilde{\lambda} - \tilde{\lambda}^{(0)} \end{bmatrix} = \begin{bmatrix} \mathbf{V}_{\theta\theta}(\tilde{\theta}^{(0)}) & \mathbf{V}_{\theta\lambda}(\tilde{\theta}^{(0)}) \\ \mathbf{V}'_{\theta\lambda}(\tilde{\theta}^{(0)}) & \mathbf{V}_{\lambda\lambda}(\tilde{\theta}^{(0)}) \end{bmatrix} \begin{bmatrix} \mathbf{d}_n(\tilde{\theta}^{(0)}) - \mathbf{R}'\tilde{\lambda}^{(0)} \\ -n(\mathbf{R}\tilde{\theta}^{(0)} - \mathbf{b}) \end{bmatrix} + o_p(1) \quad (19.117)$$

where

$$\mathbf{V}_{\theta\theta}(\tilde{\theta}) = \mathbf{J}_n^{-1}(\tilde{\theta}) - \mathbf{J}_n^{-1}(\tilde{\theta})\mathbf{R}'(\mathbf{R}\mathbf{J}_n^{-1}(\tilde{\theta})\mathbf{R}')^{-1}\mathbf{R}\mathbf{J}_n^{-1}(\tilde{\theta}) \qquad (19.118)$$

$$\mathbf{V}_{\theta\lambda}(\tilde{\theta}) = \mathbf{J}_n^{-1}(\tilde{\theta})\mathbf{R}'(\mathbf{R}\mathbf{J}_n^{-1}(\tilde{\theta})\mathbf{R}')^{-1}$$

$$\mathbf{V}_{\lambda\lambda}(\tilde{\theta}) = (\mathbf{R}\mathbf{J}_n^{-1}(\tilde{\theta})\mathbf{R}')^{-1}$$

---

[19]In general, the Newton–Raphson algorithm gives the same solution when $\mathbf{R}$ instead of $\mathbf{R}_A$ is used in the construction of $\mathbf{J}_n(\tilde{\theta})$. See Pesaran and Shin (1995b) for more details.

Hence, we obtain the following generalized version of the Newton–Raphson algorithm:

$$\begin{bmatrix} \tilde{\theta}^{(i)} \\ \tilde{\lambda}^{(i)} \end{bmatrix} = \begin{bmatrix} \tilde{\theta}^{(i-1)} \\ \tilde{\lambda}^{(i-1)} \end{bmatrix} \begin{bmatrix} \mathbf{V}_{\theta\theta}(\tilde{\theta}^{(i-1)}) & \mathbf{V}_{\theta\lambda}(\tilde{\theta}^{(i-1)}) \\ \mathbf{V}'_{\theta\lambda}(\tilde{\theta}^{(i-1)}) & \mathbf{V}_{\lambda\lambda}(\tilde{\theta}^{(i-1)}) \end{bmatrix} \begin{bmatrix} \mathbf{n}^{-1}\{\mathbf{d}_n(\tilde{\theta}^{(i-1)}) - \mathbf{R}'\tilde{\lambda}^{(i-1)}\} \\ -n(\mathbf{R}\tilde{\theta}^{(i-1)} - \mathbf{b}) \end{bmatrix} \tag{19.119}$$

For the initial estimates, $\tilde{\theta}^{(0)}$, we use the linearized exactly identified estimators given by (19.104), and for $\tilde{\lambda}^{(0)}$ we start from zero. Our experience with using this algorithm in a number of applications suggests that the generalized Newton–Raphson algorithm based on (19.119) has good convergence properties, and converges reasonably fast on a standard 486 machines. Finally, a consistent estimator of the asymptotic variance of $\tilde{\theta}$ is given by (19.118).

### 19.8.3 Log-likelihood ratio statistics for tests of over-identifying restrictions on the cointegrating relations

Consider now the problem of testing over-identifying restrictions on the coefficients of the cointegrating (or long-run) relations. Suppose there are $r$ cointegrating relations and that you want to test the restrictions

$$\mathbf{R}\mathrm{vec}(\beta) = \mathbf{b} \tag{19.120}$$

where $\mathbf{R}$ is a $k \times mr$ matrix and $\mathbf{b}$ is a $k \times 1$ vector of known constants such that $\mathrm{Rank}(\mathbf{R}) = k > r^2$. As before, let $\theta = \mathrm{vec}(\beta)$ and decompose the $k$ restriction defined by (19.120) into $r^2$ and $k - r^2$ sets of restrictions:

$$\underset{r^2 \times rm}{\mathbf{R}_A} \quad \underset{rm \times 1}{\theta} \quad = \quad \underset{r^2 \times 1}{\mathbf{b}_A} \tag{19.121}$$

$$\underset{(k-r^2) \times rm}{\mathbf{R}_B} \quad \underset{rm \times 1}{\theta} \quad = \quad \underset{(k-r^2) \times 1}{\mathbf{b}_B} \tag{19.122}$$

where $\mathbf{R} = (\mathbf{R}'_A, \mathbf{R}'_B)'$ and $\mathbf{b} = (\mathbf{b}_A, \mathbf{b}_B)$, such that $\mathrm{Rank}(\mathbf{R}_A) = r^2$, $\mathrm{Rank}(\mathbf{R}_B) = k - r^2$, and $\mathbf{b}_A \neq 0$. Without loss of generality the restriction, characterized by (19.121), can be viewed as the just-identifying restriction, and the remaining restriction defined by (19.122) will then constitute the $k - r^2$ over-identifying restriction. Let $\hat{\theta}$ be the ML estimators of $\theta$ obtained subject to the $r^2$ exactly-identifying restrictions, and $\tilde{\theta}$ be the ML estimators of $\theta$ obtained under all the $k$ restrictions in (19.120). Then, the log-likelihood ratio statistic for testing the over-identifying restrictions is simply given by

$$\mathcal{LR}(\mathbf{R}|\mathbf{R}_A) = 2\{\ell_n^c(\hat{\theta}; r) - \ell_n^c(\tilde{\theta}; r)\}, \tag{19.123}$$

where $\ell_n^c(\hat{\theta}; r)$ is given by (19.89) and represents the maximized value of the log-likelihood function under the just-identifying restriction, (say

$\mathbf{R}_A\theta = \mathbf{b}_A$), and $\ell_n^c(\tilde{\theta}; r)$ is the maximized value of the log-likelihood function under the $k$ just- and over-identifying restrictions given by (19.120).

Under the null hypothesis that the restrictions (19.120) hold, the log-likelihood ratio statistic $\mathcal{LR}(\mathbf{R}|\mathbf{R}_A)$ defined by (19.123) is asymptotically distributed as a $\chi^2$ variate with degrees of freedom equal to the number of over-identifying restrictions, namely $k - r^2 > 0$.

The above testing procedure is also applicable when interest is on testing restrictions on the single cointegrating vector of a subset of cointegrating vectors. For this purpose, one simply needs to impose just-identifying restrictions on all the vectors except for the vector(s) that are to be subject to the over-identifying restrictions. The resultant test statistic will be invariant to the nature of the just-identifying restrictions. Notice that this test of the over-identifying restrictions on the cointegrating relations pre-assumes that the variables, $\mathbf{z}_t = (\mathbf{y}_t', \mathbf{x}_t')'$, are $I(1)$, and that the number of cointegrating relations, $r$, is correctly chosen.

Another application of the above log-likelihood ratio procedure is to the problem of testing the 'co-trending' restriction (19.81), discussed in Section 19.6.1. The relevant test statistic is given by

$$\mathcal{LR}(\beta'\gamma = 0) = 2\{\ell_n^c(\hat{\theta}; r) - \ell_n^c(\tilde{\theta}; r)\} \tag{19.124}$$

where as before $\ell_n^c(\hat{\theta}; r)$ is the maximized value of the log-likelihood function when the cointegrating relations are just-identified, and $\ell_n^c(\tilde{\theta}; r)$ is the maximized value of the log-likelihood function obtained subject to the just-identified restrictions plus the additional $r$ co-trending restrictions, $\beta'\gamma = \mathbf{0}$. Under the co-trending null hypothesis, $\mathcal{LR}(\beta'\gamma = \mathbf{0})$ is asymptotically distributed as a $\chi^2$ with $r$ degrees of freedom.

### 19.8.4 Impulse response analysis in cointegrating VAR models

The impulse response analysis of the cointegrating model given by the equation systems (19.64) and (19.65) can be carried out along the lines set out in Section 19.4. In the present application it is important that the parametric restrictions implied by the deficiency in the rank of the long-run multiplier matrix, $\mathbf{\Pi}$, is taken into account. It is also important to note that due to the rank deficiency of the long-run multiplier matrix, shocks (whether equation-specific or system-wide) will have persistence effects on the individual variables in the model, and their effects do not generally die out.

The computation of the impulse response function for the cointegrating VAR model can be based on the VECM (19.68), which combines the equation systems for $\mathbf{y}_t$ and $\mathbf{x}_t$ given by (19.64) and (19.65), respectively. The solution of the combined model is given by (19.69), and the orthogonalized impulse response function of the effect of a unit shock to the $i$th variable at time $t$ in (19.68) on the $j$th variable at time $t + N$ is given by

$$OI_{ijN} = \mathbf{e}_j'(\mathbf{C}(1) + \mathbf{C}_N^*)\mathbf{T}\mathbf{e}_i \tag{19.125}$$

where, as before, $\mathbf{T}$ is a lower triangular matrix such that $\mathbf{\Sigma} = \mathbf{TT}'$, $\mathbf{e}_i$ is the selection vector defined by (19.47), and $\mathbf{C}(1)$ and $\mathbf{C}_N^*$ are defined by relations (19.74) to (19.76). Alternatively, let

$$\mathbf{A}_i = \mathbf{C}(1) + \mathbf{C}_i^* \tag{19.126}$$

Then substituting $\mathbf{C}_i^* = \mathbf{A}_i - \mathbf{C}(1)$ in (19.75) and using (19.76) it also follows that

$$\mathbf{A}_i = \mathbf{A}_{i-1}\mathbf{\Phi}_i + \cdots + \mathbf{A}_{i-p}\mathbf{\Phi}_p, \qquad i = 1,2, \ldots \tag{19.127}$$

where $\mathbf{A}_0 = \mathbf{I}_m$, and $\mathbf{A}_i = \mathbf{0}$, for $i < 0$.[20] However, from (19.126) it is clear that

$$\lim_{i \to \infty} \mathbf{A}_i = \mathbf{C}(1) \tag{19.128}$$

which is a non-zero matrix with rank $m - r$.[21] Therefore, the orthogonalized impulse responses for the cointegrating VAR model can be computed in exactly the same way as in the case of stationary VAR models. The main difference is that the matrices, $\mathbf{A}_i$, in the moving-average representation of the $\mathbf{z}_t$-process tend to zero when the underlying VAR model is trend-stationary, and tend to a non-zero rank deficient matrix $\mathbf{C}(1)$, when the underlying VAR model is first-difference stationary.[22]

The generalized impulse response function, and the orthogonalized and the generalized forecast error variance decompositions can also be computed for the cointegrating VAR models, along similar lines as in Sections 19.4.2 and 19.5.

### 19.8.5 Impulse response functions of cointegrating relations

We saw in the previous section that effects of shocks on individual variables in a cointegrating VAR model do not die out and persist for ever! An alternative approach would be to consider the effect of system-wide shocks or variable-specific shocks on the cointegrating relations, $\boldsymbol{\beta}'\mathbf{z}_t$, rather than on the individual variables in the model. The effect of shocks on cointegrating relations is bound to die out, and their time profile contains useful information on the speed of convergence of the model to its cointegrating (or 'equilibrium') relations. See Lee and Pesaran (1993), and Pesaran and Shin (1996).

Consider first the time profile of the effect of a unit shock to the variable in $\mathbf{z}_t$ on the $j$th cointegrating relation, namely $\boldsymbol{\beta}_i'\mathbf{z}_t$. Once again we can obtain such a time profile both using Sims' (1981) orthogonalization method or the generalized impulse response approach. Using (19.78), we have

---

[20]For an alternative derivation of this result, see Appendix A in Pesaran and Shin (1996). Also note that the recursive relations defined by (19.127) and (19.43) produce the same results.

[21]The matrices $\mathbf{C}_n^*$, $n = 0,1,2, \ldots$ belong to the stationary component of $\mathbf{z}_t$ and tend to zero as $n \to \infty$.

[22]See Lütkepohl and Reimers (1992) and Mellander *et al.* (1992) for more details and a derivation of the asymptotic distribution of the estimators of the orthogonalized impulse responses.

$$OI_i(\beta_j'\mathbf{z}_t, N) = \beta_j'\mathbf{A}_N\mathbf{T}\mathbf{e}_i \tag{19.129}$$

for $i = 1,2, \ldots, m, j = 1,2, \ldots, r, N = 0,1,2, \ldots$ which give the responses of a unit change in the $i$th orthogonalized shock (equal to $\sqrt{\sigma_{ii}}$) on the $j$th cointegrating relation $\beta_j'\mathbf{z}_t$.[23] The corresponding generalized impulse responses are given by

$$GI_i(\beta_j'\mathbf{z}_t, N) = \frac{\beta_j'\mathbf{A}_N\Sigma\mathbf{e}_i}{\sqrt{\sigma_{ii}}} \tag{19.130}$$

for $i = 1,2, \ldots, m, j = 1,2, \ldots, r$, and $N = 0,1,2, \ldots$. Once again, the two impulse response functions coincide either if $\Sigma$ is diagonal, or if $i = 1$.

### 19.8.6 Persistence profiles for cointegrating relations and speed of convergence to equilibrium

Given the ambiguities that surround the impulse response analysis with respect to variable-specific shocks, it is of some interest to consider the effect of system-wide shocks on cointegrating relations. Such a time profile, referred to as the persistence profile, has been proposed in Pesaran and Shin (1996). The (scaled) persistence profile of the effect of system-wide shocks on the $j$th cointegrating relationship is given by

$$h(\beta_j'\mathbf{z}_t, N) = \frac{\beta_j'\mathbf{A}_N\Sigma\mathbf{A}_N'\beta_j}{\beta_j'\Sigma\beta_j} \tag{19.131}$$

for $j = 1, 2, \ldots, r$, and $N = 0,1,2, \ldots$. The value of this profile is equal to unity on impact, but should tend to zero as $N \to \infty$, if $\beta_j$ is indeed a cointegrating vector. The persistence profile, $h(\beta_j'\mathbf{z}_t, N)$, viewed as a function of $N$ provides important information on the speed with which the effect of system-wide shocks on the cointegrating relation, $\beta_j'\mathbf{z}_t$, disappears, even though these shocks generally have lasting impacts on the individual variables in $\mathbf{z}_t$. This is a useful addition to the long-run structural modelling techniques advanced in *Microfit* and provides the users with estimates of the speed with which the economy or the markets under consideration return to their equilibrium states.

The persistence profiles are also useful in the case of time series that are close to being $I(1)$ or 'near integrated'. The persistence profiles of near integrated variables eventually converge to zero, but can be substantially different from zero for protracted periods.

[23]Notice that $\beta_j'\mathbf{C}_N^* = \beta_j'(\mathbf{A}_N - \mathbf{C}(1)) = \beta_j'\mathbf{A}_N$. See (19.126) and recall that $\beta_j'\mathbf{C}(1) = 0$.

# Part VI

# Appendices

# A

# Size Limitations

This version of *Microfit* is subject to the following limits:

1. **At the data processing stage**

   NV = Total number of variables $\leqslant 200$
   NO = Total number of observations $\leqslant 3{,}100$
   NV∗NO $\leqslant 124{,}000$

2. **At the linear and non-linear estimation and hypothesis testing stage**

   IK = Total number of regressors (including an intercept if one is included) $\leqslant 102$
   IN = Total number of observations in the estimation period $\leqslant 3{,}000$
   IP = Total number of parameters of the autoregressive (AR) error process $\leqslant 12$
   Stack = Size of the stack for the specification of non-linear restrictions or equations $\leqslant 600$. This allows you to type 600 'items' in the screen editor provided. An item may be a bracket, a variable name, an arithmatic operator, or a function name
   MAR = Maximum order of the AR error process $\leqslant 50$
   MMA = Maximum order of the MA error process $\leqslant 12$
   INP = Number of observations used in the predictive failure/structural stability tests

   $\text{IN} + \text{INP} \leqslant 3{,}000; \qquad \text{INP} \leqslant 500$

   $(\text{IP} + \text{IK}) * (\text{IN} - \text{MAR}) \leqslant 150{,}000$

3. **At the forecasting stage**

   For non-linear least squares, non-linear two-stage least squares, ARDL, unrestricted VAR, cointegrating VAR, and SURE estimation:

   IQ = Number of observations in the forecast period $\leqslant 500$

   $\text{IN} + \text{IQ} \leqslant 3{,}100$

   For all other options:

   $\text{IQ} \leqslant \text{Min}(500, 3{,}000/\text{IK})$

   $\text{IN} + \text{IQ} \leqslant 3{,}100$

4. **At the cointegrating VAR estimation stage**

   $q =$ Number of $I(0)$ variables $\leqslant 18$

$m$ = Number of endogeneous $I(1)$ variables $\leqslant 12$
$k$ = Number of exogeneous $I(1)$ variables $\leqslant 5$
MP = Maximum lag order of the VAR model

$$MP \leqslant Min\left(\frac{100-s-m}{m+k}, 24\right)$$

5. **Unrestricted VAR**
$q$ = Number of deterministic/exogeneous variables $\leqslant 18$
$m$ = Number of variables in the VAR $\leqslant 12$

$$MP \leqslant Min\left(\frac{102-s}{m}, 24\right)$$

6. **ARDL Estimation**
$s$ = Number of deterministic/fixed lag regressors $\leqslant 18$
$m$ = Number of variables in the ARDL model $\leqslant 10$

$$MP \leqslant Min\left(\frac{102-s}{m}, 24\right)$$

7. **SURE estimation**
NEQ = Number of equations in the SURE model $\leqslant 10$
MPARM = Maximum number of total parameters in the SURE model $\leqslant 200$
MPEQ = Maximum number of regressors in each equation $\leqslant 102$

8. **GARCH, EGARCH, and absolute GARCH estimation**
MAR = Maximum order of AR $\leqslant 99$
MMA = Maximum order of MA $\leqslant 99$
Maximum number of parameters in the AR part $\leqslant 12$
Maximum number of parameters in the MA part $\leqslant 12$
Maximum number of parameters included in the GARCH model (inclusive of the number of parameters in regression) $\leqslant 102$

9. **Graphics**
There is a combined limit of 6000 points on any graph and a maximum of 50 plots per graph. This means that a graph with one line can have up to 6000 points, a graph with two lines can have up to 3000 points, and so on.

10. **Copying and Pasting Data**
There is a 32K limit on the size of data that can be copied from the clipboard into *Microfit* and vice versa.

11. **Limitations of Student Version**

| | Standard | Student |
|---|---|---|
| Maximum number of observations | 3100 | 110 |
| Maximum sample size for estimation | 3000 | 100 |
| Maximum number of variables | 200 | 50 |
| Maximum number of regressors | 102 | 10 |
| Maximum number of regressors times sample size | 124000 | 2000 |

# B

# Error Messages

*Microfit* can generate up to 120 warnings and error messages, most of which are self-explanatory. In this appendix we list some of the important error messages. Messages are listed *alphabetically*.

*Note:* Some words and numbers appear in angle brackets < >. These are substitutes for specific names and numbers which *Microfit* will display. For example, <filename> in a printed error message represents an actual filename on your screen; <variable name> in a printed example represents an actual variable name on your screen.

## B.1 Error messages: letter A

### A REORDER command has not been issued. Cannot RESTORE!

The use of the RESTORE command is only meaningful if the original ordering of the variables has already been changed using a REORDER command.

### A GARCH(p,0) is not identified!

A GARCH(p,0) specifies the conditional variance of the error term to depend only on its own passed values. In particular, the conditional variance will not depend on the past values of the residuals of the underlying regression. In such a model there is no feedback from the conditional mean to the conditional variance and vice versa, and hence the model is not identified.

### All variables have titles!

If the ENTITLE command is issued on its own, all variables without a description will be presented to you so that you can type in descriptions for them. If all the variables in the workspace have descriptions assigned to them, you get the above error message. If you wish to change the description of one or more variable names, you should issue the following command:

ENTITLE <variable list>

## An almost exact relationship exists between regressors and their lagged values!

In a VAR or ARDL model when the lagged and differences of variables are created by the program and internal regressions are run, the above error message appears when the regressors of these internal regressors are collinear. This also happens if deterministic variables such as the intercept term or trend are included amongst the main variables of the VAR or ARDL model. An invalid operation has been carried out or a very large number has been calculated. Either initial values of parameters are not appropriate or variables need to be scaled! Try again.

You should check the non-linear regression formula and make sure that all the parameters are identified. You should also make sure that, given the initial values of the parameters, the regression formula is defined over the estimation period.

## At least <number> additional instruments needed

Generally there should be at least as many instruments as there are parameters to be estimated.

## At least a restriction is not linear!

It should be an easy task to make sure that all the specified restriction(s) are linear.

## At least one derivative or fitted value is not defined!

You are presented with the above error message when you attempt to carry out a non-nested test by simulation and some of the calculations are not defined over the specified sample period.

## At least one restriction is not homogeneous!

Check that all the restrictions are homogeneous.

## B.2 Error messages: letter C

### Chosen initial values imply −ve unconditional variance!

The sum of AR and MA coefficients in the GARCH process must be less than one. If this condition is not satisfied the unconditional variance of the regression will become negative and hence it will not be possible to carry out the GARCH estimation.

### Correlation matrix near singular (possible multicollinearity)! **CALCULATIONS ABANDONED**

This is due to multicollinearity amongst the regressors. If you cannot detect the source of multicollinearity you should run regressions in each of which one of the regressors is regressed on the remaining regressors. The source of collinearity will be revealed when a regression is successfully computed but the fit of the regression is perfect. The exact nature of multicollinearity can be deduced from the estimated coefficients.

## B.3 Error messages: letter D

### Data sets do not match, data not added!

Make sure that both data sets have the same frequency.

### Dependent variable contains number(s) other than zeros and ones!

In a Probit or Logit model, the dependent variable should be a binary zero or one number. Remember that you can use the SIGN function to transform a variable with positive and negative values to such a binary number.

### Dependent variable in model M2 is not defined over your sample period!

Non-nested tests are carried out over the same sample period for both models and you should make sure all the variables in the second model are defined over this common sample period.

## B.4 Error messages: letter E

### Eigenvalues cannot be calculated accurately! This is due to near multicollinearity or the presence of very small numbers

This usually happens when the variables included in the VAR are very small or the scales of some of the variables are very different from the rest. This problem also occurs when the number of observations relative to the number of estimated parameters is small.

### Equality sign is missing or misplaced!

Obviously the equality sign cannot be placed at the beginning or at the end of the formula.

### Error in batch file! Operations only partially completed.

By inspecting the last variable created in the workspace you should be able to pinpoint the command or formula in the batch file which is causing the error.

### Error in formula or command or ';' missing

The more common mistake is to forget to include the semicolon between two separate commands and/or formulae. In the case of more than one command or formula correctly separated by semicolon(s), you should check the current sample period set by the program or note the last variable created on your workspace in order to detect the error. You should also read the on-line help on typing formulae or commands.

### Error in non-linear regression formula!

You should make sure that your non-linear regression formula follows the rules which are also applicable at the data transformation stage for creating new variables.

### Error in the specification of parameter restriction(s)!

Apart from the obvious errors you could make, the most common error is to forget to type a semicolon between any two restrictions.

### Error while attempting to read observation < >! Error while attempting to read variable <name>!

The above errors will be reported when a raw data file is read into *Microfit*. You should check that there are as many observations and/or variables present on the file.

### Error while processing the restriction(s)! Please correct using the box editor.

Correct the error using the box editor. Apart from the obvious errors, the most common error is to forget to type a semicolon between any two restrictions.

### Exactly <number> variable(s) needed!

Specify the correct number of variables and try again.

## B.5 Error messages: letters F and G

### File name should have extension < >!

*Microfit* requires you to use pre-defined extensions for the different file types that it uses. The only exception is that for raw data files any extension is allowed. Also, equation (.EQU) files and list (.LST) files are interchangeable. This is a useful facility because once you have estimated a linear regression and saved it a list file, you can move to the data transformation stage, retrieve the file, and modify the contents in order to list the regression variables and find out which variable (if any) might not be defined in the estimation or forecast period.

### First <number> observations are collinear! First regressions are collinear!

This is due to multicollinearity amongst the regressors. If you cannot detect the source of muticollinearity, you should run regressions in each of which one of the regressors is regressed on the remaining regressors. The source of collinearity will be revealed when a regression is successfully computed but the fit of the regression is perfect. The exact nature of multicollinearity can be deduced from the estimated coefficients.

### Gaps in observations for <variable>, can't estimate!

This situation arises when the variables included in the regression are defined at the beginning and the end of the specified sample period but when one or more variable(s) are not defined for some observations in the middle of the estimation period. This usually occurs at the data transformation stage when an operation has been carried out on a variable and the operation is not valid for some of the data points (e.g. logarithm of a number which is negative at that data point).

## B.6 Error messages: letter I

### Incomplete information recorded as disk is either write protected or is full!

If this error occurs, the results or the information about typing in the box editor presented will be incomplete. While in such a situation the program does not crash, you should remedy the problem and redo your task. It is wise to save any data or the contents of the box editors to a different disk/directory. If you are writing to a diskette, make sure it is not write-protected and is properly placed in the disk drive. If you are trying to write to a network drive without having the privilege to do so, try to write to a different drive/directory.

### Initial values of GARCH parameters are not appropriate! The sum of AR and MA coefficients must be less than one.

If the above condition is not satisfied, the unconditional variance of the regression will become negative and hence it will not be possible to carry out the GARCH estimation.

### Invalid or non-existent variable name specified, try again! Invalid variable name <variable> specified, try again!

A variable name should be at most nine characters long. It should be alphanumeric and start with a letter. The underscore character (_) is also allowed in a variable name. When *Microfit* reads Excel files it automatically truncates any variable name which is longer than nine characters to nine characters and allocates the rest of the name to the description of the variable. Duplicate names are obviously not allowed; when there are two or more variables whose first nine characters are identical the program also produces the above error message.

### It is not possible to carry out analysis for a single variable only!

An ARDL model cannot be estimated when a single variable only is specified. Remember to include another variable such as an intercept in the ARDL model (after the ampersand).

### It is not possible to display single equation results! Please delete at least <number> variables from workspace and re-estimate.

*Microfit* automatically creates temporary variables, such as lags, differences, and error correction terms, and adds them to the workspace. These temporary variables will be automatically deleted from the workspace after the relevant task is finished. If the sum of the main variables plus these temporary variables exceeds 200, you will be presented with the above error message. The solution to this problem is to proceed to the data transformation stage and delete unwanted variables from the workspace before proceeding to repeat your task.

## B.7 Error messages: letter L

### Large d.f. for t, try a normal distribution!

If the degrees of freedom of a standardized *t*-distribution is larger than about 25, the *t*-distribution will become indistinguishable from a normal distribution. If this happens, it is obviously advisable to assume a normal distribution for the underlying (conditional) error distribution.

### Length of expression is too long!

A maximum number of 600 items is allowed in any one formula. An item may be a variable name, a bracket, a number, an arithmetic operator, or the name of a function.

## B.8 Error messages: letter M

### Method fails. Derivatives of residuals are collinear!

This is because some of the variables in the model are collinear and/or initial values of parameters are not appropriate. This error message will be displayed during non-linear estimation. You should make sure that, given the initial values of the parameters, the non-linear regression is defined. You should also make sure that the parameters of the model are identified.

## Method fails. Residuals and their lags are collinear! **CALCULATIONS ABANDONED** Method fails. The regressors are collinear! **CALCULATIONS ABANDONED**

It is possible that you are running regressions that contain perfectly collinear regressors, or that the derivatives of the non-linear function that you are trying to estimate are perfectly collinear.

## Missing observation in period < >. Can't calculate autocorrelations! Missing value for variable < > at observation < >!

*Microfit* automatically adjusts the specified sample period so that any missing observations at the beginning and at the end of the specified period are discarded. However, if after these adjustments there are missing values in the middle of the sample period, the above error messages may be displayed. This usually happens when an invalid operation has been carried out (such as taking the logarithm of a variable which contains zero or negative values for some of the observations).

## Model M1+M2 contains more than <number> regressors, can't test!

The total number of regressors allowed in the combined model M1 + M2 should not exceed 102.

## Model M1/M2 fits exactly and/or the regressors are multicollinear. Check your model specification and try again!

This is due to mutlticollinearity amongst the regressors. If you cannot detect the source of multicollinearity, you should run regressions in each of which one of the regressors is regressed on the remaining regressors. The source of collinearity will be revealed when a regression is successfully computed but the fit of the regression is perfect. The exact nature of multicollinearity can be deduced from the estimated coefficients.

## Models are not non-nested, can't test!

If the models are nested, you should be able to compare the two rival models by estimating one initially. You can then carry out either a variable addition or variable deletion test to compare the two models.

### Multicollinear regressors and their lagged values!

This is due to mutlticollinearity amongst the regressors. If you cannot detect the source of multicollinearity you should run regressions in each of which one of the regressors is regressed on the remaining regressors. The source of collinearity will be revealed when a regression is successfully computed but the fit of the regression is perfect. The exact nature of multicollinearity can be deduced from the estimated coefficients.

## B.9 Error messages: letter N

### Name <variable> is common to both data sets, data not added!

When you attempt to add a special *Microfit* file to the workspace, if a name is common to both sets of data, in order for the data not to be overwritten accidentally, *Microfit* does not allow the new set to be added to the workspace. You are effectively forced to delete the common variable from one of the data sets before attempting to merge them.

### No observation is available for forecasting!

It is possible that your estimation period covers the whole of the available data periods and you might need to extend your data set before trying to forecast. Alternatively, the above error message might be displayed because one or more variables have missing values over the forecast period and hence forecasts cannot be computed. Either go to the data processing stage and input values (forecasting assumption) for the regressors, or try to carry out the forecast over a shorter sample period over which data for the regressors are available. One common mistake is to have a deterministic variable, such as an intercept or time trend, which is not defined over the forecast period.

### Near singular variance-covariance matrix!

This arises when the variance–covariance matrix of the estimated parameters obtained after a numerical optimization is not positive definite. This implies that the achieved optimum is not well defined (a flat likelihood surface) or the optimum is only a local one. It is sometimes possible to remedy this problem by starting the optimization problem from a different set of initial values of the parameters. The problem also arises when one of the equations in a system of equations (a VAR or SURE model, for example) fits exactly.

### Non-stationarity encountered! Do you want to continue?

In the process of estimation of GARCH parameters, this error message is displayed when the implied unconditional variance of the error term in the regression becomes (temporarily) negative during the iterations. If you answer in the affirmative, the iterations will continue and if at convergence the unconditional variance is still negative, a warning will be displayed after the presentation of results.

### NORMAL/UNIFORM cannot be used with simulation commands!

It is not possible to use either of the NORMAL or UNIFORM functions while the SIM or SIMB commands are in use. The solution to the problem is very simple. First create variables such as E = NORMAL (123) or U = UNIFORM (427) where 123 and 427 are seeds of generating these random variables. Now you can use either of these variables (E or U) with the SIM or SIMB commands.

### Not enough observations available for < >, can't estimate! Not enough observations available, can't estimate! Not enough observations for model M1+M2, can't test! Not enough observations to carry out the computations! Not enough observations! Can't estimate. Not enough observations, can't test!

The above error messages will be displayed when there are too few observations available for estimation or testing. You should bear in mind that *Microfit* automatically adjusts the beginning and end of your specified sample period so that all the variables are defined over the adjusted sample period. Also remember that any invalid transformation (such as the logarithm of zero or a negative number) on a variable at the data processing stage will result in missing values.

### Not enough restrictions on CV <number>!

You should be able to see the required number of restrictions in the window above the box editor. You can use **Tab** to move between the box editor and the top window

### Not enough space for creating additional temporary lagged variables! Not enough storage to carry out calculations! you need to delete at least <number> variable(s). Not enough store available, can't estimate! Not enough store on your workspace, you must delete at least <number> variables!

*Microfit* automatically creates temporary variables such as lags, differences, and error correction terms and adds them to the workspace. These temporary variables will be automatically deleted from the workspace after the relevant task is finished. If the sum of the main variables plus these temporary variables exceeds 200, you may be presented with any of the above error messages. The solution to this problem is to proceed to the data transformation stage and delete unwanted variables from the workspace before proceeding to repeat your task.

## B.10 Error messages: letters O and P

### One or more observations in the specified sample period are missing! Re-set the sample period and try again.

This may arise because your formula contains one or more of the following functions: MEAN, STD, PTTEST, or HPF. Each of the above functions has the property that it can only be calculated if the argument of the function is defined over the entire specified sample period. Otherwise these functions return missing values for the whole of the sample period. You should, therefore, take special care to set the sample period so that the variables used by these functions are defined for the whole of that period.

### Optimization method failed to converge! Retry by changing the initial parameter estimates.

You should check the non-linear regression formula and make sure that all the parameters are identified. Also, you should make sure that, given the initial values of the parameters, the regression formula is defined over the estimation period.

### Option not available for this estimation method!

This is because either the computations have become intractable or no theory has been developed for this particular option, or simply because the option has not been implemented in *Microfit*.

### Please do not include an intercept or a trend term!
### Please do not include an intercept term among your regressors!

Some estimation methods, such as the cointegrating VAR estimation or Phillips–Hansen fully modified estimators, require the intercept and/or the trend term to be specified separately. You will be asked to supply this information at a later stage.

### Please specify r, the number of cointegrating vectors!

After carrying out the maximum likelihood estimation of a cointegrating VAR model, *Microfit* does not allow you to proceed without specifying the number of cointegrating vectors. You can specify the number of cointegrating vectors by choosing option 2 in the Cointegrating VAR Post Estimation Menu (see Section 7.5.2).

### Please type the lags in ascending order!

The lags involved in an MA or a GARCH model should be specified in ascending order. They need not be consecutive numbers, however.

## B.11 Error messages: letter R

### Regressors are collinear!

This is due to multicollinearity amongst the regressors. If you cannot detect the source of multicollinearity, you should run regressions in each of which one of the regressors is regressed on the remaining regressors. The source of collinearity will be revealed when a regression is successfully computed but the fit of the regression is perfect. The exact nature of multicollinearity can be deduced from the estimated coefficients.

### Restrictions are collinear!

Imposing or testing the restrictions will not be possible unless they are all linearly independent.

## B.12 Error messages: letter S

### Singular variance covariance matrix!

This arises when the variance–covariance matrix of the estimated parameters obtained after a numerical optimization is not positive definite.

This implies that the achieved optimum is not well defined (a flat likelihood surface) or that the optimum is only a local one. It is sometimes possible to remedy this problem by starting the optimization problem from a different set of initial values of the parameters. The problem also arises when one of the equations in a system of equations (a VAR or SURE model, for example) fits exactly.

### Small d.f. for *t*-distribution encountered!

The degrees of freedom of a *t*-distribution used in the estimation of GARCH models should at least be 2.0. If during iterations the degrees of freedom becomes equal to or smaller than 2.0, the above error message will be displayed.

### Small or −ve standard error. Please use another lag window!

When the equal weights are used in the calculation of the Newey–West adjusted variance–covariance matrix, there is a possibility that the adjusted variance–covariance matrix may become non-positive definite. The remedy to the problem is to use another lag window as suggested by the above message.

### Small or missing value for <variable>.

If the above condition is encountered, the calculations cannot be carried out. You should list the variable and inspect its values.

### Small or negative conditional variance/standard errors encountered!

In the process of estimating or forecasting GARCH models, it is possible that the values of the estimated GARCH parameters are such that the conditional variance or the conditional standard errors become very small or negative. In that case the calculations will be abandoned and the above error message will be displayed.

## B.13 Error messages: letter T

### The calculated variance of the statistic is too small, test not carried out!

Obviously the calculations cannot be carried out in such a situation. If this happens, it is usually an indication that the test of hypothesis does not make any sense.

### The combined model M1+M2 has collinear regressors. The non-nested tests cannot be carried out. It is possible that the two models are nested.

If you are presented with the above error message, apart from the possibility that the regressors of model M2 might be collinear, it is most likely that the two models M1 and M2 are nested and hence that the non-nested tests are inapplicable. In such a situation the more standard nested tests should be applied to compare the two models.

### The commenting out square brackets are not properly positioned!

At the data processing stage you are able to comment out one whole section of the box editor. You can do this by enclosing a section of this screen editor within square brackets, namely [ and ]. As long as a left bracket appears first and is matched by another right bracket, the bracketed section of the editor will be ignored when you press the **End** key. If the brackets do not follow the above rule, the above error message will be displayed.

### The conditional variance is not defined during the forecast period!

In the process of forecasting from GARCH models, it is possible that the values of the estimated GARCH parameters are such that the conditional variance or the conditional standard errors become very small or negative. In that case the calculations will be abandoned and the above error message will be displayed.

### The dependent variable in model M2 cannot be created. Log of −ve values!

When carrying out non-nested tests, if the dependent variable of model M2 is specified by you to be the logarithm of an existing variable and this variable is not positive for one or more of the observations over the sample period, the above error message will be displayed.

## The derivatives of log-likelihood w.r.t. parameters are collinear!

*Microfit* displays the following list of possible reasons for the error:

The failure of the GARCH estimation procedure may be due to:

1. Inappropriate initial values. Change initial values and try again.
2. Large damping factor. Retry with a smaller damping factor if possible.
3. Existence of serial correlation in the residuals of the regression. Retry by adding lagged values of the dependent variable to the model.
4. There may be no ARCH effects in the model. Use option 2 of the Hypothesis Testing Menu after running an OLS regression to check for the presence of ARCH effects in your regression.
5. Inappropriate assumption about the conditional distribution of errors. Change the conditional distribution of the errors from normal (or *t*-distribution) and re-estimate.

## The expression is too long!

A maximum number of 600 items are allowed in any one formula. An item may be a variable name, a bracket, a number, an arithmetic operator, or the name of a function.

## The file <name> is not on your Default Directory. The file specified is of the wrong type or there are too many observations and/or variables, data not entered!

The above error messages will be displayed when there is a problem with reading special *Microfit* files with the extension .FIT into *Microfit*. The error could occur when the data file contains too many observations and/or variables for the version of *Microfit* that you are using. There is also a possibility that the file has become corrupt. Another possibility is that you are trying to read a file which might have been given the extension .FIT but which in reality is not a special *Microfit* file! In this case *Microfit* will not be able to recognize the file as a special *Microfit* data file.

## The formula can't be evaluated due to lack of space!

When a formula is being calculated, *Microfit* uses a stack to store the intermediate results. If the formula is very complicated, *Microfit* might run out of the space allocated to it for calculations. This happens when there are a lot of variables present on the workspace or the formula is unduly complicated. You should break down the formula into simpler components when possible and at the same time delete unwanted variables from the workspace.

### The instruments and/or regressors are collinear! **CALCULATIONS ABANDONED**

This is due to multicollinearity amongst the regressors/instruments. If you cannot detect the source of multicollinearity, you should run regressions in each of which one of the regressors (instruments) is regressed on the remaining regressors (instruments). The source of collinearity will be revealed when a regression is successfully computed but the fit of the regression is perfect. The exact nature of multicollinearity can be deduced from the estimated coefficients.

### The inverse functions for both models must map into (give) the same variable!

When carrying out non-nested tests by simulation, the dependent variables of both rival models should be functions of the same variable. If not, the above error message will be displayed and the non-nested tests will not be carried out.

### The Johansen ML procedure cannot be implemented. This may be due to lack of enough observations or multicollinearity. One or more eigenvalues have been computed to be almost equal to or greater than unity.

Apart from the above reasons, it is also possible that the one or more of the variables in the cointegrating VAR contain(s) very small values.

### The likelihood function is not defined! The log-likelihood is not defined, cannot test!

When the above error messages are displayed, it will not be possible to report the maximized value of the log-likelihood function or carry out any related log-likelihood ratio as well as non-nested tests.

### The predetermined variables in the model are multicollinear!

This is because one or more of the regressors are exact linear combinations of the remaining regressors.

### The regression equation you have specified fits (almost) exactly. Please try the OLS option.
### The regression equation you have specified fits (almost) exactly. Recursive residuals cannot be computed!

If the regression equation fits (almost) exactly so that the residuals of the regression are (almost) identically zero, it is most likely that you are estimating an identity. Check you regression and try again!

### The regressors/instruments are collinear, can't test!

This error message appears when one or more of the regressors (instruments) are exact linear combinations of the remaining regressors (instruments).

### The restrictions are linearly dependent!

Imposing or testing the restrictions will not be possible unless they are all linearly independent.

### The variables in the error correction model are constructed synthetic variables and cannot be deleted!

When error correction models are presented by *Microfit* as ordinary least squares regressions, the program uses constructed temporary variables representing the error correction terms and differences of variables. These constructed variables are not directly accessible to the user. There is, however, a solution to this problem. It is possible to use the Wald test (option 7 in the Hypothesis Testing Menu) to carry out the required tests of hypothesis. The coefficients of these variables are referred to as A1, A2, A3, and so on. For example, the test of hypothesis of deleting a subset of variables included in the regression would be to test to see if a subset of these coefficients (A1, A2, A3, etc.) are jointly zero.

### The variance-covariance matrix of estimates is not positive definite!

This arises when the variance–covariance matrix of the estimated parameters obtained after a numerical optimization is not positive definite. This implies that the achieved optimum is not well defined (a flat likelihood surface) or that the optimum is only a local one. It is sometimes possible to remedy this problem by starting the optimization problem from a different set of initial values of the parameters. The problem also arises when one of the equations in a system of equations (a VAR or SURE model, for example) fits exactly.

## There are gaps in observations, can't estimate!

This situation arises when the variables included in the regression are defined at the beginning and at the end of the specified sample period but one or more variable(s) are not defined for some observations in the middle of the estimation period. This usually occurs at the data transformation stage when an operation has been carried out on a variable and the operation is not valid for some of the data points (e.g. logarithm of a number which is negative at that data point).

## There are invalid or duplicate names in your special *Microfit* file! The program cannot read it. This has arisen because you have used a converter which has incorrectly allowed invalid or duplicate names. The problem was encountered when <variable> was read!

If you encounter this error message, *Microfit* will not be able to read the special *Microfit* file since the file is internally inconsistent.

## There are no binding restrictions that can be imposed on the cointegrating vectors. This number of homogenous restriction(s) can always be satisfied by linear combinations of the cointegrating vectors.

The above error message is displayed when you attempt to carry out certain tests of hypotheses on the parameters of the cointegrating vectors after a Johansen maximum likelihood estimation. We recommend that you always choose option 4 in the Long Run Structural Modelling Menu in order to just identify and/or test the over-identifying restrictions on the cointegrating vectors.

## There are no deterministic/exogenous variables!

This error message will be displayed when you try to test for the joint significance of a subset of deterministic and/or exogenous variables in an unrestricted VAR, but the VAR model does not contain any such variables.

## There are no variables on your workspace, can't estimate!

You should input some data into your workspace from a file, from the keyboard, or by typing formulae at the data transformation stage in order to create series that can subsequently be used in a regression model.

## There is a small chance of the simulation method breaking down. At least one simulation test statistic cannot be calculated!

In the calculation of non-nested tests by simulation, the dependent variable of either of the two models will be generated randomly. If there is a small chance of generating a variable whose transformation is not defined (such as generating a negative number whose logarithm is not defined), the above error message will be displayed.

## There is no help available for this topic.

If you encounter this error message, there is a possibility that the help files supplied on the installation diskettes of *Microfit* have not been copied to your hard disk or that they have been copied to the wrong directory. If you consistently get this error message, you should try to re-install *Microfit*.

## There is no non-homogeneous (normalization) restriction on CV <number>!

At least one of the restrictions on the coefficients of each of the cointegrating vectors should be a normalization restriction. This is usually in the form of setting the coefficients of one of the variables on the cointegrating vector as either 1 or −1.

## There is not enough free hard disk to carry out computations!

*Microfit* dynamically allocates space when carrying out certain calculations. In the first place, *Microfit* tries to use the free random access memory (RAM) available to it. Failing that, some of the free hard disk will be used instead. If this is not possible, the above error message will be displayed. The solution to the problem is to free up some hard disk by deleting some of the unwanted files from the hard disk.

**These tests are not applicable for your choice of r. Choose r to be less than <number> and try again.**
**These tests are not applicable in the one variable case!**

The above two error messages are displayed when you attempt to carry out certain tests of hypotheses on the parameters of the cointegrating vectors after a Johansen maximum likelihood estimation. We recommend that you always choose option 4 in the Long Run Structural Modelling Menu in order to just identify and/or test the over-identifying restrictions on the cointegrating vectors.

**This option is not available when I(1) exogenous variables are present!**

It is planned to implement this option in the next version of *Microfit*.

**To test linear/non-linear restrictions on the parameters of the error correction model, choose option 7 in this menu.**

When error correction models are estimated internally by *Microfit*, the program uses constructed temporary variables representing the error correction terms and differences of variables. These constructed variables are not directly accessible by the user. There is, however, a solution to this problem. It is possible to use the Wald test (option 7 in the Hypothesis Testing Menu) to carry out the required tests of hypothesis. The coefficients of these variables are referred to as A1, A2, A3, and so on. For example, the test of hypothesis of deleting a subset of variables included in the regression would be to test to see if a subset of these coefficients (A1, A2, A3, etc.) are jointly zero.

**Too few variables. You need <number> variables!**

Obviously you need to type the required number of variables.

Too many equations!
Too many observations and/or variables, data not entered!
Too many observations!
Too many observations. A max. of <number> allowed! A customized version of *Microfit* can handle many more observations. For more information get in touch with Camfit Data (North America and Mexico) and Oxford University Press (elsewhere).
Too many regressors! Delete at least one.
Too many restrictions!
Too many restrictions/relationships!
Too many variables! A maximum number of <number> variables allowed!
Too many variables! Please delete at least <number> from workspace.
Total number of parameters in the model is more than <number> the maximum allowed!

The above error messages refer to the various limits imposed by *Microfit*. See Appendix A for more information on these limits.

Two or more CV's are collinear! Specify another set of restrictions.

Imposing or testing the restrictions will not be possible unless they are all linearly independent.

Two or more regressors are collinear!

This is due to multicollinearity amongst the regressors. If you cannot detect the source of multicollinearity, you should run regressions in each of which one of the regressors is regressed on the remaining regressors. The source of collinearity will be revealed when a regression is successfully computed but the fit of the regression is perfect. The exact nature of multicollinearity can be deduced from the estimated coefficients.

## B.14 Error messages: letters U and V

Unable to create file as disk is either write protected or is full!

Make sure that the disk you are trying the save the file to is not write-protected, has enough free space, and is properly placed in the disk drive.

You should also make sure that when you are saving to a network drive, you have enough privilege to write to the disk. Also refer to the explanation for the Error in file specification! error message.

## <variable> is either not a valid name or is a duplicate name!

A variable name should be at most nine characters long. It should be alphanumeric and start with a letter. The underscore character (_) is also allowed in a variable name. When *Microfit* reads Excel files it automatically truncates any variable name which is longer than nine characters to nine characters and allocates the rest of the name to the description of the variable. Duplicate names are obviously not allowed and when there are two or more variables whose first nine characters are identical, the program produces the above error message.

## <variable> already exists!

If you attempt to add an existing variable to your workspace, you see this message. The program does not allow you to give a name to an intercept, a trend, or a seasonal dummy if the name already exists as a variable.

## <variable> has no variation!

In case of plotting variable(s) against another (the XPLOT command) or producing the scatter plot of one variable against another (the SCATTER command), the last variable specified should not be constant over the specified sample period.

## <variable> is included twice!

Try again. Obviously you cannot include the same variable more than once in a command or regression equation.

## <variable> is not a valid name!

Try again. A variable name should be at most nine characters long. It should be alphanumeric and start with a letter. The underscore character (_) is also allowed in a variable name.

## <variable> is not defined at observation <observation>, can't forecast!

The variable has a missing value at the specified observation and hence forecasts cannot be computed. Either go to the data processing stage and input a value (forecasting assumption) for the variable or try to carry out the forecast over a shorter sample period for which data on the variable is available.

## <variable> is used in your current model!

When you attempt to save residuals, fitted values, or other variables derived from your current model, you cannot overwrite an existing variable used in your model.

## Variable <name> does not exist or is not valid!
## Variable <variable> does not exist!

A variable name should be at most nine characters long. It should be alphanumeric and start with a letter. The underscore character (_) is also allowed in a variable name. When *Microfit* reads Excel files it automatically truncates any variable name which is longer than nine characters to nine characters and allocates the rest of the name to the description of the variable. Duplicate names are obviously not allowed and when there are two or more variables whose first nine characters are identical, the program produces the above error message.

## Variable <name> included more than once!
## Variable <variable> is chosen as the dependent variable more than once!

Obviously you cannot include a variable in a regression or list more than once!

## Variable <name> is not defined over the forecast period!

The above error message will be displayed because the variable has missing value(s) over the forecast period and hence forecasts cannot be computed. Either go to the data processing stage and input values (forecasting assumption) for the variable or try to carry out the forecast over a shorter sample period for which data on the variable are available. One common mistake is to have a deterministic variable such as an intercept or time trend which is not defined over the forecast period.

## Variable <name> is not on your workspace! Please create it.

The non-nested test procedure requires <variable> to exist on the workspace.

## Variable <name> is not valid for inclusion in the ARDL! Variable <name> is not valid for inclusion in the VAR!

These error messages appear if you try to include lagged values of variables on the workspace in the ARDL or VAR models. You can include lagged values in these models by constructing them first at the Data Processing Stage and then using the constructed lagged variables in the ARDL or the VAR models. However, you cannot then include the current values of these variables in the model!

## Variable <name> does not exist on your workspace!

The non-nested test procedure requires <variable> to exist on the workspace.

## Very large conditional variance/standard errors encountered!

In the process of estimation of GARCH parameters, this error message is displayed when the conditional variance of the error term in the regression becomes very large. This means that the GARCH process is unstable and hence that the estimation is not possible.

## Very large derivatives of residuals have been calculated during iterations. Either initial values of parameters are not appropriate or variables need to be scaled! Try again.

This error message will be displayed during non-linear estimation. You should make sure that, given the initial values of the parameters, the non-linear regression is defined. You should also make sure that the parameters of the model are identified. Another source of error is when the variables appearing in the non-linear regression have very different scales.

## Very large values encountered!

Restart with another damping factor. Usually starting with a smaller damping factor cures the problem. Failing that, there is also the possibility that the model is misspecified.

### Very large values encountered! Try the modified Newton Raphson algorithm.

From our experience the modified Newton–Raphson algorithm is superior to the back substitution method.

### Very large values of H due to instability of GARCH encountered!

In the process of estimation of GARCH parameters, this error message is displayed when the conditional variance of the error term in the regression becomes very large. This means that the GARCH process is unstable and hence that the estimation is not possible.

## B.15 Error messages: letter Y

### You can only delete deterministic/exogenous variables!

The above error message will be displayed when you try to test for the joint significance of a subset of deterministic and/or exogenous variables in an unrestricted VAR model but you specify a variable which is one of the jointly determined variables in the unrestricted VAR model.

### You can't delete all regressors!

The above error message will be displayed when, in the process of a variable deletion test, you specify all the regressors in the regression to be deleted.

### You cannot include any of the deterministic/exogenous variables!

The above error message will be displayed when you specify a set of variables for the block non-causality test among the jointly determined variables in an unrestricted VAR model and, by mistake, specify a variable from the deterministic/exogenous variables.

### You cannot test for block non-causality of all the variables in the VAR!

Obviously you cannot test for the deletion of all the jointly determined variables in an unrestricted VAR model.

## You have created a maximum number of <number> variables and you must overwrite an existing variable not included in your model!

*Microfit* automatically creates temporary variables such as lags, differences, and error correction terms and adds them to the workspace. These temporary variables will be automatically deleted from the workspace after the relevant task is finished. If the sum of the main variables plus these temporary variables exceeds 200, you will be presented with the above error message. The solution to this problem is to overwrite an existing variable in the workspace which is not in use by your current model.

## You have included too many observations/variables. A maximum of <number> observations can be included in this regression. Try another option in the next menu. A customized version of *Microfit* can handle many more observations. For more information get in touch with Camfit Data (North America and Mexico) and Oxford University Press (elsewhere).

See Appendix A for more information on various size limits of the package.

## You have too many parameters in the SURE model. A maximum of <number> parameters can be estimated.

See Appendix A for more information on various size limits of the package.

# C

# Statistical Tables

The critical value bounds reported in Tables F and W below are computed using stochastic simulation for $T = 500$ and 20,000 replications in the case of Wald and F statistics for testing the joint null hypothesis of $\phi = \gamma_1 = \gamma_2 = \ldots = \gamma_k = 0$ in the following models:

**Case I:** No trend and no intercept

$$\Delta y_t = \phi y_{t-1} + \sum_{i=1}^{k} \gamma_i x_{i,t-1} + u_t$$

**Case II:** With intercept, but without a trend

$$\Delta y_t = a_0 + \phi y_{t-1} + \sum_{i=1}^{k} \gamma_i x_{i,t-1} + u_t$$

**Case III:** With an intercept and a linear trend

$$\Delta y_t = a_0 + a_1 t + \phi y_{t-1} + \sum_{i=1}^{k} \gamma_i x_{i,t-1} + u_t$$

where $t = 1, \ldots, T$, and $k$ is the number of the forcing variables.

The critical values for $k = 0$ are the same as the square of the critical values of the Dickey–Fuller unit root $t$-statistic. The columns headed 'I(0)' refer to the lower-bound critical values, computed when all the $k$ regressors are I(0); the figures in the columns headed 'I(1)' refer to the upper-bound critical values, and are computed assuming all the $k$ regressors are I(1).

**Table F:** Testing the existence of a long-run relationship: critical value bounds of the F statistic

**Case I: no intercept and no trend**

| | 90% | | 95% | | 97.5% | | 99% | |
|---|---|---|---|---|---|---|---|---|
| k | I(0) | I(1) | I(0) | I(1) | I(0) | I(1) | I(0) | I(1) |
| 0.000 | 3.016 | 3.016 | 4.136 | 4.136 | 5.347 | 5.347 | 7.381 | 7.381 |
| 1.000 | 2.458 | 3.342 | 3.145 | 4.153 | 3.893 | 4.927 | 5.020 | 6.006 |
| 2.000 | 2.180 | 3.211 | 2.695 | 3.837 | 3.258 | 4.458 | 3.939 | 5.341 |
| 3.000 | 2.022 | 3.112 | 2.459 | 3.625 | 2.901 | 4.161 | 3.372 | 4.797 |
| 4.000 | 1.919 | 3.016 | 2.282 | 3.474 | 2.618 | 3.924 | 3.061 | 4.486 |
| 5.000 | 1.825 | 2.943 | 2.157 | 3.340 | 2.481 | 3.722 | 2.903 | 4.261 |
| 6.000 | 1.760 | 2.862 | 2.082 | 3.247 | 2.367 | 3.626 | 2.744 | 4.124 |
| 7.000 | 1.718 | 2.827 | 2.003 | 3.199 | 2.288 | 3.536 | 2.595 | 3.909 |
| 8.000 | 1.678 | 2.789 | 1.938 | 3.133 | 2.198 | 3.445 | 2.481 | 3.826 |
| 9.000 | 1.640 | 2.774 | 1.873 | 3.072 | 2.122 | 3.351 | 2.396 | 3.725 |
| 10.000 | 1.606 | 2.738 | 1.849 | 3.026 | 2.076 | 3.291 | 2.319 | 3.610 |

**Case II: intercept and no trend**

| | 90% | | 95% | | 97.5% | | 99% | |
|---|---|---|---|---|---|---|---|---|
| k | I(0) | I(1) | I(0) | I(1) | I(0) | I(1) | I(0) | I(1) |
| 0.000 | 6.597 | 6.597 | 8.199 | 8.199 | 9.679 | 9.679 | 11.935 | 11.935 |
| 1.000 | 4.042 | 4.788 | 4.934 | 5.764 | 5.776 | 6.732 | 7.057 | 7.815 |
| 2.000 | 3.182 | 4.126 | 3.793 | 4.855 | 4.404 | 5.524 | 5.288 | 6.309 |
| 3.000 | 2.711 | 3.800 | 3.219 | 4.378 | 3.727 | 4.898 | 4.385 | 5.615 |
| 4.000 | 2.425 | 3.574 | 2.850 | 4.049 | 3.292 | 4.518 | 3.817 | 5.122 |
| 5.000 | 2.262 | 3.367 | 2.649 | 3.805 | 3.056 | 4.267 | 3.516 | 4.781 |
| 6.000 | 2.141 | 3.250 | 2.476 | 3.646 | 2.823 | 4.069 | 3.267 | 4.540 |
| 7.000 | 2.035 | 3.153 | 2.365 | 3.553 | 2.665 | 3.871 | 3.027 | 4.296 |
| 8.000 | 1.956 | 3.085 | 2.272 | 3.447 | 2.533 | 3.753 | 2.848 | 4.126 |
| 9.000 | 1.899 | 3.047 | 2.163 | 3.349 | 2.437 | 3.657 | 2.716 | 3.989 |
| 10.000 | 1.840 | 2.964 | 2.099 | 3.270 | 2.331 | 3.569 | 2.607 | 3.888 |

**Case III: intercept and trend**

| | 90% | | 95% | | 97.5% | | 99% | |
|---|---|---|---|---|---|---|---|---|
| k | I(0) | I(1) | I(0) | I(1) | I(0) | I(1) | I(0) | I(1) |
| 0.000 | 9.830 | 9.830 | 11.722 | 11.722 | 13.503 | 13.503 | 16.133 | 16.133 |
| 1.000 | 5.649 | 6.335 | 6.606 | 7.423 | 7.643 | 8.451 | 9.063 | 9.786 |
| 2.000 | 4.205 | 5.109 | 4.903 | 5.872 | 5.672 | 6.554 | 6.520 | 7.584 |
| 3.000 | 3.484 | 4.458 | 4.066 | 5.119 | 4.606 | 5.747 | 5.315 | 6.414 |
| 4.000 | 3.063 | 4.084 | 3.539 | 4.667 | 4.004 | 5.172 | 4.617 | 5.786 |
| 5.000 | 2.782 | 3.827 | 3.189 | 4.329 | 3.573 | 4.782 | 4.011 | 5.331 |
| 6.000 | 2.578 | 3.646 | 2.945 | 4.088 | 3.277 | 4.492 | 3.668 | 4.978 |
| 7.000 | 2.410 | 3.492 | 2.752 | 3.883 | 3.044 | 4.248 | 3.418 | 4.694 |
| 8.000 | 2.290 | 3.383 | 2.604 | 3.746 | 2.882 | 4.081 | 3.220 | 4.411 |
| 9.000 | 2.192 | 3.285 | 2.467 | 3.614 | 2.723 | 3.898 | 3.028 | 4.305 |
| 10.000 | 2.115 | 3.193 | 2.385 | 3.524 | 2.607 | 3.812 | 2.885 | 4.135 |

**Table W:** Testing the existence of a long-run relationship: critical value bounds of the W statistic

**Case I: no intercept and no trend**

| | 90% | | 95% | | 97.5% | | 99% | |
|---|---|---|---|---|---|---|---|---|
| k | I(0) | I(1) | I(0) | I(1) | I(0) | I(1) | I(0) | I(1) |
| 0.000 | 3.016 | 3.016 | 4.136 | 4.136 | 5.347 | 5.347 | 7.381 | 7.381 |
| 1.000 | 4.916 | 6.684 | 6.291 | 8.307 | 7.786 | 9.853 | 10.040 | 12.011 |
| 2.000 | 6.541 | 9.632 | 8.086 | 11.512 | 9.774 | 13.374 | 11.816 | 16.023 |
| 3.000 | 8.086 | 12.449 | 9.836 | 14.501 | 11.603 | 16.645 | 13.489 | 19.189 |
| 4.000 | 9.593 | 15.078 | 11.412 | 17.370 | 13.092 | 19.622 | 15.305 | 22.429 |
| 5.000 | 10.949 | 17.657 | 12.940 | 20.042 | 14.888 | 22.330 | 17.417 | 25.565 |
| 6.000 | 12.323 | 20.036 | 14.575 | 22.729 | 16.566 | 25.385 | 19.207 | 28.866 |
| 7.000 | 13.742 | 22.616 | 16.025 | 25.590 | 18.301 | 28.290 | 20.759 | 31.272 |
| 8.000 | 15.100 | 25.105 | 17.444 | 28.196 | 19.779 | 31.003 | 22.325 | 34.434 |
| 9.000 | 16.405 | 27.738 | 18.730 | 30.724 | 21.215 | 33.509 | 23.958 | 37.245 |
| 10.000 | 17.671 | 30.116 | 20.339 | 33.289 | 22.839 | 36.203 | 25.507 | 39.715 |

**Case II: intercept and no trend**

| | 90% | | 95% | | 97.5% | | 99% | |
|---|---|---|---|---|---|---|---|---|
| k | I(0) | I(1) | I(0) | I(1) | I(0) | I(1) | I(0) | I(1) |
| 0.000 | 6.597 | 6.597 | 8.199 | 8.199 | 9.679 | 9.679 | 11.935 | 11.935 |
| 1.000 | 8.085 | 9.576 | 9.867 | 11.528 | 11.552 | 13.463 | 14.114 | 15.630 |
| 2.000 | 9.546 | 12.378 | 11.380 | 14.566 | 13.211 | 16.571 | 15.864 | 18.926 |
| 3.000 | 10.844 | 15.199 | 12.875 | 17.512 | 14.907 | 19.591 | 17.540 | 22.460 |
| 4.000 | 12.124 | 17.868 | 14.252 | 20.247 | 16.460 | 22.591 | 19.085 | 25.612 |
| 5.000 | 13.569 | 20.205 | 15.896 | 22.831 | 18.339 | 25.601 | 21.097 | 28.689 |
| 6.000 | 14.989 | 22.751 | 17.330 | 25.520 | 19.760 | 28.486 | 22.868 | 31.783 |
| 7.000 | 16.279 | 25.223 | 18.920 | 28.421 | 21.322 | 30.965 | 24.215 | 34.367 |
| 8.000 | 17.601 | 27.766 | 20.448 | 31.021 | 22.797 | 33.774 | 25.634 | 37.136 |
| 9.000 | 18.993 | 30.466 | 21.634 | 33.488 | 24.368 | 36.574 | 27.158 | 39.891 |
| 10.000 | 20.238 | 32.609 | 23.087 | 35.967 | 25.640 | 39.262 | 28.673 | 42.766 |

**Case III: intercept and trend**

| | 90% | | 95% | | 97.5% | | 99% | |
|---|---|---|---|---|---|---|---|---|
| k | I(0) | I(1) | I(0) | I(1) | I(0) | I(1) | I(0) | I(1) |
| 0.000 | 9.830 | 9.830 | 11.722 | 11.722 | 13.503 | 13.503 | 16.133 | 16.133 |
| 1.000 | 11.299 | 12.670 | 13.212 | 14.847 | 15.286 | 16.902 | 18.126 | 19.571 |
| 2.000 | 12.616 | 15.326 | 14.710 | 17.617 | 17.017 | 19.661 | 19.561 | 22.752 |
| 3.000 | 13.936 | 17.831 | 16.264 | 20.477 | 18.423 | 22.989 | 21.259 | 25.655 |
| 4.000 | 15.316 | 20.420 | 17.694 | 23.335 | 20.022 | 25.861 | 23.085 | 28.932 |
| 5.000 | 16.690 | 22.963 | 19.135 | 25.971 | 21.441 | 28.692 | 24.066 | 31.984 |
| 6.000 | 18.047 | 25.521 | 20.614 | 28.617 | 22.942 | 31.443 | 25.678 | 34.844 |
| 7.000 | 19.282 | 27.936 | 22.013 | 31.065 | 24.354 | 33.984 | 27.347 | 37.553 |
| 8.000 | 20.611 | 30.443 | 23.432 | 33.715 | 25.940 | 36.727 | 28.979 | 39.697 |
| 9.000 | 21.924 | 32.846 | 24.666 | 36.138 | 27.225 | 38.985 | 30.280 | 43.050 |
| 10.000 | 23.262 | 35.126 | 26.240 | 38.760 | 28.682 | 41.928 | 31.738 | 45.482 |

# Part VII
# References

# References


Acton, F.S. (1970), *Numerical Methods That Work*, Harper and Row, New York.

Akaike, H. (1973), 'Information Theory and the Extension of the Maximum Likelihood Principle' in *Proceeding of the Second International Symposium on Information Theory*, eds B.N. Petrov and F. Csaki, Budapest, pp. 267–81.

Akaike, H. (1974), 'A New Look at the Statistical Identification Model', *IEEE: Trans. Auto. Control*, 19, pp. 716–23.

Albert, A. and J.A. Anderson (1984), 'On the Existence of Maximum Likelihood Estimates in Logistic Regression Models', *Biometrika*, 71, pp. 1–10.

Almon, S. (1965), 'The Distributed Lag Between Capital Appropriations and Expenditures', *Econometrica*, 33, pp. 178–96.

Alogoskoufis G.S. and R. Smith (1991a), 'The Phillips Curve, The Persistence of Inflation, and the Lucas Critique: Evidence from Exchange-Rate Regimes', *American Economic Review*, 81, pp. 1254–75.

Alogoskoufis G.S. and R. Smith (1991b), 'On Error Correction Models: Specification, Interpretation, Estimation', *Journal of Economic Surveys*, 5, pp. 97–128.

Amemiya, T. (1974), 'The Nonlinear Two-Stage Least Squares Estimator', *Journal of Econometrics*, 2, pp. 105–10.

Amemiya, T. (1980), 'Selection of Regressors', *International Economic Review*, 21, pp. 331–54.

Amemiya, T. (1981), 'Qualitative Response Models: A Survey', *Journal of Economic Literature*, 19, pp. 1483–536.

Amemiya, T. (1985), *Advanced Econometrics*, Basil Blackwell, Oxford.

Andrews, D.W.K. (1991), 'Heteroskedasticity and Autocorrelation Consistent Covariance Matrix Estimation', *Econometrica*, 59, pp. 817–58.

Andrews, D.W.K. and J.C. Monahan (1992), 'An Improved Heteroskedasticity and Autocorrelation Consistent Covariance Matrix Estimator', *Econometrica*, 60, pp. 953–66.

Anscombe, F.J. (1961), 'Examination of Residuals', in *Proceedings of the Fourth Berkeley Symposium on Mathematical Statistics and Probability*, 4, University of California Press, Berkeley, pp. 1–36.

Banerjee, Dolado, Galbraith and D.F. Hendry (1993), *Cointegration, Error Correction and the Econometric Analysis of Non-stationary Data*, Oxford University Press, Oxford.

Barlett, M.S. (1946), 'On the Theoretical Specification and Sampling Properties of Autocorrelated Time-Series', *Journal of the Royal Statistical Society*, (Supplement), 9, pp. 27–85.

Beach, C.M. and J.G. MacKinnon (1978), 'A Minimum Likelihood Procedure for Regression with Autocorrelated Errors', *Econometrica*, 46, pp. 51–8.

Beaudry, P. and G. Koop (1993), 'Do Recessions Permanently Change Output?', *Journal of Monetary Economics*, 31, pp. 149–63.

Belsley, D.A., E. Kuh, and R.E. Welsch (1980), *Regression Diagnostics: Identifying Influential Data and Sources of Collinearity*, John Wiley, New York.

Bera, A.K. and C.M. Jarque (1981), 'An Efficient Large-Sample Test for Normality of Observations and Regression Residuals', *Australian National University Working Papers in Econometrics*, 40, Canberra.

Bera, A.K. and M. McAleer (1989), 'Nested and Non-Nested procedures for Testing Linear and Log-Linear Regression Models'. *Sankhya B: The Indian Journal of Statistics*, 51, pp. 212–24.

Bewley, R. (1979), 'The Direct Estimation of the Equilibrium Response in a Linear Dynamic Model', *Economics Letters*, 55, pp. 251–76.

Bollerslev, T. (1986), 'Generalized Autoregressive Conditional Heteroskedasticity', *Journal of Econometrics*, 31, pp. 307–27.

Bollerslev, T. (1987), 'A Conditionally Heteroskedastic Time Series Model for Speculative Prices and Rates of Return', *Review of Economics and Statistics*, pp. 542–47

Bollerslev, T., R.Y. Chou, and K.F. Kroner (1992), 'ARCH Modeling in Finance: A Review of the Theory and Empirical Evidence', *Journal of Econometrics*, 52, pp. 5–59.

Box, G.E.P. and G.M. Jenkins (1970), *Time Series Analysis: Forecasting and Control*, Holden-Day, San Francisco. (Revised edition 1976).

Box, G.E.P. and D.A. Pierce (1970), 'Distribution of Residual Autocorrelations in Autoregressive-Integrated-Moving Average Time Series Models', *Journal of American Statistical Association*, 65, pp. 1509–26.

Breen, W., L.R. Glosten, and R. Jagannathan, (1990), 'Predictable Variations in Stock Index Returns', *Journal of Finance*, 44, pp. 1177–89.

Brent, R.P. (1973), *Algorithms for Minimization Without Derivatives*, Prentice-Hall, Englewood Cliffs, New Jersey.

Breusch, T.S. and L.G. Godfrey (1981), 'A Review of Recent Work on Testing for Autocorrelation in Dynamic Simultaneous Models', in *Macroeconomic Analysis: Essays in Macroeconomics and Econometrics*, eds D. Currie, R. Nobay, and D. Peel, Croom Helm, London.

Breusch, T.S. and A.R. Pagan (1980), 'The Lagrange Multiplier Test and its Application to Model Specifications in Econometrics', *Review of Economic Studies*, 47, pp. 239–53.

Brockwell, P.J. and R.A. Davis (1987), *Time Series: Theory and Methods*, Springer, New York.

Brown, R.L., J. Durbin, and J.M. Evans (1975), 'Techniques for Testing the Constancy of Regression Relations Over Time (with discussion)', *Journal of the Royal Statistical Society B*, 37, pp. 149–92.

Campbell, J.Y. (1987), 'Stock Returns and the Term Structure', *Journal of Financial Economics*, 18, pp. 373–99.

Campbell, J.Y. and N.G. Mankiw (1987), 'Are Output Fluctuations Transitory?', *Quarterly Journal of Economics*, 102, pp. 875–80.

Canova (1995), 'Vector Autoregresive Models: Specification, Estimation, Inference and Forecasting', in *Handbook of Applied Econometrics*, eds M.H. Pesaran and M. Wickens, Basil Blackwell, Oxford.

Chatfield, C. (1989), *The Analysis of Time Series: An Introduction*, (4th edition), Chapman and Hall, London.

Champernowne, D.G. (1960), 'An Experimental Investigation of the Robustness of Certain Procedures for Estimating Means and Regression coefficients', *Journal of the Royal Statistical Society*, Series A, CXIII, pp. 398–412.

Chesher, A. and I. Jewitt (1987), 'The Bias of Heteroskedasticity Consistent Covariance Matrix Estimator', *Econometrica*, 55, pp. 1217–22.

Chow, G.C. (1960), 'Test of Equality Between Sets of Coefficients in Two Linear Regressions', *Econometrica*, 28, pp. 591–605.

Cobb, C.W. and P.H. Douglas (1928), 'A Theory of Production', *American Economic Review*, 18, pp. 139–65.

Cochrane, J.H. (1988), 'How Big is the Random Walk Component in GNP?', *Journal of Political Economy*, 96, pp. 893–920.

Cochrane, D. and G.H. Orcutt (1949), 'Application of Least Squares Regression to Relationship Containing Autocorrelated Error Terms', *Journal of the American Statistical Association*, 44, pp. 32–61.

Cogley, J. (1995), 'Effects of Hodrick-Prescott Filter on Trend and Difference Stationary Time Series: Implications for Business Cycle Research', *Journal of Economic Dynamics and Control*, 19, pp. 253–78.

Cook, R.D. and S. Weisberg (1982), *Residuals and Influence in Regression*, Chapman and Hall, New York.

Cox, D.R. (1961), 'Tests of Separate Families of Hypotheses', in *Proceedings of the Fourth Berkeley Symposium on Mathematical Statistics and Probability*, Vol. 1, University of California Press, Berkeley.

Cox, D.R. (1962), 'Further Results on Tests of Separate Families of Hypotheses', *Journal of the Royal Statistical Society*, Series B, 24, pp. 406–24.

Cramer, (1991), *The Logit Model: An Introduction for Economists*, Edward Arnold, London.

D'Agostino, R.B., A. Belanger, and R.B. D'Agostino, Jr (1990), 'A Suggestion for Using Powerful and Informative Tests of Normality', *The American Statistician*, 44, pp. 316–21.

Dastoor, N.K. (1983), 'Some Aspects of Testing Non-nested Hypothesis', *Journal of Econometrics*, 21, pp. 213–28.

Davidson, R. and J.G. MacKinnon (1981), 'Several Tests for Model Specification in the Presence of Alternative Hypothesis', *Econometrica*, 49, pp. 781–93.

Davidson, R. and J.G. MacKinnon (1984), 'Model Specification Tests Based on Artificial Linear Regressions', *International Economic Review*, 25, pp. 485–502.

Davidson, R. and J.G. MacKinnon (1993), *Estimation and Inference in Econometrics*, Oxford University Press, Oxford.

Deaton, A.S. (1977), 'Involuntary Saving Through Unanticipated Inflation', *American Economic Review*, 67, pp. 899–910.

Deaton, A.S. (1982), 'Model Selection Procedures, or Does the Consumption Function Exist?', in *Evaluating the Reliability of Macroeconometric Models*, eds G.C. Chow and P. Corsi, John Wiley, New York.

Deaton, A. and J. Muellbauer (1980), 'An Almost Ideal Demand System', *American Economic Review*, 70, pp. 312–36.

Dhrymes, P.J. (1971), *Distributed Lags: Problems of Estimation and Formulation*, Holden-Day, San Francisco.

Dickey, D.A. and W.A. Fuller (1979), 'Distribution of the Estimators for Autoregressive Time Series with a Unit Root', *Journal of the American Statistical Association*, 74, pp. 427–31.

Diebold, F.X. and T. Schuermann (1992), 'Exact Maximum Likelihood Estimation of ARCH Models', (Manuscript), Department of Economics, University of Pennsylvania.

Dufour, J.M. (1980), 'Dummy Variables and Predictive Tests for Structural Change', *Economics Letters*, 6, pp. 241–7.

Durbin, J. (1970), 'Testing for Serial Correlation in Least-Squares Regression when Some of the Regressors are Lagged Dependent Variables', *Econometrica*, 38, pp. 410–21.

Durbin, J. and G.S. Watson, (1950), 'Testing for Serial Correlation in Least Squares Regression I', *Biometrika*, 37, pp. 409–28.

Durbin, J. and G.S. Watson, (1951), 'Testing for Serial Correlation in Least Squares Regression II', *Biometrika*, 38, pp. 159–78.

Eicker, F. (1963), 'Asymptotic Normality and Consistency of the Least Squares Estimators for Families of Linear Regressions', *The Annals of Mathematical Statistics*, 34, pp. 447–56.

Eicker, F. (1967), 'Limit Theorems for Regressions with Unequal and Dependent

Errors', in *Fifth Berkeley Symposium on Mathematical Statistics and Probability*, eds L.M. LeCam and J. Neyman, 1, University of California, Berkeley, pp. 59–82.

Engle, R.F. (1982), 'Autoregressive Conditional Heteroscedasticity with Estimates of the Variance of United Kingdom Inflation', *Econometrica*, 50, pp. 987–1007.

Engle, R.F. and C.W.J. Granger, (1987), 'Co-integration and Error Correction: Representation, Estimation and Testing', *Econometrica*, 55, pp. 251–76.

Engle, R.F. and C.W.J. Granger (1991), *Long-Run Economic Relationships: Readings in Cointegration*, Oxford University Press, Oxford.

Engle, R.F. and B.S. Yoo (1987), 'Forecasting and Testing in Co-integrated Systems', *Journal of Econometrics*, 35, pp. 143–59.

Engle, R.F., D.F. Hendry, and J.F. Richard (1983), 'Exogeneity', *Econometrica*, 51, pp. 277–304.

Engle, R.F., D.M. Lillien, and R.P. Robins (1987), 'Estimating Time Varying Risk Premia in the Term Structure: The ARCH-M Model', *Econometrica*, 55, pp. 391–407.

Fabiani, S. (1995), 'Technological Change and Output Fluctuations: An Empirical Analysis for the G7 Countries', (unpublished PhD thesis), University of Cambridge.

Fama, E.F. and K.R. French (1989), 'Business Conditions and Expected Returns on Stocks and Bonds', *Journal of Financial Economics*, 25, pp. 23–49.

Fisher, G.R. and M. McAleer, (1981), 'Alternative Procedures and Associated Tests of Significance for Non-Nested Hypotheses', *Journal of Econometrics*, 16, pp. 103–19.

Fuller, W.A. (1976), *Introduction to Statistical Time Series*, Wiley, New York.

Gallant, A.R. (1987), *Nonlinear Statistical Models*, John Wiley, New York.

Glosten, C.R., R. Jagannathan, and D.E. Runkle (1993), 'On the Relation Between the Expected Value and the Volatility of the Nominal Excess Returns on Stocks', *Journal of Finance*, 48, pp. 1779–1802.

Godfrey, L.G. (1978a), 'Testing Against General Autoregressive and Moving Average Error Models when the Regressors Include Lagged Dependent Variables', *Econometrica*, 46, pp. 1293–301.

Godfrey, L.G. (1978b), 'Testing for Higher Order Serial Correlation in Regression Equations when the Regressors Include Lagged Dependent Variables', *Econometrica*, 46, pp. 1303–10.

Godfrey, L.G. (1978c), 'A Note on the Use of Durbin's h Test When the Equation is Estimated by Instrumental Variables', *Econometrica*, 46, pp. 225–8.

Godfrey, L.G. (1988), *Misspecification Test in Econometrics: The Lagrange Multiplier Principle and Other Approaches*, Cambridge University Press, Cambridge.

Godfrey, L.G. and M.H. Pesaran (1983), 'Test of Non-Nested Regression Models: Small Sample Adjustments and Monte Carlo Evidence', *Journal of Econcometrics*, 21, pp. 133–54.

Gourierous, C., A. Holly, and A. Monfort, (1982), 'Likelihood Ratio Test, Wald Test, and Kuhn–Tucker Test in Linear Models with Inequality Constraints on the Regression Parameters', *Econometrica*, 50, pp. 63–80.

Granger, C.W.J. (1969), 'Investigating Causal Relations by Econometric Models and Cross-Spectral Methods', *Econometrica*, 37, pp. 424–38.

Granger, C.W.J. (1986), 'Developments in the Study of Cointegrated Variables', *Oxford Bulletin of Economics and Statistics*, 48, pp. 213–27.

Granger, C.W.J. and P. Newbold (1974), 'Spurious Regressions in Econometrics', *Journal of Econometrics*, 2, pp. 111–20.

Greene, W.H. (1993), *Econometric Analysis, Macmillan*, (2nd edition), New York,

Gregory, A.W. and M.R. Veall (1985), 'On Formulating Wald Test for Nonlinear Restrictions', *Econometrica*, 53, pp. 1465–8.

Gregory, A.W. and M.R. Veall (1987), 'Formulating Wald Tests of the Restrictions Implied by the Rational Expectations Hypothesis', *Journal of Applied Econometrics*, 2, pp. 61–8.

Grossman, S.J. and R.J. Shiller (1981), 'The Determinants of the Variability of Stock Market Prices', *American Economic Review*, 71, pp. 222–7.

Grunfeld, Y. (1958), 'The Determinants of Corporate Investment', (unpublished manuscript), University of Chicago, Chicago.

Grunfeld, Y. and Z. Griliches (1960), 'Is Regression Necessarily Bad?' *Review of Economics and Statistics*, 42, pp. 1–13.

Hall, A.D., H.M. Anderson, and C.W.J. Granger (1992), 'A Cointegration Analysis of Treasury Bill Yields', *Review of Economics and Statistics*, 44, pp. 116–26.

Hall, S.R. (1978), 'Stochastic Implications of the Life Cycle Permanent Income Hypothesis: Theory and Evidence', *Journal of Political Economy*, 86, pp. 971–87.

Hamilton, J.D. (1994), *Time Series Analysis*, Princeton University Press, Princeton, New Jersey.

Hannan, E.J. and B.G. Quinn (1979), 'The Determination of the Order of an Autoregression', *Journal of Royal Statistical Society B*, 41, pp. 190–5.

Hansen, L.P. (1982), 'Large Sample Properties of Generalized Methods of Moments Estimators', *Econometrica*, 50, pp. 1029–53.

Hansen, B. (1992), 'Efficient Estimation and Testing of Cointegrating Vectors in the Presence of Deterministic Trends', *Journal of Econometrics*, 53, pp. 87–121.

Hansen, L.P. and K.J. Singleton (1983), 'Stochastic Consumption, Risk Aversion, and the Temporal Behavior of Asset Returns', *Journal of Political Economy*, 91, pp. 249–65.

Harvey, A.C. (1981), *The Econometric Analysis of Time Series*, Philip Allan, London.

Harvey, A.C. (1989), *Forecasting Structural Time Series Models and the Kalman Filter*, Cambridge University Press, Cambridge.

Harvey, A.C. and A. Jaeger (1993), 'Detrending, Stylized Facts and the Business Cycle', *Journal of Applied Econometrics*, pp. 231–47.

Hausman, J.A. (1978), 'Specification Tests in Econometrics', *Econometrica*, 46, pp. 251–72.

Hayashi, F. and C. Sims (1983), 'Nearly Efficient Estimation of Time Series Models with Predetermined, but not Exogenous, Instruments', *Econometrica*, 51, pp. 783–98.

Hendry, D.F., A.R. Pagan, and J.D. Sargan (1984), 'Dynamic Specification', in *Handbook of Econometrics*, Vol. II, eds Z. Griliches and M.D. Intriligator, Elsevier, Amsterdam, pp. 1023–1100.

Heutschel, L. (1991), 'The Absolute Value GARCH Model and the Volatility of U.S. Stock Returns', (mimeo), Princeton University.

Hildreth, C. and W. Dent (1974), 'An Adjusted Maximum Likelihood Estimator', in *Econometrics and Economic Theory: Essays in Honour of Jan Tinbergen*, ed. W. Sellekaert, Macmillan, London.

Hildreth, C. and J.Y. Lu (1960), 'Demand Relations with Autocorrelated Disturbances', *Michigan State University Agricultural Experiment Station Technical Bulletin 276*, East Lansing, Michigan.

Hodrick, R. and E. Prescott (1980), 'Post-war U.S. Business Cycles: An Empirical Investigation', (unpublished manuscript), Carnegie Mellon University.

Jarque, C.M. and A.K. Bera (1980), 'Efficient Tests for Normality, Homoscedasticity and Serial Independence of Regression Residuals', *Economics Letters*, 6, pp. 255–9.

Johansen, S. (1988), 'Statistical Analysis of Cointegrated Vectors', *Journal of Economic Dynamics and Control*, 12, pp. 231–54.

Johansen, S. (1991), 'Estimation and Hypothesis Testing of Cointegrating Vectors in Gaussian Vector Autoregressive Models', *Econometrics*, 59, pp. 1551–80.

Johansen, S. (1995), *Likelihood Based Inference on Cointegration in the Vector Autoregressive Model*, Oxford University Press, Oxford.

Johansen, S. and K. Juselius (1992), 'Testing Structural Hypotheses in a Multivariate Cointegration Analysis of the PPP and UIP for UK', *Journal of Econometrica*, 53, pp. 211–44.

Judge, G.G., W.E. Griffiths, R.C. Hill, H. Lütkepohl, and T.C. Lee (1985), *The Theory and Practice of Econometrics*, (2nd edition), John Wiley, New York.

Kendall, M., A. Stuart, and J.K. Ord (1983), *The Advanced Theory of Statistics*, Vol. 3, Charles Griffin & Co, London.

King, R.G., C.I. Plosser, S.H. Stock, and M.W. Watson (1991), 'Stochastic Trends and Economic Fluctuations', *American Economic Review*, 81, pp. 819–40.

Kiviet, J.F. (1986), 'On the Rigour of Some Misspecification Tests for Modelling Dynamic Relationships', *Review of Economic Studies*, 53, pp. 241–61.

Koenker, R. (1981), 'A Note on Studentizing a Test for Heteroskedasticity', *Journal of Econometrics*, 17, pp. 107–12.

Koop, G., M.H. Pesaran, and S.M. Potter (1996), 'Impulse Response Analysis in Nonlinear Multivariate Models', *Journal of Econometrics*, 74, pp. 119–147.

Kullback, S. and R.A. Leibler, (1951), 'On Information and Sufficiency', *Annals of Mathematical Statistics*, 22, pp. 79–86.

Kwiatkowski, D., P.C.B. Phillips, P. Schmidt, and Y. Shin (1992), 'Testing the Null Hypothesis of Stationarity Against the Alternative of a Unit Root: How Sure are We that Economic Time Series Have a Unit Root?', *Journal of Econometrics*, 54, pp. 159–178.

Lee, K. and M.H. Pesaran (1993), 'Persistence Profiles and Business Cycle Fluctuations in a Disaggregated Model of UK Output Growth', *Richerche Economiche*, 47, pp. 293–322.

Lütkepohl, H. (1991), *Introduction to Multiple Time Series Analysis*, Springer-Verlag, New York.

Lütkepohl, H. and H.E. Reimers (1992), 'Impulse Response Analysis of Cointegrated Systems', *Journal of Economic Dynamics and Control*, 16, pp. 53–78.

Ljung, G.M. and G.E.P. Box (1978), 'On a Measure of Lack of Fit in Time Series Models', *Biometrika*, 65, pp. 297–303.

Maddala, G.S. (1983), *Limited-Dependent and Qualitataive Variables in Econometrics*, Cambridge University Press, Cambridge.

Maddala, G.S. (1988), *Introduction to Econometrics*, Macmillan, New York.

Magnus, J.R. and H. Neudecker (1988), *Matrix Differential Calculus with Applications in Statistics and Econometrics*, John Wiley and Sons, New York.

McAleer, M. and M.H. Pesaran (1986), 'Statistical Inference in Non-Nested Econometric Models', *Applied Mathematics and Computation*, 20, pp. 271–311.

McCallum, B.T. (1976), 'Rational Expectations and the Natural Rate Hypothesis: Some Consistent Estimates', *Econometrica*, 44, pp. 43–52.

McFadden, D. (1976), 'Quantal Choice Analysis: A Survey', *Annals of Economic and Social Measurement*, 5, pp. 363–90.

MacKinnon, J.G. (1991), 'Critical Values for Cointegration Tests', Ch. 13, in *Long-Run Economic Relationships: Readings in Cointegration*, eds R.F. Engle and C.W.J. Granger, Oxford University Press, Oxford.

MacKinnon, J.G. and H. White (1985), 'Some Heteroskedasticity-Consistent Matrix Estimators with Improved Finite Sample Properties', *Journal of Econometrics*, 29, pp. 305–25.

MacKinnon, J.G., H. White, and R. Davidson (1983), 'Tests for Model Specification in the Presence of Alternative Hypothesis: Some Further Results', *Journal of Econometrics*, 21, pp. 53–70.

Mellander, E., A. Vredin, and A. Warne (1992), 'Stochastic Trends and Economic Fluctuations in a Small Open Economy', *Journal of Applied Econometrics*, 7, pp. 369–394.

Merton, R.C. (1980), 'On Estimating the Expected Return on the Market: An Exploratory Investigation', *Journal of Financial Economics*, 8, pp. 323–61.

Mizon, G.E. and J.F. Richard (1986), 'The Encompassing Principle and its Application to Non-Nested Hypotheses', *Econometrica*, 54, pp. 657–78.

Muellbauer J. (1983), 'Surprises in the Consumption Function', *Economic Journal*, 43, (Supplement), pp. 34–50.

Nakamura, A. and M. Nakamura (1981), 'On the Relationships Between Several

Specification Tests Presented by Durbin, Wu and Hausman', *Econometrica*, 49, pp. 1583–8.

Nelson, D.B. (1991), 'Conditional Heteroskedasticity in Asset Returns: a New Approach,' *Econometrica*, 59, pp. 347–70.

Nelson, D.B. and C.Q. Cao (1992), 'Inequality Constraints in the Univariate GARCH Model', *Journal of Business and Economic Statistics*, 10, pp. 229–35.

Newey, W.K. and K.D. West (1987), 'A Simple, Positive Semi-Definite, Heteroskedasticity and Autocorrelation Consistent Covariance Matrix', *Econometrica*, 55, pp. 703–8.

Ogaki, M. (1992), 'Engle's Law and Cointegration', *Journal of Political Economy*, 100, pp. 1027–46.

Osterwald-Lenum, M. (1992), 'A Note with Quantiles of the Asymptotic Distribution of the Maximum Likelihood Cointegration Rank Test Statistics', *Oxford Bulletin of Economics and Statistics*, 54, pp. 461–72.

Pagan, A.R. (1984), 'Econometric Issues in the Analysis of Regression with Generated Regressors', *International Economic Review*, 22, pp. 221–47.

Pagan, A.R. (1996), 'The Econometrics of Financial markets', *Journal of Empirical Finance*, 3, pp. 15–102.

Pagan, A.R. and A.D. Hall (1983), 'Diagnostic Tests and Residual Analysis', *Econometric Reviews*, 2, pp. 159–218.

Pagan, A.R. and D.F. Nicholls (1984), 'Estimating Predictions, Prediction Errors and their Standard Deviation Using Constructed Variables', *Journal of Econometrics*, 24, pp. 293–310.

Pagan, A.R. and G.W. Schwert (1990), 'Alternative Models for Conditional Stock Volatility', *Journal of Econometrics*, 45, pp. 267–90.

Park, J.Y. (1992), 'Canonical Cointegratng Regressions', *Econometrica*, 60, pp. 119–43.

Perron, P. (1989), 'The Great Crash, the Oil Price Shock, and the Unit Root Hypothesis', *Econometrica*, 57, pp. 1361–1401.

Perron, P. and J.Y. Campbell (1993), 'A Note on Johansen's Cointegration Procedure when Trends are Present', *Empirical Economics*, 18, pp. 777–89.

Pesaran, B. (1988), 'Exact Maximum Likelihood Estimation of Regression Models with Invertible General order Moving Disturbances', *National Institute of Economic and Social Research, Discussion Paper No. 136*.

Pesaran, B. (1990), 'Instrumental Variable Estimation of Regression Models with Invertible General order Moving Average Disturbances', (unpublished manuscript).

Pesaran, B. and G. Wright (1995), 'The Use of Spreads in Forecasting Medium Term U.K. Interest Rates', mimeo, University of East London.

Pesaran, M.H. (1972), *Small Sample Estimation of Dynamic Economic Models*, (unpublished PhD Thesis), Cambridge University.

Pesaran, M.H. (1974), 'On the General Problem of Model Selection', *Review of Economic Studies*, 41, pp.153–71.

Pesaran, M.H. (1981), 'Diagnostic Testing and Exact Maximum Likelihood Estimation of Dynamic Models', in *Proceedings of the Econometric Society European Meeting, 1979, Selected Econometric Papers in memory of Stefan Valvanis*, ed. E.G. Charatsis, North-Holland, Amsterdam, pp. 63–87.

Pesaran, M.H. (1982a), 'A Critique of the Proposed Tests of the Natural Rate-Rational Expectations Hypothesis', *Economic Journal*, 92, pp. 529–54.

Pesaran, M.H. (1982b), 'Comparison of Local Power of Alternative Tests of Non-Nested Regression Models', *Econometrica*, 50, pp. 1287–305.

Pesaran, M.H. (1987a), *The Limits to Rational Expectations*, Basil Blackwell, Oxford, Reprinted with corrections (1989).

Pesaran, M.H. (1987b), 'Global and Partial Non-Nested Hypotheses and Asymptotic Local Power', *Econometric Theory*, 3, pp. 69–97.

Pesaran, M.H. (1988), 'On the Policy Ineffectiveness Proposition and a Keynesian Alternative: A Rejoinder', *Economic Journal*, 98, pp. 504–8

Pesaran, M.H. (1991), 'On the Volatility and Efficiency of Stock Prices', *Cuadernos Economicos*, 49, pp. 121–55 (in Spanish).

Pesaran, M.H. (1997), 'The Role of Economic Theory in Modelling the Long Run', *Economic Journal*, 107, pp. 178–91.

Pesaran, M.H. and R.A. Evans (1984), 'Inflation, Capital Gains and UK Personal Savings: 1953–81', *Economic Journal*, 94, pp. 237–57.

Pesaran, M.H. and B. Pesaran (1991), *Microfit 3.0: An Interactive Econometric Software Package*, Oxford University Press, Oxford.

Pesaran, M.H. and B. Pesaran (1993), 'A Simulation Approach to the Problem of Computing Cox's Statistic for Testing Non-nested Models', *Journal of Econometrics*, 57, pp. 377–92.

Pesaran, M.H. and B. Pesaran (1995), 'A Non-nested Test of Level-Differenced Versus Log-Differenced Stationary Models', *Econometric Reviews*, 14, pp. 213–27.

Pesaran, M.H., and Y. Shin, (1995a), 'An Autoregressive Distributed Lag Modelling Approach to Cointegration Analysis', *DAE Working Paper No. 9514*, Department of Applied Economics, University of Cambridge. Forthcoming in S. Strom, A. Holly and P. Diamond (Eds.), *Centennial volume of Rangar Frisch*, Econometric Society Monograph, Cambridge, Cambridge University Press.

Pesaran, M.H. and Y. Shin, (1995b), 'Long Run Structural Modelling', (unpublished manuscript), University of Cambridge.

Pesaran, M.H., and Y. Shin, (1996), 'Cointegration and the Speed of Convergence to Equilibrium', *Journal of Econometrics*, 71, pp. 117–43.

Pesaran, M. H. and Y. Shin (1997) 'Generalized Impulse Response Analysis in Linear Multivariate Models', unpublished manuscript, Cambridge University.

Pesaran, M H. and L.J. Slater (1980), *Dynamic Regression: Theory and Algorithms*, Ellis Horwood, Chichester.

Pesaran, M.H. and R.P. Smith (1985), 'Evaluation of Macroeconometric Models', *Economic Modelling*, 2, pp. 125–34.

Pesaran, M.H. and R.J. Smith (1990), 'A Unified Approach to Estimation and Orthogonality Tests in Linear Single Equation Econometric Models', *Journal of Econometrics*, 44, pp. 41–66.

Pesaran, M.H. and R.J. Smith (1994), 'A Generalized $\bar{R}^2$ Criterion for Regression Models Estimated by the Instrumental Variables Method', *Econometrica*, 62, pp. 705–10.

Pesaran, M. H. and L. W. Taylor (1997), 'Diagnostics for IV Regressions', DAE Working Paper No. 9709, Department of Applied Economics, University of Cambridge.

Pesaran, M.H. and A. Timmermann (1992), 'A Simple Nonparametric Test of Predictive Performance', *Journal of Business and Economic Statistics*, 10, pp. 461–65.

Pesaran, M.H. and A. Timmermann (1994), 'Forecasting Stock Returns: An Examination of Stock Market Trading in the Presence of Transaction Costs', *Journal of Forecasting*, 13, pp. 335–67.

Pesaran, M.H. and A. Timmermann (1995), 'Predictability of Stock Returns: Robustness and Economic Significance', *Journal of Finance*, 50, pp. 1201–28.

Pesaran, M.H., R.G. Pierce, and K.C. Lee (1993), 'Persistence, Cointegration and Aggregation: A Disaggregated Analysis of Output Fluctuations in the U.S. Economy', *Journal of Econometrics*, 56, pp. 57–88.

Pesaran, M.H., Y. Shin, and R.J. Smith (1996a), 'Testing for the Existence of a Long-Run Relationship', DAE Working Paper No. 9622, Department of Applied Economics, University of Cambridge.

Pesaran, M.H., Y. Shin, and R.J. Smith (1996b), 'Structural Analysis of Vector Error Correction Models with Exogenous I(1) Variables', DAE Working Paper No. 9706, Department of Applied Economics, University of Cambridge.

Pesaran, M.H., R.P. Smith, and S. Yeo (1985) 'Testing for Structural Stability and Predictive Failure: A Review', *Manchester School*, 53, pp. 280–95.

Phillips, A.W. (1958), 'The Relation Between Unemployment and the Rate of

Change of Money Wage Rates in the United Kingdom, 1861–1957, *Economica*, pp. 283–99.

Phillips, P.C.B. (1986), 'Understanding Spurious Regressions in Econometrics', *Journal of Econometrics*, 33, pp. 311–40.

Phillips, P.C.B. (1987), 'Time Series Regression with a Unit Root'. *Econometrica*, 55, pp. 277–301.

Phillips, P.C.B. and B.E. Hansen (1990), 'Statistical Inference in Instrumental Variables Regression with *I*(1) Processes', *Review of Economic Studies*, 57, pp. 99–125.

Phillips, P.C.B. and S. Ouliaris (1990), 'Asymptotic Properties of Residal Based Tests for Cointegration', *Econometrica*, 578, pp. 165–93.

Phillips, P.C.B. and P. Perron (1988), 'Testing for a Unit Root in Time Series Regression', *Biometrika*, 75, pp. 335–46.

Potter, S.M. (1995), 'A Nonlinear Approach to US GNP', *Journal of Applied Econometrics*, 10, pp. 109–25.

Powell, M.J.D. (1964), 'An Efficient Method of Finding the Minimum of a Function of Several Variables without Calculating Derivative', *The Computer Journal*, 7, pp. 155–62.

Power, S. (1990), 'An Exact Transformation Matrix for Use with Rational Expectations Models with MA(1) Composite Disturbance', *Oxford Bulletin of Economics and Statistics*, 52, pp. 89–94.

Press, W.H., B.P. Flannery, S.A. Teukolsky, and W.T. Vetterling (1989), *Numerical Recipes: The Art of Scientific Computing* (FORTRAN version), Cambridge University Press, Cambridge.

Priestley, M.B. (1981), *Spectral Analysis and Time Series*, Academic Press, London.

Ramsey, J.B. (1969), 'Test for Specification Errors in Classical Linear Least Squares Regression Analysis', *Journal of the Royal Statistical Society B*, pp. 350–71.

Ramsey, J.B. (1970), 'Models, Specification Error and Inference: A Discussion of Some Problems in Econometric Methodology', *Bulletin of the Oxford Institute of Economics and Statistics*, 32, pp. 301–18.

Rao, C.R. (1948), 'Large Sample Tests of Statistical Hypotheses Concerning Several Parameters with Applications to Problems of Estimation', *Proceedings of the Cambridge Philosophical Society*, 44, pp. 50–7.

Rao, C.R. (1970), 'Estimation of Heteroskedastic Variances in Linear Models', *Journal of the American Statistical Association*, 65, pp. 161–72.

Rush, M. and D. Waldo (1988), 'On the Policy Ineffectiveness Proposition and a Keynesian Alternative', *Economic Journal*, 98, pp. 498–503.

Said, E.S. and D. Dickey (1984), 'Testing for Unit Roots in Autoregressive Moving Average Model of Unknown Order', *Biometrika*, 71, pp. 599–607.

Salkever, D.S. (1976), 'The Use of Dummy Variables to Compute Predictions, Prediction Errors and Confidence Intervals', *Journal of Econometrics*, 4, pp. 393–7.

Sargan, J.D. (1958), 'The Estimation of Economic Relationships Using Instrumental Variables', *Econometrica*, 26, pp. 393–415.

Sargan, J.D. (1959), 'The Estimation of Relationships with Autocorrelated Residuals by the Use of Instrumental Variables', *Journal of the Royal Statistical Society B*, 21, pp. 91–105.

Sargan, J.D. (1964), 'Wages and Prices in the United Kingdom: A Study in Econometric Methodology', in *Econometrics Analysis for National Economic Planning*, eds P.E. Hart, G. Mills, and J.K. Whitaker, Butterworth, London.

Sargan, J.D. (1976), 'Testing for Misspecification after Estimation Using Instrumental Variables', (unpublished manuscript), London School of Economics.

Sargan, J.D. and A. Bhargava (1983), 'Testing Residuals from Least Squares Regression for Being Generated by a Gaussian Random Walk', *Econometrica*, 51, pp. 153–74.

Scheffe, H. (1959), *The Analysis of Variance*, John Wiley, New York.

Schwarz, G. (1978), 'Estimating the Dimension of a Model', *Annals of Statistics*, 6, pp. 461–4.

Serfling, R.J. (1980), *Approximation Theorems of Mathematical Statistics*, Wiley, New York.

Sims, C. (1980), 'Macroeconomics and Reality,' *Econometrica*, 48, pp. 1–48.

Sims, C. (1981), 'An Autoregressive Index Model for the US 1948–1975', in *Large-Scale Econometric Models*, ed. J.B. Ramsey, North-Holland, The Netherlands.

Söderlind, P. (1994), 'Cyclical Properties of a Read Business Cycle Model', *Journal of Applied Econometrics*, 9, pp. 113–22.

Spanos, A. (1986), *Statistical Foundations of Econometric Modelling*, Cambridge University Press, Cambridge.

Stock, J.M. (1987), 'Asymptotic Properties of the Least Squares Estimators of the Cointegrating Vectors', *Econometrica*, 55, pp. 1035–56.

Stock, J.M. (1994), 'Unit Roots, Structural Breaks and Trends', in *Handbook of Econometrics*, eds R.F. Engle and D. McFadden, North Holland, pp. 2738–841.

Stock, J.M. and M.W. Watson (1988), 'Testing for Common Trends', *Journal of the American Statistical Association*, 83, pp. 1097–107.

Theil, H. (1971), *Principle of Econometrics*, John Wiley, New York.

Tong, H. (1990), *Non-Linear Time Series*, Oxford University Press, Oxford.

Vuong, Q.H. (1989), 'Likelihood Ratio Tests for Model Selections and Non-Nested Hypotheses', *Econometrica*, 57, pp. 307–33.

Watson, M.W. (1994), 'Vector Autoregression and Cointegration', in *Handbook of Econometrics*, eds R.F. Engle and D. MacFadden, North Holland, pp. 843–915.

White, H. (1980), 'A Heteroskedasticity-Consistent Covariance Matrix Estimator and a Direct Test for Heteroskedasticity', *Econometrica*, 48, pp. 817–38.

White, H. (1982), 'Maximum Likelihood Estimation of Misspecified Models', *Econometrica*, 50, pp. 1–25.

Wickens, M.R. (1982), 'The Efficient Estimation of Econometric Models with Rational Expectations', *Review of Economic Studies*, 49, pp. 55–67.

Wu, D.M. (1973), 'Alternative Tests of Independence Between Stochastic Regressors and Disturbances', *Econometrica*, 41, pp. 733–50.

Yule, G.U. (1926), 'Why do We Sometimes Get Nonsense-correlations between Time Series? A Study in Sampling and the Nature of Time-Series', *Journal of the Royal Statistical Society*, pp. 1–64.

Zellner, A. (1962), 'An Efficient Method of Estimating Seemingly Unrelated Regressions, and Tests for Aggregation Bias', *Journal of the American Statistical Association*, 57, pp. 348–68.

# Author Index

# Subject Index